# Scarcity
## Humanity's Final Chapter?

Published by Booklocker.com, Inc., Port Charlotte, Florida.

Printed in the United States of America on acid-free paper.

Booklocker.com, Inc.
2012

First Edition

# Scarcity

## Humanity's Final Chapter?

The realities, choices, and likely outcomes associated with
ever-increasing nonrenewable natural resource scarcity

## Christopher O. Clugston

To Matt, Becca, Sarah, and Luke—

it would appear that **Scarcity** and scarcity
will be my legacies to you

# Acknowledgements

To the very few who supported my research and analytical efforts through your insights, comments, criticisms, and words of encouragement; I cannot possibly thank you enough.

# Preface

The message put forth in *Scarcity* is simple and straightforward:

Humanity's industrial lifestyle paradigm is enabled almost exclusively by enormous and ever-increasing quantities of finite and non-replenishing nonrenewable natural resources (NNRs)—fossil fuels, metals, and nonmetallic minerals—which serve as the raw material inputs to our industrialized economies, as the building blocks that comprise our industrialized infrastructure and support systems, and as the primary energy sources that power our industrialized societies.

As a result of our ever-increasing exploitation since the inception of our industrial revolution over 200 years ago, economically viable supplies associated with the vast majority of the earth's NNRs are becoming increasingly scarce, both domestically (US) and globally. In fact, NNR scarcity had become epidemic by 2008, immediately prior to the Great Recession, to the extent that there are **not enough economically viable NNRs** to perpetuate our industrial lifestyle paradigm going forward.

Absent some combination of immediate and drastic reductions in our global NNR utilization levels, continuous major discoveries of economically viable NNR deposits, and continuous major improvements in our NNR exploration, extraction, production, and processing technologies—none of which appear to be even remotely possible—we will experience escalating international and intranational conflicts during the coming decades over increasingly scarce NNRs, which will devolve into global societal collapse, almost certainly by the year 2050.

Before dismissing this message out of hand, I strongly encourage you to consider the evidence presented in *Scarcity* and to conduct your own research into NNR scarcity. Then ask yourself how can it be that we are facing the most daunting challenge ever to confront our species, yet nobody seems to be paying attention.

# Preface

# Foreword
## by William R. Catton Jr.

By temperament and upbringing, I have been an optimist all my life, inclined to approach any challenge with high hopes. I consider myself also a realist, unwilling to deny or ignore facts just because they may be uncomfortable or inconvenient. This book will confront readers with many inconvenient and uncomfortable facts, which it would be unwise to disregard. I try to hope that a widely prevalent denial tendency will subside.

Way back in 1941, when our country was at last emerging from the Great Depression, most of my young friends were similarly endowed with an optimistic attitude about life. On a December Sunday afternoon several of us, all teen-agers, were playing a game of touch football. Our game that afternoon was interrupted by a high school classmate who came by to tell us a bit of stunning news: "Hey, Japan has just bombed Pearl Harbor!" None of us realized then how much world geography we would soon be learning from daily news stories. After our first reaction, "Where's Pearl Harbor?" our second reaction was to assure each other that with our country now drawn into what was already known as the second World War, it would soon be over. Incendiary bombs our airplanes would drop, we assumed, would quickly destroy those "paper homes" of that far-away enemy. We had no inkling of the looming duration and devastation of the war, nor even any notion of how all of us would be personally involved. Nor did we anticipate what delusions of near-omnipotence our side's eventual victory would nurture.

In 1941 an American teen-ager with a dollar in his pocket could buy (to put into his ten- or twenty-dollar used car) several gallons of gasoline. Being mobile and adolescent afforded a sense of indomitability. Spending a dollar that way brought no thoughts of being a participant in the soon-to-accelerate depletion of one of this planet's non-renewable resources. And if the jalopy's engine badly needed new piston rings, its teen-age owner who always checked the oil dipstick whenever he bought gasoline, had no sense of guilt about the blue smoke that poured from his rusty exhaust pipe as the lubricating oil in the car's crankcase joined gasoline flowing from its carburetor into its cylinders. "You can buy an awful lot of motor-oil for the price of a ring-job," he often muttered, as if that resolved any problem. None of us playing football that day had yet heard of the word "ecology" nor did we think about this planet or any part of it as "the environment." Human impact upon it never worried us.

In the 21st century we still reckon a problem's significance largely in terms of the monetary cost of coping with it. Most of us have yet to out-grow such narrow views of life and the world we live in. Some today might at least feel a few guilt pangs if their car's tailpipe were so conspicuously polluting the atmosphere we all share.

Today, there are more than seven billion people using this planet as home, supply depot, and disposal site. With so many, each doing the sorts of things our "advanced" equipment enables us to do, it gets ever harder to separate the activity space, supply depot, and disposal site functions of the environment, global or local. We passed the seven billion mark only twelve years after we hit six billion. And that was only 20 years after I published a book depicting four billion as a serious overload, and less than six decades after a news report broke up that touch football game -- when we lived aboard a planet with only about two and a half billion human users of its resources.

Probably even in 1941 most students in American high schools were aware something called "the industrial revolution" had happened. If they thought about it at all, most were probably glad to be its beneficiaries, supposing its major effect was the enabling of a modern lifestyle based on possession of some "very neat" gadgets. Even our parents and other adults gave little thought in those days to how much of the planet's substance was being extracted and transformed annually into the equipment that supported all the activities we knew as normal. Hardly anyone spent any time wondering how long we could continue the "progress" that became possible when devices had been invented for using the energy in "fossil fuels" to greatly augment the muscular energy of domesticated animals (or human workers, or even slaves).

Coal, petroleum, and natural gas were abundant. Escalating use of them seemed "a good thing." We paid little attention to the fact that it was the very basis for our having become "modern," and we didn't even bother to think about the difference between renewable and non- renewable "resources." There seemed to be plenty. Times were improving.

The atmosphere and the oceans seemed enormous enough that it seemed silly to worry about the eventual effects of using them as a disposal site. Smoke from that tail-pipe obligingly blew "away." Oil didn't run out; previously unknown deposits were always being discovered. Discovery was easy to regard as replenishment as older wells "played out."

How much of the planet's goodies did we willingly use up in winning that war? How thoroughly have we outdone ourselves ever since? And now, how much remains?

In the most recent decade or two, most adult Americans have learned to deplore our dependence on imported oil -- i.e. energy from elsewhere, not recognizing that our use of even "domestic" oil has made us dependent on energy from elsewhen -- the solar energy captured by prehistoric plant life, some of which got geologically converted into underground deposits of petroleum and other "fossil fuels." Almost no one has learned to regard those underground stocks of accumulated prehistoric energy-rich substances as nature's sequestration of the carbon component that made Earth's original atmosphere unsuitable for animals or humans to breathe.

To whatever extent people contemplate such historic events as "the agricultural revolution" and "the industrial revolution," most of us have assumed both should be seen as welcome progress, making life better for human beings --and enabling this planet to support more and more of us. If it was progress when humans learned to manage the growth of humanly-useful plant species, becoming farmers rather than foragers, then we ought to be concerned about the industrial revolution -- because one of its effects was the reversal of that advancement from foraging to farming.  Industrialism has made us again dependent on "resources" whose availability we do not control and cannot renew. We ought to recognize those offshore oil platforms in the Gulf of Mexico (American) and in the North Sea (British, or Norwegian) as the tools of modern foraging. Was it progress to return to foraging (on a massive scale)? Or was it a tragically retrograde step?

Human societies have been making themselves increasingly dependent on nonrenewable natural resources (NNRs in this book), so ever since the industrial revolution, eventual scarcity has been our destiny. Every pound or kilogram of metallic ore we extracted, smelted, and used, diminished what's left; every quart or liter of petroleum we extracted, refined, and burned, made Earth that much oil-poorer and pushed its atmosphere back toward the primordial state that prevailed before the stuff got buried -- long prior to Homo "sapiens" existence.

Chris Clugston has pulled together such an array of facts about the path ravenous humanity has trod and the consequences we now confront that no person who fails to read this book should be eligible for election to high office. Politicians speak of "the American dream," a phrase that involves a birth-right expectation of ever more and more. What we have done to the planet on which we and all our neighbors depend has now committed us to a future of ever less and less. That transition from one expectation to its opposite is a change to which we will find it very difficult to adjust. We have brought upon ourselves a future very unlike our habitual assumptions. But adjust to it we must.

In terms of self-inflicted diminishing availability of NNRs, the predicament humanity now confronts cannot be dispelled by patriotic slogans or glowing political and corporate promises. Pretending we can perpetuate our habitual extravagant prodigality by striving for "resource self-sufficiency" is flagrant self-deception, based on obstinate avoidance of ecological wisdom. It worsens rather than mitigates our real predicament. Our leaders mislead us when they speak of today's predicament as if it were only a cluster of soluble problems. The problems will not go away if we just "throw the rascals out" and replace them with other leaders no more ecologically sophisticated. Following that tempting course might feel like a return to the innocence of our adolescent years, but it will aggravate, not alleviate, the hardships toward which we are rushing.

Reading what Clugston has written can at least endow us with some maturity, a sense of realism about our situation as inhabitants of a planet we have fundamentally altered. That could dissuade us from playing a misleading blame game. A futile search for villains to hold accountable for having condemned us to a declining future will persuade us to act in ways that make matters worse than they have to be.

Facing a real carrying capacity deficit, we and our posterity must endure the self-inflicted transition to a destiny of ever less and less. Understanding and accepting its factual basis will help. We, the heirs of the industrial revolution, (with little or no thought of limits), privileged recently to behave as creatures with gigantic powers by virtue of all the fossil fuel that energized our mechanical muscles, were unwittingly committed to a Faustian bargain. The only way of ameliorating its day of reckoning is to accept that bargain for what it was, to savor joyful memories of the blessings we have had, to understand their real basis, and to educate our descendants to live with less hubris on a resource-depleted planet.


William R. Catton, Jr.
Professor Emeritus
Washington State University

# Contents

# Introduction—Human Misperceptions

**Unfolding today among humankind is
the most colossal self-inflicted tragedy in the history of the world.**

During the course of human history, there have been two fundamental shocks to humanity's prevailing worldview. The first occurred when Pythagoras discovered that the earth is not flat; the second occurred when Copernicus discovered that the earth is not the center of the universe.

The third and potentially fatal fundamental shock to humanity's worldview is about to occur. We will soon discover that we can no longer provide continuously improving material living standards for ever-increasing numbers of our ever-expanding global human population. The earth no longer contains "enough" nonrenewable natural resources.

*Scarcity* is a comprehensive, multidisciplinary assessment of the realities, choices, and likely outcomes associated with ever-increasing nonrenewable natural resource scarcity.

*Scarcity* is also the story of a species, Homo sapiens, whose superior intellect should have caused it to eschew natural resource utilization behavior through which lower order species often experience population "irruptions" followed by "die-offs". No such luck...

## Industrialism and NNRs

It is understandable that we human beings would seek to improve our societal wellbeing—the material living standards enjoyed by our human populations—through industrialism. The material living standards associated with industrialized lifestyles such as those enjoyed by Americans and Western Europeans are far superior to the material living standards afforded by pre-industrial agrarian and hunter-gatherer lifestyles.

Seemingly unnoticed, however, is the fact that our industrial lifestyle paradigm is enabled almost exclusively by enormous and ever-increasing quantities of nonrenewable natural resources (NNRs)—fossil fuels, metals, and nonmetallic (industrial and construction) minerals—which serve as the raw material inputs to our industrialized economies, as the building blocks that comprise our industrialized infrastructure and support systems, and as the primary energy sources that power our industrialized societies.

As an example, NNRs comprise approximately 95% of the raw material inputs to the US economy each year. America currently (2008) uses nearly 6.5 billion tons of newly mined NNRs per annum—an almost inconceivable 162,000% increase since the year 1800—which equates to approximately 43,000 pounds yearly per US citizen.

## NNR Scarcity

Unfortunately, NNRs are finite; and as their name implies, NNR reserves are not replenished on a time scale that is relevant from the perspective of a human lifespan. More unfortunately, economically viable supplies associated with the vast majority of NNRs that enable our industrialized way of life are becoming increasingly scarce, both domestically (US) and globally.

1

In fact, NNR scarcity had become epidemic by 2008, immediately prior to the onset of the Great Recession:

- Sixty eight (68) of the 89 NNRs that enable our modern industrial existence—including bauxite, copper, iron/steel, manganese, natural gas, oil, phosphate rock, potash, rare earth minerals, and zinc—were scarce domestically in 2008.

- Sixty three (63) of the 89 NNRs that enable our modern industrial existence—including aluminum, coal, copper, iron/steel, manganese, natural gas, oil, phosphate rock, potash, rare earth minerals, uranium, and zinc—were scarce globally in 2008.

While there will always be "plenty of NNRs" in the ground, there are **"not enough economically viable NNRs"** in the ground to perpetuate our industrial lifestyle paradigm going forward.

The episode of NNR scarcity that occurred immediately prior to the onset of the Great Recession marked transition points for both America and the world. The number of permanently scarce NNRs had become sufficiently large by 2008 to permanently depress future economic growth trajectories and societal wellbeing trajectories at both the domestic (US) and global levels.

**Implications of NNR Scarcity**

Domestically, US economic output (GDP) and societal wellbeing levels "peaked" permanently prior to the Great Recession. As a result, US economic output (GDP) and societal wellbeing levels will trend generally downward going forward, forever.

Globally, future worldwide economic output (GDP) and societal wellbeing trajectories "diverged" permanently from pre-recession trajectories. As a result, global economic output (GDP) and societal wellbeing levels will trend upward at a continuously declining rate (at best) over the near term, peak in the not-too-distant future, and trend downward thereafter.

Ironically, through our incessant pursuit of global industrialism, we have been eliminating— persistently and systematically—the finite and non-replenishing NNRs upon which our industrialized way of life and our very existence depend.

Because this natural resource utilization behavior, which enables our current "success"—our industrialized way of life—and which is essential to perpetuating our success, is simultaneously undermining our very existence, neither our natural resource utilization behavior nor our industrial lifestyle paradigm is sustainable. This is our "predicament".

So while global industrialism and its extraordinary levels of societal wellbeing are understandable human objectives, they are also physically impossible objectives. Our historical reality of "continuously more and more", which we have experienced since the dawn of industrialism, is being displaced by our new reality of "continuously less and less", as NNR scarcity becomes increasingly pervasive.

## Consequences of NNR Scarcity

Humanity's fate was sealed in the 18th century, at the inception of our industrial revolution. The NNR genie had been let out of the bottle and could not be put back. The episode of epidemic NNR scarcity that occurred in 2008, immediately prior to the Great Recession, was merely a harsh reminder that the historically unprecedented population levels and material living standards associated with our temporary era of industrialism are coming to an end.

Humanity's transition to a sustainable lifestyle paradigm, a pre-industrial lifestyle paradigm within which a drastically reduced human population will experience subsistence level material living standards derived exclusively from renewable natural resources (RNRs)—water, soil (farmland), forests, and other naturally occurring biota—is therefore inevitable. Our choice is not whether we "wish to be sustainable"; our choice involves the process by which we "will become sustainable".

We can choose to alter fundamentally our existing unsustainable natural resource utilization behavior and transition voluntarily to a sustainable lifestyle paradigm over the next several decades. In the process, we would cooperate globally in utilizing remaining accessible NNRs to orchestrate a relatively gradual—but horrifically painful nonetheless—transition, thereby optimizing our population level and material living standards both during our transition and at sustainability.

Alternatively, we can choose to squander Earth's dwindling NNR supplies in futile attempts to perpetuate our unsustainable industrial lifestyle paradigm, perhaps for a few decades (at most). In the process, we will deplete remaining NNR reserves to levels at which they will become insufficient to support the economic output (GDP) levels, population levels, and material living standards associated with our industrialized and industrializing nations.

Global competition for increasingly scarce natural resources will escalate into resource wars, which will escalate into global societal collapse by the middle of the 21st century, under the most optimistic scenario.

It would appear that we have made our choice, if only by default.

## The NNR Scarcity Analysis

At the core of **Scarcity** is the NNR Scarcity Analysis (Analysis), which assesses current and future NNR scarcity, both domestically (US) and globally. The Analysis provides overwhelming if not irrefutable evidence to support the preceding assertions.

The Analysis is based on comprehensive quantitative and qualitative criticality and scarcity evaluations associated with the 89 NNRs that enable our modern industrial existence, and for which the US Geological Survey (USGS) and the US Energy Information Administration (EIA) maintain detailed information regarding domestic (US) and global NNR demand, supply, pricing, and utilization.

The criticality and scarcity associated with each of the 89 analyzed NNRs are thoroughly profiled in Appendix A.

**Scarcity** is essential reading for those who correctly perceive that the world, especially the industrialized world, is in a state of decline—decline that cannot possibly be reversed by our relentless barrage of misguided economic and political "fixes". **Scarcity** will enable you to make sense of a world that is experiencing the most profound paradigm shift in human history.

**In viewing the world from our firmly entrenched anthropocentric (human-centered) perspective[1], there is always hope for a brighter future, because the implicit assumption underlying our anthropocentric perspective is that there will always be "enough" NNRs to enable a brighter future—and that humankind need only be concerned with using these NNRs to provide ever-improving material living standards for ever-increasing numbers of our ever-expanding global population.**

**In viewing the world from the broader ecological perspective[2], however, there is no hope for a brighter future, because the fundamental assumption underlying our limited anthropocentric perspective is wrong.**

# I. Nature's Role in Human Existence

**We do not inherit the earth from our ancestors; we borrow it from our children.**
– Native American Proverb

- **Ecological Resources—the Fundamental Enablers**
- **Natural Resources and Human Evolution**

## Ecological Resources—the Fundamental Enablers

From the human-centered anthropocentric perspective, boundless human ingenuity, innovation, and resulting economic activity have enabled the historically unprecedented level of societal wellbeing associated with our industrialized way of life.

**Nature's Perspective—the Broader Ecological Perspective**

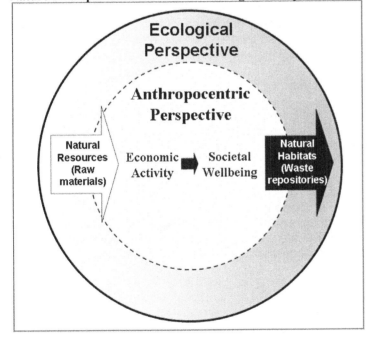

From the broader ecological perspective— Nature's[1] perspective— natural resources and natural habitats enable all life on earth, including the unprecedented level of societal wellbeing associated with humanity's industrialized way of life.

### Natural Habitats (NHs)

A habitat is the natural environment in which an organism lives, or the physical environment that surrounds (influences and is utilized by) a species population.[2] Atmospheric, aquatic, and terrestrial habitats are critical to human existence, both as areas that we physically occupy and as regenerating repositories for our wastes.

Natural habitats experience degradation both from natural phenomena such as volcanoes, fires, and floods; and from human exploitation. Fortunately, natural habitats regenerate over time through various physical and biological processes. Barring major disasters, an existing habitat will remain sufficiently robust to support life so long as periodic degradation does not exceed periodic regeneration on a persistent basis.

## Natural Resources (NRs)

A natural resource is a biotic (living or once living) entity or abiotic (nonliving) entity that exists "naturally"; that is, independent of human action.[3] Natural resources are typically classified as "renewable" and "nonrenewable".

### *Renewable Natural Resources (RNRs)*

Renewable natural resources[4]—i.e., air, water, soil (farmland), forests, and other naturally occurring biota—enable all life, including human life. RNRs provide all or most of the life supporting essentials—water, food, energy, shelter, and clothing—in pre-industrial societies.

RNR reserves are depleted by natural phenomena such as drought, soil erosion, disease, and predation; and by human exploitation. As is the case with natural habitats, RNR reserves replenish through various physical and biological processes. Barring major disasters, RNR reserves will remain sufficient to support life so long as periodic depletion does not exceed periodic replenishment on a persistent basis.

### *Nonrenewable Natural Resources (NNRs)*

Nonrenewable natural resources[5]—fossil fuels, metals, and nonmetallic (industrial and construction) minerals—enable industrialized human life.[6] [The term "industrial" as used here includes all post-agrarian societal designations such as "advanced", "modern", "developed", and "post-industrial"; all of which describe human populations that rely heavily upon nonrenewable natural resources.]

The support infrastructure within industrialized societies, the raw material inputs to industrialized economies, and the primary energy sources that power industrialized societies consist almost entirely of NNRs. NNRs are the principal sources of the tremendous real wealth[7] surpluses required to perpetuate industrialized societies.

**Industrial Lifestyle Paradigm Model**

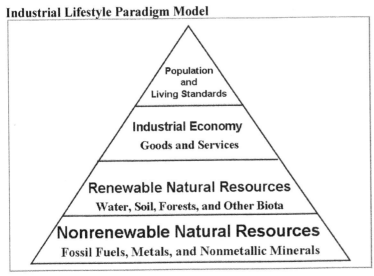

The historically unprecedented population levels and material living standards associated with our industrial lifestyle paradigm are enabled by continuous access to enormous and ever-increasing quantities of nonrenewable natural resources.

NNRs play two critical roles in enabling industrialized human existence:

- NNRs enable RNRs—water, soil (farmland), forests, and other naturally occurring biota—to be exploited in ways and at levels that are necessary to support the extraordinary population levels and material living standards associated with industrialized human societies; and
- NNRs enable the production and provisioning of manmade goods and infrastructure—e.g., airplanes, computers, skyscrapers, super-highways, refrigerators, light bulbs, communication networks, etc.—that differentiate industrialized societies from pre-industrial societies; goods and infrastructure that are inconceivable through the exclusive utilization of RNRs.

NNR reserves are depleted primarily through human exploitation; and since NNRs are not replenished through natural physical or biological processes on a timescale that is relevant from the perspective of a human lifespan[8], persistent NNR depletion will result in exhaustion.

# Natural Resources and Human Evolution

**Human Societal Wellbeing and Natural Resource Utilization**

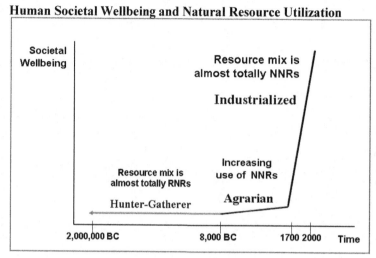

During the past 2+ million years, humanity—Homo sapiens and our hominid predecessors—evolved through three major lifestyle paradigms: hunter-gatherer, agrarian, and industrial.

Each of the three paradigms is readily distinguishable from the other two in terms of its worldview, natural resource utilization behavior, and resulting level of societal wellbeing—i.e., attainable population levels and material living standards.[9]

## The Hunter-Gatherer Lifestyle Paradigm

The hunter-gatherer (HG) lifestyle paradigm spanned over 2 million years, from the time that our hominid ancestors first stood erect on the continent of Africa to approximately 8,000 BC. HG societies consisted of small nomadic clans, typically numbering between 50 and 100 individuals, who subsisted primarily on naturally occurring vegetation and wildlife.[10]

The HG lifestyle can best be described as subsistence living for a relatively constant population that probably never exceeded 5 million globally.[11] Hunter-gatherers produced few manmade goods beyond the necessities required for their immediate survival, and they generated no appreciable wealth surplus.

The HG worldview revered Nature as the provider of life and subsistence, a perspective that fostered a passive lifestyle orientation through which hunter-gatherers sought to live—albeit somewhat exploitatively—within the environmental context defined by Nature. The HG resource mix consisted almost entirely of renewable natural resources such as water and naturally-occurring edible plant life and wildlife.[12]

## The Agrarian Lifestyle Paradigm

The agrarian lifestyle paradigm commenced in approximately 8,000 BC and lasted until approximately 1700 AD, when England initiated what was to become the industrial revolution. Agrarian societies existed primarily by raising cultivated crops and domesticated livestock.[13]

The agrarian worldview perceived Nature as something to be augmented through human effort, by domesticating naturally occurring plant and animal species. The agrarian lifestyle orientation was proactive in the sense that it sought to improve upon what Nature provided.

While modest wealth surpluses were sometimes generated by agrarian populations, agrarian existence typically offered little more in the way of material living standards for the vast majority of agrarian populations than did the HG lifestyle[14]—although the global agrarian population did increase significantly, reaching nearly 800 million by 1750 AD.[15]

The agrarian resource mix consisted primarily of RNRs, which were increasingly overexploited by ever-expanding, permanently-settled agrarian populations. As agrarian cultivation and grazing practices became increasingly intensive, renewable natural resource reserves were increasingly depleted and natural habitats were increasingly degraded as well.[16]

**The Industrial Lifestyle Paradigm**

The inception of the industrial lifestyle paradigm occurred with England's industrial revolution in the early 18th century, less than 300 years ago.[17] Today, over 1.5 billion people[18]— approximately 22% of the world's 6.9 billion total population[19]—is considered "industrialized"; and nearly three times that many people actively aspire to an industrialized way of life.[20]

Our industrialized world is characterized by an incomprehensibly complex mosaic of interdependent yet independently operating human and non-human entities and infrastructure.

**Industrial Mosaic**

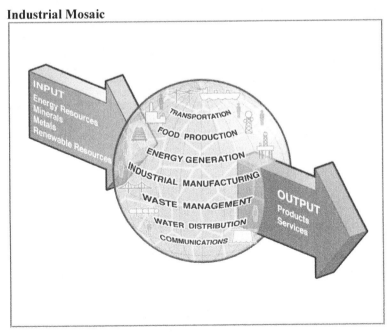

These entities must function continuously, efficiently, and collectively at the local, regional, national, and global levels in order to convert natural resource inputs into the myriad goods and services that enable our modern industrial way of life.

[Note that failures within the industrial mosaic can disrupt, temporarily or permanently, the flow of societal essentials—water, food, energy, shelter, and clothing—to broad segments of our global population.]

Tremendous wealth surpluses are typically generated by industrialized societies; such wealth surpluses are actually required to enable the historically unprecedented material living standards enjoyed by increasingly large segments of ever-expanding industrialized populations.

The industrialized worldview perceives Nature as something to be harnessed through industrial processes and infrastructure, in order to enhance the human condition. It is an exploitive worldview that seeks to use natural resources and natural habitats as the means to continuously improve human societal wellbeing—that is, to provide continuously improving material living standards for ever-increasing numbers of ever-expanding human populations.

The resource mix associated with today's industrialized societies is heavily oriented toward nonrenewable natural resources, which, in addition to renewable natural resources and natural habitats, have been increasingly overexploited since the dawn of the industrial revolution.

It is precisely this persistent overexploitation of natural resources and natural habitats—especially NNRs—that has enabled the "success" associated with the industrial lifestyle paradigm—success being defined here as continuous increases in both human population levels and human material living standards.

## America—A Unique Industrialized Society

Prior to Columbus's "discovery of America", approximately 8-10 million Amerindians resided in what is now the United States. These Amerindians and their predecessors had occupied America for over 30,000 years, living essentially as hunter-gatherers.[21] The Amerindian lifestyle paradigm was essentially sustainable; and the country was "full" in 1491 from a hunter-gatherer population perspective.[22]

American industrialism, which commenced in the late early 19th century[23], has existed for less than 200 years—less than 8 of the 80,000+ generations during which hominids have occupied the earth and the 1,000+ generations during which humans have occupied America. America is a unique industrialized society—an extreme case with regard to its worldview, resource utilization behavior, and resulting level of societal wellbeing.

### *America's Worldview*

Most Americans believe that through their heroic efforts, determination, and resolve, early American pioneers settled a vast, essentially uninhabited landmass and took control of its enormous bounty of natural resources. During the 500 years since Columbus "discovered" America, the continuously expanding American population dramatically improved its material living standards through hard work, courage, innovation, and ingenuity—they "earned it".[24]

Most Americans further believe that in the process of settling this bountiful land, they rightfully exploited Amerindians and Nature, both through divine justification[25] and self-bestowed justification. [26] Americans perceive themselves to be "exceptional" people[27]—in fact, they believe that they are the Christian god's chosen people.[28] Americans see America as the greatest nation the world has ever known, and believe that it will remain so forever.

The American worldview perceives Nature as something to be conquered, as Americans seek to achieve perpetual economic growth, population expansion, and material living standard improvement through their ever-increasing utilization of the earth's "unlimited" natural resources.

This distorted cornucopian worldview[29], which is being adopted increasingly by other industrialized and industrializing nations, is the logical outgrowth of a misinformed historical perspective and an inaccurate understanding of Nature's role in human existence.

### America's Natural Resource Utilization Behavior

America's lifestyle paradigm evolution from hunter-gatherer to agrarian to industrial has been enabled not by divine ordination or by American exceptionalism, but by fundamental shifts in America's resource utilization behavior over time, especially during the past 200 years.

**US Natural Resource Mix**

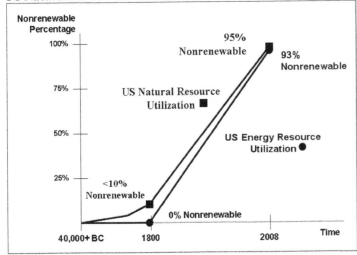

During the past 8-10 thousand years, but especially since the inception of the American industrial revolution, the mix of natural resources flowing into the US economy has shifted from "almost exclusively renewable" to "almost exclusively nonrenewable".[30, 31, 32, 33]

**US Natural Resource Utilization Levels**

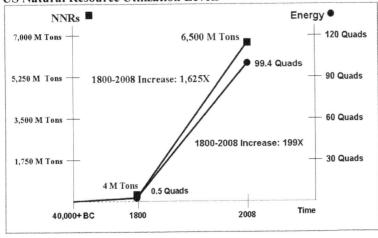

Between the years 1800 and 2008, total US NNR utilization increased over 1600 times—from nearly 4 million tons to 6,500 million tons.[34, 35]

During the same period, total US energy utilization increased by nearly 200 times—from 0.5 quadrillion BTUs to 99.4 quadrillion BTUs.[36, 37]

11

This shift in US natural resource utilization behavior has enabled Americans to continuously and dramatically expand both the mix and levels of natural resources and derived goods and services available to them, thereby establishing and perpetuating the American way of life to which most Americans currently feel entitled.

### American Societal Wellbeing

The shift in US natural resource utilization behavior has enabled the meteoric increase in American societal wellbeing over the past 200 years—ever-increasing material living standards enjoyed by an ever-increasing population.

**US Population Level and Material Living Standards**

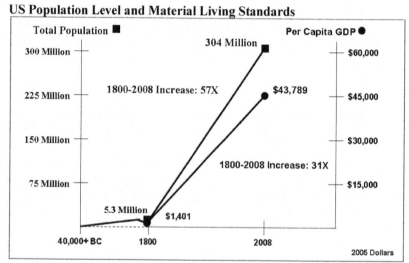

Between the years 1800 and 2008, the total US population increased by a factor of 57—from 5.3 million to 304 million.[38, 39]

During the same period, the average US material living standard (annual per capita GDP) increased by a factor of 31—from $1,401 per year to $43,789 per year.[40, 41]

While industrialized nations—especially the US—have certainly experienced historically unprecedented increases in societal wellbeing over the past several hundred years, their continued "success" is predicated upon continued access to sufficient supplies of essential natural resources, especially NNRs.

# II. NNRs

*Original sin had nothing to do with a garden and an apple; it occurred the first time one of our hominid ancestors used a nonrenewable natural resource.*

- **NNR Applications**
- **NNR Significance**
- **NNR Physical Appearance**
- **NNR Occurrence**
- **NNR "Production"**

NNRs are useful to the populations of modern industrialized and industrializing societies to the extent that they enable us to improve our societal wellbeing—the material living standards enjoyed by our industrialized and industrializing populations.

All else being equal, greater NNR quantities (economic input) enable greater levels of goods and services (economic output), which enable greater levels of societal wellbeing.

**NNRs (Economic Input) → Goods and Services (Economic Output) → Societal Wellbeing (Population Level and Material Living Standards)**

Therefore, in order to provide ever-improving material living standards for ever-increasing segments or our ever-expanding global population, we must obtain ever-increasing quantities of NNRs—specifically, "economically viable" NNRs.

## NNR Applications

All systems, networks, structures, products, and processes associated with industrialized societies are enabled, either exclusively or nearly exclusively, by NNRs. Specific NNR applications vary widely, but share common attributes as a function of NNR type: fossil fuels, metals, and nonmetallic (industrial and construction) minerals.

**Fossil Fuels**: 3 of the 89 NNRs analyzed in the NNR Scarcity Analysis are fossil fuels: coal, natural gas, and oil. Fossil fuels are carbon based energy sources that currently provide approximately 85% of the world's primary energy (2007), and are expected by the US Energy Information Administration to provide over 80% of global primary energy in the year 2035.[1]

Coal generated 27% of the world's primary energy in 2007, a percentage that is expected to increase to 28% by 2035. (EIA) Coal is used in industrial applications such as steel making, but is used primarily to generate electricity; 44% of global electricity in 2007 was generated by coal, which accounted for 64% of global coal utilization during the year.[2]

Natural gas generated 23% of global primary energy during 2007, and is expected to provide 22% of global primary energy in 2035. (EIA) Globally, 40% of natural gas is used for industrial applications and 36% is used for electricity generation (2007).[3]

"Oil" (including natural gas liquids and biofuels) provided over 35% of global primary energy in 2007, a percentage that is expected to decline to approximately 30% by 2035. (EIA) Oil is the world's leading source of transportation energy, which accounted for 53% of global oil use in 2007, and is expected to account for 61% of global oil use in 2035.[4]

Petroleum (oil and natural gas) also serves as the "feedstock" for thousands of products that are indispensible to modern industrial existence, including fertilizers, plastics, pharmaceuticals, paints, insecticides, herbicides, and various synthetic fabrics.[5]

**Metals**: 49 of the 89 NNRs analyzed in the NNR Scarcity Analysis are metals, which are elements, compounds, or alloys characterized by high electrical conductivity.[6] Metals are ideally suited to structural, electrical conductivity, and thermal (heat) conductivity applications. Specific examples include:

| Metal | Applications |
|---|---|
| Aluminum | Aluminum is used in myriad transportation, packaging, building, electrical, machinery, and consumer durables applications. |
| Cobalt | Cobalt is used as a super-alloy in gas turbine blades and jet aircraft engines; in lithium-ion, nickel-cadmium, and nickel-metal-hydride batteries; as a catalyst in liquid fuels refining; and in super magnets. |
| Copper | Copper is used as a thermal conductor, an electrical conductor (including super conducting), a building material, and a constituent of various metal alloys. |
| Germanium | Germanium is used in fiber-optic, infrared optic, thermal imaging, and semiconductor applications; and as a catalyst and in the manufacture of satellite based solar cells. |
| Magnesium | Magnesium is used as an aluminum alloy in cars, aerospace equipment, electronic devices, and beverage cans; as a zinc alloy in die casting; in the desulfurization of iron/steel; as a reducing agent in uranium production; and in titanium production. |
| Nickel | Nickel is used as an alloy in nickel steels (stainless steel) and nickel cast irons; as the cathode in rechargeable batteries including nickel-cadmium, nickel-iron, nickel hydrogen, and nickel-metal hydride; and in plating, coinage, and magnet applications. |
| Platinum Group Metals | Platinum group metals are used as components of catalytic converters, fuel cells, electronic computer and communication devices, and nuclear reactors. |
| Rare Earth Minerals | Rare earth minerals are used in batteries, lasers, magnets, oil refining, superconductors, and phosphors; also used as alloys and catalysts. |
| Titanium | Titanium is used as an alloy (with iron, molybdenum, vanadium, and aluminum); in aerospace (in jet engines, missiles, and spacecraft); in industrial processes (chemical and petro-chemical, desalination, and pulp and paper); and in medical prostheses, orthopedic implants, dental and endodontic instruments and files, dental implants, sporting goods, jewelry, and mobile phones. |
| Vanadium | Vanadium is used as an iron and steel alloy, in high speed tool steels, as a catalyst in the production of sulfuric acid, in superconducting magnets, and in surgical instruments. |

**Nonmetallic Minerals**: 37 of the 89 NNRs analyzed in the NNR Scarcity Analysis are nonmetallic minerals, also known as industrial minerals and construction minerals. Nonmetallic minerals are geological materials that have commercial value in industrial and construction applications, and are neither fossil fuels nor metals.[7] Specific examples include:

| Nonmetallic Mineral | Applications |
|---|---|
| Abrasives | Abrasives are used in grinding, polishing, buffing, honing, cutting, drilling, sharpening, lapping, and sanding applications. |
| Clays | Clays are used in making tile, ceramics, pottery, bricks, and paper; also used as oil/gas well drilling mud, as refractory agents, and as sealants. |
| Diamond (industrial) | Diamond is used in industrial cutting, grinding, and polishing applications; and in niche semiconductor applications. |
| Fluorspar | Fluorspar is used as flux in steel and aluminum production, in petroleum refining, in opalescent glass manufacture, and as the feedstock for hydrofluoric acid (used in pharmaceuticals and polymers). |
| Gypsum | Gypsum is used in the production of wallboard, plaster, and cement; also used as a soil conditioner. |
| Nitrogen (ammonia) | Nitrogen (anhydrous ammonium sulfate and urea) is one of the primary components of inorganic NPK (Nitrogen, Phosphorous, [K] Potassium) fertilizers; also used in pharmaceuticals, explosives, and cleaning products. |
| Quartz Crystal | Quartz crystal is used in computer and communication electronics applications (filters, frequency controls, and timers); also used in optical applications. |
| Sand & Gravel (construction) | Construction sand and gravel are used in brick making, road base and coverings, and concrete production. |
| Sand & Gravel (industrial) | Industrial sand and gravel are used in glassmaking, in hydraulic fracturing applications, in foundries (casting), as an abrasive (sandblasting), on icy highways, and in water filtration applications. |
| Vermiculite | Vermiculite is used as an insulator in refractories and buildings; and as a soil conditioner, packing material, fireproofing agent, absorbent, and lightweight concrete/plaster aggregate. |

Information regarding the specific applications associated with each of the 89 NNRs analyzed in the NNR Scarcity Analysis is contained in Appendix A.

## NNR Significance

As discussed in the previous chapter, NNR utilization by industrialized and industrializing nations has increased dramatically during the past several hundred years. As an example:

- America currently (2008) uses approximately 6.5 billion tons of newly mined NNRs each year, which equates to nearly 43,000 pounds per US citizen. This compares with approximately 4 million tons of total NNR utilization, or 1,500 pounds per person, in the year 1800.[8, 9]
- NNRs, as a percentage of raw material inputs to the US economy, increased from less than 10% in the year 1800 to approximately 95% today.[10, 11]

As a result of these spectacular increases in NNR utilization, the size of the US economy (GDP) increased from approximately $7.4 billion (2005 USD) in 1800 to $13.2 trillion (2005 USD) in 2008—an increase of nearly 1800 times![12]

During 2008, approximately $80 billion of nonfuel NNR inputs to the US economy were converted into nearly $2.3 trillion in finished goods output[13]—a "value added multiplier" of

15

nearly 29 times. In the case of cement alone, $10.5 billion of US cement was used to produce over $50 billion of concrete in 2008.[14]

As the following NNR extraction/production data[15] clearly indicate, global NNR utilization has increased dramatically as well.

**1958-2008 Global NNR Extraction/Production Increases (Metric Tons)**

| NNR | Annual Global NNR Extraction/Production Levels | | |
|---|---|---|---|
| | **1958** | **2008** | **1958-2008 % Increase** |
| Aluminium | 3,510,000 | 39,000,000 | 1011% |
| Bauxite | 21,400,000 | 205,000,000 | 858% |
| Cement | 262,500,000 | 2,840,000,000 | 982% |
| Copper | 3,190,000 | 15,400,000 | 383% |
| Iron Ore | 405,000,000 | 2,220,000,000 | 448% |
| Oil* | 7,661,000,000 | 26,897,000,000 | 251% |
| Phosphate Rock | 33,700,000 | 161,000,000 | 378% |
| Potash | 7,980,000 | 34,800,000 | 336% |
| Titanium Concentrates | 1,650,000 | 9,640,000 | 484% |
| Zinc | 2,950,000 | 11,600,000 | 293% |

*Oil production data are measured in barrels/year; 1960 data used instead of 1958 data.

Despite continuous improvement in efficiency, productivity, and technology; and despite NNR recycling, conservation, and reuse; global NNR extraction/production levels have increased up to ten fold during the past 50 years. And given our incessant quest for global industrialization, it is almost certain that our future NNR requirements will increase unabated in most cases.

## NNR Physical Appearance

NNRs can be obtained in various forms and grades, as determined by the extent to which they have been refined or processed. Raw, partially refined, and refined NNR forms include ores, oxides, sludge, slimes, concentrates, compounds, alloys, powders, liquids, gases, slabs, sticks, lumps, rods, granules, bars, strips, tubes, sheets, and wire—among others.[16]

Chromium, for example, can be obtained in the form of chromite ore, chromium chemicals, chromium ferroalloys, chromium metal, and stainless steel.[17] ASTM International, which develops international standards for materials, products, systems, and services used in construction, manufacturing, and transportation, recognizes 31 grades of titanium metal and alloys.[18]

## NNR Occurrence

While NNRs are essentially ubiquitous, useful or "economically viable" NNR supplies are rare in most cases.

- **Crustal Occurrences**: Huge quantities of nearly all NNRs exist in the undifferentiated earth's crust—earth's outer rocky shell, which ranges in thickness from approximately 3 miles to 30 miles.[19] Crustal NNR concentrations range from 27% for silicon and 8% for aluminum, to 60 parts per million for copper and 2 parts per million for tin, to 5 parts per billion for platinum and 0.3 parts per billion for indium.[20]

Because the mass of the earth's crust is enormous, even NNRs with very small crustal concentrations exist in large quantities within the entire undifferentiated earth's crust.

Unfortunately, crustal NNR concentrations are too small in all cases to be economically viable. For example, economically viable iron ore concentrations are at least 6 times greater than average crustal concentrations; in the case of zinc, economically viable concentrations are 30 times greater than crustal concentrations; for titanium 25-100 times greater, for copper 100-200 times greater, and for chromium 4000-5000 times greater.[21]

Mining the undifferentiated earth's crust is not a viable solution for perpetuating our industrial lifestyle paradigm.

- **Resources**: Slightly greater NNR concentrations exist in mineral deposits classified as "resources". The USGS defines a resource as a "concentration of naturally occurring solid, liquid, or gaseous material in or on the Earth's crust in such form and amount that economic extraction of a commodity from the concentration is currently or potentially feasible."[22]

As is the case with NNR occurrences in the undifferentiated earth's crust, only tiny percentages of NNRs classified as resources are currently economically viable. While some currently "sub-economic" resources might someday "become economical" through technology improvements and/or price increases, these lower quality NNRs will also generate lower economic output (GDP) and societal wellbeing levels than currently mined NNRs, owing to their higher exploration, extraction/production, and processing costs.

- **Reserves**: Economically viable NNR concentrations exist in proven deposits that the USGS classifies as "reserves" An NNR reserve is "(t)hat part of the reserve base which could be economically extracted or produced at the time of determination."[23]

NNR reserves are typically very small in comparison with NNR resources and crustal occurrences. While the size of an NNR reserve can be increased through new discoveries and through improvements in NNR exploration, extraction/production, and processing technologies, NNR reserves are also depleted through persistent extraction/production.

The salient points regarding NNR occurrence:

- While sub-economic NNR quantities are enormous, the economically viable NNR quantities that enable us to operate and perpetuate our industrialized and industrializing societies are extremely small in nearly all cases;
- The highest quality NNR occurrences are typically discovered and exploited first, leaving continuously lower quality occurrences for subsequent exploitation; and
- Globally available, economically viable NNR supplies are determined by two diametrically opposing forces that compete within an environment of ever-increasing global NNR requirements: continuously declining NNR quality—i.e., decreasing NNR deposit size, accessibility, and ore concentrations; versus continuously improving technology—increasingly cost effective NNR exploration, extraction/production, processing, and utilization techniques.

Technological improvements, which are subject to diminishing marginal investment returns, inevitably lose the battle of opposing forces—i.e., beyond some point, each incremental unit of technology investment yields smaller quantities of economically viable NNRs. The real wealth surpluses generated by successive NNR exploration and production investments decrease continuously from that point forward—initially in individual deposits, then in nations, ultimately globally.

Examples of ever-increasing extraction/production cost factors that cause diminishing marginal NNR investment returns include:

- The average depth of US oil and natural gas wells was 3,742 feet in 1950; by 2008 the average well depth increased to 5,964 feet;[24]
- The real (inflation adjusted) average cost per US oil and natural gas well was $261,000 in 1960; by 2007 the average well cost increased to $3,482,000;[25] and
- The real (inflation adjusted) average drilling cost per foot associated with US oil and natural gas wells was $62 in 1960; by 2007 the average cost per foot increased to $574.[26]

The following statement from the US Department of Energy regarding future US natural gas supplies is generally applicable to nearly all NNRs: "In the future, more of our domestic [US] natural gas supplies must come from technically challenging [expensive] resources and settings, continuing the historical trend from onshore to offshore marine environments, from shallow to deeper formations, and from conventional to more unconventional resources."[27]

# NNR "Production"

## "Production"

The term "production" when applied to NNRs is a misnomer in the sense that humans do not actually "produce" NNRs—we extract and process naturally occurring materials, from which we recover NNRs.

Because the term "production" has become widely accepted in the industry, it is used synonymously with the more accurate term "extraction" to describe the various processes by which we recover NNRs from the earth. [Note that the term "production" as used here refers to newly mined NNRs, exclusive of recycling, unless otherwise specified.]

NNRs can be produced as primary products, as is the case when iron ore is mined from an iron ore deposit; as coproducts, as is the case when silver is recovered in the process of mining copper, lead, or zinc; and as byproducts, as is the case when sulfur is recovered from petroleum refining or bismuth is recovered from tungsten, tin, or copper processing.[28]

## The NNR Production Process

NNR exploration, extraction, and processing are complex, costly, risky, and hazardous endeavors that require significant investments of financial resources, energy resources, and non-energy natural resources (such as water and infrastructure), in addition to specialized facilities, equipment, expertise, technology, and processes—which are typically unique for every NNR.

While specific production processes vary among NNRs, some or all of the following activities are generally involved in producing NNRs that are useful to humans as inputs to our industrialized economies.[29]

1.  **Exploration**: Before an NNR can be produced, it must be discovered—exploration processes must be undertaken to identify mineral concentrations that are economically viable to mine. Exploration processes range from remote sensing via satellites and aircraft, to ground based geophysical and geochemical analyses using specialized scientific instrumentation, to old time prospecting.
2.  **Pre-production**: Activities such as test drilling, feasibility studies, mine planning, environmental impact analyses, permitting, and infrastructure development must be conducted prior to the commencement of actual mining activities.
3.  **Extraction**: The extraction of "unrefined" or "raw" minerals is typically accomplished through placer mining, in which targeted minerals are found among the sediments in existing or ancient stream beds; through hard rock mining, in which targeted minerals are recovered from surface or sub-surface mining activities; or through drilling, in which fluids such as oil and natural gas are recovered from "wells".
4.  **Crushing**: Extracted materials are often pulverized, milled, or ground through mechanical processes into smaller particles to facilitate further processing.
5.  **Separation**: The isolation of the useable NNR minerals from the waste material (gangue) is typically accomplished by one or more of the following methods:
    a.  **Physical**—physical separation techniques include flotation, centrifugal force, washing, leaching, jigging, tabling, heavy media separation, and magnetic separation.
    b.  **Chemical**—chemical separation techniques involve the "reduction" of the mined material through the introduction of catalysts, reagents, and/or electricity, which isolate the NNR by causing chemical changes to the originally mined ore.
    c.  **Thermal**—thermal separation techniques facilitate NNR isolation through melting, boiling, smelting, or roasting; which are often accomplished at extremely high temperatures.
6.  **Refinement**: The purity of the separated NNR is often enhanced through various physical, chemical, and/or thermal processes to achieve the grade required by the intended application.
7.  **Alloying**: In applications involving metals, one or more complementary metals or alloys is often mixed with a primary metal such as aluminum, steel, or titanium to achieve application specific performance characteristics such as hardness, temperature resistance, corrosion resistance, and malleability.

While the preceding generalized NNR production process is by no means universally applicable or all inclusive, one NNR production trend is becoming increasingly pervasive: as NNR quality decreases due to ever-increasing exploitation, the costs, complexity, and risks associated with all NNR production activities are increasing.

# III. NNR Scarcity

*The world is flat; the earth is the center of the universe;*
*and there will always be "enough" NNRs.*

- **Economically Viable NNRs**
- **NNR Scarcity Dynamics**
- **NNR Scarcity Impacts**
- **Nature's Limits**
- **Pre-recession NNR Scarcity**

In a general sense, NNR scarcity exists whenever there is "not enough"—that is, whenever a population's NNR requirement exceeds available NNR supply.

**NNR Scarcity**

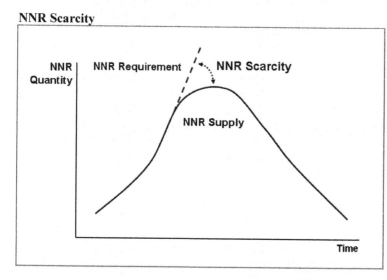

For purposes of the NNR Scarcity Analysis, NNR scarcity exists when the economically viable NNR supply available to a society is insufficient to completely address the society's NNR requirement.

That is, NNR scarcity exists when the NNR quantity (economic input) necessary to generate the mix and levels of goods and services (economic output) is insufficient to enable the society's "expected" level of societal wellbeing.

NNR scarcity negatively impacts societal wellbeing—i.e., some combination of a society's population level and average material living standard is diminished by NNR scarcity. All else being equal, the greater the incidence of NNR scarcity, the greater the negative impact on societal wellbeing

## Economically Viable NNRs

Economically viable NNRs positively impact economic output (GDP) levels, thereby improving societal wellbeing levels attainable by industrialized and industrializing nations.

## Economic Viability

**Economically Viable NNR Scenarios**

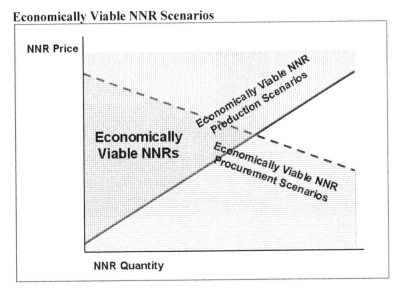

As discussed previously, total NNR quantities in the earth are enormous in all cases. The vast majority of these NNRs, however, are not economically viable. In order to be economically viable, an NNR must be economical to produce and economical to procure.

**Economically Viable NNR Production Scenarios**: the solid line defines the minimum price at which NNR producers are willing to supply each of the corresponding NNR quantities; i.e., the lowest price at which NNR producers can profitably cover the operating costs and expenses associated with supplying each NNR quantity.

At prices above the solid line, NNR producers would make additional profits. At prices below the solid line, NNR producers would suffer financial losses in the process of supplying the corresponding NNR quantity.

The solid line slopes upward because NNR producers must exploit increasingly marginal—and expensive—NNR deposits as quantities increase. NNR producers therefore require higher prices at these greater quantities to cover their operating costs and expenses.

**Economically Viable NNR Procurement Scenarios**: the dashed line defines the maximum price that NNR users are willing to pay for each of the corresponding NNR quantities; i.e., the highest price at which NNR users can profitably employ the NNR as an input to targeted investment opportunities.

At prices below the dashed line, the financial returns on targeted investment opportunities would exceed minimum requirements. At prices above the dashed line, users would suffer financial losses on their targeted investment opportunities.

The dashed line slopes downward because NNR users will initially target investment opportunities offering the highest returns; these are the investment opportunities that can profitably support the highest NNR prices. As investment returns on subsequent investment opportunities decline, the NNR prices that can be profitably supported decline as well.

## Maximum Economically Viable NNR Quantity

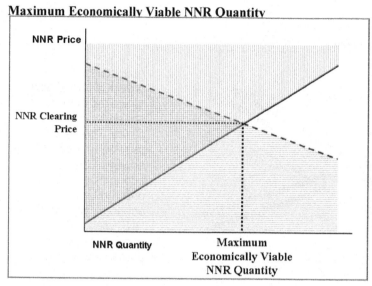

The point at which the solid line and the dashed line intersect defines the "maximum economically viable NNR quantity" and the associated clearing price level; that is, the maximum NNR quantity that is both economically viable to produce and economically viable to procure, given market conditions at a given point in time.

## Sub-economic NNRs

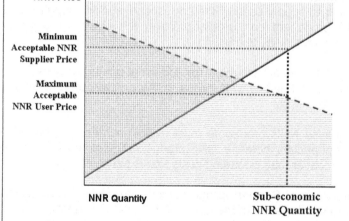

At NNR quantities greater than the "maximum economically viable NNR quantity", the minimum NNR price acceptable to NNR suppliers exceeds the maximum price acceptable to NNR users. These NNR quantities are "sub-economic"; they are neither economically viable to produce nor economically viable to procure.

In the event that NNR suppliers produce and users procure beyond the "maximum economically viable NNR quantity", human resources, natural resources, and/or financial resources are suboptimally allocated—and resulting economic output (GDP) and societal wellbeing levels are suboptimal as well.

## NNR Sufficiency and Scarcity

The terms "NNR sufficiency" and "NNR scarcity" require a reference point—i.e., an NNR quantity can only be "sufficient" or "scarce" with respect to some specified quantity. As used here, the reference point is the society's "NNR requirement"—that is, the NNR quantity required to generate the economic output (GDP) level necessary to enable the society's prevailing or "expected" level of societal wellbeing.

## NNR Sufficiency

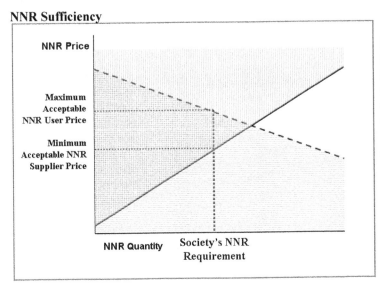

In cases where the society's NNR requirement is less than or equal to the maximum economically viable NNR quantity, the available NNR supply is "sufficient". At these quantities, the maximum prices that NNR users are willing to pay are greater than or equal to the minimum prices that NNR suppliers must charge in order to remain profitable.

Given the favorable NNR pricing structure that exists within an NNR sufficiency (surplus) scenario, NNR users would likely expand their operations and seek additional investment opportunities that employ the NNR as an input, thereby increasing their demand for the "affordable" NNR.

## NNR Scarcity

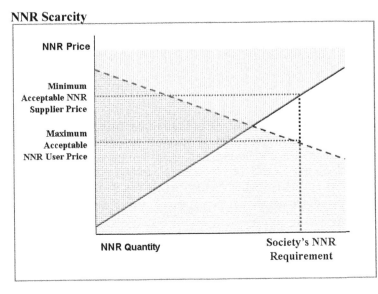

In cases where the society's NNR requirement exceeds the maximum economically viable NNR quantity, the available NNR supply is "scarce". At these quantities, the maximum prices that NNR users are willing to pay are lower than the minimum prices that NNR suppliers must charge in order to remain profitable.

Given the unfavorable NNR pricing structure that exists within an NNR scarcity scenario, NNR users would likely curtail operations and cancel or postpone marginal investment opportunities that employ the NNR as an input, thereby reducing their demand for the "overpriced" NNR.

**Physical NNR Production Limit**

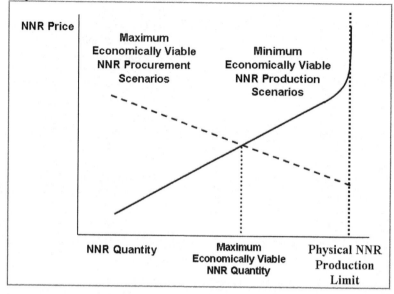

At some NNR quantity, it becomes physically impossible to increase NNR production at any price; this quantity is the physical NNR production limit.

Because economic NNR supply constraints occur well prior to the point at which incremental NNR extraction/production becomes physically impossible, and because a society's economic output (GDP) level and societal wellbeing are determined by available supplies of economically viable NNRs, the NNR Scarcity Analysis is concerned with maximum economically viable NNR quantities.

## NNR Scarcity Dynamics

### NNR Depletion

NNRs are finite; and as their name implies, NNR reserves are not replenished on a time scale that is relevant from the perspective of a human lifespan.[1] And while supplies associated with most NNRs are practically unlimited in the undifferentiated earth's crust and are typically abundant in occurrences classified by the USGS as "resources", economically viable NNR supplies—those that improve human societal wellbeing—are small and rare in most cases, extremely small and extremely rare in many cases.

**NNR Depletion Cycle**

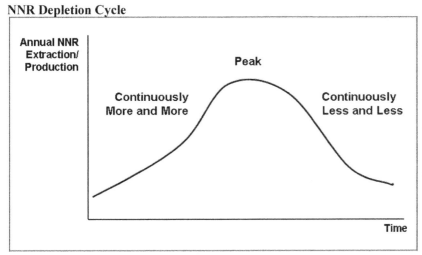

Persistent exploitation (extraction/production) will therefore deplete economically viable NNR supplies to exhaustion. The typical NNR depletion cycle is characterized by:[2]

**"Continuously More and More"**: as NNR discoveries increase and NNR exploration, extraction, production, and processing technologies improve, the large, easily accessible, high quality NNR deposits are exploited, and annual NNR extraction/production levels increase continuously.

**"Peak Extraction/Production"**: assuming unfettered—unconstrained and increasing—exploitation over time, the annual NNR extraction/production level reaches its maximum.

**"Continuously Less and Less"**: as NNR exploitation activities are relegated to fewer, smaller, less accessible, lower quality deposits, annual NNR extraction/production levels decline continuously—ultimately to exhaustion.

England offers an excellent example of "peak NNRs"—and of the associated consequences. Because England was the first nation to industrialize and to heavily exploit its domestic NNR reserves, annual extraction/production levels associated with British NNRs were among the first to peak. Lead extraction within England peaked in 1856, copper in 1863, tin in 1871, iron ore in 1882, and coal in 1913.[3]

Note that England lost its position as the world's preeminent economic and military power by the 1920s.

**NNR Lifecycle**

The NNR lifecycle is determined by both the NNR discovery cycle and the NNR depletion cycle—NNRs cannot be extracted or produced unless and until they are first discovered.[4]

## NNR Lifecycle

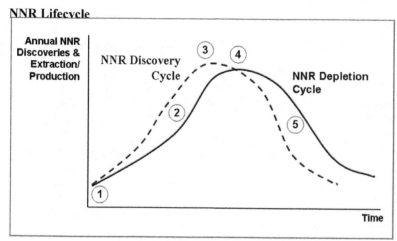

As is the case with NNR depletion, annual NNR discoveries increase initially, as the highest quality deposits are found. NNR discoveries then peak and subsequently decline, as remaining deposits decrease in terms of quantity and quality.

Note that annual NNR extraction/production levels continue to increase even after annual discoveries have peaked.

**1. First Discovery**: NNR extraction/production and NNR utilization commence with the initial NNR discovery.

**2. Increasing Reserves**: the NNR reserve level increases or "grows", as annual NNR discovery levels exceed annual NNR extraction/production levels.

**3. Peak Discovery**: the annual NNR discovery level reaches its maximum or "peak" level.

**4. Peak Extraction/Production**: the annual NNR extraction/production level reaches its maximum or "peak" level.

**5. Decreasing Reserves**: the NNR reserve level decreases, as annual NNR extraction/production levels exceed annual NNR discovery levels.

Note that the following relationship holds true with respect to NNRs individually, in combination, and in the aggregate: declining NNR discoveries beget declining NNR extraction/production levels, which beget declining NNR economic input levels, which cause declining economic output (GDP) levels, which cause declining societal wellbeing levels.

**Declining NNR Discoveries → Declining NNR Extraction/Production Levels →
Declining NNR Input → Declining Economic Output (GDP) →
Declining Societal Wellbeing (Population Level and Material Living Standards)**

**Declining NNR Quality**

The "bell shaped" NNR discovery and depletion functions result from the fact that the higher quality—i.e., the most economically viable to produce—NNR deposits are typically discovered and exploited initially, leaving the lower quality—i.e., the least economically viable to produce—deposits for subsequent discovery and exploitation.[5]

NNR quality—typically defined in terms of the ore concentration and purity associated with NNR deposits—therefore declines, on average, over time. For example:

- The average grade of US copper ores declined from 4% in 1900 to 1.2% in 1940, to 0.47% in 1980, to 0.44% in 2000.[6]
- The average grade of Australian lead ores declined from 16% in 1900 to 4% in 2000; Australian zinc ore quality declined from 12% to 7% during the same period.[7]
- Iron ore mined in the US prior to WWII consisted primarily of hematite ores, which ranged in grade from 60%-70% iron ore concentration. As these deposits were mined out, the US was forced to rely increasingly on lower quality taconite deposits, which average approximately 30% iron ore concentration.[8]
- USSR manganese ore grades declined from 35.8% to 31.2% in only 10 years, between 1970 and 1980.[9]

As NNR quality declines, each incremental unit of NNR becomes increasingly expensive to extract/produce, which is reflected in increasing NNR prices and decreasing NNR demand. As this process unfolds, annual NNR extraction/production levels increase at a decreasing rate, peak, and then decline—causing the NNR depletion function to approximate the shape of a bell curve.

[Note that if NNRs were homogeneous in terms of quality and extraction costs, NNRs would deplete in a linear manner with a positive (upward) slope, assuming increasing demand over time. As the last unit of NNR was extracted, total exhaustion would occur and NNR extraction would fall to zero instantaneously. This, of course, is not the case.]

## NNR Scarcity Impacts

While NNR scarcity is always detrimental to societal wellbeing, some instances of NNR scarcity are more detrimental than others.

- Every instance of NNR scarcity adversely impacts one or more economic outputs, and consequently adversely impacts societal wellbeing as well;
- Scarcity associated with an indispensible NNR, such as oil, is obviously more detrimental to economic output and societal wellbeing levels than scarcity associated with a less critical NNR, such as cesium; and
- NNR scarcity can be causal or compounding—that is, scarcity associated with NNR "A" can cause scarcity associated with NNR "B"; or, scarcity associated with NNR "A" can amplify the impact of scarcity associated with NNR "B".

## Nature's Limits

As NNR exploitation continues unabated, instances of NNR scarcity become increasingly severe.

## Temporary NNR Scarcity

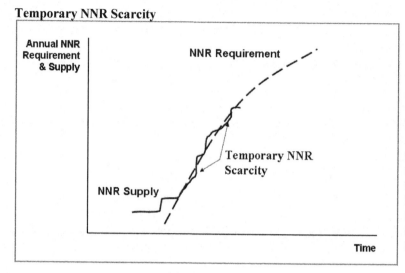

**Temporary NNR Scarcity**

Temporary NNR scarcity occurs when the economically viable supply associated with an NNR becomes temporarily insufficient to generate the level of economic output (GDP) that is required to enable a society's prevailing or expected level of societal wellbeing.

That is, when the economically viable NNR supply level temporarily falls short of the society's "required" NNR level.

Temporary NNR scarcity is exemplified by the "commodity boom/bust cycles" that have characterized most NNRs since the inception of our industrial revolution.[10]

- Increasing user demand during a "boom" phase causes increasing NNR price levels, as available NNR supplies become increasingly constrained.
- Increasing NNR price levels spur increased mining activity, typically at increasingly marginal sites, in an effort to bring on the incremental supply necessary to completely fulfill increasing demand.
- The incremental NNR supply, which is typically more costly to produce, further increases NNR price levels.
- Increasing NNR prices force prospective users to postpone or cancel marginally profitable investment opportunities, thereby reducing NNR demand.
- Reduced user demand causes NNR price levels to decrease, sometimes dramatically.
- A "bust" phase commences, as NNR suppliers are faced with declining prices, excess production capacity, and excess inventories.

Historically, as NNR prices reached sufficiently low levels, user demand would again increase, thereby triggering a subsequent boom phase and precipitating another round of temporary NNR scarcity.

Temporary NNR scarcity also results from exogenous events such as earthquakes, hurricanes, mine floods, mine cave-ins, power shortages, and worker strikes; and from geopolitical actions such as export/import quotas, tariffs, and embargos.

Fortunately, because the shortfalls associated with economically viable NNR supplies are temporary, the detrimental impacts to the society's economic output (GDP) level and societal wellbeing are temporary as well.

## Permanent NNR Scarcity

**Permanent NNR Scarcity**

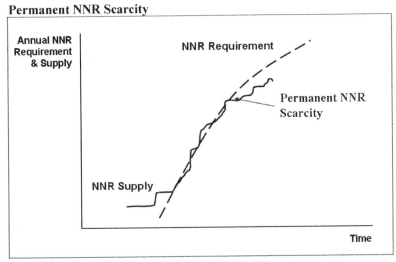

Permanent NNR scarcity occurs when the economically viable supply associated with an NNR will never again be sufficient to generate the level of economic output (GDP) that is required to enable a society's prevailing or expected level of societal wellbeing.

That is, when the economically viable NNR supply level permanently falls short of the society's "required" NNR level.

Permanent NNR scarcity typically occurs at the pre-peak inflection point on the NNR depletion curve, at which time the annual growth rate associated with economically viable NNR supply begins to decline, while the required NNR level continues to increase at its prevailing rate. From that point forward, there is no longer "enough".

Because the economically viable NNR supply level never fully recovers to the required NNR level, the society's economic output (GDP) and societal wellbeing levels never completely recover to their expected levels.

## Permanent Peak NNR Extraction/Production

**Permanent Peak NNR Extraction/Production**

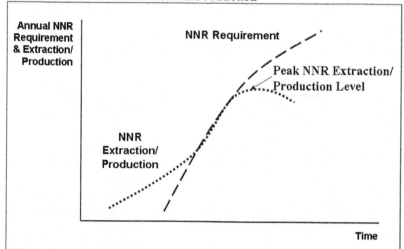

NNR extraction/ production reaches its maximum or peak level when the economically viable NNR quantity extracted/produced during the "peak year" can no longer be exceeded in subsequent years.

Peak NNR extraction/production is the consequence of diminishing marginal investment returns on NNR deposits of continuously declining quality. As NNR deposits become fewer, smaller, less accessible, and of lower grade and purity; the total annually recoverable quantities of economically viable NNRs increase at a decreasing rate, and ultimately peak (reach their maximum).

Beyond the point of peak NNR extraction/production, the annually recoverable quantities of economically viable NNRs go into terminal decline. Attempts to recover NNR quantities equal to or greater than the peak economically viable quantity, while physically possible, will result in suboptimal NNR investment returns, suboptimal aggregate economic output (GDP), and suboptimal societal wellbeing.

## Permanent Peak NNR Utilization

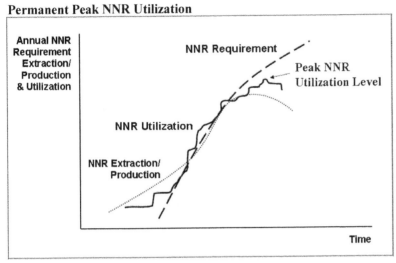

**Permanent Peak NNR Utilization**

NNR utilization reaches its maximum or peak level when the total economically viable supply of an NNR obtained from all sources—extraction/production, recycling, reuse, stocks, and inventories—during the "peak year" can no longer be exceeded in subsequent years.

Continuously declining post peak NNR utilization levels equate to continuously decreasing NNR inputs to a society's economy, which generate continuously decreasing economic output (GDP) and societal wellbeing levels.

The severity associated with decreases in economic output (GDP) and societal wellbeing resulting from declining post peak NNR utilization is determined by NNR criticality, the post peak decline rate, and the availability of technically and economically viable NNR substitutes.

## Pre-recession NNR Scarcity

NNR scarcity was epidemic at both the domestic (US) level and the global level in 2008, immediately prior to the onset of the Great Recession.

### Domestic (US) Pre-recession NNR Scarcity

America's declining industrial preeminence, declining global economic competitiveness, and declining societal wellbeing should come as no surprise. Historically abundant NNRs—the enablers of the American way of life—are becoming increasingly scarce.

**Domestic NNR Scarcity** The vast majority of the 89 analyzed NNRs were scarce domestically (US) in 2008; and, barring future reductions in domestic NNR requirement trajectories and/or major new domestic economically viable discoveries, nearly all of these NNRs will likely or almost certainly remain scarce permanently going forward.

### Domestic (US) NNR Scarcity Incidence

| Domestic (US) NNR Scarcity | Quantity | Examples of Domestic (US) NNR Scarcity |
|---|---|---|
| Scarce in 2008 | 68 (76%) | Bauxite, Chromium, Cobalt, Copper, Gypsum, |
| Almost Certain or Likely to Remain Scarce Permanently | 63 (71%) | Iron/Steel, Magnesium, Manganese, Natural Gas, Oil, Phosphate Rock, Platinum Group Metals, Potash, Rare Earth Minerals, Silicon, Titanium, Uranium, Zinc |

By 2008, immediately prior to the Great Recession, domestically available, economically viable supplies associated with 68 (76%) of the 89 analyzed NNRs were unable to completely address domestic (US) NNR requirements. 63 (71%) of the analyzed NNRs are "likely" or "almost certain" to remain scarce permanently.

NNRs that were scarce domestically (US) in 2008 and that are expected to remain scarce permanently going forward include most of the primary energy resources, metals, and nonmetallic minerals that are indispensible to perpetuating the American way of life.

**US NNR Import Reliance** The US relied on imported NNRs in the vast majority of cases in 2008.

### 2008 US NNR Import Reliance

| Domestic (US) NNR Imports | Quantity | Examples of US NNR Import Reliance |
|---|---|---|
| US Imported Some Quantity in 2008 | 69 (77%) | Chromium (66%), Cobalt (81%), Copper (31%), Magnesium (50%), Natural Gas (13%), Oil (57%), Potash (84%), Silicon (52%), Tin (80%), Titanium (54%), Uranium (78%), Zinc (71%) |
| US Imported 100% in 2008 | 19 (21%) | Bauxite, Graphite, Fluorspar, Indium, Manganese, Niobium, Quartz Crystal, Rare Earth Minerals, Tantalum, Vanadium |

The US imported some quantity of 69 (77%) of the 89 analyzed NNRs in 2008; imports in 19 (21%) of the cases accounted for 100% of 2008 US supply.

## Global Pre-recession NNR Scarcity

While the US has been able to rely on foreign imports to offset ever-increasing domestic NNR scarcity, the world has no such "safety net"—there is only one earth.

**Global NNR Scarcity** The following NNRs were scarce globally in 2008; and, barring future reductions in global NNR requirement trajectories and/or major new economically viable discoveries, the majority will likely or almost certainly remain scarce permanently going forward.

### Global NNR Scarcity Incidence

| Global NNR Scarcity | Quantity | Examples of Global NNR Scarcity |
|---|---|---|
| Scarce in 2008 | 63 (71%) | Coal, Chromium, Cobalt, Copper, Iron/Steel, |
| Almost Certain or Likely to Remain Scarce Permanently | 44 (49%) | Magnesium, Manganese, Natural Gas, Oil, Phosphate Rock, Potash, Rare Earth Minerals, Silicon, Titanium, Uranium, Zinc |

By 2008, immediately prior to the Great Recession, 63 (71%) of the 89 analyzed NNRs were scarce globally, as evidenced by upward trending price levels between 2000 and 2008. 44 (49%) of the analyzed NNRs are "likely" or "almost certain" to remain scarce permanently.

NNRs that were scarce globally in 2008 and that are expected to remain scarce permanently going forward include most of the primary energy resources, metals, and nonmetallic minerals that are indispensible to all industrialized and industrializing nations.

**Going Forward—Increasing NNR Scarcity**

So long as 1.5 billion people seek to perpetuate their industrialized lifestyles and billions more actively aspire to an industrialized way of life, global NNR requirements will increase unabated, while globally available, economically viable NNR supplies will become increasingly constrained as they approach, reach, and pass peak extraction/production and peak utilization/supply levels. NNR scarcity will become increasingly prevalent, both domestically (US) and globally.

Note that NNR scarcity does not involve "running out" of NNRs, it involves "running short" of NNRs. While there will always be "plenty of NNRs" in the ground, there will not always be "plenty of economically viable NNRs" in the ground. In fact, there are no longer "enough economically viable NNRs" in the ground, as is clearly demonstrated by the following NNR Scarcity Analysis.

# IV. Evidence: The NNR Scarcity Analysis

**Many thanks to the USGS, EIA, BEA, BLS, Fed, CBO, FBI, IEA, UN, World Bank, and countless NGOs and industry associations for providing the data "dots". I merely connected them.**

- **NNR Scarcity Analysis Overview**
- **NNR Criticality and Scarcity**
- **Domestic (US) NNR Scarcity Analysis**
- **Global NNR Scarcity Analysis**
- **NNR Scarcity and Modern Industrial Existence**
- **2008 was Different**

Because NNR scarcity has been increasing domestically (US) for decades and is now occurring with increasing frequency globally[1], and because NNR scarcity will undermine, if not preclude, the population levels and material living standards associated with today's industrialized and industrializing nations, it is critical that we understand the extent to which NNR scarcity exists today and the extent to which it is likely to exist in the immediate future.

## NNR Scarcity Analysis Overview

### NNR Scarcity Analysis Purpose

The purpose of the NNR Scarcity Analysis (Analysis) is to illustrate the extent to which NNR scarcity existed domestically (US) and globally in 2008, following the period of rapid global economic growth that immediately preceded the Great Recession; and to assess the likelihood that NNR scarcity is permanent—that is, that NNR scarcity will persist indefinitely going forward.

The Analysis consists of three sub-analyses:

- Domestic (US) NNR Scarcity Analysis;
- Global NNR Scarcity Analysis; and
- NNR Scarcity and Modern Industrial Existence.

Note that all industrialized and industrializing nations are vulnerable to NNR scarcity. No nation, with the possible exception of Russia, is even remotely close to being self-sufficient with respect to economically viable NNR supplies. The US is the subject of the NNR Scarcity Analysis because it is the extreme case.

### NNR Scarcity Analysis Data Sources

The Analysis is based on comprehensive evaluations of 89 nonrenewable natural resources (NNRs)—fossil fuels, metals, and nonmetallic (industrial and construction) minerals—that enable our modern industrial existence, and for which extensive extraction/production, utilization/consumption, and pricing data are maintained by the USGS, EIA, IEA, other credible governmental agencies, non-governmental agencies, and mineral commodity industry sources.

Detailed Profiles associated with the 89 analyzed NNRs are contained in Appendix A.

**NNR Profiles**

Associated with each NNR is an NNR Profile (See Appendix A), which contains detailed information regarding NNR criticality and scarcity. NNR Profiles follow a common format:

| NNR Profile | | | |
|---|---|---|---|
| **NNR Uses and Critical Applications** | | | |
| **Primary Uses** | | | |
| **Critical Applications** | | | |
| **NNR Criticality** | | **NNR Criticality Classification:** | |
| **Substitutes** | | | |
| **Criticality Assessment** | | | |
| **US NNR Scarcity** | **Scarce in 2008:** | **Permanently Scarce:** | |
| **2008 US Import Reliance:** | | **2008 Domestic US Supply:** | |
| **Historical US Import Trends** | | | |
| **Historical US Usage Trends** | | | |
| **US Peak Extraction Year (thru 2008):** | | **US Peak Utilization Year (thru 2008):** | |
| **Potential Geopolitical US Supply Constraints** | | | |
| **US Scarcity Assessment** | | | |
| **Global NNR Scarcity** | **Scarce in 2008:** | **Permanently Scarce:** | |
| **Historical Global Extraction Trends** | | | |
| **Global Peak Extraction Year (thru 2008):** | | **Years to Global Reserve Exhaustion:** | |
| **Projected Global Peak Extraction Year:** | | **Projected Global Peak Supply Year:** | |
| **Interdependencies** | | | |
| **Global Scarcity Assessment** | | | |

## NNR Criticality and NNR Scarcity

NNR "criticality" considers the importance associated with each NNR in perpetuating our modern industrial existence, while NNR "scarcity" considers the relationship between a population's requirement for an NNR and its availability (supply).

An NNR can be critical to modern industrial existence, yet be sufficiently abundant (not scarce)—bauxite in 2008 is a case in point. On the other hand, an NNR can be scarce, yet play only a peripheral (non-critical) role in perpetuating our industrialized way of life—barite in 2008 is an example.

## NNR Criticality Classifications

Each NNR plays an important role in perpetuating our modern industrial existence; some NNRs, however, play more important roles than others. The NNR criticality assessment considers the role played by each NNR in producing, provisioning, and supporting the infrastructure, goods, and services that enable global industrialism.

Information sources used in determining NNR criticality include the NNR Profiles and several recent domestic (US) and international studies and forums pertaining to NNR criticality.[2] The following NNR criticality classifications are used in the NNR Scarcity Analysis:

- **Indispensible**: used ubiquitously to provide one or more societal essentials—water, food, energy, and infrastructure—to an entire industrialized population; substitutes are extremely limited or nonexistent.
- **Critical**: used extensively to provide one or more societal essentials—water, food, energy, and infrastructure—to broad segments of an industrialized population; substitutes are limited.
- **Important**: used to provide one or more societal essentials—water, food, energy, and infrastructure—to limited segments of an industrialized population; technically viable substitutes are typically available.
- **Declining**: use is in general decline, typically due to toxicity, safety issues, or adverse environmental impacts.

## NNR Scarcity Definitions

In a general sense, NNR scarcity exists when the economically viable NNR supply available to a society is insufficient to completely address the society's NNR requirement, which is the NNR quantity (economic input) necessary to generate the mix and levels of goods and services (economic output) required to enable the society's "expected" level of societal wellbeing, which for industrialized humanity equates to ever-improving material living standards for ever-increasing numbers of our ever-expanding global population.

For purposes of the Analysis, scarcity associated with each of the 89 analyzed NNRs was assessed during the year 2008—the culmination of the global economic growth period from approximately 2000 to 2008 that immediately preceded the Great Recession.

The Analysis also considers the likelihood that scarcity associated with each of the 89 analyzed NNRs is permanent; that is, the likelihood that the episode of NNR scarcity evidenced in 2008 will persist indefinitely going forward.

### *Domestic (US) NNR Scarcity Definition*

An NNR is considered "scarce" domestically (US) in the event that domestically available, economically viable NNR supplies were insufficient to completely address domestic requirements in 2008. In such cases, the US relied on (net) foreign NNR imports in 2008 to completely address domestic requirements.

An NNR is considered "permanently scarce" domestically (US) in the event that domestically available, economically viable NNR supplies will likely or almost certainly never be sufficient to completely address future domestic NNR requirements on a continuous basis. The US will be forced to rely on (net) foreign NNR imports indefinitely.

### Global NNR Scarcity Definition

An NNR is considered "scarce" globally in the event that globally available NNR supplies[3] between the years 2000 and 2008 were insufficient to prevent an inflation adjusted NNR price level increase[4] during the 2000-2008 period. In such cases, the 2008 globally available, economically viable NNR supply was insufficient to completely address the 2008 global NNR requirement.

(See Appendix B for 2000 and 2008 global extraction/production levels, 2000 and 2008 price levels, and 2000-2008 percentage changes in the extraction/production levels and price levels associated with each of the 89 analyzed NNRs.)

Specifically:

If the annual global NNR supply level increased between 2000 and 2008, and:

- The NNR price level increased between 2000 and 2008 as well, the NNR was considered "scarce" in 2008 because global NNR supplies, while increasing between 2000 and 2008, remained insufficient to prevent a price level increase during the period.
- The NNR price level decreased or remained unchanged between 2000 and 2008, the NNR was considered "not scarce" because increasing global NNR supplies were sufficient to prevent a price level increase during the period.

If the annual global NNR supply level decreased between 2000 and 2008, and:

- The NNR price level increased between 2000 and 2008, the NNR was considered "scarce" in 2008 because global NNR supplies could not be increased during the period, much less increased sufficiently to prevent a price level increase.
- The NNR price level decreased between 2000 and 2008, the NNR was considered "not scarce" in 2008 because global NNR supplies, while decreasing between 2000 and 2008, remained sufficient to prevent a price level increase during the period.

An NNR is considered "permanently scarce" globally in the event that globally available, economically viable NNR supplies will likely or almost certainly never be sufficient to completely address future global requirements on a continuous basis.

As we attempt to reestablish our pre-recession global economic growth rate, the NNR price level will increase as increasingly marginal and expensive NNR deposits are exploited, thereby curbing global NNR demand and rendering globally available, economically viable NNR supplies insufficient to completely address our global NNR requirement.

## Domestic (US) NNR Scarcity Analysis

The following table summarizes domestic (US) criticality and scarcity associated with each of the 89 analyzed NNRs; salient findings include:

- An overwhelming majority—68 of the 89 analyzed NNRs—were considered "scarce" domestically (US) in 2008, immediately prior to the Great Recession; most (58) are almost certain to remain scarce permanently; (See Appendix C for Permanent US NNR Scarcity Definitions.)
- The US imported some quantity of 69 of the 89 analyzed NNRs in 2008; imports associated with 19 of the NNRs accounted for 100% of 2008 US supply;
- Annual domestic (US) extraction/production levels associated with a sizeable majority, 61 of the 89 analyzed NNRs, have almost certainly peaked permanently; (See Appendix C for Permanent US Peak NNR Extraction/Production Level Definitions.) and
- Annual domestic (US) utilization levels associated with a majority, 50 of the 89 analyzed NNRs, have likely peaked permanently. (See Appendix C for Permanent US Peak NNR Utilization Level Definitions.)

2008 Domestic (US) NNR Scarcity Summary

| Nonrenewable Natural Resource (NNR) | NNR Criticality | Domestic (US) Scarcity | | 2008 US Import Percent | US NNR Limits | | | |
|---|---|---|---|---|---|---|---|---|
| | | In 2008 | Permanent | | US Extraction/ Production Peak | | US Utilization Peak | |
| | | | | | Year | Permanent | Year | Permanent |
| Abrasives (Manufactured) | Critical | Yes | Almost Certain | 76% | 1974 | Almost Certain | 1974 | Likely |
| Abrasives (Natural) | Declining | No | Unlikely | 0% | 2008 | Unclear | 1979 | Likely |
| Aluminum | Indispensible | Yes | Almost Certain | 24% | 1980 | Almost Certain | 1999 | Likely |
| Antimony | Critical | Yes | Almost Certain | 93% | 1948 | Almost Certain | 1997 | Likely |
| Arsenic | Critical | Yes | Almost Certain | 100% | 1944 | Almost Certain | 1942 | Likely |
| Asbestos | Important | Yes | Unclear | 100% | 1973 | Almost Certain | 1973 | Likely |
| Barite | Important | Yes | Almost Certain | 80% | 1981 | Almost Certain | 1981 | Likely |
| Bauxite | Indispensible | Yes | Almost Certain | 100% | 1943 | Almost Certain | 1974 | Likely |
| Beryllium | Critical | Yes | Unclear | 17% | 1980 | Almost Certain | 1999 | Likely |
| Bismuth | Critical | Yes | Almost Certain | 94% | -0- | Almost Certain | 2007 | Unlikely |
| Boron | Critical | No | Unclear | 0% | 1995 | Unclear | 1978 | Likely |
| Bromine | Important | Yes | Likely | 12% | 1997 | Almost Certain | 2005 | Unlikely |
| Cadmium | Important | No | Unclear | 0% | 1969 | Likely | 1969 | Likely |
| Cement | Indispensible | Yes | Unclear | 11% | 2005 | Unclear | 2005 | Unlikely |
| Cesium | Important | Yes | Almost Certain | 100% | -0- | Almost Certain | 1984 | Inconclusive |
| Chromium | Indispensible | Yes | Almost Certain | 66% | 1956 | Almost Certain | 1965 | Likely |
| Clays | Indispensible | No | Unlikely | 0% | 1973 | Unclear | 1973 | Likely |
| Coal | Indispensible | No | Unclear | 0% | 2008 | Unlikely | 2007 | Unlikely |
| Cobalt | Indispensible | Yes | Almost Certain | 81% | 1958 | Almost Certain | 2005 | Unlikely |
| Copper | Indispensible | Yes | Almost Certain | 31% | 1998 | Almost Certain | 1999 | Likely |
| Diamond (Industrial) | Important | Yes | Almost Certain | 91% | 2008 | Unclear | 2008 | Unlikely |
| Diatomite | Important | No | Unlikely | 0% | 2006 | Unlikely | 2006 | Unlikely |
| Feldspar | Important | Yes | Almost Certain | 32% | 1997 | Almost Certain | 1997 | Likely |

2008 Domestic (US) NNR Scarcity Summary (continued)

| Nonrenewable Natural Resource (NNR) | NNR Criticality | US NNR Limits | | | | | | |
| --- | --- | --- | --- | --- | --- | --- | --- | --- |
| | | Domestic (US) Scarcity | | 2008 US Import Percent | US Extraction/ Production Peak | | US Utilization Peak | |
| | | In 2008 | Permanent | | Year | Permanent | Year | Permanent |
| Fluorspar | Critical | Yes | Almost Certain | 100% | 1944 | Almost Certain | 1973 | Likely |
| Gallium | Critical | Yes | Almost Certain | 99% | 1978 | Almost Certain | 2000 | Unclear |
| Garnet | Important | Yes | Almost Certain | 37% | 1998 | Almost Certain | 2007 | Unlikely |
| Gemstones | Important | Yes | Almost Certain | 99% | 1991 | Almost Certain | 2007 | Unlikely |
| Germanium | Critical | Yes | Almost Certain | 90% | 1981 | Almost Certain | 2007 | Unlikely |
| Gold | Important | No | Unclear | 0% | 1998 | Likely | 1998 | Likely |
| Graphite (Natural) | Critical | Yes | Almost Certain | 100% | 1907 | Almost Certain | 1978 | Likely |
| Gypsum | Indispensible | Yes | Almost Certain | 24% | 2006 | Unclear | 2006 | Unlikely |
| Hafnium | Important | Yes | Unclear | 8% | 1983 | Almost Certain | 2003 | Unclear |
| Helium | Important | No | Unlikely | 0% | 1967 | Unclear | 2000 | Unclear |
| Indium | Critical | Yes | Almost Certain | 100% | 1966 | Almost Certain | 2008 | Unlikely |
| Iodine | Critical | Yes | Almost Certain | 72% | 1992 | Almost Certain | 2002 | Unclear |
| Iron Ore | Indispensible | No | Unclear | 0% | 1953 | Likely | 1954 | Likely |
| Iron/Steel | Indispensible | Yes | Likely | 13% | 1973 | Almost Certain | 1973 | Likely |
| Kyanite | Important | No | Unlikely | 0% | 2007 | Unlikely | 2008 | Unlikely |
| Lead | Critical | Yes | Almost Certain | 16% | 1970 | Almost Certain | 1999 | Likely |
| Lime | Critical | No | Unlikely | 1% | 2006 | Unlikely | 2006 | Unlikely |
| Lithium | Critical | Yes | Almost Certain | >50% | 1954 | Almost Certain | 1974 | Likely |
| Magnesium Compounds | Critical | Yes | Almost Certain | 54% | 1966 | Almost Certain | 1966 | Likely |
| Magnesium Metal | Indispensible | Yes | Almost Certain | 50% | 1943 | Almost Certain | 1997 | Likely |
| Manganese | Indispensible | Yes | Almost Certain | 100% | 1918 | Almost Certain | 1973 | Likely |
| Mercury | Declining | No | Unclear | 0% | 1943 | Likely | 1964 | Likely |

2008 Domestic (US) NNR Scarcity Summary (continued)

| Nonrenewable Natural Resource (NNR) | NNR Criticality | US NNR Limits | | | | | | |
| --- | --- | --- | --- | --- | --- | --- | --- | --- |
| | | Domestic (US) Scarcity | | 2008 US Import Percent | US Extraction/ Production Peak | | US Utilization Peak | |
| | | In 2008 | Permanent | | Year | Permanent | Year | Permanent |
| Mica (Scrap and Flake) | Important | Yes | Almost Certain | 18% | 1984 | Almost Certain | 2006 | Unlikely |
| Mica (Sheet) | Declining | Yes | Almost Certain | 100% | 1943 | Almost Certain | 1950 | Likely |
| Molybdenum | Critical | No | Unclear | 0% | 1980 | Unclear | 2006 | Unlikely |
| Natural Gas | Indispensible | Yes | Likely | 13% | 1973 | Unclear | 2008 | Unlikely |
| Nickel | Critical | Yes | Almost Certain | 34% | 1997 | Almost Certain | 1974 | Likely |
| Niobium | Critical | Yes | Almost Certain | 100% | -0- | Almost Certain | 2006 | Unlikely |
| Nitrogen (Ammonia) | Indispensible | Yes | Almost Certain | 42% | 1980 | Almost Certain | 1998 | Likely |
| Oil | Indispensible | Yes | Almost Certain | 57% | 1970 | Almost Certain | 2005 | Unclear |
| Peat | Declining | Yes | Almost Certain | 57% | 1987 | Almost Certain | 2005 | Unlikely |
| Perlite | Important | Yes | Almost Certain | 26% | 1999 | Almost Certain | 2000 | Unclear |
| Phosphate Rock | Indispensible | Yes | Likely | 4% | 1980 | Almost Certain | 1998 | Likely |
| Platinum Group Metals (PGM) | Indispensible | Yes | Almost Certain | 89% | 2002 | Unclear | 2008 | Unlikely |
| Potash | Indispensible | Yes | Almost Certain | 84% | 1967 | Almost Certain | 1979 | Likely |
| Pumice | Important | Yes | Unclear | 6% | 2006 | Unlikely | 2004 | Unclear |
| Quartz Crystal | Critical | Yes | Almost Certain | 100% | 1984 | Almost Certain | 1943 | Likely |
| Rare Earth Minerals (REM) | Indispensible | Yes | Almost Certain | 100% | 1984 | Almost Certain | 1990 | Likely |
| Rhenium | Critical | Yes | Almost Certain | 85% | 1991 | Almost Certain | 2008 | Unlikely |
| Rubidium | Important | Yes | Almost Certain | 100% | ? | Almost Certain | Inconclusive | |
| Salt | Critical | Yes | Likely | 21% | 2008 | Unclear | 2008 | Unlikely |
| Sand & Gravel (Construction) | Indispensible | No | Unlikely | 0% | 2006 | Unlikely | 2006 | Unlikely |
| Sand & Gravel (Industrial) | Indispensible | No | Unlikely | 0% | 2005 | Unlikely | 1979 | Likely |
| Selenium | Important | No | Unclear | 0% | 1969 | Likely | 1969 | Likely |

2008 Domestic (US) NNR Scarcity Summary (continued)

| Nonrenewable Natural Resource (NNR) | NNR Criticality | Domestic (US) Scarcity | | US NNR Limits | | | | |
|---|---|---|---|---|---|---|---|---|
| | | In 2008 | Permanent | 2008 US Import Percent | US Extraction/ Production Peak | | US Utilization Peak | |
| | | | | | Year | Permanent | Year | Permanent |
| Silicon | Indispensible | Yes | Almost Certain | 52% | 1979 | Almost Certain | 2000 | Unclear |
| Silver | Critical | Yes | Almost Certain | 67% | 1916 | Almost Certain | 2003 | Unclear |
| Soda Ash | Important | No | Unlikely | 0% | 2008 | Unlikely | 1990 | Likely |
| Sodium Sulfate | Important | No | Unclear | 0% | 1968 | Likely | 1973 | Likely |
| Stone (Crushed) | Indispensible | No | Unlikely | 1% | 2006 | Unlikely | 2006 | Unlikely |
| Stone (Dimension) | Important | Yes | Almost Certain | 87% | 1931 | Almost Certain | 2007 | Unlikely |
| Strontium | Important | Yes | Almost Certain | 100% | 1943 | Almost Certain | 1999 | Likely |
| Sulfur | Indispensible | Yes | Almost Certain | 25% | 1981 | Almost Certain | 1995 | Likely |
| Talc | Declining | No | Unclear | 0% | 1979 | Likely | 1990 | Likely |
| Tantalum | Critical | Yes | Almost Certain | 100% | -0- | Almost Certain | 1974 | Likely |
| Tellurium | Critical | Yes | Almost Certain | 40% | 1960 | Almost Certain | 1979 | Inconclusive |
| Thallium | Important | Yes | Almost Certain | 100% | 1977 | Almost Certain | 1970 | Likely |
| Thorium | Declining | Yes | Almost Certain | 100% | 1961 | Almost Certain | 1972 | Likely |
| Tin | Critical | Yes | Almost Certain | 80% | 1945 | Almost Certain | 1950 | Likely |
| Titanium Mineral Con. | Indispensible | Yes | Almost Certain | 78% | 1964 | Almost Certain | 1997 | Likely |
| Titanium Metal | Indispensible | Yes | Almost Certain | 71% | 1989 | Almost Certain | 2007 | Unlikely |
| Tungsten | Critical | Yes | Almost Certain | 60% | 1955 | Almost Certain | 1954 | Likely |
| Uranium | Critical | Yes | Almost Certain | 65% | 1981 | Almost Certain | 1960 | Likely |
| Vanadium | Critical | Yes | Almost Certain | 100% | 1981 | Almost Certain | 2005 | Unclear |
| Vermiculite | Declining | Yes | Almost Certain | 40% | 1973 | Almost Certain | 1973 | Likely |
| Zinc | Indispensible | Yes | Almost Certain | 71% | 1969 | Almost Certain | 1999 | Likely |
| Zirconium | Critical | No | Unclear | 0% | 1989 | Likely | 1988 | Likely |

**Domestic (US) NNR Scarcity**

**2008 Domestic (US) NNR Scarcity Summary**

| Domestic (US) NNR Scarcity | NNR Criticality | | | | Total |
|---|---|---|---|---|---|
| | Indispensible | Critical | Important | Declining | |
| **2008 US NNR Scarcity** | | | | | |
| Scarce | 22 | 26 | 16 | 4 | **68** |
| Not Scarce (Sufficient) | 6 | 4 | 8 | 3 | **21** |
| Inconclusive | 0 | 0 | 0 | 0 | **0** |
| **Totals** | **28** | **30** | **24** | **7** | **89** |
| | | | | | |
| **Permanent US NNR Scarcity** | | | | | |
| Almost Certain | 18 | 24 | 12 | 4 | **58** |
| Likely | 3 | 1 | 1 | 0 | **5** |
| Unclear | 3 | 4 | 7 | 2 | **16** |
| Unlikely | 4 | 1 | 4 | 1 | **10** |
| Inconclusive | 0 | 0 | 0 | 0 | **0** |
| **Totals** | **28** | **30** | **24** | **7** | **89** |

68 of the 89 analyzed NNRs were "scarce" domestically (US) in 2008—i.e., domestically available, economically viable NNR supplies were insufficient to completely address domestic requirements. The US was therefore reliant to some extent on (net) foreign NNR imports in 2008.

Of the 68 domestically scarce NNRs:

- 22 NNRs—including aluminum, copper, iron/steel, natural gas, oil, phosphate rock, potash, rare earth minerals, titanium, and zinc—are indispensible to modern industrial existence; and
- 26 NNRs—including gallium, graphite, indium, lithium, niobium, tin, uranium, and vanadium—are critical to modern industrial existence.

21 of the 89 analyzed NNRs were "not scarce"[5] domestically (US) in 2008—the US was not reliant on net foreign NNR imports in 2008.

Of the 21 domestically sufficient NNRs:

- 6 NNRs—including clays, coal, iron ore, sand and gravel, and crushed stone—are indispensible to modern industrial existence; and
- 4 NNRs—including boron, lime, and molybdenum—are critical to modern industrial existence.

Barring future reductions in domestic (US) NNR requirement trajectories and/or major new domestic economically viable discoveries, 63 of the 89 analyzed NNRs are either "almost certain" or "likely" to remain scarce permanently going forward:

- 58 NNRs—including aluminum, copper, lithium, oil, potash, rare earth minerals, tin, titanium, uranium, and zinc—are "almost certain" to remain scarce domestically; and
- 5 NNRs—including iron/steel, natural gas, and phosphate rock—are "likely" to remain scarce domestically.

Only 10 of the 89 analyzed NNRs—including clays, helium, lime, sand and gravel, soda ash, and crushed stone—are "unlikely" to become permanently scarce domestically (US) in the immediate future.

## Domestic (US) NNR Import Reliance

US NNR import reliance increased steadily during the 20th century and into the 21st century. By 2008, the US imported some amount of 69 NNRs, and imported 100% of 19 NNRs.

**2008 US NNR Import Reliance**

| US Import Percentage | NNR # | NNRs Imported by the US |
|---|---|---|
| 1%-20% | 10 | Beryllium, **Cement**, **Iron/Steel**, Lead, Lime, Mica (sheet), **Natural Gas**, **Phosphate Rock**, Pumice, **Stone (crushed)** |
| 21%-40% | 11 | **Aluminum**, Bromine, **Copper**, Feldspar, Garnet, **Gypsum**, Nickel, Perlite, Salt, **Sulfur**, Vermiculite |
| 41%-60% | 9 | Lithium, Magnesium Compounds, **Magnesium Metal**, **Nitrogen (ammonia)**, **Oil**, Peat, **Silicon**, **Titanium Metal**, Tungsten |
| 61%-80% | 7 | Barite, **Chromium**, Silver, Tin, **Titanium Concentrates**, Uranium, **Zinc** |
| 81%-99% | 11 | Antimony, Bismuth, **Cobalt**, Diamond, Gallium, Gemstones, Germanium, **Platinum Group Metals**, **Potash**, Rhenium, Stone (dimension) |
| 100% | 19 | Arsenic, Asbestos, **Bauxite**, Cesium, Fluorspar, Graphite, Indium, **Manganese**, Mica (sheet), Niobium, Quartz Crystal, **Rare Earth Minerals**, Rubidium, Strontium, Tantalum, Tellurium, Thallium, Thorium, Vanadium |
| N/A (Insufficient data)* | 2 | Hafnium, Selenium |
| **Total Imported NNRs** | **69** | |

*The US produced no Hafnium or Selenium in 2008; some of each must have been imported.
**Bold: indispensible to modern industrial existence**

## Peak Domestic (US) NNR Extraction/Production

**2008 Annual Domestic (US) Peak NNR Extraction/Production Summary**

| US NNR Extraction/Production | NNR Criticality | | | | Total |
|---|---|---|---|---|---|
| | Indispensible | Critical | Important | Declining | |
| Almost Certainly Peaked Permanently | 18 | 25 | 14 | 4 | **61** |
| Likely Peaked Permanently | 1 | 1 | 4 | 2 | **8** |
| Unclear | 5 | 3 | 2 | 1 | **11** |
| Unlikely Peaked Permanently | 4 | 1 | 4 | 0 | **9** |
| Inconclusive | 0 | 0 | 0 | 0 | **0** |
| **Totals** | **28** | **30** | **24** | **7** | **89** |

Annual domestic (US) extraction/production levels associated with 69 of the 89 analyzed NNRs have "almost certainly" or "likely" peaked permanently.

- Annual domestic (US) extraction/production levels associated with 61 of the 69 NNRs—including aluminum, chromium, cobalt, copper, iron/steel, magnesium, manganese, oil, phosphate rock, potash, rare earth minerals, titanium, and zinc—have "almost certainly" peaked permanently; and

- Annual domestic (US) extraction/production levels associated with 8 of the 69 NNRs—including gold, iron ore, selenium, and zirconium—have "likely" peaked permanently.

It is "unlikely" that annual domestic (US) extraction/production levels associated with 9 of the 89 analyzed NNRs—including coal, diatomite, lime, pumice, sand and gravel, soda ash, and crushed stone—have peaked permanently.

Peak (to date) domestic (US) extraction/production occurred prior to the new millennium in 74 of the 89 analyzed cases; only 15 of the 89 analyzed NNRs had not reached domestic (US) peak (to date) extraction/production levels by the year 2000.

**Domestic (US) Peak NNR Extraction/Production Incidence**

| US Peak-to-Date 1900-1950 | US Peak-to-Date 1951-1975 | US Peak-to-Date 1976-1999 | US Peak-to-Date 2000-2008 |
|---|---|---|---|
| 13 NNRs | 28 NNRs | 33 NNRs | 15 NNRs |

[Note: it is assumed that if domestic (US) economically viable NNR extraction/production levels could be increased beyond current levels, such would be the case.[6] Doing so would:

1. Decrease US foreign NNR dependence by reducing NNR imports and associated trade deficits; and
2. Increase American economic performance (and societal wellbeing) by increasing US NNR exports, US finished goods exports, and associated trade surpluses.]

**Peak Domestic (US) NNR Utilization**

**2008 Annual Domestic (US) Peak NNR Utilization Summary**

| US NNR Utilization | NNR Criticality | | | | Total |
|---|---|---|---|---|---|
| | Indispensible | Critical | Important | Declining | |
| Likely Peaked Permanently | 17 | 17 | 10 | 6 | 50 |
| Unclear | 2 | 4 | 4 | 0 | 10 |
| Unlikely Peaked Permanently | 9 | 8 | 8 | 1 | 26 |
| Inconclusive | 0 | 1 | 2 | 0 | 3 |
| Totals | 28 | 30 | 24 | 7 | 89 |

It is "likely" that annual domestic (US) utilization levels associated with 50 of the 89 analyzed NNRs—including aluminum, clays, copper, iron ore, magnesium, manganese, phosphate rock, potash, rare earth minerals, sulfur, and zinc—have peaked permanently.

It is "unlikely" that annual domestic (US) utilization levels associated with 26 of the 89 analyzed NNRs—including coal, cobalt, gypsum, lime, molybdenum, natural gas, platinum group metals, and titanium—have peaked permanently.

## Domestic (US) NNR Scarcity Summary Assessment

Total US NNR requirements—i.e., the NNR quantities (economic inputs) necessary to perpetuate the American way of life—increasingly exceeded domestically available, economically viable NNR supplies throughout the latter half of the 20th century.

By 2008, in a sizeable majority of cases, total US NNR requirements permanently exceeded domestically available, economically viable NNR supplies. And in a majority of cases, total US NNR requirements permanently exceeded domestic (US) and imported economically viable NNR supplies combined.

- 68 of the 89 analyzed NNRs were scarce domestically (US) in 2008; 58 of these NNRs are "almost certain" to remain scarce permanently, barring future reductions in domestic NNR requirement trajectories and/or major new domestic economically viable discoveries. The US will be perennially reliant on foreign suppliers—often few in number, geographically remote, politically unstable, geopolitically adversarial, and/or increasingly unwilling or unable to fulfill American demand—for these NNRs.
- Annual domestic (US) extraction/production levels associated with 61 of the 89 analyzed NNRs have "almost certainly" peaked permanently. Going forward, US import reliance associated with these NNRs will increase as domestically available, economically viable supplies decline continuously.
- Annual domestic (US) utilization levels associated with 50 of the 89 analyzed NNRs "likely" peaked permanently. For these 50 NNRs, total annual input quantities to the US economy, from domestic (US) and foreign sources combined, are likely in terminal decline.

Going forward, 47 of the 89 analyzed NNRs are considered "at risk" domestically (US). That is, combined domestic (US) and imported economically viable supplies associated with these NNRs will likely experience increasingly severe shortages, as America attempts to reestablish and maintain its pre-recession economic output (GDP) level and growth rate on a continuous basis.

### Domestic (US) "At Risk" NNRs

| Nonrenewable Natural Resource (NNR) | NNR Criticality | Permanent US NNR Scarcity | Permanent US Peak Extraction/ Production | Permanent US Peak Utilization | Potential Geopolitical Supply Constraints |
|---|---|---|---|---|---|
| Abrasives (Manufactured) | Critical | Almost Certain | Almost Certain | Likely | 83% of US fused aluminum oxide and crude silicon carbide imports come from China. |
| Aluminum | Indispensible | Almost Certain | Almost Certain | Likely | 56% of US aluminum imports come from Canada. |
| Antimony | Critical | Almost Certain | Almost Certain | Likely | 51% of US antimony imports come from China; over 50% of the proven global antimony reserves are located in China and Russia (combined). |

**Domestic (US) "At Risk" NNRs (continued)**

| Nonrenewable Natural Resource (NNR) | NNR Criticality | Permanent US NNR Scarcity | Permanent US Peak Extraction/ Production | Permanent US Peak Utilization | Potential Geopolitical Supply Constraints |
|---|---|---|---|---|---|
| Arsenic | Critical | Almost Certain | Almost Certain | Likely | 86% of US arsenic metal imports and 47% of trioxide imports come from China. |
| Barite | Important | Almost Certain | Almost Certain | Likely | 93% of US barite imports come from China. |
| Bauxite | Indispensible | Almost Certain | Almost Certain | Likely | Over 50% of proven global bauxite reserves are located in Australia and Guinea. |
| Beryllium | Critical | | Almost Certain | Likely | 58% of US beryllium imports come from Kazakhstan. |
| Bismuth | Critical | Almost Certain | Almost Certain | | Over two thirds of proven global bismuth reserves are located in China. |
| Chromium | Indispensible | Almost Certain | Almost Certain | Likely | Over 75% of proven global chromium reserves are located in South Africa and Kazakhstan (combined). |
| Cobalt | Indispensible | Almost Certain | Almost Certain | | Over half of the proven global cobalt reserves are located in the Congo. |
| Copper | Indispensible | Almost Certain | Almost Certain | Likely | 40% of US copper imports come from Chile. |
| Fluorspar | Critical | Almost Certain | Almost Certain | Likely | 52% of US fluorspar imports come from China. |
| Gallium | Critical | Almost Certain | Almost Certain | | China, Kazakhstan, and the Ukraine are 3 of the top 4 producers of unrefined gallium. |
| Germanium | Critical | Almost Certain | Almost Certain | | China produces a majority of the world's germanium. |
| Graphite (Natural) | Critical | Almost Certain | Almost Certain | Likely | 47% of US graphite imports come from China; nearly 80% of proven global reserves are located in China. |
| Gypsum | Indispensible | Almost Certain | | | China is by far the leading producer of gypsum in the world. |

**Domestic (US) "At Risk" NNRs (continued)**

| Nonrenewable Natural Resource (NNR) | NNR Criticality | Permanent US NNR Scarcity | Permanent US Peak Extraction/ Production | Permanent US Peak Utilization | Potential Geopolitical Supply Constraints |
|---|---|---|---|---|---|
| Indium | Critical | Almost Certain | Almost Certain | | 40% of US indium imports come from China; half of the proven global indium reserves are located in China. |
| Iodine | Critical | Almost Certain | Almost Certain | | 60% of proven global iodine reserves are located in China. |
| Iron/Steel | Indispensible | Likely | Almost Certain | Likely | China accounts for more than half of annual global iron ore extraction. |
| Lead | Critical | Almost Certain | Almost Certain | Likely | China accounts for 40% of global lead mine production. |
| Lithium | Critical | Almost Certain | Almost Certain | Likely | 63% of US lithium imports come from Chile; 76% of proven global lithium reserves are located in Chile. |
| Magnesium Compounds | Critical | Almost Certain | Almost Certain | Likely | 79% of US magnesium compound imports come from China. |
| Magnesium Metal | Indispensible | Almost Certain | Almost Certain | Likely | 40% of US magnesium metal imports come from Canada. |
| Manganese | Indispensible | Almost Certain | Almost Certain | Likely | Over 50% of proven global manganese reserves are located in South Africa and the Ukraine (combined). |
| Nickel | Critical | Almost Certain | Almost Certain | Likely | Nearly 40% of proven global nickel reserves are located in Australia. |
| Niobium | Critical | Almost Certain | Almost Certain | | 85% of US niobium imports come from Brazil; Brazil produces about 75% of the world's supply of niobium. |

**Domestic (US) "At Risk" NNRs (continued)**

| Nonrenewable Natural Resource (NNR) | NNR Criticality | Permanent US NNR Scarcity | Permanent US Peak Extraction/ Production | Permanent US Peak Utilization | Potential Geopolitical Supply Constraints |
|---|---|---|---|---|---|
| Nitrogen (Ammonia) | Indispensable | Almost Certain | Almost Certain | Likely | 55% of US ammonia imports come from Trinidad and Tobago. |
| Oil | Indispensable | Almost Certain | Almost Certain | ???? | Approximately 80% of the world's proven oil reserves are located in the Middle East. |
| Phosphate Rock | Indispensable | Likely | Almost Certain | Likely | 100% of US phosphate rock imports come from Morocco. |
| Platinum Group Metals (PGM) | Indispensable | Almost Certain | | | The US produces only 2% of global platinum and 6% of global palladium. |
| Potash | Indispensable | Almost Certain | Almost Certain | Likely | Over 50% of proven global potash reserves are located in Canada. |
| Quartz Crystal | Critical | Almost Certain | Almost Certain | Likely | Most US quartz crystal (cultured) imports come from China, Japan, and Russia. |
| Rare Earth Minerals (REM) | Indispensable | Almost Certain | Almost Certain | Likely | 91% of US REM imports come from China; China accounts for 95% of global REM extraction. |
| Rhenium | Critical | Almost Certain | Almost Certain | | Chile has the largest proven rhenium reserves and is the world's largest rhenium producer. |
| Silicon | Indispensable | Almost Certain | Almost Certain | | China produced 65% of the world's silicon in 2008. |
| Silver | Critical | Almost Certain | Almost Certain | | 54% of US silver imports come from Mexico. |
| Sulfur | Indispensable | Almost Certain | Almost Certain | Likely | 71% of US elemental sulfur imports and 77% of US sulfuric acid imports come from Canada. |

49

**Domestic (US) "At Risk" NNRs (continued)**

| Nonrenewable Natural Resource (NNR) | NNR Criticality | Permanent US NNR Scarcity | Permanent US Peak Extraction/ Production | Permanent US Peak Utilization | Potential Geopolitical Supply Constraints |
|---|---|---|---|---|---|
| Tantalum | Critical | Almost Certain | Almost Certain | Likely | The vast majority of proven global tantalum reserves are located in Australia (36%) and Brazil (59%). |
| Tellurium | Critical | Almost Certain | Almost Certain | | 43% of US tellurium imports come from China. |
| Thallium | Important | Almost Certain | Almost Certain | Likely | 78% of US thallium imports come from Russia. |
| Tin | Critical | Almost Certain | Almost Certain | Likely | 47% of US tin imports come from Peru. |
| Titanium Mineral Concentrates | Indispensible | Almost Certain | Almost Certain | Likely | 51% of US titanium mineral concentrate imports come from South Africa. |
| Titanium Metal | Indispensible | Almost Certain | Almost Certain | | 52% of US titanium sponge metal imports come from Kazakhstan. |
| Tungsten | Critical | Almost Certain | Almost Certain | Likely | 43% of US tungsten imports come from China; 64% of proven global reserves are located in China. |
| Uranium | Critical | Almost Certain | Almost Certain | Likely | Canada, Australia, and Kazakhstan each produce approximately one quarter of the world's annual uranium supply. |
| Vanadium | Critical | Almost Certain | Almost Certain | | China and South Africa each account for approximately 40% of proven global vanadium reserves. |
| Zinc | Indispensible | Almost Certain | Almost Certain | Likely | 68% of US zinc ore and concentrate imports come from Peru. |

The Great Recession marked a tipping point in US history. The epidemic incidence of permanent domestic (US) NNR supply constraints—i.e., permanent NNR scarcity, permanent peak NNR extraction/production levels, and permanent peak NNR utilization levels—experienced by the onset of the Great Recession, imposed permanent limits on future US economic output (GDP) and societal wellbeing levels.

# Global NNR Scarcity Analysis

The following table summarizes global criticality and scarcity associated with each of the 89 analyzed NNRs; salient findings include:

- An overwhelming majority, 63 of the 89 analyzed NNRs, were considered "scarce" globally in 2008, immediately prior to the Great Recession;
- A significant number, 28 of the 89 analyzed NNRs, is almost certain to remain permanently scarce globally going forward; and a sizeable number, 16 of the 89 analyzed NNRs, is likely to remain scarce permanently; (See Appendix C for Permanent Global NNR Scarcity Definitions.) and
- Global extraction/production levels associated with a small but significant number, 8 of the 89 analyzed NNRs, have likely peaked permanently. (See Appendix C for Permanent Global Peak NNR Extraction/Production Level Definitions.)

## 2008 Global NNR Criticality and Scarcity Summary

| Nonrenewable Natural Resource (NNR) | NNR Criticality | Global NNR Limits | | | |
|---|---|---|---|---|---|
| | | Global Scarcity | | Global Extraction/ Production Peak | |
| | | In 2008 | Permanent | Year | Permanent |
| Abrasives (Manufactured) | Critical | No | Unclear | Inconclusive | |
| Abrasives (Natural) | Declining | No | Unlikely | 1974 | Unclear |
| Aluminum | Indispensible | Yes | Unclear | 2008 | Unlikely |
| Antimony | Critical | Yes | Almost Certain | 2008 | Unlikely |
| Arsenic | Critical | No | Unclear | 2003 | Unlikely |
| Asbestos | Important | Yes | Unclear | 1977 | Unclear |
| Barite | Important | Yes | Almost Certain | 1981 | Unlikely |
| Bauxite | Indispensible | No | Likely | 2008 | Unlikely |
| Beryllium | Critical | Yes | Likely | 1961 | Likely |
| Bismuth | Critical | Yes | Almost Certain | 2008 | Unlikely |
| Boron | Critical | No | Unclear | 2004 | Unlikely |
| Bromine | Important | Yes | Unclear | 2006 | Unlikely |
| Cadmium | Important | Yes | Likely | 1988 | Unlikely |
| Cement | Indispensible | Yes | Unclear | 2008 | Unlikely |
| Cesium | Important | No | Unclear | 1982 | Likely |
| Chromium | Indispensible | Yes | Almost Certain | 2008 | Unlikely |
| Clays | Indispensible | Yes | Unclear | Inconclusive | |
| Coal | Indispensible | Yes | Almost Certain | 2008 | Unlikely |
| Cobalt | Indispensible | Yes | Almost Certain | 2008 | Unlikely |
| Copper | Indispensible | Yes | Almost Certain | 2008 | Unlikely |
| Diamond (Industrial) | Important | No | Unclear | 2007 | Unlikely |
| Diatomite | Important | No | Unlikely | 2008 | Unlikely |
| Feldspar | Important | No | Unclear | 2008 | Unlikely |
| Fluorspar | Critical | Yes | Likely | 2008 | Unlikely |
| Gallium | Critical | No | Unclear | 2008 | Unlikely |
| Garnet | Important | No | Unclear | 2006 | Unlikely |
| Gemstones | Important | No | Unlikely | 2006 | Unlikely |
| Germanium | Critical | No | Unclear | 2008 | Unlikely |
| Gold | Important | Yes | Almost Certain | 2001 | Likely |
| Graphite (Natural) | Critical | Yes | Likely | 2008 | Unlikely |
| Gypsum | Indispensible | Yes | Likely | 2007 | Unlikely |

**2008 Global NNR Criticality and Scarcity Summary (continued)**

| Nonrenewable Natural Resource (NNR) | NNR Criticality | Global NNR Limits | | | |
|---|---|---|---|---|---|
| | | Global Scarcity | | Global Extraction/ Production Peak | |
| | | In 2008 | Permanent | Year | Permanent |
| Hafnium | Important | Yes | Unclear | 1963 | Unlikely |
| Helium | Important | No | Unlikely | 2008 | Unlikely |
| Indium | Critical | Yes | Almost Certain | 2006 | Unlikely |
| Iodine | Critical | Yes | Unclear | 2006 | Unlikely |
| Iron Ore | Indispensible | Yes | Almost Certain | 2008 | Unlikely |
| Iron/Steel | Indispensible | Yes | Almost Certain | 2007 | Unlikely |
| Kyanite | Important | Yes | Unclear | 2008 | Unlikely |
| Lead | Critical | Yes | Almost Certain | 2008 | Unlikely |
| Lime | Critical | Yes | Unclear | 2008 | Unlikely |
| Lithium | Critical | Yes | Likely | 2006 | Unlikely |
| Magnesium Compounds | Critical | Yes | Unclear | 2008 | Unlikely |
| Magnesium Metal | Indispensible | Yes | Likely | 2007 | Unlikely |
| Manganese | Indispensible | Yes | Almost Certain | 2008 | Unlikely |
| Mercury | Declining | Yes | Unclear | 1971 | Unlikely |
| Mica (Scrap and Flake) | Important | Yes | Unclear | 2005 | Unclear |
| Mica (Sheet) | Declining | No | Unclear | 1975 | Unlikely |
| Molybdenum | Critical | Yes | Almost Certain | 2008 | Unlikely |
| Natural Gas | Indispensible | Yes | Almost Certain | 2008 | Unlikely |
| Nickel | Critical | Yes | Likely | 2007 | Unlikely |
| Niobium | Critical | Yes | Almost Certain | 2008 | Unlikely |
| Nitrogen (Ammonia) | Indispensible | Yes | Almost Certain | 2008 | Unlikely |
| Oil | Indispensible | Yes | Almost Certain | 2005 | Unclear |
| Peat | Declining | No | Unlikely | 1984 | Unlikely |
| Perlite | Important | Yes | Unclear | 1999 | Likely |
| Phosphate Rock | Indispensible | Yes | Almost Certain | 1988 | Unclear |
| Platinum Group Metals (PGM) | Indispensible | No | Unclear | 2006 | Unlikely |
| Potash | Indispensible | Yes | Likely | 2007 | Unlikely |
| Pumice | Important | No | Unlikely | 2007 | Unlikely |
| Quartz Crystal | Critical | Inconclusive | | 1966 | Likely |
| Rare Earth Minerals (REM) | Indispensible | Yes | Unclear | 2006 | Unlikely |
| Rhenium | Critical | Yes | Almost Certain | 2008 | Unlikely |
| Rubidium | Important | Inconclusive | | Inconclusive | |
| Salt | Critical | Yes | Unclear | 2006 | Unlikely |
| Sand & Gravel (Construction) | Indispensible | Yes | Unclear | Inconclusive | |
| Sand & Gravel (Industrial) | Indispensible | Yes | Likely | 2007 | Unlikely |
| Selenium | Important | Yes | Almost Certain | 1996 | Likely |
| Silicon | Indispensible | Yes | Likely | 2008 | Unlikely |
| Silver | Critical | Yes | Almost Certain | 2008 | Unlikely |
| Soda Ash | Important | Yes | Unclear | 2008 | Unlikely |
| Sodium Sulfate | Important | No | Unlikely | 2008 | Unlikely |
| Stone (Crushed) | Indispensible | Yes | Unclear | Inconclusive | |
| Stone (Dimension) | Important | No | Unlikely | Inconclusive | |
| Strontium | Important | Yes | Likely | 2004 | Unclear |
| Sulfur | Indispensible | Yes | Almost Certain | 2008 | Unlikely |

**2008 Global NNR Criticality and Scarcity Summary (continued)**

| Nonrenewable Natural Resource (NNR) | NNR Criticality | Global NNR Limits | | | |
|---|---|---|---|---|---|
| | | Global Scarcity | | Global Extraction/ Production Peak | |
| | | In 2008 | Permanent | Year | Permanent |
| Talc | Declining | No | Unclear | 1997 | Unlikely |
| Tantalum | Critical | No | Unlikely | 2004 | Unlikely |
| Tellurium | Critical | No | Unclear | 1974 | Likely |
| Thallium | Important | Yes | Almost Certain | 1989 | Likely |
| Thorium | Declining | Yes | Unclear | 1972 | Inconclusive |
| Tin | Critical | Yes | Almost Certain | 2007 | Unlikely |
| Titanium Mineral Con. | Indispensible | Yes | Likely | 2007 | Unlikely |
| Titanium Metal | Indispensible | Yes | Unclear | Inconclusive | |
| Tungsten | Critical | Yes | Almost Certain | 2004 | Unclear |
| Uranium | Critical | Yes | Almost Certain | 1982 | Inconclusive |
| Vanadium | Critical | Yes | Likely | 2007 | Unlikely |
| Vermiculite | Declining | No | Unlikely | 1987 | Unlikely |
| Zinc | Indispensible | Yes | Likely | 2008 | Unlikely |
| Zirconium | Critical | Yes | Almost Certain | 2007 | Unlikely |

## Global NNR Scarcity

**2008 Global NNR Scarcity Summary**

| Global NNR Scarcity | NNR Criticality | | | | Totals |
|---|---|---|---|---|---|
| | Indispensible | Critical | Important | Declining | |
| **2008 Global NNR Scarcity** | | | | | |
| Scarce | 26 | 22 | 13 | 2 | 63 |
| Not Scarce (Sufficient) | 2 | 7 | 10 | 5 | 24 |
| Inconclusive | 0 | 1 | 1 | 0 | 2 |
| **Totals** | 28 | 30 | 24 | 7 | 89 |
| | | | | | |
| **Permanent Global NNR Scarcity** | | | | | |
| Almost Certain | 12 | 12 | 4 | 0 | 28 |
| Likely | 8 | 6 | 2 | 0 | 16 |
| Unclear | 8 | 10 | 11 | 4 | 33 |
| Unlikely | 0 | 1 | 6 | 3 | 10 |
| Inconclusive | 0 | 1 | 1 | 0 | 2 |
| **Totals** | 28 | 30 | 24 | 7 | 89 |

63 of the 89 analyzed NNRs were "scarce" globally in 2008—i.e., the (inflation adjusted) price levels associated with these NNRs increased between 2000 and 2008.

In some cases, the 2000-2008 price level increases were significant (50%-100%):

| 2000-2008 Price Increases for Globally Scarce NNRs | 2000-2008 Price Increases for Globally Scarce NNRs |
|---|---|
| Coal: 52% | Rare Earth Minerals: 58% |
| Cobalt: 84% | Rhenium: 86% |
| Magnesium: 99% | Silicon: 59% |
| Nickel: 96% | Zirconium: 68% |

In other cases, the 2000-2008 price level increases were extraordinary (100%+):

| 2000-2008 Price Increases for Globally Scarce NNRs | 2000-2008 Price Increases for Globally Scarce NNRs | 2000-2008 Price Increases for Globally Scarce NNRs |
|---|---|---|
| Antimony: 243% | Lead: 121% | Selenium: 572% |
| Bismuth: 175% | Manganese: 227% | Silver: 146% |
| Chromium: 266% | Molybdenum: 795% | Sulfur: 750% |
| Copper: 190% | Natural Gas: 156% | Thallium: 202% |
| Gypsum: 115% | Nitrogen (ammonia): 179% | Tin: 145% |
| Indium: 192% | Oil: 244% | Tungsten: 239% |
| Iron Ore: 132% | Phosphate Rock: 145% | Uranium: 215% |
| Iron and Steel: 105% | Potash: 230% | Vanadium: 547% |

Of the 63 NNRs that were scarce globally in 2008:

- 26 NNRs—including aluminum, chromium, coal, cobalt, copper, gypsum, iron ore, natural gas, nitrogen (ammonia), oil, phosphate rock, potash, rare earth minerals, silicon, and zinc—are indispensible to modern industrial existence; and
- 22 NNRs—including antimony, bismuth, indium, lead, lithium, molybdenum, nickel, niobium, rhenium, tin, tungsten, uranium, and vanadium—are critical to modern industrial existence.

24 of the 89 analyzed NNRs were "not scarce" globally in 2008—i.e., globally available, economically viable supplies were sufficient between 2000 and 2008 to prevent price level increases during the period.

Of the 24 globally sufficient NNRs:

- 2 NNRs—bauxite and platinum group metals (PGM)—are indispensible to modern industrial existence; and
- 7 NNRs—including boron, gallium, germanium, tantalum, and tellurium—are critical to modern industrial existence.

Barring future reductions in global NNR requirement trajectories and/or major new economically viable discoveries, 44 of the 89 analyzed NNRs are either "almost certain" or "likely" to remain scarce permanently going forward:

- 28 NNRs—including chromium, coal, cobalt, copper, gypsum, iron, ore, manganese, natural gas, oil, phosphate rock, tin, and uranium—are "almost certain" to remain scarce globally; and
- 16 NNRs—including fluorspar, graphite, lithium, magnesium, nickel, potash, vanadium, and zinc—are "likely" to remain scarce globally.

Globally available, economically viable supplies associated with 10 of the 89 analyzed NNRs—including diatomite, helium, peat, pumice, sodium sulfate, tantalum, and vermiculite—are "unlikely" to become permanently scarce globally in the immediate future.

## Peak Global NNR Extraction/Production

### 2008 Annual Global Peak NNR Extraction/Production Summary

| Global NNR Extraction/Production | NNR Criticality | | | | Total |
|---|---|---|---|---|---|
| | Indispensible | Critical | Important | Declining | |
| Almost Certainly Peaked Permanently | 0 | 0 | 0 | 0 | 0 |
| Likely Peaked Permanently | 0 | 3 | 5 | 0 | 8 |
| Unclear | 2 | 1 | 3 | 2 | 8 |
| Unlikely Peaked Permanently | 22 | 24 | 14 | 4 | 64 |
| Inconclusive | 4 | 2 | 2 | 1 | 9 |
| Totals | 28 | 30 | 24 | 7 | 89 |

Annual global extraction/production levels associated with 18 of the 89 analyzed NNRs peaked (to date) prior to 2000. Annual extraction/production levels associated with 8 of the 18 NNRs—beryllium, cesium, gold, perlite, quartz crystal, selenium, tellurium, and thallium—have "likely" peaked permanently on the global level. Beryllium, quartz crystal, and tellurium are critical to modern industrial existence.

## Increasing Global NNR Scarcity

The following three indicators of increasing global NNR scarcity underscore the challenges facing industrialized and industrializing nations as they attempt to reestablish and exceed pre-recession economic output (GDP) levels and growth rates going forward.

### *Required Global NNR Extraction/Production Growth Rates*

A "doubling time" is the number of years within which annual NNR extraction or production will double assuming a specified compound annual growth rate (CAGR) in extraction/production—in this case the CAGR that existed prior to the Great Recession.

Following are the pre-recession CAGRs and approximate doubling times associated with 22 indispensible and critical NNRs.

### Pre-recession NNR Extraction/Production Level CAGRs and Doubling Times

| NNR | 2000-2008 CAGR | NNR Extraction/ Production Level Doubling Time | Critical NNR Applications |
|---|---|---|---|
| Antimony | 6.6% | 11 Years | Starter-lights-ignition batteries used in cars and trucks |
| Bauxite | 6.3% | 13.5 Years | The only economically viable feedstock for aluminum |
| Beryllium | 6.5% | 11 Years | Satellites, military aircraft, nuclear power generation equipment |
| Bismuth | 9.4% | 7.5 Years | Nontoxic substitute for lead in solder and plumbing fixtures |
| Cement | 6.8% | 11 Years | Ubiquitous building material |
| Chromium | 4.9% | 14.5 Years | Stainless steel, jet engines, and gas turbines |
| Coal | 5.1% | 14 Years | Largest source of electricity generation in the world |

**Pre-recession NNR Extraction/Production Level CAGRs and Doubling Times (continued)**

| NNR | 2000-2008 CAGR | NNR Extraction/ Production Level Doubling Time | Critical NNR Applications |
|---|---|---|---|
| Cobalt | 8.6% | 8.5 Years | Gas turbine blades, jet aircraft engines, batteries |
| Fluorspar | 4.3% | 16.5 Years | Feedstock for fluorine bearing chemicals, aluminum and uranium processing |
| Germanium | 9.1% | 8 Years | Fiber optics, thermal imaging, wireless communications |
| Gypsum | 5.0% | 14 Years | Wallboard, plaster, cement |
| Indium | 6.9% | 10.5 Years | LCDs, touchscreens, thin film solar cells |
| Iron Ore | 9.4% | 7.5 Years | The only feedstock for iron and steel |
| Lithium | 8.2% | 9 Years | Aircraft parts, mobile phones, batteries for electric vehicles |
| Magnesium | 6.0% | 12 Years | Aerospace equipment, electronic devices, beverage cans |
| Manganese | 5.1% | 9 Years | Stainless steel, gasoline additive, dry cell batteries |
| Molybdenum | 6.2% | 11.5 Years | Aircraft parts, electrical contacts, industrial motors, tool steels |
| Niobium | 12.3% | 6 Years | Jet and rocket engines, turbines, superconducting magnets |
| REMs | 5.0% | 14 Years | Permanent magnets, electric vehicle batteries, superconductors |
| Rhenium | 5.9% | 12 Years | Petroleum refining, jet engines, gas turbine blades |
| Silicon | 7.3% | 10 Years | Primary component of glass, concrete, and semiconductors |
| Uranium | 4.3% | 16.5 Years | Primary energy source, weapons |
| Zirconium | 7.3% | 10 Years | Nuclear power plants, jet engines, gas turbine blades |

In order to reestablish and maintain pre-recession global extraction/production CAGRs, coal extraction must double every 14 years, cobalt extraction must double every 8.5 years, iron ore extraction must double every 7.5 years, manganese extraction must double every 9 years, and niobium extraction must double every 6 years—forever!

While it is possible that pre-recession global NNR extraction/production CAGRs can be reestablished and maintained in some cases for limited periods of time, it is impossible that these CAGRs can be reestablished and maintained in all or even most cases for an indefinite period of time.

### Global NNR Reserves Adequacy

"Years to Exhaustion" is the number of years that proven global NNR reserves would last assuming the reestablishment of pre-recession (2000-2008) compound annual growth rates (CAGRs) in annual NNR extraction/production.

**Years to Exhaustion Associated with Proven Global NNR Reserves**

| Years Until Exhaustion* | NNR # | NNRs |
|---|---|---|
| 1-10 Years | 4 | Antimony, Diamond (industrial), Garnet, Lithium |
| 11-20 Years | 13 | Arsenic, Barite, Bismuth, Iron Ore, Lead, Manganese, Molybdenum, Niobium, Silver, Strontium, Tin, Zinc, Zirconium |
| 21-30 Years | 7 | Cadmium, Chromium, Cobalt, Copper, Fluorspar, Nickel, Rhenium |
| 31-40 Years | 12 | Bauxite, Boron, Coal, Gold, Graphite, Mercury, Natural Gas, Oil, Thallium, Titanium Concentrates, Tungsten, Uranium |

*Reserve to production (R/P) data used for NNRs with negative 2000-2008 CAGRs: thallium, mercury, gold, cadmium, and boron.

In the event that pre-recession CAGRs are reestablished going forward, proven global reserves associated with 36 of the 89 analyzed NNRs would exhaust within 40 years (by 2048)—including bauxite in 40 years, coal in 40 years, cobalt in 26 years, copper in 27 years, iron ore in 15 years, manganese in 17 years, molybdenum in 20 years, natural gas in 34 years, nickel in 30 years, oil in 39 years, tin in 18 years, uranium in 34 years, and zinc in 13 years.

While it is extremely unlikely that global reserves associated with any of these NNRs will exhaust completely by 2048, barring major new economically viable NNR discoveries and/or new technologies that dramatically increase recoverable NNR quantities, many of these NNRs will likely become increasingly scarce going forward.

### Impending Global NNR Extraction/Production Peaks

The annual global extraction/production levels associated with the following 18 NNRs, which are either critical or indispensible to modern industrial existence, are projected to peak by the year 2035.[7]

**Projected Global Peak NNR Extraction/Production Years**

| NNR and Projected Peak Extraction/Production Year | NNR and Projected Peak Extraction/Production Year | NNR and Projected Peak Extraction/Production Year |
|---|---|---|
| Chromium – 2035 | Magnesium Metal – 2010 | Phosphate Rock* – 1988 |
| Coal – 2030 | Manganese – 2024 | Platinum Group Metals* – 2005 |
| Cobalt – 2035 | Molybdenum – 2025 | Tin – 2018 |
| Copper – 2030 | Natural Gas – 2025 | Titanium Concentrates – 2025 |
| Indium – 2018 | Nickel – 2025 | Tungsten – 2010 |
| Iron Ore – 2015 | Oil – 2017 | Zinc – 2020 |

*Possibly already reached global peak extraction.

While it is unlikely that all of these global extraction/production peak projections will be realized, it is likely that many or most of these NNRs will become increasingly scarce in the immediate future.

### Global NNR Scarcity Summary Assessment

Total global NNR requirements—i.e., the NNR quantities (economic inputs) necessary to perpetuate pre-recession global economic output (GDP) and growth—had put increasing pressure on globally available, economically viable NNR supplies since the beginning of the new millennium.

By 2008, global NNR requirements exceeded globally available, economically viable NNR supplies in the vast majority of cases.

- 63 of the 89 analyzed NNRs were scarce globally in 2008.
- 28 of the 89 analyzed NNRs are "almost certain" to remain scarce permanently, barring future reductions in global NNR requirement trajectories and/or major new economically viable discoveries.
- 16 of the 89 analyzed NNRs will "likely" remain scarce permanently, barring future reductions in global NNR requirement trajectories and/or major new economically viable discoveries.

Going forward, 39 of the 89 analyzed NNRs are considered "at risk" globally. That is, globally available, economically viable supplies associated with these NNRs will likely experience increasingly severe shortages, as industrialized and industrializing nations attempt to reestablish and exceed pre-recession global economic output (GDP) levels and growth rates on a continuous basis.

**Global "At Risk" NNRs**

| Nonrenewable Natural Resource (NNR) | NNR Criticality | Permanent Global NNR Scarcity | Permanent Global Peak Extraction/ Production | Years to Global Reserves Exhaustion (from 2008) |
|---|---|---|---|---|
| Antimony | Critical | Almost Certain | | 8 years |
| Bauxite | Indispensible | Likely | By 2038 | 40 years |
| Beryllium | Critical | Likely | Likely in 1961 | |
| Bismuth | Critical | Almost Certain | | 17 years |
| Cadmium | Important | Likely | By 1988* | 25 years** |
| Chromium | Indispensible | Almost Certain | By 2035 | 26 years |
| Coal | Indispensible | Almost Certain | By 2030 | 40 years |
| Cobalt | Indispensible | Almost Certain | By 2035 | 26 years |
| Copper | Indispensible | Almost Certain | By 2030 | 27 years |
| Fluorspar | Critical | Likely | | 23 years |
| Graphite (Natural) | Critical | Likely | | 38 years |
| Indium | Critical | Almost Certain | By 2018 | |
| Iron Ore | Indispensible | Almost Certain | By 2015 | 15 years |
| Iron/Steel | Indispensible | Almost Certain | | |
| Lead | Critical | Almost Certain | By 1990* | 17 years |
| Lithium | Critical | Likely | | 8 years |
| Magnesium Metal | Indispensible | Likely | By 2010 | |
| Manganese | Indispensible | Almost Certain | By 2024 | 17 years |
| Molybdenum | Critical | Almost Certain | By 2025 | 20 years |
| Natural Gas | Indispensible | Almost Certain | By 2025 | 34 years |
| Nickel | Critical | Likely | By 2025 | 30 years |
| Niobium | Critical | Almost Certain | | 15 years |
| Nitrogen (Ammonia) | Indispensible | Almost Certain | | |
| Oil | Indispensible | Almost Certain | By 2017 | 39 years |
| Phosphate Rock | Indispensible | Almost Certain | By 1988* | |
| Platinum Group Metals (PGM) | Indispensible | | By 2005* | |

**Global "At Risk" NNRs (continued)**

| Nonrenewable Natural Resource (NNR) | NNR Criticality | Permanent Global NNR Scarcity | Permanent Global Peak Extraction/ Production | Years to Global Reserves Exhaustion (from 2008) |
|---|---|---|---|---|
| Potash | Indispensible | Likely | | |
| Rhenium | Critical | Almost Certain | | 22 years |
| Selenium | Important | Almost Certain | Likely in 1996 | |
| Silver | Critical | Almost Certain | By 2010 | 11 years |
| Sulfur | Indispensible | Almost Certain | | |
| Tellurium | Critical | | Likely in 1974 | |
| Thallium | Important | Almost Certain | Likely in 1989 | 38 years** |
| Tin | Critical | Almost Certain | By 2018 | 18 years |
| Titanium Mineral Concentrates | Indispensible | Likely | By 2025 | 37 years |
| Tungsten | Critical | Almost Certain | By 2010 | 32 years |
| Uranium | Critical | Almost Certain | By 1982* | 34 years |
| Zinc | Indispensible | Likely | By 2020 | 13 years |
| Zirconium | Critical | Almost Certain | | 19 years |

*The (Verhulst) logistics curve fitting analysis projected global peak extraction/production prior to the year 2010. However, either the projected peak was subsequently exceeded or it is currently unclear whether the pre-2010 peak is permanent. While the Verhulst methodology is naturally subject to inaccuracy with regard to precise peak NNR extraction/production timing, it is a viable indicator of existing or impending NNR scarcity.

**2008 reserve to production (R/P) data were used in lieu of extrapolated extraction/production projections because the 2000-2008 compound annual growth rate (CAGR) associated with annual global extraction/production was negative.

The Great Recession marked a tipping point in world history as well. Epidemic permanent global NNR scarcity experienced by the onset of the Great Recession permanently depressed the future growth trajectories associated with global economic output (GDP) and societal wellbeing.

## NNR Scarcity and Modern Industrial Existence

Water comes from turning on a faucet; electricity comes from a wall socket; light comes from flipping a switch; heat and air conditioning come from adjusting a thermostat; food comes from a grocery store; gasoline comes from a gas station; and instantaneous global communication comes from pressing buttons on a handheld electronic device—right?

Actually, these essential attributes of our modern industrial existence, in addition to nearly all others, are enabled by enormous and ever-increasing quantities of NNRs.

The following analysis considers NNR scarcity as it relates to five critical NNR-enabled application areas, each of which is essential to modern industrial existence:

- Essential Infrastructure
- Primary Energy Generation
- Industrial Agriculture
- Computers and Other High Technology Electronic Devices

- Emerging "Green" Technologies (Electric Cars, Wind Turbines, and Solar Cells)

Consider in each case the domestic (US) peak (to date) NNR extraction/production year, the domestic (US) NNR import percentage, the likelihood regarding permanent NNR scarcity, and the potential geopolitical NNR supply constraints.

Given America's extraordinary levels of foreign NNR dependence and vulnerability, and the fact that all industrialized and industrializing nations are similarly dependent and vulnerable, the potential for conflict—resource wars—will certainly increase going forward as these NNRs become increasingly scarce.

## NNRs Used in Essential Infrastructure

The physical foundation of every industrialized nation is infrastructure—buildings, roads, systems, and networks. Infrastructure consists almost entirely of NNRs; and it is produced, provisioned, and maintained almost exclusively through the utilization of NNRs.

**NNRs Used in Essential Infrastructure**

| Infrastructure NNR | Peak US Extraction/ Production Year (to date) | 2008 US Import Percent | Permanent Scarcity | | Potential Geopolitical Supply Constraints |
|---|---|---|---|---|---|
| | | | US | Global | |
| Abrasives | 1974 | 76% | Almost Certain | Unclear | 83% of US fused aluminum oxide and crude silicon carbide are imported from China |
| Aluminum | 1980 | 24% | Almost Certain | Unclear | 56% of US aluminum imports come from Canada |
| Boron | 1995 | 0% | Unclear | Unclear | 72% of proven global boron reserves are located in Turkey |
| Cement | 2005 | 11% | Unclear | Unclear | |
| Chromium | 1956 | 66% | Almost Certain | Almost Certain | Over 75% of proven global reserves are located in South Africa and Kazakhstan |
| Clays | 1973 | 0% | Unlikely | Unclear | 84% of US clay imports come from Brazil |
| Cobalt | 1958 | 81% | Almost Certain | Almost Certain | Over half of the proven global cobalt reserves are located in the Congo |
| Copper | 1998 | 31% | Almost Certain | Almost Certain | 40% of US copper imports come from Chile |
| Gypsum | 2006 | 24% | Almost Certain | Likely | China is the world's second largest gypsum producer |

**NNRs Used in Essential Infrastructure (continued)**

| Infrastructure NNR | Peak US Extraction/ Production Year (to date) | 2008 US Import Percent | Permanent Scarcity | | Potential Geopolitical Supply Constraints |
|---|---|---|---|---|---|
| | | | US | Global | |
| Iron/Steel | 1973 | 13% | Likely | Almost Certain | China is the world's leading steel producer |
| Lead | 1970 | 0% | Almost Certain | Almost Certain | China accounts for 40% of global lead mine production |
| Magnesium | 1943 | 50% | Almost Certain | Likely | 40% of US magnesium metal imports come from Canada |
| Manganese | 1918 | 100% | Almost Certain | Almost Certain | Over 50% of proven global manganese reserves are located in South Africa and the Ukraine |
| Molybdenum | 1980 | 0% | Unclear | Almost Certain | Nearly 40% of proven global molybdenum reserves are located in China |
| Nickel | 1997 | 34% | Almost Certain | Likely | Nearly 40% of proven global nickel reserves are located in Australia |
| Sand and Gravel | 2006 | 0% | Unlikely | Unclear | 75% of US construction sand and gravel imports come from Canada |
| Silicon | 1979 | 52% | Almost Certain | Likely | China produces 65% of the world's silicon |
| Stone (Crushed) | 2006 | 1% | Unlikely | Unclear | 43% of US crushed stone imports come from Canada |
| Tin | 1945 | 80% | Almost Certain | Almost Certain | China and Indonesia each produce over 40% of the world's tin |
| Titanium | 1989 | 54% | Almost Certain | Unclear | 52% of US titanium sponge metal imports come from Kazakhstan |
| Vanadium | 1981 | 100% | Almost Certain | Likely | China and South Africa each account for approximately 40% of global vanadium production |

## NNRs Used In Primary Energy Generation

Nothing moves in the absence of energy. Currently, 90% of the primary energy that powers our industrialized and industrializing world is provided by nonrenewable energy sources[8]—and none of the emerging renewable primary energy converters could exist in the absence of NNRs.

**NNRs Used In Primary Energy Generation**

| Primary Energy NNR | Peak US Extraction/ Production Year (to date) | 2008 US Import Percent | Permanent Scarcity | | Potential Geopolitical Supply Constraints |
|---|---|---|---|---|---|
| | | | US | Global | |
| Coal (27%) | 2008 | 0% | Unclear | Almost Certain | |
| Natural Gas (23%) | 1973 | 13% | Likely | Almost Certain | Nearly 100% of US natural gas imports come from Canada |
| Oil (35%) | 1970 | 57% | Almost Certain | Almost Certain | Approximately 80% of proven world oil reserves are in the Middle East |
| Uranium (5%) | 1981 | 78% | Almost Certain | Almost Certain | Canada, Australia, and Kazakhstan each produce approximately one quarter of the world's annual uranium supply |

## NNRs Used in Industrial Agriculture

Industrialized populations could not exist in the absence of industrial agriculture; and industrial agriculture could not exist in the absence of NNRs.[9] NNRs are the primary components of agricultural machinery, agricultural facilities, agricultural fuels, fertilizers, pesticides, herbicides, and fungicides.

**NNRs Used in Industrial Agriculture**

| Industrial Agriculture NNR | Peak US Extraction/ Production Year (to date) | 2008 US Import Percent | Permanent Scarcity | | Potential Geopolitical Supply Constraints |
|---|---|---|---|---|---|
| | | | US | Global | |
| Boron | 1995 | 0% | Unclear | Unclear | 72% of proven global boron reserves are located in Turkey |
| Copper | 1998 | 31% | Almost Certain | Almost Certain | 40% of US copper imports come from Chile |

**NNRs Used in Industrial Agriculture (continued)**

| Industrial Agriculture NNR | Peak US Extraction/ Production Year (to date) | 2008 US Import Percent | Permanent Scarcity | | Potential Geopolitical Supply Constraints |
|---|---|---|---|---|---|
| | | | US | Global | |
| Iron | 1953 | 0% | Unclear | Almost Certain | China accounts for more than half of annual global iron ore extraction |
| Magnesium | 1943 | 50% | Almost Certain | Likely | 40% of US magnesium metal imports currently come from Canada |
| Manganese | 1918 | 100% | Almost Certain | Almost Certain | Over 50% of proven global manganese reserves are located in South Africa and the Ukraine |
| Molybdenum | 1980 | 0% | Unclear | Almost Certain | Nearly 40% of proven global molybdenum reserves are located in China |
| Natural Gas | 1973 | 13% | Likely | Almost Certain | |
| Nitrogen (Ammonia) | 1980 | 42% | Almost Certain | Almost Certain | 55% of US ammonia imports come from Trinidad and Tobago |
| Oil | 1970 | 57% | Almost Certain | Almost Certain | Approximately 80% of the world's proven oil reserves are located in the Middle East |
| Phosphate Rock | 1980 | 4% | Likely | Almost Certain | 100% of US phosphate rock imports come from Morocco |
| Potash | 1967 | 84% | Almost Certain | Likely | over 50% of proven global potash reserves are located in Canada |
| Selenium | 1969 | 0% | Unclear | Almost Certain | 46% of US selenium imports come from Belgium |
| Sulfur | 1981 | 25% | Almost Certain | Almost Certain | 71% of US elemental sulfur imports from Canada |
| Zinc | 1969 | 71% | Almost Certain | Likely | 68% of US zinc ore and concentrate imports come from Peru |

## NNRs Used in Computers and Other High Tech Electronic Devices

NNRs are the primary components of computers[10] and of all electrical and electronic communication, medical, defense, and consumer devices that enable modern industrial existence.

### NNRs Used in Computers and Other High Tech Electronic Devices

| Computer and High Tech NNR | Peak US Extraction/ Production Year (to date) | 2008 US Import Percent | Permanent Scarcity | | Potential Geopolitical Supply Constraints |
|---|---|---|---|---|---|
| | | | US | Global | |
| Aluminum | 1980 | 24% | Almost Certain | Unclear | |
| Antimony | 1948 | 93% | Almost Certain | Almost Certain | 51% of US antimony imports come from China |
| Arsenic | 1944 | 100% | Almost Certain | Unclear | 86% of US arsenic metal imports come from China |
| Barite | 1981 | 80% | Almost Certain | Almost Certain | 93% of US barite imports come from China |
| Beryllium | 1980 | 17% | Unclear | Likely | 58% of US beryllium imports come from Kazakhstan |
| Bismuth | Never Mined in the US | 94% | Almost Certain | Almost Certain | Over 2/3 of proven global bismuth reserves are located in China |
| Cadmium | 1969 | 0% | Unclear | Likely | |
| Chromium | 1956 | 66% | Almost Certain | Almost Certain | Over 75% of proven global reserves are located in South Africa and Kazakhstan |
| Cobalt | 1958 | 81% | Almost Certain | Almost Certain | Over half of the proven global cobalt reserves are located in the Congo |
| Copper | 1998 | 31% | Almost Certain | Almost Certain | 40% of US copper imports come from Chile |
| Europium (REM) | 1984 | 100% | Almost Certain | Unclear | China accounts for 95% of global REM extraction |
| Gallium | 1978 | 99% | Almost Certain | Unclear | China, Kazakhstan, and the Ukraine are 3 of the top 4 producers of unrefined gallium |
| Germanium | 1981 | 90% | Almost Certain | Unclear | China produces a majority of the world's germanium |

**NNRs Used in Computers and Other High Tech Electronic Devices (continued)**

| Computer and High Tech NNR | Peak US Extraction/ Production Year (to date) | 2008 US Import Percent | Permanent Scarcity | | Potential Geopolitical Supply Constraints |
|---|---|---|---|---|---|
| Gold | 1998 | 0% | Unclear | Almost Certain | China is the leading gold producing nation |
| Indium | 1966 | 100% | Almost Certain | Almost Certain | Half of the proven global indium reserves are located in China |
| Iron (Ore) | 1953 | 0% | Unclear | Almost Certain | |
| Lead | 1970 | 0% | Almost Certain | Almost Certain | China accounts for 40% of global lead mine production |
| Manganese | 1918 | 100% | Almost Certain | Almost Certain | Over 50% of proven global manganese reserves are located in South Africa and the Ukraine |
| Mercury | 1943 | 0% | Unclear | Unclear | China accounts for 2/3 of global mercury extraction |
| Nickel | 1997 | 34% | Almost Certain | Likely | Nearly 40% of proven global nickel reserves are located in Australia |
| Niobium | Never Mined in the US | 100% | Almost Certain | Almost Certain | Brazil produces about 75% of the world's supply of niobium |
| Palladium (PGM) | 2002 | 79% | Almost Certain | Unclear | 46% of US palladium imports come from Russia |
| Plastics (Oil) | 1970 | 57% | Almost Certain | Almost Certain | Approximately 80% of the world's proven oil reserves are located in the Middle East |
| Platinum (PGM) | 2002 | 89% | Almost Certain | Unclear | South Africa produces about 79% of the world's platinum |
| Ruthenium (PGM) | 2002 | 89%* | Almost Certain | Unclear | |
| Rhodium (PGM) | 2002 | 89%* | Almost Certain | Unclear | |
| Selenium | 1969 | 0% | Unclear | Almost Certain | 46% of US selenium imports come from Belgium |
| Silicon | 1979 | 52% | Almost Certain | Likely | China produces 65% of the world's silicon |

**NNRs Used in Computers and Other High Tech Electronic Devices (continued)**

| Computer and High Tech NNR | Peak US Extraction/ Production Year (to date) | 2008 US Import Percent | Permanent Scarcity | | Potential Geopolitical Supply Constraints |
|---|---|---|---|---|---|
| Silver | 1916 | 67% | Almost Certain | Almost Certain | 54% of US silver imports come from Mexico |
| Tantalum | Never Mined in the US | 100% | Almost Certain | Unlikely | A vast majority of proven global tantalum reserves are located in Australia (36%) and Brazil (59%) |
| Terbium (REM) | 1984 | 100% | Almost Certain | Unclear | China accounts for 95% of global REM extraction |
| Tin | 1945 | 80% | Almost Certain | Almost Certain | China and Indonesia each produce over 40% of the world's tin |
| Titanium | 1989 | 54% | Almost Certain | Unclear | 52% of US titanium sponge metal imports come from Kazakhstan |
| Vanadium | 1981 | 100% | Almost Certain | Likely | China and South Africa each account for approximately 40% of global vanadium production |
| Yttrium (REM) | 1984 | 100% | Almost Certain | Unclear | China accounts for 95% of global REM extraction |
| Zinc | 1969 | 71% | Almost Certain | Likely | 68% of US zinc ore and concentrate imports come from Peru |

\* Platinum import data; specific data for ruthenium and rhodium are not available.

## NNRs Used in Emerging Technologies

In addition to many of the above listed NNRs, emerging technologies often require additional "exotic" NNRs to address specialized energy storage, electric motor, and integrated circuit applications.[11]

**NNRs Used in Emerging Technologies**

| Emerging Technology NNR | Peak US Extraction/ Production Year (to date) | 2008 US Import Percent | Permanent Scarcity | | Potential Geopolitical Supply Constraints |
|---|---|---|---|---|---|
| | | | US | Global | |
| Dysprosium (REM) [Permanent Magnets] | 1984 | 100% | Almost Certain | Unclear | 91% of US REM imports come from China; China accounts for 95% of global REM extraction |
| Lanthanum (REM) [Batteries] | 1984 | 100% | Almost Certain | Unclear | 91% of US REM imports come from China; China accounts for 95% of global REM extraction |
| Lithium [Batteries] | 1954 | >50% | Almost Certain | Likely | 63% of US lithium imports come from Chile, 76% of proven global lithium reserves are located in Chile |
| Neodymium (REM) [Permanent Magnets] | 1984 | 100% | Almost Certain | Unclear | 91% of US REM imports come from China; China accounts for 95% of global REM extraction |
| Phosphorous [Solar Cells] | 1980 | 4% | Likely | Almost Certain | 100% of US phosphate rock imports come from Morocco |
| Samarium (REM) [Permanent Magnets] | 1984 | 100% | Almost Certain | Unclear | 91% of US REM imports come from China; China accounts for 95% of global REM extraction |
| Tellurium [Solar Cells] | 1960 | 100% | Almost Certain | Unclear | 43% of US tellurium imports come from China |
| Terbium (REM) [Permanent Magnets] | 1984 | 100% | Almost Certain | Unclear | 91% of US REM imports come from China; China accounts for 95% of global REM extraction |

## NNR Scarcity and Modern Industrial Existence Summary Assessment

NNRs enable literally every aspect of our modern industrial existence; and most NNRs, especially those that are indispensible to our industrialized way of life, are now likely or almost certainly scarce permanently, both domestically (US) and globally.

We may be able to mitigate or even overcome NNR scarcity in some cases through technical innovation, substitution, conservation, recycling, efficiency improvements, and productivity enhancements. We cannot, however, possibly mitigate or overcome NNR scarcity in all or even most cases.

NNR scarcity is epidemic, domestically (US) and globally; and it is increasing both in terms of incidence and severity despite our efforts and hopes to the contrary. Our incessant quest for global industrialization—and our consequent ever-increasing requirements for nearly all NNRs within an environment of increasingly constrained economically viable NNR supplies—will overwhelm our efforts to mitigate the ultimately devastating effects of NNR scarcity.

## 2008 was Different

The period of rapid global economic growth prior to the Great Recession differed fundamentally from the "boom" phases associated with historical commodity (NNR) "boom/bust" cycles.

### Historical NNR Scarcity

Episodes of NNR scarcity have occurred periodically since the inception of our industrial revolution. NNRs typically became scarce during economic boom periods, which were characterized by heavy NNR demand. As NNR prices increased, sufficient additional economically viable NNR supplies were brought online to completely address our then-existing requirements, and NNR scarcity subsided.

Because these episodes of NNR scarcity were temporary—i.e., sufficient quantities of economically viable NNRs were readily available to be brought online—the economic output (GDP) levels and growth rates that existed prior to the NNR scarcity episode were reestablished, or exceeded.

### NNR Scarcity in 2008

The NNR scarcity episode that occurred in 2008, immediately prior to the Great Recession, was different.

#### *2008 Global NNR Requirements*

Both the scope and the magnitude associated with global NNR requirements were historically unprecedented by 2008.

**Global Industrialism**: By 2008, nearly 5 billion people lived in industrialized or industrializing nations, an increase of nearly 4 billion since 1975[12]—industrialism had transitioned from a "Western" phenomenon to a global phenomenon.

Global GDP, which is a viable proxy for NNR demand/utilization[13], increased from $39.3 trillion (2005 USD) in 2000 to $49.4 trillion (2005 USD) in 2008—an extraordinary 26% increase in only 8 years.[14]

**Global NNR Demand**: "Until 2000, global output of minerals on average had increased fivefold since 1950. Until 2007, production again grew by 17% in the case of precious metals, by 33% percent in the case of mass consumables, and by 46% percent in the case of doping agents."[15]

**NNR Prices**: "While [NNR] prices have fallen for over two decades after spiking sharply in the 1980's, this trend has reversed over the past couple of years. Real prices have more than doubled sine 2002 and have reached a level they haven't seen since the second oil shock nearly three decades ago."[16]

## 2008 Global NNR Supply

Global NNR supplies were severely strained in the vast majority of cases by 2008.

**Peak NNR Discoveries**: Global discoveries associated with numerous indispensible and critical NNRs—including coal, copper, iron ore, lead, natural gas, nickel, oil, platinum group metals, uranium, and zinc—peaked (to date) during the 1960s and 1970s.

Global discoveries associated with some or all of the coproducts and byproducts of these NNRs—including bismuth, cadmium, cobalt, gallium, gold, mercury, molybdenum, rhenium, scandium, selenium, silver, sulfur, thallium, and vanadium—likely peaked during the 1960s and 1970s as well.[17]

**Aggregate Global NNR Discovery Levels and Extraction/Production Levels**

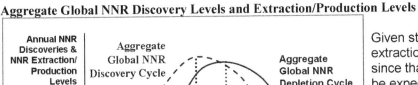
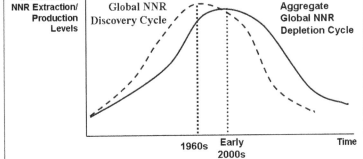

Given steadily increasing extraction/production since that time, it was to be expected that permanent scarcity and permanent peak extraction/production would follow peak discovery by 40-50 years.[18]

**Declining NNR Quality**: "Future mining will face an increasing geological distance. This means mining deposits of lower ore grade, which are found in deeper and less accessible layers in the planet's crust. Deposits are to be found at greater geographic distance from centres of consumption and in less accessible environments (e.g. offshore)."[19]

**Diminishing NNR Investment Returns**: "This global [NNR] search temporarily increased the success rate of global exploration efforts as new lands opened up in the 1990s, but in recent years exploration seems to have become increasingly unsuccessful again. Specifically, the massive increase in exploration budgets during the commodities boom from 2003 to 2008 was not mirrored by a massive increase in metals discovery during this period. Quite the opposite."[20]

## 2008 Global NNR Scarcity

It is therefore not surprising that by the middle of the first decade of the new millennium, NNR producers were finding it increasingly difficult to bring online sufficient economically viable NNR supplies to completely address global requirements—despite the fact that the price levels associated with the vast majority of NNRs trended upward since the year 2000 or before.

By 2008, the earth could no longer keep pace with ever-increasing global NNR requirements. Sufficient NNR quantities could not be physically extracted from the earth in a timely and cost-effective manner to perpetuate global pre-recession economic output (GDP) levels and growth rates—half of the analyzed NNRs had likely or almost certainly become permanently scarce globally.

The Great Recession—which should be understood more broadly as an ecological phenomenon, rather than simply as an economic phenomenon—ensued.

## 2008 in Retrospect

Permanent NNR scarcity did not become epidemic "in" 2008, it became epidemic "by" 2008. 2008 marked the culmination of a historically unprecedented period of sustained global economic growth that put historically unprecedented strain on remaining economically viable NNR supplies. An extraordinary number of NNR users were demanding extraordinary NNR quantities from fewer, smaller, less accessible, lower quality NNR deposits.

Yet permanent NNR scarcity had been increasingly evident in industrialized nations such as the UK and the US for generations. 2008 was simply the transition point, the year during which the number of permanently scarce NNRs became sufficiently large to permanently depress future economic growth trajectories and societal wellbeing improvement trajectories associated with America and the world.

## Going Forward

While we are not about to "run out" of any NNR, we are in the process of running critically short of many.

**Future NNR Requirements**: "Continued industrialization of the developing world will lead to rising global demand for scarce minerals. According to the OECD, global demand for minerals is expected to double over the next 25 years [by 2035]."[21]

**Future NNR Prices**: "It should be no surprise to anyone, though, that current declining mineral discovery trends will likely continue, that ever-growing mineral commodity consumption will become harder to sustain, and that mineral and metal prices will increase."[22]

**Future NNR Supply**: "In the past century the increase in demand has been equalled by an increase in mining and extraction of the required material resources. Exploration of new locations and technological innovation in mining and extraction has kept the available and known material reserves on par with the increase in demand. Will this continue in the 21st century as well? It is difficult to predict a century ahead, but looking at a number of developments, we are afraid the answer is: no."[23]

All indications are that we will attempt to reestablish and maintain or exceed pre-recession economic output (GDP) levels and growth rates, both domestically (US) and globally. We will soon discover, however, that ever-increasing NNR scarcity has rendered these goals physically impossible, and that the implications and consequences for human societal wellbeing associated with this reality are catastrophic.

# V. Implications of NNR Scarcity

**The fundamental cause of our predicament is ecological—it is not economic or political. Our attempted economic and political "solutions" are therefore irrelevant.**

- **Natural Resource Utilization Behavior and Societal Wellbeing**
- **Implications of NNR Scarcity for US Societal Wellbeing**
- **Implications of NNR Scarcity for Global Societal Wellbeing**
- **The Significance of 2008**
- **Sustainability is Inevitable**

The reality that we have known since the inception of our industrial revolution—exponentially improving material living standards for ever-increasing segments of our ever-expanding global population—no longer exists. Sufficient economically viable NNR supplies are no longer available to perpetuate this reality.

Our societal wellbeing will be compromised going forward, both domestically (US) and globally.

## Natural Resource Utilization Behavior and Societal Wellbeing

### Human Natural Resource Utilization and Societal Wellbeing

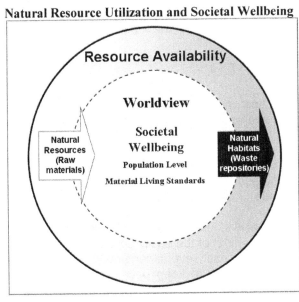

Natural Resource Utilization and Societal Wellbeing

The level of societal wellbeing attainable by a human population—i.e., the population level and the average per capita material living standard enjoyed by that population—is determined by the population's natural resource utilization behavior—i.e., the mix and levels of natural resources utilized by the population.

A population's natural resource utilization behavior is determined by natural resource availability and by the population's worldview.

As discussed in Chapter 1, the worldviews and natural resource utilization behavior associated with hunter-gatherer, agrarian, and industrialized populations differ dramatically.

## Industrialized Natural Resource Utilization and Societal Wellbeing

Industrialized Natural Resource Utilization and Societal Wellbeing

The level of societal wellbeing attainable by an industrialized nation is determined almost exclusively by the mix and levels of nonrenewable natural resources (NNRs) utilized by the nation's population.

NNR inputs to the nation's economic system are converted into infrastructure, goods, and services outputs, which enable the nation's level of societal wellbeing.

All else being equal, the greater the mix and levels of NNR inputs to an industrialized nation's economy, the greater the level of economic output (typically defined as Gross Domestic Product—GDP) generated by that nation, and the higher the nation's level of societal wellbeing.

## Industrialism is Not Sustainable[1]

Since the inception of our industrial revolution, humanity has been the beneficiary of "continuously more and more" with respect to available NNR supplies and resulting economic output (GDP) levels, human population levels, and average material living standards.

Unfortunately, in the process of reaping the benefits associated with "continuously more and more", we have been eliminating—persistently and increasingly—the very natural resources upon which our industrialized way of life depends.

As clearly demonstrated by the NNR Scarcity Analysis, historically abundant and cheap NNRs are becoming increasingly scarce and expensive—most of the easily accessible, high quality, low cost NNR deposits have been exploited over the past several centuries. Less accessible, lower quality, higher cost NNR supplies are struggling to keep pace with ever-increasing requirements, both domestically (US) and globally.

**Societal Wellbeing "Evolution"**

As economically viable supplies associated with an ever-increasing number of NNRs transition from "continuously more and more" to "continuously less and less", societal wellbeing levels transition as well—initially at the national level, ultimately at the global level.

**1. Continuous Growth**: during the period of NNR abundance, the mix and levels of economically viable NNR inputs to an industrializing society's economy are sufficient to enable continuously increasing economic output (GDP) levels and continuously improving societal wellbeing. The society establishes its (ultimately erroneous) expectation regarding future economic growth and societal wellbeing improvement by simply extrapolating their experience with "continuously more and more" indefinitely into the future.

**2. Pre-peak Divergence**: as economically viable supplies associated with an increasing number of NNRs become permanently scarce, peak, and decline, the mix and levels of NNR inputs to the society's economy become insufficient to enable economic growth and societal wellbeing improvement at prevailing or "expected" rates. Actual economic output (GDP) and societal wellbeing trajectories diverge permanently from "expected" trajectories.

**3. Peak Societal Wellbeing**: as economically viable supplies associated with a critical number of NNRs become permanently scarce, peak, and decline, the society's economic output (GDP) and societal wellbeing reach their maximum or peak levels.

**4. Terminal Decline**: as economically viable supplies associated with remaining NNRs peak permanently and go into terminal decline, the society's economic output (GDP) and societal wellbeing levels go into terminal decline—"continuously less and less"—as well.

### Humanity's Predicament[2]

In our unrelenting quest for global industrialization—and our consequent ever-increasing utilization of the earth's increasingly scarce NNRs—we have been undermining both our industrial lifestyle paradigm and our very existence as a species.

Ironically, the natural resource utilization behavior that has enabled our historically unprecedented success—our industrial lifestyle paradigm—and that is essential to our continued success, is also pushing us toward our imminent demise.[3]

[Note that humanity's predicament is not unique among species, as William Catton points out in "Overshoot", "We need to see that, in each case, the organisms using their habitat unavoidably reduce its capacity to support their kind by what they necessarily do to it in the process of living. ... This is what mankind has been doing. We have overshot environmental limits and have begun inflicting serious damage upon *our* habitat's capacity to support *our* species."[4]]

## Implications of NNR Scarcity for US Societal Wellbeing

The meteoric rise in American societal wellbeing that occurred during the past 200 years was an anomaly, a one time event enabled by America's ever-increasing utilization of finite and non-replenishing nonrenewable natural resources. The onset of the Great Recession marked the permanent transition from America's old reality of "continuously more and more" to its new reality of "continuously less and less".

**American Societal Wellbeing**

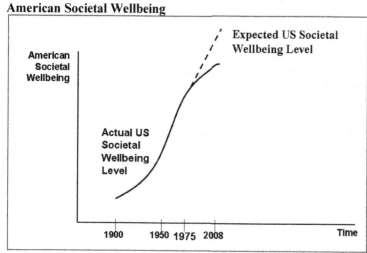

The economic "miracles" that became an American trademark during "continuously more and more", will be impossible during "continuously less and less". Available economically viable NNR supplies will be insufficient to perpetuate the American way of life going forward, much less to improve upon it.

American societal wellbeing has peaked permanently.

### US Societal Wellbeing Evolution

#### *US Societal Wellbeing 1900-1950: Continuously More and More*

The US industrial revolution was well underway by the turn of the 20th century—Americans were migrating from the farms to the cities, and foreign immigrants were flooding into America in search of better lives. America, which was a veritable treasure trove of natural resources, was nearly self-sufficient with respect to NNRs, especially NNRs that were essential to the emerging US industrial economy.

Despite (or as a result of) two world wars and the Great Depression, America became the production engine of the world during the first half of the 20th century. In addition to sufficient domestically available, economically viable NNR supplies in most cases, America also possessed state-of-the-art manufacturing facilities and infrastructure, and a low cost, willing, and appropriately skilled workforce, which were necessary to convert NNR inputs into world leading finished good outputs.

The tremendous financial wealth generated by America's industrializing economy during the 1900-1950 period remained within US borders for the most part—Americans were buying American manufactured goods. In addition, vast amounts of foreign wealth flowed into the US as a result of American (net) exports to foreign countries—foreigners were buying American manufactured goods as well.

America's NNR input, economic output (GDP), population, and material living standard levels increased rapidly during the first half of the 20th century:

- NNR input to the US economy increased from 293 million tons in 1900 to 1,971 million tons in 1950.[5]
- US economic output (GDP) increased from $423 billion (2005 USD) in 1900 to $2.0 trillion (2005 USD) in 1950.[6]
- America's population level increased from 76 million in 1900 to 152 million in 1950.[7]
- America's average material living standard, as defined by per capita GDP, increased from $5,600 (2005 USD) in 1900 to $13,200 (2005 USD) in 1950.[8]

However, even as America was experiencing its heydays of emerging industrialization, an increasing number of NNRs were becoming scarce domestically (US).

- As early as 1928, America was (net) importing some quantities associated with 39 of the 89 NNRs analyzed in the NNR Scarcity Analysis; and
- Between 1900 and 1950, domestic (US) extraction/production levels associated with the following indispensible NNRs peaked permanently (to date): manganese (1918), bauxite (1943), and magnesium (1943).

### US Societal Wellbeing 1950-1975: Changes

By the middle of the 20th century, the US and much of the industrialized world were fully ensconced in the post war building boom, which resulted in steadily increasing domestic (US) demand for nearly all NNRs.

However, domestic (US) extraction/production levels associated with many NNRs were near, at, or past peak, and the US was forced to import increasing quantities of foreign NNRs in order to enable its increasing economic output (GDP) levels. Increasing amounts of US financial wealth flowed beyond US borders to pay for the ever-increasing NNR import inflows.

While America retained its position as the leading global production engine, declining domestic NNR supplies in combination with ever-increasing US labor costs and other manufacturing costs began to undermine America's global economic preeminence. Rapidly industrializing nations such as Japan and Germany, which had lower manufacturing costs and ready access to affordable NNRs, became increasingly viable competitors—both Americans and foreigners continuously increased their purchases of non-American manufactured goods.

The US reacted to the changing environment by:

- Transitioning from a "manufacturing economy" to a "service economy", which requires fewer NNR inputs, but also generates less real wealth;

- Transitioning from a "production economy" to a "consumption economy", which featured the creation of "suburbia", the NNR enablers of which have been increasingly imported;
- Establishing a global military presence to insure continuous access to foreign NNR supplies at favorable prices; and
- Relying increasingly on "pseudo purchasing power" (PPP)[9] to compensate for the increasing gap between American creation of real wealth and American consumption.

Pseudo purchasing power enables a society to increase its "current" procurement levels of natural resources and derived goods and services through unsustainable economic behavior—that is, by:

- Liquidating previously accumulated economic asset (wealth) reserves,
- Exchanging ever-increasing quantities of fiat currency for real wealth,
- Incurring ever-increasing levels of unrepayable debt, and
- Underfunding investments critical to its future wellbeing.

As a result of these adaptations, America's NNR input, economic output (GDP), population, and material living standard levels continued to increase through 1975:

- NNR inputs to the US economy increased from 1,971 million tons in 1950 to 4,008 million tons in 1975.[10]
- US economic output (GDP) increased from $2.0 trillion (2005 USD) in 1950 to $4.9 trillion (2005 USD) in 1975.[11]
- America's population level increased from 152 million in 1950 to 216 million in 1975.[12]
- America's average material living standard, as defined by per capita GDP, increased from $13,200 (2005 USD) in 1950 to $22,600 (2005 USD) in 1975.[13]

However, America's growing prosperity was being built on an increasingly shaky foundation.

- By 1968, America was importing 54 of the 89 analyzed NNRs, including 100% of 6 NNRs; and
- Between 1950 and 1975, domestic (US) extraction/production levels associated with the following indispensible NNRs peaked permanently (to date): iron ore (1953), chromium (1956), cobalt (1958), potash (1961), zinc (1969), oil, 1970), and iron/steel (1973).

US President Richard Nixon understood all too well the inherent dangers associated with America's dependence on foreign NNRs, "The Soviet leaders have their eyes on the economic under-pinnings of modern society. Their aim is to pull the plug on the Western industrial machine. The Western industrial nations' dependence on foreign sources of vital raw materials is one of our chief vulnerabilities."[14]

### US Societal Wellbeing 1975-2000: Divergence

As domestic (US) extraction/production and utilization (supply) levels associated with an increasing number of NNRs reached their peaks during the latter part of the 20th century, America's position as the world's leading producer of both commodity goods and high-end goods continued to erode.

America's response was to:

- "Offshore" its corporate manufacturing operations, through US-owned multinational corporations, to production facilities located in foreign countries that offered lower labor costs and overall operating costs;
- Expand its international military presence;
- Increase its reliance on pseudo purchasing power; and
- Invent the "financial sector", which creates even less real wealth than the "service sector".

Ever-increasing amounts of US financial wealth flowed beyond US borders to pay for foreign labor, foreign production facilities, and foreign NNRs.

Foreign outsourcing did, however, enable the US to further increase its societal wellbeing between 1975 and 2000:

- NNR input to the US economy increased from 4,008 million tons in 1975 to 6,765 million tons in 2000.[15]
- US economic output (GDP) increased from $4.9 trillion (2005 USD) in 1975 to $11.2 trillion (2005 USD) in 2000.[16]
- America's population level increased from 216 million in 1975 to 281 million in 2000.[17]
- America's average material living standard, as defined by per capita GDP, increased from $22,600 (2005 USD) in 1975 to $39,900 (2005 USD) in 2000.[18]

Yet improvement in US societal wellbeing had begun to slow by the 1970s.[19] The annual growth rates in total US NNR utilization, economic output (GDP), and energy utilization—three indicators of societal wellbeing—all declined during the 1975-2000 period when compared with the 1950-1975 period.

**Domestic (US) Societal Wellbeing Indicators**

| US Societal Wellbeing Indictor | Compound Annual Growth Rate | |
|---|---|---|
| | 1950 to 1975 | 1975 to 2000 |
| Total US NNR Utilization | 2.88% | 2.04% |
| US Economic Output (GDP) | 3.62% | 3.39% |
| Total US Energy Utilization | 3.01% | 1.24% |

By 1975, the trajectory associated with US societal wellbeing improvement had diverged from the "expected" or "normal" trajectory, which had prevailed until that time.

Underlying this "divergence" was the fact that domestic (US) extraction/production levels associated with the following indispensible NNRs peaked permanently (to date) between 1975 and 2000: silicon (1979), aluminum (1980), nitrogen/ammonia (1980), potash (1980), sulfur (1981), rare earth minerals (1984), titanium (1989), and copper (1998).

Following the 1970s oil shocks and the 1980 commodity price spikes, the notion of NNR scarcity began to emerge in academic press, if not yet in the general public consciousness.

- "Therefore, if scarcity is measured by relative prices, the evidence indicates that nonrenewable natural-resource commodities are becoming scarce." (M. Slade, 1982[20])

- "The view that [NNR] scarcity is static or diminishing deserves reconsideration. It is no longer supported by the data and has not been supported by the data for a decade." (Hall and Hall, 1984[21])

### *US Societal Wellbeing 2000-2008: Peaking Societal Wellbeing*

As America transitioned from the 20th century to the 21st century, domestically available, economically viable NNR supplies continued to decrease—even as US demand for manufactured goods continued to increase unabated. In order to satisfy this demand, Americans resorted increasingly to imported finished goods produced entirely by foreign-owned companies.

The inevitable consequence was continuously declining American ownership and control of the NNR inputs, the production facilities and processes, and the goods and services outputs that enable America's way of life. Abundant best-in-class manufacturing capacity and low cost labor existed in newly industrializing nations—nations in which manufacturers could remain profitable despite continuously increasing NNR prices.

Year after year, the US produced fewer products that could not be produced less expensively elsewhere; to a disturbing degree, America was becoming a distribution outlet for foreign manufacturers. (As recently as December 2010, nearly 20% of US private sector jobs were in wholesaling and retailing.[22])

America's value-added contribution to the product provisioning process had diminished continuously for decades, as had its remaining pool of real wealth and its capacity to generate real purchasing power with which to procure NNRs and derived goods and services.

Staggering amounts of US financial wealth—much of it derived from pseudo purchasing power—flowed beyond US borders to pay for the entire product and service provisioning mix: raw materials (NNRs), marketing, engineering, production, distribution, customer service, administration, and profit. America's reign as the preeminent global production engine had come to an end.

America's response to its continuously eroding global economic dominance was to rely increasingly on pseudo purchasing power in increasingly desperate attempts to perpetuate its way of life.[23] Increasingly, Americans:

- Depleted their previously accumulated economic asset (wealth) reserves—home equity, savings, and physical assets;
- Exchanged ever-increasing quantities of fiat currency—"printed money" that has no intrinsic value—for real wealth;
- Incurred levels of debt at the individual, corporate, and government levels that they have neither the capacity nor the intention to repay; and
- Underfunded investments critical to their future wellbeing—"social entitlements" (Social Security and Medicare), pension funds, retirement funds, and infrastructure upgrades and repairs.

Due primarily to its ever-increasing fiscal profligacy—i.e., its ever-increasing reliance on pseudo purchasing power—America was able to overcome the bursting dot.com bubble and the 9/11 attacks and to further increase its economic output (GDP), population, and material living standard levels between 2000 and 2008:

- NNR input to the US economy **decreased** from 6,765 million tons in 2000 to 6,493 million tons in 2008.[24]
- US economic output (GDP) increased from $11.2 trillion (2005 USD) in 2000 to $13.3 trillion (2005 USD) in 2008.[25]
- America's population level increased from 281 million in 2000 to 304 million in 2008.[26]
- America's average material living standard, as defined by per capita GDP, increased from $39,900 (2005 USD) in 2000 to $43,800 (2005 USD) in 2008.[27]

US reliance on NNR imports continued to increase unabated during the early years of the new millennium. By 2008, America was (net) importing 68 of the 89 analyzed NNRs, including 100% of 19 NNRs. [Note that these figures do not include foreign NNRs used by US "offshore" manufacturers, or foreign NNRs contained in goods imported by the US—"direct" US NNR import figures significantly understate America's total reliance on foreign NNRs.]

Improvement in US societal wellbeing continued to slow between 2000 and 2008 as well, to the point where it was approaching peak.[28]

**Domestic (US) Compound Annual Growth Rates in Societal Wellbeing**

| US Societal Wellbeing Indictor | Compound Annual Growth Rate | | |
|---|---|---|---|
| | 1950 to 1975 | 1975 to 2000 | 2000 to 2008 |
| Total US NNR Utilization | 2.88% | 2.04% | -0.51% |
| US Economic Output (GDP) | 3.62% | 3.39% | 2.15% |
| Total US Energy Utilization | 3.01% | 1.24% | 0.05% |

### *US Societal Wellbeing in 2008: Peak Societal Wellbeing*

By the onset of the Great Recession:

- Domestic (US) NNR scarcity was epidemic—68 of the 89 analyzed NNRs had become scarce domestically by 2008; 58 of the 89 NNRs are "almost certain" to remain scarce permanently.

- American industrial preeminence[29] and global economic competitiveness[30] had declined steadily since the 1950s, as exemplified by America's declining manufacturing orientation.

## Declining US Manufacturing Presence

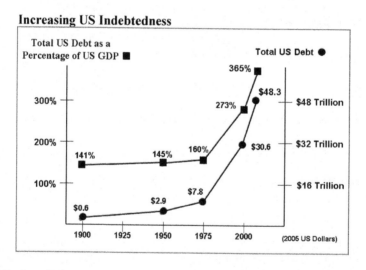

US Mfg. as a % of Global Mfg. Peaked in 1955

US Mfg. as a % of US GDP Peaked in 1963

- The American way of life was being financed to an ever-increasing extent by pseudo purchasing power. Increases in US debt levels[31] and declines in US savings rates[32] and home owners' equity levels[33] illustrate this trend.

## Increasing US Indebtedness

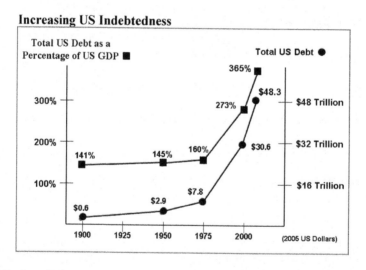

## Declining US Savings Rate

## Declining US Homeowner's Equity

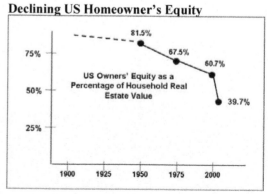

- Increases in US economic output (GDP)—and improvement in US societal wellbeing—which slowed dramatically between 2000 and 2008, peaked during 2008.

  Domestic (US) GDP [2005 USD] increased at a compound annual rate of 2.15% between 2000 and 2008, compared with a 3.49% compound annual growth rate between 1950 and 2000. US GDP increased 1.5% between 2006 and 2007, 0% between 2007 and 2008, and minus 2.2% between 2008 and 2009.[34]

The divergence between total US NNR requirements and domestically available, economically viable NNR supplies had increased since the middle of the 20th century. Through its ever-increasing reliance on pseudo purchasing power, the US filled its ever-widening "domestic NNR gap" with foreign NNRs—directly, through NNR imports; and indirectly, through offshoring and the importation of foreign-made finished goods.

During the decades preceding the Great Recession, foreign governments and businesses in export driven nations had been willing to trade their NNRs and finished goods for increasingly questionable US debt and continuously devaluing US dollars, in order to provide a seemingly unlimited market for their exports.

By the end of 2008, NNR scarcity had become epidemic globally and this arrangement broke down. US pseudo purchasing power, in the form of the "credit bubble", burst; and America plummeted into the Great Recession. The US, which had not been able to afford its way of life in real terms for decades, could no longer afford its way of life under any circumstances—even through its ever-increasing recourse to pseudo purchasing power.

**Peak US Societal Wellbeing**

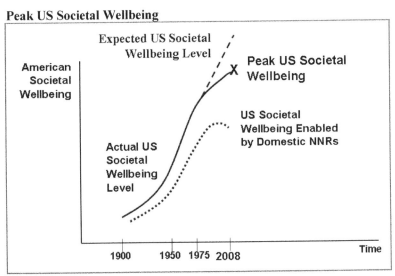

The Great Recession marked the peak in American societal wellbeing; the US will never again be able to obtain sufficient economically viable NNR supplies—domestic and foreign combined—to enable continuous increases in its economic output (GDP) level and societal wellbeing level.

While material living standards will improve for a continuously decreasing minority of Americans over the near term—as has been the case during the past several decades—aggregate US societal wellbeing has peaked.

## Indicators of Peaking US Societal Wellbeing

Since the middle of the 20th century, the US has resorted increasingly to unsustainable economic behavior to reinforce its centuries of unsustainable natural resource utilization behavior, in increasingly desperate attempts to perpetuate its unsustainable American way of life.

Indicators of America's impending peak in societal wellbeing, which have been in evidence for generations, have become increasingly pronounced in recent years.

**Continuously Devaluing US Dollar** – using the year 1950 as a baseline, each US dollar provided $1 worth of purchasing power in 1950. By the year 1975, the purchasing power provided by a US dollar declined to 43.6 cents; by 2008, the purchasing power of a US dollar further declined to 13.5 cents—only 13.5% of a dollar's value in 1950.[35]

**US Transition to a Service Economy** – 1957 was the last year in which the "goods" sector of the US economy (GDP) was larger than the "services" sector; by 2008 the "goods" sector comprised only 26% of the total US economy.[36]

**US Foreign Oil Dependence** – domestic US oil production peaked in 1970, and has declined at an average annual rate of 1.7% since that time; 1995 was the last year in which domestic (US) oil production exceeded imports; the US currently imports approximately two thirds of its oil and refined petroleum products.[37]

**US Dollar Becomes a Fiat Currency** – Richard Nixon closed the "gold window" in 1971, thereby reneging on America's pledge to exchange gold for US dollars on the international level, and relegating US currency to intrinsically valueless pieces of paper.[38]

**US Transition to a Net Importer** – 1975 was the last year in which the value of US exports exceeded the value of US imports; the 2008 annual US foreign trade deficit was $669 billion.[39]

**US Transition to a Debtor Nation** – 1981 was the last year in which the amount of money owed by the rest of the world to the US exceeded the amount of money owed by the US to the rest of the world; by the end of 2008, the US, now the world's largest debtor nation by far, owed the rest of the world over $6 trillion more than the world owed to the US.[40]

**US Transition to a Net Asset Seller** – 1985 was the last year in which US ownership of foreign assets exceeded foreign ownership of US assets; by the end of 2008, foreigners owned $3.5 trillion more US assets than US citizens owned of foreign assets.[41]

**Declining US Real Median Family Income** – real (inflation adjusted) US median family income peaked at $61,000 in the year 2000, despite the economic boom that occurred between the 2000 and 2008.[42]

**Unfunded US "Social Entitlement" Programs** – the amount by which projected future cash outflows associated with Social Security, Medicare, and Medicaid exceeded projected future cash inflows, expressed in today's dollars (present value), totaled over $70 trillion at the end of 2008; this unfunded liability is increasing by nearly $3 trillion per year.[43]

**Unrepayable US Debt** – total US debt exceeded $ 52 trillion at the end of June 2009, which was 3.7 times the size of annual US economic output (GDP); total US debt amounted to "only" 2.6 times the size of US GDP in 1929, at the onset of the Great Depression.[44]

**Increasingly Costly US Military Presence** – as of 31 March 2008, the US maintained a foreign military presence of 290,000+ personnel, on 820 installations, located in 158 countries; prior to WWII, America was an "isolationist" nation.[45]

**Aging Physical Infrastructure**—from airports to bridges to dams to the power grid to railroads to roadways to waterways, America's 2009 "Infrastructure GPA (Grade Point Average)" was a "D", and the estimated cost to fix the problem is $2.2 trillion.[46]

**Post-peak US NNRs** – 69 of the 89 NNRs analyzed in the NNR Scarcity Analysis have "almost certainly" or "likely" reached permanent domestic (US) extraction/production levels; 19 of these NNRs are indispensable to modern industrial existence.

**Domestic (US) Peak (To Date) NNR Extraction/Production Timing**

| Domestic (US) Peak (To Date) NNR Extraction/Production Years | | |
|---|---|---|
| **1900-1950** | **1951-1975** | **1976-1999** |
| Graphite - 1907 | **Iron Ore - 1953** | Thallium – 1977 |
| Silver - 1916 | Lithium - 1954 | Gallium - 1978 |
| **Manganese - 1918** | **Chromium - 1956** | **Silicon - 1979** |
| Stone (Dimension) - 1931 | **Cobalt - 1958** | Talc - 1979 |
| **Bauxite - 1943** | Cesium – pre-1959 | **Aluminum – 1980** |
| **Magnesium Metal - 1943** | Niobium – pre-1959 | Beryllium - 1980 |
| Mercury - 1943 | Rubidium – pre-1959 | Molybdenum - 1980 |
| Mica (Sheet) - 1943 | Tantalum – pre-1959 | **Nitrogen (Ammonia) - 1980** |
| Strontium - 1943 | Tellurium - 1960 | **Phosphate Rock - 1980** |
| Arsenic - 1944 | Thorium - 1961 | Barite -1981 |
| Fluorspar - 1944 | **Titanium Concentrates - 1964** | Germanium - 1981 |
| Antimony - 1948 | Indium - 1966 | **Sulfur - 1981** |
| | Magnesium Compounds - 1966 | Uranium - 1981 |
| | Helium - 1967 | Vanadium - 1981 |
| | **Potash - 1967** | Hafnium - 1983 |
| | Sodium Sulfate - 1968 | Mica (Scrap/Flake) - 1984 |
| | Cadmium - 1969 | Quartz Crystal - 1984 |
| | Selenium - 1969 | **Rare Earth Minerals - 1984** |
| | **Zinc - 1969** | Peat - 1987 |
| | Lead - 1970 | **Titanium Metal - 1989** |
| | **Oil - 1970** | Zirconium - 1989 |
| | Asbestos – 1973 | Gemstones - 1991 |
| | **Iron and Steel - 1973** | Rhenium - 1991 |
| | Vermiculite - 1973 | Iodine - 1992 |
| | Abrasives (Manufactured) - 1974 | Boron - 1995 |
| | | Bismuth – pre-1997 |
| | | Bromine – 1997 |
| | | Feldspar - 1997 |
| | | Nickel - 1997 |
| | | **Copper -1998** |
| | | Garnet (Industrial) - 1998 |
| | | Perlite - 1999 |

**Bold: Indispensable to Modern Industrial Existence**

## Future US Societal Wellbeing: A Bumpy Plateau into Continuous Decline

**US NNR Utilization Levels**

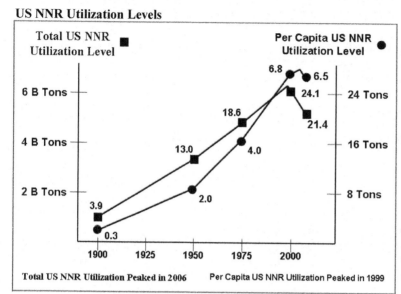

After increasing meteorically throughout the 20th century, total US NNR utilization levels plateaued and per capita US NNR utilization levels declined during the new millennium.[47] As NNR inputs to the US economy decline, US economic output (GDP) and societal wellbeing levels must decline as well.

America is caught in an NNR-scarcity-induced death spiral:

- Reduced levels of domestically available, economically viable NNR inputs to the US economy generate a reduced US economic output (GDP) level;
- A reduced US economic output (GDP) level yields a reduced wealth surplus with which to procure foreign (imported) NNR inputs to the US economy; the result...
- Continuously declining domestic (US) and foreign economically viable NNR inputs to the US economy generate continuously declining US economic output (GDP) levels—and continuously declining societal wellbeing!

### Declining NNR Inputs → Declining Economic Output (GDP) → Declining Societal Wellbeing (Population Level and Material Living Standards)

Assuming, however, that the US remains successful to some extent in "buying GDP with PPP" over the near term, it is unlikely that US economic output (GDP) and societal wellbeing will decline continuously from 2008 onward. It is more likely that US economic output (GDP) and aggregate societal wellbeing will move along a bumpy plateau, possibly for a decade or so, as the US desperately attempts to obtain sufficient NNRs and derived goods and services to perpetuate its American way of life.

Going forward, economic viability will be less of a consideration for American procurements of both imported NNRs and imported goods, as the US no longer has any illusions regarding the repayment of its "IOUs"; nor does the US have any reservations regarding the "printing" of whatever quantities of USD are required to obtain necessary imports.

America will pursue a strategy of "extend and pretend"—i.e., Americans will attempt to perpetuate their way of life at all costs, while professing immunity from the laws of economics and (more importantly) from the laws of Nature—in order to defer the inevitable—economic and societal collapse—for as long as its human and Natural benefactors will permit it to do so.

**America's Future Societal Wellbeing Trajectory**

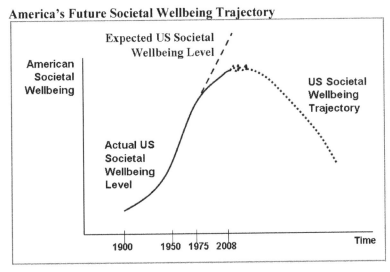

America's fate will be determined by its capacity to obtain sufficient NNRs and derived goods and services through pseudo purchasing power, military intervention, and the threat of military intervention. As these tactics fail in the not-to-distant future, America will fail as well.

Note that all industrialized nations are heavily reliant on imported NNRs and face similar fates—America is simply the most vulnerable.

## Implications of NNR Scarcity for Global Societal Wellbeing

As is the case with America, the vast majority of NNRs did not become scarce globally "in" 2008; they became scarce globally "by" 2008. The Great Recession marked milestones in global NNR scarcity and global industrialism, and a transition point—actually an inflection point—in global societal wellbeing.

### Global Societal Wellbeing Evolution

#### *Global Societal Wellbeing 1900-1950: Emerging "Western" Industrialization*

The global human population in the year 1900 was approximately 1.7 billion, of which approximately 200 million resided in nations that were industrialized or in the process of becoming industrialized.[48] Western Europe—specifically the UK, Germany, France, and Italy—and the US accounted for a majority of the world's industrialized and industrializing population in 1900; with Russia, Austria, and Japan accounting for most of the remainder.[49]

Total annual global economic output (GDP) in 1900 was approximately $2.1 trillion (2005 USD).[50]

By 1950, the global human population had increased to approximately 2.5 billion, of which approximately 500 million lived in nations that were industrialized or in the process of becoming industrialized.[51] By mid-century, much of Western Europe had joined the ranks of industrialized and industrializing nations.[52]

Total annual global economic output (GDP) increased to $6.6 trillion (2005 USD) by 1950.[53]

## Global Societal Wellbeing 1950-2000: Emerging "Eastern" Industrialization

Between 1950 and 2000, the global human population increased to approximately 6.1 billion[54], of which 4+ billion lived in nations that were industrialized or in the process of becoming industrialized.[55]

During the second half of the 20th century, industrialism spread to the Four Asian Tigers—South Korea, Hong Kong, Singapore, and Taiwan; to Latin America, most notably Brazil; and to Southern Africa, the Persian Gulf, and Eastern/South Eastern Asia, with China, India, Indonesia, Malaysia, and Thailand emerging toward the end of the 20th century.

Total annual global economic output (GDP) increased to $39.3 trillion (2005 USD) by 2000.[56]

Yet juxtaposed against these tremendous increases in global industrialization and economic output was the specter of looming global NNR scarcity. Annual global discovery levels associated with coal, copper, iron ore, natural gas, nickel, and oil peaked (to date) during the 1960s. Annual global lead, platinum group metals, uranium, and zinc discoveries peaked (to date) during the 1970s.[57]

## Global Societal Wellbeing 2000-2008: The Quest for Global Industrialization

Between 2000 and 2008, the global human population further increased to approximately 6.7 billion[58], of which nearly 5 billion were living in industrialized or industrializing nations. An increasing number of countries in Latin America, South America, and the Middle East were becoming industrialized.[59]

Total annual global economic output (GDP) increased to a historically unprecedented level of $49.4 trillion (2005 USD) by 2008.[60] Not surprisingly, global NNR demand and supply also reached historically unprecedented levels during the 2000-2008 period.

Global extraction/production levels associated with 66 of the 89 NNRs analyzed in the NNR Scarcity Analysis increased between 2000 and 2008. In some cases, 2000-2008 global extraction/production level increases were significant (40%-80%):

| 2000-2008 Global NNR Extraction/Production Increases | 2000-2008 Global NNR Extraction/Production Increases |
|---|---|
| Aluminum: 60% | Indium: 71% |
| Antimony: 67% | Iron/Steel: 63% |
| Bauxite: 51% | Magnesium: 59% |
| Beryllium: 65% | Molybdenum: 61% |
| Cement: 71% | Rare Earth Minerals: 47% |
| Chromium: 47% | Rhenium: 58% |
| Coal: 49% | Silicon: 76% |
| Gypsum: 47% | Zirconium: 75% |

In other cases, 2000-2008 global extraction/production level increases were extraordinary (80+%):

| 2000-2008 Global NNR Extraction/Production Increases | 2000-2008 Global NNR Extraction/Production Increases |
|---|---|
| Bismuth: 105% | Lime: 145% |
| Cobalt: 93% | Lithium: 87% |
| Germanium: 100% | Manganese: 91% |
| Iron Ore: 106% | Niobium: 154% |

The fact that annual global extraction/production associated with 62 of the 89 analyzed NNRs reached peak (to date) levels between 2000 and 2008, confirms the historically unprecedented levels of global NNR demand and corresponding global NNR supply that existed during the period of rapid global economic growth prior to the Great Recession.

### Global Societal Wellbeing in 2008: Divergence

Between 1900 and 2008, the number of people residing in industrialized and industrializing nations increased by a factor of 25—from approximately 200 million to nearly 5 billion. During that time, the level of global economic output as measured by GDP increased by a factor of 25 as well, from approximately $2 trillion to nearly $50 trillion (2005 USD).

Enabling this extraordinary increase in global industrialization over the past century were commensurate increases in global NNR utilization. While global NNR utilization data spanning the entire 1900-2008 interval are not available in most cases, the following representative examples demonstrate the magnitude by which global NNR utilization, as approximated by annual global NNR extraction/production levels, increased between 1900 and 2008.

**1900 and 2008 Annual Global NNR Extraction/Production Levels (Metric Tons)**

| NNR | 1900 Global Extraction/Production | 2008 Global Extraction/Production | 1900-2008 Increase |
|---|---|---|---|
| Aluminum | 6,800 | 39,000,000 | 5700 times |
| Bauxite | 88,000 | 205,000,000 | 2300 times |
| Cement | 62,400,000* | 2,840,000,000 | 46 times |
| Copper | 495,000 | 15,400,000 | 31 times |
| Iron Ore | 95,000,000** | 2,220,000,000 | 23 times |
| Manganese | 592,000 | 13,300,000 | 22 times |
| Molybdenum | 10 | 218,000 | 2100 times |
| Nickel | 9,290 | 1,570,000 | 169 times |
| Phosphate Rock | 3,150,000 | 161,000,000 | 51 times |
| Zinc | 479,000 | 11,600,000 | 24 times |

\* 1925 data
\*\* 1904 data

Total annual global NNR extraction/production levels increased dramatically in all cases between 1900 and 2008; increases in some cases were spectacular. More importantly, from the perspective of future global NNR requirements, billions of people residing in newly industrializing nations have yet to utilize NNRs at per capita levels that remotely approximate the levels at which NNRs are used by residents of currently industrialized nations.

For example, annual US per capita GDP was nearly 6 times larger in 2008 than annual global per capita GDP—$43,000 (2005 USD) in the US versus $7,400 (2005 USD) globally. Assuming that GDP scales in proportion to NNR utilization, which has been the case with

America since the inception of its industrial revolution[61], total global NNR utilization (economically viable NNR supplies) must increase approximately six fold to provide the global populace with an American living standard.

Unfortunately, this NNR utilization increase cannot possibly be achieved…

## Future Global Societal Wellbeing: Not Enough

By 2008, it was not only impossible for global NNR suppliers to completely address ever-increasing global NNR requirements in a timely manner; it was impossible for NNR suppliers to completely address ever-increasing global NNR requirements—period. The NNR quantities that were required to perpetuate the level of global economic output (GDP) and the rate of global economic growth that existed in 2008 could not be supplied at prices that were economically viable for both suppliers and buyers.

The vast majority of NNRs—63 of the 89 analyzed NNRs—were scarce globally in 2008. [Note: It is reasonable to assume that had incremental globally available, economically viable NNR supplies been available in any of the 63 cases for which global NNR scarcity existed in 2008, these supplies would have been brought online at some point between 2000 and 2008, thereby preventing the dramatic NNR price increases—and the Great Recession—that resulted in their absence.]

The increased price levels associated with these globally scarce NNRs made unprofitable many of the investment opportunities that were to be targeted beyond 2008, and that were required to maintain the then-prevailing global economic growth rate into 2009 and beyond. As ever-increasing numbers of these investment opportunities were postponed or canceled, global demand for the vast majority of NNRs declined as well—in many cases precipitously.

The tangible manifestation associated with the "destruction" of global NNR demand by the end of 2008 was the Great Recession. The less well understood but far more devastating implication associated with wide scale NNR scarcity by the end of 2008—given that scarcity in most cases is likely or almost certainly permanent—is the permanent divergence of future growth rates in global economic output (GDP) and societal wellbeing from their pre-recession (expected) rates.

**Future Global Societal Wellbeing Trajectory**

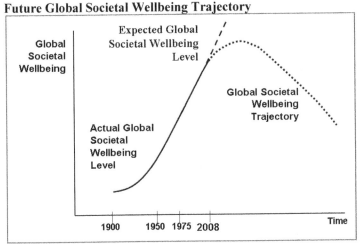

Sufficient economically viable NNR supplies should remain available globally to enable the reestablishment of pre-recession economic growth rates for some nations over the near term, and to enable global economic growth in the aggregate over the near term as well.

However, the overall global economic growth rate experienced prior to the Great Recession will never again be reestablished on a continuous basis. Rather, the size of the global economy—and the global societal wellbeing level—will increase at continuously declining rates, peak, and go into terminal decline within the next few decades.

## The Significance of 2008

Remaining globally available, economically viable NNR supplies are simply no longer sufficient in the aggregate to enable pre-recession growth rates in global economic output (GDP) and global societal wellbeing. NNRs that were scarce globally in 2008 will become increasingly scarce through continued exploitation; and an increasing number of NNRs for which supplies remained sufficient in 2008 will become scarce going forward through continued exploitation.

The upper limits to growth in global economic output (GDP) and global societal wellbeing have been reached. As attempts are made to recover from the Great Recession and restore global economic output levels and growth rates to pre-recession levels, and as global demand for NNR inputs approaches pre-recession levels, the economically debilitating effects of epidemic NNR scarcity will again be felt globally.

NNR price levels will increase as they did between 2000 and 2008, and the global economy will encounter a "growth ceiling" created by NNR scarcity, and experience a "Greater Recession".

In the likely event that global NNR exploitation continues unabated going forward, thereby further depleting remaining economically viable reserves, the global "growth ceiling" will become lower—i.e., the global NNR demand thresholds necessary to induce epidemic global NNR scarcity and trigger subsequent global economic recessions will decline continuously.

The stark conclusion to be derived from the NNR Scarcity Analysis is that 2008 marked the permanent "peak" in US societal wellbeing and the permanent "divergence from expected" global societal wellbeing. This assertion will be proven false only in the event that the US and global economies fully recover from the Great Recession and reestablish—for at least a decade—the economic output (GDP) levels and growth rates that existed prior to the Great Recession.

While it is possible that 2008 was a "false alarm" and that the permanent peak in US societal wellbeing and/or the permanent divergence from expected global societal wellbeing have yet to occur, what is known with certainty:

- The vast majority of NNRs had become scarce by the onset of the Great Recession—reaching the societal wellbeing limits posited by the Analysis is a question of "when", not "if"; and
- Neither our NNR-dependent natural resource utilization behavior nor our resulting industrial lifestyle paradigm is sustainable—their demise is also a question of "when", not "if".

**Humanity's Divergence from Sustainability**

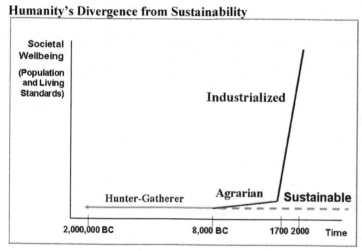

Humanity's fate was sealed in the 18th century, at the inception of our industrial revolution. The NNR genie had been let out of the bottle and could not be put back. Our insatiable appetite for the extraordinary improvements in societal wellbeing enabled by NNRs increased continuously from that point forward.

The episode of epidemic NNR scarcity in 2008 was merely a harsh reminder that the historically unprecedented population levels and material living standards associated with our temporary era of industrialism are coming to an end.

## Sustainability is Inevitable

"Business as usual" (industrialism), "stasis" (no growth), "downscaling" (reduced NNR utilization), and "moving toward sustainability" (feel good initiatives) are not options going forward; we will be sustainable...

### Unintended Consequences

It is difficult to argue that our incessant quest for global industrialization and the natural resource utilization behavior that enables our quest are inherently evil. We have simply applied our ever-expanding knowledge and technology over the past several centuries toward dramatically improving our level of societal wellbeing, through our ever-increasing utilization of NNRs.

However, despite our possibly justifiable naïveté during our meteoric rise to "exceptionalism", and despite the fact that our predicament is undoubtedly an unintended consequence of our efforts to continuously improve the material living standards enjoyed by our ever-expanding global population[62]; globally available, economically viable supplies associated with the NNRs required to perpetuate our industrial lifestyle paradigm will not be sufficient going forward.

## Our Transition to Sustainability

Humanity's transition to a sustainable lifestyle paradigm, within which a drastically reduced human population will rely exclusively on renewable natural resources (RNRs)[63]—water, soil (farmland), forests, and other naturally occurring biota—is therefore inevitable. Our choice is not whether we "wish to be sustainable"; our choice involves the process by which we "will become sustainable".

We can choose to alter fundamentally our existing unsustainable natural resource utilization behavior and transition voluntarily to a sustainable lifestyle paradigm over the next several decades. In the process, we would cooperate globally in utilizing remaining accessible NNRs to orchestrate a relatively gradual—but horrifically painful nonetheless—transition, thereby optimizing our population level and material living standards both during our transition and at sustainability.

Or, we can refrain from taking preemptive action and allow Nature to orchestrate our transition to sustainability through societal collapse, thereby experiencing catastrophic reductions in our population level and material living standards.

**Humanity's Choice**

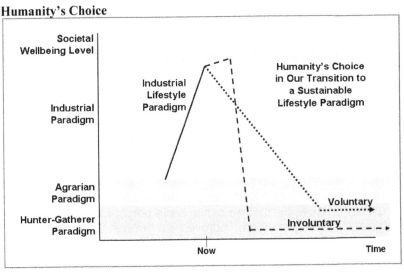

There are no other alternatives—we "will be" sustainable, either voluntarily or involuntarily; and we will be sustainable soon.

# VI. Consequences of NNR Scarcity

**We are the pathetic victims of tragic circumstances of our own inadvertent creation, which are beyond our capacity to resolve.**

- **What Happens Next?**
- **Humanity's Unraveling**
- **The "Squeeze" is On**
- **Was 2008 Different?**

As human beings, we want to believe that "for every problem, there is a solution". At worst, we want to believe that we can mitigate the risks, exposure, and/or damage associated with any problem, by taking preemptive or preparatory action.

In the case of problems related to renewable natural resource scarcity—water shortages, soil loss, crop shortages, etc.—and in the case of problems related to natural habitat degradation—pollution, biodiversity loss, climate change, etc.—solutions do exist, solutions that may involve little or no adverse impacts on our industrialized way of life.

Unlike problems related to RNRs and NHs, however, NNR scarcity cannot be solved. Rather, NNR scarcity will be resolved, inevitably through global societal collapse, which while not ecologically inevitable, is culturally inevitable. As a species that has been conditioned over hundreds of years to expect "continuously more and more", we will not accept gracefully our new reality of "continuously less and less".

We will not, therefore, seek to optimize our transition to sustainability as a global community, thereby cooperatively maximizing our global population level and material living standards both during our transition and at sustainability. We will attempt to optimize our wellbeing at the national level and ultimately at the individual level—each seeking to maximize his or her advantage at the expense of others, through conflict.

## What Happens Next?

We will make a catastrophic situation worse…

Regrettably, we are culturally incapable of transitioning voluntarily to a sustainable lifestyle paradigm. During the course of our industrialized epoch, we developed our cornucopian worldview—we believe, explicitly or implicitly, that we can achieve perpetual economic growth, population expansion, and material living standard improvement through our ever-increasing utilization of the earth's "unlimited" NNR supplies.

Our cornucopian worldview has rendered us unable to acknowledge our predicament—that our industrial lifestyle paradigm is <u>not sustainable</u> precisely because globally available, economically viable NNR supplies are <u>not unlimited</u>—much less to face the inevitably painful consequences associated with its resolution.

**Humanity's Paradox: We are the Unwitting Orchestrators of Our Own Demise**

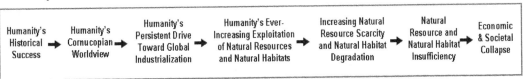

It is inconceivable that our increasingly industrialized global population will voluntarily adopt an unimaginably painful resolution to a predicament that our distorted cornucopian worldview will not permit us to acknowledge in the first place—even though a voluntary transition to sustainability is far preferable to the only available alternative.

Instead, we will squander earth's remaining accessible NNRs in futile attempts to perpetuate our unsustainable industrial lifestyle paradigm for as long as possible, thereby depleting remaining NNR reserves to levels at which they will become insufficient to support the economic output (GDP) levels, population levels, and material living standards associated with our industrialized and industrializing nations—a scenario that is unfolding now.

# Humanity's Unraveling

## Misperceptions

While we may not actually believe that global NNR supplies are truly "unlimited", we certainly behave as though we believe that there will always be "enough" NNRs to satisfy our ever-increasing global requirements—perpetual NNR sufficiency is presumed without question. This fundamental misperception, which gives rise to a series of related misperceptions, will lead to our demise.

Going forward, increasing global NNR scarcity will induce a series of increasingly frequent and severe economic recessions punctuated by increasingly brief and anemic recoveries, a trend that will be especially pronounced for the NNR-deficient—but highly NNR-dependent—nations in the industrialized "West".

Continuously increasing NNR prices combined with decreasing willingness by industrializing nations to exchange their real wealth—natural resources and derived goods and services—for unrepayable debt and continuously devaluing currencies from the industrialized West, will cause continuous declines in total purchasing power among Western nations.

As global NNR scarcity becomes increasingly pervasive, the previously improving material living standards associated with industrializing nations will stagnate; and the previously stagnant material living standards associated with industrialized nations will converge toward those of industrializing nations.

Because most global "opinion leaders" will continue to misperceive our situation from the human-centered anthropocentric perspective, they will erroneously attribute our ongoing decline in societal wellbeing to factors such as insufficient financial investment, insufficient technical innovation, and ineffective leadership.

The prevailing view will be that our predicament can and will be "fixed" through fiscal "stimulus", technology, education, and sound government policies (which will become increasingly protectionist and nationalistic).

Our situation will continue to deteriorate, however, despite our ongoing attempts to "fix" it. NNR scarcity will devolve into increasingly severe temporary NNR supply shortages, as ever-tightening NNR supplies fail increasingly to completely address global requirements. We will react with shocked disbelief—and increasing desperation—as our economic and political solutions fail dismally and completely to resolve our predicament.

**The Ecological Perspective**

By this time, increasingly larger segments of the global populace will come to understand our situation correctly, from the broader ecological perspective.

The Ecological Perspective

We will realize that our ever-expanding industrial lifestyle paradigm is enabled by earth's finite natural resources and natural habitats; we will realize that our economic woes are actually rooted in the increasingly scarce NNR supplies that are thwarting our incessant attempts to achieve global industrialization; and we will realize that increasing NNR scarcity is a Nature-imposed, geological absolute over which we have no control and that we cannot "fix".

We will realize, too late, that human economics and politics are irrelevant to Nature.

As we come to grips with this reality, and as our fiscal profligacy exacerbates our already deteriorating economic circumstances, we will resort increasingly to conflict in futile attempts to obtain the incremental natural resources required to preserve our faltering national economies.

Escalating natural resource wars in combination with our declining economic output levels will reduce our material living standards and population levels—a situation that will worsen as war related destruction disrupts our critical natural resource supplies and our critical societal support systems such as water distribution, food production and distribution, energy generation and distribution, sanitation, healthcare, transportation, communications, and law enforcement.

## Economic and Societal Collapse

As NNR scarcity becomes severe and NNR supply shortages become permanent, industrialized nations will be unable to maintain the economic output levels necessary to fund their ballooning debt service, social entitlement, and social services obligations—nor will they be able to obtain additional credit with which to offset their declining real wealth generation capabilities.

Interdependent national economies—initially those with large fiscal deficits and balance of payments deficits such as the US—will experience cascading defaults.

As permanent NNR supply shortages become ubiquitous, we will be unable to produce and provision societal essentials[1]—clean water, food, energy, shelter, clothing, and infrastructure—at levels sufficient to support our national populations. Nor will we be able to effect a voluntary transition to sustainability, should we even consider it, as excessively depleted natural resource reserves and excessively damaged societal support systems will no longer permit it.

**Global Societal Collapse**

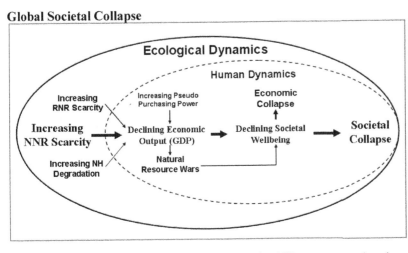

All industrialized and industrializing nations, irrespective of their economic and political orientations, will collapse, taking the aid-dependent, non-industrialized world with them.

Nature will orchestrate our transition to sustainability—remorselessly and horrifically—through famine, disease, and pestilence.

## The Aftermath

Under the best case scenario, a surviving global human population of a few million will remain to scavenge among the remnants of decimated natural resource reserves and severely degraded natural habitats. Under the worst case scenario, we will annihilate ourselves through global nuclear war.

Ironically, the more vigorously we strive to perpetuate our unsustainable industrialized way of life through ever-increasing NNR exploitation, the more quickly and thoroughly we will deplete NNR/RNR reserves and degrade natural habitats, thereby hastening and exacerbating our global societal collapse.

# The "Squeeze" is On

It would be convenient if our unraveling were to occur in 1,000 years, or 500 years, or even 50 years. We could then dismiss it as a concern for future generations and go busily about improving our national and global societal wellbeing levels in the meantime.

Unfortunately, this is not the case. The Great Recession was a tangible manifestation of our predicament—NNR scarcity was epidemic in 2008, both domestically (US) and globally. Our unraveling is in process.

At present, however, only an extremely small minority of the global populace understands that NNR scarcity is the fundamental cause underlying our predicament and its derivative economic and political problems. When the general public becomes aware of this fact and of the fact that NNR scarcity is a permanent, ever-increasing, and unsolvable phenomenon, collapse will ensue in short order.

## Public Ignorance

In the past, globally available, economically viable supplies associated with most NNRs were generally sufficient; NNR scarcity, when it occurred, was a temporary phenomenon. Incremental economically viable NNR supplies were available to be brought online, thereby restoring economic output (GDP) and growth to "expected" levels.

Because episodes of NNR scarcity have occurred periodically since the inception of our industrial revolution, they are considered temporary "inconveniences", which are interspersed with the boom phases of "normal" commodity boom/bust cycles.

Today, despite the fact that NNR scarcity is becoming increasingly prevalent—as clearly demonstrated by the NNR Scarcity Analysis—and despite the fact that the impact associated with NNR scarcity has certainly been felt—as an underlying cause of the Great Recession—the general public remains almost completely unaware. This is understandable, as it is obviously in nobody's interest to see humanity fail.

Our opinion leaders—i.e., the political, economic, and other societal elites who have the greatest vested interest in preserving the status quo—continue to preach that historically robust levels of economic growth can be sustained indefinitely. Some of our opinion leaders may still believe this to be true, although it is difficult to believe that many or most do.

[There currently exists considerable speculation regarding the extent to which our opinion leaders actually understand our predicament and its consequences, and are merely conducting a charade in order to perpetuate "business as usual", from which most of them benefit disproportionately, for as long as possible. At the end of the day, the awareness levels and motives associated with our opinion leaders are irrelevant; the outcome—societal collapse—remains unchanged.]

The general public—given their cornucopian worldview and their almost complete lack of understanding regarding the enablers of their industrialized existence—adheres steadfastly to the notion that "every generation will have it better than the last". The vast majority of the general public undoubtedly still believes this to be true, despite stagnant or declining material living standards in much of the industrialized world.

So long as myth supersedes reality and the general public remains ignorant regarding the nature of our predicament and of the fact that our predicament cannot be solved, complete societal collapse is unlikely. It is likely, however, that as our situation devolves, the general public will become increasingly frustrated, angry, and scared.

"We" will blame "them"—the government, corporations, foreigners, capitalists, communists, Christians, Muslims, the rich, the poor, anybody who is not "us"—for our continuously deteriorating circumstances. And we will become increasingly susceptible to the empty rhetoric of Hitleresque demagogues who promise—and fail—to restore "normalcy", at the expense of our remaining freedoms.

Through their ignorance, the general public will exacerbate our already deteriorating situation. They will fail to understand that "we"—all of us—are the problem.[2] We in the industrialized world have been and continue to be the all-too-willing beneficiaries of the unsustainable societal wellbeing levels afforded by our unsustainable industrial lifestyle paradigm.

**Public Awareness**

Within the next few years, however, NNR scarcity will become:

- "Noticeable"—NNR supplies will become increasingly constrained and NNR prices will rise continuously; then
- "Inconvenient"—periodic and temporary shortages and rationing associated with NNRs and derived goods and services will occur with increasing frequency; then
- "Disruptive"—shortages and rationing associated with ever-increasing numbers of NNRs and derived goods and services will become permanent; and finally,
- "Debilitating"—supplies associated with ever-increasing numbers of NNRs and derived goods and services will become permanently unavailable.

As this scenario unfolds, increasingly large segments of humanity will become aware of the fact that NNRs enable our industrialized way of life, and that ever-increasing NNR scarcity is the fundamental cause underlying our continuously declining economic output (GDP) and societal wellbeing levels, both domestically (US) and, by that time, globally as well.

Historically prevalent public attitudes of generosity and forbearance, which were made possible by abundant and cheap NNRs during our epoch of "continuously more and more", will be displaced by public intolerance:

- Childbirth will be condemned rather than celebrated;
- All immigration will be outlawed;
- Traditionally unquestioned resource uses—from "social entitlements" and universally accessible healthcare, to professional sports and cosmetics—will be considered "unfair" or "wasteful", and ultimately eliminated; and
- "Excessive wealth" will be appropriated for "the public good".

Ultimately, the general public will become aware of the fact that our predicament has no solution; and the following "trigger" conditions for societal collapse will be met:

- NNR scarcity will become "disruptive"—the available mix and levels associated with economically viable NNRs and derived goods and services will become insufficient to enable "tolerable" day-to-day existence; and
- Sufficiently large segments of society will:
  - Become aware of the fact that ever-increasing NNR scarcity is a permanent phenomenon; and
  - Acknowledge the fact that our predicament cannot be "fixed"; "continuously less and less"—continuously declining societal wellbeing—is our new reality.

Previously sporadic social unrest and resource wars will degenerate—seemingly instantaneously—into full fledged conflicts among nations, classes, and ultimately individuals for remaining natural resources and real wealth.

It will become universally understood that the only way to "stay even" within a continuously contracting operating environment—much less to improve one's lot—is to take from someone else. Life will become a "negative sum game" within the "shrinking pie" of "continuously less and less".

**Global Societal Collapse**

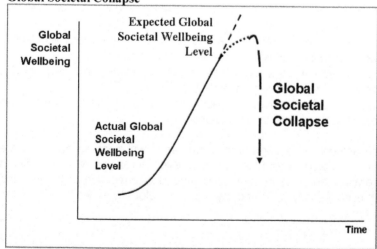

Social institutions will dissolve; law and order will cease to exist; and chaos will fill the void—nations will collapse.

## The Catalyst

The primary triggering event leading to humanity's demise will be the point at which NNR scarcity becomes "disruptive"—that is, when day-to-day existence for a sufficiently large segment of society becomes "intolerable".

Given the complexities associated with human nature, and the fact that industrialized Homo sapiens have never experienced "continuously less and less", it is impossible to define precisely the level of NNR scarcity at which continuously devolving human existence will become "intolerable"; nor is it possible to define precisely the "sufficiently large" segment of society for whom day-to-day existence must become intolerable in order to trigger collapse.

It is certain, however, that within an operating environment characterized by continuously contracting economic output (GDP) and societal wellbeing levels, this threshold will be reached—"continuously less and less" is a relentless, remorseless "squeeze" that will intensify interminably until humanity cracks.

## Timing

It is possible that the US experience can provide some guidance regarding the point at which the squeeze will become intolerable globally. In 1975, the approximate year during which US economic output (GDP) and societal wellbeing levels permanently diverged from historical growth trajectories, the global industrialized/industrializing population was approximately 1 billion.[3]

By 2008, less than 35 years later, US economic output (GDP) and societal wellbeing levels had peaked permanently. In the absence of ever-increasing NNR imports between 1975 and 2008, day-to-day existence for a sufficiently large segment of American society would surely have become sufficiently "intolerable" to induce significant social unrest, if not total societal collapse.

Given that half of the 89 analyzed NNRs are either likely or almost certain to remain scarce permanently at the global level; that no extraterrestrial source NNR imports exists for the world as a whole, and that the global industrialized/industrializing population has increased nearly 5 fold since 1975...

### Likely Global Societal Collapse Timing

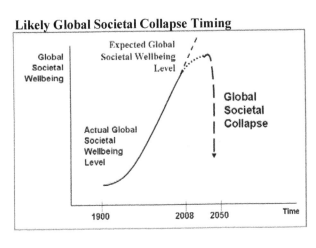

...it is highly likely that the interval between global societal wellbeing "divergence" in 2008 and global societal collapse will be 35 years or less.

Absent some combination of immediate and drastic reductions in our global NNR utilization levels, continuous major new economically viable NNR discoveries, and continuous major improvements in our NNR exploration, extraction, production, and processing technologies— none of which appear remotely possible—global societal collapse will almost certainly occur before the year 2050.

## Till Then

As NNRs become increasingly scarce and expensive going forward, some nations will fare better than others during the near term. Successful "economically viable" nations will be those that have ongoing access to their required mix and levels of economically viable NNRs, either within their borders or through importation, and that are able to maximize "added value" by profitably converting those NNRs into "demanded" finished goods at globally competitive prices.

Economically viable nations will experience upward trending economic output (GDP) and societal wellbeing levels, possibly for a decade or more. Nations that are unable to compete effectively at the global level will experience downward trending economic output (GDP) and societal wellbeing trajectories, a scenario that is currently unfolding within an ever-increasing number of nations.

Critical success factors associated with economically viable nations include:

- Sufficient "state-of-the-art" production capacity with which to generate sufficient real purchasing power with which to procure sufficient increasingly scarce NNRs;
- A workforce that is appropriately educated, trained, and skilled to produce targeted products;
- Production facilities and processes that are optimized to produce targeted products;
- Comparatively low business expenses including rents, wages, benefits, utilities, regulatory compliance, and taxes;
- A stable and comparatively unfettered economic operating environment unburdened by onerous government regulations and intervention; and
- Minimal reliance on pseudo purchasing power as a funding source for economic activity.

All else being equal, nations adhering most closely to these critical success factors will remain economically viable for the longest period of time, as they will be able to accommodate continuously increasing price levels associated with increasingly scarce NNRs for the longest period of time.

Nations such as Germany, which produce best-in-class, high priced goods; nations such as Japan, which produce high quality, reasonably priced goods; and nations such as China, which produce good quality, low priced, mass market goods, are likely to remain economically viable over the near term.

The US and other economically-overextended "developed" nations, which, for the most part, produce overpriced goods at various quality levels, are likely to experience continuously eroding global competitiveness.

It is essential to note, however, that while NNRs will be "relatively scarcer" for the less competitive nations in the near term, the vast majority of NNRs will continue to become "absolutely scarcer" for all nations, irrespective of their near term economic viability.

So while some industrialized and industrializing nations will remain economically viable over the near term, none are sustainable. All industrialized and industrializing nations will collapse in the not-too-distant future, as we resort increasingly to conflict as the primary means by which to allocate earth's dwindling nonrenewable and renewable natural resources and derived real wealth.

### What Can We Do?

The relevant question is "what will we do"? The answer is "nothing meaningful". We will continue to behave as we have during the past several centuries, until Nature intervenes; we are culturally incapable of behaving differently. And since our "best case" scenario going forward differs only marginally from our "worst case" scenario, there is no compelling reason to modify our unsustainable economic and ecological behavior at this point.

Through industrialism, humanity set out to accomplish great things; and we have accomplished great things. Unfortunately, we have obviated ourselves in the process.

## Was 2008 Different?

It is my contention that "2008 was different"—that 2008 was a pivotal year for both the US and the world with respect to future economic growth and societal wellbeing.

Specifically, globally available, economically viable NNR supplies will be insufficient going forward to enable pre-recession domestic (US) and global economic growth trajectories and societal wellbeing improvement trajectories on a continuous basis—there are not enough affordable NNRs.

If my contention is wrong, it is either premature or inaccurate.

**Premature**: In this case, my assertions regarding future US and global economic growth and societal wellbeing trajectories are correct; they will simply be validated at a later date. The actual "peak" (US) and "divergence" (global) points were not reached in 2008, but will be reached at some time in the future.

**Inaccurate**: In this case, the pre-recession NNR scarcity episode simply coincided with the boom phase associated with another commodity boom/bust cycle—NNR scarcity evidenced in 2008 was temporary, as has been the case for the past 200 years.

Sufficient globally available, economically viable NNR supplies will be brought online to restore pre-recession economic output levels and growth rates, domestically (US) and globally, and to enable the next economic "boom"; and the next, and the next...

If my assertions are premature, then the issue is one of timing, not outcome; and the only open issue is "when" my assertions regarding peak domestic (US) societal wellbeing and diverging global societal wellbeing will be validated.

If my assertions are inaccurate, then the fundamental cause associated with our "predicament" is strictly economic—there is no underlying ecological cause, there are no current or imminent geologically imposed NNR supply limits. Globally available, economically viable NNR supplies will remain sufficient to enable pre-recession (or better) economic output (GDP) levels, economic growth rates, and societal wellbeing improvement trajectories for the indefinite future.

In either case, notwithstanding global societal collapse in the meantime, the validity associated with my assertions will be known with certainty only in the next 10-20 years, as attempts are made to reestablish and ultimately exceed pre-recession domestic (US) and global economic output (GDP) levels and growth rates over an extended period of time.

In the event that pre-recession domestic (US) and global economic output (GDP) levels and economic growth rates can be reestablished or exceeded through the year 2025, and proven NNR reserve levels at that time remain sufficient to perpetuate global industrialism indefinitely from that point forward, I will stand corrected regarding my contention that "2008 was different".

While nothing would make me happier than being wrong about 2008, what remains beyond dispute is the fact that our definition of "enough" NNRs increases continuously, as our quest for global industrialism continues unabated, even as NNR quality declines continuously and economically viable NNR supplies tighten continuously. This scenario cannot end well.

# VII. Myths and Reality

**If we proceed from erroneous assumptions, we will arrive at erroneous conclusions.**

As a result of our extraordinarily positive experience with industrialism, we have developed a set of myths to reinforce our cornucopian worldview and our belief that our industrial lifestyle paradigm will exist in perpetuity. These myths are now unquestioned and are transmitted as part of our "cultural DNA".

Unfortunately, while we may find comfort, confidence, and strength in the rationalizations provided by our myths, they will not shield us from reality.

### Human Ingenuity and Initiative Can Solve Any Problem

**Myth:** Somebody will think of something; they always have, and they always will.

**Reality**: We tend to attribute our ever-improving industrialized societal wellbeing—which we achieved through our ever-increasing utilization of NNRs during our era of "continuously more and more"—almost exclusively to human ingenuity and initiative. We therefore tend to believe that through continued human ingenuity and initiative, we will continue to obtain "enough" NNRs to enable ever-expanding global industrialization and continuously improving societal wellbeing going forward.

We seem to overlook the fact that our good fortune was enabled by the historically abundant NNR reserves that existed, completely independent of any human involvement, during our era of "continuously more and more"; and that in the absence of said NNR abundance, human ingenuity and initiative would have availed us nothing.

While human ingenuity and initiative were necessary and significant facilitators of our industrialized "success" during our historical era of "continuously more and more", human ingenuity and initiative cannot possibly compensate for increasingly scarce NNRs during our new reality of "continuously less and less".

Going forward, the limiting factor is not insufficient human ingenuity and initiative; it is insufficient economically viable NNRs.

### Economic and Political Solutions Can Solve Any Problem

**Myth**: Through enlightened economic and political policies and initiatives at the national and global levels, we will overcome all obstacles to global industrialism and enable a continuously improving industrialized lifestyle for our ever-increasing global population.

**Reality**: Unfortunately, the fundamental cause underlying our predicament is ecological—ever-increasing NNR scarcity—it is not economic or political. The economic and political issues that we address and attempt to resolve are merely manifestations of our predicament—they are symptoms, not the disease.

To paraphrase Thoreau, we are "thrashing at the economic and political branches of our predicament, rather than hacking at the ecological root".

103

Since none of the economic and political expedients that we employ to solve these problems can create additional economically viable NNRs—which are the primary enablers of our industrialized existence—our economic and political "solutions" are irrelevant.

In fact, from the broader ecological perspective, all human economics and politics are irrelevant. Ownership of the means of production—from private ownership to state ownership; the methods by which scarce resources are allocated—from free markets to central planning; and our forms of government—from democracy to autocracy—have no bearing on industrial humanity's ultimate destiny.

All industrialized and industrializing nations, irrespective of their economic systems and political orientations, are unsustainable and will collapse in the not-too-distant future as a consequence of their dependence upon increasingly scarce NNRs.

## We Will Grow Our Way Out of It

**Myth**: Large industrialized nations such as the US can incur enormous debt obligations at the individual, corporate, and government levels because their robust and resilient economies will enable them to generate future economic growth and corresponding wealth surpluses with which to repay the debt. They can thereby "grow their way out" of seemingly exorbitant debt obligations.

**Reality**: "Growing our way out" of debt was a plausible—although not always practiced—strategy during our historical reality of "continuously more and more", in which NNRs were generally abundant and cheap.

During "continuously more and more", ever-increasing supplies of economically viable NNRs were available as inputs to the economies of industrialized nations such as the US. These NNR inputs generated increasing economic output (GDP) levels and increasing wealth surpluses with which to repay previously incurred debt—or at least to assure creditors that outstanding debt obligations could be repaid if necessary.

As an increasing number of NNRs have become increasingly scarce over the past several decades, economically viable NNR supplies available to nations such as the US have become constrained, and the uses of debt by these nations has changed dramatically as a result.

Historically, debt was typically used to fund collateralized investments and wealth producing investments, which would generate economic growth and create sufficient wealth surpluses (investment returns) to repay the debt. While total debt levels were seldom paid down, much less totally repaid, creditors remained convinced that sufficient wealth surpluses existed to repay the debt in the event that it was called in.

During the past several decades, debt has been used increasingly by nations such as America to finance current consumption—as an offset against flat or declining real growth in economic output and wealth creation—thereby generating no wealth surpluses with which to repay the debt, or to maintain the illusion that existing debt obligations can be discharged.

In the case of the US, the vast majority of debt—incurred increasingly from foreign sources—is used to finance consumer spending, wars, social entitlements, welfare and other transfer payments, pensions, and interest on previously incurred debt. Such uses of funds may produce short term increases in economic output; but they do not produce positive investment returns—wealth surpluses with which to repay the loans through which the funds were originally obtained.

Too, current debt-funded "investments" in areas such as education, research, technical innovation, infrastructure, and bailouts often lack well-defined and clearly articulated economic justification. It is therefore unclear to what extent, if any, these "investments" actually generate economic growth and wealth surpluses with which to repay debt.

It is becoming increasingly clear that economically stagnating nations such as the US can no longer "grow their way out" of excessive indebtedness. Economically viable NNR supplies available as inputs to their economies are no longer sufficient to produce the real wealth surpluses necessary to repay existing—much less continuously increasing—debt.

The result is a growing crisis in confidence regarding the creditworthiness associated with nations such as the US, which seek to offset anemic, flat, or declining economic output levels with ever-increasing debt in order to perpetuate the material living standards to which they feel entitled.

As existing and prospective creditors become increasingly wary, interest rates—and interest payments—incurred by these nations will increase, ultimately to levels at which interest obligations will become too onerous to be discharged. The resulting instances of fiscal insolvency will be addressed through "debt monetization" (central bank procurement of treasury issuance), "debt restructuring" (partial default) or "capitulation" (total default).

The only open issue at this point is the duration of the debt "confidence game"—more precisely, "sucker's game". How long will creditors remain willing to hold this obviously unrepayable debt?

## Everything is Cyclical—with an Upward Bias

**Myth**: Commodity (NNR) supplies and economic growth experience cyclical "ups and downs", but NNR supplies and national economies always recover from the down phases; and they always establish "higher highs" than previously—they "ratchet up".

**Reality**: Our experience with "continuously more and more" since the inception of our industrial revolution has created false impressions regarding NNR supplies and economic growth.

It was to be expected that the prevailing trends in NNR supplies, economic output (GDP), and societal wellbeing would be "up" during our historical period of "continuously more and more". "Continuously more and more" was characterized by a "requirements driven" environment, in which NNR utilization levels—and economic growth—were generally determined by ever-increasing NNR requirements.

These trends are reversing themselves as we transition to our new reality of "continuously less and less". "Continuously less and less" is characterized by a "supply constrained" environment, in which NNR utilization levels—and economic growth—are determined by continuously tightening, increasingly expensive NNR supplies.

As NNR scarcity becomes increasingly pervasive, NNR supplies, economic output (GDP), and societal wellbeing will peak and decline—they will "ratchet down", both nationally and globally.

## Plentiful NNR Supplies Remain to be Discovered

**Myth**: The earth is a virtual treasure trove of nonrenewable natural resources; abundant untapped NNR supplies remain available for generations to come.

**Reality**: While enormous quantities of nearly all NNRs exist in the undifferentiated earth's crust, an extremely high percentage of these NNRs are sub-economic, and will remain so. Economically viable NNRs—those that enable us to perpetuate our industrial lifestyle paradigm—are neither abundant nor widely distributed; and they occur only in well understood geological formations.

Because geologists have been using increasingly sophisticated techniques to search for these formations since the inception of our industrial revolution, the vast majority of the earth's surface has been explored and most of the high quality NNR deposits have been discovered and exploited.

Additional economically viable NNR deposits undoubtedly remain to be discovered, but such discoveries will be fewer in number, smaller in size, less accessible, and of lower grade and purity. All NNRs, with the possible exception of a few "practically inexhaustible" minerals such as sand, gravel, and stone, are becoming increasingly scarce—and even "practically inexhaustible" NNRs are not always sufficiently available when and where they are needed.

NNR scarcity does not involve "running out" of NNRs, it involves "running short" of NNRs. While there will always be "plenty of NNRs" in the ground, there will not always be "plenty of economically viable NNRs" in the ground.

In fact, there are no longer "enough economically viable NNRs" in the ground to perpetuate our industrial lifestyle paradigm going forward, as evidenced by the epidemic incidence of permanent NNR scarcity that precipitated the Great Recession.

## "Official" NNR Reserve Estimates Typically Understate Remaining Reserve Quantities

**Myth:** During the 20th century, official government estimates regarding remaining NNR reserves often understated actually remaining reserve levels. In many cases, additional investment brought forth new NNR discoveries, and new technologies increased the quantities of economically viable NNRs recoverable from known deposits. NNR reserve estimates thereby "grew" as a result.

**Reality:** It was to be expected that new discoveries and new technologies would increase ("grow") NNR reserves during our historical period of "continuously more and more". Many large, easily accessible, high quality NNR deposits remained to be discovered; and rudimentary NNR exploration and production technologies were subject to tremendous improvement.

As new discoveries were made and technologies were improved during the early years of relatively light NNR utilization, NNR reserves "grew" in nearly every case.

More recently:

- Remaining NNR deposits have become fewer in number, smaller in size, less accessible, and of lower grade and purity—NNR discoveries associated with an increasing number of NNRs are approaching, reaching, and passing peak levels;
- Incremental investments in new NNR exploitation technologies are experiencing diminishing returns—each incremental dollar invested in new technology generates fewer incremental NNRs; and
- NNR utilization levels, which draw down NNR reserves, are greater than ever in most cases—and are expected to increase dramatically in the future.

Going forward, economically viable NNR reserve levels will contract as a natural consequence of peaking/declining annual NNR discovery levels juxtaposed against ever-increasing annual NNR extraction/production levels.

## Increasing NNR Prices Always Bring About Sufficient NNR Supplies

**Myth**: NNR availability is determined by supply and demand; as users demand more NNRs and bid up the prices, additional NNR supplies are brought online.

**Reality**: Total NNR supplies in the earth's crust are enormous in nearly all cases. The preponderance of these supplies, however, is not economically viable. To be economically viable, an NNR must be both economically viable to produce and economically viable to procure.

As NNR demand increases, suppliers must exploit increasingly marginal—lower quality, higher cost—deposits to fulfill incremental demand. As NNR suppliers increase prices to cover their increasing costs, NNR prices reach levels at which they curb demand from users who cannot profitably employ these higher priced NNRs in available investment opportunities.

So while "plentiful" economically viable NNR supplies may exist from the producers' perspective, these increasingly expensive NNR supplies are not economically viable from the users' perspective—which accounts for the fact that the overwhelming majority of most NNRs remain in the ground, and always will.

Note too that economic output (GDP) and societal wellbeing do not increase as a result of increasingly expensive NNRs—i.e., the "value" provided by an NNR does not increase as its cost/price increases. The actual effect is just the opposite—higher priced NNRs diminish economic output (GDP) and societal wellbeing levels.

As NNR (input) prices increase, the number of profitable investment opportunities available to NNR users (buyers) decreases. NNR users therefore reduce NNR procurements (demand), target fewer investment opportunities, and generate lower levels of economic output (GDP) and societal wellbeing.

## We Can Always Produce Additional NNRs

**Myth**: Economic viability is irrelevant; so long as NNRs physically exist and we continue to need them, we will produce them irrespective of cost.

**Reality**: While it is certainly physically possible to extract/produce NNRs at levels greater than those that are economically viable, such a course of action is "suboptimal" from both economic output (GDP) and societal wellbeing perspectives—i.e., the incremental resources allocated to extracting/producing the sub-economic NNRs would generate greater economic output (GDP) and produce higher levels of societal wellbeing if they were invested elsewhere.

The inevitable consequences associated with producing sub-economic NNRs—as with any suboptimal investment—are suboptimal economic output (GDP) and suboptimal societal wellbeing.

So while sub-economic NNR supplies can certainly be extracted or produced—and certain segments of a society's population may benefit as a result—the net effect will be lower total economic output (GDP) and overall societal wellbeing levels than would be the case if the sub-economic NNRs were not extracted or produced.

## Legal Restrictions Currently Limit Access to Plentiful NNR Supplies

**Myth**: Abundant economically viable NNR supplies exist in countries such as the US, but are currently inaccessible due to legal restrictions or environmental regulations.

**Reality**: While it is true that restrictions and regulations in countries such as the US currently limit access to economically viable NNR deposits, both the size and quality associated with these off-limit reserves are often overstated—both by those who stand to gain through their exploitation and by uninformed "optimists" seeking panaceas—as is the capacity of these currently restricted NNRs to enable countries such as the US to become "independent" from foreign NNR imports.

That being said, the assumption regarding plentiful currently restricted economically viable NNR supplies is almost certain to be tested in the not-too-distant future, as NNRs become increasingly scarce globally, as surplus NNRs available for export to countries such as the US decrease, and as heavily import-dependent countries such as the US become increasingly desperate to perpetuate their way of life at all costs—including the abolition of existing restrictions on domestic NNR exploitation.

Only time will tell to what extent and over what period of time the exploitation of currently restricted NNR reserves can cost-effectively offset declining and increasingly expensive NNR imports for nations such as the US. It is likely that the relaxation of restrictions will have a meaningful positive impact in a few cases, while in most cases it will not.

## NNR Substitution will Eliminate NNR Scarcity

**Myth:** NNR substitutes have displaced scarce NNRs historically and will continue to do so going forward, thereby dramatically reducing requirements (and demand) for today's increasingly scarce NNRs.

**Reality:** Technically viable NNR substitutes exist in many cases; however, the vast majority of these technically viable substitutes are not economically viable—that is, the technically viable NNR substitutes are inferior from a price/performance perspective. [Note that both silver and aluminum are price/performance inferior substitutes for copper in the manufacture of electrical wire; each for a different reason!]

In other cases, substitutes that are both technically viable and economically viable exist, but are becoming increasingly scarce as well. In the remainder of cases, NNR substitutes simply do not exist.

It is safe to assume that if technically and economically viable substitutes for increasingly scarce NNRs were readily available, they would be in use today.

Note too that "forced substitution"—substituting a price/performance inferior NNR for a price/performance superior NNR—while physically possible in some cases, constitutes a suboptimal allocation of resources, and always suboptimizes total economic output (GDP) and overall societal wellbeing.

## Technical Innovation Will Insure Sufficient Incremental NNR Supplies

**Myth:** New technologies will enable us to discover additional NNRs and to recover greater quantities from the NNR deposits that we discover.

**Reality:** It is true that new technologies have enabled NNR discoveries in increasingly remote and difficult to access regions; and it is true that new technologies have enabled the recovery of increasing NNR quantities from existing NNR deposits.

However, because remaining NNR deposits are of continuously declining quality, technical innovation is subject to diminishing marginal investment returns—i.e., after some point, each incremental unit of technology investment yields continuously smaller quantities of economically viable NNRs—initially in individual deposits, then in nations, and ultimately globally.

So despite continuous technical innovation, technology must always play catch-up to declining NNR quality; and technology inevitably falls further behind.

That we must resort to increasingly complex and expensive "just-in-time" technologies to discover, extract, process, and provision sufficient supplies of dwindling "low ROI" NNRs—the only remaining NNRs—is the most telling evidence of increasing NNR scarcity.

Unfortunately, perpetuating our industrial lifestyle paradigm requires ever-increasing quantities of "high ROI" NNRs.

Note too that while technology can enable us to discover additional NNRs, recover additional NNR quantities from existing deposits, conserve NNRs, and use NNRs more efficiently; it cannot create additional NNRs. Technology is limited both in terms of its marginal effectiveness and its absolute effectiveness.

## Incremental Financial Investment Will Insure Sufficient NNR Supplies

**Myth:** Remaining NNR supplies are virtually unlimited, or are certainly sufficient to address our current and long term requirements. We need only make sufficient financial investments in NNR exploration and production to insure sufficient NNR supplies for centuries to come.

**Reality:** Financial investments of all types, including investments in NNR exploration and production, are subject to diminishing marginal returns—that is, after some point, each incremental unit of investment generates fewer incremental units of NNR output.

As remaining NNR deposits become fewer in number, smaller in size, less accessible, and of lower grade and purity, financial investments in NNR exploration and production are reaching the point of diminishing marginal returns in an increasing number of cases. Economically viable NNR supplies, which are required to perpetuate our industrial lifestyle paradigm, are becoming increasingly constrained—even as global requirements for these NNRs increase unabated.

## Recycling Will Extend NNR Supplies Indefinitely

**Myth:** Recycling will enable us to reuse previously extracted NNRs indefinitely, thereby greatly reducing or eliminating our future requirements for newly mined NNRs.

**Reality:** NNR recycling is currently employed extensively, both domestically and globally. In the US, recycled (old scrap) copper constitutes 6% of total domestic utilization; recycled aluminum, 30%; and recycled tin, 20%.[1] Yet mine production—new extraction—associated with these and other currently recycled NNRs increases unabated.

Recycled NNRs currently account for between 5% and 8% of total domestic (US) NNR utilization.[2] While recycling percentages can likely be increased both domestically and globally, it is also likely that the upside potential associated with such increases is small. Much of the economically viable recycling that can occur already occurs; and many indispensible NNRs, such as fossil fuels and fertilizer components, cannot be recycled at all.

The effectiveness associated with recycling is also limited by the fact that NNR loss results during each successive recycling iteration.

So while recycling certainly reduces our requirements for newly mined NNRs, future recycling will never eliminate our requirements for newly mined NNRs, nor is it likely in most cases to eliminate continuous increases in our requirements for newly mined NNRs.

## NNR Conservation Will Enable US to Reduce NNR Utilization Levels

**Myth**: We will dramatically reduce our global NNR requirement, demand, and utilization levels through NNR conservation and "green" initiatives.

**Reality**: Really—when? To date, we have shown no inclination toward adopting meaningful self-limiting natural resource utilization behavior. And it is unlikely that we will ever do so, since reducing our NNR utilization levels would reduce our corresponding economic output (GDP) and societal wellbeing levels—which we continuously strive to increase.

[For those who claim that we "waste" tremendous NNR quantities, and that simply "eliminating waste" would significantly reduce our NNR utilization levels, keep in mind that "waste" to one person is "livelihood" to another—or, more likely, to many. Reduced NNR inputs always generate reduced economic output (GDP) and societal wellbeing levels.]

Even in the event that we were to launch meaningful domestic (US) and global NNR conservation initiatives, reducing our NNR utilization levels would merely defer societal collapse, not avert it. We would simply deplete remaining NNR reserves more slowly and collapse at a slightly later date.

Notwithstanding the temporary NNR demand destruction that will accompany increasingly frequent and severe economic recessions going forward, so long as 1.5 billion people seek to perpetuate their industrialized way of life and at least 3 times that many actively aspire to an industrialized lifestyle, global NNR requirements and utilization levels will increase unabated.

Any minor decreases in NNR requirements accruing from human feel-good initiatives will be dwarfed by the unrelenting overall increases in NNR requirements and the resulting increases in global NNR utilization levels required to perpetuate ever-expanding global industrialization.

We will increase continuously both our NNR and RNR utilization levels, until geological factors (Nature) intervene to constrain supplies and limit our use.

## Increased Efficiency and Enhanced Productivity Will Reduce NNR Requirements, Demand, and Utilization

**Myth:** We will reduce our NNR requirements, demand, and utilization levels through increased efficiency and enhanced productivity solutions such as state-of-the-art machinery, factory automation, process improvements, computerization, and advanced digital communications.

**Reality:** We tend to think in terms of human efficiency and productivity, not in terms of NNR utilization efficiency and productivity. As a result, our efficiency improving and productivity enhancing solutions typically save human labor (and inconvenience) at the expense of additional NNR utilization.

Too, contrary to conventional wisdom, efficiency improving and productivity enhancing solutions devised specifically to reduce NNR utilization typically reduce "per unit" NNR utilization, while increasing "total" NNR utilization.[3]

## Population Stabilization Will Solve our NNR Scarcity Problem

**Myth:** Voluntary population stabilization or population reduction will dramatically reduce our NNR utilization levels, thereby "saving sufficient NNRs for future generations".

**Reality:** Population stabilization or reduction, assuming that either could be successfully implemented, would only defer our inevitable societal collapse, not avert it. Suppose that we could magically reduce our population level by 50%—instantaneously. All else being equal, we would reduce our NNR utilization levels by 50% as well—thereby merely doubling the time interval between now and societal collapse, from approximately 25 years to approximately 50 years.

Reducing our utilization of newly mined NNRs through population reduction, recycling, conservation, efficiency increases, productivity enhancements, or by any other means, affords us a temporary "stay of execution", at best, not a "pardon". So long as we use NNRs on a continuous basis, the result is the same—ever-increasing NNR scarcity culminating in societal collapse.

**"Stopping Growth", "Downscaling", or "Moving toward Sustainability" Are Viable Solutions to NNR Scarcity**

**Myth**: By voluntarily stabilizing or reducing our NNR utilization levels, we will enjoy a "simpler life"—a downscaled industrialized lifestyle paradigm—and enable future generations to do the same.

**Reality**: As is the case with population reduction, voluntarily stabilizing or reducing our NNR utilization levels through "halfway" measures—should we even consider such measures—would merely defer global societal collapse, not avert it. Slowing our pace would not alter our destination; we would simply deplete remaining NNR reserves more slowly and collapse at a slightly later date.

Achieving a sustainable lifestyle paradigm through unsustainable natural resource utilization behavior—i.e., through persistent use of finite and non-replenishing NNRs—is an oxymoron; it is physically impossible. A lifestyle paradigm that is enabled by unsustainable NNR utilization behavior—even at reduced levels—is unsustainable as well.

Attempting to justify our ongoing exploitation and utilization of nonrenewable natural resources—at any level—is simply self-serving hypocrisy. In truth, we hope that sufficient quantities of essential NNRs remain available to support <u>our</u> generation at a comfortable material living standard through the remainder of <u>our</u> lives; future generations are on their own.

Note too that modern industrialism is a global phenomenon; industrial existence at any level requires continuous access to NNRs from around the world. No nation—much less a state, province, city, or town—is even remotely close to being self-sufficient with respect to the economically viable NNRs required to perpetuate its existence. Self-contained, self-sufficient, industrialized "microcosms" are therefore physically impossible.

Finally, those who insist that "growth is the culprit", create the impression that humanity's current impact on the earth is somehow "OK"; and that it is our attempt to "grow" this impact that is "not OK".

In other words, were we to voluntarily "stabilize" our impact on the planet at existing levels—i.e., to maintain current levels of RNR utilization, NNR utilization, and NH degradation—our industrial lifestyle paradigm would somehow be sustainable, or "nearly sustainable". Nothing could be further from the truth.

Our modern industrial existence is enabled almost exclusively by finite and non-replenishing NNRs. NNRs serve as the raw material inputs to our industrialized economies, as the building blocks that comprise our industrialized infrastructure and support systems, and as the primary energy sources that power our industrialized societies.

NNRs have also enabled us to temporarily exploit RNRs and NHs at historically unprecedented levels, thereby enabling our species to temporarily overshoot earth's carrying capacity by orders of magnitude.

Stabilizing our levels of RNR utilization, NNR utilization, and NH degradation—should such an unlikely course of action ever be implemented—would slightly reduce future NNR depletion rates, temporarily delay the effects of increasing NNR scarcity, and briefly postpone our inevitable societal collapse. Stabilization—no growth—is only marginally preferable to continuous growth.

Humanity's aggregate impact on the planet has not been "OK" since our hunter-gatherer ancestors subsisted exclusively on RNRs; and our aggregate impact on the planet will not again be "OK" until our hunter-gather successors subsist exclusively on RNRs.

## We Can Avert Societal Collapse through a "Soft Landing"

**Myth:** Global societal collapse is not inevitable; we can "contract gradually"—i.e., reduce our population levels and material living standards gradually over time—as available NNR supplies contract.

**Reality:** Populations of existing industrialized nations such as the US, who take for granted "continuously more and more", will not accept gracefully our new reality of "continuously less and less". Nor will populations of industrializing nations, who aspire to "continuously more and more", accept gracefully the reality that they will never realize the improved material living standards afforded by an industrialized way of life.

The inevitable result of the shattered hopes and dreams to come will be escalating international and intranational conflicts over remaining natural resources, which will devolve into global societal collapse.

Our only alternative course of action involves a voluntary, globally-adopted, and well-orchestrated transition to a sustainable lifestyle paradigm—which must be initiated immediately and implemented quickly. Such a transition would culminate in a few hundred million people at most, living quasi agrarian/hunter-gatherer lifestyles at best.

While far preferable to global societal collapse, a voluntary transition to sustainability will not be seriously considered. As a species, we could never agree on how to allocate increasingly scarce natural resources during our transition; nor could we agree on how to reduce our population level and material living standards rapidly and continuously during our transition.

There can be no soft landing.

## Humanity's Real Problem Is the Unequal Distribution of Wealth

**Myth:** A majority of the world's wealth is currently held by a small elite minority. If the world's economic output were distributed equally among the world's population, everyone would enjoy a relatively comfortable living standard.

**Reality:** It is true that current global economic wealth and economic output, if divided equally, would provide a comfortable living standard for the world's population. Today's global average per capita GDP approximates that of Brazil—certainly a comfortable material living standard, and actually an improvement for the populations of 123 of the world's nations.[4]

Unfortunately, the redistribution of natural resources, wealth, and/or income would not resolve our predicament—which is caused by increasing NNR scarcity—the global demand/supply dynamics associated with future NNR availability remain unchanged. Globally available, economically viable NNR supplies will become increasingly scarce going forward, irrespective of who owns, controls, or derives benefit from them.

## "Advanced" Nations Such as the US Are Less Dependent on NNRs

**Myth:** NNR utilization levels in "advanced" nations such as the US are declining naturally, because "post-industrial economies" require fewer NNRs than emerging "production economies".

**Reality:** NNR inputs to the US economy have certainly declined during the past several decades in parallel with America's transition from a production economy to a "post-industrial" economy.

This transition was brought about not by choice, however, but by continuously decreasing domestically available, economically viable NNR supplies. The US did not "evolve" into a post-industrial economy; it "devolved" into a post-industrial economy. The US did not choose to become a post industrial economy in order to use fewer NNRs; it became a post industrial economy because it had access to fewer economically viable NNRs.

As domestically available, economically viable NNR supplies decreased, the US resorted initially to foreign NNR imports, followed by foreign offshoring and foreign goods imports, both of which utilize foreign NNRs. In addition, the US resorted increasingly to pseudo purchasing power, especially ever-increasing debt and continuous money printing (currency debasement), to pay for their ever-increasing reliance on foreign NNRs.

Current US NNR utilization levels are likely greater than ever; the mix has simply shifted increasingly toward foreign NNRs. This shift, in conjunction with America's ever-increasing "costs of doing business"—inordinately high wages, benefits, social entitlements, taxes, and regulatory compliance costs—have significantly undermined America's global economic competitiveness.

## Pre-collapse Preparation is the Answer

**Myth**: We have prepared successfully for disasters in the past, and we will prepare successfully for NNR scarcity.

**Reality**: Disasters with which we are familiar and for which we are accustomed to preparing—either natural disasters such as earthquakes, floods, volcanic eruptions, and hurricanes, or manmade disasters such as oil spills and nuclear leakages—are typically:

- Precipitated by a single, well-defined, catastrophic event; and
- Limited in terms of frequency and geographical scope.

Preparation for these natural and manmade disasters has been possible because:

- The preparatory requirements associated with each disaster type are generally well understood (although not always fully implemented); and

- Sufficient surplus human resources and natural resources have been available during our era of "continuously more and more" to enable thorough preparation and effective response—i.e., rapid emergency response and eventual total recovery.

Disaster victims have known that "help is on the way", typically within days, if not hours. They have also known that "things will return to some semblance of normalcy", typically within months, if not weeks or days—almost always through tremendous contributions of "outside assistance" (surplus resources).

As a result of our preparatory efforts, disaster related disruptions to critical societal support systems—such as water distribution, food distribution, energy generation and distribution, sanitation, healthcare, transportation, communications, and law enforcement—have been limited in terms of severity and duration.

Imminent disasters related to ever-increasing NNR scarcity, with which we are totally unfamiliar, will be:

- Precipitated by a currently unpredictable series of increasingly severe shortages associated with an ever-increasing number of NNRs, goods, and services; and
- Continuously increasing in terms of frequency, geographic scope, severity, and duration.

Attempts to prepare for disasters related to NNR scarcity are therefore futile because:

- The specific "unraveling" scenario associated with ever-increasing NNR scarcity cannot possibly be known in advance; and
- Surplus resources, especially NNRs, will not be available during our new era of "continuously less and less" to address ever-worsening shortages, outages, disruptions, and resulting conflicts.

As disasters related to NNR scarcity become increasingly prevalent and severe, and as the general public becomes aware of the fact that "help is not on the way" and that "things will not return to normal", social order will completely disintegrate and societal collapse will ensue.

Disruptions resulting from disasters that occurred during our historical era of "continuously more and more" were temporary—impacted populations recovered, and preparation facilitated the recovery processes. Disruptions resulting from ever-increasing NNR scarcity will be permanent—humanity will not recover, and no amount of preparation will alter that reality or its inevitable consequences.

## Post-collapse Preparation Is the Answer

**Myth:** Well-prepared individuals, groups, and communities will survive our impending collapse and maintain healthy, fulfilling, and productive lives in its aftermath.

**Reality:** Those who survive our collapse will be those who can obtain sufficient life sustaining essentials—especially clean water and food—on a continuous basis, both during and after collapse. Those who store large quantities of these essentials and those who attempt to produce food, either individually or in communities, will be easy targets for the vast majority who have neither the foresight to store nor the skills to produce.

No matter how remote or secluded your sanctuary, somebody will know about it; and they will come to call when they become desperate; and they will be well armed and devoid of compassion. You can prepare for a last stand, but you cannot prepare for post-collapse survival.

## Post-collapse Life Will Be Preferable to Our Industrial Lifestyle Paradigm

**Myth:** Industrialization has brought nothing but misery and degradation to the human race; our quality of life (and spiritual wellbeing) will improve substantially in a post-collapse world.

**Reality:** The post-collapse lifestyle awaiting the few who survive will, under the best of circumstances, share many attributes with pre-Columbian America. Unfortunately, the realities associated with subsistence level existence bear little semblance to the Hollywood accounts.

Those who anxiously await our post-collapse world will be disappointed, assuming they live to experience it. The fact that nobody is opting to jettison the amenities afforded by an industrialized way of life in favor of a hunter-gatherer lifestyle today should be sufficient proof that our future way of life is not something to be anticipated.

Industrialism is not inherently "evil" or immoral; it is simply unsustainable and physically impossible going forward.

# VIII. Humanity's Final Chapter?

**NNR scarcity is the most daunting challenge ever to confront humanity.
Should we fail to meet the challenge, "Scarcity" will become
"Humanity's Final Chapter".**

- Possibly...
- Probably...

## Possibly...

### Humanity's Predicament

During the course of our unrelenting pursuit of global industrialization, and our consequent ever-increasing utilization of the earth's increasingly scarce NNRs, we have been eliminating—persistently and systematically—the very natural resources upon which our industrialized way of life and our very existence depend.

Ironically, the natural resource utilization behavior that has enabled our historically unprecedented "success"—our industrial lifestyle paradigm—and that is essential to our continued success, is also pushing us toward our imminent demise. This is humanity's predicament.

### Humanity's Limited Perspective

To date, our distorted cornucopian worldview and limited anthropocentric perspective have rendered us incapable of understanding our predicament and its fundamental cause, which is ecological—ever-increasing NNR scarcity—not economic or political. The economic and political problems with which we concern ourselves are merely manifestations of our predicament—they are symptoms, not the disease.

Because none of the economic and political expedients that we employ to solve these problems can create additional NNRs, our attempted economic and political "solutions" are irrelevant. Metaphorically, our well is running dry, yet we insist on tinkering with the pump.

### Humanity's Ultimate Challenge

If humanity is to avert the global societal collapse scenario outlined in *Scarcity* and perpetuate our industrial lifestyle paradigm going forward, we must extract continuously increasing quantities of economically viable NNRs from deposits of continuously declining quality, thereby enabling us to provide ever-improving material living standards for ever-increasing numbers of our ever-expanding global population.

To accomplish this objective, we must:

- Continuously discover and successfully exploit major new economically viable deposits of nearly all NNR types—assuming that such deposits exist—from the earth's few remaining unexplored and less hospitable, higher cost, greater risk regions such as the ocean floor, beneath the ocean floor, beneath the polar ice caps, and in politically unstable nations; and

- Continuously develop major new NNR exploration, extraction, production, processing, and provisioning technologies that will enable us to cost-effectively extract and utilize continuously increasing quantities of economically viable NNRs from fewer, smaller, less accessible, and lower concentration deposits.

Simply put, we must obtain more and more from less and less at existing or lower costs—forever.

# Probably...

### Why 2008 was Different

City-states, nation-states, and international empires have collapsed throughout human history. Yet because previous instances of societal collapse occurred within the context of our historical reality of "continuously more and more", the detrimental impacts proved to be temporary for humanity as a whole.

Available natural resource supplies were sufficient to enable humanity to recover, and to actually increase our population levels and improve our material living standards following each collapse.

Our impending global collapse will be the first human societal collapse to occur within the context of our new reality of "continuously less and less". Because increasingly scarce natural resource supplies, especially economically viable NNR supplies, will be insufficient to enable a post collapse recovery, our impending collapse will be our last.

### Hitting the Ceiling—Again

The Great Recession and the sputtering post-recession recovery—despite massive central government "fiscal stimulus" programs and "accommodative" central bank monetary policies—clearly demonstrate the pervasiveness and permanence associated with both domestic (US) and global NNR scarcity. During the spring of 2011 as *Scarcity* goes to press, increasing NNR prices are threatening once again to throttle US and global economic output (GDP) and societal wellbeing levels.

(Note that this economic slowdown scenario did in fact occur in 2011, as evidenced by the global economic malaise that became increasingly prevalent during the year. Moreover, consensus end-of-the-year economic forecasts[1] call for a recession in Europe and continued economic sluggishness in the rest of the world going into 2012. The fledgling post-recession economic recovery of 2009/2010 was aborted in 2011 by NNR scarcity.)

Given the rapidity with which our "next" economic slowdown occurred, and given our in-process transition to "continuously less and less", our global economic/political situation could easily deteriorate quickly, as public frustration and anger over continuously declining material living standards manifest themselves in increasing social unrest.

If prevailing trends continue, global societal collapse will almost certainly occur well before the year 2050.

**"The 'developed' nations have been widely regarded as previews of the future condition of the 'underdeveloped' countries. It would have been more accurate to reverse the picture..."** – William Catton Jr., "Overshoot"

# IX. Postscript: Thoughts on Humanity's Predicament

### It's the ecology, stupid...

The following short essays expand upon three critical themes addressed in "Scarcity": 1) the ecological cause underlying our predicament; 2) our misguided attempts to "fix" our predicament through economic and political expedients; and 3) our failure as a species to respond intelligently to our predicament.

- Essay 1: Ecological and Economic Reality
- Essay 2: Nature's Ultimate Con
- Essay 3: Humanity's Fatal Distraction

## Essay 1: Ecological and Economic Reality

**Our persistent global economic malaise is rooted in ecology. As a consequence of our ever-increasing exploitation since the inception of our industrial revolution, the vast majority of the earth's finite and non-replenishing nonrenewable natural resources (NNRs), which serve as the primary inputs to our industrialized and industrializing economies, are becoming increasingly scarce globally.**

**The result is diminishing real economic output (GDP) levels, currently for NNR deficient Western nations with high material living standards, correspondingly high societal support costs, and consequent declining global economic competitiveness—such as the US and most of the industrialized West—and soon for the world at large.**

**NNRs**: NNRs—fossil fuels, metals, and non-metallic minerals—enable our industrialized way of life. They serve as the building blocks that comprise our industrialized infrastructure and societal support systems, as the raw material inputs to our industrialized economies, and as the primary energy sources that power our industrialized societies.

Unfortunately, through our incessant pursuit of global industrialism, we have been systematically eliminating the finite and non-replenishing NNRs upon which our industrialized way of life and our very existence depend.

**Humanity's Predicament**: the Great Recession marked a transition point in humanity's industrial lifestyle paradigm—going forward, there will not be "enough" globally available, economically viable NNRs to restore our global economic growth trajectory to its pre-recession level on a continuous basis. Under the best case scenario, global economic output (GDP) will increase at a declining rate, peak, and go into terminal decline within the next few decades.

**The Cause**: increasingly, the cost reductions associated with our ongoing improvements in NNR exploration, extraction, production, and processing technologies are no longer sufficient to offset the cost increases associated with continuously declining NNR quality—newly discovered NNR deposits are fewer, smaller, less accessible, and of lower grade and purity.

Ironically, while human ingenuity and technical innovations that increase economically viable NNR supply levels are experiencing diminishing returns, human ingenuity and technical innovations that increase our NNR requirement levels appear to be unlimited. Our global requirements for newly mined NNRs of nearly every type continue to increase unabated.

**The Result**: as industrialized and industrializing nations attempt to recover economically from the Great Recession—i.e., to reestablish their pre-recession economic output (GDP) levels and growth trajectories:

- Global NNR demand levels will increase,
- Which will cause increasingly costly NNR supplies to be exploited,
- Which will cause NNR price levels to increase,
- Which will cause NNR demand levels to decrease (demand destruction),
- Which will cause economic output (GDP) levels to diminish and the economic recovery to stall.

This "start-stop" economic recovery scenario manifested itself between 2009 and 2011. And, as global NNR scarcity becomes increasingly pervasive during successive economic recovery attempts, NNR demand destruction will occur at ever-lower "ceilings" or thresholds, and global economic output (GDP) levels and societal wellbeing levels—our population and material living standard levels—will ratchet downward.

**The Implications**: both our natural resource utilization behavior, which is heavily oriented toward enormous and ever-increasing quantities of finite, non-replenishing, and increasingly scarce NNRs, and our industrial lifestyle paradigm, which is enabled by our natural resource utilization behavior, are unsustainable—actually physically impossible—going forward.

Furthermore, because the fundamental cause underlying our predicament is ecological—not economic or political—our attempted economic and political "fixes" cannot possibly work. No combination of private and public "investments", "policies", and "initiatives" can enable us to extract enough economically viable NNRs to perpetuate our industrial lifestyle paradigm.

**The Consequence**: our transition to a sustainable lifestyle paradigm, within which a drastically reduced subset of our current global population will experience pre-industrial, subsistence level material living standards, is both inevitable and imminent.

And, because we are culturally incapable of implementing a voluntary transition to sustainability, our transition will occur catastrophically, through self-inflicted global societal collapse. As a species that has been conditioned since the inception or our industrial revolution to expect "continuously more and more", we will not accept gracefully our new reality of "continuously less and less".

# Essay 2: Nature's Ultimate Con

**Nature suckered us in with temporary abundance; a condition that we misconstrued as permanent...**

## The Set Up

Enabled by abundant and inexpensive domestic nonrenewable natural resources (NNRs)—fossil fuels, metals, and nonmetallic minerals—times were SO GOOD for Americans between the inception of our industrial revolution and the middle of the 20th century, that we came to believe that our domestic NNR supplies were unlimited and that our resulting prosperity was permanent.

This belief—formally articulated by our mantra "every American generation will have it better than the last"—became so firmly ingrained in our culture that we promised ourselves and our descendents the "American way of life"—continuously improving material living standards for our ever-expanding population—to be enabled by our "unlimited" NNRs.

## The Sting

Unfortunately, NNR supplies are not unlimited; they are finite and non-replenishing. And, by the mid/late 20th century, domestically available, economically viable supplies associated with the vast majority of the NNRs that enable our industrial existence had become scarce, and were no longer sufficient to fulfill the promises made by our ancestors during the era of American NNR abundance.

In response to ever-increasing domestic NNR scarcity, we relied increasingly on foreign subsidization in the form of imported NNRs, imported goods and services, and imported credit to perpetuate our American way of life through the mid/late 20th century and into the 21st century.

Today, as a consequence of living increasingly beyond our means over the past 150 years, both economically and ecologically, we are now "rolling over" in terms of our societal wellbeing level—i.e., our American way of life is entering a state of terminal decline.

## Read'em and Weep

Because NNRs are now becoming increasingly scarce globally as well as domestically, we in the US can no longer perpetuate our American way of life through imported NNRs, imported NNR-derived products and services, and imported credit.

We no longer possess adequate real wealth to offer in return for these imports, and the rest of the world is becoming increasingly wary with regard to accepting our unrepayable debt and continuously devaluing currency in exchange for their real wealth.

## Suckers...

America is Nature's greatest con to date because virtually nobody in America currently understands that we have been conned. We continue to believe unquestioningly that perceived "structural flaws in the American economy" can be "fixed" through "enlightened economic and political policies and programs".

Unfortunately, America's predicament cannot be "fixed" through economic and political expedients, because the underlying cause associated with our predicament is ecological—ever-increasing NNR scarcity—it is not economic or political.

Most unfortunately, America's predicament cannot be "fixed" at all, because we will never have access to "enough" economically viable NNRs—from domestic and imported sources combined—to enable us to deliver on the physically impossible promises made by our ancestors back when times were SO GOOD for Americans, temporarily.

Next sucker—the world…

# Essay 3: Humanity's Fatal Distraction

**Metaphorically, our well is running dry, yet we insist on tinkering with the pump.**

### Anthropocentric Viewpoints

Our anthropocentric (human-centered) perspective offers two conflicting viewpoints regarding the underlying cause and appropriate solution associated with the economic malaise that persists throughout most of the industrialized world.

Anthropocentric Viewpoints

| Viewpoints | "Right" Viewpoint | "Left" Viewpoint |
|---|---|---|
| **Perceived Problem** | Excessive Government Intervention | Unfettered Free Markets |
| **Proposed Solution** | Unfettered Free Markets | More Government Intervention |

**"Conservative Right" Viewpoint**: excessive government intervention in the economy causes resource misallocation—malinvestment—thereby causing suboptimal societal wellbeing (the material living standards enjoyed by our industrialized populations).

The solution is unfettered free markets, which will optimize resource allocation and maximize wealth creation, thereby maximizing societal wellbeing.

**"Liberal Left" Viewpoint**: unfettered free market capitalism causes resource misallocation toward the wealthy minority, thereby causing suboptimal societal wellbeing.

The solution is government sponsored economic policies and programs, which will mandate the "equitable" allocation of resources and promote "social justice", thereby maximizing societal wellbeing.

While the right is primarily concerned with "optimum" resource allocation and the left is primarily concerned with "equitable" resource allocation, both sides advocate the perpetuation of our industrial lifestyle paradigm; and both sides thereby advocate the ongoing exploitation of natural resources, especially nonrenewable natural resources (NNRs), in order to achieve this objective.

Further, each side believes that our economic malaise will be resolved—possibly following a major economic crisis—only when people "come to their senses" and implement its proposed solution.

## Flaws in Our Anthropocentric Perspective

Unfortunately, both anthropocentric viewpoints are inherently flawed...

- Both sides believe that economic/political "structural flaws"—which, ironically, are diametrically opposed—within the context of our existing industrial lifestyle paradigm, are responsible for our economic malaise. Both sides further believe that their recommended economic/political "structural changes"—which, ironically, are diametrically opposed—will remedy the situation and optimize global societal wellbeing going forward;
- Both sides focus exclusively on our economic/political behavior, and fail to consider our natural resource utilization behavior; and
- Neither side considers the sufficiency or sourcing of enabling natural resources, especially NNRs, going forward.

...because the underlying cause associated with our persistent economic malaise is ecological—it is not economic or political.

## Ecological Reality—Nature's Perspective

Our economic/political behavior is irrelevant within the broader context of our unsustainable natural resource utilization behavior—which is the real cause of our persistent economic malaise.

Specifically:

- The vast majority of NNRs—the fossil fuels, metals, and nonmetallic minerals that enable our industrial lifestyle paradigm—are becoming increasingly scarce globally. That is, there are not "enough" economically viable NNRs to perpetuate our industrial lifestyle paradigm going forward; and
- Implementing economic and political structural changes within the context of our industrial lifestyle paradigm is futile because our industrial lifestyle paradigm, which is enabled by our unsustainable natural resource utilization behavior, is also unsustainable—actually physically impossible—going forward, under any economic/political system.

## Our Fatal Distraction

We have allowed ourselves to become distracted by an irrelevant argument between two diametrically opposed, physically impossible, economic/political viewpoints, rather than attempting to address the most daunting ecological challenge ever to confront humanity—ever-increasing NNR scarcity.

We argue over tinkering with the pump, when our real problem is that our well is running dry.

## Why?

For reasons ranging from ignorance to denial, we as a species have failed to respond intelligently to our predicament—that is, by attempting to resolve our predicament in such a way that we avert global societal collapse.

- Most people are completely unaware of the fact that our industrial lifestyle paradigm and our industrialized economies are enabled almost exclusively by enormous and ever-increasing quantities of finite, non-replenishing, and increasingly scarce NNRs. They cannot, therefore, possibly understand that ever-increasing NNR scarcity is responsible for our current economic malaise, and, more importantly, for the imminent demise of our industrialized way of life.

- Too, most people have a strong vested interest, either as current participants or as aspirants, in perpetuating our industrial lifestyle paradigm. Those who are aware of ever-increasing NNR scarcity and of its catastrophic consequences often choose to deny a reality that they consider too unpleasant or too inconvenient to contemplate.

Regrettably, the vast majority of our influential "thought leaders"—business executives, politicians, academics, economic/political analysts, media commentators, social activists, and other "concerned citizens"—remain ignorant or in denial; and thereby perpetuate ignorance on the part of the general public, either unintentionally or intentionally.

Most regrettably, while the probability that we can avert or significantly mitigate the catastrophic consequences associated with our predicament through an intelligent response is certainly very small, the probability that we will experience imminent global societal collapse in the event that we remain ignorant or in denial and fail to respond intelligently is 100%.

# X. Epilog: An Intelligent Response to Humanity's Predicament

**It is not clear to me that an intelligent response to our predicament exists.**

In my six years of researching human sustainability and NNR scarcity, I have yet to encounter a prospective "solution" to our predicament that appears even remotely plausible; but I cannot say with certainty at this point that an "intelligent response" does not exist.

It is clear, however, that if we fail to formulate an intelligent response to our predicament soon; humanity's in-process unraveling will devolve into global societal collapse, essentially as described in **Scarcity**. It is also clear that we cannot possibly formulate an intelligent response if we remain ignorant or in denial regarding our predicament and its consequences.

And while the probability that we can formulate and implement an intelligent response to our predicament, thereby mitigating its catastrophic consequences, is certainly very small; the probability that we will experience imminent global societal collapse in the event that we remain ignorant or in denial and fail to respond intelligently is 100%.

**NNR scarcity is the most daunting challenge ever to confront humanity.**
**If we Homo sapiens are truly exceptional, now is the time to prove it.**

Chris Clugston
October 2011

# XI. End Notes and References

## Introduction

1. The anthropocentric perspective considers the philosophy, processes, and activities by which natural resource inputs to a society's economy are converted into goods and services outputs (wealth creation). It also considers the philosophy, processes, and activities by which goods and services (wealth) are allocated among a society's population. The fundamental assumption underlying the prevailing anthropocentric perspective is that notwithstanding periodic temporary shortfalls, natural resource inputs and natural habitat waste absorption capacities will remain sufficient to perpetuate global industrialism indefinitely. For an overview of anthropocentrism, see - http://en.wikipedia.org/wiki/Anthropocentrism.

2. The ecological perspective considers natural resource inputs and natural habitat waste absorption capacities as the ultimate limiting factors governing a society's economic/political processes and activities, its attainable economic output (GDP) level, and its attainable level of societal wellbeing—i.e., the material living standards enjoyed by the society's population.

## Chapter 1

1. The term "Nature", as used here, refers to the inestimable number of physical and biological processes and phenomena that define the physical world in which we live; neither consciousness nor a physical manifestation is ascribed to "Nature".

2. "Habitat", Wikipedia, 2009 - http://en.wikipedia.org/wiki/Habitat.

3. "Natural Resource", Wikipedia, 2011 - http://en.wikipedia.org/wiki/Natural_resource.

4. "Renewable Resource", Wikipedia, 2011 - http://en.wikipedia.org/wiki/Renewable_resources.

5. "Nonrenewable Resource", Wikipedia, 2011 - http://en.wikipedia.org/wiki/Non-renewable_resources.

6. US Senator Larry Craig summed up the role played by NNRs in enabling our modern industrial existence: "Without the thousands of materials derived from minerals, society would be unable to provide food, fuel, shelter, clothing, potable water, treatment and disposal of sewage and industrial wastes, garbage removal and processing, medicines and medical services, communications, facilities to produce and deliver electricity, construction and manufacturing facilities and equipment to build and maintain our places of business an our jobs, and the transportation systems that deliver these products to our homes and businesses and then remover our wastes. Moreover, we would be unable to maintain law and order and a national defense. Most of us would die." "Geodestinies", page 29; W. Youngquist, National Book Company, Portland, OR, 1997; originally from "Government Support for Geologic Research Faces an Uncertain Future", Geotimes, 1996) – http://www.geotimes.org/gtmar96.html.

7. The basis for real wealth creation exists:

- In the ground—crops;
- On the ground—livestock; and
- Under the ground—fossil fuels, metals, and nonmetallic minerals (NNRs).

Renewable natural resources (RNRs) are the basis for real wealth creation in both agrarian and industrialized societies. Human labor and RNRs in combination generate real wealth in the form of farm produce.

Nonrenewable natural resources (NNRs) are the primary basis for real wealth creation in industrialized societies. Human labor and NNRs in combination generate the vast array of infrastructure and products that differentiate industrialized societies from pre-industrial societies.

The "service sector" provides "added value", at best, in the process of real wealth creation. At worst, the service sector merely redistributes existing real wealth (surplus) and creates nothing.

8. "Mineral commodities refer to resources produced through geological events spanning time scales that are orders of magnitude greater than the time scales typically considered of relevance to the human race, millions of years vs. thousands of years." "Mineral Economics: Overview of a Discipline", J. Tilton and R. Gordon, Resources Policy, 2008.
9. Societal wellbeing involves a "tradeoff" between a society's population level and its average per capita material living standard. At a given a natural resource mix (and levels), there exists an array of possible population level and material living standard combinations. In general, a higher average material living standard necessitates a lower population level; a lower average material living standard enables a higher population level. For a more detailed discussion of the population level/living standard tradeoff, see "On American Sustainability—Anatomy of a Societal Collapse", pages 21-22 and accompanying notes; C. Clugston, 2009 – http://www.wakeupamerika.com/PDFs/On-American-Sustainability.pdf.
10. "The World of Hunter Gatherers", The TimeMap of World History, 2010 – http://www.timemaps.com/hunter-gatherer/.
11. "World Population", Wikipedia, 2011 - http://en.wikipedia.org/wiki/World_population.
12. "The World of Hunter Gatherers", The TimeMap of World History, 2010 – http://www.timemaps.com/hunter-gatherer/.
13. "The Coming of Farming", The TimeMap of World History, 2010 – http://www.timemaps.com/farming/.
14. Human life expectancy during the Upper Paleolithic (2.5 million BC to 10,000 BC) averaged approximately 33 years; human life expectancy varied considerably during the agrarian epoch, ranging from 18 years to the mid-30s – "Life Expectancy", Wikipedia, 2011 http://en.wikipedia.org/wiki/Life_expectancy.
15. "World Population", Wikipedia, 2011 - http://en.wikipedia.org/wiki/World_population.
16. For an explanation regarding the unsustainable nature of the agrarian lifestyle paradigm, see "Agriculture: Unsustainable Resource Depletion Began 10,000 Years Ago", Peter Salonius, 2008 - http://www.theoildrum.com/node/4628#more.
17. "The Industrial Revolution", Wikipedia, 2011 – http://en.wikipedia.org/wiki/Industrial_revolution; and "Industrialization", Wikipedia, 2011 – http://en.wikipedia.org/wiki/Industrialisation.
18. The current "global industrialized" population estimate includes the majority of people in Europe, North America, Russia, Japan, Australia, Singapore, Hong Kong, Taiwan, South Korea, South Africa, and Israel; plus population clusters in a multitude of nations in various stages of industrial development.
19. "US and World Population Clocks", US Census Bureau, 2011 – http://www.census.gov/main/www/popclock.html.
20. With very few exceptions—possibly some nations in sub-Sahara Africa and Latin America—essentially every currently non-industrialized nation is in the process of becoming industrialized.

21. For an overview of the timing and circumstances associated with the original settlement of the US, see David Stannard's "American Holocaust – The Conquest of the New World", pages 9-11; Oxford University Press, NY, NY, 1992.

22. William Catton explains this seeming paradox as follows: "The Europeans who began taking over the New World in the sixteenth and seventeenth centuries were not ecologists. Although they soon were compelled to realize that the Americas were not quite *un*-inhabited, they were not prepared to recognize that these new lands really were, in an ecological sense, much more than "sparsely" inhabited. This second hemisphere was, in fact, essentially "full". As we have seen, the world supported fewer people when they were at the hunter-gatherer level than when they advanced to the agrarian level. In the same way, a continent that was (ecologically speaking) "full" of hunters and gatherers was bound to seem almost empty to invaders coming from an agrarian culture and accustomed to that culture's greater density of settlement." "Overshoot", page 26; William Catton Jr. University of Illinois Press, Chicago, IL, 1982.

23. "Technological and Industrial History of the United States", Wikipedia, 2011 - http://en.wikipedia.org/wiki/American_Industrial_Revolution.

24. The vast majority of Americans rely upon high school text books and Hollywood for their US history education—it is loosely based on a true story. The mainstream historical perspective is consequently naïve, simplistic, myth-based, faith-based, superficial, and generally misinformed. For a more realistic depiction of America's heritage, especially as it pertains to the relationship between European settlers, American pioneers, and Native Americans, see David Stannard's "American Holocaust". For a more realistic depiction of America's current "predicament" and its inevitable consequences, see William Catton's "Overshoot".

25. Since the time of the Puritans, Americans have derived divine justification for their exploitive worldview and resource utilization behavior from the Bible: "And God said, Let us make man in our image after our likeness: and let them have dominion over the fish of the sea, and over the fowl of the air, and over the cattle, and over all the earth, and over every creeping thing that creepeth upon the earth." Genesis 1:26 (Bible)

26. Examples of European Settler and American pioneer self-bestowed justification for America's exploitive worldview and resource utilization behavior abound; for a representative sample see John Winthrop's bio - http://en.wikipedia.org/wiki/John_Winthrop; John Cotton's sermon to Winthrop and his Puritans prior to their departure to the New World - http://www.spartacus.schoolnet.co.uk/USABmapM.htm; and the perspectives of Presidents Washington, Jefferson, and Jackson in David Stannard's "American Holocaust", pgs 119-124.

27. Deborah Madsen offers an excellent explanation of the Puritan's view of American exceptionalism in "American Exceptionalism", pg 3 – http://books.google.com/books?hl=en&id=hOW1KB026LcC&dq=american+exceptionalism&printsec=frontcover&source=web&ots=i4rxAwjo5L&sig=aFA-SPBjbBcJS0moYd67XeH0ZYc&sa=X&oi=book_result&resnum=2&ct=result#PPA3,M1; see also the Wikipedia overview – http://www.google.com/search?hl=en&q=american+exceptionalism.

28. See John Winthrop's "City upon a Hill" sermon: "wee shall finde that the God of Israell is among us, when tenn of us shall be able to resist a thousand of our enemies [Native Americans], when hee shall make us a prayse and glory, that men shall say of succeeding plantacions: the lord make it like that of New England: for wee must Consider that wee shall be as a Citty upon a Hill, the eies of all people are uppon us;" – http://www.mtholyoke.edu/acad/intrel/winthrop.htm.

29 For a general explanation of the cornucopian worldview see Wikipedia –

http://en.wikipedia.org/wiki/Cornucopian; for a critical assessment of the cornucopian worldview see "The Cornucopian Fallacies" by Lindsey Grant - http://dieoff.org/page45.htm.
30. Estimated US nonrenewable materials (minerals) as a percentage of total US mineral utilization in the year 1800: US per capita mineral use in 1800 was ~1500 lbs. – http://www.mii.org/pdfs/Minerals1776vsToday.pdf. Total US energy consumption in 1800 was 0.47 quadrillion BTUs, all generated from biomass [wood] – http://www.eia.doe.gov/emeu/aer/txt/stb1701.xls. Given that the energy content of wood averages ~20 million BTUs per cord – http://hearth.com/econtent/index.php/articles/heating_value_wood, ~23.5 million cords of wood were used that year for "energy generation" purposes alone; this equates to ~4.43 cords/person on average, given an 1800 US population of 5.3 million – http://www.measuringworth.com/. A cord of hardwood weighs ~5000 lbs.; a cord of soft wood weighs ~3000 lbs - http://www.csgnetwork.com/logweight.html; assuming only 3,000 lbs./cord, the 4.43 cords/person equates to 13,300 lbs. of energy-related wood use per capita in 1800. The 13,300 lbs. figure does not include wood used for building and construction purposes; nor does it include agricultural material flows into the economy that year. Even so, the 1,500 lbs. of mineral use combined with the 13,300 lbs. of energy-related wood use produce a total of nearly 15,000 lbs. of material resources used per person in 1800, of which approximately 90% were renewable. It can be readily asserted that with the inclusion of "non-energy" wood use and agricultural material use, well over 90% of the material resources flowing into the US economy in 1800 were renewable; less than 10% were nonrenewable.
31. Estimated US nonrenewable materials (minerals) as a percentage of total US mineral utilization in the year 2008: the 2006 percentage of renewable materials flowing into the US economy from the Wagner USGS study was ~5% (see "the Mineral Mountain" and pgs. 20-24)—a percentage that had been relatively constant since the 1960s. Nonrenewables accounted for approximately 95% of the materials flowing into the US economy that year. "Economic Drivers of Mineral Supply", Lori Wagner et al., USGS, 2002 – http://pubs.usgs.gov/of/2002/of02-335/of02-335.pdf.
32. Estimated US energy derived from nonrenewable sources as a percentage of total US energy use in the year 1800: 0%; 0.47 quadrillion BTUs (Quads) of total US energy consumption in 1800 (average of 1795 and 1805), all of which was derived from renewable primary energy sources (biomass) - http://www.eia.doe.gov/emeu/aer/txt/stb1701.xls.
33. Estimated US energy derived from nonrenewable sources as a percentage of total US energy use in the year 2008: 92.6%; 99.4 Quads (quadrillion BTUs) of total energy consumption, of which 92.0 Quads were derived from nonrenewable primary energy sources – http://www.eia.doe.gov/emeu/aer/pdf/pages/sec1_9.pdf.
34. Estimated total US mineral (NNR) utilization in the year 1800: per capita US mineral utilization in 1776 was about 1200 lbs./year – http://www.mii.org/pdfs/Minerals1776vsToday.pdf; I increased the per capita number to 1500 lbs. for the year 1800; so total US mineral utilization was 1500 lbs. times 5.3 million people, equals (3,975,000 tons) ~ 4 million tons.
35. Estimated US total mineral (NNR) utilization in the year 2008: per capita US mineral utilization in 2008 was ~42,719 pounds, per Mineral Industry Information, pg. 2 - http://www.mii.org/pdfs/Baby_Info.pdf; times 304 million people, equals ~6.5 billion tons total.
36. Estimated US total energy use in the year 1800: 0.47 quadrillion BTUs; US EIA, "Estimated Primary Energy Consumption in the United States, Selected Years, 1635-1945" - http://www.eia.doe.gov/emeu/aer/txt/stb1701.xls.
37. Estimated US total energy use in the year 2008: 99.4 quadrillion BTUs; US EIA, "Primary Energy Consumption by Source", Annual Energy Review 2010 – http://www.eia.doe.gov/emeu/aer/pdf/pages/sec1_9.pdf.

38. Estimated US population level in the year 1800: 5.3 million; from Measuring Worth – http://www.measuringworth.com/.
39. Estimated US population level in the year 2008: 302 million; from Measuring Worth – http://www.measuringworth.com/.
40. Estimated US average annual per capita GDP (material living standard) in the year 1800: $1,398; from Measuring Worth - http://www.measuringworth.com/.
41. Estimated US average annual per capita GDP (material living standard) in the year 2008: $43,789; from Measuring Worth - http://www.measuringworth.com/.

# Chapter 2

1. "World Total Energy Consumption by Region and Fuel, Reference Case, 2005-2035" International Energy Outlook 2010, US EIA, 2010 – http://www.eia.gov/oiaf/ieo/excel/ieoreftab_2.xls.
2. "Coal", International Energy Outlook 2010, US EIA, 2010 – http://www.eia.gov/oiaf/ieo/coal.html.
3. "Natural Gas", International Energy Outlook 2010, US EIA, 2010 – http://www.eia.gov/oiaf/ieo/nat_gas.html.
4. "World Liquids Consumption by Sector", Figure 31 data, US EIA, 2010 – http://www.eia.gov/oiaf/ieo/excel/figure_31data.xls.
5. "Petroleum Based Products: A Long List", Save and Conserve, 2007 – http://www.saveandconserve.com/2007/05/petroleum_based_products_a_long_list.html.
6. "Metal", Wikipedia, 2011 - http://en.wikipedia.org/wiki/Metal.
7. "Industrial Mineral", Wikipedia, 2011 - http://en.wikipedia.org/wiki/Industrial_mineral
8. Estimated total US mineral utilization in the year 1800: per capita US mineral utilization in 1776 was about 1200 lbs./year - http://www.mii.org/pdfs/Minerals1776vsToday.pdf; I increased the per capita number to 1500 lbs. for the year 1800; so total US mineral utilization was 1500 lbs. times 5.3 million people, equals (3,975,000 tons) ~ 4 million tons.
9. Estimated US total mineral utilization in the year 2008: per capita US mineral utilization in 2008 was ~42,719 pounds, per Mineral Industry Information, pg. 2 – http://www.mii.org/pdfs/Baby_Info.pdf; times 304 million people, equals ~6.5 billion tons total.
10. Estimated US nonrenewable materials (minerals) as a percentage of total US mineral utilization in the year 1800: US per capita mineral use in 1800 was ~1500 lbs. – http://www.mii.org/pdfs/Minerals1776vsToday.pdf. Total US energy consumption in 1800 was .47 quadrillion BTUs, all generated from biomass [wood] – http://www.eia.doe.gov/emeu/aer/txt/stb1701.xls. Given that the energy content of wood averages ~20 million BTUs per cord – http://hearth.com/econtent/index.php/articles/heating_value_wood, ~23.5 million cords of wood were used that year for "energy generation" purposes alone; this equates to ~4.43 cords/person on average, given an 1800 US population of 5.3 million - http://www.measuringworth.com/. A cord of hardwood weighs ~5000 lbs.; a cord of soft wood weighs ~3000 lbs - http://www.csgnetwork.com/logweight.html; assuming only 3,000 lbs./cord, the 4.43 cords/person equates to 13,300 lbs. of energy-related wood use per capita in 1800. The 13,300 lbs. figure does not include wood used for building and construction purposes; nor does it include agricultural material flows into the economy that year. Even so, the 1,500 lbs. of mineral use combined with the 13,300 lbs. of energy-related wood use produce a total of nearly 15,000 lbs. of material resources used per person in 1800, of which approximately 90% were renewable. It can be readily asserted that with the inclusion of "non-energy" wood use

and agricultural material use, well over 90% of the material resources flowing into the US economy in 1800 were renewable; less than 10% were nonrenewable.

11. Estimated US nonrenewable materials (minerals) as a percentage of total US mineral utilization in the year 2008: the 2006 percentage of renewable materials flowing into the US economy from the Wagner USGS study was ~5% (see "the Mineral Mountain" and pgs. 20-24)—a percentage that had been relatively constant since the 1960s; nonrenewables accounted for approximately 95% of the materials flowing into the US economy that year; "Economic Drivers of Mineral Supply", Lori Wagner et al., USGS, 2002 – http://pubs.usgs.gov/of/2002/of02-335/of02-335.pdf.

12. From Measuring Worth - http://www.measuringworth.com/.

13. "Mineral Commodities Summary 2009", page 5; USGS, 2009 – http://minerals.usgs.gov/minerals/pubs/mcs/2009/mcs2009.pdf.

14. "Mineral Commodities Summary 2009", page 40; USGS, 2009 – http://minerals.usgs.gov/minerals/pubs/mcs/2009/mcs2009.pdf.

15. For all listed NNRs except oil - "Historical Statistics for Mineral and Material Commodities in the United States (various profiles), USGS, 2010 - http://minerals.usgs.gov/ds/2005/140/; for oil – "World Crude Oil Production 1960-2008, US EIA, 2010 - http://www.eia.doe.gov/emeu/aer/txt/stb1105.xls.

16. "Mineral Commodity Summaries 2010", various NNR profiles; US Geological Survey, 2010 - http://minerals.usgs.gov/minerals/pubs/mcs/2010/mcs2010.pdf.

17. "Mineral Commodities Summary 2009", page 44; USGS, 2009 – http://minerals.usgs.gov/minerals/pubs/mcs/2009/mcs2009.pdf.

18. "Titanium", Wikipedia, 2011 - http://en.wikipedia.org/wiki/Titanium.

19. "Crust", Wikipedia, 2011 - http://en.wikipedia.org/wiki/Crust_(geology).

20. "Abundance of Elements in Earth's Crust", Wikipedia, 2010 – http://en.wikipedia.org/wiki/Abundance_of_elements_in_Earth's_crust.

21. "Mineral and Energy Resources", Professor S. A. Nelson, Tulane University – http://earthsci.org/education/teacher/basicgeol/resource/resource.html.

22. "Mineral Commodities Summary 2009", page 191; USGS, 2009 – http://minerals.usgs.gov/minerals/pubs/mcs/2009/mcs2009.pdf.

23. "Mineral Commodities Summary 2009", page 192; USGS, 2009 – http://minerals.usgs.gov/minerals/pubs/mcs/2009/mcs2009.pdf.

24. "U.S. Average Depth of Crude Oil, Natural Gas, and Dry Exploratory and Developmental Wells Drilled (Feet per Well)", US EIA, 2011 – http://www.eia.gov/dnav/pet/hist/LeafHandler.ashx?n=PET&s=E_ERTW0_XWD0_NUS_FW&f=A.

25. "U.S. Real Cost per Crude Oil, Natural Gas, and Dry Well Drilled (Thousand Dollars per Well)", US EIA, 2011 – http://www.eia.gov/dnav/pet/hist/LeafHandler.ashx?n=PET&s=E_ERTW0_XWWR_NUS_MDW&f=A.

26. "U.S. Real Cost per Foot of Crude Oil, Natural Gas, and Dry Wells Drilled (Dollars per Foot)", US EIA, 2011 – http://www.eia.gov/dnav/pet/hist/LeafHandler.ashx?n=PET&s=E_ERTW0_XWPR_NUS_DF&f=A.

27. "Finding and Producing Natural Gas", page 4, US DOE, 2003 – http://www.fossil.energy.gov/programs/oilgas/publications/naturalgas_general/gas_fundamentals.pdf.

28. "Mineral Commodity Summaries 2010", various NNR profiles; US Geological Survey, 2010 - http://minerals.usgs.gov/minerals/pubs/mcs/2010/mcs2010.pdf.

29. An overview of mining in general and NNR production (with multiple references) can be found at - "Mining", Wikipedia, 2011 - http://en.wikipedia.org/wiki/Mining; additional detail regarding various NNR extraction and separation processes can be found at MineEngineer.com - http://www.mine-engineer.com/.

# Chapter 3

1. "Mineral commodities refer to resources produced through geological events spanning time scales that are orders of magnitude greater than the time scales typically considered of relevance to the human race, millions of years vs. thousands of years." From "Mineral economics: Overview of a discipline.", J. Tilton and R. Gordon; Resources Policy, 2008 - http://msl1.mit.edu/msl/students/msl_theses/Alonso_E-thesis.pdf.
2. Colin Campbell explains the depletion function associated with nonrenewable resources and provides examples pertaining to oil depletion in "The Coming Oil Crisis", pages 95-97; Colin J. Campbell, Multi-Science Publishing Company & Petroconsultants S.A., 1988.
3. "Geodestinies", page 19; W. Youngquist, National Book Company, Portland, OR, 1997.
4. For an NNR lifecycle example, see Figures 4 and 5 in - "World Oil Production Forecast – Update May 2009", Oil Drum, 2009 - http://www.theoildrum.com/node/5395; global (conventional) oil discoveries peaked in the mid 1960s, annual production exceeded annual discoveries in the mid 1980s, and global extraction peaked (to date) in 2008.
5. "When considering peak minerals, production follows the typical Hubbert [bell shaped] curve. However, well before peak production, mining operations start to become characterised by lower costs (with high ore grades, simple ores and low mine waste), but as the peak is approached and passed, the costs associated with production increase (because of falling average ore grades, deeper mines, complex ores and greater mine waste)." – "Peak Minerals", Wikipedia, 2010 - http://en.wikipedia.org/wiki/Peak_minerals.
6. "Natural Resource Economics", Wikipedia, 2011 – http://en.wikipedia.org/wiki/Natural_resource_economics.
7. "The Arrival of Peak Lead—Peak Environmental Impacts", Dr. Gavin Mudd, Lead Action News, 2010 - http://www.lead.org.au/lanv11n1/lanv11n1-8.html.
8. "Iron Ore", Wikipedia, 2011 - http://en.wikipedia.org/wiki/Iron_ore; and "Iron Ore", Mineral Information Institute", 2011 - http://www.mii.org/Minerals/photoiron.html.
9. "Soviet Natural Resources in the World Economy", page 265; Jensen, Shabad, and Wright - http://books.google.com/books?id=GiOU4EGyt_0C&pg=PA265&lpg=PA265&dq=declining+m etal+ore+grades&source=bl&ots=UPzRPL_6qT&sig=fgy0q58v3YMalucU0ZRtHrbxYxl&hl=en& ei=h3jJTMSJF4GglAfKzrnxAQ&sa=X&oi=book_result&ct=result&resnum=3&ved=0CCAQ6AE wAjgK#v=onepage&q&f=false.
10. "200 Years of Commodity Prices", Barry Bannister, 2010 - http://www.japaninc.com/files/images/mgz_72_commo-price-cycles.JPG.

# Chapter 4

1. Following is a sample of credible sources noting increasing NNR scarcity over the past several decades:
   - "Therefore, if scarcity is measured by relative prices, the evidence indicates that nonrenewable natural-resource commodities are becoming scarce." - 'Trends in Natural Resources Commodity Prices: An Analysis of the Time Domain', page 136; Margaret Slade; JOURNAL OF ENVIRONMENTAL ECONOMICS AND MANAGEMENT, 1982 –

- http://www.colorado.edu/Economics/vjcourses/resource/slade.pdf.
- "The view that [NNR] scarcity is static or diminishing deserves reconsideration. It is no longer supported by the data and has not been supported by the data for a decade." - "Concepts and Measures of Natural Resource Scarcity with a Summary of Recent Trends", page 373; Hall and Hall; JOURNAL OF ENVIRONMENTAL ECONOMICS AND MANAGEMENT, 1984 –
- http://www.csulb.edu/~dhall/Concepts%20and%20Measurements%20of%20Natural%20Resource%20Scarcity.pdf.
- "The overall [mineral] discovery rate rose throughout the 1950s and 1960s, peaked in the late 1970s, and evidently fell during the 1980s and 1990s." – "Fifty Year Trends in Mineral Discovery – Commodity and Ore Type Targets", Chris Blain, page 10; 'Exploration Mining Geology', Canadian Institute of Mining, Metallurgy, and Petroleum, 2000 - http://emg.geoscienceworld.org/cgi/content/abstract/9/1/1 (abstract).
- "[NNR] Consumption growth has in recent decades been fed by larger, more mechanized mining operations at the world's great ore bodies—those discovered, in most cases, many years ago. Application of technology and economies of scale are enabling more productive mining, overcoming the failure of exploration to sustain the resources mined. But this is temporary and it is unsustainable. I believe these great ore bodies are being discovered less frequently because they are getting scarcer." – "The Declining Discovery Trend – People, Science, or Scarcity?" page 1; Ross Beaty, Society of Economic Geologists Newsletter, 2010 –
- http://www.segweb.org/newsviews/81VIEWS_I_Apr2010.pdf.
- "There are some important factors that create serious concerns about to what extent mineral production can be expanded at the same rates as in the past. Two key factors are the increasing *geological* and *geographical distance* to minerals. Past mining has concentrated on picking the 'low-hanging fruit' and depleted those resources that were of the highest quality, easiest to extract and closest to consumers." - "Scarcity of Minerals", page 16; The Hague Centre for Strategic Studies, 2010 –
- http://www.georisq.nl/HCSS_Scarcity%20of%20Minerals.pdf.
- "Exploration of new locations and technological innovation in mining and extraction has kept the available and known material reserves on par with the increase in demand. Will this continue in the 21st century as well? It is difficult to predict a century ahead, but looking at a number of developments, we are afraid the answer is: no." - "Mineral Scarcity", page 3; Stichting Materials Innovation Institute (M2i), 2009 - http://www.m2i.nl/images/stories/m2i%20material_scarcity%20report.pdf.

2. Recent studies and analyses highlighting critical NNRs include:
- "Strategic Metals: An Introduction", Seeking Alpha, 2010 –
- http://seekingalpha.com/article/225173-strategic-metals-an-introduction.
- "Declaration of the World Resources Forum – September 16, 2009", World Resources Forum, 2009 - http://www.worldresourcesforum.org/wrf_declaration.
- "Minerals, Critical Minerals, and the US Economy", Committee on Critical Mineral Impacts of the U.S. Economy, Committee on Earth Resources, National Research Council, 2008 - http://books.nap.edu/catalog.php?record_id=12034.
- "Scarcity of Minerals", The Hague Centre for Strategic Studies, 2010 –
- http://www.georisq.nl/HCSS_Scarcity%20of%20Minerals.pdf.
- "Critical Raw Materials for the EU", Raw Materials Study Group/European Commission, 2010 –
- http://ec.europa.eu/enterprise/policies/raw-materials/files/docs/report_en.pdf.

3. Global NNR extraction/production levels are used as proxies for global NNR supply levels because reliable global NNR supply data (including recycled NNRs, reused NNRs, and NNR stock and inventory reductions) are generally unavailable. The annual NNR extraction/production level closely approximates the annual NNR supply level, and actually understates total supply in cases where recycled NNRs contribute to total supply. NNR extraction/production is considered a fair proxy for supply, given that the data were used only to determine the directional change in NNR supply between 2000 and 2008.

4. An NNR price level increase can result from "demand pull", in which case an NNR price is "bid up" by buyers; or from "cost push", in which case increased supplier capital costs and/or operating expenses are passed along to buyers. Note that both demand pull and cost push NNR price increases occur within an operating environment characterized by NNR scarcity.

In the former case, buyers willingly bid up NNR prices in an environment where available supplies are insufficient to completely address requirements. Higher prices serve as a rationing mechanism for scarce NNRs.

In the latter case, a cost push NNR price increase will only "stick" in the event that buyers are willing (and able) to pay the increased price for scarce NNR supplies. In the event that NNR supplies are abundant, one or more NNR suppliers will inevitably lower their prices as user demand declines (as a result of the attempted price increase), and the attempted price increase will fail.

5. While domestically available, economically viable NNR supplies associated with each of the 21 NNRs considered "not scarce" in the Analysis were sufficient to fulfill 2008 domestic (US) demand—the US did not (net) import these NNRs in 2008—it cannot be stated with certainty that domestically available, economically viable NNR supplies associated with each of these NNRs was sufficient to completely address domestic requirements in 2008.

The Analysis errs on the side of conservatism by characterizing these 21 NNRs as "not scarce" domestically in 2008, when any or all of them could have been scarce in the sense that while the domestically available, economically viable supply associated with each of the 21NNRs was sufficient to fulfill domestic demand in 2008, it may not have been sufficient to enable the societal wellbeing level "expected" by Americans in 2008.

6. The following excerpts from a 2008 Industry Week article support the contention that the US is physically unable to increase domestic economically viable extraction/production levels associated with most NNRs. "The preliminary estimated value of U.S. non-fuel mine production grew to $68 billion in 2007, a 2.9% increase over the previous year, according to the U.S. Geological Survey. The increase in value resulted from higher prices for many minerals rather than increased production. For most mineral commodities, the quantity produced [in the US] decreased." Yet, "…global consumption of metals and minerals rose, driven by the economies of China and India…" J. Jusko, "Value of U.S. Mineral Production Grew to $68 Billion in 2007", Industry Week, 2008 –
http://www.industryweek.com/articles/value_of_u-s-
_mineral_production_grew_to_68_billion_in_2007_15806.aspx.

7. Global peak NNR extraction/production projections are based on US Geological Survey (USGS) and US Energy Information Administration (EIA) NNR reserve estimates, in combination with (Verhulst) logistics curve fitting analyses contained in "Minerals Depletion", Dr. L. David Roper, 2010 - http://www.roperld.com/science/minerals/minerals.htm; projected peak global NNR extraction levels in the Analysis were determined by applying Verhulst logistics modeling (curve fitting) to historic annual global NNR extraction/production data and the USGS global NNR "reserve base" estimate (the larger of the two USGS estimates of

ultimately recoverable resources). For an explanation of the Verhulst logistics function and its applicability to projecting NNR depletion see – "Depletion Theory", Dr. L. David Roper, 1976 - http://www.roperld.com/science/minerals/DepletTh.pdf and "Verhulst Function for Modeling Mineral Depletion", Dr. L. David Roper, 2009 – http://www.roperld.com/science/minerals/VerhulstFunction.htm.

8. "World Total Energy Consumption by Region and Fuel, Reference Case, 2005-2035, Table A2; International Energy Outlook 2010, US EIA, 2010 – http://www.eia.doe.gov/oiaf/ieo/excel/ieoreftab_2.xls.

9. "Fertilizer", Wikipedia, 2011 - http://en.wikipedia.org/wiki/Fertilizer.

10. "The Evolution of Materials Used in Personal Computers", A. Monchamp (EIA), Second OECD Workshop on Environmentally Sound Management of Wastes Destined for Recovery Operations, 2000 - http://www.oecd.org/dataoecd/44/46/2741576.pdf; and "Innovative Technologies and Strategic Resources", slide 21; A. Reller, Environment Science Center, 2009 - http://www.lisboncivicforum.org/lisbon09/reller_pr.pdf.

11. "Theme: Material Demand Impact of Electric Cars", Seeking Alpha, 2010 – http://seekingalpha.com/article/185304-theme-materials-demand-impact-of-electric-cars; "Oil Scarcity Leads Us to Electric Cars, Which Leads Us to Neodymium Scarcity", Herron, Examiner.com, 2009 - http://www.examiner.com/green-transportation-in-national/oil-scarcity-leads-us-to-electric-cars-which-leads-us-to-neodymium-scarcity; "Electric Motor", Wikipedia, 2011 – http://en.wikipedia.org/wiki/Electric_motor; and "Solar Cell", Wikipedia, 2011- http://en.wikipedia.org/wiki/Solar_cell.

12. The 1975 global industrialized population of approximately 1 billion is estimated at roughly 20% of the 4.1 billion 1975 global population; industrialized regions at the time included most of Europe, Russia, North America, Japan, and the four Asian tigers.

13. Between the years 1800 and 2008, total US NNR utilization increased by a factor of 1625 times (from 4 million tons to 6.5 billion tons). During the same period, US GDP increased by a factor of 1799 times (from $7.4 billion [2005 USD] to $13.312 trillion [2005 USD]. The close correlation between increases in US NNR utilization and US GDP since the year 1800 is remarkable.

14. "Real Historical Gross Domestic Product (GDP) and Growth Rates of GDP", World Bank - http://www.ers.usda.gov/Data/Macroeconomics/Data/HistoricalRealGDPValues.xls.

15. "Scarcity of Minerals", page 15; The Hague Centre for Strategic Studies, 2010 – http://www.georisq.nl/HCSS_Scarcity%20of%20Minerals.pdf.

16. "Scarcity of Minerals", page 15; The Hague Centre for Strategic Studies, 2010 – http://www.georisq.nl/HCSS_Scarcity%20of%20Minerals.pdf.

17. "Fifty Year Trends in Mineral Discovery – Commodity and Ore Type Targets", Chris Blain, page 4 and Figure 18 on page 10 (the "bell shaped" NNR discovery plot peaked in 1969); Exploration Mining Geology, Canadian Institute of Mining, Metallurgy, and Petroleum, 2000 - http://emg.geoscienceworld.org/cgi/content/abstract/9/1/1 (abstract); "Mineral Commodity Summaries 2010", USGS NNR profiles contain coproduct and byproduct relationships; US Geological Survey, 2010 - http://minerals.usgs.gov/minerals/pubs/mcs/2010/mcs2010.pdf; "World Oil Production Forecast – Update May 2009", Figures 4 and 5; Oil Drum, 2009 - http://www.theoildrum.com/node/5395; http://www.theoildrum.com/node/5395; "Future of Natural Gas Supply", page 11, Figure 13; J. Laherrere (and Exxon) - http://www.peakoil.net/JL/BerlinMay20.pdf; and Colin Campbell explain peak NNR discovery as it pertains to oil: "The picture shows that there are now virtually no new major [oil] provinces left to find, and that efforts will have to concentrate on ever smaller and obscure prospects in established basins, and on trying to increase the recovery from what has already been

discovered. The law of diminishing returns applies very much to the discovery of oil." "The Coming Oil Crisis", page 77; Colin J. Campbell, Multi-Science Publishing Company & Petroconsultants S.A., 1988.

18. Colin Campbell explains the relationship between NNR discovery and NNR depletion in "The Coming Oil Crisis", pages 95-97. See also Appendix III (Production Profiles), pages 197-200, in which Campbell profiles the discovery/extraction profiles associated with oil in 22 countries. The intervals between peak discovery and peak extraction range between 20 and 60 years. Colin J. Campbell, Multi-Science Publishing Company & Petroconsultants S.A., 1988.

19. "Scarcity of Minerals", page 16; The Hague Centre for Strategic Studies, 2010 – http://www.georisq.nl/HCSS_Scarcity%20of%20Minerals.pdf.

20. "The Declining Discovery Trend – People, Science, or Scarcity?" page 2; Ross Beaty, Society of Economic Geologists Newsletter, 2010 – http://www.segweb.org/newsviews/81VIEWS_I_Apr2010.pdf.

21. "Scarcity of Minerals", page 15; The Hague Centre for Strategic Studies, 2010 – http://www.georisq.nl/HCSS_Scarcity%20of%20Minerals.pdf.

22. "The Declining Discovery Trend – People, Science, or Scarcity?" page 3; Ross Beaty, Society of Economic Geologists Newsletter, 2010 – http://www.segweb.org/newsviews/81VIEWS_I_Apr2010.pdf.

23. "Mineral Scarcity", page 3; Stichting Materials innovation institute (M2i), 2009 – http://www.m2i.nl/images/stories/m2i%20material_scarcity%20report.pdf.

# Chapter 5

1. Fred Cottrell described "sustainability" in 1955, before the term was even conceived, as "a type of persistent equilibrium between men and their environment" in "Energy and Society", page 33; Fred Cottrell, Greenwood Press, Westport, CT, 1955. For a broader explanation of "sustainability", see "Sustainability Defined", C. Clugston, 2009 - http://www.wakeupamerika.com/PDFs/Sustainability-Defined.pdf.

2. William Catton first described humanity's "predicament": "Human beings, in two million years of cultural evolution, have several times succeeded in taking over additional portions of the earth's total life-supporting capacity, at the expense of other creatures. Each time, human population has increased. But man has now learned to rely on a technology that augments human carrying capacity in a necessarily temporary way—as temporary as the extension of life by eating the seeds needed to grow next year's food. Human population, organized into industrial societies and blind to the temporariness of carrying capacity supplements based on exhaustible resource dependence, responded by increasing more exuberantly than ever, even though this meant overshooting the number our planet could support. Something akin to bankruptcy was the inevitable sequel." From "Overshoot", page 5; William Catton Jr. University of Illinois Press, Chicago, IL, 1982.

3. William Catton offers a general explanation of detritus ecosystems, in which organisms, detritovores, consume the finite food supply available within their habitat, bloom in the process, then crash (die-off) once the food supply becomes exhausted. He then goes on to explain detritovoric behavior as it pertains to humans, "It is therefore understandable that people welcomed ways of becoming colossal, not recognizing as a kind of detritus the transformed organic remains called "fossil fuels," and not noticing that Homo colossus was in fact a detritovore, subject to the risk of crashing as a consequence of blooming."; "Overshoot", pages 168-169; also - http://dieoff.org/page15.htm.

4. "Overshoot", page 96; William Catton Jr. University of Illinois Press, Chicago, IL, 1982.

5. Mineral Information Institute (Historic US NNR utilization information compiled by the Mineral Information Institute is available upon request from coclugston at Comcast dot net.) – www.mii.org.
6. Measuring Worth - http://www.measuringworth.com/.
7. Measuring Worth - http://www.measuringworth.com/.
8. Measuring Worth - http://www.measuringworth.com/.
9. For a more detailed discussion of Pseudo Purchasing Power, see "On American Sustainability—Anatomy of a Societal Collapse", page 19 and accompanying notes; C. Clugston, 2009 - http://www.wakeupamerika.com/PDFs/On-American-Sustainability.pdf.
10. Mineral Information Institute (Historic US NNR utilization information compiled by the Mineral Information Institute is available upon request from coclugston at Comcast dot net.) – www.mii.org.
11. Measuring Worth - http://www.measuringworth.com/.
12. Measuring Worth - http://www.measuringworth.com/.
13. Measuring Worth - http://www.measuringworth.com/.
14. "Geodestinies", page 62; W. Youngquist, National Book Company, Portland, OR, 1997; originally from "The Real War", page 341; R. Nixon, Warner Books, Inc. 1980.
15. Mineral Information Institute (Historic US NNR utilization information compiled by the Mineral Information Institute is available upon request from coclugston at Comcast dot net.) – www.mii.org.
16. Measuring Worth - http://www.measuringworth.com/.
17. Measuring Worth - http://www.measuringworth.com/.
18. Measuring Worth - http://www.measuringworth.com/.
19. Total US NNR Utilization—from the Mineral Information Institute (Historic US NNR utilization information compiled by the Mineral Information Institute is available upon request from coclugston at Verizon dot net.) - www.mii.org; US Economic Output (GDP)—from "Flow of Funds Accounts of the United States", US Federal Reserve, 2010 – http://www.federalreserve.gov/releases/z1/Current/data.htm; and Total US Energy Utilization—from "Primary Energy Consumption by Source, 1949-2009", Table 1.3; US EIA, 2009 - http://www.eia.doe.gov/emeu/aer/pdf/pages/sec1_9.pdf.
20. 'Trends in Natural Resources Commodity Prices: An Analysis of the Time Domain', page 136; Margaret Slade; JOURNAL OF ENVIRONMENTAL ECONOMICS AND MANAGEMENT, 1982 - http://www.colorado.edu/Economics/vjcourses/resource/slade.pdf.
21. "Concepts and Measures of Natural Resource Scarcity with a Summary of Recent Trends", page 373; Hall and Hall; JOURNAL OF ENVIRONMENTAL ECONOMICS AND MANAGEMENT, 1984 – http://www.csulb.edu/~dhall/Concepts%20and%20Measurements%20of%20Natural%20Resource%20Scarcity.pdf.
22. "The Employment Situation – December 2010", US Bureau of Labor Statistics, table B.1, 2011 - http://www.bls.gov/news.release/pdf/empsit.pdf).
23. For specific examples of 2007 domestic (US) consumption enabled by pseudo purchasing power, see notes 3-18 through 3-22 on page 70 of "On American Sustainability—Anatomy of a Societal Collapse"; C. Clugston, 2009 - http://www.wakeupamerika.com/PDFs/On-American-Sustainability.pdf.
24. Mineral Information Institute (Historic US NNR utilization information compiled by the Mineral Information Institute is available upon request from coclugston at Comcast dot net.) – www.mii.org.
25. Measuring Worth - http://www.measuringworth.com/.
26. Measuring Worth - http://www.measuringworth.com/.
27. Measuring Worth - http://www.measuringworth.com/.

28. Total US NNR Utilization—from the Mineral Information Institute (Historic US NNR utilization information compiled by the Mineral Information Institute is available upon request from coclugston at Verizon dot net.) - www.mii.org; US Economic Output (GDP)—from "Flow of Funds Accounts of the United States", US Federal Reserve, 2010 - http://www.federalreserve.gov/releases/z1/Current/data.htm; and Total US Energy Utilization—from "Primary Energy Consumption by Source, 1949-2009", Table 1.3; US EIA, 2009 - http://www.eia.doe.gov/emeu/aer/pdf/pages/sec1_9.pdf.

29. "The 2009 National Income and Product Account", US Bureau of Economic Analysis, 2010 - http://www.bea.gov/industry/xls/GDPbyInd_VA_NAICS_1998-2009.xls; and "GDP by Industry 1947 to 1997", US Bureau of Economic Analysis, 2010 - C:\Documents and Settings\Administrator\Local Settings\Temporary Internet Files\Content.IE5\G9N9ZIGD\GDPbyInd_VA_NAICS_1947-1997[1].xls.

30. "GDP Breakdown at Current Prices in US Dollars", United Nations UNStats, 2010 - C:\Documents and Settings\Administrator\Local Settings\Temporary Internet Files\Content.IE5\W88033OT\Download-GDPcurrent-USD-all[1].xls.

31. "Flow of Funds Accounts of the United States", Table L.1; US Federal Reserve, 2010 - http://www.federalreserve.gov/releases/z1/Current/data.htm.

32. "Flow of Funds Accounts of the United States", Table F.10; US Federal Reserve, 2010 - http://www.federalreserve.gov/releases/z1/Current/data.htm.

33. "Flow of Funds Accounts of the United States", Table B.100; US Federal Reserve, 2010 - http://www.federalreserve.gov/releases/z1/Current/data.htm.

34. "Flow of Funds Accounts of the United States", Table F.6; US Federal Reserve, 2010 - http://www.federalreserve.gov/releases/z1/Current/data.htm.

35. "Measuring Worth" - http://www.measuringworth.com/calculators/uscompare/result.php.

36. "GDP by Major Product Type", Table 1.2.5, US Bureau of Economic Analysis, 2009 - http://www.bea.gov/national/nipaweb/TableView.asp?SelectedTable=19&ViewSeries=NO&Java=no&Request3Place=N&3Place=N&FromView=YES&Freq=Year&FirstYear=1950&LastYear=2008&3Place=N&Update=Update&JavaBox=no.

37. "Petroleum Overview 1949-2008", Table 5.1, US Energy Information Administration, 2009 - http://www.eia.doe.gov/emeu/aer/txt/stb0501.xls.

38. "The Bretton Woods System", Wikipedia, 2011 – http://en.wikipedia.org/wiki/Bretton_Woods_system.

39. "US Federal Reserve Flow of Funds Accounts of the United States", Table F.107, 2009; 1975 data - http://www.federalreserve.gov/releases/z1/Current/annuals/a1975-1984.pdf; 2008 data - http://www.federalreserve.gov/releases/z1/Current/annuals/a2005-2008.pdf.

40. "US Federal Reserve Flow of Funds Accounts of the United States", Table L.1, 2009; 1981 data -http://www.federalreserve.gov/releases/z1/Current/annuals/a1975-1984.pdf ; 2008 data - http://www.federalreserve.gov/releases/z1/Current/annuals/a2005-2008.pdf.

41. "International Investment Position of the United States at Yearend 1976-2008", Table 2, US Bureau of Economic Analysis, 2009 - http://www.bea.gov/international/xls/intinv08_t2.xls.

42. "For Many, a Boom that Wasn't", The New York Times, 9 April 2008 - http://www.nytimes.com/2008/04/09/business/09leonhardt.html?ex=1365393600&en=83a62b21dfe6f807&ei=5124&partner=permalink&exprod=permalink.

43. "Fiscal and Generational Imbalances: An Update", pg. 26; Gokhale and Smetters, 2005 - http://www.philadelphiafed.org/research-and-data/events/2005/fed-policy-forum/papers/Smetters-Assessing_the_Federal_Government.pdf.

44. Year 2008 data ($52,793/$14,143) from "US Federal Reserve Flow of Funds Accounts of the United States", Tables f.6 and L1, 2009 – http://www.federalreserve.gov/releases/z1/Current/z1.pdf; 1929 data from; "Gold: Back to the Future?", Downs and Matlack, 2004 –

http://www.gold-eagle.com/editorials_04/matlack072304.html.

45. "Active Duty Personnel Strengths by Regional Area and by Country", US Department of Defense, 2008 - http://siadapp.dmdc.osd.mil/personnel/MILITARY/history/hst0803.pdf; and "United States Armed Forces", Wikipedia, 2009 – http://en.wikipedia.org/wiki/United_States_armed_forces.

46. "Report Card for America's Infrastructure", American Society of Civil Engineers - http://www.asce.org/reportcard/2009/.

47. Mineral Information Institute (Historic US NNR utilization information compiled by the Mineral Information Institute is available upon request from coclugston at Comcast dot net.) – www.mii.org.

48. "World Population", Wikipedia, 2011 - http://en.wikipedia.org/wiki/World_population.

49. "Relative Share of World Manufacturing Output, 1750 to 1900", Wikipedia, 2004 - http://en.wikipedia.org/wiki/File:Graph_rel_share_world_manuf_1750_1900_02.png.

50. Global GDP estimates consist of the averages between Kemmer's and Maddison's estimates, adjusted to 2005 USD – Kemmer - http://www.ier.hit-u.ac.jp/~kitamura/data/Source/WorldPopulationData.xls; Maddison – http://www.ggdc.net/Maddison/Historical_Statistics/horizontal-file_03-2007.xls.

51. "World Population", Wikipedia, 2011 - http://en.wikipedia.org/wiki/World_population.

52. "Industrialization", Wikipedia, 2011 - http://en.wikipedia.org/wiki/Industrialisation.

53. Global GDP estimates consist of the averages between Kemmer's and Maddison's estimates, adjusted to 2005 USD – Kemmer - http://www.ier.hit-u.ac.jp/~kitamura/data/Source/WorldPopulationData.xls; Maddison – http://www.ggdc.net/Maddison/Historical_Statistics/horizontal-file_03-2007.xls.

54. "World Population", Wikipedia, 2011 - http://en.wikipedia.org/wiki/World_population.

55. "Industrialization", Wikipedia, 2011 - http://en.wikipedia.org/wiki/Industrialisation.

56. "Real Historical Gross Domestic Product (GDP) and Growth Rates of GDP" [adjusted to 2005 USD], World Bank, 2010 – http://www.ers.usda.gov/Data/Macroeconomics/Data/HistoricalRealGDPValues.xls.

57. "Fifty Year Trends in Mineral Discovery – Commodity and Ore Type Targets", Chris Blain, page 4; 'Exploration Mining Geology', Canadian Institute of Mining, Metallurgy, and Petroleum, 2000 - http://emg.geoscienceworld.org/cgi/content/abstract/9/1/1 (abstract); "World Oil Production Forecast – Update May 2009", Figures 4 and 5; Oil Drum, 2009 - http://www.theoildrum.com/node/5395; http://www.theoildrum.com/node/5395; "Future of Natural Gas Supply", page 11, Figure 13; J. Laherrere (and Exxon) – http://www.peakoil.net/JL/BerlinMay20.pdf.

58. "World Population", Wikipedia, 2011 - http://en.wikipedia.org/wiki/World_population.

59. "Industrialization", Wikipedia, 2011 - http://en.wikipedia.org/wiki/Industrialisation.

60. "Real Historical Gross Domestic Product (GDP) and Growth Rates of GDP" [adjusted to 2005 USD], World Bank, 2010 – http://www.ers.usda.gov/Data/Macroeconomics/Data/HistoricalRealGDPValues.xls.

61. Between the years 1800 and 2008, total US NNR utilization increased by a factor of 1625 times (from 4 million tons to 6.5 billion tons). During the same period, US GDP (in 2005 USD) increased by a factor of 1799 times ($7.4 billion to $13,312 billion).

62. "Using the ecological paradigm to think about human history, we can see instead that the end of exuberance was the summary result of all our separate and innocent decisions to have a baby, to trade a horse for a tractor, to avoid illness by getting vaccinated, to move from a farm to a city, to live in a heated home, to buy a family automobile and not depend on public transit, to specialize, exchange, and thereby prosper.". "Overshoot", page 177; William Catton Jr. University of Illinois Press, Chicago, IL, 1982.

63. Conceptually, it is possible for a sustainable population to make use of previously extracted (recycled, reused, or stockpiled) NNRs, if such NNRs are processed and provisioned through the exclusive utilization of RNRs and previously extracted NNRs. In practice, such "sustainable NNR utilization" would be quite limited, and would become increasingly limited over time as previously extracted NNR supplies were depleted through reuse or continued recycling.

## Chapter 6

1. To paraphrase Liebig's Law of the Minimum (http://en.wikipedia.org/wiki/Liebig's_law_of_the_minimum): our capacity to perpetuate our industrial lifestyle paradigm is controlled not by all NNRs in our current NNR mix, but by the scarcest NNR or NNR combination (the limiting factor). Per William Catton, "The fundamental principal [of Liebig's Law] is this: whatever necessity is least abundantly available (relative to per capita requirements) sets an environment's carrying capacity [the total population level supportable by a given natural resource mix]." "Overshoot", page 158; William Catton Jr. University of Illinois Press, Chicago, IL, 1982.

Permanent disruptions to the supplies associated with one or a few NNRs will be sufficient to permanently impair our capacity to produce and provision societal essentials, thereby causing societal collapse.
2. "We will need to keep in mind that to a very large extent the horrible aspects of life in a future beset with a deepening carrying capacity deficit will have come about because of the things *almost everyone* hopefully and innocently did in the past. It wasn't just decisions and actions by someone in particular that inflicted grievous circumstances upon us, and subjected us to horrendous experiences. To single out supposed perpetrators of our predicament, resort to anger, and attempt to retaliate, will be the ultimate folly." "Bottleneck: Humanity's Pending Impasse", pages 124-125; William Catton Jr. Xlibris Corporation, 2009.
3. The 1975 global industrialized population of approximately 1 billion is estimated at roughly 20% of the 4.1 billion 1975 global population; industrialized regions at the time included most of Europe, Russia, North America, Japan, and the four Asian tigers.

## Chapter 7

1. "Mineral Commodity Summaries 2009", various NNR profiles; US Geological Survey, 2009 - http://minerals.usgs.gov/minerals/pubs/mcs/2009/mcs2009.pdf.
2. "Sociocultural and Institutional Drivers and Constraints to Mineral Supply", Brown, USGS 2002, pg. 41 (recycled metals) - http://pubs.usgs.gov/of/2002/of02-333/of02-333.pdf; and "Recycled Aggregates—Profitable Resource Conservation", USGS 2000, pg. 1 (recycled industrial minerals) - http://pubs.usgs.gov/fs/fs-0181-99/fs-0181-99so.pdf.
3. Jevons Paradox explains this seemingly counter intuitive phenomenon. "Jevons Paradox", Wikipedia, 2011 - http://en.wikipedia.org/wiki/Jevons_paradox.
4. "List of Countries by GDP (PPP) Per Capita", Wikipedia, 2011- http://en.wikipedia.org/wiki/List_of_countries_by_GDP_(PPP)_per_capita.

## Chapter 8

1. Example 2012 economic forecasts: Goldman Sachs - http://www2.goldmansachs.com/our-thinking/global-economic-outlook/outlook-2012/index.html; IHS -

http://www.ihs.com/info/ecc/a/economic-predictions-2012.aspx?ocid=top10-2012-pdsrch:globalinsight:ppc:0001&s_kwcid=TC|1026151|u.s.%20economic%20forecast||S|b|17398405538; IMF – http://money.cnn.com/2011/09/20/news/economy/imf_economic_outlook/index.htm/; Morgan Stanley - http://www.morganstanley.com/views/gef/; PIMCO – http://www.zerohedge.com/news/pimco-releases-2012-economic-forecasts-presenting-wall-street-2011-market-forecast-track-record; Reuters – http://www.reuters.com/article/2011/12/25/us-wrapup-2012-polls-idUSTRE7BM1BN20111225; United Nations - http://www.un.org/en/development/desa/policy/wesp/index.shtml.

# XII. Appendixes

- **Appendix A: NNR Profiles**
- **Appendix B: 2000 and 2008 Global NNR Extraction/Production Levels and Price Levels**
- **Appendix C: NNR Scarcity Definitions**

## Appendix A: NNR Profiles

Appendix A contains comprehensive criticality and scarcity assessments associated with each of the 89 NNRs that enable our industrial existence and that serve as the basis for the NNR Scarcity Analysis.

Note that NNR Profiles are not encyclopedic compendia of geological NNR information. NNR Profiles are comprehensive summaries of domestic (US) and global NNR demand, supply, and utilization information, from which meaningful assessments regarding pre-recession (2008) and future NNR scarcity can be derived.

The following "common" information sources are used in many, most, or all of the profiles:

1. "Mineral Commodity Summaries 2010" (USGS, 2010), US Geological Survey, 2010 - http://minerals.usgs.gov/minerals/pubs/mcs/2010/mcs2010.pdf.

2. "Mineral Commodity Summaries 2009" (USGS, 2009), US Geological Survey, 2009 - http://minerals.usgs.gov/minerals/pubs/mcs/2009/mcs2009.pdf..

3. "Mineral Commodity Summaries 2008" (USGS, 2008), US Geological Survey, 2008 - http://minerals.usgs.gov/minerals/pubs/mcs/2008/mcs2008.pdf.

4. "Historical Statistics for Mineral and Material Commodities in the United States"; US Geological Survey, 2010 - http://minerals.usgs.gov/ds/2005/140/.

5. "US Minerals Databrowser", MAZAMA Science, 2010 – http://mazamascience.com/Minerals/USGS/index.html.

6. "Minerals Depletion", L. David Roper, 2010 (Source of Projected Global Peak Extraction/Production Year and Projected Global Peak Supply Year) - http://www.roperld.com/science/minerals/minerals.htm.

Information sources applicable to each individual profile are referenced with the specific profile.

| NNR Profile | Abrasives (Manufactured) |
|---|---|

| **NNR Uses and Critical Applications** | |
|---|---|
| **Primary Uses** | Manufactured abrasives are hard, synthetically-produced industrial materials used in grinding, polishing, buffing, honing, cutting, drilling, sharpening, lapping, and sanding applications. |
| **Critical Applications** | Manufactured abrasives are widely used in a variety of industrial, consumer, and technological applications to shape, finish, or polish a workpiece through rubbing. |

| **NNR Criticality** | **NNR Criticality Classification: Critical** |
|---|---|
| **Substitutes** | Natural and manufactured (synthetic) abrasives are often substituted for each other; a variety of abrasives exist for nearly all applications. |
| **Criticality Assessment** | Abrasives, both manufactured and natural, are pervasive and play a key role as finishing agents in a multitude of industrial and construction applications. |

| **US NNR Scarcity** | **Scarce in 2008: Yes** | **Permanently Scarce: Almost Certain** |
|---|---|---|
| **2008 US Import Reliance:** 76% | | **2008 Domestic US Supply:** 24% |
| **Historical US Import Trends** | US reliance on manufactured abrasives imports increased steadily during the 20th century and into the 21st century. | |
| **Historical US Usage Trends** | Annual US manufactured abrasives utilization levels increased steadily during the first three quarters of the 20th century, peaking temporarily in 1918, 1929, 1937, 1943, 1957, and 1966, before peaking permanently (to date) in 1974. Domestic manufactured abrasives utilization generally declined during the latter decades of the 20th century and into the 21st century; the 2008 US manufactured abrasives utilization level amounted to only 70% of the 1974 peak utilization level. | |
| **US Peak Production Year (thru 2008):** 1974 | **US Peak Utilization Year (thru 2008):** 1974 | |
| **Potential Geopolitical US Supply Constraints** | 83% of US fused aluminum oxide and crude silicon carbide imports come from China. | |

| NNR Profile | Abrasives (Manufactured) [continued] |
|---|---|
| **US Scarcity Assessment** | That annual domestic manufactured abrasives utilization decreased by 30% since peaking (to date) in 1974, is a significant indicator of declining American industrial preeminence and global economic competitiveness.<br><br>The US currently relies heavily on imported manufactured abrasives, the overwhelming majority (83%) of which comes from China. The quantity of manufactured abrasives supplied by foreign sources during 2008 accounted for 76% of the total 2008 US utilization level.<br><br>Available evidence supports the contention that domestic manufactured abrasives supplies will remain insufficient to completely address domestic requirements going forward:<br><br>• The annual US manufactured abrasives production level decreased by 61% since peaking (to date) in 1974—a compelling indicator that domestic economically viable manufactured abrasives production has peaked permanently;<br>• The US has been heavily reliant on imported natural abrasives since the late 1940s; and<br>• The quantity of manufactured abrasives produced domestically during 2008 amounted to only 41% of the total 2008 US utilization level—a significant indicator of America's increasing dependence on foreign NNRs.<br><br>Barring future reductions in the domestic (US) manufactured abrasives requirement trajectory and/or major new domestic economically viable discoveries, manufactured abrasives will almost certainly remain scarce domestically in the future. |

| Global NNR Scarcity | Scarce in 2008: No | Permanently Scarce: Unclear |
|---|---|---|
| **Historical Global Production Trends** | "Imports and higher operating costs continued to challenge abrasives producers in the United States and Canada [in 2009]. Foreign competition, particularly from China, is expected to persist and further curtail production in North America." (USGS, 2010)<br><br>Global USGS manufactured abrasives production data are not available. | |

| Global Peak Production Year (thru 2008): N/A | Years to Global Reserve Exhaustion: N/A |
|---|---|
| Projected Global Peak Production Year: N/A | Projected Global Peak Supply Year: N/A |

| Interdependencies | None identified. |
|---|---|
| **Global Scarcity Assessment** | While annual global production data associated with manufactured abrasives are unavailable from the USGS for the 2000-2008 pre-recession period, manufactured abrasives prices decreased by 4% between 2000 and 2008, indicating that global manufactured abrasives supplies were sufficient to completely address global requirements during 2008.<br><br>Given the lack of recent global manufactured abrasives production data and current proven reserves information, it is unclear whether globally available, economically viable manufactured abrasives supplies will remain sufficient to completely address future global requirements, or whether manufactured abrasives will become scarce globally in the not-too-distant future. |

1. "Abrasive", Wikipedia, 2011 - http://en.wikipedia.org/wiki/Abrasive.

2. "Manufactured Abrasives Statistics", Historical Statistics for Mineral and Material Commodities in the United States, USGS, 2010 - http://minerals.usgs.gov/ds/2005/140/abrasivesmanufactured.xls.

| NNR Profile | Abrasives (Natural) | |
|---|---|---|
| **NNR Uses and Critical Applications** | | |
| **Primary Uses** | Natural abrasives are hard, naturally-occurring stones, which vary in shape and chemical composition, that are used in grinding, polishing, buffing, honing, cutting, drilling, sharpening, lapping, and sanding applications. | |
| **Critical Applications** | Natural abrasives are widely used in a variety of industrial, consumer, and technological applications to shape, finish, or polish a workpiece through rubbing. | |
| **NNR Criticality** | **NNR Criticality Classification: Declining** | |
| **Substitutes** | Manufactured (synthetic) abrasives derived from fused aluminum oxide and silicon carbide can be substituted for natural abrasives; a variety of both natural and manufactured abrasives exist for nearly all applications. | |
| **Criticality Assessment** | While abrasives play a key role as finishing agents in a multitude of industrial and construction applications, the utilization of natural abrasives has been declining in favor of manufactured abrasives. | |
| **US NNR Scarcity** | Scarce in 2008: No | **Permanently Scarce: Unlikely** |
| **2008 US Import Reliance:** 0% | | **2008 Domestic US Supply:** 100% |
| **Historical US Import Trends** | Historically, the US was primarily a net importer of natural abrasives; however, net US natural abrasives imports have remained at zero (0) since 1994. | |
| **Historical US Usage Trends** | Annual US natural abrasives utilization levels generally increased during the first three quarters of the 20th century, peaking temporarily in 1905, 1920, 1941, and 1950, before peaking permanently (to date) in 1979. Domestic natural abrasives utilization levels generally declined in a fluctuating manner since that time; the 2008 US natural abrasives utilization level amounted to 94% of the 1979 peak utilization level. | |
| **US Peak Extraction Year (thru 2008):** 2008* | | **US Peak Utilization Year (thru 2008):** 1979 |
| **Potential Geopolitical US Supply Constraints** | None identified. | |

| NNR Profile | Abrasives (Natural) [continued] |
|---|---|
| **US Scarcity Assessment** | That annual domestic natural abrasives utilization decreased by 6% since peaking (to date) in 1979, is an indicator of declining American industrial preeminence and global economic competitiveness.<br><br>The US is, however, currently addressing its total requirements for natural abrasives through domestic supplies.<br><br>Available evidence supports the contention that domestic natural abrasives supplies will likely remain sufficient to completely address domestic requirements for the foreseeable future:<br><br>• Domestic natural abrasives supplies were sufficient to completely address domestic requirements during the 2000-2008 period of rapid economic growth prior to the Great Recession; and<br>• 2008 US natural abrasives demand, which spiked by 36% from the 2007 level, was completely addressed by domestic supplies.<br><br>Barring future increases in the domestic (US) natural abrasives requirement trajectory, domestically available, economically viable natural abrasives supplies will likely remain sufficient to completely address domestic requirements going forward. |

| Global NNR Scarcity | Scarce in 2008: No | Permanently Scarce: Unclear |
|---|---|---|
| **Historical Global Extraction Trends** | Annual global natural abrasives extraction levels fluctuated widely during the first three quarters of the 20th century, peaking temporarily in 1925 before peaking permanently (to date) in 1974. Annual global extraction levels declined in a fluctuating manner since that time. Annual global natural abrasives extraction data for the 2000-2008 period is unavailable from the USGS. | |

| Global Peak Extraction Year (thru 2008): 1974 | Years to Global Reserve Exhaustion: N/A |
|---|---|
| **Projected Global Peak Extraction Year: N/A** | **Projected Global Peak Supply Year: N/A** |

| Interdependencies | None identified. |
|---|---|
| **Global Scarcity Assessment** | While annual global extraction data associated with natural abrasives are unavailable from the USGS for the 2000-2008 pre-recession period, natural abrasives prices decreased by a substantial 53% between 2000 and 2008, indicating that global natural abrasives supplies were sufficient to completely address global requirements during 2008.<br><br>Given the lack of recent global natural abrasives extraction data and current proven reserves information, it is unclear whether globally available, economically viable natural abrasives supplies will remain sufficient to completely address future global requirements, or whether natural abrasives will become scarce globally in the future. |

1. "Abrasive", Wikipedia, 2011 - http://en.wikipedia.org/wiki/Abrasive.
2. "Natural Abrasives Statistics", Historical Statistics for Mineral and Material Commodities in the United States, USGS, 2010 - http://minerals.usgs.gov/ds/2005/140/abrasivesnatural.xls.

| NNR Profile | Aluminum |
|---|---|
| **NNR Uses and Critical Applications** | |

| | |
|---|---|
| **Primary Uses** | Aluminum is a soft, malleable, durable, lightweight, silvery-white metal used in a variety of transportation, packaging, building, electrical, machinery, and consumer durables applications. |
| **Critical Applications** | Its low weight, corrosion resistance, malleability, and strength (when alloyed), make aluminum an ideal construction material across a wide variety of industrial, construction, defense, and consumer product applications. |

| **NNR Criticality** | **NNR Criticality Classification: Indispensible** |
|---|---|
| **Substitutes** | Materials such as composites, glass, paper, plastics, steel, magnesium, titanium, vinyl, and copper can "technically" substitute for aluminum; none offer the price/performance characteristics associated with aluminum across such a wide range of applications. |
| **Criticality Assessment** | Aluminum is the most widely used non-ferrous metal in the world; aluminum is indispensible to modern industrial existence. |

| **US NNR Scarcity** | **Scarce in 2008: Yes** | **Permanently Scarce: Almost Certain** |
|---|---|---|
| **2008 US Import Reliance:** 24% | | **2008 Domestic US Supply:** 76% |

| | |
|---|---|
| **Historical US Import Trends** | Historically, the US has been primarily a net importer of aluminum; net US aluminum imports have increased dramatically and steadily over the past several decades. |
| **Historical US Usage Trends** | Annual US aluminum utilization levels generally increased during the 20th century, peaking temporarily in 1920, 1929, 1943, 1978, and 1987 before peaking permanently (to date) in 1999. Domestic aluminum utilization decreased significantly during the early years of the 21st century; the 2008 US aluminum utilization level amounted to only 71% of the 1999 peak utilization level. |

| **US Peak Production Year (thru 2008):** 1980 | **Peak US Utilization Year (thru 2008):** 1999 |
|---|---|
| **Potential Geopolitical US Supply Constraints** | 56% of US aluminum imports come from Canada. |

| NNR Profile | Aluminum (continued) |
|---|---|
| **US Scarcity Assessment** | "Domestic resources of bauxite [the only economically viable feedstock for aluminum] are inadequate to meet long-term U.S. demand…" (USGS, 2010)<br><br>That annual domestic aluminum utilization decreased by 29% since peaking (to date) in 1999, is a primary indicator of declining American industrial preeminence and global economic competitiveness.<br><br>The US currently relies considerably on imported aluminum, the majority (56%) of which comes from Canada. The quantity of aluminum supplied by foreign sources during 2008 accounted for 24% of the total 2008 US utilization level.<br><br>Available evidence supports the contention that domestic aluminum supplies will remain insufficient to completely address domestic requirements going forward:<br><br>• The annual US aluminum production level decreased by 43% since peaking (to date) in 1980—a compelling indicator that domestic economically viable aluminum production has peaked permanently;<br>• The US has become increasingly reliant on aluminum imports since 1992; and<br>• The quantity of aluminium produced domestically during 2008 amounted to only 70% of the total 2008 US utilization level—a primary cause of America's lack of economic self-sufficiency.<br><br>Barring future reductions in the domestic (US) aluminum requirement trajectory and/or major new domestic economically viable discoveries, aluminum will almost certainly remain scarce domestically in the future. |

| Global NNR Scarcity | Scarce in 2008: Yes | Permanently Scarce: Unclear |
|---|---|---|

| **Historical Global Production Trends** | "World primary aluminum production continued to increase [in 2007] as capacity expansions outside the United States were brought onstream." (USGS, 2008)<br><br>Annual global aluminum production levels generally increased during the 20th and 21st centuries, peaking temporarily in 1918, 1929, 1943, 1974, and 1980; annual global aluminum production increased 60% between 2000 and 2008.<br><br>"China is the world's biggest aluminum producer…" (China Daily, 2010) |
|---|---|

| Global Peak Production Year (thru 2008): 2008 | Years to Global Reserve Exhaustion: N/A |
|---|---|
| Projected Global Peak Production Year: N/A | Projected Global Peak Supply Year: N/A |

| **Interdependencies** | Aluminum is almost always produced from bauxite ores because other aluminum sources, while often abundant, are not economically viable. |
|---|---|

| NNR Profile | Aluminum (continued) |
|---|---|
| **Global Scarcity Assessment** | A 60% increase in the annual global aluminum production level between 2000 and 2008 implies an increase in global aluminum demand during the pre-recession period, and a corresponding increase in global aluminum supply in response to increased global demand.<br><br>The fact that the price of aluminum increased by 30% during the 2000-2008 period indicates that global aluminium supply, while increasing during the eight year period, remained insufficient to completely address global requirements in 2008.<br><br>Available evidence regarding the likelihood that global aluminum supplies will remain insufficient to completely address global requirements going forward is conflicting:<br><br>• An increase in the price of aluminum during the 2000-2008 period induced an insufficient increase in aluminum supply—compelling evidence of tight global supply in 2008; and<br>• Evidence contained in the Bauxite Profile indicates that global bauxite supplies are likely to remain scarce going forward; however<br>• Proven global bauxite reserves are considered by the USGS to be "sufficient to meet world demand for metal [aluminum] well into the future".<br><br>It is therefore unclear whether aluminum will remain scarce globally in the future, or whether globally available, economically viable aluminum supplies will be sufficient to completely address future global requirements.<br><br>"Global demand for primary aluminum may almost double in the next decade [by 2020] led by growth in China, leading to a supply shortage of about 8 million metric tons…" (China Mining Association, 2010) |

1. "Aluminum", Wikipedia, 2011 - http://en.wikipedia.org/wiki/Aluminium.
2. "Aluminum Statistics", Historical Statistics for Mineral and Material Commodities in the United States, USGS, 2010 – http://minerals.usgs.gov/ds/2005/140/aluminum.xls.
3. "Power Cuts Take Sheen off Aluminum Producers", China Daily, 2010 - http://www.chinadaily.com.cn/business/2010-01/21/content_9353984.htm.
4. "Global Aluminum Demand May Double by 2020 on China", China Mining Association, 2010 - http://www.chinamining.org/News/2010-06-23/1277272014d37202.html.

| NNR Profile | Antimony |
|---|---|
| **NNR Uses and Critical Applications** | |
| **Primary Uses** | Antimony is a lustrous, brittle, silvery-gray metalloid used in applications such as flame retardants, transportation (including batteries), chemicals, ceramics, and glass. |
| **Critical Applications** | Antimony is used as a dopant for ultra-high conductivity silicon wafers (electronics); as a flame retardant for aircraft and clothing; and as an alloy to increase the hardness of lead in batteries. |

| NNR Profile | Antimony (continued) | |
|---|---|---|
| **NNR Criticality** | **NNR Criticality Classification: Critical** | |
| **Substitutes** | Ample technically viable substitutes, including chromium, tin, titanium, zinc, zirconium, copper, cadmium, and sulfur, exist for various antimony applications. Price/performance characteristics associated with the substitutes vary per application.<br><br>"…the trend to low-maintenance batteries has tilted the balance of consumption away from antimony and toward calcium as an additive." (USGS, 2010) | |
| **Criticality Assessment** | Antimony is used primarily in niche applications, which improve the effectiveness of other NNRs and manufactured goods—lead hardening in lead/acid batteries being the most pervasive antimony application. | |
| **US NNR Scarcity** | **Scarce in 2008: Yes** | **Permanently Scarce: Almost Certain** |
| **2008 US Import Reliance:** 93% | | **2008 Domestic US Supply:** 7% |
| **Historical US Import Trends** | The US has consistently relied heavily on antimony imports, as very little antimony has ever been extracted in the US. | |
| **Historical US Usage Trends** | Annual US antimony utilization generally increased during the 20th century—often in a widely fluctuating manner—peaking temporarily in 1917, 1929, 1941, and 1973, before peaking permanently (to date) in 1997. Domestic antimony utilization then declined significantly during the early years of the 21st century; the 2008 US antimony utilization level amounted to only 46% of the 1997 peak utilization level. | |
| **US Peak Extraction Year (thru 2008):** 1948 | | **Peak US Utilization Year (thru 2008):** 1997 |
| **Potential Geopolitical US Supply Constraints** | 51% of US antimony imports come from China—67% of metal, 37% of ores and concentrates, and 50% of oxides; China accounted for 84% of world production (2005); over 50% of the proven global antimony reserves are located in China and Russia (combined).<br><br>In 2010, China imposed a 57,500 metric ton quota on antimony exports. (Hague, 2010) | |

| NNR Profile | Antimony (continued) |
|---|---|
| **US Scarcity Assessment** | "No mines are currently producing antimony ore in the U.S...." (MII, 2010)<br><br>That annual domestic antimony utilization decreased by 54% since peaking (to date) in 1997, is a significant indicator of declining American industrial preeminence and global economic competitiveness.<br><br>The US currently relies almost exclusively on imported antimony, the majority (51%) of which comes from China. The quantity of antimony supplied by foreign sources during 2008 accounted for 93% of the total 2008 US utilization level.<br><br>Available evidence supports the contention that domestic antimony supplies will remain insufficient to completely address domestic requirements going forward:<br><br>• Annual US antimony extraction ceased entirely in 2000—a compelling indicator that domestic economically viable antimony extraction has peaked permanently;<br>• US antimony import levels have generally increased since the late 1940s; and<br>• The quantity of antimony extracted domestically during 1948, the year of peak (to date) domestic antimony extraction, amounted to only 27% of the 2008 total US utilization level—a significant indicator of America's increasing dependence on foreign NNRs.<br><br>Barring future reductions in the domestic (US) antimony requirement trajectory and/or major new domestic economically viable discoveries, antimony will almost certainly remain scarce domestically in the future. |

| Global NNR Scarcity | Scarce in 2008: Yes | Permanently Scarce: Almost Certain |
|---|---|---|

| **Historical Global Extraction Trends** | "China, which accounted for about 90 percent of global antimony output last year [2009], curbed exports and production of minor metals this year to shore up prices and ensure domestic supplies. The country's commerce minister last month said the controls were part of measures to protect the environment." (People's Daily Online, 2010)<br><br>Global antimony extraction levels generally increased during the 20th and 21st centuries, peaking temporarily in 1916, 1929, 1943, 1951, and 1977; annual global antimony extraction increased 67% between 2000 and 2008. |
|---|---|

| Global Peak Extraction Year (thru 2008): 2008 | Years to Global Reserve Exhaustion: 8 |
|---|---|
| Projected Global Peak Extraction Year: N/A | Projected Global Peak Supply Year: N/A |
| **Interdependencies** | None identified. |

| NNR Profile | Antimony (continued) |
|---|---|
| **Global Scarcity Assessment** | "During 2007, the world's leading antimony producer, China, continued experiencing production restraints." (USGS, 2008)<br><br>A 67% increase in the annual global antimony extraction level between 2000 and 2008 implies a robust increase in global antimony demand during the pre-recession period, and a correspondingly robust increase in global antimony supply in response to increased global demand.<br><br>The fact that the price of antimony increased by an extraordinary 243% during the 2000-2008 period indicates that global antimony supply, while increasing substantially during the eight year period, remained woefully insufficient to completely address global requirements in 2008.<br><br>Available evidence supports the contention that global antimony supplies will remain insufficient to completely address global requirements going forward:<br><br>• Proven global antimony reserves will exhaust in only 8 years, assuming the restoration of pre-recession utilization levels and growth rates;<br>• The substantial increase in global antimony supply levels between 2000 and 2008 failed to prevent an extraordinary price increase during the period—compelling evidence of unaddressed global requirements in 2008; and<br>• It is questionable whether the robust 6.6% compound annual growth rate (CAGR) in global antimony extraction evidenced between 2000 and 2008—an interval during which antimony became scarce globally despite a significant increase in extraction—can be reestablished, much less increased, going forward. A 6.6% CAGR would necessitate a continuous doubling in the annual global extraction level of antimony every 11 years.<br><br>Barring future reductions in the global antimony requirement trajectory and/or major new economically viable discoveries, antimony will almost certainly remain scarce globally in the future. |

1. "Antimony", Wikipedia, 2011 - http://en.wikipedia.org/wiki/Antimony.
2. "Antimony Statistics", Historical Statistics for Mineral and Material Commodities in the United States, USGS, 2010 – http://minerals.usgs.gov/ds/2005/140/antimony.xls.
3. "Objective Capital Rare Earth and Minor Metals Investment Summit: Strategic Metals – Policy and Power", slide 5; J. Kooroshy, The Hague Centre for Strategic Studies, 2010 - http://www.slideshare.net/objectivecapital/objective-capital-rare-earth-and-minor-metals-investment-summit-strategic-metals-policy-and-power-jaakko-kooroshy.
4. "Antimony", Minerals Information Institute, 2010 - http://www.mii.org/Minerals/photoant.html.
5. "Antimony Set to Scale New Peak on China Moves", People's Daily Online, 2010 - http://english.peopledaily.com.cn/90001/90778/90860/7133571.html.

| NNR Profile | Arsenic |
|---|---|
| **NNR Uses and Critical Applications** | |
| **Primary Uses** | Arsenic is a yellow, black, or gray metalloid used in wood preservatives, pesticides, herbicides, insecticides, alloys, medicines, pigments, and semiconductors. |

| NNR Profile | Arsenic (continued) |
|---|---|
| **Critical Applications** | High purity arsenic is a feedstock for high performance semiconductors—used in solar cell, telecommunication, optical, and infrared applications. |

| NNR Criticality | NNR Criticality Classification: Critical |
|---|---|
| **Substitutes** | Arsenic remains price/performance superior as a wood preservative, although substitutes are available for both wood treatments (typically copper based) and treated wood (concrete, steel, and plastic composites); substitutability in other arsenic applications varies as a function of price/performance characteristics. |
| **Criticality Assessment** | Because of its toxicity, arsenic has been banned by the US (in 2003) and other countries as a wood preservative in residential applications; arsenic's remaining and increasingly prevalent critical application is high performance semiconductors. |

| US NNR Scarcity | Scarce in 2008: Yes | Permanently Scarce: Almost Certain |
|---|---|---|
| **2008 US Import Reliance:** 100% | | **2008 Domestic US Supply:** 0% |
| **Historical US Import Trends** | US arsenic import reliance generally increased through the 20th century; US net arsenic imports increased dramatically during the past several decades. | |
| **Historical US Usage Trends** | Annual US arsenic utilization levels fluctuated widely during the 20th century, peaking temporarily in 1907, 1920, and 1930; peaking permanently (to date) in 1942; then peaking temporarily in 1959, 1967, 1974, and 1998. Domestic arsenic utilization declined dramatically during the early years of the 21st century; the 2008 US arsenic utilization level amounted to only 13% of the 1942 peak utilization level. | |

| US Peak Extraction Year (thru 2008): 1944 | Peak US Utilization Year (thru 2008): 1942 |
|---|---|
| **Potential Geopolitical US Supply Constraints** | 86% of US arsenic metal imports and 47% of trioxide imports come from China; China accounted for 50% of world arsenic production (2005). |

| **US Scarcity Assessment** | "There has been no domestic production of arsenic trioxide or arsenic metal since 1985." (USGS, 2010)

That annual domestic arsenic utilization decreased by 87% since peaking (to date) in 1942, is an indicator of declining American industrial preeminence and global economic competitiveness; and of arsenic's toxicity.

The US currently relies exclusively on imported arsenic, the majority (86% of arsenic metal) of which comes from China.

Available evidence supports the contention that domestic arsenic supplies will remain insufficient to completely address domestic requirements going forward:

• Annual US arsenic extraction ceased entirely in 1986—a compelling indicator that domestic economically viable arsenic extraction has peaked permanently; and
• US arsenic import levels have generally increased since the late 1970s—an indicator of America's increasing dependence on foreign NNRs.

Barring future reductions in the domestic (US) arsenic requirement trajectory and/or major new domestic economically viable discoveries, arsenic will almost certainly remain scarce domestically in the future.

"In response to human health issues, the wood-preserving industry made a voluntary decision to stop using CCA [chromated copper arsenate] to treat wood used for decks and outdoor residential use by yearend 2003." (USGS, 2010) |
|---|---|

| NNR Profile | Arsenic (continued) | |
|---|---|---|
| **Global NNR Scarcity** | **Scarce in 2008: No** | **Permanently Scarce: Unclear** |
| **Historical Global Extraction Trends** | Annual global arsenic extraction levels fluctuated widely during the 20th and 21st centuries, peaking temporarily in 1905, 1911, 1932, 1968, and 1989, before peaking permanently (to date) in 2003; annual global arsenic extraction increased 11% between 2000 and 2008. | |
| **Global Peak Extraction Year (thru 2008):** 2003 | | **Years to Global Reserve Exhaustion:** 18 |
| **Projected Global Peak Extraction Year:** N/A | | **Projected Global Peak Supply Year:** N/A |
| **Interdependencies** | Arsenic is naturally occurring, but is also co-produced with copper, gold, and lead. | |
| **Global Scarcity Assessment** | An 11% increase in the annual global arsenic extraction level between 2000 and 2008 implies an increase in global arsenic demand during the pre-recession period, and a corresponding increase in global arsenic supply in response to increased global demand. | |

**Global Scarcity Assessment** (continued):

The fact that the price of arsenic decreased by a substantial 22% during the 2000-2008 period indicates that the global supply of arsenic in 2008 was sufficient to completely address 2008 global requirements.

Available evidence regarding the likelihood that global arsenic supplies will remain sufficient to completely address global requirements going forward is conflicting:

- A declining arsenic price level between 2000 and 2008 indicates that global arsenic supplies were sufficient to completely address global requirements in 2008; and
- Arsenic is coming under increasing scrutiny due to its toxicity, which could adversely impact global demand going forward; however
- Proven global arsenic reserves would exhaust in only 18 years, assuming the restoration of pre-recession utilization levels and growth rates.

It is therefore unclear whether globally available, economically viable arsenic supplies will remain sufficient to completely address future global requirements, or whether arsenic will become scarce globally in the not-too-distant future.

1. "Arsenic", Wikipedia, 2011 - http://en.wikipedia.org/wiki/Arsenic.
2. "Arsenic Statistics", Historical Statistics for Mineral and Material Commodities in the United States, USGS, 2010 – http://minerals.usgs.gov/ds/2005/140/arsenic.xls.

| NNR Profile | Asbestos | |
|---|---|---|
| **NNR Uses and Critical Applications** | | |
| **Primary Uses** | Asbestos is a family of six fibrous minerals used in roofing products, insulation, and heat and flame retardants. | |
| **Critical Applications** | None identified. | |
| **NNR Criticality** | | **NNR Criticality Classification: Important** |
| **Substitutes** | Ample technically and economically viable and asbestos substitutes exist for both fibrous and non-fibrous applications. | |

| NNR Profile | Asbestos (continued) | |
|---|---|---|
| **Criticality Assessment** | Asbestos has been banned by the EU and other jurisdictions, due to its toxicity. Transitions to non-toxic substitutes are currently underway in most nations. | |
| **US NNR Scarcity** | **Scarce in 2008: Yes** | **Permanently Scarce: Unclear** |
| **2008 US Import Reliance:** 100% | | **2008 Domestic US Supply:** 0% |
| **Historical US Import Trends** | The US has been a consistent net importer of asbestos, a trend that continues despite dramatic declines in total US utilization levels. | |
| **Historical US Usage Trends** | "Much of the decline in [asbestos] imports and consumption probably can be attributed to reduced commercial building construction where asbestos-based roofing compounds are used." (USGS, 2010)  Annual US asbestos utilization levels generally increased during the first three quarters of the 20th century, peaking temporarily in 1905, 1929, and 1955, before peaking permanently (to date) in 1973. Domestic asbestos utilization declined dramatically since that time, and is currently (2008) less than 1% of its 1973 peak level. | |
| **US Peak Extraction Year (thru 2008):** 1973 | | **Peak US Utilization Year (thru 2008):** 1973 |
| **Potential Geopolitical US Supply Constraints** | 89% of US asbestos imports come from Canada; China and Russia (combined) accounted for 60% of world asbestos extraction (2006). | |
| **US Scarcity Assessment** | "Asbestos has not been mined in the United States since 2002..." (USGS, 2010)  That annual domestic asbestos utilization decreased by 99% since peaking (to date) in 1973, is an indicator of declining American industrial preeminence and global economic competitiveness; and, more importantly, of asbestos' toxicity.  The US currently relies exclusively on imported asbestos, the overwhelming majority of which (89%) comes from Canada.  Available evidence regarding the likelihood that domestic asbestos supplies will remain insufficient to completely address domestic requirements going forward is conflicting:  • Annual US asbestos extraction ceased entirely in 2003; and  • The USGS considers proven US asbestos reserves to be "small"; however  • Domestic asbestos demand has decreased dramatically over the past several decades, due primarily to asbestos' toxicity.  It is therefore unclear whether asbestos will remain scarce domestically in the future, or whether domestically available, economically viable asbestos supplies will be sufficient to completely address future domestic requirements, given the unusual demand/supply characteristics associated with asbestos. | |
| **Global NNR Scarcity** | **Scarce in 2008: Yes** | **Permanently Scarce: Unclear** |
| **Historical Global Extraction Trends** | Annual global asbestos extraction levels generally increased during the first three quarters of the 20th century, peaking temporarily in 1929 and 1937, before peaking permanently (to date) in 1977, and declining significantly until the new millennium, at which time global asbestos extraction increased slightly until 2003. Annual global asbestos extraction declined 1% between 2000 and 2008. | |
| **Global Peak Extraction Year (thru 2008):** 1977 | | **Years to Global Reserve Exhaustion:** N/A |
| **Projected Global Peak Extraction Year:** N/A | | **Projected Global Peak Supply Year:** N/A |
| **Interdependencies** | None identified. | |

| NNR Profile | Asbestos (continued) |
|---|---|
| **Global Scarcity Assessment** | A 1% decrease in the annual global asbestos extraction level between 2000 and 2008 implies either a decrease in global asbestos demand or insufficient global asbestos supplies during the pre-recession period.<br><br>The fact that the price of asbestos increased by an extraordinary 247% during the 2000-2008 period, indicates that the declining global supply of asbestos was woefully insufficient to completely address global requirements in 2008.<br><br>Available evidence regarding the likelihood that global asbestos supplies will remain insufficient to completely address global requirements going forward is conflicting:<br><br>• Sufficient asbestos supply could not be brought online between 2000 and 2008 to prevent an extraordinary price increase during the period—compelling evidence of unaddressed global requirements in 2008; however<br>• The annual global asbestos extraction level decreased by 56% since reaching its peak (to date) level in 1977. It is unclear to what extent this phenomenon resulted from declining global requirements, insufficient globally available, economically viable supply, or a combination of both.<br><br>It is therefore unclear whether asbestos will remain scarce globally in the future, or whether globally available, economically viable asbestos supplies will be sufficient to completely address future global requirements. |

1. "Asbestos", Wikipedia, 2011 - http://en.wikipedia.org/wiki/Asbestos.
2. "Asbestos Statistics", Historical Statistics for Mineral and Material Commodities in the United States, USGS, 2010 – http://minerals.usgs.gov/ds/2005/140/asbestos.xls.

| NNR Profile | Barite | |
|---|---|---|
| **NNR Uses and Critical Applications** | | |
| **Primary Uses** | Barite is a white or colorless mineral used as a weighting agent in gas and oil well drilling fluids; as a filler, extender, or weighting agent in products such as paints, plastics, and rubber; and as a radiation shield. | |
| **Critical Applications** | The most critical barite (barium) applications are drilling fluid (mud) and radiation shielding. | |
| **NNR Criticality** | **NNR Criticality Classification: Important** | |
| **Substitutes** | While barite substitutes exist, including celestite, ilmenite, iron ore, and synthetic hematite, their price/performance characteristics are generally inferior, especially in the case of the drilling fluid application. | |
| **Criticality Assessment** | Despite its declining importance as a component of faceplate glass in the cathode-ray tubes of televisions and computer monitors, barite plays a supporting role in several niche applications, including oil/gas well drilling and radiation intensive healthcare. | |
| **US NNR Scarcity** | **Scarce in 2008: Yes** | **Permanently Scarce: Almost Certain** |
| **2008 US Import Reliance:** 80% | | **2008 Domestic US Supply:** 20% |
| **Historical US Import Trends** | US reliance on barite imports has generally increased during both the 20th and 21st centuries. | |

| NNR Profile | Barite (continued) |
|---|---|
| **Historical US Usage Trends** | Annual US barite utilization levels generally increased during the first three quarters of the 20th century, peaking temporarily in 1907, 1920, 1929, 1937, 1957, and 1969 before peaking permanently (to date) in 1981. Domestic barite utilization declined during the 1980s and early 1990s; despite resuming its upward trend into the 21st century, the 2008 US barite utilization level amounted to only 75% of the 1981 peak utilization level. |

| US Peak Extraction Year (thru 2008): 1981 | Peak US Utilization Year (thru 2008): 1981 |
|---|---|

| **Potential Geopolitical US Supply Constraints** | 93% of US barite imports come from China. |
|---|---|
| **US Scarcity Assessment** | That annual domestic barite utilization decreased by 25% since peaking (to date) in 1981, is an indicator of declining American industrial preeminence and global economic competitiveness.<br><br>The US currently relies almost exclusively on imported barite—the majority (93%) of which comes from China. The quantity of barite supplied by foreign sources during 2008 accounted for 80% of the total 2008 US utilization level.<br><br>Available evidence supports the contention that domestic barite supplies will remain insufficient to completely address domestic requirements going forward:<br><br>• The annual US barite extraction level decreased by 75% since peaking (to date) in 1981—a compelling indicator that domestic economically viable barite extraction has peaked permanently;<br>• The US has become increasingly reliant on barite imports since WWII;<br>• The quantity of barite extracted domestically during 2008 amounted to only 20% of the total 2008 US utilization level—an indicator of America's increasing dependence on foreign NNRs; and<br>• The quantity of barite extracted domestically during 1981, the year of peak (to date) domestic barite extraction, amounted to only 80% of the 2008 total US utilization level.<br><br>Barring future reductions in the domestic (US) barite requirement trajectory and/or major new domestic economically viable discoveries, barite will almost certainly remain scarce domestically in the future. |

| Global NNR Scarcity | Scarce in 2008: Yes | Permanently Scarce: Almost Certain |
|---|---|---|

| **Historical Global Extraction Trends** | Annual global barite extraction levels generally increased during the first three quarters of the 20th century, peaking temporarily in 1929 and 1957, before peaking permanently (to date) in 1981. Following declines in the 1980s, global barite extraction levels resumed their upward trend into the 21st century; annual global barite extraction increased 23% between 2000 and 2008. |
|---|---|

| Global Peak Extraction Year (thru 2008): 1981 | Years to Global Reserve Exhaustion: 19 |
|---|---|
| Projected Global Peak Extraction Year: 2000 | Projected Global Peak Supply Year: 2000 |
| **Interdependencies** | None identified. |

| NNR Profile | Barite (continued) |
|---|---|
| **Global Scarcity Assessment** | "Almost all barite consumed for drilling in the major U.S. oil and gas producing regions (excluding the Rocky Mountain region) is supplied by imports from China and India." (USGS, 2008)<br><br>A 23% increase in the annual global barite extraction level between 2000 and 2008 implies an increase in global demand during the pre-recession period, and a corresponding increase in barite supply in response to increased global demand.<br><br>The fact that the price of barite increased by 23% during the 2000-2008 period indicates that global barite supply, while increasing during the eight year period, remained insufficient to completely address global requirements in 2008.<br><br>Available evidence supports the contention that global barite supplies will remain insufficient to completely address global requirements going forward:<br><br>• Proven global barite reserves would exhaust in only 19 years, assuming the restoration of pre-recession utilization levels and growth rates;<br>• The global barite extraction level was projected to peak in approximately 2000;<br>• The global barite supply level was projected to peak in approximately 2000 as well; and<br>• The increased global barite supply brought online between 2000 and 2008 failed to prevent a price increase during the period—evidence of unaddressed global requirements in 2008.<br><br>Barring future reductions in the global barite requirement trajectory and/or major new economically viable discoveries, barite will almost certainly remain scarce globally in the future. |

1. "Barite", Wikipedia, 2011 - http://en.wikipedia.org/wiki/Baryte.
2. "Barite Statistics", Historical Statistics for Mineral and Material Commodities in the United States, USGS, 2010 – http://minerals.usgs.gov/ds/2005/140/barite.xls.

| NNR Profile | Bauxite (and Alumina) |
|---|---|
| **NNR Uses and Critical Applications** | |
| **Primary Uses** | Bauxite is a multiple mineral ore that serves as the primary feedstock for the production of aluminum; it is also used in the production of non-metallurgical products such as abrasives, chemicals, and refractories. |
| **Critical Applications** | The only economically viable aluminum feedstock. |
| **NNR Criticality** | **NNR Criticality Classification: Indispensible** |
| **Substitutes** | Materials such as clay, alunite, anorthosite, coal wastes, and oil shales are technically feasible substitutes for bauxite in the production of alumina, but are significantly inferior from a price/performance perspective. |
| **Criticality Assessment** | Bauxite is by far the most price/performance effective source of alumina and aluminum; bauxite is indispensible to modern industrial existence. |

| NNR Profile | Bauxite (and Alumina) [continued] | |
|---|---|---|
| US NNR Scarcity | Scarce in 2008: Yes | Permanently Scarce: Almost Certain |
| 2008 US Import Reliance: 100% | | 2008 Domestic US Supply: 0% |
| Historical US Import Trends | US reliance on bauxite imports has generally increased during both the 20th and 21st centuries. | |
| Historical US Usage Trends | Annual US bauxite utilization levels generally increased during the first three quarters of the 20th century, peaking temporarily in 1918, 1930, and 1943, before peaking permanently (to date) in 1974. After experiencing dramatic declines during the 1980s, domestic bauxite utilization levels increased slightly during the early years of the 21st century; the 2008 US bauxite utilization level amounted to only 56% of the 1974 peak utilization level. | |
| US Peak Extraction Year (thru 2008): 1943 | | Peak US Utilization Year (thru 2008): 1974 |
| Potential Geopolitical US Supply Constraints | 32% of US bauxite imports come from Jamaica; 41% of US alumina imports come from Australia; over 50% of proven global bauxite reserves are located in Australia and Guinea.<br><br>"…on June 23 [2009], the EU announced that both it and the U.S. 'had requested WTO consultations with China regarding China's export restrictions on a number of key raw materials, which it considers are in clear breach of international trade rules.'<br><br>In the words of the EU announcement: 'European industries have raised concerns for a number of years on export restrictions - quotas, export duties and minimum export prices - which China applies on key raw materials, such as yellow phosphorous, bauxite, coke, fluorspar, magnesium, manganese, silicon metal, silicon carbide and zinc. Some of these resources cannot be found elsewhere.'" (Seeking Alpha, 2009) | |

| NNR Profile | Bauxite (and Alumina) [continued] |
|---|---|
| **US Scarcity Assessment** | "Domestic resources of bauxite [the only economically viable feedstock for aluminum] are inadequate to meet long-term U.S. demand..." (USGS, 2010)<br><br>That annual domestic bauxite utilization decreased by 44% since peaking (to date) in 1974, is a primary indicator of declining American industrial preeminence and global economic competitiveness.<br><br>The US currently relies exclusively on imported bauxite, large percentages of which come from Jamaica and Australia.<br><br>Available evidence supports the contention that domestic bauxite supplies will remain insufficient to completely address domestic requirements going forward:<br><br>• Annual US bauxite extraction ceased entirely in 1989—a compelling indicator that domestic economically viable bauxite extraction has peaked permanently; and<br>• The quantity of bauxite extracted domestically during 1943, the year of peak (to date) domestic bauxite extraction, amounted to only 66% of the 2008 total US utilization level—a primary indicator of America's increasing dependence on foreign NNRs.<br><br>Barring future reductions in the domestic (US) bauxite requirement trajectory and/or major new domestic economically viable discoveries, bauxite will almost certainly remain scarce domestically in the future.<br><br>"The energy costs of metals such as silver, bauxite, and iron ore show their increasing scarcity in the US..." (Handbook, 2002) |

| Global NNR Scarcity | Scarce in 2008: No | Permanently Scarce: Likely |
|---|---|---|
| **Historical Global Extraction Trends** | "Australia was one of the top producers of bauxite [in 2008] with almost one-third world share, followed by China, Brazil, Guinea, and Jamaica." (Australian Bauxite, 2010)<br><br>Annual global bauxite extraction levels generally increased during both the 20th and 21st centuries, peaking temporarily in 1917, 1929, 1943, and 1980; annual global bauxite extraction increased 51% between 2000 and 2008. | |

| Global Peak Extraction Year (thru 2008): 2008 | Years to Global Reserve Exhaustion: 40 |
|---|---|
| Projected Global Peak Extraction Year: 2038 | Projected Global Peak Supply Year: 2040 |
| **Interdependencies** | None identified. |

| NNR Profile | Bauxite (and Alumina) [continued] |
|---|---|
| **Global Scarcity Assessment** | "Demand for bauxite is growing at a faster rate than the growth in global industrial production. In the emerging economies of Asia, in particular China and India, bauxite demand is particularly strong…" (Australian Bauxite, 2010)<br><br>A 51% increase in the annual global bauxite extraction level between 2000 and 2008 implies a robust increase in global bauxite demand during the pre-recession period, and a correspondingly robust increase in global bauxite supply in response to increased global demand.<br><br>The fact that the price of bauxite decreased by 9% during the 2000-2008 period indicates that the global supply of bauxite in 2008 was sufficient to completely address 2008 global requirements.<br><br>Available evidence, albeit somewhat conflicting, supports the contention that global bauxite supplies will likely become insufficient to completely address global requirements going forward:<br><br>• While global bauxite extraction levels have generally increased since the early 20th century, bauxite price levels have generally decreased since that time, albeit in a fluctuating manner—evidence of sufficient global bauxite supplies; however<br>• Proven global bauxite reserves would exhaust in only 40 years, assuming the restoration of pre-recession utilization levels and growth rates;<br>• The global bauxite extraction level is projected to peak in approximately 2038;<br>• The global bauxite supply level is projected to peak in approximately 2040;<br>• The price of bauxite increased by almost 9% between 2002 and 2008, which indicates bauxite scarcity on the global level in 2008; and<br>• It is unclear whether the robust 5.3% compound annual growth rate (CAGR) in global bauxite extraction evidenced between 2000 and 2008—which was required to enable pre-recession global economic growth—can be reestablished and maintained going forward. A 5.3% CAGR would necessitate a continuous doubling in the annual global extraction level of bauxite every 13.5 years.<br><br>Barring future reductions in the global bauxite requirement trajectory and/or major new economically viable discoveries, bauxite will likely become scarce globally in the not-too-distant future. |

1. "Bauxite", Wikipedia, 2011 - http://en.wikipedia.org/wiki/Bauxite.
2. "Bauxite Statistics", Historical Statistics for Mineral and Material Commodities in the United States, USGS, 2010 – http://minerals.usgs.gov/ds/2005/140/bauxitealumina.xls.
3. "Fluorspar: The Cool Mineral", T. Vulcan, Seeking Alpha, 2009 - http://seekingalpha.com/article/160670-fluorspar-the-cool-mineral.
4 "Handbook of Environmental and Resource Economics", page 100; J. van den Bergh, Edward Elgar Publishing, Inc., 2002 – http://books.google.com/books?id=L9yA5gHwKn4C&pg=PA100&lpg=PA100&dq=us+bauxite+scarcity&source=bl&ots=1IFAumgFED&sig=ZcRMlo3vgkoLm5dtQk1UL7oH41Y&hl=en&ei=KP

6yTK3pJYH_8Aaet6WeCQ&sa=X&oi=book_result&ct=result&resnum=5&sqi=2&ved=0CCAQ
6AEwBA#v=onepage&q=us%20bauxite%20scarcity&f=false.
5. "Market Overview" (Bauxite Demand), Australian Bauxite Limited, 2010 -
http://www.australianbauxite.com.au/marketindustry1.html.

| NNR Profile | Beryllium |
|---|---|

| **NNR Uses and Critical Applications** ||
|---|---|
| **Primary Uses** | Beryllium is a strong, lightweight, brittle, steel-gray metal used as a hardening agent in alloys (e.g., beryllium-copper). Application areas include computers and telecommunications, aerospace and defense, appliances, automotive electronics, and industrial components; beryllium is also used in particle physics experiments. |
| **Critical Applications** | High technology applications requiring high temperature metal alloys— e.g., satellite and space vehicle structures, inertial guidance systems, military aircraft brakes, and space optical systems components; also nuclear weaponry and power generation applications. |

| **NNR Criticality** | **NNR Criticality Classification: Critical** |
|---|---|
| **Substitutes** | Substitute materials possessing the temperature related performance characteristics of beryllium are not available in its niche application areas. |
| **Criticality Assessment** | "Although only two-thirds the weight of aluminum and a quarter of the weight of steel, on a kilogram-for-kilogram basis, beryllium is actually six times stronger than steel." (Seeking Alpha, 2098) <br><br> Because of its stability at high temperatures, beryllium is ideal for critical niche aerospace and defense applications. (The DOD formed a partnership with an Ohio-based beryllium producer to insure adequate domestic supplies). <br><br> "Because the cost of beryllium is high compared with that of other materials, it is used in applications in which its properties are crucial." (USGS, 2010) |

| **US NNR Scarcity** | **Scarce in 2008: Yes** | **Permanently Scarce: Unclear** |
|---|---|---|
| **2008 US Import Reliance: 17%** || **2008 Domestic US Supply: 83%** |
| **Historical US Import Trends** | Historically, the US has been both a net importer and a net exporter of beryllium; over the past two decades the US has become primarily a beryllium net exporter. ||
| **Historical US Usage Trends** | "In addition to being the world's largest beryllium miner, the U.S. is also the world's largest producer of beryllium products." (Seeking Alpha, 2008) <br><br> Annual US beryllium utilization levels fluctuated widely during the 20th century, in a generally increasing manner, peaking temporarily in 1943, 1960, and 1971, before peaking permanently (to date) in 1999. While domestic beryllium utilization generally increased during the early years of the 21st century, the 2008 US beryllium utilization level amounted to only 55% of the 1999 peak utilization level. ||
| **US Peak Extraction Year (thru 2008): 1980** || **Peak US Utilization Year (thru 2008): 1999** |
| **Potential Geopolitical US Supply Constraints** | 58% of US beryllium imports come from Kazakhstan. <br><br> "Because of the toxic nature of beryllium, various international, national, and State guidelines and regulations have been established regarding beryllium in air, water, and other media." (USGS, 2010) ||

| NNR Profile | Beryllium (continued) |
|---|---|
| **US Scarcity Assessment** | "The United States has very little beryl that can be economically hand sorted from pegmatite deposits." However, "World resources in known deposits of beryllium have been estimated to be more than 80,000 tons. About 65% of these resources [are] in nonpegmatite deposits in the United States…" (USGS, 2010)<br><br>That annual domestic beryllium utilization decreased by 45% since peaking (to date) in 1999, is an indicator of declining American industrial preeminence and global economic competitiveness; and of beryllium's toxicity.<br><br>The US currently relies marginally on imported beryllium, the majority (58%) of which comes from Kazakhstan. The quantity of beryllium supplied by foreign sources during 2008 accounted for 17% of the total US utilization level.<br><br>Available evidence regarding the likelihood that domestic beryllium supplies will remain insufficient to completely address domestic requirements going forward is conflicting:<br><br>• The annual US beryllium extraction level decreased by 35% since peaking (to date) in 1980—a compelling indicator that domestic economically viable beryllium extraction has peaked permanently; and<br>• The quantity of beryllium extracted domestically during 2008 amounted to only 83% of the total 2008 US utilization level—a significant indicator of America's increasing dependence on foreign NNRs; however<br>• As a result of generally declining domestic requirements for beryllium, the US has become a consistent net beryllium exporter since the 1990s; and<br>• US beryllium (bertrandite) resources are considered by the USGS to be substantial.<br><br>It is therefore unclear whether beryllium will remain scarce domestically in the future or whether domestically available, economically viable beryllium supplies will be sufficient to completely address future domestic requirements. |

| Global NNR Scarcity | Scarce in 2008: Yes | Permanently Scarce: Likely |
|---|---|---|
| **Historical Global Extraction Trends** | "The majority of the world's currently mined beryllium comes from the U.S. (100 tonnes, or nearly 77% of world mine production in 2007, according to the USGS), in particular from Utah, where it is mined as bertrandite ore. The only other countries in which it is currently mined in any quantity are China (20 tonnes) and Mozambique (6 tonnes)." (Seeking Alpha, 2008)<br><br>Annual global beryllium extraction levels fluctuated widely during the 20th and 21st centuries, peaking temporarily in 1943, before peaking permanently (to date) in 1961, and experiencing lower level peaks in 1981 and 1998; however, annual global beryllium extraction increased 65% between 2001 and 2008. | |

| | | |
|---|---|---|
| **Global Peak Extraction Year (thru 2008):** 1961 | | **Years to Global Reserve Exhaustion:** N/A |
| **Projected Global Peak Extraction Year:** N/A | | **Projected Global Peak Supply Year:** N/A |
| **Interdependencies** | None identified. | |

| NNR Profile | Beryllium (continued) |
|---|---|
| **Global Scarcity Assessment** | "Finding the [beryllium] ores in sufficient concentration to make them economically viable to mine and process is the difficulty." (Seeking Alpha, 2008)<br><br>A 65% increase in the annual global beryllium extraction level between 2001 and 2008 implies a robust increase in global beryllium demand during the pre-recession period, and a correspondingly robust increase in global beryllium supply in response to increased global demand.<br><br>The fact that the price of beryllium increased by a substantial 74% during the 2001-2008 period indicates that global beryllium supply, while increasing considerably during the eight year period, remained insufficient to completely address global requirements in 2008.<br><br>Available evidence supports the contention that global beryllium supplies will likely remain insufficient to completely address global requirements going forward:<br><br>• The annual global beryllium extraction level decreased by 58% since reaching its peak (to date) level in 1961;<br>• The considerable increase in global beryllium supply levels between 2001 and 2008 failed to prevent a substantial price increase during the period—compelling evidence of unaddressed global requirements in 2008; and<br>• It is questionable whether the robust 6.5% compound annual growth rate (CAGR) in global beryllium extraction evidenced between 2000 and 2008—an interval during which beryllium became scarce globally despite a significant increase in extraction—can be reestablished, much less increased, going forward. A 6.5% CAGR would necessitate a continuous doubling in the annual global extraction level of beryllium every 11 years.<br><br>Barring future reductions in the global beryllium requirement trajectory and/or major new economically viable discoveries, beryllium will likely remain scarce globally in the future. |

1. "Beryllium", Wikipedia, 2011 - http://en.wikipedia.org/wiki/Beryllium.
2. "Beryllium Statistics", Historical Statistics for Mineral and Material Commodities in the United States, USGS, 2010 – http://minerals.usgs.gov/ds/2005/140/beryllium.xls.
3. "Beryllium: Bombs and More (Much More), Seeking Alpha, 2008 - http://seekingalpha.com/article/108644-beryllium-bombs-and-more-much-more.

| NNR Profile | Bismuth | |
|---|---|---|
| **NNR Uses and Critical Applications** | | |
| **Primary Uses** | Bismuth is a heavy, brittle, silvery-white metal serving a broad range of uses including cosmetics, pharmaceuticals (anti-diarrheal), and medical procedures; also used as a nontoxic replacement for lead, and in electronics, superconductor, soldering, alloying, and ammunition applications. | |
| **Critical Applications** | As a replacement for lead in applications involving drinking water—water meters, plumbing supplies, fixtures, and solders; zinc-bismuth alloys may also emerge as a superior galvanizing solution (thinner). | |

| NNR Profile | Bismuth (continued) |
|---|---|

| NNR Criticality | NNR Criticality Classification: Critical |
|---|---|
| Substitutes | Technically viable substitutes exist for most bismuth applications; price/performance characteristics vary. |
| Criticality Assessment | "In recent years, several new uses for bismuth have been developed as a nontoxic substitute for lead. These include the use of bismuth in brass plumbing fixtures, fire assaying, ceramic glazes, crystal ware, fishing weights, shot for waterfowl hunting, lubricating greases, pigments, and solders." (Bismuth, 2003)<br><br>In addition to addressing a wide range of existing applications, bismuth is assuming an increasing role as a nontoxic replacement for lead.<br><br>"The Safe Drinking Water Act Amendment of 1996 required that all new and repaired fixtures and pipes for potable water supply be lead free after August 1998." (USGS, 2010) |

| US NNR Scarcity | Scarce in 2008: Yes | Permanently Scarce: Almost Certain |
|---|---|---|
| **2008 US Import Reliance:** 94% | | **2008 Domestic US Supply:** 6% |
| Historical US Import Trends | US reliance on bismuth imports has typically been extensive, as US extraction has been negligible; domestic bismuth supplies are generally derived from recycling. | |
| Historical US Usage Trends | Annual US bismuth utilization levels generally increased during both the 20<sup>th</sup> and 21<sup>st</sup> centuries, peaking temporarily in 1907, 1918, 1942, 1966, 1987, and 1995, before increasing in a fluctuating manner during the early years of the new millennium. | |

| US Peak Production Year (thru 2008): pre-1997 | Peak US Utilization Year (thru 2008): 2007 |
|---|---|
| Potential Geopolitical US Supply Constraints | China accounted for 40% of global bismuth extraction (2005); over two thirds of proven global bismuth reserves are located in China. |
| US Scarcity Assessment | "The United States ceased production of primary refined bismuth in 1997 and is thus highly import dependent for its supply." (USGS, 2010)<br><br>The US currently relies almost exclusively on imported bismuth; the quantity of bismuth supplied by foreign sources during 2008 accounted for 94% of the total US utilization level.<br><br>Available evidence supports the contention that domestic bismuth supplies will remain insufficient to completely address domestic requirements going forward:<br><br>• While US bismuth utilization increased into the new millennium, annual US bismuth extraction ceased entirely in 1998—a compelling indicator that domestic economically viable bismuth extraction has peaked permanently; and<br>• US bismuth import levels have increased significantly since WWII—a significant indicator of America's increasing dependence on foreign NNRs.<br><br>Barring future reductions in the domestic (US) bismuth requirement trajectory and/or major new domestic economically viable discoveries, bismuth will almost certainly remain scarce domestically in the future. |

| NNR Profile | Bismuth (continued) | |
|---|---|---|
| **Global NNR Scarcity** | **Scarce in 2008: Yes** | **Permanently Scarce: Almost Certain** |
| **Historical Global Production Trends** | "About, 90%-95% of the bismuth produced worldwide is as a byproduct of lead refining. The world refined bismuth output is about 12,500 tons in 2008 with an excess of 50% supply from China followed by Mexico, Belgium, Peru, and Canada." (Global Bismuth, 2009)<br><br>Annual global bismuth extraction levels generally increased during the 20th and 21st centuries, peaking temporarily in 1915, 1942, 1974, and 1999; annual global bismuth extraction increased 105% between 2000 and 2008.<br><br>"The major driver for the bismuth market is Asia dominated by China." (Global Bismuth, 2009) | |
| **Global Peak Production Year (thru 2008):** 2008 | | **Years to Global Reserve Exhaustion:** 17 |
| **Projected Global Peak Production Year:** N/A | | **Projected Global Peak Supply Year:** N/A |
| **Interdependencies** | Bismuth is typically produced as a byproduct of processing lead, tungsten, tin, copper, and silver. | |

| NNR Profile | Bismuth (continued) |
|---|---|
| **Global Scarcity Assessment** | "The estimated average [bismuth] price for 2007 was about 173% above that for 2006. Industry sources attributed the substantial price increases to a moderate increase in world demand combined with flat world production..." (USGS, 2008)<br><br>A 105% increase in the annual global bismuth extraction/production level between 2000 and 2008 implies a significant increase in global bismuth demand during the pre-recession period, and a correspondingly significant increase in global bismuth supply in response to increased global demand.<br><br>The fact that the price of bismuth increased by an extraordinary 175% during the 2000-2008 period indicates that global bismuth supply, while increasing significantly during the eight year period, remained woefully insufficient to completely address global requirements in 2008.<br><br>Available evidence supports the contention that global bismuth supplies will remain insufficient to completely address global requirements going forward:<br><br>• Proven global bismuth reserves would exhaust in only 17 years, assuming the restoration of pre-recession utilization levels and growth rates;<br>• The significant increase in global bismuth supply levels between 2000 and 2008 failed to prevent an extraordinary price increase during the period—compelling evidence of unaddressed global requirements in 2008; and<br>• It is questionable whether the extremely robust 9.4% compound annual growth rate (CAGR) in global bismuth extraction evidenced between 2000 and 2008—an interval during which bismuth became scarce globally despite a significant increase in extraction—can be reestablished, much less increased, going forward. A 9.4% CAGR would necessitate a continuous doubling in the annual global extraction level of bismuth every 7.5 years.<br><br>Barring future reductions in the global bismuth requirement trajectory and/or major new economically viable discoveries, bismuth will almost certainly remain scarce globally in the future. |

1. "Bismuth", Wikipedia, 2011 - http://en.wikipedia.org/wiki/Bismuth.
2. "Bismuth Statistics", Historical Statistics for Mineral and Material Commodities in the United States, USGS, 2010 – http://minerals.usgs.gov/ds/2005/140/bismuth.xls.
3. "Bismuth", M. George, page 121; US Geological Survey Minerals Yearbook – 2003, USGS, 2003 - http://minerals.usgs.gov/minerals/pubs/commodity/bismuth/bismumyb03.pdf Bismuth
4. "Global Bismuth Metal Market", page 22; B. Raja, Steel Authority of India Ltd., 2009 - http://www.metalworld.co.in/analysis0909.pdf.

| NNR Profile | Boron |
|---|---|

## NNR Uses and Critical Applications

| | |
|---|---|
| **Primary Uses** | Boron is a hard, non-conductive, brown or black metalloid used as a dopant in the semiconductor industry; and in insulation fiberglass, detergents, glass (Pyrex), ceramics, aerospace materials, insecticides, preservatives, and high-hardness compounds; boron is also an essential plant nutrient. |
| **Critical Applications** | Semiconductor dopant, component of neodymium magnets (wind turbines), fuel ignition material in jet engines, and superconductivity material (magnesium diboride). |

| NNR Criticality | NNR Criticality Classification: Critical |
|---|---|
| **Substitutes** | Technically viable substitutes are available in detergent, enamel, insulation, and soap applications; price/performance trade-offs vary. Substitutes are not as readily available in high technology applications. |
| **Criticality Assessment** | Boron fulfills a wide variety of niche roles in a multitude of industrial, commercial, and aerospace application areas.<br><br>"Industrially, very pure isolated boron is produced with difficulty, as boron tends to form refractory materials containing small amounts of carbon or other elements." (Wikipedia) |

| US NNR Scarcity | Scarce in 2008: No | Permanently Scarce: Unclear |
|---|---|---|

| 2008 US Import Reliance: 0% | 2008 Domestic US Supply: 100% |
|---|---|

| | |
|---|---|
| **Historical US Import Trends** | Historically, the US has been a net exporter of boron. |
| **Historical US Usage Trends** | Annual US boron utilization levels increased during the first three quarters of the 20th century, peaking temporarily in 1906, 1917, 1923, and 1936, before peaking permanently (to date) in 1978. Domestic boron utilization levels generally declined during the 1980s and early 1990s before resuming their upward trend into the 21st century; however, the 2005 (latest year for available data) US boron utilization level amounted to only 75% of the 1978 peak utilization level. |

| US Peak Extraction Year (thru 2008): 1995* | Peak US Utilization Year (thru 2008): 1978* |
|---|---|

| | |
|---|---|
| **Potential Geopolitical US Supply Constraints** | 72% of proven global boron reserves are located in Turkey; 59% of US (boric acid) imports come from Turkey; however, the US is a net exporter of boron. |

| NNR Profile | Boron (continued) |
|---|---|
| **US Scarcity Assessment** | That annual domestic boron utilization (2005) decreased by 25% since peaking (to date) in 1978, is a significant indicator of declining American industrial preeminence and global economic competitiveness.<br><br>The US is however currently addressing its total requirement for boron through domestic supplies.<br><br>Available evidence regarding the likelihood that domestic boron supplies will remain sufficient to completely address domestic requirements going forward is conflicting:<br><br>• The 2005 US boron extraction level exceeded the 2005 US domestic utilization level by 39%; and<br>• The US has generally been a net boron exporter since the early 20th century; however<br>• While US boron utilization increased into the new millennium, the domestic boron extraction level decreased by 16% since peaking (to date) in 1995—an indicator that domestic economically viable boron supplies have likely peaked permanently.<br><br>It is therefore unclear whether domestically available, economically viable boron supplies will remain sufficient to completely address future domestic requirements, or whether boron will become scarce domestically in the not-too-distant future. |

| Global NNR Scarcity | Scarce in 2008: No | Permanently Scarce: Unclear |
|---|---|---|
| **Historical Global Extraction Trends** | "Turkey [47% of 2009 global production] and the United States [2009 production data not available] are the world's largest producers of boron. Turkey has almost 72% of the world's boron reserves." (Wikipedia; USGS, 2010 [figures])<br><br>Annual global boron extraction levels generally increased during the latter decades of the 20th century and into the early 21st century, peaking temporarily in 1977 and 1989, before peaking permanently (to date) in 2004; however, annual global boron extraction decreased 5% between 2000 and 2008.<br><br>"U.S. processed [boron] products had fewer impurities and were produced with lower emissions than in other countries." (USGS, 2008) | |

| Global Peak Extraction Year (thru 2008): 2004 | Years to Global Reserve Exhaustion: 39** |
|---|---|
| Projected Global Peak Extraction Year: N/A | Projected Global Peak Supply Year: N/A |
| **Interdependencies** | None identified. |

| NNR Profile | Boron (continued) |
|---|---|
| **Global Scarcity Assessment** | A 5% decrease in the annual global boron extraction level between 2000 and 2008 implies either a decrease in global boron demand or insufficient global boron supplies during the pre-recession period.<br><br>The fact that the price of boron decreased by 21% during the 2000-2008 period indicates generally declining global demand, and that 2008 global boron supplies were likely sufficient to completely address global requirements at that time.<br><br>Available evidence regarding the likelihood that global boron supplies will remain sufficient to completely address global requirements going forward is conflicting:<br><br>• Both the global boron extraction level and the boron price level decreased between 2000 and 2008—compelling evidence of sufficient global supply in 2008; however<br>• Proven global boron reserves would exhaust in only 39 years, assuming that future annual utilization levels remain constant at the 2008 level.<br><br>It is therefore unclear whether globally available, economically viable boron supplies will remain sufficient to completely address future global requirements, or whether boron will become scarce globally in the not-too-distant future.<br><br>"China, Eastern Europe, and India are favorable areas for increased borates consumption because of their growing economies." (USGS, 2008) |

*1995 was an outlier for US extraction; previous peak was 1979.
*2005 was latest year for US utilization data.
** Reserve to Production data.

1. "Boron", Wikipedia, 2011 - http://en.wikipedia.org/wiki/Boron.
2. "Boron Statistics", Historical Statistics for Mineral and Material Commodities in the United States, USGS, 2010 – http://minerals.usgs.gov/ds/2005/140/boron.xls.

| NNR Profile | Bromine |
|---|---|
| **NNR Uses and Critical Applications** | |
| **Primary Uses** | Bromine is a dense, mobile, reddish-brown liquid (at room temperature) mineral used as a fire retardant, and in oil/gas well drilling fluids, dyes, and pharmaceuticals; bromine was formerly used a pesticide and gasoline additive (banned in many jurisdictions as toxic). |
| **Critical Applications** | Removing mercury from coal powered power plants; oil/gas well drilling fluid. |
| **NNR Criticality** | **NNR Criticality Classification: Important** |
| **Substitutes** | Viable bromine substitutes exist for all but the oil and gas well completion and packer (drilling) applications. |

| NNR Profile | Bromine (continued) |
|---|---|
| **Criticality Assessment** | "Canada has joined the European Union in prohibiting decabromodiphenyl ether (Deca-BDE), a widely used flame retardant, from being used in televisions, computers, and textiles." (USGS, 2010)<br><br>Bromine plays a role in several niche applications, for which technically and economically viable substitutes are readily available in most cases.<br><br>"Other companies intended to market bromine and brominated derivatives to be used in the removal of mercury from [coal powered electricity generation] plant emissions." (USGS, 2010) |

| US NNR Scarcity | Scarce in 2008: Yes | Permanently Scarce: Likely |
|---|---|---|

| 2008 US Import Reliance: 12%* | 2008 Domestic US Supply: 88% |
|---|---|

| **Historical US Import Trends** | Prior to 1988, the US had been primarily a net exporter of bromine; since 1988, the US has become primarily a net importer of bromine. |
|---|---|
| **Historical US Usage Trends** | Annual US bromine utilization levels generally increased during the 20th and 21st centuries, peaking temporarily in 1907, 1919, 1930, 1944, 1956, 1979, and 1997, before peaking permanently (to date) in 2005. |

| US Peak Extraction Year (thru 2008): 1997* | Peak US Utilization Year (thru 2008): 2005* |
|---|---|

| **Potential Geopolitical US Supply Constraints** | 91% of US bromine imports come from Israel; however, the US is the world's largest bromine producer. |
|---|---|
| **US Scarcity Assessment** | "Although still the leading bromine producer in the world, the U.S. dominance has decreased as other countries, such as China, Israel, Japan, and Jordan, have strengthened their positions as world producers of elemental bromine." (USGS, 2010)<br><br>The US currently relies marginally on imported bromine, the vast majority (91%) of which comes from Israel. The quantity of bromine supplied by foreign sources during 2008 accounted for 12% of the total 2008 US utilization level.<br><br>Available evidence supports the contention that domestic bromine supplies will likely remain insufficient to completely address domestic requirements going forward:<br><br>• While US bromine utilization increased into the new millennium, the annual (2006) US bromine extraction level decreased by 2% since peaking (to date) in 1997—an indicator that domestic bromine extraction has possibly peaked permanently;<br>• The US has become increasingly reliant on bromine imports since the late 1980s;<br>• The quantity of bromine extracted domestically during 2006 amounted to only 88% of the total 2006 US utilization level—an indicator of America's increasing dependence on foreign NNRs; and<br>• The quantity of bromine extracted domestically during 1997, the year of peak (to date) domestic bromine extraction, amounted to only 90% of the 2006 total US utilization level.<br><br>Barring future reductions in the domestic (US) bromine requirement trajectory and/or major new domestic economically viable discoveries, bromine will likely remain scarce domestically in the future. |

| NNR Profile | Bromine (continued) | |
|---|---|---|
| **Global NNR Scarcity** | **Scarce in 2008: Yes** | **Permanently Scarce: Unclear** |
| **Historical Global Extraction Trends** | Annual global bromine extraction levels generally increased during the latter decades of the 20th century and into the 21st century, peaking temporarily in 1990 and 2000; annual global bromine extraction increased 23% between 2000 and 2006. | |
| **Global Peak Extraction Year (thru 2008): 2006** | | **Years to Global Reserve Exhaustion: N/A** |
| **Projected Global Peak Extraction Year: N/A** | | **Projected Global Peak Supply Year: N/A** |
| **Interdependencies** | None identified. | |
| **Global Scarcity Assessment** | A 23% increase in the annual global bromine extraction level between 2000 and 2006, implies an increase in global bromine demand during the pre-recession period, and a corresponding increase in global bromine supply in response to increased global demand.<br><br>The fact that the price of bromine increased by 31% during the 2000-2006 period indicates that global bromine supply, while increasing during the six year period, remained insufficient to completely address global requirements in 2006.<br><br>Available evidence regarding the likelihood that global bromine supplies will remain insufficient to completely address global requirements going forward is conflicting:<br><br>• An increase in the price of bromine during the 2000-2006 period induced an insufficient increase in bromine supply—evidence of tight global supply in 2006; and<br>• The annual global bromine extraction level decreased by 38% between 2006 and 2008, although it is unclear whether this phenomenon resulted from declining global demand, insufficient global supply, or a combination of both; however<br>• Proven global bromine reserves are considered by the USGS to be "large".<br><br>It is therefore unclear whether bromine will remain scarce globally in the future, or whether globally available, economically viable bromine supplies will be sufficient to completely address future global requirements. | |

*2006 was latest available historical data; 2006 through 2008 summary data are reported as <25%. (USGS, 2010 Mineral Summaries)

1. "Bromine", Wikipedia, 2011 - http://en.wikipedia.org/wiki/Bromine.
2. "Bromine Statistics", Historical Statistics for Mineral and Material Commodities in the United States, USGS, 2010 – http://minerals.usgs.gov/ds/2005/140/bromine.xls.

| NNR Profile | Cadmium |
|---|---|
| **NNR Uses and Critical Applications** | |
| **Primary Uses** | Cadmium is a soft, malleable, ductile, bluish-white metal used historically as a pigment, a plastic stabilizer, and in corrosion-resistant plating; cadmium is currently used as an alloy and in high tech electronics applications. |
| **Critical Applications** | Nickel cadmium batteries and cadmium telluride solar panels. |

| NNR Profile | Cadmium (continued) |
|---|---|
| **NNR Criticality** | **NNR Criticality Classification: Important** |
| Substitutes | Lithium ion and nickel metal hydride batteries are displacing nickel cadmium batteries in high-cost, high-performance products. While cadmium is encountering increasing resistance due to its toxicity, NiCd is still the battery option of choice for low cost applications. |
| Criticality Assessment | As battery applications account for nearly 90% of cadmium utilization, cadmium's importance is generally declining. Note that should Ni-Cad battery usage in industrial and "off-grid" electrical storage applications increase, cadmium's criticality could increase as well.<br><br>"The percentage of cadmium consumed globally for NiCd battery production has been increasing, while the percentages for the other traditional end uses of cadmium—specifically coatings, pigments, and stabilizers—have gradually decreased, owing to environmental and health concerns." (USGS, 2010) |

| US NNR Scarcity | Scarce in 2008: No | Permanently Scarce: Unclear |
|---|---|---|
| **2008 US Import Reliance: 0%** | | **2008 Domestic US Supply: 100%** |

| | |
|---|---|
| Historical US Import Trends | The US was primarily a net importer of cadmium since the beginning of the 20th century; the US has become primarily a net cadmium exporter since 2001, although current US cadmium supplies are recovered primarily from scrap rather than from new production. |
| Historical US Usage Trends | Annual US cadmium utilization levels generally increased through the first three quarters of the 20th century, peaking temporarily in 1907, 1917, 1939, 1944, and 1956, before peaking permanently (to date) in 1969; domestic cadmium utilization declined steadily thereafter, and is currently only 8% of its 1969 peak level. |

| US Peak Production Year (thru 2008): 1969 | Peak US Utilization Year (thru 2008): 1969 |
|---|---|

| | |
|---|---|
| Potential Geopolitical US Supply Constraints | None identified. |
| US Scarcity Assessment | That annual domestic cadmium utilization decreased by 92% since peaking (to date) in 1964, is an indicator of declining American industrial preeminence and global economic competitiveness; and of cadmium's toxicity.<br><br>However, as a result of continuously declining domestic demand for cadmium, the US is currently addressing its total cadmium requirement through domestic supplies, although this has only been the case since 2001.<br><br>Available evidence regarding the likelihood that domestic cadmium supplies will remain sufficient to completely address domestic requirements going forward is conflicting:<br><br>• The 2008 US cadmium production level exceeded the 2008 US domestic utilization level by 41%; however<br>• The domestic cadmium production level decreased by 86% since peaking (to date) in 1969—an indicator that domestic economically viable cadmium production has peaked permanently; and<br>• The US was a consistent net cadmium importer until 2001.<br><br>It is therefore unclear whether domestically available, economically viable cadmium supplies will remain sufficient to completely address future domestic requirements, or whether cadmium will become scarce domestically in the not-too-distant future. |

| NNR Profile | Cadmium (continued) | |
|---|---|---|
| **Global NNR Scarcity** | **Scarce in 2008: Yes** | **Permanently Scarce: Likely** |
| **Historical Global Production Trends** | "Most of the world's primary cadmium was produced in Asia and the Pacific [2009]—specifically China, Japan, and the Republic of Korea…" (USGS, 2010)<br><br>Annual global cadmium production levels increased during most of the 20th century, peaking temporarily in 1917, 1930, 1943, and 1979, before peaking permanently in 1988 and declining slowly since that time. Annual global cadmium production decreased 3% between 2000 and 2008. | |

| Global Peak Production Year (thru 2008): 1988 | Years to Global Reserve Exhaustion: 25* |
|---|---|
| Projected Global Peak Production Year: 1988 | Projected Global Peak Supply Year: 2002 |

| **Interdependencies** | Cadmium is produced primarily as a byproduct of zinc, lead, and copper processing. |
|---|---|
| **Global Scarcity Assessment** | A 3% decrease in the annual global cadmium production level between 2000 and 2008 implies either a decrease in global cadmium demand or insufficient global cadmium supplies during the pre-recession period.<br><br>The fact that the price of cadmium increased by a phenomenal 1206% during the 2000-2008 period, indicates that the declining global supply of cadmium was woefully insufficient to completely address global requirements in 2008.<br><br>Available evidence, while somewhat conflicting, supports the contention that global cadmium supplies will likely remain insufficient to completely address global requirements going forward:<br><br>• The annual global cadmium extraction level decreased by 11% since reaching its peak (to date) level in 1988, although it is unclear whether this phenomenon resulted from declining global demand, insufficient global supply, or a combination of both;<br>• Proven global cadmium reserves would exhaust in only 25 years, assuming that future annual utilization levels remain constant at the 2008 level;<br>• The global cadmium production level was projected to peak in 1988;<br>• The global cadmium supply level was projected to peak in 2002;<br>• Annual global cadmium production peaked (to date) in 1988—compelling evidence that globally available, economically viable cadmium production may be near, at, or past its permanent peak level; and<br>• A phenomenal increase in the price of cadmium during the 2000-2008 period could not induce an increase in global cadmium supply—compelling evidence of unaddressed global requirements in 2008.<br><br>Barring future reductions in the global cadmium requirement trajectory and/or major new economically viable discoveries, cadmium will likely remain scarce globally in the future.<br><br>"If recent [European Union] legislation involving cadmium dramatically reduces long-term demand, a situation could arise, such as has been recently seen with mercury, where an accumulating oversupply of byproduct cadmium will need to be permanently stockpiled." (USGS, 2010) |

*Reserve to Production data.

1. "Cadmium", Wikipedia, 2011 - http://en.wikipedia.org/wiki/Cadmium.

2. "Cadmium Statistics", Historical Statistics for Mineral and Material Commodities in the United States, USGS, 2010 – http://minerals.usgs.gov/ds/2005/140/cadmium.xls.

| NNR Profile | Cement |
|---|---|
| **NNR Uses and Critical Applications** | |
| **Primary Uses** | Cement is an anhydrous, powdery, grayish-white construction material used as a binder in mortar and concrete. |
| **Critical Applications** | Cement is an almost ubiquitous building material. |

| NNR Criticality | NNR Criticality Classification: Indispensible |
|---|---|
| **Substitutes** | Concrete substitutes in the construction sector include aluminum, asphalt, clay brick, rammed earth, fiberglass, glass, steel, stone, and wood; price/performance attributes associated with each substitute vary with the application. |
| **Criticality Assessment** | The infrastructure and construction requirements associated with industrial nations could not be met in the absence of cement; cement is indispensible to modern industrial existence.<br><br>"The [US] cement industry is the building block of the nation's construction industry. Few construction projects can take place without utilizing cement somewhere in the design." (Portland, 2009) |

| US NNR Scarcity | Scarce in 2008: Yes | Permanently Scarce: Unclear |
|---|---|---|
| **2008 US Import Reliance:** 11% | | **2008 Domestic US Supply:** 89% |
| **Historical US Import Trends** | US reliance on cement imports increased during the past several decades, and periodically exceeded 25% of total annual US utilization during the years prior to the Great Recession. | |
| **Historical US Usage Trends** | Annual US cement utilization levels generally increased during the 20th and 21st centuries, peaking temporarily in 1928, 1942, 1973, and 1987, before peaking permanently (to date) in 2005. | |
| **US Peak Production Year (thru 2008):** 2005 | | **Peak US Utilization Year (thru 2008):** 2005 |
| **Potential Geopolitical US Supply Constraints** | None identified. | |

| NNR Profile | Cement (continued) |
|---|---|
| **US Scarcity Assessment** | "Heavy reliance on imports to satisfy consumption subjects the United States' market to sometimes volatile global economic conditions regarding the availability of foreign cement…" (Portland, 2009)<br><br>The US currently relies marginally on imported cement—the quantity of cement supplied by foreign sources during 2008 accounted for 11% of the total 2008 US utilization level.<br><br>Available evidence regarding the likelihood that domestic cement supplies will remain insufficient to completely address domestic requirements going forward is conflicting:<br><br>• Net US cement imports increased steadily over the past several decades—an indicator of declining American industrial preeminence and global economic competitiveness; however<br>• Annual US cement production levels increased into the new millennium (until the US housing and construction slowdown began in 2006); and<br>• The USGS considers cement raw materials (especially limestone) to be "geologically widespread and abundant".<br><br>It is therefore unclear whether cement will remain scarce domestically in the future, or whether domestically available, economically viable cement supplies will be sufficient to completely address future domestic requirements.<br><br>"A new [US] emissions limitation protocol for cement plants was released in 2009 that would significantly lower the acceptable emissions levels of mercury and some other pollutants. It was unclear how many plants would be able to comply with the new limits…" (USGS, 2010) |

| Global NNR Scarcity | Scarce in 2008: Yes | Permanently Scarce: Unclear |
|---|---|---|
| **Historical Global Production Trends** | "In 2006 it was estimated that China manufactured 1.235 billion metric tons of cement, which was 44% of the world total cement production." [The US produced less than 4% of the world cement total in 2006.] (Wikipedia)<br><br>Annual global cement production levels peaked temporarily in 1929 and 1939, then generally increased in an almost uninterrupted manner through the remainder of the 20th century and into the 21st century; annual global cement production increased 71% between 2000 and 2008. | |

| | | | |
|---|---|---|---|
| Global Peak Production Year (thru 2008): 2008 | | Years to Global Reserve Exhaustion: N/A | |
| Projected Global Peak Production Year: N/A | | Projected Global Peak Supply Year: N/A | |
| **Interdependencies** | None identified. | | |

177

| NNR Profile | Cement (continued) |
|---|---|
| **Global Scarcity Assessment** | A 71% increase in the annual global cement production level between 2000 and 2008 implies a significant increase in global demand during the pre-recession period, and a correspondingly significant increase in global cement supply in response to increased global demand.<br><br>The fact that the price of cement increased by 5% during the 2000-2008 period indicates that global cement supply, while increasing during the eight year period, remained insufficient to completely address global requirements in 2008.<br><br>Available evidence regarding the likelihood that global cement supplies will remain insufficient to completely address global requirements going forward is conflicting:<br><br>• The increased global cement supply brought online between 2000 and 2008 failed to prevent a price increase during the period—evidence of unaddressed global requirements in 2008; and<br>• It is questionable whether the robust 6.8% compound annual growth rate (CAGR) in global cement production evidenced between 2000 and 2008—an interval during which cement became scarce globally despite a significant increase in production—can be reestablished, much less increased, going forward. A 6.8% CAGR would necessitate a continuous doubling in the annual global production level of cement every 11 years; however<br>• Proven global supplies of the raw materials (especially limestone) required to manufacture cement are considered by the USGS to be "widespread and abundant".<br><br>It is therefore unclear whether cement will remain scarce globally in the future, or whether globally available, economically viable cement supplies will be sufficient to completely address future global requirements.<br><br>"A return to cement sales volumes more in line with the 2005-06 record years was expected to take about 5 years." (USGS, 2010) |

1. "Cement", Wikipedia, 2011 - http://en.wikipedia.org/wiki/Cement.
2. "Cement Statistics", Historical Statistics for Mineral and Material Commodities in the United States, USGS, 2010 – http://minerals.usgs.gov/ds/2005/140/cement.xls.
3. "Cement and Concrete Basics", Portland Cement Association, 2009 - http://www.cement.org/basics/cementindustry.asp.

| NNR Profile | Cesium |
|---|---|
| **NNR Uses and Critical Applications** | |
| **Primary Uses** | Cesium is a very soft, very ductile, silvery-gold metal (is a liquid at 83 degrees F) used in oil/gas well drilling fluids (cesium formate), atomic clocks, photoelectric cells, and various niche chemical, medical, and nuclear applications. |
| **Critical Applications** | Drilling fluid and nuclear medicine are the most pervasive, and growing, cesium applications. |

| NNR Profile | Cesium (continued) |
|---|---|
| **NNR Criticality** | **NNR Criticality Classification: Important** |

| | |
|---|---|
| **Substitutes** | Germanium, rubidium, selenium, silicon, tellurium, and several other metals can substitute for cesium in photosensitive materials; rubidium is a viable substitute in many applications. |
| **Criticality Assessment** | "Cost and reactivity of the [cesium] metal point to continued limited applications." (USGS, 2008)<br><br>Cesium is used in a variety of niche applications, although its cost and reactivity have limited its viability in more broad based applications. |

| **US NNR Scarcity** | Scarce in 2008: Yes | Permanently Scarce: Almost Certain |
|---|---|---|
| **2008 US Import Reliance:** 100% | | **2008 Domestic US Supply:** 0% |

| | |
|---|---|
| **Historical US Import Trends** | The US has always been nearly 100% reliant on imported cesium. |
| **Historical US Usage Trends** | Annual US cesium utilization levels generally increased from the 1960s, peaking temporarily in 1972 before peaking permanently (to date) in 1984 (USGS data is not available past 1988).<br><br>"Mine production, consumption, import, and export data for cesium have not been available since the late 1980s. There is no trading of cesium…" (USGS, 2010) |

| **US Peak Extraction Year (thru 2008):** N/A* | **Peak US Utilization Year (thru 2008):** 1984** |
|---|---|

| | |
|---|---|
| **Potential Geopolitical US Supply Constraints** | Canada operates the only currently economically viable cesium mining operation in the world, and is the main supplier of cesium to the US.<br><br>"Pollucite, the ore mineral of cesium with the most commercial importance, may be found in zoned pegmatites worldwide, with the largest deposit at Bernic Lake in Canada." (USGS, 2010) |
| **US Scarcity Assessment** | "Domestic cesium occurrences will remain uneconomic unless there is a change in the market, such as new or increased end uses." (USGS, 2008)<br><br>The US currently relies exclusively on imported cesium, nearly all of which is imported from Canada.<br><br>Given that cesium has never been mined in the US in commercial quantities, cesium will almost certainly remain scarce domestically in the future, barring major new domestic economically viable discoveries. |

| **Global NNR Scarcity** | Scarce in 2008: No | Permanently Scarce: Unclear |
|---|---|---|

| | |
|---|---|
| **Historical Global Extraction Trends** | Global cesium extraction data are very limited, ceasing after 1977. Limited quantities of cesium were extracted globally during the 1960s, with the global extraction level peaking (to date) in 1972. |

| **Global Peak Extraction Year (thru 2008):** 1972 | **Years to Global Reserve Exhaustion:** N/A |
|---|---|
| **Projected Global Peak Extraction Year:** N/A | **Projected Global Peak Supply Year:** N/A |

| | |
|---|---|
| **Interdependencies** | Pollucite, the mineral within which cesium occurs, is mined as a byproduct of lithium extraction. |

| NNR Profile | Cesium (continued) |
|---|---|
| **Global Scarcity Assessment** | "World resources of cesium have not been estimated." (USGS, 2010) <br><br> While annual global production data associated with cesium are unavailable from the USGS for the 2000-2008 pre-recession period, cesium prices decreased by 26% between 2000 and 2008, indicating that global cesium supplies were sufficient to completely address global requirements during 2008. <br><br> Given that global cesium resources have not been estimated by the USGS, it is unclear whether globally available, economically viable cesium supplies will remain sufficient to completely address future global requirements, or whether cesium will become scarce globally in the future. |

*Apparently never mined in the US.
** Last year of available data was 1988.

1. "Cesium", Wikipedia, 2011 - http://en.wikipedia.org/wiki/Cesium.
2. "Cesium Statistics", Historical Statistics for Mineral and Material Commodities in the United States, USGS, 2010 – http://minerals.usgs.gov/ds/2005/140/cesium.xls.

| NNR Profile | Chromium | |
|---|---|---|
| **NNR Uses and Critical Applications** | | |
| **Primary Uses** | Chromium is a hard, malleable, lustrous steel-gray metal used as an alloy and in electroplating and anodizing applications; chromium is also used as a pigment, in dyes, as a wood preservative and tanning agent, and as a catalyst. | |
| **Critical Applications** | Stainless steel, due to its corrosion resistance and hardness; chromium-nickel superalloys, which are used in jet engines and gas turbines. | |
| **NNR Criticality** | **NNR Criticality Classification: Indispensible** | |
| **Substitutes** | There are no viable chromium substitutes in stainless steel and superalloys. | |
| **Criticality Assessment** | "While chromium is used extensively in the refractory and chemical industries, its criticality derives from its role in the metallurgical industry and particularly in the production of defense equipment." (GeoJournal, 1995) <br><br> Chromium plays a key support role in a wide variety of critical industrial, aerospace, and defense applications; as such, chromium is indispensible to modern industrial existence. | |
| **US NNR Scarcity** | **Scarce in 2008: Yes** | **Permanently Scarce: Almost Certain** |
| **2008 US Import Reliance:** 66% | **2008 Domestic US Supply:** 34% | |
| **Historical US Import Trends** | Historically, the US has been a net importer of chromium. | |
| **Historical US Usage Trends** | Annual US chromium utilization levels generally increased during the first two thirds of the 20th century, peaking temporarily in 1905, 1918, 1930, and 1941, before peaking permanently (to date) in 1965. Domestic chromium utilization fluctuated in a downward direction since that time; the 2008 US chromium utilization level amounted to only 48% of the 1965 peak utilization level. | |
| **US Peak Extraction Year (Thru 2008):** 1956 | **Peak US Utilization Year (thru 2008):** 1965 | |

| NNR Profile | Chromium (continued) |
|---|---|
| **Potential Geopolitical US Supply Constraints** | South Africa accounts for approximately 40% of global chromite ore extraction; over 75% of proven global chromium reserves are located in South Africa and Kazakhstan (combined). <br><br> "South Africa, which accounts for about 40% of world chromite ore and ferrochromium production, experienced electrical power shortages that South Africa's electrical power utility dealt with by rationing." (USGS, 2010) |
| **US Scarcity Assessment** | "According to the USGS, however, there is, at present, but a single company mining chromite ore in the U.S." (Seeking Alpha, 2008) <br><br> That annual domestic chromium utilization decreased by 52% since peaking (to date) in 1965, is a major indicator of declining American industrial preeminence and global economic competitiveness. <br><br> The US currently relies heavily on imported chromium, a large percentage (40%) of which comes from South Africa. The quantity of chromium supplied by foreign sources during 2008 accounted for 66% of the total 2008 US utilization level. <br><br> Available evidence supports the contention that domestic chromium supplies will remain insufficient to completely address domestic requirements going forward: <br><br> • Annual US chromium extraction ceased entirely in 1962—a compelling indicator that domestic economically viable chromium extraction has peaked permanently; and <br> • The quantity of chromium extracted domestically during 1956, the year of peak (to date) domestic chromium extraction, amounted to only 13% of the 2008 total US utilization level—a primary indicator of America's increasing dependence on foreign NNRs. <br><br> Barring future reductions in the domestic (US) chromium requirement trajectory and/or major new domestic economically viable discoveries, chromium will almost certainly remain scarce domestically in the future. |
| **Global NNR Scarcity** | **Scarce in 2008: Yes**    **Permanently Scarce: Almost Certain** |
| **Historical Global Extraction Trends** | "South Africa remains the world's largest producer of chromite ore and concentrates, followed by Kazakhstan and India. Together they account for around 80% of the world's production of chromite ore." (Seeking Alpha, 2008) <br><br> Annual global chromium extraction levels generally increased during both the 20th and 21st centuries, peaking temporarily in 1906, 1918, 1929, 1942, 1957, 1978, and 1989; annual global chromium extraction increased 47% between 2000 and 2008. |
| **Global Peak Extraction Year (thru 2008): 2008** | **Years to Global Reserve Exhaustion: >26** |
| **Projected Global Peak Extraction Year: 2035** | **Projected Global Peak Supply Year: 2048** |
| **Interdependencies** | None identified. |

181

| NNR Profile | Chromium (continued) |
|---|---|
| **Global Scarcity Assessment** | "The price of ferrochromium reached historical levels in 2007, not least because of China's growing demand as a consumer." (Seeking Alpha, 2008)<br><br>A 47% increase in the annual global chromium extraction level between 2000 and 2008 implies a robust increase in global chromium demand during the pre-recession period, and a correspondingly robust increase in global chromium supply in response to increased global demand.<br><br>The fact that the price of chromium increased by an extraordinary 266% during the 2000-2008 period indicates that global chromium supply, while increasing substantially during the eight year period, remained woefully insufficient to completely address global requirements in 2008.<br><br>Available evidence supports the contention that global chromium supplies will remain insufficient to completely address global requirements going forward:<br><br>• The global chromium extraction level is projected to peak in approximately 2035;<br>• The global chromium supply level is projected to peak in approximately 2048;<br>• The substantial increase in global chromium supply levels between 2000 and 2008 failed to prevent an extraordinary price increase during the period—compelling evidence of unaddressed global requirements in 2008; and<br>• It is questionable whether the robust 4.9% compound annual growth rate (CAGR) in global chromium extraction evidenced between 2000 and 2008—an interval during which chromium became scarce globally despite a significant increase in extraction—can be reestablished, much less increased, going forward. A 4.9% CAGR would necessitate a continuous doubling in the annual global extraction level of chromium every 14.5 years.<br><br>Barring future reductions in the global chromium requirement trajectory and/or major new economically viable discoveries, chromium will almost certainly remain scarce globally in the future.<br><br>"China's growth was generally recognized as the leading cause of increased chromium demand. Chinese stainless steel production exceeded that of the United States beginning in 2004 and by 2007 was 142% greater than that of the United States." (USGS, 2008) |

1. "Chromium", Wikipedia, 2011 - http://en.wikipedia.org/wiki/Chromium.
2. "Chromium Statistics", Historical Statistics for Mineral and Material Commodities in the United States, USGS, 2010 – http://minerals.usgs.gov/ds/2005/140/chromium.xls.
3. "Geopolitics and the Cold War Environment: The Case for Chromium", GeoJournal, page 209, L. Anderson, 1995 - http://www.springerlink.com/content/n2nh1050607q4213/.
4. "Chromium: More than Fancy Trim", Tom Vulcan, Seeking Alpha, 2008 - http://seekingalpha.com/article/96172-chromium-more-than-fancy-trim.

| NNR Profile | Clay |
|---|---|

## NNR Uses and Critical Applications

| Primary Uses | Clay is a family of fine grained minerals, including bentonite, fire clay, Fuller's earth, and kaolin, which exhibit plasticity when moistened and harden when fried or dried, and are used in making tile, ceramics, pottery, bricks, and paper; clays are also used as oil/gas well drilling mud, as refractory agents, and as sealants. |
|---|---|
| Critical Applications | Bricks, ceramics, tile, and refractory agents. |

| NNR Criticality | NNR Criticality Classification: Indispensible |
|---|---|
| Substitutes | Other building, construction, and production materials may be effectively substituted for clay in some applications, although clay's unique properties often preclude price/performance effective substitutes. |
| Criticality Assessment | The derivatives of clay are found in nearly every construction project and are involved in a wide range of industrial processes; clays are indispensible to modern industrial existence. |

| US NNR Scarcity | Scarce in 2008: No | Permanently Scarce: Unlikely |
|---|---|---|
| 2008 US Import Reliance: 0% | | 2008 Domestic US Supply: 100% |
| Historical US Import Trends | Historically, the US has been a net exporter of clays. | |
| Historical US Usage Trends | Annual US clay utilization levels generally increased during the first three quarters of the 20th century (especially during and after WWII), peaking temporarily in 1929, 1943, and 1956, before peaking permanently (to date) in 1973. Domestic clay utilization trended downward since that time; the 2008 US clay utilization level amounted to only 45% of the 1973 peak utilization level. | |
| US Peak Extraction Year (thru 2008): 1973 | | Peak US Utilization Year (thru 2008): 1973 |
| Potential Geopolitical US Supply Constraints | 84% of US clay imports come from Brazil; however, the US is currently a net exporter of clay. | |

| NNR Profile | Clay (continued) |
|---|---|
| **US Scarcity Assessment** | "Total sales or use of clays declined as the U.S. economy slowed and housing starts declined in 2007." (USGS, 2008)<br><br>That annual domestic clay utilization decreased by 45% since peaking (to date) in 1973, is a major indicator of declining American industrial preeminence and global economic competitiveness.<br><br>However, as a result of continuously declining domestic demand for clay, the US is currently addressing its total requirement for clay through domestic supplies.<br><br>Available evidence supports the contention that domestic clay supplies will likely remain sufficient to completely address domestic requirements for the foreseeable future:<br><br>• Domestic clay supplies were sufficient to completely address domestic requirements during the 2000-2008 period of rapid economic growth prior to the Great Recession;<br>• The US has been a net clay exporter since 1938; and<br>• Proven domestic clay reserves are considered by the USGS to be "extremely large".<br><br>Barring future increases in the domestic (US) clay requirement trajectory, domestically available, economically viable clay supplies will likely remain sufficient to completely address domestic requirements going forward.<br><br>"In 2009, [US] clay and shale production was reported in 41 States. About 190 companies operated approximately 830 clay pits or quarries." (USGS, 2010) |

| Global NNR Scarcity | Scarce in 2008: Yes | Permanently Scarce: Unclear |
|---|---|---|
| **Historical Global Extraction Trends** | Because global clay reserves are very large and widely dispersed, the USGS does not monitor annual global extraction levels. | |

| Global Peak Extraction Year (thru 2008): N/A | Years to Global Reserve Exhaustion: N/A |
|---|---|
| **Projected Global Peak Extraction Year:** N/A | **Projected Global Peak Supply Year:** N/A |

| Interdependencies | None identified. |
|---|---|

| NNR Profile | Clay (continued) |
|---|---|
| Global Scarcity Assessment (2000-2008) | While annual global extraction data associated with clays are unavailable from the USGS for the 2000-2008 pre-recession period, clay prices increased by 25% between 2000 and 2008, indicating that global clay supplies were insufficient to completely address global requirements during 2008.<br><br>Available evidence regarding the likelihood that global clay supplies will remain insufficient to completely address global requirements going forward is conflicting:<br><br>• An increase in the price of clays during the 2000-2008 period indicates global scarcity in 2008; however<br>• Proven global clay resources are considered by the USGS to be "extremely large".<br><br>It is therefore unclear whether clays will remain scarce globally in the future, or whether globally available, economically viable clay supplies will be sufficient to completely address future global requirements.<br><br>(Given that each of the various clays possesses unique demand/supply characteristics, it is likely that some clay types will experience temporary scarcity, locally and/or regionally, going forward.) |

1. "Clays", Wikipedia, 2011 - http://en.wikipedia.org/wiki/Clays.
2. "Clays Statistics", Historical Statistics for Mineral and Material Commodities in the United States, USGS, 2010 – http://minerals.usgs.gov/ds/2005/140/clay.xls.

| NNR Profile | Coal |
|---|---|

## NNR Uses and Critical Applications

| Primary Uses | Coal is readily combustible black or brownish-black "fossil fuel" used as a primary energy source both domestically and globally. Coal (coking coal) is also used in iron and steel making, and coal can be gasified and liquefied in order to broaden its applicability as a fuel source. |
|---|---|
| Critical Applications | Coal is the largest source of energy for electricity generation, both domestically (~50%) and globally (~40%); coal is also a critical source of fuel in some areas for space heating and cooking. (EIA, 2010) |

| NNR Criticality | NNR Criticality Classification: Indispensable |
|---|---|
| Substitutes | Other nonrenewable and renewable energy sources can be substituted for coal in most applications; although price/performance, general availability, and scalability vary per application. |
| Criticality Assessment | Unless and until alternative or renewable energy sources prove viable on a large scale, coal will remain an indispensible domestic and global primary energy source. |

| US NNR Scarcity | Scarce in 2008: No | Permanently Scarce: Unclear |
|---|---|---|
| **2008 US Import Reliance:** 0% | | **2008 Domestic US Supply:** 100% |
| Historical US Import Trends | The US has been a net exporter of coal since the middle of the 20th century. | |
| Historical US Usage Trends | After peaking temporarily in 1951, annual US coal utilization levels generally increased on an uninterrupted basis during the remainder of the 20th century and into the 21st century. | |
| **US Peak Extraction Year (thru 2008):** 2008 | | **US Peak Utilization Year (thru 2008):** 2007 |

| NNR Profile | Coal (continued) |
|---|---|
| **Potential Geopolitical US Supply Constraints** | "…on June 23 [2009], the EU announced that both it and the U.S. 'had requested WTO consultations with China regarding China's export restrictions on a number of key raw materials, which it considers are in clear breach of international trade rules.' <br><br> In the words of the EU announcement: 'European industries have raised concerns for a number of years on export restrictions - quotas, export duties and minimum export prices - which China applies on key raw materials, such as yellow phosphorous, bauxite, coke [coal], fluorspar, magnesium, manganese, silicon metal, silicon carbide and zinc. Some of these resources cannot be found elsewhere.'" (Seeking Alpha, 2009) |
| **US Scarcity Assessment** | "Coal production in the United States, currently the world's second largest producer, has undergone multiple peaks and declines, but total coal energy output peak was reached in 1998…" (Peak Coal, 2010) <br><br> The US is currently addressing its total requirement for coal through domestic supplies. <br><br> Both domestic coal extraction levels and utilization levels increased into the new millennium, indicating that while US coal requirements are generally increasing, domestic coal supplies are sufficient to completely address domestic requirements. <br><br> However, while the US ranks number one globally in terms of proven coal reserves, a large portion of US reserves consist of low grade (lower-energy-content) sub-bituminous and lignite coals. It is quite possible that while the US will extract larger physical quantities of domestic coal in the future, US coal supply has already peaked in terms of energy content, and that domestic requirements for coal "energy" will exceed domestic supply going forward. <br><br> It is therefore unclear whether domestically available, economically viable coal supplies will remain sufficient to completely address future domestic requirements, or whether coal will become scarce domestically in the not-too-distant future. <br><br> "…it is very likely that bituminous coal production in the US has already peaked, and that total (volumetric) coal production will peak between 2020 and 2030." (EWG, 2007) |

| Global NNR Scarcity | Scarce in 2008: Yes | Permanently Scarce: Almost Certain |
|---|---|---|
| **Historical Global Extraction Trends** | "…the top five hard coal producers [2009] are China [2,971 metric tonnes], the USA [919 metric tonnes], India, Australia and Indonesia." (World Coal Institute, 2010) <br><br> Global coal extraction levels generally increased during the latter portion of the 20th century; annual global coal extraction increased 49% between 2000 and 2008. | |

| Global Peak Extraction Year (thru 2008): 2008 | Years to Global Reserve Exhaustion: 40** |
|---|---|
| Projected Global Peak Extraction Year: 2030* | Projected Global Peak Supply Year: 2030* |

| NNR Profile | Coal (continued) |
|---|---|
| **Interdependencies** | None identified. |
| **Global Scarcity Assessment** | "Collective projections generally predict that global peak coal production may occur sometime around 2025 at 30 percent above current production in the best case scenario…" (Peak Coal, 2010)<br><br>A 49% increase in the annual global coal extraction level between 2000 and 2008 implies a robust increase in global demand during the pre-recession period, and a correspondingly robust increase in global coal supply in response to increased global demand.<br><br>The fact that the price of coal increased by a considerable 52% during the 2000-2008 period indicates that global coal supply, while increasing robustly during the eight year period, remained insufficient to completely address global requirements in 2008.<br><br>Available evidence supports the contention that global coal supplies will remain insufficient to completely address global requirements going forward:<br><br>• Proven global coal reserves would exhaust in only 40 years, assuming the restoration of pre-recession utilization levels and growth rates;<br>• The global coal extraction (supply) level is projected to peak in approximately 2030;<br>• The robust increase in global coal supply brought online between 2000 and 2008 failed to prevent a considerable price increase during the period—compelling evidence of unaddressed global requirements in 2008; and<br>• It is questionable whether the robust 5.1% compound annual growth rate (CAGR) in global coal extraction evidenced between 2000 and 2008—an interval during which coal became scarce globally despite a significant increase in extraction—can be reestablished, much less increased, going forward. A 5.1% CAGR would necessitate a continuous doubling in the annual global extraction level of coal every 14 years.<br><br>Barring future reductions in the global coal requirement trajectory and/or major new economically viable discoveries, coal will almost certainly remain scarce globally in the future.<br><br>"The global peak of coal production from existing coalfields is predicted to occur close to the year 2011." (Patzek, 2009)<br><br>"The projection is that we will have consumed half of the ultimate world oil, gas, and coal production by 2019." (Rutledge, 2008) |

*From "On American Sustainability" (a synthesis of various projections)
**Reserve to Production analyses of remaining global coal reserves vary depending upon underlying assumptions; the most optimistic is WEC/EIA at approximately 130 years; a more conservative estimate by Dr. David Rutledge is 28 years.

1. "Coal", Wikipedia, 2011 - http://en.wikipedia.org/wiki/Coal.
2. "Peak Coal"; Wikipedia, 2010 - http://en.wikipedia.org/wiki/Peak_coal.

3. "Fluorspar: The Cool Mineral", T. Vulcan, Seeking Alpha, 2009 -
http://seekingalpha.com/article/160670-fluorspar-the-cool-mineral.
4. "Coal Overview, 1949-2008", Table 7.1; US EIA -
http://www.eia.doe.gov/emeu/aer/txt/stb0701.xls.
5. "World Coal Production 1997-2008, Table 11.14; US EIA, 2010 -
http://www.eia.doe.gov/emeu/aer/txt/stb1114.xls.
6. "Coal Prices 1949-2009, Table 7.8; US EIA -2010 -
http://www.eia.doe.gov/emeu/aer/txt/stb0708.xls.
7. "How Much Coal is Left?" US EIA, 2010 -
http://www.eia.doe.gov/neic/infosheets/coalreserves.html.
8. "Where is Coal Found?" World Coal Association, 2010 -
http://www.worldcoal.org/coal/where-is-coal-found/.
9. "Coal Reserves", Source Watch, 2010 -
http://www.sourcewatch.org/index.php?title=Coal_reserves.
10. "Coal: Resources and Future Production", page 39; Energy Watch Group (EWG), 2007 -
http://www.energywatchgroup.org/fileadmin/global/pdf/EWG_Report_Coal_10-07-2007ms.pdf
EWG
11. "Hubbert's Peak, the Coal Question, and Climate Change", Dr. David Rutledge, Caltech,
2008 - http://www.its.caltech.edu/~rutledge/AGU%20abstract.pdf.
12. "A Global Coal Production Forecast with Multi-Hubbert Cycle Analysis", T. Patzek and G.
Croft, Department of Petroleum & Geosystems Engineering, The University of Texas, 2009 -
http://www.sciencedirect.com/science?_ob=ArticleURL&_udi=B6V2S-50338NC-
1&_user=108429&_coverDate=08%2F31%2F2010&_rdoc=2&_fmt=high&_orig=browse&_src
h=doc-
info(%23toc%235710%232010%23999649991%232163742%23FLA%23display%23Volume)
&_cdi=5710&_sort=d&_docanchor=&_ct=41&_acct=C000059713&_version=1&_urlVersion=0
&_userid=108429&md5=789d52395d34e83b4e2b03acd6b5073b

| NNR Profile | Cobalt |
|---|---|
| **NNR Uses and Critical Applications** ||
| **Primary Uses** | Cobalt is a hard, lustrous gray metal used in the preparation of magnetic, wear-resistant, high-strength alloys; cobalt is also used as a pigment, as a cancer treatment agent, and is the basis for vitamin B-12 (essential to all life). |
| **Critical Applications** | "The fastest growing use of cobalt is in the production of rechargeable batteries. Virtually all mainstream battery chemistries require significant amounts of cobalt." (Senate Hearing, 2010) <br><br> Cobalt is used as a super-alloy in gas turbine blades and jet aircraft engines; in lithium-ion, nickel-cadmium, and nickel-metal-hydride batteries; as a catalyst (in liquid fuels refining); and in prostheses and super magnets. <br><br> "Cobalt is also the essential element needed in almost every form of clean energy production technology being developed today." (Senate Hearing, 2010) |
| **NNR Criticality** | **NNR Criticality Classification: Indispensible** |
| **Substitutes** | Substitutes for cobalt, where available, are typically price/performance inferior. |
| **Criticality Assessment** | Cobalt is a major contributor across a broad range of critical niche and specialty industrial, aerospace, defense, medical, and renewable energy applications; cobalt is indispensible to modern industrial existence. |

| NNR Profile | Cobalt (continued) | |
|---|---|---|
| **US NNR Scarcity** | **Scarce in 2008: Yes** | **Permanently Scarce: Almost Certain** |
| **2008 US Import Reliance:** 81% | | **2008 Domestic US Supply:** 19% |
| **Historical US Import Trends** | The US has relied heavily on cobalt imports since WWII; only very small amounts of byproduct cobalt are typically produced in the US each year. | |
| **Historical US Usage Trends** | Annual US cobalt utilization levels generally increased during the 20$^{th}$ century—in a fluctuating manner—(especially after WWII), peaking temporarily in 1912, 1918, 1929, 1941, 1959, and 1974, before peaking permanently (to date) in 2005. | |
| **US Peak Production Year (thru 2008):** 1958 | | **US Peak Utilization Year (thru 2008):** 2005* |
| **Potential Geopolitical US Supply Constraints** | The Congo accounts for approximately 40% of global cobalt ore and partially refined cobalt—over half of the proven global cobalt reserves are located in the Congo; China is the leading global producer of refined cobalt.<br><br>"In 2006, the Government of Congo (Kinshasa) began to enforce a ban on exports of unprocessed cobalt." (USGS, 2008) | |
| **US Scarcity Assessment** | "The United States did not mine or refine cobalt in 2009; however, negligible amounts of byproduct cobalt were produced as intermediate products from some mining operations. U.S. supply comprised imports, stock releases, and secondary materials, such as cemented carbide scrap, spent catalysts, and superalloy scrap. " (USGS, 2010)<br><br>The US currently relies almost exclusively on imported cobalt—the quantity of cobalt supplied by foreign sources during 2008 accounted for 81% of the total 2008 US utilization level.<br><br>Available evidence supports the contention that domestic cobalt supplies will remain insufficient to completely address domestic requirements going forward:<br><br>• While US cobalt utilization increased into the new millennium, annual US (primary) cobalt production ceased entirely in 1972—a compelling indicator that domestic economically viable cobalt production has peaked permanently; and<br>• The quantity of (primary) cobalt produced domestically during 1958, the year of peak (to date) domestic cobalt production, amounted to only 18% of the 2008 total US utilization level—a primary indicator of America's increasing dependence on foreign NNRs.<br><br>Barring future reductions in the domestic (US) cobalt requirement trajectory and/or major new domestic economically viable discoveries, cobalt will almost certainly remain scarce domestically in the future.<br><br>"The vulnerability of the United States to disruptions in the supply of imported materials considered essential to industrial production has been of concern to policymakers throughout the post-World War II era. Cobalt is a prime example of such a 'strategic mineral.'" (CBO, 1982) | |

| NNR Profile | Cobalt (continued) | |
|---|---|---|
| **Global NNR Scarcity** | **Scarce in 2008: Yes** | **Permanently Scarce: Almost Certain** |
| **Historical Global Production Trends** | "In recent years, China has become the world's leading producer of refined cobalt, and much of its production has been from cobalt-rich ores imported from Congo (Kinshasa)." (USGS, 2008)<br><br>Annual global cobalt production levels generally increased during the 20th century, peaking temporarily in 1909, 1929, 1940, 1974, and 1986; annual global cobalt production increased 93% between 2000 and 2008. | |
| **Global Peak Production Year (thru 2008): 2008** | | **Years to Global Reserve Exhaustion: 26** |
| **Projected Global Peak Production Year: 2030** | | **Projected Global Peak Supply Year: 2065** |
| **Interdependencies** | Cobalt is mainly produced as a byproduct of copper and nickel mining. | |
| **Global Scarcity Assessment** | "Cobalt had been in an iffy supply status ever since the Belgian Congo (world's only significant source of cobalt) was given a hasty independence in 1960 and the cobalt-producing province seceded as Katanga, followed by several wars and insurgencies, local government removals, railroads destroyed, and nationalizations." (NR Economics, 2011)<br><br>A 93% increase in the annual global cobalt production level between 2000 and 2008 implies a significant increase in global demand during the pre-recession period, and a correspondingly significant increase in global cobalt supply in response to increased global demand.<br><br>The fact that the price of cobalt increased by a considerable 84% during the 2000-2008 period indicates that global cobalt supply, while increasing considerably during the eight year period, remained insufficient to completely address global requirements in 2008.<br><br>Available evidence supports the contention that global cobalt supplies will remain insufficient to completely address domestic requirements going forward:<br><br>• Proven global cobalt reserves would exhaust in only 26 years, assuming the restoration of pre-recession utilization levels and growth rates;<br>• The global cobalt production level is projected to peak in approximately 2030;<br>• The global cobalt supply level is projected to peak in approximately 2065;<br>• The significant increase in global cobalt supply brought online between 2000 and 2008 failed to prevent a considerable price increase during the period—compelling evidence of unaddressed global requirements in 2008; and<br>• It is questionable whether the extremely robust 8.6% compound annual growth rate (CAGR) in global cobalt production evidenced between 2000 and 2008—an interval during which cobalt became scarce globally despite an extraordinary increase in production—can be reestablished, much less increased, going forward. An 8.6% CAGR would necessitate a continuous doubling in the annual global production level of cobalt every 8.5 years.<br><br>Barring future reductions in the global cobalt requirement trajectory and/or major new economically viable discoveries, cobalt will almost certainly remain scarce globally in the future.<br><br>"Health, safety, and environmental issues are becoming increasingly significant with respect to such metals as cobalt." (USGS, 2008) | |

*Tied the peak level set in 2001; 1959 and 1974 peaks were close to the 2005 peak in terms of volume.

1. "Cobalt", Wikipedia, 2011 - http://en.wikipedia.org/wiki/Cobalt.
2. "Cobalt Statistics", Historical Statistics for Mineral and Material Commodities in the United States, USGS, 2010 – http://minerals.usgs.gov/ds/2005/140/cobalt.xls.
3. "Natural Resource Economics", Wikipedia, 2011 - http://en.wikipedia.org/wiki/Natural_resource_economics.
4. Cobalt: Policy Options for a Strategic Mineral", US Congressional Budget Office, 1982 - http://www.cbo.gov/doc.cfm?index=5126&type=0.
5. "Senate Energy and Natural Resources Hearing", 2010 - http://www.tradingmarkets.com/news/stock-alert/fcacf_senate-energy-and-natural-resources-committee-hearing-1203810.html.

| NNR Profile | Copper | |
|---|---|---|
| **NNR Uses and Critical Applications** | | |
| **Primary Uses** | Copper is a soft, malleable, ductile, peach-colored metal used as a thermal conductor, an electrical conductor, a building material, and a constituent of various metal alloys (brass and bronze being the most common). | |
| **Critical Applications** | Thermal and electrical conducting applications, including super-conducting; copper is also used in antibacterial applications, and is essential to all plant and animal life. | |
| **NNR Criticality** | **NNR Criticality Classification: Indispensable** | |
| **Substitutes** | Copper substitutes are technically available in many application areas; most substitutes, however, are price/performance inferior. | |
| **Criticality Assessment** | Copper, in its native form or as an alloy, is used in a broad range of critical industrial, construction, biomedical, and consumer product applications; copper is indispensible to modern industrial existence. | |
| **US NNR Scarcity** | **Scarce in 2008: Yes** | **Permanently Scarce: Almost Certain** |
| **2008 US Import Reliance:** 31% | **2008 Domestic US Supply:** 69% | |
| **Historical US Import Trends** | The US has transitioned from a net exporter of copper in the early/middle years of the 20th century, to an increasingly reliant net importer today. | |
| **Historical US Usage Trends** | Annual US copper utilization levels generally increased during the 20th century, peaking temporarily in 1918, 1929, 1941, 1966, and 1979, before peaking permanently (to date) in 1999. Domestic copper utilization declined steadily since that time; the 2008 US copper utilization level amounted to only 65% of the 1999 peak utilization level. "Refined copper consumption declined slightly [in 2009], as double digit declines in the European Union, Japan, and the United States were mostly offset by growth in China's apparent consumption of more than 25%." (USGS, 2010) | |
| **US Peak Extraction Year (thru 2008):** 1998 | **US Peak Utilization Year (thru 2008):** 1999 | |
| **Potential Geopolitical US Supply Constraints** | 40% of US copper imports come from Chile; Chile produces over one third of the world's copper. | |

| NNR Profile | Copper (continued) |
|---|---|
| **US Scarcity Assessment** | That annual domestic copper utilization decreased by 35% since peaking (to date) in 1999, is a primary indicator of declining American industrial preeminence and global economic competitiveness.<br><br>The US currently relies considerably on imported copper, a large percentage (40%) of which comes from Chile. The quantity of copper supplied by foreign sources during 2008 accounted for 31% of the total 2008 US utilization level.<br><br>Available evidence supports the contention that domestic copper supplies will remain insufficient to completely address domestic requirements going forward:<br><br>• The annual US copper extraction level decreased by 43% since peaking (to date) in 1998—a compelling indicator that domestic economically viable copper extraction has peaked permanently;<br>• The US has become increasingly reliant on copper imports since the early 1990s; and<br>• The quantity of copper extracted domestically during 2008 amounted to only 61% of the total 2008 US utilization level—a primary cause of America's lack of economic self-sufficiency.<br><br>Barring future reductions in the domestic (US) copper requirement trajectory and/or major new domestic economically viable discoveries, copper will almost certainly remain scarce domestically in the future. |

| Global NNR Scarcity | Scarce in 2008: Yes | Permanently Scarce: Almost Certain |
|---|---|---|
| **Historical Global Extraction Trends** | Annual global copper extraction levels increased almost continuously during the 20th century and early 21st century, peaking temporarily in 1918, 1929, and 1943; annual global copper extraction increased 17% between 2000 and 2008. | |

| Global Peak Extraction Year (thru 2008): 2008 | Years to Global Reserve Exhaustion: 27 |
|---|---|
| **Projected Global Peak Extraction Year:** 2030 | **Projected Global Peak Supply Year:** 2040 |
| **Interdependencies** | None identified. |

| NNR Profile | Copper (continued) |
|---|---|
| **Global Scarcity Assessment** | "Globally, economic copper resources are being depleted with the equivalent production of three world-class copper mines being consumed annually; meanwhile, copper demand is increasing by more than 575,000 tons annually and accelerating." Furthermore, "only 56 new copper discoveries have been made during the past three decades," and "21 of the 28 largest copper mines in the world are not amenable to expansion, while many large copper mines will be exhausted between 2010 and 2015." (Salon, 2006)<br><br>A 17% increase in the annual global copper extraction level between 2000 and 2008 implies an increase in global copper demand during the pre-recession period, and a corresponding increase in global copper supply in response to increased global demand.<br><br>The fact that the price of copper increased by an extraordinary 190% during the 2000-2008 period indicates that global copper supply, while increasing during the eight year period, remained woefully insufficient to fully address global requirements in 2008.<br><br>Available evidence supports the contention that global copper supplies will remain insufficient to completely address global requirements going forward:<br><br>• World copper discoveries peaked (to date) in 1996; (Wikipedia, 2010)<br>• Proven global copper reserves would exhaust in only 27 years, assuming the restoration of pre-recession utilization levels and growth rates;<br>• The global copper extraction level is projected to peak in approximately 2030;<br>• The global copper supply level is projected to peak in approximately 2040; and<br>• An extraordinary increase in the price of copper during the 2000-2008 period could induce only a nominal increase in copper supply—compelling evidence that globally available, economically viable copper extraction may be near or at its permanent peak level.<br><br>Barring future reductions in the global copper requirement trajectory and/or major new economically viable discoveries, copper will almost certainly remain scarce globally in the future.<br><br>"…imports of refined copper by China [in 2007], the world's leading copper consumer, gave rise to concern over supply adequacy." (USGS, 2008)<br><br>"Copper is extensively mined and has a huge reserve base, but recent analysis has found that for the world population to attain North American affluence by 2100, more copper would be required than exists in the Earth's crust." (IEEE Spectrum, 2008) |

1. "Copper", Wikipedia, 2011 - http://en.wikipedia.org/wiki/Copper.
2. "Copper Statistics", Historical Statistics for Mineral and Material Commodities in the United States, USGS, 2010 – http://minerals.usgs.gov/ds/2005/140/copper.xls.
3. "Metal Stocks and Sustainability", T. Graedel etal. Department of Geology and Geophysics, Yale University, 2005 - http://www.eco-info.org/IMG/pdf/Metal_stocks_and_sustainability.pdf.

4. "Supply Risk, Scarcity, and Cellphones", S. Moore, IEEE Spectrum, 2008 - http://spectrum.ieee.org/telecom/wireless/supply-risk-scarcity-and-cellphones.
5. "Peak Copper?" A. Leonard, Salon, 2006 - http://www.salon.com/technology/how_the_world_works/2006/03/02/peak_copper/index.html.
6. Peak Copper", Wikipedia, 2010 - http://en.wikipedia.org/wiki/Peak_copper.

| NNR Profile | Diamond (Industrial) |
|---|---|
| **NNR Uses and Critical Applications** | |
| **Primary Uses** | Diamond (in its pure form) is a hard colorless carbon allotrope used in industrial cutting, grinding, and polishing applications; diamond is also the most popular gemstone, and is used in niche semiconductor applications. |
| **Critical Applications** | None identified. |

| NNR Criticality | NNR Criticality Classification: Important |
|---|---|
| **Substitutes** | Synthetic diamonds and diamond simulants such as zirconium and carborundum are viable substitutes for natural diamonds (98% of the industrial diamonds in the US market are synthetic). |
| **Criticality Assessment** | While diamond is the hardest known industrial material and possesses the highest thermal conductivity of any industrial mineral, its industrial applications are limited and readily available substitutes for natural diamonds exist. |

| US NNR Scarcity | Scarce in 2008: Yes | Permanently Scarce: Almost Certain |
|---|---|---|
| **2008 US Import Reliance: 91%/56%**** | | **2008 Domestic US Supply: 9%/44%**** |
| **Historical US Import Trends** | Historically, the US has been both a net importer and a net exporter of industrial diamonds (natural stones are not produced domestically); the US has become increasingly reliant on industrial diamond net imports since 1992. | |
| **Historical US Usage Trends** | "U.S. demand for industrial diamond [for tips of cement cutting saw blades]. is likely to continue in the construction sector as the United States continues building and repairing the Nation's highway system. (USGS 2010)<br><br>Annual US industrial diamond utilization levels generally increased during both the 20th and 21st centuries, peaking temporarily in 1920, 1944, 1956, and 1966, before increasing relatively steadily into the new millennium.<br><br>"The United States will continue to be the world's leading market for industrial diamond into the next decade and will remain a significant producer and exporter of industrial diamond as well." (USGS, 2008) | |
| **US Peak Production Year (thru 2008): 2008** | | **US Peak Utilization Year (thru 2008): 2008** |
| **Potential Geopolitical US Supply Constraints** | 57% of US imports of synthetic diamond materials come from China; 74% of natural diamond stone imports come from countries in Africa. | |

| NNR Profile | Diamond (Industrial) [continued] |
|---|---|
| **US Scarcity Assessment** | The US currently relies almost exclusively on imported natural industrial diamonds, the large majority (74%) of which comes from countries in Africa, including Botswana, South Africa, and Namibia. The quantity of natural industrial diamonds supplied by foreign sources during 2008 accounted for 91% of the total 2008 US utilization level.<br><br>The US also relies heavily on imported manufactured (synthetic) diamonds, the majority (57%) of which comes from China. The quantity of manufactured industrial diamonds supplied by foreign sources during 2008 accounted for 56% of the total 2008 US utilization level.<br><br>While both the annual US industrial diamond utilization level and the annual US industrial diamond extraction/production level increased into the new millennium, net US industrial diamond imports increased steadily since 1992—an indicator of America's increasing dependence on foreign NNRs.<br><br>Barring future reductions in the domestic (US) industrial diamond requirement trajectory and/or major new domestic economically viable discoveries, industrial diamonds will almost certainly remain scarce domestically in the future. |

| Global NNR Scarcity | Scarce in 2008: No | Permanently Scarce: Unclear |
|---|---|---|
| **Historical Global Production Trends** | Annual global diamond extraction/production levels increased gradually during the early/mid 20<sup>th</sup> century, peaking temporarily in 1967 and 1980, before increasing dramatically in 1988, and increasing phenomenally in 2004; annual global industrial diamond extraction/production increased by 871% between 2000 and 2008. [Based on USGS data.]<br><br>"China is the world's leading producer of synthetic industrial diamond [in 2009]..." (USGS 2010) | |

| Global Peak Production Year (thru 2008): 2007 | Years to Global Reserve Exhaustion: 4* |
|---|---|
| Projected Global Peak Production Year: N/A | Projected Global Peak Supply Year: N/A |

| Interdependencies | None identified. |
|---|---|

| NNR Profile | Diamond (Industrial) [continued] |
|---|---|
| **Global Scarcity Assessment** | An 871% increase in the annual global industrial diamond extraction/production level between 2000 and 2008 implies a meteoric increase in global industrial diamond demand during the pre-recession period, and a corresponding increase in global industrial diamond supply in response to increased global demand.<br><br>The fact that the price of industrial diamond decreased by an extraordinary 56% during the 2000-2008 period indicates that the global supply of industrial diamonds in 2008 was sufficient to completely address 2008 global requirements.<br><br>Assuming that the USGS 2000-2008 global industrial diamond extraction/production figures are accurate, available evidence regarding the likelihood that global industrial diamond supplies will remain sufficient to completely address global requirements going forward is conflicting:<br><br>• While global industrial diamond extraction/production levels have generally increased since the early 1960s, industrial diamond price levels have generally decreased since that time—compelling evidence of sufficient global industrial diamond supplies; however<br>• Proven global industrial diamond reserves would exhaust in only 4 years, assuming the restoration of pre-recession utilization levels and growth rates (and the accuracy of USGS global industrial diamond extraction/production data); and<br>• It is unclear whether the inordinately robust 32.9% compound annual growth rate (CAGR) in global industrial diamond extraction/production evidenced between 2000 and 2008 (again, assuming the accuracy of USGS global industrial diamond extraction/production data)—which was required to enable pre-recession global economic growth—can be reestablished and maintained going forward. A 32.9% CAGR would necessitate a continuous doubling in the annual global extraction/production level of industrial diamond every 2.5 years.<br><br>It is therefore unclear whether globally available, economically viable industrial diamond supplies will remain sufficient to completely address future global requirements, or whether industrial diamonds will become scarce in the not-too-distant future.<br><br>"…the decline [in prices for synthetic industrial diamonds] is even more likely if competition from low-cost producers in China and Russia continues increasing." (USGS, 2008) |

*Natural industrial diamond years to exhaustion.

**Natural industrial diamonds/Synthetic industrial diamonds.

1. "Diamond", Wikipedia, 2011 - http://en.wikipedia.org/wiki/Diamond.
2. "Industrial Diamond Statistics", Historical Statistics for Mineral and Material Commodities in the United States, USGS, 2010 – http://minerals.usgs.gov/ds/2005/140/diamondindustrial.xls.

| NNR Profile | Diatomite |
|---|---|

## NNR Uses and Critical Applications

| | |
|---|---|
| **Primary Uses** | Diatomite is a soft, very light, porous, white mineral used as a mild abrasive, filtration aid, cement additive, insecticide, absorbent, and as a component of dynamite (which is nitroglycerin packed in diatomite). |
| **Critical Applications** | None identified. |

| NNR Criticality | NNR Criticality Classification: Important |
|---|---|
| **Substitutes** | Substitutes for diatomite exist in all application areas, but price/performance characteristics are inferior to those of diatomite in some cases. |
| **Criticality Assessment** | Diatomite is useful in a variety of niche applications for which viable substitutes are generally available. |

| US NNR Scarcity | Scarce in 2008: No | Permanently Scarce: Unlikely |
|---|---|---|

| 2008 US Import Reliance: 0% | 2008 Domestic US Supply: 100% |
|---|---|

| | |
|---|---|
| **Historical US Import Trends** | The US has been a net exporter of diatomite since the early 1960s. |
| **Historical US Usage Trends** | Annual US diatomite utilization levels generally increased during the 20<sup>th</sup> and 21<sup>st</sup> centuries, peaking temporarily in 1909, 1929, 1957, 1966, 1979, and 1997, before peaking permanently (to date) in 2006. |

| US Peak Extraction Year (thru 2008): 2006 | US Peak Utilization Year (thru 2008): 2006 |
|---|---|

| | |
|---|---|
| **Potential Geopolitical US Supply Constraints** | None identified. |
| **US Scarcity Assessment** | The US is currently addressing its total requirement for diatomite through domestic supplies.<br><br>Available evidence supports the contention that domestic diatomite supplies will likely remain sufficient to completely address domestic requirements for the foreseeable future:<br><br>• Domestic diatomite supplies were sufficient to completely address domestic requirements during the 2000-2008 period of rapid economic growth prior to the Great Recession; and<br>• Proven domestic diatomite reserves are sufficient to last for over 50 years (assuming the restoration of pre-recession utilization levels and growth rates).<br><br>Barring future increases in the domestic (US) diatomite requirement trajectory, domestically available, economically viable diatomite supplies will likely remain sufficient to completely address domestic requirements going forward. |

| Global NNR Scarcity | Scarce in 2008: No | Permanently Scarce: Unlikely |
|---|---|---|

| | |
|---|---|
| **Historical Global Extraction Trends** | Annual global diatomite extraction levels generally increased during the 20<sup>th</sup> and 21<sup>st</sup> centuries, peaking temporarily in 1920, 1968, 1974, 1986, and 1994; annual global diatomite extraction increased by 15% between 2000 and 2008. |

| Global Peak Extraction Year (thru 2008): 2008 | Years to Global Reserve Exhaustion: >100 |
|---|---|
| Projected Global Peak Extraction Year: N/A | Projected Global Peak Supply Year: N/A |
| **Interdependencies** | None identified. |

| NNR Profile | Diatomite (continued) |
|---|---|
| **Global Scarcity Assessment** | A 15% increase in the annual global diatomite extraction level between 2000 and 2008 implies an increase in global diatomite demand during the pre-recession period, and a corresponding increase in global diatomite supply in response to increased global demand.<br><br>The fact that the price of diatomite decreased by a substantial 30% during the 2000-2008 period indicates that the global supply of diatomite in 2008 was sufficient to completely address 2008 global requirements.<br><br>Available evidence supports the contention that global diatomite supplies will remain sufficient to completely address global requirements going forward:<br><br>• While global diatomite extraction levels have generally increased since the early 1990s, diatomite price levels have generally decreased since that time—compelling evidence of sufficient global diatomite supplies; and<br>• Proven global diatomite reserves are sufficient to last for over 100 years (assuming the restoration of pre-recession utilization levels and growth rates).<br><br>Barring future increases in the global diatomite requirement trajectory, globally available, economically viable diatomite supplies will likely remain sufficient to completely address global requirements going forward. |

1. "Diatomite", Wikipedia, 2011 - http://en.wikipedia.org/wiki/Diatomite.
2. "Diatomite Statistics", Historical Statistics for Mineral and Material Commodities in the United States, USGS, 2010 – http://minerals.usgs.gov/ds/2005/140/diatomite.xls.

| NNR Profile | Feldspar | |
|---|---|---|
| **NNR Uses and Critical Applications** | | |
| **Primary Uses** | Feldspars are a group of minerals that comprise 60% of the earth's crust, which are used in the production of glass, ceramics, and geopolymers; feldspars are also used as fillers, insulators, and abrasives. | |
| **Critical Applications** | None identified. | |
| **NNR Criticality** | **NNR Criticality Classification: Important** | |
| **Substitutes** | Viable feldspar substitutes, including clays, electric furnace slag, feldspar-silica mixtures, pyrophyllite, spodumene, and talc, are available for most applications; nepheline syenite is the primary feldspar substitute. | |
| **Criticality Assessment** | Feldspar is extremely pervasive, both in its occurrence and in its use; however, suitable alternatives to feldspar-provided solutions are generally available. | |
| **US NNR Scarcity** | **Scarce in 2008: Yes** | **Permanently Scarce: Almost Certain** |
| **2008 US Import Reliance:** 32% | **2008 Domestic US Supply:** 68% | |
| **Historical US Import Trends** | The US has been a net importer of feldspar, particularly nepheline syenite (which contains feldspar), over the past several decades.<br><br>"…80% of [feldspar based] ceramic tiles and 50% of the plumbing fixtures sold in the United States were imported." (USGS, 2008) | |

| NNR Profile | Feldspar (continued) |
|---|---|
| **Historical US Usage Trends** | Annual US feldspar utilization levels generally increased during the early/mid 20th century, peaking temporarily in 1906, 1917, 1926, and 1956; domestic utilization then increased dramatically in 1975, peaked temporarily in 1979, peaked permanently (to date) in 1997, and declined generally since that time. The 2008 US feldspar utilization level amounted to only 77% of the 1997 peak utilization level.<br><br>"Domestic feldspar consumption is moving away from ceramics toward glass markets…" (USGS, 2010) |

| US Peak Extraction Year (thru 2008): 1997 | US Peak Utilization Year (thru 2008): 1997 |
|---|---|

| **Potential Geopolitical US Supply Constraints** | 54% of US feldspar imports come from Turkey. |
|---|---|
| **US Scarcity Assessment** | That annual domestic feldspar utilization decreased by 23% since peaking (to date) in 1997, is an indicator of declining American industrial preeminence and global economic competitiveness.<br><br>The US currently relies considerably on imported feldspar, the majority (54%) of which comes from Turkey. The quantity of feldspar supplied by foreign sources during 2008 accounted for 32% of the total 2008 US utilization level.<br><br>Available evidence supports the contention that domestic feldspar supplies will remain insufficient to completely address domestic requirements going forward:<br><br>• The annual US feldspar extraction level decreased by 28% since peaking (to date) in 1997—an indicator that domestic economically viable feldspar extraction has peaked permanently;<br>• The US has become increasingly reliant on feldspar imports since 1975;<br>• The quantity of feldspar extracted domestically during 2008 amounted to only 68% of the total 2008 US utilization level—a significant indicator of America's increasing dependence on foreign NNRs; and<br>• The quantity of feldspar extracted domestically during 1997, the year of peak (to date) domestic feldspar extraction, amounted to only 94% of the 2008 total US utilization level.<br><br>Barring future reductions in the domestic (US) feldspar requirement trajectory and/or major new domestic economically viable discoveries, feldspar will almost certainly remain scarce domestically in the future. domestically in the future. |

| Global NNR Scarcity | Scarce in 2008: No | Permanently Scarce: Unclear |
|---|---|---|

| **Historical Global Extraction Trends** | "China reportedly was the leading producing country of ceramics, including sanitaryware, tableware, and tile." (USGS, 2008)<br><br>Annual global feldspar extraction levels increased consistently during both the 20th and 21st centuries, pausing only briefly in 1911, 1928, and 1941; annual global feldspar extraction increased by 12% between 2000 and 2008. |
|---|---|

| Global Peak Extraction Year (thru 2008): 2008 | Years to Global Reserve Exhaustion: N/A |
|---|---|
| Projected Global Peak Extraction Year: N/A | Projected Global Peak Supply Year: N/A |

| **Interdependencies** | None identified. |
|---|---|

| NNR Profile | Feldspar (continued) |
|---|---|
| **Global Scarcity Assessment** | A 130% increase in the annual global feldspar extraction level between 2000 and 2008 implies a significant increase in global feldspar demand during the pre-recession period, and a correspondingly significant increase in global feldspar supply in response to increased global demand.<br><br>The fact that the price of feldspar decreased by 12% during the 2000-2008 period indicates that the global supply of feldspar in 2008 was sufficient to completely address 2008 global requirements.<br><br>Available evidence regarding the likelihood that global feldspar supplies will remain sufficient to completely address global requirements going forward is conflicting:<br><br>• While global feldspar extraction levels have generally increased since the early 20th century, feldspar price levels have generally decreased since that time—compelling evidence of sufficient global feldspar supplies; and<br>• Global feldspar resources are considered by the USGS to be "large"; however<br>• It is unclear whether the extremely robust 11% compound annual growth rate (CAGR) in global feldspar extraction evidenced between 2000 and 2008—which was required to enable pre-recession global economic growth—can be reestablished and maintained going forward. An 11% CAGR would necessitate a continuous doubling in the annual global extraction level of feldspar every 6.5 years.<br><br>It is therefore unclear whether globally available, economically viable feldspar supplies will remain sufficient to completely address future global requirements, or whether feldspar will become scarce globally in the not-too-distant future. |

1. "Feldspar", Wikipedia, 2011 - http://en.wikipedia.org/wiki/Feldspar.
2. "Feldspar Statistics", Historical Statistics for Mineral and Material Commodities in the United States, USGS, 2010 – http://minerals.usgs.gov/ds/2005/140/feldspar.xls.

| NNR Profile | Fluorspar |
|---|---|
| **NNR Uses and Critical Applications** | |
| **Primary Uses** | Fluorspar (fluorite) is a widely occurring colorful mineral used as flux in steel and aluminum production; fluorspar is also used in petroleum refining, in opalescent glass manufacture, and as the feedstock for hydrofluoric acid (used in pharmaceuticals and polymers). |
| **Critical Applications** | Used in the production of hydrofluoric acid, as the feedstock for fluorine bearing chemicals (refrigerant and thermoplastic applications); in processing aluminum and uranium; in water fluoridation; and in petroleum refining. |
| **NNR Criticality** | **NNR Criticality Classification: Critical** |
| **Substitutes** | Fluorspar substitutes are available in some application areas, but price/performance attributes tend to be inferior. |

| NNR Profile | Fluorspar (continued) |
|---|---|
| **Criticality Assessment** | Fluorspar plays a significant contributory role in a diverse range of industrial applications, many of which are critical.<br><br>"HF [hydrofluoric acid] is the primary feedstock for the manufacture of virtually all fluorine-bearing chemicals and is also a key ingredient in the processing of aluminum and uranium." (USGS, 2010) |

| **US NNR Scarcity** | Scarce in 2008: Yes | Permanently Scarce: Almost Certain |
|---|---|---|

| **2008 US Import Reliance:** 100% | **2008 Domestic US Supply:** 0% |
|---|---|

| **Historical US Import Trends** | The US has been increasingly reliant on fluorspar imports since the 1940s. |
|---|---|
| **Historical US Usage Trends** | Annual US fluorspar utilization levels generally increased during the first three quarters of the 20$^{th}$ century, peaking temporarily in 1905, 1918, 1926, 1944, and 1957, before peaking permanently (to date) in 1973. Domestic fluorspar utilization declined dramatically during the 1980s and fluctuated at relatively constant level thereafter; the 2008 US fluorspar utilization level amounted to only 39% of the 1973 peak utilization level.<br><br>"As a result of accidental releases of HF at three U.S. petroleum refineries in Illinois, Pennsylvania, and Texas, [in 2009] the largest industrial union in North America called for the phaseout of HF used in petroleum alkylation units at refineries [15% of US HF utilization]." (UGSS, 2010) |

| **US Peak Extraction Year (thru 2008):** 1944 | **US Peak Utilization Year (thru 2008):** 1973 |
|---|---|

| **Potential Geopolitical US Supply Constraints** | 52% of US fluorspar imports come from China.<br><br>"The West's growing concerns about China's dominance of the fluorspar market (among others), including possible export restrictions, came to a head earlier this year [2009] when, on June 23, the EU announced that both it and the U.S. "had requested WTO consultations with China regarding China's export restrictions on a number of key raw materials, which it considers are in clear breach of international trade rules.<br><br>In the words of the EU announcement: 'European industries have raised concerns for a number of years on export restrictions - quotas, export duties and minimum export prices - which China applies on key raw materials, such as yellow phosphorous, bauxite, coke, fluorspar, magnesium, manganese, silicon metal, silicon carbide and zinc. Some of these resources cannot be found elsewhere.'" (Seeking Alpha, 2009) |

| NNR Profile | Fluorspar (continued) |
|---|---|
| **US Scarcity Assessment** | "The U.S. produces no primary fluorspar, although a tiny amount is produced as a by-product of limestone quarrying in Illinois." (Seeking Alpha, 2009)<br><br>That annual domestic fluorspar utilization decreased by 61% since peaking (to date) in 1973, is a significant indicator of declining American industrial preeminence and global economic competitiveness.<br><br>The US currently relies exclusively on imported fluorspar—the majority (52%) of which comes from China.<br><br>Available evidence supports the contention that domestic fluorspar supplies will remain insufficient to completely address domestic requirements going forward:<br><br>• Annual US fluorspar extraction ceased entirely in 1997—a compelling indicator that domestic economically viable fluorspar extraction has peaked permanently; and<br>• The quantity of fluorspar extracted domestically during 1944, the year of peak (to date) domestic fluorspar extraction, amounted to only 71% of the 2008 total US utilization level—a significant indicator of America's increasing dependence on foreign NNRs.<br><br>Barring future reductions in the domestic (US) fluorspar requirement trajectory and/or major new domestic economically viable discoveries, fluorspar will almost certainly remain scarce domestically in the future.<br><br>"…the U.S. Institute for Defense Analyses undertook an 'initial risk review' for various materials to determine if shortages or near-shortages 'in meeting defense-essential demands' could arise; the agency named fluorspar as one such mineral that could possibly suffer shortages." (Seeking Alpha, 2009) |

| Global NNR Scarcity | | Scarce in 2008: Yes | Permanently Scarce: Likely |
|---|---|---|---|
| **Historical Global Extraction Trends** | | "Five countries, China [52% of 2007 global extraction], Mexico [17%], Mongolia [8%], South Africa [6%] and Russia [4%], accounted for 86% of world [fluorspar] production in 2007." (Roskill, 2009; USGS, 2008 [figures])<br><br>Annual global fluorspar extraction levels generally increased during the 20th and 21st centuries, peaking temporarily in 1918, 1929, 1944, 1974, 1981, and 1989, before declining dramatically in the 1990s. Global extraction levels resumed their upward trend into the new millennium; annual global fluorspar extraction increased 29% between 2000 and 2008. | |

| Global Peak Extraction Year (thru 2008): 2008 | Years to Global Reserve Exhaustion: 23 |
|---|---|
| Projected Global Peak Extraction Year: N/A | Projected Global Peak Supply Year: N/A |

| **Interdependencies** | Fluorspar is recovered as a byproduct of limestone quarrying, and as a byproduct of phosphate rock production (fluorosilicic acid). |
|---|---|

| NNR Profile | Fluorspar (continued) |
|---|---|
| **Global Scarcity Assessment** | "Over the past decade as a whole, demand for fluorspar has grown by just over 2.2%py but in the years from 2003 to 2007, growth rates exceeded 4%py as the industry started to recover from the effects of restrictions on the use of some fluorocarbons [Montreal protocol of 1989]." (Roskill, 2009)<br><br>A 29% increase in the annual global fluorspar extraction level between 2000 and 2008 implies an increase in global fluorspar demand during the pre-recession period, and a corresponding increase in global fluorspar supply in response to increased global demand.<br><br>The fact that the price of fluorspar increased by 39% during the 2000-2008 period indicates that global fluorspar supply, while increasing during the eight year period, remained insufficient to completely address global requirements in 2008.<br><br>Available evidence supports the contention that global fluorspar supplies will likely remain insufficient to completely address global requirements going forward:<br><br>• Proven global fluorspar reserves would exhaust in only 23 years, assuming the restoration of pre-recession utilization levels and growth rates;<br>• The increase in global fluorspar supply levels between 2000 and 2008 failed to prevent a price increase during the period—evidence of unaddressed global requirements in 2008; and<br>• It is questionable whether the 4.3% compound annual growth rate (CAGR) in global fluorspar extraction evidenced between 2000 and 2008—an interval during which fluorspar became scarce globally despite a significant increase in extraction—can be reestablished, much less increased, going forward. A 4.3% CAGR would necessitate a continuous doubling in the annual global extraction level of fluorspar every 16.5 years.<br><br>Barring future reductions in the global fluorspar requirement trajectory and/or major new economically viable discoveries, fluorspar will likely remain scarce globally in the future. |

1. "Fluorspar", Wikipedia, 2011 - http://en.wikipedia.org/wiki/Fluorspar.
2. "Fluorspar Statistics", Historical Statistics for Mineral and Material Commodities in the United States, USGS, 2010 – http://minerals.usgs.gov/ds/2005/140/fluorspar.xls.
3. "The Economics of Fluorspar" (10th edition), Roskill, 2009 - http://www.roskill.com/reports/industrial-minerals/fluorspar.
4. "Fluorspar: The Cool Metal, T. Vulcan, Seeking Alpha, 2009 - http://seekingalpha.com/article/160670-fluorspar-the-cool-mineral.

| NNR Profile | Gallium |
|---|---|

### NNR Uses and Critical Applications

| Primary Uses | Gallium is a brittle, soft, silvery metal, which is a liquid at or near room temperature (86 degrees F), used in high-temperature thermometric applications and as a stability enabling metal alloy (plutonium being one application); currently used primarily in electronic components (semiconductors, microwave, infrared, LEDs, solar cells, and fuel cells). |
|---|---|
| Critical Applications | High performance semiconductors (integrated circuits and optoelectronic devices), stabilizing alloys, and potentially in solar cells and fuel cells. |

| NNR Criticality | NNR Criticality Classification: Critical |
|---|---|
| Substitutes | Viable substitutes for gallium are available in most applications, although price/performance is often an issue; substitutes are typically not available in defense related applications.<br><br>"Because of their unique properties, there are currently, in a range of defense-related applications [radar, active array antenna, and infrared cameras], no effective substitutes for either GaAs [gallium arsenide] or GaN [gallium nitride]." (Seeking Alpha, 2009) |
| Criticality Assessment | Gallium currently addresses niche requirements in semiconductor and alloying applications; if its use in fuel cells and solar cells (CIGS—copper indium gallium [di]selenide.) becomes widely adopted, gallium will become increasingly critical.<br><br>"Some of the most critical [minerals] are found in cell phones. The ones to worry about, says Graedel, are difficult to find substitutes for and are produced only as by-products of something else, so their own supplies are constrained. Gallium and indium fall into that category." (IEEE Spectrum, 2008) |

| US NNR Scarcity | Scarce in 2008: Yes | Permanently Scarce: Almost Certain |
|---|---|---|
| 2008 US Import Reliance: 99% | | 2008 Domestic US Supply: 1% |
| Historical US Import Trends | With the exception of a few years during the late 1970s and early 1980s, the US has relied almost exclusively on gallium imports. | |
| Historical US Usage Trends | Annual US gallium utilization levels generally increased during the latter decades of the 20th century, peaking temporarily in 1979 and 1986, before peaking permanently (to date) in 2000. US gallium utilization levels rebounded following post 2000 declines, but not to year 2000 levels; the 2008 US gallium utilization level amounted to only 72% of the 2000 peak utilization level.<br><br>"Gallium arsenide (GaAs) and gallium nitride (GaN) electronic components represented about 98% of domestic gallium consumption [in 2009]." (UGSS, 2010) | |
| US Peak Production Year (thru 2008): 1978 | | US Peak Utilization Year (thru 2008): 2000 |
| Potential Geopolitical US Supply Constraints | China, Kazakhstan, and the Ukraine are 3 of the top 4 producers of unrefined gallium. | |

| NNR Profile | Gallium (continued) |
|---|---|
| **US Scarcity Assessment** | "No domestic primary gallium recovery was reported in 2009." (USGS, 2010)<br><br>That annual domestic gallium utilization decreased by 28% since peaking (to date) in 2000, is an indicator of declining American industrial preeminence and global economic competitiveness.<br><br>The US currently relies almost exclusively on imported gallium; the quantity of gallium supplied by foreign sources during 2008 accounted for 99% of the total 2008 US utilization level.<br><br>Available evidence supports the contention that domestic gallium supplies will remain insufficient to completely address domestic requirements going forward:<br><br>• US gallium production ceased in 1987—a significant indicator of America's increasing dependence on foreign NNRs, and a compelling indicator that domestic economically viable gallium production has peaked permanently; and<br>• The quantity of gallium produced domestically during 1978, the year of peak (to date) domestic gallium production, amounted to only 19% of the 2008 total US utilization level.<br><br>Barring future reductions in the domestic (US) gallium requirement trajectory and/or major new domestic economically viable discoveries, gallium will almost certainly remain scarce domestically in the future.<br><br>"There is, currently, no primary gallium recovery in the U.S. And, unfortunately, any prospect of there being any soon, seems, in today's economic environment, to be receding rapidly." (Seeking Alpha, 2009) |

| Global NNR Scarcity | Scarce in 2008: No | Permanently Scarce: Unclear |
|---|---|---|
| **Historical Global Production Trends** | "The major primary gallium-producing countries [in 2007] are China, Germany, Japan, and Ukraine." (Seeking Alpha, 2009)<br><br>Annual global gallium production levels generally increased during the later decades of the 20th century and into the 21st century, peaking temporarily in 1973, 1986, and 1998; annual global gallium production increased 23% between 2000 and 2008. | |

| Global Peak Production Year (thru 2008): 2008 | Years to Global Reserve Exhaustion: N/A |
|---|---|
| **Projected Global Peak Production Year:** N/A | **Projected Global Peak Supply Year:** N/A |

| Interdependencies | Most gallium is produced as a byproduct of bauxite and zinc ore processing.<br><br>"Economic deposits of gallium rarely occur, and production is almost entirely as a by-product of alumina production where gallium is extracted, in an impure form, from the caustic liquor that is generated during bauxite processing." (MMTA) |
|---|---|

| NNR Profile | Gallium (continued) |
|---|---|
| **Global Scarcity Assessment** | "Producers in China claimed that there was a shortage of supply [in 2007], which was the principal reason for the increase in prices." (USGS, 2008)<br><br>A 23% increase in the annual global gallium production level between 2000 and 2008 implies an increase in global gallium demand during the pre-recession period, and a corresponding increase in global gallium supply in response to increased global demand.<br><br>The fact that the price of gallium decreased by a substantial 28% during the 2000-2008 period indicates that the global supply of gallium in 2008 was sufficient to completely address 2008 global requirements.<br><br>Available evidence regarding the likelihood that global gallium supplies will remain sufficient to completely address global requirements going forward is conflicting:<br><br>• A declining gallium price level between 2000 and 2008 indicates that global gallium supplies were sufficient to completely address global requirements in 2008; however<br>• The USGS statement (above) regarding China's assessment of global gallium demand/supply dynamics in 2007 indicates global gallium scarcity toward the end of the 2000-2008 period.<br><br>It is therefore unclear whether globally available, economically viable gallium supplies will remain sufficient to completely address future global requirements, or whether gallium will become scarce globally in the not-too-distant future.<br><br>"The world bauxite reserves are so large that much of them will not be mined for many decades; hence, most of the gallium in the bauxite reserves cannot be considered to be available in the short term." (USGS, 2010) |

1. "Gallium", Wikipedia, 2011 - http://en.wikipedia.org/wiki/Gallium.
2. "Gallium Statistics", Historical Statistics for Mineral and Material Commodities in the United States, USGS, 2010 – http://minerals.usgs.gov/ds/2005/140/gallium.xls.
3. "Supply Risk, Scarcity, and Cellphones", S. Moore, IEEE Spectrum, 2008 - http://spectrum.ieee.org/telecom/wireless/supply-risk-scarcity-and-cellphones.
4. "Gallium", MMTA, UK - http://www.mmta.co.uk/uploaded_files/GalliumMJ.pdf.
5. "Gallium: the Slippery Metal", Seeking Alpha, 2009 - http://seekingalpha.com/article/117894-gallium-the-slippery-metal.

| NNR Profile | Garnet (Industrial) |
|---|---|
| **NNR Uses and Critical Applications** | |
| **Primary Uses** | Garnet is a group of six minerals, which range in hardness and color, used primarily as abrasives—sand blasting, water jet cutting, and polishing—in industrial applications; garnet is also used as a water filtration medium and to determine the genesis and time histories associated with many igneous and metamorphic rocks—garnet is also a gemstone. |
| **Critical Applications** | None identified. |

| NNR Profile | Garnet (Industrial) [continued] | |
|---|---|---|
| **NNR Criticality** | **NNR Criticality Classification: Important** | |
| **Substitutes** | Natural or synthetic substitutes exist for nearly all niche garnet applications, but are often price/performance inferior. | |
| **Criticality Assessment** | While abrasives play an important role in many industrial and construction applications, viable alternatives exist for all applications in which garnet is used. | |
| **US NNR Scarcity** | **Scarce in 2008: Yes** | **Permanently Scarce: Almost Certain** |
| **2008 US Import Reliance:** 37% | | **2008 Domestic US Supply:** 63% |
| **Historical US Import Trends** | The US, at one time a net exporter of garnet, has become an increasingly reliant net importer over the past several decades. | |
| **Historical US Usage Trends** | Annual US garnet utilization levels increased slowly during the first three quarters of the 20$^{th}$ century, peaking temporarily in 1907, 1916, 1924, 1954, and 1974. Domestic garnet utilization increased significantly in the mid 1980s, peaked temporarily in 1992, then increased dramatically into the new millennium. | |
| **US Peak Extraction Year (thru 2008):** 1998 | | **US Peak Utilization Year (thru 2008):** 2007 |
| **Potential Geopolitical US Supply Constraints** | India and Australia each account for 35% of US industrial garnet imports. | |
| **US Scarcity Assessment** | "Garnet imports have displaced U.S. production in the domestic market, with Australia, Canada, China, and India being major garnet suppliers." (USGS, 2008)<br><br>The US currently relies considerably on imported garnet, the majority of which comes from India (35%) and Australia (35%). The quantity of garnet supplied by foreign sources during 2008 accounted for 37% of the total 2008 US utilization level.<br><br>Available evidence supports the contention that domestic garnet supplies will remain insufficient to completely address domestic requirements going forward:<br><br>• While US garnet utilization increased into the new millennium, the annual US garnet extraction level decreased by 15% since peaking (to date) in 1998—an indicator that domestic economically viable garnet extraction has peaked permanently;<br>• The US has become increasingly reliant on garnet imports since 1998;<br>• The quantity of garnet extracted domestically during 2008 amounted to only 63% of the total 2008 US utilization level—an indicator of America's increasing dependence on foreign NNRs; and<br>• The quantity of garnet extracted domestically during 1998, the year of peak (to date) domestic garnet extraction, amounted to only 74% of the 2008 total US utilization level.<br><br>Barring future reductions in the domestic (US) garnet requirement trajectory and/or major new domestic economically viable discoveries, garnet will almost certainly remain scarce domestically in the future. | |
| **Global NNR Scarcity** | **Scarce in 2008: No** | **Permanently Scarce: Unclear** |
| **Historical Global Extraction Trends** | Annual global garnet extraction levels increased very slowly during much of the 20$^{th}$ century, peaking temporarily in 1923; extraction levels then increased phenomenally since the late 1980s; annual global garnet extraction increased 187% between 2000 and 2008. | |

| NNR Profile | Garnet (Industrial) [continued] | |
|---|---|---|
| Global Peak Extraction Year (thru 2008): 2007 | | Years to Global Reserve Exhaustion: N/A |
| Projected Global Peak Extraction Year: N/A | | Projected Global Peak Supply Year: N/A |
| Interdependencies | None identified. | |
| Global Scarcity Assessment | A 187% increase in the annual global garnet extraction level between 2000 and 2008 implies a significant increase in global garnet demand during the pre-recession period, and a correspondingly significant increase in global garnet supply in response to increased global demand. The fact that the price of garnet decreased by a substantial 20% during the 2000-2008 period indicates that the global supply of garnet in 2008 was sufficient to completely address 2008 global requirements. Available evidence regarding the likelihood that global garnet supplies will remain sufficient to completely address global requirements going forward is conflicting:<br><br>• While global garnet extraction levels have generally increased since the 1960s, garnet price levels have generally decreased since that time—compelling evidence of sufficient global garnet supplies; and<br>• Global garnet reserves are considered by the USGS to be "moderate to large"; however<br>• It is unclear whether the extremely robust 14.1% compound annual growth rate (CAGR) in global garnet extraction evidenced between 2000 and 2008—which was required to enable pre-recession global economic growth—can be reestablished and maintained going forward. A 14.1% CAGR would necessitate a continuous doubling in the annual global extraction level of garnet every 5 years.<br><br>It is therefore unclear whether globally available, economically viable garnet supplies will remain sufficient to completely address future global requirements, or whether garnet will become scarce globally in the not-too-distant future.<br><br>"The garnet market is very competitive. To increase profitability and remain competitive with foreign imported material, other salable mineral products that occur with garnet, such as kyanite, marble, mica minerals, sillimanite, staurolite, wollastonite, or metallic ores, may be produced." (USGS, 2010) | |

1. "Garnet", Wikipedia, 2011 - http://en.wikipedia.org/wiki/Garnet.
2. "Garnet Statistics", Historical Statistics for Mineral and Material Commodities in the United States, USGS, 2010 – http://minerals.usgs.gov/ds/2005/140/garnet.xls.

| NNR Profile | Gemstones |
|---|---|
| **NNR Uses and Critical Applications** | |
| Primary Uses | A gemstone is an "attractive" mineral, which is typically hard, lustrous, and rare, used to make jewelry or other items of adornment; gemstones are characterized as precious and semi-precious. |
| Critical Applications | None identified. |

| NNR Profile | Gemstones (continued) | |
|---|---|---|
| **NNR Criticality** | **NNR Criticality Classification: Important** | |
| **Substitutes** | Synthetically manufactured gemstones, which possess the same chemical and physical properties as naturally occurring stones, are viable natural gemstone substitutes, as are "simulants", which differ from natural gemstones in chemical and physical properties. | |
| **Criticality Assessment** | Since gemstones are valued primarily for their aesthetic and cosmetic qualities, they are not considered critical to industrialization. | |
| **US NNR Scarcity** | **Scarce in 2008: Yes** | **Permanently Scarce: Almost Certain** |
| **2008 US Import Reliance:** 99% | | **2008 Domestic US Supply:** 1% |
| **Historical US Import Trends** | The US has always relied almost exclusively on imported gemstones. | |
| **Historical US Usage Trends** | Annual US gemstone utilization levels increased slowly during most of the 20th century, peaking temporarily in 1929 and 1946, before increasing dramatically from the 1990s into the new millennium. "The U.S. market for unset gem-quality diamonds was estimated to have exceeded $17.7 billion, accounting for more than an estimated 35% of world demand." (USGS, 2008) | |
| **US Peak Extraction Year (thru 2008):** 1991* | | **US Peak Utilization Year (thru 2008):** 2007 |
| **Potential Geopolitical US Supply Constraints** | 48% of US gemstone imports come from Israel. | |
| **US Scarcity Assessment** | The US currently relies almost exclusively on imported gemstones, a large percentage (48%) of which comes from Israel. The quantity of gemstones supplied by foreign sources during 2008 accounted for 99% of the total 2008 US utilization level. Available evidence supports the contention that domestic gemstone supplies will remain insufficient to completely address domestic requirements going forward: • The value of annual US gemstone extraction decreased by 86% since peaking (to date) in 1991—a compelling indicator that domestic economically viable gemstone extraction has peaked permanently; and • The US has become increasingly reliant on gemstone imports since the 1960s. Barring future reductions in the domestic (US) gemstone requirement trajectory and/or major new domestic economically viable discoveries, gemstones will almost certainly remain scarce domestically in the future. | |
| **Global NNR Scarcity** | **Scarce in 2008: No** | **Permanently Scarce: Unlikely** |
| **Historical Global Extraction Trends** | "Mine production of diamond in 2007 for Canada, Congo (Kinshasa), and Russia increased, while production for South Africa decreased..." USGS, 2008) Annual global gemstone extraction levels increased slowly during most of the 20th century, peaking temporarily in 1946 and 1970, before increasing rapidly since the early 1980s; annual global gemstone extraction increased 30% between 2000 and 2008. | |
| **Global Peak Extraction Year (thru 2008):** 2006 | | **Years to Global Reserve Exhaustion:** N/A |
| **Projected Global Peak Extraction Year:** N/A | | **Projected Global Peak Supply Year:** N/A |
| **Interdependencies** | None identified. | |

| NNR Profile | Gemstones (continued) |
|---|---|
| **Global Scarcity Assessment** | A 30% increase in the annual global gemstone extraction level between 2000 and 2008 implies an increase in global gemstone demand during the pre-recession period, and a corresponding increase in global gemstone supply in response to increased global demand.<br><br>The fact that the price of gemstones decreased by 5% during the 2000-2008 period indicates that the global supply of gemstones in 2008 was sufficient to completely address 2008 global requirements.<br><br>Given that no evidence was identified to the contrary, barring future increases in the global gemstone requirement trajectory, globally available, economically viable gemstone supplies will likely remain sufficient to completely address global requirements going forward. |

*Production value rather than volume.

1. "Gemstones", Wikipedia, 2011 - http://en.wikipedia.org/wiki/Gemstones.
2. "Gemstones Statistics", Historical Statistics for Mineral and Material Commodities in the United States, USGS, 2010 – http://minerals.usgs.gov/ds/2005/140/gemstones.xls.

| NNR Profile | Germanium |
|---|---|
| **NNR Uses and Critical Applications** | |
| **Primary Uses** | Germanium is a hard, brittle, lustrous, silvery-white metalloid used in fiber-optic, infrared optic, thermal imaging, and semiconductor applications; germanium is also used as a catalyst and in the manufacture of satellite based solar cells. |
| **Critical Applications** | Optical fiber cores, thermal imaging applications, (phase change) semiconductor memories, and wireless communications applications; nanowires is a potentially significant emerging application.<br><br>"Demand for germanium continued to grow in 2007 as fiber optic network construction was begun in many parts of the world." AND: "…use of germanium in night vision lenses for automobiles continued to grow, as did its commercial use in gamma ray detection instrumentation…" (USGS, 2008) |

| NNR Criticality | NNR Criticality Classification: Critical |
|---|---|
| **Substitutes** | Substitutes for germanium are available, but most are inferior from a price/performance perspective. |
| **Criticality Assessment** | Germanium plays a key role in several high technology application areas; in the event that germanium based solar cells become viable terrestrial sources of electricity, germanium will become increasingly critical. |

| US NNR Scarcity | Scarce in 2008: Yes | Permanently Scarce: Almost Certain |
|---|---|---|
| **2008 US Import Reliance:** 90% | | **2008 Domestic US Supply:** 10% |
| **Historical US Import Trends** | The US is heavily reliant on germanium imports; a trend that has increased during the new millennium. | |
| **Historical US Usage Trends** | Annual US germanium utilization levels fluctuated widely during the mid-late 20th century, peaking temporarily in 1960 and 1982; domestic germanium utilization levels increased dramatically after 2005. | |
| **US Peak Production Year (thru 2008):** 1981 | | **US Peak Utilization Year (thru 2008):** 2007 |

| NNR Profile | Germanium (continued) |
|---|---|
| **Potential Geopolitical US Supply Constraints** | "Next time, by the way, you wonder why a company like Intel is building its next big "chip" plant in China you might ask yourself how much of the reason for that is to insure access to critical-no build without-supplies of indium, tellurium, antimony and germanium." (Byproducts, 2007)<br><br>46% of US germanium imports come from Belgium; 24% come from China; China produces a majority of the world's germanium.<br><br>"China removed toll trading tax benefits for germanium and most other minor metals in April [2007], effectively decreasing the supply of germanium to the world market." (USGS, 2008) |
| **US Scarcity Assessment** | "Germanium production in the United States comes from either the refining of imported germanium compounds or industry-generated scrap." (USGS, 2010)<br><br>The US currently relies almost exclusively on imported germanium, the majority (70%) of which comes from Belgium and China. The quantity of germanium supplied by foreign sources during 2008 accounted for 90% of the total 2008 US utilization level.<br><br>Available evidence supports the contention that domestic germanium supplies will remain insufficient to completely address domestic requirements going forward:<br><br>• While US germanium utilization increased into the new millennium, the annual US germanium production level decreased by 84% since peaking (to date) in 1981—a compelling indicator that domestic economically viable germanium production has peaked permanently;<br>• The US has become increasingly reliant on germanium imports since 2003;<br>• The quantity of germanium produced domestically during 2008 amounted to only 9% of the total 2008 US utilization level—a significant indicator of America's increasing dependence on foreign NNRs; and<br>• The quantity of germanium produced domestically during 1981, the year of peak (to date) domestic germanium production, amounted to only 52% of the 2008 total US utilization level.<br><br>Barring future reductions in the domestic (US) germanium requirement trajectory and/or major new domestic economically viable discoveries, germanium will almost certainly remain scarce domestically in the future. |
| **Global NNR Scarcity** | **Scarce in 2008: No**     **Permanently Scarce: Unclear** |
| **Historical Global Production Trends** | "While the U.S. does produce some primary [germanium] metal [5 metric tons in 2007, which includes secondary production], once again, China dominates [100 metric tons in 2007]." (HardAssets, 2009); [BGS is #s source]<br><br>Annual global germanium production levels fluctuated widely during the mid-late 20th century, peaking temporarily in 1963, 1969, and 1981, before generally declining into the new millennium; however, annual global germanium production increased 100% between 2000 and 2008. |

211

| NNR Profile | Germanium (continued) |
|---|---|
| **Global Peak Production Year (thru 2008):** 2008* | **Years to Global Reserve Exhaustion:** N/A |
| **Projected Global Peak Production Year:** N/A | **Projected Global Peak Supply Year:** N/A |

| | |
|---|---|
| **Interdependencies** | Germanium is produced primarily as a byproduct of zinc, silver, lead, and copper ore processing; germanium is also produced as a byproduct of coal combustion.<br><br>"There is no commercially abundant ore from which germanium can be extracted primarily." (Byproducts, 2007) |
| **Global Scarcity Assessment** | "Germanium prices continued to move upward in 2007 as demand grew and supplies remained tight." (USGS, 2008)<br><br>A 100% increase in the annual global germanium production level between 2000 and 2008 implies a significant increase in global germanium demand during the pre-recession period, and a correspondingly significant increase in global germanium supply in response to increased global demand.<br><br>The fact that the price of germanium decreased by 4% during the 2000-2008 period indicates that the global supply of germanium in 2008 was sufficient to completely address 2008 global requirements.<br><br>Available evidence regarding the likelihood that global germanium supplies will remain sufficient to completely address global requirements going forward is conflicting:<br><br>• A declining germanium price level between 2000 and 2008 indicates that global germanium supplies were sufficient to completely address global requirements in 2008; however<br>• The price of germanium increased by 38% between 2001 and 2008, which indicates germanium scarcity on a global level in 2008; and<br>• It is unclear whether the extremely robust 9.1% compound annual growth rate (CAGR) in global germanium production evidenced between 2000 and 2008—which was required to enable pre-recession global economic growth—can be reestablished and maintained going forward. A 9.1% CAGR would necessitate a continuous doubling in the annual global production level of germanium every 8 years.<br><br>It is therefore unclear whether globally available, economically viable germanium supplies will remain sufficient to completely address future global requirements, or whether germanium will become scarce globally in the not-too-distant future. |

*2008 global peak production was very likely a one year "spike".

1. "Germanium", Wikipedia, 2011 - http://en.wikipedia.org/wiki/Germanium.
2. "Germanium Statistics", Historical Statistics for Mineral and Material Commodities in the United States, USGS, 2010 – http://minerals.usgs.gov/ds/2005/140/germanium.xls.
3. "Byproducts II: Another Germanium Rush?" J. Lifton, Resource Investor, 2007 - http://www.resourceinvestor.com/News/2007/4/Pages/Byproducts-II--Another-Germanium-Rush-.aspx.
4. "Germanium: Winkler's Metal", T. Vulcan, HardAssets Investor, 2009 - http://www.hardassetsinvestor.com/features-and-interviews/1487.html?start=1.

| NNR Profile | Gold |
|---|---|

## NNR Uses and Critical Applications

| | |
|---|---|
| **Primary Uses** | Gold is a dense, soft, malleable, ductile, shiny, yellow precious metal used in coinage and jewelry, and as a store of value; industrial uses for gold include dentistry and electronics. |
| **Critical Applications** | None identified, although niche alloying, electrical conductivity, and corrosion resistance applications are important. |

| NNR Criticality | NNR Criticality Classification: Important |
|---|---|
| **Substitutes** | Other precious metals such as PGMs and silver can substitute for gold as a store of value; viable substitutes in dental and most electronic applications exist as well. From an investment perspective, however, gold remains the precious metal of choice. |
| **Criticality Assessment** | While gold is a universally sought after store of value, its contributions to industrialization are marginal. |

| US NNR Scarcity | Scarce in 2008: No | Permanently Scarce: Unclear |
|---|---|---|
| **2008 US Import Reliance: 0%** | | **2008 Domestic US Supply: 100%** |
| **Historical US Import Trends** | Historically, the US has been both a net importer and a net exporter of gold; for the past decade, the US has been primarily a net exporter. | |
| **Historical US Usage Trends** | Annual US gold utilization levels fluctuated within a narrow but generally increasing range during both the 20th century, peaking temporarily in 1920, 1946, and 1969, before peaking permanently (to date) in 1998. Domestic utilization levels generally declined since that time; the 2008 US gold utilization level amounted to only 27% of the 1998 peak utilization level. | |

| US Peak Extraction Year (thru 2008): 1998 | US Peak Utilization Year (thru 2008): 1998 |
|---|---|

| **Potential Geopolitical US Supply Constraints** | China is the leading gold producing nation; however, the US is currently a gold exporter. |
|---|---|
| **US Scarcity Assessment** | That annual domestic gold utilization decreased by 73% since peaking (to date) in 1998, is an indicator declining American industrial preeminence and global economic competitiveness. |
| | The US is however currently addressing its total requirement for gold through domestic supplies. |
| | Available evidence regarding the likelihood that domestic gold supplies will remain sufficient to completely address domestic requirements going forward is conflicting: |
| | • Domestic gold supplies were sufficient to completely address domestic requirements during the 2000-2008 period of rapid economic growth prior to the Great Recession; and<br>• The US has been generally a net gold exporter since 1988; however<br>• The domestic gold extraction level decreased by 36% since peaking (to date) in 1998—an indicator that domestic economically viable gold extraction has peaked permanently. |
| | Because the demand/supply dynamics associated with gold, which is considered an "investment asset", differ from those of strictly industrial metals, it is difficult to assess domestic scarcity going forward. It is therefore unclear whether domestically available, economically viable gold supplies will remain sufficient to completely address future domestic requirements, or whether gold will become scarce domestically in the not-too-distant future. |

| NNR Profile | Gold (continued) | |
|---|---|---|
| Global NNR Scarcity | Scarce in 2008: Yes | Permanently Scarce: Almost Certain |
| Historical Global Extraction Trends | "Steadily increasing gold mining in China raised it to the third leading producer of gold worldwide from fourth in 2006." [US is now 4th ](USGS, 2008)<br><br>Annual gold extraction levels generally increased in a cyclical manner during the 20th and 21st centuries, peaking temporarily in 1912, 1940, and 1970, before peaking permanently (to date) in 2001; annual global gold extraction decreased 13% between 2000 and 2008. | |

| Global Peak Extraction Year (thru 2008): 2001 | Years to Global Reserve Exhaustion: 21* |
|---|---|
| Projected Global Peak Extraction Year: 2012 | Projected Global Peak Supply Year: 2030 |

| Interdependencies | Gold can be recovered as a byproduct of processing base metals such as copper. |
|---|---|
| Global Scarcity Assessment | A 13% decrease in the annual global gold extraction level between 2000 and 2008 implies either a decrease in global gold demand or insufficient global gold supplies during the pre-recession period.<br><br>The fact that the price of gold increased by an extraordinary 149% during the 2000-2008 period, indicates that the declining global gold supply was woefully insufficient to completely address global requirements in 2008.<br><br>Available evidence supports the contention that global gold supplies will remain insufficient to completely address global requirements going forward:<br><br>• Proven global gold reserves would exhaust in only 21 years, assuming that future annual utilization levels remain constant at the 2008 level;<br>• The global gold extraction level is projected to peak in approximately 2012;<br>• The global gold supply level is projected to peak in approximately 2030;<br>• Annual global gold extraction peaked (to date) in 2001—evidence that globally available, economically viable gold extraction may be at or near its permanent peak level; and<br>• An extraordinary increase in the price of gold during the 2000-2008 period could not induce a sufficient increase in global gold supply—compelling evidence of unaddressed global requirements in 2008.<br><br>Barring future reductions in the global gold requirement trajectory and/or major new economically viable discoveries, gold will almost certainly remain scarce globally in the future..<br><br>"Jewelry consumption continued to drop as the price of gold continued to increase." AND: "…investment in gold has increased, with investors seeking safe haven investments…" (USGS, 2010) |

\* Reserve to Production data.

1. "Gold", Wikipedia, 2011 - http://en.wikipedia.org/wiki/Gold.
2. "Gold Statistics", Historical Statistics for Mineral and Material Commodities in the United States, USGS, 2010 – http://minerals.usgs.gov/ds/2005/140/gold.xls.

| NNR Profile | Graphite (Natural) |
|---|---|
| **NNR Uses and Critical Applications** | |
| **Primary Uses** | Natural graphite is a black, conductive carbon allotrope used in "lead" pencils, in refractories and foundries, in brake linings, in semiconductors, in zinc-carbon batteries, and as a lubricant. |
| **Critical Applications** | High technology applications—composites (carbon fibers), electronics, lubricants, batteries and fuel cells—and refractory applications. |

| NNR Criticality | NNR Criticality Classification: Critical |
|---|---|
| **Substitutes** | Natural graphite substitutes, such as synthetic graphite (coke and pitch), exist in most cases, although substitutes are often price/performance inferior. |
| **Criticality Assessment** | If emerging applications for natural graphite become viable, especially applications related to fuel cells, natural graphite will become more critical.<br><br>"It [graphite] is unique in that it has properties of both a metal and a non-metal. It is flexible but not elastic, has a high thermal and electrical conductivity, and is highly refractory and chemically inert." (Graphite, 2011) |

| US NNR Scarcity | Scarce in 2008: Yes | Permanently Scarce: Almost Certain |
|---|---|---|
| **2008 US Import Reliance: 100%** | | **2008 Domestic US Supply: 0%** |
| **Historical US Import Trends** | Except for brief periods during the early and middle decades of the 20th century, the US has been totally reliant on imported natural graphite. | |
| **Historical US Usage Trends** | Annual US natural graphite utilization levels generally increased during the first three quarters of the 20th century—in a widely fluctuating manner—peaking temporarily in 1907, 1918, 1929, and 1948, before peaking permanently (to date) in 1978. Domestic graphite utilization generally declined through the 1980s and 1990s, before recovering slightly during the early 21st century; the 2008 US natural graphite utilization level amounted to only 61% of the 1978 peak utilization level. | |
| **US Peak Extraction Year (thru 2008): 1907** | | **US Peak Utilization Year (thru 2008): 1978** |
| **Potential Geopolitical US Supply Constraints** | 47% of US graphite imports come from China; China produces over 70% of the world's natural graphite, and nearly 80% of proven global reserves are located in China. | |

| NNR Profile | Graphite (Natural) [continued] |
|---|---|
| **US Scarcity Assessment** | "Although natural graphite was not produced in the United States in 2009, approximately 100 U.S. firms, primarily in the Northeastern and Great Lakes regions, used it for a wide variety of applications." (USGS, 2010)<br><br>That annual domestic graphite utilization decreased by 39% since peaking (to date) in 1978, is an indicator of declining American industrial preeminence and global economic competitiveness.<br><br>The US currently relies exclusively on imported natural graphite, a considerable percentage (47%) of which comes from China.<br><br>Available evidence supports the contention that domestic graphite supplies will remain insufficient to completely address domestic requirements going forward:<br><br>• Annual US graphite extraction ceased entirely in 1954—a compelling indicator that domestic economically viable graphite extraction has peaked permanently; and<br>• The quantity of graphite extracted domestically during 1907, the year of peak (to date) domestic graphite extraction, amounted to only 53% of the 2008 total US utilization level—a significant indicator of America's increasing dependence on foreign NNRs.<br><br>Barring future reductions in the domestic (US) graphite requirement trajectory and/or major new domestic economically viable discoveries, graphite will almost certainly remain scarce domestically in the future.<br><br>"The major North American graphite mine in Quebec has a remaining lifespan of just a few years." (Mineweb, 2010) |

| Global NNR Scarcity | | Scarce in 2008: Yes | Permanently Scarce: Likely |
|---|---|---|---|
| **Historical Global Extraction Trends** | | "China [71% of 2009 global mine production] and India [12% of 2009 global mine production] are the leading producers of graphite in the world, accounting for nearly 80% of global graphite production." (Top News, 2008; USGS, 2010)<br><br>Annual global natural graphite extraction levels generally increased in a cyclical manner during the 20th and 21st centuries, peaking temporarily in 1907, 1917, 1929, 1943, 1963, and 1989; annual global natural graphite extraction increased by 32% between 2000 and 2008.<br><br>"China's graphite production is expected to continue growing as producers there collaborate with western graphite producers." (USGS, 2010) | |

| Global Peak Extraction Year (thru 2008): 2008 | Years to Global Reserve Exhaustion: 38 |
|---|---|
| Projected Global Peak Extraction Year: N/A | Projected Global Peak Supply Year: N/A |
| **Interdependencies** | None identified. |

| NNR Profile | Graphite (Natural) [continued] |
|---|---|
| **Global Scarcity Assessment** | "Over the last decade, the development of thermal and chemical processes to produce high-purity natural graphite has enabled a more effective use of graphite resources, as lower grade ores and fines can be transformed into grades suitable for use in demanding applications such as batteries." (Roskill, 2010)<br><br>A 32% increase in the annual global graphite extraction level between 2000 and 2008 implies an increase in global graphite demand during the pre-recession period, and a corresponding increase in global graphite supply in response to increased global demand.<br><br>The fact that the price of graphite increased by 24% during the 2000-2008 period indicates that global graphite supply, while increasing during the eight year period, remained insufficient to completely address global requirements in 2008.<br><br>Available evidence supports the contention that global graphite supplies will likely remain insufficient to completely address global requirements going forward:<br><br>• Proven global graphite reserves would exhaust in only 38 years, assuming the restoration of pre-recession utilization levels and growth rates; and<br>• The increase in global graphite supply levels between 2000 and 2008 failed to prevent a price increase during the period—evidence of unaddressed global requirements in 2008.<br><br>Barring future reductions in the global graphite requirement trajectory and/or major new economically viable discoveries, graphite will likely remain scarce globally in the future.<br><br>"Large-scale fuel-cell applications are being developed that could consume as much graphite as all other uses combined." (USGS, 2010) |

1. "Graphite", Wikipedia, 2011 - http://en.wikipedia.org/wiki/Graphite.
2. "Graphite Statistics", Historical Statistics for Mineral and Material Commodities in the United States, USGS, 2010 – http://minerals.usgs.gov/ds/2005/140/graphite.xls.
3. "Graphite – Classifications, Applications, and Properties of Graphite", A to Z of Materials, 2011 - http://www.azom.com/details.asp?ArticleID=1630.
4. "Western Industrial Users Seen as Hopeless at Securing Specialty Metals Supplies", Mineweb, 2010 - http://www.mineweb.com/mineweb/view/mineweb/en/page72102?oid=107698&sn=Detail&pid=65
5. "Global Carbon & Graphite Market to Exceed $8.1 Billion by 2012", Mining Top News, 2008 - http://www.miningtopnews.com/global-carbon-graphite-market-to-exceed-81-billion-by-2012-according-to-new-report-by-global-industry-analysts-inc.html.
6. "The Economics of Natural Graphite", Roskill, 2010 - http://www.prnewswire.co.uk/cgi/news/release?id=264189.

| NNR Profile | Gypsum |
|---|---|
| **NNR Uses and Critical Applications** | |
| **Primary Uses** | Gypsum is a very soft, often chalky colored mineral used primarily in the production of wallboard, plaster, and cement; also used as a soil conditioner. |
| **Critical Applications** | Gypsum is used in the manufacture of portland cement; it is also nearly ubiquitous as an economical building material. |

| NNR Criticality | NNR Criticality Classification: Indispensible |
|---|---|
| **Substitutes** | Synthetic gypsum (57% of US utilization in 2009) and other substitutes exist for natural gypsum applications, with the exception of a portland cement additive, although substitutes may be price/performance inferior. |
| **Criticality Assessment** | Gypsum enables both residential and commercial construction on a scale that would be unattainable in its absence; gypsum is indispensible to modern industrial existence.<br><br>"Gypsum is one of the most widely used minerals in the world. Most is used to make wall board, also know as sheet rock. It is estimated that the average American home contains seven metric tons of gypsum." (Bray, 2002) |

| US NNR Scarcity | Scarce in 2008: Yes | Permanently Scarce: Almost Certain |
|---|---|---|
| **2008 US Import Reliance:** 24% | | **2008 Domestic US Supply:** 76% |
| **Historical US Import Trends** | The US has become an increasingly heavy net importer of gypsum since the mid 20th century.<br><br>"In 2007, small, local shortages in wallboard supplies were met by increased imports." (USGS, 2008) | |
| **Historical US Usage Trends** | Annual US gypsum utilization levels generally increased during the 20th and 21st centuries (especially following WWII), peaking temporarily in 1916, 1926, 1941, 1964, 1973, 1978, 1989, and 1999.<br><br>"Demand for gypsum depends principally on the strength of the construction industry—particularly in the United States, where about 95% of the gypsum consumed is used for building plasters, the manufacture of portland cement, and wallboard products." (USGS, 2010) | |
| **US Peak Extraction Year (thru 2008):** 2006 | | **US Peak Utilization Year (thru 2008):** 2006 |
| **Potential Geopolitical US Supply Constraints** | 67% of US gypsum imports come from Canada; China is the world's second largest gypsum producer, Iran is third. | |

218

| NNR Profile | Gypsum (continued) |
|---|---|
| **US Scarcity Assessment** | "Overall, 46 companies produced gypsum in the United States at 55 mines in 18 States, and 9 companies calcined gypsum at 57 plants in 29 States." (USGS, 2010)<br><br>The US currently relies to an increasing extent on imported gypsum, the majority (67%) of which comes from Canada. The quantity of gypsum supplied by foreign sources during 2008 accounted for 24% of the total 2008 US utilization level.<br><br>While both the annual US gypsum utilization level and the annual US gypsum extraction level increased into the new millennium, net US gypsum imports increased steadily since 1946—a significant indicator of America's increasing dependence on foreign NNRs.<br><br>Barring future reductions in the domestic (US) gypsum requirement trajectory and/or major new domestic economically viable discoveries, gypsum will almost certainly remain scarce domestically in the future. |

| Global NNR Scarcity | Scarce in 2008: Yes | Permanently Scarce: Likely |
|---|---|---|
| **Historical Global Extraction Trends** | | "The United States was the world's leading producer of gypsum in 2007." (USGS, 2008)<br><br>Annual global gypsum extraction levels generally increased during the 20th century (especially since WWII), peaking temporarily in 1929, 1942, 1979, 1990, and 1999; annual global gypsum extraction increased 47% between 2000 and 2008.<br><br>"China produced more than three times the annual amount [of gypsum] of the United States [in 2009], the world's second ranked producer." (USGS, 2010) |

| Global Peak Extraction Year (thru 2008): 2007 | Years to Global Reserve Exhaustion: N/A |
|---|---|
| **Projected Global Peak Extraction Year:** N/A | **Projected Global Peak Supply Year:** N/A |

| Interdependencies | None identified. |
|---|---|

| NNR Profile | Gypsum (continued) |
|---|---|
| **Global Scarcity Assessment** | A 47% increase in the annual global gypsum extraction level between 2000 and 2008 implies a relatively robust increase in global gypsum demand during the pre-recession period, and a correspondingly robust increase in global gypsum supply in response to increased global demand.<br><br>The fact that the price of gypsum increased by a substantial 115% during the 2000-2008 period indicates that global gypsum supply, while increasing considerably during the eight year period, remained insufficient to completely address global requirements in 2008.<br><br>Available evidence supports the contention that global gypsum supplies will likely remain insufficient to completely address global requirements going forward:<br><br>• A relatively robust increase in global gypsum supply levels between 2000 and 2008 failed to prevent a substantial price increase during the period—compelling evidence of unaddressed global requirements in 2008; and<br>• It is questionable whether the robust 5% compound annual growth rate (CAGR) in global gypsum extraction evidenced between 2000 and 2008—an interval during which gypsum became scarce globally despite a significant increase in extraction—can be reestablished, much less increased, going forward. A 5% CAGR would necessitate a continuous doubling in the annual global extraction level of gypsum every 14 years.<br><br>Barring future reductions in the global gypsum requirement trajectory and/or major new economically viable discoveries, gypsum will likely remain scarce globally in the future.<br>Unless:<br><br>"The construction of wallboard plants designed to use synthetic gypsum as feedstock will result in less use of natural gypsum…" (USGS, 2010)<br><br>In any event:<br><br>"As more cultures recognize the economics and efficiency of wallboard, worldwide production of gypsum [natural and/or synthetic] is expected to increase." (USGS, 2010) |

1. "Gypsum", Wikipedia, 2011 - http://en.wikipedia.org/wiki/Gypsum.
2. "Gypsum Statistics", Historical Statistics for Mineral and Material Commodities in the United States, USGS, 2010 – http://minerals.usgs.gov/ds/2005/140/gypsum.xls.
3. "The Mineral Gypsum", J. Bray, Emporium State University, 2002 - http://www.emporia.edu/earthsci/amber/go336/bray/index.htm.

| NNR Profile | Hafnium |
|---|---|
| **NNR Uses and Critical Applications** | |

| | |
|---|---|
| **Primary Uses** | Hafnium is a shiny, ductile, corrosion-resistant, silver-gray metal used in filaments, electrodes, and (very small) semiconductors; hafnium is also used as a superalloy. |
| **Critical Applications** | Used as cladding material for nuclear fuel rods; and as an alloy in rocket fuel nozzles (Apollo).<br><br>"As an example of the increasing importance of Hafnium, Intel Corporation has begun commercial production of its Hafnium based high-K metal gate 45 nm [nanometer] chips, which has been called by Intel Co-Founder Gordon Moore 'the biggest transistor advancement in 40 years'." (Canadian International Minerals, 2010) |

| **NNR Criticality** | **NNR Criticality Classification: Important** |
|---|---|
| **Substitutes** | Zirconium and other minerals can substitute for hafnium in most applications, generally with price/performance degradation; in other applications (some superalloys), hafnium has no viable substitute. |
| **Criticality Assessment** | While hafnium plays a key role in several niche applications, some of which lack viable hafnium substitutes, its current contribution to global industrialism is relatively small—a situation that could change in the future. |

| **US NNR Scarcity** | **Scarce in 2008: Yes** | **Permanently Scarce: Unclear** |
|---|---|---|
| **2008 US Import Reliance:** 8% (2003 data) | **2008 Domestic US Supply:** 92% (2003 data) | |

| | |
|---|---|
| **Historical US Import Trends** | US hafnium imports fluctuated from the middle of the 20th century onward, peaking in 2008; net imports as a percentage of total domestic utilization never exceeded 20%. |
| **Historical US Usage Trends** | Annual US hafnium utilization levels increased during the latter half of the 20th century and into the 21st century, peaking temporarily in 1964 before peaking permanently (to date) in 2003 (the last year of data availability). |

| **US Peak Production Year (thru 2008):** 1983* | **US Peak Utilization Year (thru 2008):** 2003** |
|---|---|

| | |
|---|---|
| **Potential Geopolitical US Supply Constraints** | 60% of US unwrought hafnium imports come from France; 42% of the proven global hafnium reserves are located in South Africa, 35% are located in Australia. |
| **US Scarcity Assessment** | "Two firms produced zircon [the primary source of hafnium] from surface-mining operations in Florida and Virginia [in 2009]. Zirconium and hafnium metal were produced from zircon by two domestic producers…" (USGS, 2010)<br><br>Based on limited USGS data, the US currently relies marginally on imported hafnium, the majority (60%) of which comes from France. The quantity of hafnium supplied by foreign sources during 2003 accounted for 8% of the total 2003 US utilization level.<br><br>Evidence regarding the likelihood that domestic hafnium supplies will remain insufficient to completely address domestic requirements going forward is unavailable.<br><br>It is therefore unclear whether hafnium will remain scarce domestically in the future, or whether domestically available, economically viable hafnium supplies will be sufficient to completely address future domestic requirements. |

| NNR Profile | Hafnium (continued) | |
|---|---|---|
| Global NNR Scarcity | Scarce in 2008: Yes | Permanently Scarce: Unclear |
| Historical Global Production Trends | "…world producers of hafnium-bearing minerals include Germany, the United Kingdom, Brazil, China, India, Russia, South Africa, Ukraine, and the United States." (MII, 2011)  USGS annual global production data for hafnium are not available. | |
| Global Peak Production Year (thru 2008): 1963 | | Years to Global Reserve Exhaustion: N/A |
| Projected Global Peak Production Year: N/A | | Projected Global Peak Supply Year: N/A |
| Interdependencies | Hafnium is refined from zirconium minerals (zircon); both hafnium and zirconium are coproducts of titanium ore processing. | |
| Global Scarcity Assessment | While annual global production data associated with hafnium are unavailable from the USGS for the 2000-2008 pre-recession period, hafnium prices increased by 47% between 2000 and 2008, indicating that global hafnium supplies were insufficient to completely address global requirements during 2008.  Given the lack of USGS data, it is unclear whether hafnium will remain scarce globally in the future, or whether globally available, economically viable hafnium supplies will be sufficient to completely address future global requirements.  (It is worth noting that hafnium prices generally decreased dramatically between 1963 and 2001, despite generally increasing annual global hafnium production levels during that period. Hafnium prices then increased between 2001 and 2008, albeit in a fluctuating manner. The initial instance of global hafnium scarcity therefore coincided with the period of rapid global economic growth prior to the Great Recession.)  "Cohen cites the work of researchers like Armin Reller ["New Scientist" article], a materials chemist at the University of Augsburg in Germany, who has predicted that supplies of indium, used in liquid-crystal displays, and of hafnium, a critical element for next-generation semiconductors, could be exhausted by 2017." (Information Week, 2007; New Scientist, 2007) | |

*1987 was the last year of USGS data availability.
** 2003 was the last year of USGS data availability.
***Peak "unit value" (not total value) of global production (1998 dollars);

1. "Hafnium", Wikipedia, 2011 - http://en.wikipedia.org/wiki/Hafnium.
2. "Hafnium Statistics", Historical Statistics for Mineral and Material Commodities in the United States, USGS, 2010 – http://minerals.usgs.gov/ds/2005/140/hafnium.xls.
3. "Diamond Drill Permits for Carbo Rare Earth Project Received", Canadian International Minerals, Inc. (Press Release), 2010 - http://finance.yahoo.com/news/Canadian-International-cnw-715999117.html?x=0&.v=1.
4. "Dwindling of Rare Metals Imperils Innovation", R. Martin, Information Week, 2007 - http://www.informationweek.com/news/global-cio/showArticle.jhtml?articleID=199703110.
5. "Hafnium", Minerals Information Institute (MII), 2011 - http://www.mii.org/Minerals/photohafn.html.
6. "Earth's Natural Wealth: An Audit", D. Cohen, New Scientist, 2007 - http://www.newscientist.com/article/mg19426051.200-earths-natural-wealth-an-audit.html.

| NNR Profile | Helium |
|---|---|

## NNR Uses and Critical Applications

| Primary Uses | Helium is a colorless, odorless, non-toxic, inert gas used in cryogenics (cooling), arc welding, controlled atmosphere, and leak detection applications; helium is also used as a pressuring/purging gas. |
|---|---|
| Critical Applications | Cooling superconducting magnets in MRI scanners; superconductivity (electronics). |

| NNR Criticality | NNR Criticality Classification: Important |
|---|---|
| Substitutes | Viable helium substitutes generally exist, with the exception of cryogenic applications requiring temperatures below -429F. |
| Criticality Assessment | While helium plays an important role in several niche applications, especially cryogenics, its overall contribution to industrialization is relatively modest. |

| US NNR Scarcity | Scarce in 2008: No | Permanently Scarce: Unlikely |
|---|---|---|

| 2008 US Import Reliance: 0% | 2008 Domestic US Supply: 100% |
|---|---|

| Historical US Import Trends | The US has been a net exporter of helium since the early 1960s. |
|---|---|
| Historical US Usage Trends | Annual US helium utilization levels increased during the middle/later decades of the 20th century, peaking temporarily in 1944 and 1966, before peaking permanently (to date) in 2000; domestic helium utilization declined significantly since that time; the 2008 US helium utilization level amounted to only 66% of the 2000 peak utilization level. |

| US Peak Production Year (thru 2008): 1967 | US Peak Utilization Year (thru 2008): 2000 |
|---|---|

| Potential Geopolitical US Supply Constraints | None identified. |
|---|---|
| US Scarcity Assessment | That annual domestic helium utilization decreased by 34% since peaking (to date) in 2000, and domestic helium production decreased by 40% since peaking (to date) in 1967, are indicators of declining American industrial preeminence and global economic competitiveness.

However, as a result of recently declining domestic demand for helium, the US is currently addressing its total helium requirement through domestic supplies.

While it is unclear at this point whether the domestic helium production peak reached in 1967 is temporary or permanent, available evidence supports the contention that domestic helium supplies will likely remain sufficient to completely address domestic requirements for the foreseeable future:

- Domestic helium supplies were sufficient to completely address domestic requirements during the 2000-2008 period of rapid economic growth prior to the Great Recession; and
- Domestic helium reserves are considered by the USGS to be quite large.

Barring future increases in the domestic (US) helium requirement trajectory, domestically available, economically viable helium supplies will likely remain sufficient to completely address domestic requirements going forward.

(It is worth noting that helium is often produced from natural gas. Increasing scarcity associated with domestic (US) natural gas could adversely impact future US helium supplies.) |

| NNR Profile | Helium (continued) | |
|---|---|---|
| **Global NNR Scarcity** | **Scarce in 2008: No** | **Permanently Scarce: Unlikely** |
| **Historical Global Production Trends** | Annual global helium production levels fluctuated widely during the 20th and 21st centuries, peaking temporarily in 1944, increasing dramatically in the 1960s, peaking temporarily in 1971, decreasing dramatically in 1970s and early 1980s, then peaking temporarily in 1997. Annual global helium production increased 49% between 2000 and 2008. | |
| **Global Peak Production Year (thru 2008):** 2008 | **Years to Global Reserve Exhaustion:** N/A | |
| **Projected Global Peak Production Year:** 2075 | **Projected Global Peak Supply Year:** N/A | |
| **Interdependencies** | Helium is found in the minerals containing uranium and thorium, and is produced commercially as a byproduct of natural gas (methane) extraction. | |
| **Global Scarcity Assessment** | A 49% increase in the annual global helium production level between 2000 and 2008 implies an increase in global helium demand during the pre-recession period, and a corresponding increase in global helium supply in response to increased global demand. The fact that the price of helium decreased by 3% during the 2000-2008 period indicates that the global supply of helium in 2008 was sufficient to completely address 2008 global requirements. Available evidence supports the contention that global helium supplies will likely remain sufficient to completely address global requirements for the foreseeable future: • While global helium production levels have generally increased since the early 1980s, helium price levels have generally decreased since that time—evidence of sufficient global helium supplies; • The global helium production level is not projected to peak until approximately 2075; and • Proven global helium reserves are considered by the USGS to be quite large. Barring future increases in the global helium requirement trajectory, globally available, economically viable helium supplies will likely remain sufficient to completely address global requirements going forward. (As is the case with helium domestically, increasing scarcity associated with global natural gas could adversely impact future global helium supplies.) | |

1. "Helium", Wikipedia, 2011 - http://en.wikipedia.org/wiki/Helium.
2. "Helium Statistics", Historical Statistics for Mineral and Material Commodities in the United States, USGS, 2010 – http://minerals.usgs.gov/ds/2005/140/helium.xls.


| NNR Profile | Indium |
|---|---|
| **NNR Uses and Critical Applications** | |
| **Primary Uses** | Indium is a very soft, malleable, easily fusible, silvery-white metal used in liquid crystal displays and computer touchscreens (indium tin oxide—ITO), and as a semiconductor component; indium is also used as a lubricant, an alloy, and as a component in lead-free solders. |

| NNR Profile | Indium (continued) |
|---|---|
| **Critical Applications** | Electrode in LCDs and touchscreens; wireless communication devices; control rods in nuclear reactors; and thin film solar cells (an emerging application).<br><br>"Production of indium tin oxide (ITO) continued to be the leading end use of indium… ITO thin-film coatings were primarily used for electrically conductive purposes in a variety of flat-panel devices—most commonly liquid crystal displays (LCDs)." (USGS, 2010) |

| NNR Criticality | | NNR Criticality Classification: Critical |
|---|---|---|
| **Substitutes** | Due to its scarcity, viable substitutes for all indium applications are under development; while some substitutes are technically feasible, few are currently economically viable.<br><br>"Some of the most critical [metals] are found in cell phones. The ones to worry about, says Graedel, are difficult to find substitutes for and are produced only as by-products of something else, so their own supplies are constrained. Gallium and indium fall into that category." (IEEE Spectrum, 2008) | |
| **Criticality Assessment** | Indium is used in a wide range of niche applications, some of which, such as the solar cell and nuclear fuel rod applications, are critical to addressing future energy requirements. In the event that economically viable substitutes can be developed, indium will become less critical.<br><br>"In mid-2009, the Japanese Government announced plans to include indium and gallium in its national stockpile of rare metals, which was initially created to support stable economic conditions for domestic industries that consume these raw materials." (USGS, 2010) | |

| US NNR Scarcity | Scarce in 2008: Yes | Permanently Scarce: Almost Certain |
|---|---|---|
| **2008 US Import Reliance:** 100% | | **2008 Domestic US Supply:** 0% |
| **Historical US Import Trends** | Historically, the US has been almost totally reliant on indium imports. | |
| **Historical US Usage Trends** | Annual US indium utilization levels increased during the mid/late 20$^{th}$ century (especially since the 1960s), peaking temporarily in 1944, 1951, 1973, and 1979, before increasing dramatically from the 1990s into the new millennium. | |
| **US Peak Production Year (thru 2008):** 1966 | | **US Peak Utilization Year (thru 2008):** 2008 |
| **Potential Geopolitical US Supply Constraints** | 40% of US indium imports come from China; half of the proven global indium reserves are located in China.<br><br>In 2010, China imposed a 233 metric ton quota on indium exports. (Hague, 2010) | |

| NNR Profile | Indium (continued) |
|---|---|
| **US Scarcity Assessment** | "Indium was not recovered from ores in the United States in 2009." (USGS, 2010) <br><br> The US currently relies exclusively on imported indium, a large percentage (40%) of which comes from China. <br><br> Available evidence supports the contention that domestic indium supplies will remain insufficient to completely address domestic requirements going forward: <br><br> • While US indium utilization increased into the new millennium, domestic indium production ceased entirely in 1970—a significant indicator of America's increasing dependence on foreign NNRs, and a compelling indicator that domestic economically viable indium production has peaked permanently; <br> • US indium import levels have increased dramatically since the late 1990s, as have domestic indium utilization levels; and <br> • The quantity of indium produced domestically during 1966, the year of peak (to date) domestic indium production, amounted to only 4% of the 2008 total US utilization level. <br><br> Barring future reductions in the domestic (US) indium requirement trajectory and/or major new domestic economically viable discoveries, indium will almost certainly remain scarce domestically in the future. |

| Global NNR Scarcity | Scarce in 2008: Yes | Permanently Scarce: Almost Certain |
|---|---|---|

| **Historical Global Production Trends** | "According to the USGS, the top five indium producing countries in the world in 2009 were China, Japan, Canada, Republic of Korea, and Belgium. China's refinery production of indium was approximately 300 metric tons in 2009. This is approximately 50% of the annual total global refined production of 597 metric tons." (SMG, 2010) <br><br> After peaking temporarily in 1972 and declining through most of the 1980s, annual global indium production levels increased dramatically since the late 1980s; annual global indium production increased 71% between 2000 and 2008. |
|---|---|

| Global Peak Production Year (thru 2008): 2006 | Years to Global Reserve Exhaustion: N/A |
|---|---|
| Projected Global Peak Production Year: 2018 | Projected Global Peak Supply Year: 2030 |

| **Interdependencies** | Indium is currently produced only from zinc ores (sphalerite); it is hoped that processes will be developed whereby indium production from other base metals such as tin, lead, and copper will become economically viable, thereby increasing reserves. <br><br> "The average indium content of zinc deposits from which it is recovered, ranges from less than 1 part per million to 100 parts per million. Its occurrence in nature with other base metal ores is sub-economic for indium recovery." (SMG, 2010) |
|---|---|

| NNR Profile | Indium (continued) |
|---|---|
| **Global Scarcity Assessment** | "The [2007] indium market, however, remained in deficit as demand for the metal, supported largely by ITO [indium tin oxide] demand, continued to outpace supply." (USGS, 2008) |
| | A 71% increase in the annual global indium production level between 2000 and 2008 implies a robust increase in global indium demand during the pre-recession period, and a correspondingly robust increase in global indium supply in response to increased global demand. |
| | The fact that the price of indium increased by an extraordinary 192% during the 2000-2008 period indicates that global indium supply, while increasing considerably during the eight year period, remained woefully insufficient to completely address global requirements in 2008. |
| | Available evidence supports the contention that global indium supplies will remain insufficient to completely address global requirements going forward: |
| | • The global indium production level is projected to peak in approximately 2018;<br>• The global indium supply level is projected to peak in approximately 2030;<br>• The considerable increase in global indium supply levels between 2000 and 2008 failed to prevent an extraordinary price increase during the period—compelling evidence of unaddressed global requirements in 2008; and<br>• It is questionable whether the robust 6.9% compound annual growth rate (CAGR) in global indium production evidenced between 2000 and 2008—an interval during which indium became scarce globally despite a significant increase in production—can be reestablished, much less increased, going forward. A 6.9% CAGR would necessitate a continuous doubling in the annual global production level of indium every 10.5 years. |
| | Barring future reductions in the global indium requirement trajectory and/or major new economically viable discoveries, indium will almost certainly remain scarce globally in the future. |
| | "The price of indium has shot up recently. Unless new resources are found and recycling improves, indium could be scarce by 2020." (IEEE Spectrum, 2008) |

1. "Indium", Wikipedia, 2011 - http://en.wikipedia.org/wiki/Indium.
2. "Indium Statistics", Historical Statistics for Mineral and Material Commodities in the United States, USGS, 2010 – http://minerals.usgs.gov/ds/2005/140/indium.xls.
3. "Objective Capital Rare Earth and Minor Metals Investment Summit: Strategic Metals – Policy and Power", slide 5; J. Kooroshy, The Hague Centre for Strategic Studies, 2010 - http://www.slideshare.net/objectivecapital/objective-capital-rare-earth-and-minor-metals-investment-summit-strategic-metals-policy-and-power-jaakko-kooroshy.
4."The Indium Market", SMG Indium Resource Ltd. 2010 -http://www.smg-indium.com/Market.html.
5. "Supply Risk, Scarcity, and Cellphones", S. Moore, IEEE Spectrum, 2008 - http://spectrum.ieee.org/telecom/wireless/supply-risk-scarcity-and-cellphones.

| NNR Profile | Iodine |
|---|---|
| **NNR Uses and Critical Applications** | |

| **Primary Uses** | Iodine is a bluish-black mineral used in biocides, iodine salts, liquid crystal displays (LCDs), synthetic fabric treatments, and x-ray contrast media; iodine is essential to all living organisms. |
|---|---|
| **Critical Applications** | Iodized salt; LCDs.<br><br>"An estimated 35% of children in developing countries suffer from iodine deficiency." [Countries pass laws to increase the use of iodized salt.] USGS, 2008 |

| **NNR Criticality** | **NNR Criticality Classification: Critical** |
|---|---|
| **Substitutes** | In cases where iodine substitutes do exist, they are often price/performance inferior; in some animal feed, catalytic, nutritional, pharmaceutical, and photographic applications, there are no substitutes for iodine. |
| **Criticality Assessment** | Iodine is an essential element to life; it is also used in a variety of niche applications for which viable substitutes are not readily available. |

| **US NNR Scarcity** | **Scarce in 2008: Yes** | **Permanently Scarce: Almost Certain** |
|---|---|---|
| **2008 US Import Reliance: 72%*** | | **2008 Domestic US Supply: 28%*** |

| **Historical US Import Trends** | Historically, the US has relied on imports for a majority of its iodine supplies; the US has become increasingly reliant on iodine imports over the past several decades. |
|---|---|
| **Historical US Usage Trends** | Annual US iodine utilization levels generally increased—in a fluctuating manner—during the latter two thirds of the 20th century and into the 21st century, peaking temporarily in 1937, 1943, 1981, and 1989, before peaking permanently (to date) in 2002. |

| **US Peak Production Year (thru 2008): 1992*** | **US Peak Utilization Year (thru 2008): 2002*** |
|---|---|

| **Potential Geopolitical US Supply Constraints** | 80% of US iodine imports come from Chile; Chile accounts for more than 50% of world production; 60% of proven global iodine reserves are located in China. |
|---|---|
| **US Scarcity Assessment** | The US currently relies heavily on imported iodine, the vast majority (80%) of which comes from Chile. The quantity of iodine supplied by foreign sources during 2008 accounted for 72% of the total 2008 US utilization level.<br><br>Available evidence supports the contention that domestic iodine supplies will remain insufficient to completely address domestic requirements going forward:<br><br>• While US iodine utilization increased into the new millennium, the annual US iodine production level decreased by 22% since peaking (to date) in 1992—a compelling indicator that domestic economically viable iodine production has peaked permanently;<br>• The US has been heavily reliant on iodine imports since the early 20th century;<br>• The quantity of iodine produced domestically during 2005 (the last year of available data) amounted to only 28% of the total 2005 US utilization level—a significant indicator of America's increasing dependence on foreign NNRs;<br>• The quantity of iodine produced domestically during 1967, the year of peak (to date) domestic iodine production, amounted to only 36% of the 2005 total US utilization level.<br><br>Barring future reductions in the domestic (US) iodine requirement trajectory and/or major new domestic economically viable discoveries, iodine will almost certainly remain scarce domestically in the future. |

| NNR Profile | Iodine (continued) | |
|---|---|---|
| **Global NNR Scarcity** | **Scarce in 2008: Yes** | **Permanently Scarce: Unclear** |
| **Historical Global Production Trends** | "Chile was the leading producer of iodine in the world [approximately 60% of the global total in 2008]." USGS, 2008<br><br>Annual global iodine production levels have generally increased since the middle 20th century, peaking temporarily in 1976 and 1991, before increasing into the new millennium; annual global iodine production increased 36% between 2000 and 2008. | |
| **Global Peak Production Year (thru 2008): 2006** | **Years to Global Reserve Exhaustion: >50** | |
| **Projected Global Peak Production Year: N/A** | **Projected Global Peak Supply Year: N/A** | |
| **Interdependencies** | Most iodine is produced as a byproduct of natural gas, oil, and nitrate processing. | |
| **Global Scarcity Assessment** | "Prices for iodine have increased in recent years owing to high demand…" USGS, 2010<br><br>A 36% increase in the annual global iodine production level between 2000 and 2008 implies an increase in global iodine demand during the pre-recession period, and a corresponding increase in global iodine supply in response to increased global demand.<br><br>The fact that the price of iodine increased by 18% during the 2000-2008 period indicates that global iodine supply, while increasing during the eight year period, remained insufficient to completely address global requirements in 2008.<br><br>Available evidence regarding the likelihood that global iodine supplies will remain insufficient to completely address global requirements going forward is conflicting:<br><br>• An increase in the price of iodine during the 2000-2008 period induced an insufficient increase in iodine supply—evidence of tight global supply in 2008; however<br>• Proven global iodine reserves are sufficient to last for over 50 years (assuming the restoration of pre-recession utilization levels and growth rates).<br><br>It is therefore unclear whether iodine will remain scarce globally in the future, or whether globally available, economically viable iodine supplies will be sufficient to completely address future global requirements.<br><br>"Global shipments of LCD televisions were expected to double by 2012, resulting in an anticipated increase in consumption of iodine by LCD producers." AND: "As more countries implement legislation mandating salt iodization to combat iodine deficiency, the global demand for iodized salt would be expected to increase." USGS, 2010 | |

\* USGS data is available only through 2005.

1. "Iodine", Wikipedia, 2011 - http://en.wikipedia.org/wiki/Iodine.
2. "Iodine Statistics", Historical Statistics for Mineral and Material Commodities in the United States, USGS, 2010 – http://minerals.usgs.gov/ds/2005/140/iodine.xls.

| NNR Profile | Iron Ore |
|---|---|

## NNR Uses and Critical Applications

| Primary Uses | Iron ores are gray, yellow, purple, and red rocks and minerals from which metallic iron can be extracted; metallic iron is used to make pig iron, which is used to make steel. |
|---|---|
| Critical Applications | Steel making. |

| NNR Criticality | NNR Criticality Classification: Indispensible |
|---|---|
| Substitutes | Iron ore is the only source of primary (pig) iron; besides scrap iron, primary iron is the only source of steel. |
| Criticality Assessment | Next to oil, iron (steel) is the most critical NNR in the industrialized world; iron ore is indispensible to modern industrial existence. |

| US NNR Scarcity | Scarce in 2008: No | Permanently Scarce: Unclear |
|---|---|---|
| **2008 US Import Reliance: 0%** | | **2008 Domestic US Supply: 100%** |

| Historical US Import Trends | Prior to the 1953 peak in domestic iron ore extraction, the US was essentially self-sufficient in iron ore supplies. Between the early 1950s and the early 21$^{st}$ century, the US was a net importer of iron ore, the peak years occurring in the mid/late 1970s. Given the decline in America's industrial preeminence, US iron ore requirements have declined to levels at which domestic demand can be totally addressed by domestic supplies; the US has recently become a net iron ore exporter. |
|---|---|
| Historical US Usage Trends | "The United States was estimated to have produced and consumed 1% of the world's [2009] iron ore output." (USGS, 2010)<br><br>Annual US iron ore utilization levels generally increased through the first half of the 20$^{th}$ century, peaking temporarily in 1907, 1917, 1929, 1937, and 1944, before peaking permanently (to date) 1954. Domestic iron ore utilization declined to a lower peak in 1978, before trending generally downward since that time; the 2008 US iron ore utilization level amounted to only 34% of the 1954 peak utilization level. |

| US Peak Extraction Year (thru 2008): 1953 | US Peak Utilization Year (thru 2008): 1954 |
|---|---|
| **Potential Geopolitical US Supply Constraints** | 58% of US iron ore imports come from Canada; however, the US is currently a net iron ore exporter; China accounts for more than half of annual global iron ore extraction. |

| NNR Profile | Iron Ore (continued) |
|---|---|
| **US Scarcity Assessment** | "Historically, more than 85% of the US iron ore consumed during World War II had come from the rich open-pit hematite mines in the Lake Superior region. By the end of the Vietnam War, however, most of the high grade ores in the Great Lakes region had been mined, and the industry had to turn to beneficiation of lower grade ores." (MSU)<br><br>That annual domestic iron ore utilization decreased by 66% since peaking (to date) in 1954, is a primary indicator of declining American industrial preeminence and global economic competitiveness.<br><br>However, as a result of continuously declining domestic demand for iron ore, the US is currently addressing its total iron ore requirement through domestic supplies, although this has only been the case since 2007.<br><br>Available evidence regarding the likelihood that domestic iron ore supplies will remain sufficient to completely address domestic requirements going forward is conflicting:<br><br>• The 2008 US iron ore extraction level exceeded the 2008 US domestic utilization level by nearly 8%; however<br>• The domestic iron ore extraction level decreased by 55% since peaking (to date) in 1953—a primary cause of declining American industrial preeminence and global competitiveness, and a compelling indicator that domestic economically viable iron ore extraction has peaked permanently; and<br>• The US was a consistent net iron ore importer until 2007.<br><br>It is therefore unclear whether domestically available, economically viable iron ore supplies will remain sufficient to completely address future domestic requirements, or whether iron ore will become scarce domestically in the not-too-distant future. |

| Global NNR Scarcity | Scarce in 2008: Yes | Permanently Scarce: Almost Certain |
|---|---|---|
| **Historical Global Extraction Trends** | "In 2008, China imported one-half of the world's total iron ore exports and produced about one-half of the world's pig iron." (USGS, 2010)<br><br>Annual global iron ore extraction levels generally increased during the 20th century (especially since the end of WWII), peaking temporarily in 1917, 1929, 1942, and 1979, before increasing meteorically during the early 21st century; annual global iron ore extraction increased by a phenomenal 106% between 2000 and 2008.<br><br>"International iron ore trade and production of iron ore and pig iron—key indicators of iron ore consumption—clearly show that iron ore consumption in China is the major factor upon which the expansion of the international iron ore industry depends." (USGS, 2008) | |

| Global Peak Extraction Year (thru 2008): 2008 | Years to Global Reserve Exhaustion: 15 |
|---|---|
| **Projected Global Peak Extraction Year: 2015** | **Projected Global Peak Supply Year: 2070** |
| **Interdependencies** | None identified. |

| NNR Profile | Iron Ore (continued) |
|---|---|
| **Global Scarcity Assessment** | "Following a year of almost 20% increase in worldwide price for lump and fines in 2006, increases of almost 10% in 2007 have resulted from a continuing supply deficit." AND: "Major iron-ore-mining companies continue to reinvest profits in mine development, but increases in capacity have not been keeping up with the demand growth, which is dominated by China." (USGS, 2008)<br><br>A 106% increase in the annual global iron ore extraction level between 2000 and 2008 implies a tremendous increase in global iron ore demand during the pre-recession period, and a correspondingly tremendous increase in global iron ore supply in response to increased demand.<br><br>The fact that the price of iron ore increased by an extremely robust 132% during the 2000-2008 period indicates that global iron ore supply, while increasing tremendously during the eight year period, remained insufficient to completely address global requirements in 2008.<br><br>Available evidence supports the contention that global iron ore supplies will remain insufficient to completely address global requirements going forward:<br><br>• Proven global iron ore reserves would exhaust in only 15 years, assuming the restoration of pre-recession utilization levels and growth rates;<br>• The global iron ore extraction level is projected to peak in approximately 2020; and<br>• The increased global iron ore supply brought online between 2000 and 2008 failed to prevent an extremely robust price increase during the period—compelling evidence of unaddressed global requirements in 2008; and<br>• It is questionable whether the extremely robust 9.4% compound annual growth rate (CAGR) in global iron ore extraction evidenced between 2000 and 2008—an interval during which iron ore became scarce globally despite an extraordinary increase in extraction—can be reestablished, much less increased, going forward. A 9.4% CAGR would necessitate a continuous doubling in the annual global extraction level of iron ore every 7.5 years.<br><br>Barring future reductions in the global iron ore requirement trajectory and/or major new economically viable discoveries, iron ore will almost certainly remain scarce globally in the future.<br><br>"China continued to actively invest in overseas [iron ore] ventures in Africa, Australia, and South America in order to provide raw materials for its growing urbanization. Earlier interest in importation of North American ores by China has decreased somewhat…" (USGS, 2010) |

1. "Iron Ore", Wikipedia, 2011 - http://en.wikipedia.org/wiki/Iron_ore.
2. "Iron Ore Statistics", Historical Statistics for Mineral and Material Commodities in the United States, USGS, 2010 – http://minerals.usgs.gov/ds/2005/140/ironore.xls.
3. "Iron Mining Today", Michigan State University (MSU) - http://www.geo.msu.edu/geogmich/iron_iii.html.

| NNR Profile | Iron/Steel |
|---|---|
| **NNR Uses and Critical Applications** | |
| **Primary Uses** | Iron is a lustrous silvery-gray metal that is used in making cast iron, wrought iron, and steel; it is also used as a catalyst and as a nutritional supplement. The main shortcoming associated with iron is that it oxidizes (rusts) when exposed to air. Steel is an alloy consisting of iron (primarily) with traces of other materials such as carbon, nickel, manganese, molybdenum, cobalt, chromium, vanadium, and tungsten. Steel is used in the production of infrastructure (buildings, roads, bridges, etc.), ships, machinery, tools, appliances, and weapons. |
| **Critical Applications** | Iron and steel are nearly ubiquitous. In addition to being the steel feedstock, iron is also critical as a catalyst in the Haber-Bosch process (ammonia production) and the Fischer-Tropsch process (synthetic oil production). |

| **NNR Criticality** | **NNR Criticality Classification: Indispensible** |
|---|---|
| **Substitutes** | There is no substitute for iron in steelmaking. While metallic and non-metallic substitutes exist for iron and steel in industrial and construction applications, iron and steel are typically price/performance superior. |
| **Criticality Assessment** | "Iron is the least expensive and most widely used metal." (USGS, 2010) <br><br> Iron is the most common metal on the planet; iron and steel are the world's most commonly used metals, and account for approximately 95% of all metals used globally; iron and steel are indispensible to modern industrial existence. |

| **US NNR Scarcity** | **Scarce in 2008: Yes** | **Permanently Scarce: Likely** |
|---|---|---|
| **2008 US Import Reliance: 13%** | | **2008 Domestic US Supply: 87%** |
| **Historical US Import Trends** | | The US has been a net importer of iron and steel since the late 1940s; US import reliance has increased significantly since the middle 1990s; net iron/steel imports have typically exceeded 10% of total US utilization since 2000. |
| **Historical US Usage Trends** | | Annual US iron and steel production levels generally increased during the first three quarters of the 20th century, peaking temporarily in 1906, 1916, 1929, 1944, and 1957, before peaking permanently (to date) in 1973. Domestic iron and steel production declined dramatically during the remainder of the 1970s, then remained relatively constant since the early 1980s; the 2008 US iron/steel utilization level amounted to only 41% of the 1973 peak utilization level. |
| **US Peak Production Year (thru 2008): 1973** | | **US Peak Utilization Year (thru 2008): 1973** |
| **Potential Geopolitical US Supply Constraints** | | China accounts for nearly half of global steel utilization. <br><br> "Seven U.S. steel producers and the United Steelworkers Union filed an antidumping suit against China [in 2009] with the U.S. International Trade Commission and the U.S. Department of Commerce, covering $2.7 billion of steel imports into the United States. Steel producers contended that tariff increases were needed to help them survive the global recession." (USGS, 2010) |

| NNR Profile | Iron/Steel (continued) |
|---|---|
| **US Scarcity Assessment** | That annual domestic iron and steel utilization decreased by 59% since peaking (to date) in 1973, is a primary indicator of declining American industrial preeminence and global economic competitiveness.<br><br>As a result of dramatically diminished domestic demand for iron and steel, the US currently relies only marginally on iron and steel imports. The quantity of iron and steel supplied by foreign sources during 2008 accounted for 13% of the total 2008 US utilization level.<br><br>Available evidence supports the contention that domestic iron and steel supplies will likely remain insufficient to completely address domestic requirements going forward:<br><br>• The annual US iron and steel production level decreased by 63% since peaking (to date) in 1973—a compelling indicator that domestic economically viable iron and steel production has peaked permanently;<br>• The US has become increasingly reliant on iron and steel imports since the late 1940s; and<br>• The quantity of iron and steel produced domestically during 2008 amounted to only 89% of the total 2008 US utilization level—a primary cause of America's lack of economic self-sufficiency.<br><br>Barring future reductions in the domestic (US) iron and steel requirement trajectories and/or major new domestic economically viable discoveries, iron and steel will likely remain scarce domestically in the future. |

| Global NNR Scarcity | Scarce in 2008: Yes | Permanently Scarce: Almost Certain |
|---|---|---|
| **Historical Global Production Trends** | "By 1947, the United States controlled 60 percent of the world's steelmaking potential." (Answers.com, 2010)<br><br>Annual global iron and steel production levels generally increased during the 20$^{th}$ century, peaking temporarily in 1916, 1929, 1941, and 1979, before increasing dramatically during the pre-recession years of the 21$^{st}$ century; annual global iron and steel production increased 63% between 2000 and 2008.<br><br>"According to International Iron and Steel Institute data…The three leading steel-producing countries [in 2009] were China with about 39%; Japan, 10%; and the United States, 8%." (USGS, 2010 [Kyanite article]) | |

| Global Peak Production Year (thru 2008): 2007 | Years to Global Reserve Exhaustion: N/A |
|---|---|
| **Projected Global Peak Production Year:** N/A | **Projected Global Peak Supply Year:** N/A |
| **Interdependencies** | Iron and steel production depend upon iron ore supplies. |

| NNR Profile | Iron/Steel (continued) |
|---|---|
| **Global Scarcity Assessment** | "Relentless increases in the price of steel [in 2008] are halting or slowing major construction projects world-wide and investments in shipbuilding and oil-and-gas exploration..." (WSJ, 2008)<br><br>A 63% increase in the annual global iron and steel production level between 2000 and 2008 implies a robust increase in global iron and steel demand during the pre-recession period, and a correspondingly robust increase in global iron and steel supply in response to increased global demand.<br><br>The fact that the price of iron and steel increased by a substantial 105% during the 2000-2008 period indicates that global iron and steel supply, while increasing considerably during the eight year period, remained insufficient to completely address global requirements in 2008.<br><br>Available evidence supports the contention that global iron and steel supplies will remain insufficient to completely address global requirements going forward:<br><br>• Iron ore (iron and steel feedstock) almost certain to remain scarce globally going forward (see Iron Ore Profile);<br>• The considerable increase in global iron and steel supply levels between 2000 and 2008 failed to prevent a substantial price increase during the period—compelling evidence of unaddressed global requirements in 2008; and<br>• It is questionable whether the robust 6.3% compound annual growth rate (CAGR) in global iron and steel production evidenced between 2000 and 2008—an interval during which iron and steel became scarce globally, despite significant increases in production—can be reestablished, much less increased, going forward. A 6.3% CAGR would necessitate a continuous doubling in the annual global production level of iron and steel every 11.5 years.<br><br>Barring future reductions in the global iron and steel requirement trajectories and/or major new economically viable discoveries, iron and steel will almost certainly remain scarce globally in the future.<br><br>"According to the World Steel Association... China's ASC [apparent steel consumption] was expected to increase by 5% in 2010, and was expected to account for 48% of world steel consumption." (USGS, 2010) |

1. "Iron", Wikipedia, 2011 - http://en.wikipedia.org/wiki/Iron_ore.
2. "Steel", Wikipedia, 2011 - http://en.wikipedia.org/wiki/Steel.
3. "Iron and Steel Statistics", Historical Statistics for Mineral and Material Commodities in the United States, USGS, 2010 – http://minerals.usgs.gov/ds/2005/140/ironsteel.pdf.
4. "Mineral Commodity Summaries 2005" (USGS, 2005), US Geological Survey, 2005 - http://minerals.usgs.gov/minerals/pubs/mcs/2005/mcs2005.pdf.
5. "Iron and Steel Industry", Answers.com (from Gale Encyclopedia of US History), 2010 - http://www.answers.com/topic/iron-and-steel-industry.
6. "Fast Rising Steel Prices Set Back Big Projects", G. Matthews, Wall Street Journal (WSJ), 2008 - http://www.fundmymutualfund.com/2008/05/wsj-fast-rising-steel-prices-set-back.html.

| NNR Profile | Kyanite |
|---|---|

**NNR Uses and Critical Applications**

| **Primary Uses** | Kyanite is a typically blue mineral used refractory and ceramic products, including plumbing fixtures and dishware; kyanite is also used in electronic and electrical applications (as an insulator). |
|---|---|
| **Critical Applications** | Refractory applications.<br><br>"The steel industry worldwide continued to be the leading consumer of refractories." (USGS, 2008) |

| **NNR Criticality** | **NNR Criticality Classification: Important** |
|---|---|
| **Substitutes** | Viable kyanite substitutes, including synthetic mullite, super duty fire clays, and high alumna materials, are available. |
| **Criticality Assessment** | Kyanite addresses multiple niche applications for which viable substitutes are generally available. |

| **US NNR Scarcity** | **Scarce in 2008: No** | **Permanently Scarce: Unlikely** |
|---|---|---|
| **2008 US Import Reliance: 0%** | | **2008 Domestic US Supply:** 100% |
| **Historical US Import Trends** | Historically, the US has been both a net importer and a net exporter of kyanite; the US has been a net kyanite exporter since the 1960s. | |
| **Historical US Usage Trends** | During the period of time for which USGS US kyanite utilization data are available (1998-2008), annual US kyanite utilization levels increased by 20%. | |
| **US Peak Extraction Year (thru 2008):** 2007 | | **US Peak Utilization Year (thru 2008):** 2008 |
| **Potential Geopolitical US Supply Constraints** | 89% of US kyanite imports come from South Africa; however, the US is a net exporter of kyanite. | |
| **US Scarcity Assessment** | The US is currently addressing its total requirement for kyanite through domestic supplies.<br><br>Available evidence supports the contention that domestic kyanite supplies will likely remain sufficient to completely address domestic requirements going forward:<br><br>• Domestic kyanite supplies were sufficient to completely address domestic requirements during the 2000-2008 period of rapid economic growth prior to the Great Recession; and<br>• Domestic kyanite reserves are considered by the USGS to be "large".<br><br>Barring future increases in the domestic (US) kyanite requirement trajectory, domestically available, economically viable kyanite supplies will likely remain sufficient—notwithstanding temporary local shortages—to completely address domestic requirements going forward.<br><br>"Large resources of kyanite and related minerals are known to exist in the United States. The chief resources are in deposits of micaceous schist and gneiss, mostly in the Appalachian Mountains area and in Idaho. Other resources are in aluminous gneiss in southern California. These resources are not economical to mine at present." (USGS, 2010) | |

| NNR Profile | Kyanite (continued) | |
|---|---|---|
| **Global NNR Scarcity** | **Scarce in 2008: Yes** | **Permanently Scarce: Unclear** |
| **Historical Global Extraction Trends** | Annual global kyanite extraction levels generally increased during both the 20th and 21st centuries (especially since WWII), peaking temporarily in 1930, 1937, 1957, 1980, 1989, and 1998; annual global kyanite production increased 16% between 2000 and 2008. | |
| **Global Peak Extraction Year (thru 2008):** 2008 | | **Years to Global Reserve Exhaustion:** N/A |
| **Projected Global Peak Extraction Year:** N/A | | **Projected Global Peak Supply Year:** N/A |
| **Interdependencies** | None identified. | |
| **Global Scarcity Assessment** | A 16% increase in the annual global kyanite extraction level between 2000 and 2008 implies an increase in global kyanite demand during the pre-recession period, and a corresponding increase in global kyanite supply in response to increased global demand.<br><br>The fact that the price of kyanite increased by 10% during the 2000-2008 period indicates that global kyanite supply, while increasing during the eight year period, remained insufficient to completely address global requirements in 2008.<br><br>Available evidence regarding the likelihood that global kyanite supplies will remain insufficient to completely address global requirements going forward is conflicting:<br><br>• An increase in the price of kyanite during the 2000-2008 period induced a modest yet insufficient increase in kyanite supply—evidence of tight global supply in 2008; however<br>• Proven global kyanite reserves are considered by the USGS to be "large".<br><br>It is therefore unclear whether kyanite will remain scarce globally in the future, or whether globally available, economically viable kyanite supplies will be sufficient to completely address future global requirements. | |

1. "Kyanite", Wikipedia, 2011 - http://en.wikipedia.org/wiki/Kyanite.
2. "Kyanite Statistics", Historical Statistics for Mineral and Material Commodities in the United States, USGS, 2010 – http://minerals.usgs.gov/ds/2005/140/kyanite.xls.

| NNR Profile | Lead | |
|---|---|---|
| **NNR Uses and Critical Applications** | | |
| **Primary Uses** | Lead is a dense, soft, malleable, non-conductive, bluish-white (when freshly cut), heavy metal used in building construction, batteries, ammunition, weights; lead is also used in solder, pewter, fusible alloys, and radiation shielding. | |
| **Critical Applications** | Lead-acid batteries for automotive (SLI: starting-lighting-ignition) and industrial applications (uninterruptible power supplies); also nuclear insulation (x-ray protection).<br><br>"…while the automotive industry has traditionally been the largest consumers of lead, use in electronic applications is increasing in the United States." (Doe Run, 2010) | |

| NNR Profile | Lead (continued) | |
|---|---|---|
| **NNR Criticality** | **NNR Criticality Classification: Critical** | |
| **Substitutes** | Lead substitutes, including plastics, aluminum, iron, and tin, are readily available in all application areas except batteries, which is currently the most critical lead application. | |
| **Criticality Assessment** | Lead-acid batteries represent a significant and pervasive application for lead. | |
| **US NNR Scarcity** | **Scarce in 2008: Yes** | **Permanently Scarce: Almost Certain** |
| **2008 US Import Reliance:** 16% | **2008 Domestic US Supply:** 84% | |
| **Historical US Import Trends** | While the US was a net exporter of lead during the early decades of the 20$^{th}$ century, the US has been almost exclusively a net importer of lead since the 1940s. | |
| **Historical US Usage Trends** | "Falling [lead] consumption in the United States was due in large part to diminished demand for lead by the battery industry." (Reference for Business)<br><br>Annual US lead utilization levels generally increased during the 20$^{th}$ century—in a cyclical manner—peaking temporarily in 1907, 1920, 1926, 1937, 1942, 1953, and 1974, before peaking permanently (to date) in 1999. Domestic lead utilization generally declined during the early years of the 21$^{st}$ century; the 2008 US lead utilization level amounted to only 86% of the 1999 peak utilization level.<br><br>"Operating one of the most advanced [battery recycling] facilities in the world, Doe Run recovers and recycles nearly 160,000 tons of refined lead each year. In the U.S., the battery industry is virtually a closed loop." (Doe Run, 2010) | |
| **US Peak Production Year (thru 2008):** 1970 | **US Peak Utilization Year (thru 2008):** 1999 | |
| **Potential Geopolitical US Supply Constraints** | China accounts for 40% of global lead mine production; nearly 30% of proven global reserves are located in Australia; 70% of US lead imports come from Canada.<br><br>"China removed the value-added tax rebate and imposed a 10% tax on exports of refined lead, leading to significantly decreased exports. As a result, an appreciable shortage of refined lead was evident on the world market during 2007." (USGS, 2008) | |

| NNR Profile | Lead (continued) |
|---|---|
| **US Scarcity Assessment** | That annual domestic lead utilization decreased by 14% since peaking (to date) in 1999, is a significant indicator of declining American industrial preeminence and global economic competitiveness.<br><br>The US currently relies marginally on imported lead, the majority (70%) of which comes from Canada. The quantity of lead supplied by foreign sources during 2008 accounted for 16% of the total 2008 US utilization level.<br><br>Available evidence supports the contention that domestic lead supplies will remain insufficient to completely address domestic requirements going forward:<br><br>• The annual US lead production level decreased by 78% since peaking (to date) in 1970—a compelling indicator that domestic economically viable lead production has peaked permanently;<br>• The US has remained consistently reliant on lead imports since 1940;<br>• The quantity of lead produced domestically during 2008 amounted to only 9% of the total 2008 US utilization level (although secondary lead production through recycling amounted to 77% of total US utilization)—an indicator of America's increasing dependence on foreign NNRs; and<br>• The quantity of lead extracted domestically during 1970, the year of peak (to date) domestic lead extraction, amounted to only 42% of the 2008 total US utilization level.<br><br>Barring future reductions in the domestic (US) lead requirement trajectory and/or major new domestic economically viable discoveries, lead will almost certainly remain scarce domestically in the future. |

| Global NNR Scarcity | Scarce in 2008: Yes | Permanently Scarce: Almost Certain |
|---|---|---|
| **Historical Global Production Trends** | "Given the need for batteries to support these vehicles [cars and e-bikes], China has passed North America as the world's largest producer and consumer of lead in the last six years. In 2009, China consumed 41 percent of the 8.3 million tons of lead used in the world. China was also responsible for the 42 percent of the 8.6 million tons produced. China's lead production more than doubled between 2003 and 2009 as consumption caught up to production." (Doe Run, 2010)<br><br>Annual global lead production levels generally increased during both the 20th and 21st centuries, peaking temporarily in 1908, 1928, 1939 (war years data unavailable), 1956, and 1976, before continuing to increase into the new millennium; annual global lead production increased 20% between 2000 and 2008.<br><br>"Increases in lead concentrate production are anticipated in China, Europe, and South America…" (USGS, 2008) | |

| Global Peak Production Year (thru 2008): 2008 | Years to Global Reserve Exhaustion: 17 |
|---|---|
| **Projected Global Peak Production Year: 1990** | **Projected Global Peak Supply Year: 2040** |

| Interdependencies | Lead is typically recovered as a byproduct of zinc, silver, and copper production.<br><br>"Lead is frequently recovered as a byproduct of zinc production, so lead production was affected by the downturn in the zinc market." (USGS, 2010) |
|---|---|

| NNR Profile | Lead (continued) |
|---|---|
| **Global Scarcity Assessment** | "During 2007, the average price of refined lead rose appreciably from that of 2006 on both the U.S. and world markets, approaching record highs. Consistent with this rise in price, the global supply situation for refined lead remained tight, as stocks continued to decline and demand remained strong." (USGS, 2008)<br><br>A 20% increase in the annual global lead production level between 2000 and 2008 implies an increase in global lead demand during the pre-recession period, and a corresponding increase in global lead supply in response to increased global demand.<br><br>The fact that the price of lead increased by an extremely robust 121% during the 2000-2008 period indicates that global lead supply, while increasing during the eight year period, remained insufficient to completely address global requirements in 2008.<br><br>Available evidence supports the contention that global lead supplies will remain insufficient to completely address global requirements going forward:<br><br>• Proven global lead reserves would exhaust in only 17 years, assuming the restoration of pre-recession utilization levels and growth rates;<br>• The global lead extraction level was projected to peak in approximately 1990;<br>• The global lead supply level is projected to peak in approximately 2040; and<br>• An extremely robust increase in the price of lead during the 2000-2008 period could induce only a nominal increase in lead supply—evidence that globally available, economically viable lead extraction may be at or near its permanent peak level.<br><br>Barring future reductions in the global lead requirement trajectory and/or major new economically viable discoveries, lead will almost certainly remain scarce globally in the future.<br><br>"Chinese net imports of lead concentrate rose significantly during the year, affecting the supply of concentrate on the world market." (USGS, 2008) |

1. "Lead", Wikipedia, 2011 - http://en.wikipedia.org/wiki/Lead.
2. "Lead Statistics", Historical Statistics for Mineral and Material Commodities in the United States, USGS, 2010 – http://minerals.usgs.gov/ds/2005/140/lead.xls.
3. "Lead and Zinc Ores", Reference for Business - http://www.referenceforbusiness.com/industries/Mining/Lead-Zinc-Ores.html.
4. "Emerging Economies Driving Global Lead Market", The Doe Run Company (Press Release), 2010 - http://www.doerun.com/EmergingEconomiesDrivingGlobalLeadMarket/tabid/179/language/en-US/Default.aspx.

| NNR Profile | Lime |
|---|---|

## NNR Uses and Critical Applications

| Primary Uses | Lime is a soft chalky-white mineral used in building mortar and concrete; lime is also used as a chemical feedstock, in steelmaking, in water treatment, and in pulp and paper production. |
|---|---|
| Critical Applications | Mortar, plaster, concrete. |

## NNR Criticality — NNR Criticality Classification: Critical

| Substitutes | Viable lime substitutes, including limestone, gypsum, and cement, are available for all lime applications; price/performance characteristics vary per application. |
|---|---|
| Criticality Assessment | While substitutes exist for most lime applications, the use of lime in building and construction related applications is pervasive. |

## US NNR Scarcity — Scarce in 2008: No — Permanently Scarce: Unlikely

| 2008 US Import Reliance: 1% | 2008 Domestic US Supply: 99% |
|---|---|

| Historical US Import Trends | While the US has become net importer of lime since the 1960s; net imports have seldom exceeded 3% of total annual US utilization. |
|---|---|
| Historical US Usage Trends | Annual US lime utilization levels generally increased during both the 20th and 21st centuries, peaking temporarily in 1916, 1925, 1974, 1979, and 1998, before continuing to increase during the new millennium. |

| US Peak Extraction Year (thru 2008): 2006 | US Peak Utilization Year (thru 2008): 2006 |
|---|---|

| Potential Geopolitical US Supply Constraints | 84% of US lime imports come from Canada; while the US is a net importer of lime, net imports as a percentage of total US utilization are typically low. |
|---|---|
| US Scarcity Assessment | "These [32 US lime producing] companies had 75 primary lime plants (plants operating lime kilns) in 29 States and Puerto Rico [at the end of 2009]." (USGS, 2010)<br><br>The US is essentially meeting its total requirement for lime through domestic supplies.<br><br>Given that US lime resources are considered by the USGS to be "adequate", barring future increases in the domestic (US) lime requirement trajectory, domestically available, economically viable lime supplies will likely remain sufficient—notwithstanding temporary localized shortages—to completely address domestic requirements going forward. |

## Global NNR Scarcity — Scarce in 2008: Yes — Scarce in Future: Unclear

| Historical Global Extraction Trends | Annual global lime extraction levels increased steadily during the latter decades of the 20th century, peaking temporarily in 1974, 1980, and 1989, decreased in the 1990s, then increased meteorically during the early years of the 21st century; annual global lime extraction increased 145% between 2000 and 2008. |
|---|---|

| Global Peak Extraction Year (thru 2008): 2008 | Years to Global Reserve Exhaustion: N/A |
|---|---|
| Projected Global Peak Extraction Year: N/A | Projected Global Peak Supply Year: N/A |

| Interdependencies | None identified. |
|---|---|

| NNR Profile | Lime (continued) |
|---|---|
| **Global Scarcity Assessment** | A 145% increase in the annual global lime extraction level between 2000 and 2008 implies an extremely robust increase in global lime demand during the pre-recession period, and a corresponding extremely robust increase in global lime supply in response to increased global demand.<br><br>The fact that the price of lime increased by 22% during the 2000-2008 period indicates that global lime supply, while increasing significantly during the eight year period, remained insufficient to completely address global requirements in 2008.<br><br>Available evidence regarding the likelihood that global lime supplies will remain insufficient to completely address global requirements going forward is conflicting:<br><br>• An increase in the price of lime during the 2000-2008 period induced a significant yet insufficient increase in lime supply—evidence of tight global supply in 2008; and<br>• It is unclear whether the extremely robust 11.8% compound annual growth rate (CAGR) in global lime extraction evidenced between 2000 and 2008—which was required to enable pre-recession global economic growth—can be reestablished and maintained going forward. An 11.8% CAGR would necessitate a continuous doubling in the annual global extraction level of lime every 6 years; however<br>• Proven global lime reserves are considered by the USGS to be "adequate".<br><br>It is therefore unclear whether lime will remain scarce globally in the future, or whether globally available, economically viable lime supplies will be sufficient to completely address future global demand.<br><br>"In recent years, lime companies have reported that they were unable to keep up with rising production costs, and the large 2009 price increases were lime company efforts to reestablish operating margins." (USGS, 2010) |

1. "Lime Material", Wikipedia, 2011 - http://en.wikipedia.org/wiki/Lime_(material).
2. "Lime Mortar", Wikipedia, 2011 - http://en.wikipedia.org/wiki/Lime_mortar.
3. "Lime Statistics", Historical Statistics for Mineral and Material Commodities in the United States, USGS, 2010 – http://minerals.usgs.gov/ds/2005/140/lead.xls.

| NNR Profile | Lithium |
|---|---|
| **NNR Uses and Critical Applications** | |
| **Primary Uses** | Lithium is a soft, very light, highly conductive, silvery-white metal used in heat-resistant glass and ceramics, as a high strength alloy, as a coolant in heat transfer applications, in batteries, as a lubricant, and in mood stabilizing drugs. |
| **Critical Applications** | Lithium-ion batteries (electronic vehicles), aircraft parts (alloy), and mobile phones; lithium is also used in the production of H-bombs.<br><br>"…a typical [lithium-ion] cell can generate approximately 3 volts, compared with 2.1 volts for lead/acid or 1.5 volts for zinc-carbon cells. Because of its low atomic mass, it also has a high charge-and-power-to-weight ratio." (Wikipedia) |

| **NNR Criticality** | **NNR Criticality Classification: Critical** |
|---|---|
| **Substitutes** | Substitutes for lithium, including calcium, magnesium, mercury, zinc, and boron, glass, and polymer fibers, are available in most applications; price/performance is an issue in some cases. |
| **Criticality Assessment** | Lithium is useful in a variety of niche applications; assuming that lithium-ion batteries will become a major energy source for electric vehicles, lithium will become increasingly critical.<br><br>"The emergence of new technologies and engineered materials creates the prospect of rapid increases in demand for some minerals previously used in relatively small quantities in a small number of applications—such as lithium in automotive batteries…" (Freiman, 2010) |

| **US NNR Scarcity** | **Scarce in 2008: Yes** | **Permanently Scarce: Almost Certain** |
|---|---|---|
| **2008 US Import Reliance: >50%** | | **2008 Domestic US Supply: <50%** |
| **Historical US Import Trends** | "The United States remained the leading importer of lithium minerals and compounds and the leading producer of value-added lithium materials." (USGS, 2010)<br><br>Historically, the US has been both a net exporter and a net importer of lithium; the US has become increasingly reliant on lithium imports since 1997. | |
| **Historical US Usage Trends** | Annual US lithium utilization levels increased slowly prior to WWII, peaking temporarily in 1901, 1920, 1928 and 1944; then increased rapidly following the war until peaking (to date) in 1974. Domestic lithium utilization has generally declined—in a cyclical manner—since that time; the 2008 US lithium utilization level amounted to only 48% of the 1974 peak utilization level.<br><br>"As part of the American Recovery and Reinvestment Act of 2009, the U.S. Department of Energy funded $2.4 billion in grants to accelerate the development of United States manufacturing capacity for batteries and electric-drive components and for the deployment of electric-drive vehicles." (USGS, 2010) | |
| **US Peak Extraction Year (thru 2008): 1954*** | | **US Peak Utilization Year (thru 2008): 1974** |

| NNR Profile | Lithium (continued) |
|---|---|
| **Potential Geopolitical US Supply Constraints** | 63% of US lithium imports come from Chile, 35% from Argentina; Chile is the leading lithium producer in the world; 76% of proven global lithium reserves are located in Chile.<br><br>"Exclusive dependency on Lithium Ion batteries, where the Lithium will overwhelmingly come from South America, would be like being dependent on South America for 100% of our oil supply." (Tahil, 2006) |
| **US Scarcity Assessment** | "The United States remained the leading importer of lithium minerals and compound [in 2009]..." (USGS, 2010)<br><br>That annual domestic lithium utilization decreased by 52% since peaking (to date) in 1974, is a significant indicator of declining American industrial preeminence and global economic competitiveness.<br><br>The US currently relies heavily on imported lithium, the majority of which comes from Chile (63%) and Argentina (35%). The quantity of lithium supplied by foreign sources during 2008 accounted for more than 50% of the total 2008 US utilization level.<br><br>Available evidence supports the contention that domestic lithium supplies will remain insufficient to completely address domestic requirements going forward:<br><br>• Annual US lithium extraction has decreased to negligible levels since peaking (to date) in 1954—a compelling indicator that domestic economically viable lithium extraction has peaked permanently;<br>• The US has become increasingly reliant on lithium imports since 1998;<br>• The quantity of lithium extracted domestically during 2008 was negligible in comparison to the total 2008 US utilization level—a significant indicator of America's increasing dependence on foreign NNRs; and<br>• The quantity of lithium extracted domestically during 1954, the year of peak (to date) domestic lithium extraction, amounted to only 57% of the 2008 total US utilization level.<br><br>Barring future reductions in the domestic (US) lithium requirement trajectory and/or major new domestic economically viable discoveries, lithium will almost certainly remain scarce domestically in the future. |
| **Global NNR Scarcity** | Scarce in 2008: No — Permanently Scarce: Likely |

| NNR Profile | Lithium (continued) |
|---|---|
| **Historical Global Extraction Trends** | "Chile [42% of mine production] was the leading lithium chemical producer in the world; Argentina [13%], China [13%], and the United States [data withheld by USGS] also were major [2008] producers [Australia accounted for 25% of 2008 mine production]." (USSG, 2010)<br><br>Annual global lithium extraction levels generally increased during the 20th century (especially since WWII)—in a cyclical manner—peaking temporarily in 1928, 1937, 1944, 1957, 1965, 1975, 1989 and 1996, before increasing rapidly into the new millennium; annual global lithium extraction increased 87% between 2000 and 2008.<br><br>"The greatest existing lithium carbonate deposits occur in Chile, Argentina, Bolivia and China, with other countries holding only tiny fractions of the world's known supply." (Vandervelde, 2009) |

| Global Peak Extraction Year (thru 2008): 2006 | Years to Global Reserve Exhaustion: 8 |
|---|---|
| **Projected Global Peak Extraction Year: 2060** | **Projected Global Peak Supply Year: 2075** |
| **Interdependencies** | None identified. |

| NNR Profile | Lithium (continued) |
|---|---|
| **Global Scarcity Assessment** | An 87% increase in the annual global lithium extraction level between 2000 and 2008 implies a significant increase in global lithium demand during the pre-recession period, and a correspondingly significant increase in global lithium supply in response to increased global demand.<br><br>The fact that the price of lithium decreased by 21% during the 2000-2008 period indicates that the global supply of lithium in 2008 was sufficient to completely address 2008 global requirements.<br><br>Available evidence, albeit somewhat conflicting, supports the contention that global lithium supplies will likely become insufficient to completely address global requirements going forward:<br><br>• While global lithium extraction levels have generally increased since the late 1970s, lithium price levels have generally decreased since that time, albeit in a fluctuating manner—evidence of sufficient global lithium supplies;<br>• The global lithium extraction level is not projected to peak until approximately 2060; and<br>• The global lithium supply level is not projected to peak until approximately 2075; however<br>• The price of lithium increased by an extraordinary 245% between 2001 and 2008, which indicates lithium scarcity on a global level in 2008;<br>• Proven global lithium reserves would exhaust in only 8 years, assuming the restoration of pre-recession utilization levels and growth rates; and<br>• It is questionable whether the extremely robust 8.2% compound annual growth rate (CAGR) in global lithium extraction evidenced between 2000 and 2008—an interval during which lithium became scarce globally despite an extraordinary increase in extraction—can be reestablished, much less increased, going forward. An 8.2% CAGR would necessitate a continuous doubling in the annual global extraction level of lithium every 9 years.<br><br>Barring future reductions in the global lithium requirement trajectory and/or major new economically viable discoveries, lithium will likely become scarce globally in the not-too-distant future.<br><br>Whether future lithium supplies will be sufficient to support a global electronic vehicle market is still the subject of intense debate:<br><br>• "Nevertheless, many financial analysts [not geologists] who have done studies on the outlook for future Lithium production say that worries about scarcity are overblown." Versus;<br>• "In 2008, Meridian International Research, a renewable-energy think tank in France, concluded that the world does face a [lithium] shortage when vehicle demand is added to considerable consumer electronics demand." (Vandervelde, 2009) |

• US lithium extraction data (USGS) is not available past 1954; based on USGS export, import, and "consumption" data, it is possible that US lithium extraction actually peaked in the 1970s.

1. "Lithium", Wikipedia, 2011 - http://en.wikipedia.org/wiki/Lithium.

2. "Lithium Statistics", Historical Statistics for Mineral and Material Commodities in the United States, USGS, 2010 – http://minerals.usgs.gov/ds/2005/140/lithium.xls.

3. "Analysis: Recent Panics over Rare Metal Scarcity Overblown", Ars Technica, 2008 - http://arstechnica.com/business/news/2008/07/analysis-recent-panics-over-rare-metal-scarcity-overblown.ars.

4. TESTIMONY ON MINERALS, CRITICAL MINERALS, AND THE U.S. ECONOMY FOR THE HEARING "RARE EARTH MINERALS AND 21ST CENTURY INDUSTY" (US House of Representatives), Dr. Stephen Freiman, 2010 - http://www7.nationalacademies.org/ocga/testimony/Minerals_Critical_Minerals_and_the_US_Economy.asp.

5. "The Trouble with Lithium", page 5; W. Tahil, Meridian International Research, 2006 - http://tyler.blogware.com/lithium_shortage.pdf.

6. "No Looming Lithium Shortage for EVs", J. Vandervelde, Hybrids Central, 2009 - http://www.allcarselectric.com/blog/1035532_no-looming-lithium-shortage-for-evs.

| NNR Profile | Magnesium Compounds |
|---|---|
| **NNR Uses and Critical Applications** | |
| **Primary Uses** | Magnesium compounds—e.g., periclase (magnesia), magnetite, dolomite, and olivine—are used in refractory applications (furnace linings), and in agricultural, chemical, construction, environmental, and industrial applications. |
| **Critical Applications** | Refractory applications; too, olivine might become useful as an agent in carbon dioxide sequestration. |
| **NNR Criticality** | **NNR Criticality Classification: Critical** |
| **Substitutes** | Alumina, chromite, and silica substitute for magnesia in some refractory applications. |
| **Criticality Assessment** | Magnesium compounds play critical roles in a variety of industrial, construction, agricultural, and medical applications. |
| **US NNR Scarcity** | **Scarce in 2008: Yes** | **Permanently Scarce: Almost Certain** |
| **2008 US Import Reliance:** 54% | **2008 Domestic US Supply:** 46% |
| **Historical US Import Trends** | The US has almost always been a net importer of magnesium compounds; American reliance on magnesium compound imports has increased dramatically since the 1980s. |
| **Historical US Usage Trends** | Annual US magnesium compound utilization levels generally increased—in a fluctuating manner—during the first three quarters of the 20th century, peaking temporarily in 1903, 1913, 1920, 1926, 1937, and 1943. Domestic magnesium compound utilization increased dramatically in 1958, before peaking permanently (to date) in 1966 and declining in a cyclical manner thereafter; the 2008 US magnesium compound utilization level amounted to only 50% of the 1966 peak utilization level. |
| **US Peak Extraction Year (thru 2008):** 1966 | **US Peak Utilization Year (thru 2008):** 1966 |

| NNR Profile | Magnesium Compounds (continued) |
|---|---|
| **Potential Geopolitical US Supply Constraints** | 79% of US magnesium compound imports come from China.<br><br>In 2009, China imposed a 10% duty on magnesium compound exports; in 2010, China imposed a 1,330,000 metric ton quota on magnesium compound exports. (Hague, 2010)<br><br>"...on June 23 [2009], the EU announced that both it and the U.S. 'had requested WTO consultations with China regarding China's export restrictions on a number of key raw materials, which it considers are in clear breach of international trade rules.<br><br>In the words of the EU announcement: 'European industries have raised concerns for a number of years on export restrictions - quotas, export duties and minimum export prices - which China applies on key raw materials, such as yellow phosphorous, bauxite, coke, fluorspar, magnesium, manganese, silicon metal, silicon carbide and zinc. Some of these resources cannot be found elsewhere.'" (Seeking Alpha, 2009)<br><br>Yet in other cases, the US takes diametrically opposing measures...<br><br>"The U.S. Department of Commerce, International Trade Administration, began [in 2009] an antidumping duty investigation of imports of magnesia-carbon bricks from China and Mexico and a countervailing duty investigation of imports of magnesia-carbon bricks from China." (USGS, 2010) |

| NNR Profile | Magnesium Compounds (continued) |
|---|---|
| **US Scarcity Assessment** | That annual domestic magnesium compound utilization decreased by 50% since peaking (to date) in 1966, is a major indicator of declining American industrial preeminence and global economic competitiveness.<br><br>The US currently relies heavily on imported magnesium compounds, the vast majority (79%) of which comes from China. The quantity of magnesium compounds supplied by foreign sources during 2008 accounted for 54% of the total 2008 US utilization level.<br><br>Available evidence supports the contention that domestic magnesium compound supplies will remain insufficient to completely address domestic requirements going forward:<br><br>• The annual US magnesium compound extraction level decreased by 76% since peaking (to date) in 1966—a compelling indicator that domestic economically viable magnesium compound extraction has peaked permanently;<br>• The US has become increasingly reliant on magnesium compound imports since 1981; and<br>• The quantity of magnesium compounds extracted domestically during 2008 amounted to only 46% of the total 2008 US utilization level—a significant indicator of America's increasing dependence on foreign NNRs.<br><br>Barring future reductions in the domestic (US) magnesium compound requirement trajectory and/or major new domestic economically viable discoveries, magnesium compounds will almost certainly remain scarce domestically in the future. |

| Global NNR Scarcity | Scarce in 2008: Yes | Permanently Scarce: Unclear |
|---|---|---|
| **Historical Global Extraction Trends** | Annual global magnesium compound extraction levels generally increased during the 20$^{th}$ and 21$^{st}$ centuries, peaking temporarily in 1903, 1913, 1920, 1926, 1937, and 1943. Global magnesium compound extraction increased dramatically in 1958, then peaked temporarily in 1968 and 1986, before increasing into the new millennium; annual global magnesium compound extraction increased 44% between 2000 and 2008. | |

| Global Peak Extraction Year (thru 2008): 2008 | Years to Global Reserve Exhaustion: N/A |
|---|---|
| Projected Global Peak Extraction Year: N/A | Projected Global Peak Supply Year: N/A |

| **Interdependencies** | None identified. |
|---|---|

| NNR Profile | Magnesium Compounds (continued) |
|---|---|
| **Global Scarcity Assessment** | A 44% increase in the annual global magnesium compound extraction level between 2000 and 2008 implies a robust increase in magnesium compound demand during the pre-recession period, and a correspondingly robust increase in magnesium compound supply in response to increased global demand.<br><br>The fact that the price of magnesium compounds increased by a modest 2% during the 2000-2008 period indicates that global magnesium compound supply was nearly sufficient to completely address global requirements in 2008.<br><br>Available evidence regarding the likelihood that magnesium compound supplies will remain insufficient to completely address global requirements going forward is conflicting:<br><br>• A modest increase in the price of magnesium compounds during the 2000-2008 period induced a "nearly sufficient", but still inadequate, increase in magnesium compound supply—evidence of marginally tight global supply in 2008; and<br>• It is unclear whether the robust 4.7% compound annual growth rate (CAGR) in global magnesium compound extraction evidenced between 2000 and 2008—which was required to enable pre-recession global economic growth—can be reestablished and maintained going forward. A 4.7% CAGR would necessitate a continuous doubling in the annual global extraction level of magnesium compounds every 15 years; however<br>• Magnesium compound resources are considered by the USGS to "range from large to virtually unlimited".<br><br>It is therefore unclear whether magnesium compounds will remain scarce globally in the future, or whether globally available, economically viable magnesium compound supplies will be sufficient to completely address future global requirements. |

1. "Magnesia", Wikipedia, 2011 - http://en.wikipedia.org/wiki/Magnesia_(mineral).
2. "Magnasite", Wikipedia, 2011 - http://en.wikipedia.org/wiki/Magnasite.
3. "Olivine", Wikipedia, 2011 - http://en.wikipedia.org/wiki/Olivine.
4. "Magnesium Compound Statistics", Historical Statistics for Mineral and Material Commodities in the United States, USGS, 2010 –
http://minerals.usgs.gov/ds/2005/140/magnesiumcompounds.xls.
5. "Objective Capital Rare Earth and Minor Metals Investment Summit: Strategic Metals – Policy and Power", slide 5; J. Kooroshy, The Hague Centre for Strategic Studies, 2010 - http://www.slideshare.net/objectivecapital/objective-capital-rare-earth-and-minor-metals-investment-summit-strategic-metals-policy-and-power-jaakko-kooroshy.
6. "Fluorspar: The Cool Metal, T. Vulcan, Seeking Alpha, 2009 - http://seekingalpha.com/article/160670-fluorspar-the-cool-mineral.

| NNR Profile | Magnesium Metal |
|---|---|

## NNR Uses and Critical Applications

| Primary Uses | Magnesium is a fairly strong, lightweight, silvery-white metal used primarily as an alloying agent with aluminum and zinc; magnesium is also used as a fertilizer additive, as an antacid, and in fireworks, flares, and incendiary bombs; magnesium ions are essential to all living cells. |
|---|---|
| Critical Applications | Structural applications (aluminum alloy) in cars, aerospace equipment, electronic devices, and beverage cans; die casting (zinc alloy); desulfurization of iron/steel; reducing agent (uranium production); and titanium production. |

| NNR Criticality | NNR Criticality Classification: Indispensable |
|---|---|

| Substitutes | Magnesium substitutes, primarily aluminum and zinc, exist in castings, wrought, and structural applications; however, price/performance characteristics may be inferior. |
|---|---|
| Criticality Assessment | "Magnesium is the third most commonly used structural metal, following iron and aluminium." (Wikipedia)<br><br>Magnesium is indispensable to modern industrial existence. |

| US NNR Scarcity | Scarce in 2008: Yes | Permanently Scarce: Almost Certain |
|---|---|---|
| **2008 US Import Reliance:** 50% | | **2008 Domestic US Supply:** 50% |

| Historical US Import Trends | Until the late 1990s, the US was primarily a net exporter of magnesium metal; since that time, magnesium net imports have consistently exceeded 50% of US supply. |
|---|---|
| Historical US Usage Trends | Annual US magnesium metal utilization levels generally increased during the 20th century (especially during and after WWII), peaking temporarily in 1929, 1943 (spike), 1952 (spike), and 1973, before peaking permanently (to date) in 1997. Domestic magnesium metal utilization levels declined significantly in 2000, before recovering slightly thereafter; the 2008 US magnesium metal utilization level amounted to only 76% of the 1997 peak utilization level. |

| US Peak Production Year (thru 2008): 1943 | US Peak Utilization Year (thru 2008): 1997 |
|---|---|
| Potential Geopolitical US Supply Constraints | 40% of US magnesium metal imports come from Canada. |

| NNR Profile | Magnesium Metal (continued) |
|---|---|
| **US Scarcity Assessment** | "The United States has traditionally been the major world supplier of this metal [magnesium], supplying 45% of world production even as recently as 1995. Today, the US market share is at 7%, with a single domestic producer left…" (Wikipedia)<br><br>That annual domestic magnesium metal utilization decreased by 24% since peaking (to date) in 1997, is a significant indicator of declining American industrial preeminence and global economic competitiveness.<br><br>Available evidence supports the contention that domestic magnesium metal supplies will remain insufficient to completely address domestic requirements going forward:<br><br>• Annual US magnesium metal production has decreased to negligible levels since peaking (to date) in 1943—a compelling indicator that domestic economically viable magnesium metal production has peaked permanently;<br>• The US has become increasingly reliant on magnesium metal imports since 1996; and<br>• The quantity of magnesium metal extracted domestically during 2008 was negligible in comparison to the total 2008 US utilization level—a primary indicator of America's increasing dependence on foreign NNRs.<br><br>Barring future reductions in the domestic (US) magnesium metal requirement trajectory and/or major new domestic economically viable discoveries, magnesium metal will almost certainly remain scarce domestically in the future.<br><br>"Magnesium supplies in the United States were expected to remain tight." (USGS, 2008) |

| Global NNR Scarcity | Scarce in 2008: Yes | Permanently Scarce: Likely |
|---|---|---|
| **Historical Global Production Trends** | "As of 2005, China has taken over as the dominant supplier [of magnesium metal], pegged at 60% world market share, which increased from 4% in 1995." (Wikipedia)<br><br>Global magnesium metal production levels generally increased during the 20th and 21st centuries, peaking temporarily in 1943 (spike), 1953 (spike), 1980, and 1990, before increasing into the new millennium; annual global magnesium metal production increased 59% between 2000 and 2008.<br><br>"The only new [magnesium metal production] plants that were either being constructed or planned [in 2008] were in China." (USGS, 2008) | |

| Global Peak Production Year (thru 2008): 2007 | Years to Global Reserve Exhaustion: N/A |
|---|---|
| Projected Global Peak Production Year: 2010 | Projected Global Peak Supply Year: 2010 |

| Interdependencies | None identified. |
|---|---|

| NNR Profile | Magnesium Metal (continued) |
|---|---|
| **Global Scarcity Assessment** | "Tight magnesium supplies drove prices up in 2007." (USGS, 2008)<br><br>A 59% increase in the annual global magnesium metal production level between 2000 and 2008 implies a robust increase in global magnesium metal demand during the pre-recession period, and a correspondingly robust increase in global magnesium metal supply in response to increased global demand.<br><br>The fact that the price of magnesium metal increased by a substantial 99% during the 2000-2008 period indicates that global magnesium metal supply, while increasing considerably during the eight year period, remained insufficient to completely address global requirements in 2008.<br><br>Available evidence, albeit somewhat conflicting, supports the contention that global magnesium metal supplies will likely remain insufficient to completely address global requirements going forward:<br><br>• Global magnesium metal reserves are considered by the USGS to be "sufficient to supply current and future requirements"; however<br>• The global magnesium metal extraction level is projected to peak in approximately 2010;<br>• The global magnesium metal supply level is projected to peak in approximately 2010 as well;<br>• The considerable increase in global magnesium metal supply levels between 2000 and 2008 failed to prevent a substantial price increase during the period—compelling evidence of unaddressed global requirements in 2008; and<br>• It is questionable whether the robust 6% compound annual growth rate (CAGR) in global magnesium metal production evidenced between 2000 and 2008—an interval during which magnesium metal became scarce globally despite a significant increase in production—can be reestablished, much less increased, going forward. A 6% CAGR would necessitate a continuous doubling in the annual global production level of magnesium metal every 12 years.<br><br>Barring future reductions in the global magnesium metal requirement trajectory and/or major new economically viable discoveries, magnesium metal will likely remain scarce globally in the future.<br><br>"As steel production increases it will create a demand for specialty metals thereby positively affecting the prices of all strategic metals including the three "M's", Manganese, Magnesium and Molybdenum as well as cobalt, niobium, tungsten, vanadium and titanium." (Kitco, 2010) |

1. "Magnesium", Wikipedia, 2011 - http://en.wikipedia.org/wiki/Magnesium.
2. "Magnesium Metal Statistics", Historical Statistics for Mineral and Material Commodities in the United States, USGS, 2010 – http://minerals.usgs.gov/ds/2005/140/magnesium.xls.
3. Rare Earths Pre-Curser To Other Metal Shortages Dominated By China Production? L. Reaugh, Kitco, 2010 - http://www.kitco.com/ind/Reaugh/feb052010.html.

| NNR Profile | Manganese |
|---|---|
| **NNR Uses and Critical Applications** | |
| **Primary Uses** | Manganese is a hard, brittle, difficult to fuse, silvery-gray metal used as an aluminum, iron, and steel alloy (stainless steel); manganese is also used as a gasoline additive, as a pigment, and in (disposable) dry cell batteries; manganese is required by all living organisms. |
| **Critical Applications** | Metallurgical alloy; manganese is essential to iron and steel production. "Most [manganese] ore consumption was related to steel production, directly in pig iron manufacture and indirectly through upgrading ore to ferroalloys." (USGS, 2010) |

| NNR Criticality | NNR Criticality Classification: Indispensible |
|---|---|
| **Substitutes** | "Manganese has no satisfactory substitute in its major applications." (USGS, 2010) While substitutes exist in most non-metallurgical applications, manganese has no substitutes in its critical metallurgical applications. |
| **Criticality Assessment** | "You can't make steel without Manganese and if you can't make steel, the world stops." (Reser: Gilbertson (BHP Billiton) quote, 2010) As an indispensable element in the production of iron and steel, manganese is indispensible to modern industrial existence. |

| US NNR Scarcity | Scarce in 2008: Yes | Permanently Scarce: Almost Certain |
|---|---|---|
| **2008 US Import Reliance:** 100% | | **2008 Domestic US Supply:** 0% |
| **Historical US Import Trends** | The US has been heavily reliant on manganese imports throughout the 20th and 21st centuries. | |
| **Historical US Usage Trends** | Annual US manganese utilization levels generally increased during the first three quarters of the 20th century—in a fluctuating manner—peaking temporarily in 1907, 1918 1937, 1942, 1957, and 1968, before peaking permanently (to date) in 1973 and generally declining during the remainder of the century. Domestic manganese utilization experienced a slight increase during the early years of the 21st century; however, the 2008 US manganese utilization level still amounted to only 62% of the 1973 peak utilization level. | |
| **US Peak Extraction Year (thru 2008):** 1918 | | **US Peak Utilization Year (thru 2008):** 1973 |
| **Potential Geopolitical US Supply Constraints** | 34% of US manganese imports come from South Africa, 21% (57% of US ore imports) come from Gabon; over 50% of proven global manganese reserves are located in South Africa and the Ukraine (combined). "…on June 23 [2009], the EU announced that both it and the U.S. 'had requested WTO consultations with China regarding China's export restrictions on a number of key raw materials, which it considers are in clear breach of international trade rules. In the words of the EU announcement: 'European industries have raised concerns for a number of years on export restrictions - quotas, export duties and minimum export prices - which China applies on key raw materials, such as yellow phosphorous, bauxite, coke, fluorspar, magnesium, manganese, silicon metal, silicon carbide and zinc. Some of these resources cannot be found elsewhere.'" (Seeking Alpha, 2009) | |

| NNR Profile | Manganese (continued) |
|---|---|
| **US Scarcity Assessment** | "Manganese is the most critical metal at risk to supply and restriction in the United States as there is no US production." (AMI, 2010)<br><br>That annual domestic manganese utilization decreased by 38% since peaking (to date) in 1973, is a significant indicator of declining American industrial preeminence and global economic competitiveness.<br><br>The US currently relies exclusively on imported manganese, the majority of which comes from countries located in Africa.<br><br>Available evidence supports the contention that domestic manganese supplies will remain insufficient to completely address domestic requirements going forward:<br><br>• US manganese extraction ceased entirely in 1991—a significant indicator of America's increasing dependence on foreign NNRs, and a compelling indicator that domestic economically viable manganese extraction has peaked permanently;<br>• Ores containing 35% or more manganese have not been extracted domestically since 1970; and<br>• The quantity of manganese extracted domestically during 1918, the year of peak (to date) domestic manganese extraction, amounted to only 48% of the 2008 total US utilization level.<br><br>Barring future reductions in the domestic (US) manganese requirement trajectory and/or major new domestic economically viable discoveries, manganese will almost certainly remain scarce domestically in the future. |
| **Global NNR Scarcity** | **Scarce in 2008: Yes**    **Permanently Scarce: Almost Certain** |
| **Historical Global Extraction Trends** | "China was the largest producer [in 2009] of Mn [ore] units (2.7 million mt) [25% of global total], followed by South Africa (1.9 million mt), Australia (1.8 million mt), Brazil (1 million mt), Gabon (956K mt), India (845K mt) and Kazakhstan (377K mt)." (IMI, 2010)<br><br>Annual global manganese extraction levels generally increased during the first three quarters of the 20th century, peaking temporarily in 1907, 1913, 1918, 1930, 1937, 1966, 1976, and 1989, before declining dramatically during the remainder of the century. Manganese extraction levels surged, however, between 2000 and 2008, increasing by 91% during that period.<br><br>"China continued to be the world's largest Mn [manganese] alloy producing country having produced nearly 6.6 million mt [in 2009]. It accounted for almost 57% of global output." (IMI, 2010) |

| Global Peak Extraction Year (thru 2008): 2008 | Years to Global Reserve Exhaustion: 17 |
|---|---|
| **Projected Global Peak Extraction Year:** 2024 | **Projected Global Peak Supply Year:** 2050 |
| **Interdependencies** | None identified. |

| NNR Profile | Manganese (continued) |
|---|---|
| **Global Scarcity Assessment** | "…the average weekly spot market price had tripled to $8.65 per metric ton unit during the first 10 months of 2007 owing to increased global demand for manganese ore, particularly in China and India." (USGS, 2008)<br><br>A 91% increase in the annual global manganese production level between 2000 and 2008 implies a robust increase in global manganese demand during the pre-recession period, and a correspondingly robust increase in global manganese supply in response to increased global demand.<br><br>The fact that the price of manganese increased by an extraordinary 227% during the 2000-2008 period indicates that global manganese supply, while increasing considerably during the eight year period, remained woefully insufficient to completely address global requirements in 2008.<br><br>Available evidence supports the contention that global manganese supplies will remain insufficient to completely address global requirements going forward:<br><br>• Proven global manganese reserves would exhaust in only 17 years, assuming the restoration of pre-recession utilization levels and growth rates;<br>• The global manganese extraction level is projected to peak in approximately 2024;<br>• The global manganese supply level is projected to peak in approximately 2050;<br>• The considerable increase in global manganese supply levels between 2000 and 2008 failed to prevent an extraordinary price increase during the period—compelling evidence of unaddressed global requirements in 2008; and<br>• It is questionable whether the extremely robust 8.4% compound annual growth rate (CAGR) in global manganese production evidenced between 2000 and 2008—an interval during which manganese became scarce globally despite an extraordinary increase in production—can be reestablished, much less increased, going forward. An 8.4% CAGR would necessitate a continuous doubling in the annual global production level of manganese every 9 years.<br><br>Barring future reductions in the global manganese requirement trajectory and/or major new economically viable discoveries, manganese will almost certainly remain scarce globally in the future. |

1. "Manganese", Wikipedia, 2011 - http://en.wikipedia.org/wiki/Manganese.
2. "Manganese Statistics", Historical Statistics for Mineral and Material Commodities in the United States, USGS, 2010 – http://minerals.usgs.gov/ds/2005/140/manganese.xls.
3. "[Manganese] Production", International Manganese Institute (IMI), 2010 - http://www.manganese.org/about_mn/production.
4. "Expanding Manganese Resource at Artillery Peak Grows by 45%", L. Reaugh, American Manganese, Inc. (AMI) 2010 - http://www.americanmanganeseinc.com/expanding-manganese-resource-at-artillery-peak-grows-by-45/.
5. "American Manganese Production", K. Reser, Financial Sense University, 2010 - http://www.financialsensearchive.com/fsu/editorials/2010/0126.html.

6. "Fluorspar: The Cool Metal, T. Vulcan, Seeking Alpha, 2009 - http://seekingalpha.com/article/160670-fluorspar-the-cool-mineral.

| NNR Profile | Mercury | |
|---|---|---|
| **NNR Uses and Critical Applications** | | |
| **Primary Uses** | Mercury is a heavy silvery-white metal used in chlorine-caustic soda production, and in thermometers, manometers, barometers, sphygmomanometers, float valves, electrical switches and lighting (compact florescent light bulbs), and scientific apparatus; mercury also forms amalgams with metals such as gold and aluminum. | |
| **Critical Applications** | None identified. | |
| **NNR Criticality** | **NNR Criticality Classification: Declining** | |
| **Substitutes** | Viable substitutes for mercury exist in all application areas; price/performance attributes vary. | |
| **Criticality Assessment** | Mercury use is generally declining due to its toxicity; in the event that demand for compact florescent light bulbs increases going forward, mercury will become increasingly important. | |
| **US NNR Scarcity** | **Scarce in 2008: No** | **Permanently Scarce: Unclear** |
| **2008 US Import Reliance:** 0% | | **2008 Domestic US Supply:** 100% |
| **Historical US Import Trends** | "The United States is a leading exporter of mercury…" (USGS, 2008) Historically, the US has been both a net exporter and a net importer of mercury; the US has been a mercury net exporter since 2003. | |
| **Historical US Usage Trends** | Annual US mercury utilization levels generally increased during the first two thirds of the 20th century, peaking temporarily in 1907, 1918, 1937, 1957, and 1965, before peaking permanently (to date) in 1964 and declining continuously thereafter; the 2000 (latest available data) US mercury utilization level amounted to only 7% of the 1964 peak utilization level. "Governmental regulations and environmental standards are likely to continue as major factors in domestic mercury recycling, supply, and demand." (USGS, 2010) | |
| **US Peak Extraction Year (thru 2008):** 1943 | | **US Peak Utilization Year (thru 2008):** 1964 |
| **Potential Geopolitical US Supply Constraints** | China accounts for two thirds of global mercury extraction (2005); 60% of US mercury imports come from Peru; however, the US is a net mercury exporter. | |

| NNR Profile | Mercury (continued) |
|---|---|
| **US Scarcity Assessment** | "Mercury has not been produced as a primary commodity in the United States since 1992..." (USGS, 2010)<br><br>That annual domestic mercury utilization decreased by 93% since peaking (to date) in 1964, is primarily due to mercury's toxicity.<br><br>The US is currently addressing its total requirement for mercury through domestic supplies.<br><br>Available evidence regarding the likelihood that domestic mercury supplies will remain sufficient to completely address domestic requirements going forward is conflicting.<br><br>• Annual US mercury extraction peaked (to date) in 1943, before ceasing entirely in 1993. It is unclear to what extent these phenomena resulted from declining domestic/global requirements, insufficient domestically available, economically viable supply, or a combination of both.<br><br>It is therefore unclear whether domestically available, economically viable mercury supplies will remain sufficient to completely address domestic requirements, or whether mercury will become scarce domestically in the not-too-distant future. |

| Global NNR Scarcity | Scarce in 2008: Yes | Permanently Scarce: Unclear |
|---|---|---|
| **Historical Global Extraction Trends** | Annual global mercury utilization levels generally increased during the first three quarters of the 20th century, peaking temporarily in 1906, 1911, 1929, 1941, 1958, and 1965, before peaking permanently (to date) in 1971, and declining dramatically thereafter; annual global mercury extraction decreased 3% between 2000 and 2008.<br><br>"Former mines in Italy, the United States and Mexico which once produced a large proportion of the world supply have now been completely mined out..." (Wikipedia) | |

| Global Peak Extraction Year (thru 2008): 1971 | Years to Global Reserve Exhaustion: 35* |
|---|---|
| **Projected Global Peak Extraction Year:** 1970 | **Projected Global Peak Supply Year:** N/A |
| **Interdependencies** | Mercury can be produced as a byproduct of gold and silver processing. |

| NNR Profile | Mercury (continued) |
|---|---|
| **Global Scarcity Assessment** | "The rising price of gold has driven the global demand for mercury that is used for artisanal gold mining…" (USGS, 2008) <br><br> A 3% decrease in the annual global mercury extraction level between 2000 and 2008 implies either a decrease in global mercury demand or insufficient global mercury supplies during the pre-recession period. <br><br> The fact that the price of mercury increased by an extraordinary 210% during the 2000-2008 period, indicates that the declining global supply of mercury was woefully insufficient to completely address global requirements in 2008. <br><br> Available evidence regarding the likelihood that global mercury supplies will remain insufficient to completely address global requirements going forward is conflicting: <br><br> • Proven global mercury reserves would exhaust in only 35 years, assuming that future annual utilization levels remain constant at the 2008 level; <br> • The global mercury extraction level was projected to peak in 1970; and <br> • Sufficient mercury supply could not be brought online between 2000 and 2008 to prevent an extraordinary price increase during the period—compelling evidence of unaddressed global requirements in 2008; however <br> • The annual global mercury extraction level decreased by 88% since reaching its peak (to date) level in 1971—although it is unclear whether this phenomenon resulted from declining global requirements, insufficient globally available, economically viable supply, or a combination of both. <br><br> It is therefore unclear whether mercury will remain scarce globally in the future, or whether globally available, economically viable mercury supplies will be sufficient to completely address future global requirements. <br><br> "Non-mercury technology (new technology) for the production of chlorine and caustic soda and the ultimate closure of the world's mercury-cell chlor-alkali plants will put tons of mercury on the global market for recycling, sale, or storage." (USGS, 2008) |

\* Reserve to Production data.

1. "Mercury", Wikipedia, 2011 - http://en.wikipedia.org/wiki/Mercury_(element).
2. "Mercury Statistics", Historical Statistics for Mineral and Material Commodities in the United States, USGS, 2010 – http://minerals.usgs.gov/ds/2005/140/mercury.xls.

| NNR Profile | Mica (Natural) Scrap and Flake |
|---|---|
| **NNR Uses and Critical Applications** | |
| **Primary Uses** | Micas are a group of sheet minerals having highly perfect basal cleavage; scrap and flake mica, which are more abundant than sheet mica, are used in joint (drywall) compound, oil-well drilling additives, paint, roofing, and rubber products. |
| **Critical Applications** | None identified. |

| NNR Profile | Mica (Natural) Scrap and Flake (continued) | |
|---|---|---|
| **NNR Criticality** | **NNR Criticality Classification: Important** | |
| **Substitutes** | Technically and economically viable scrap and flake mica substitutes, including synthetic micas, diatomite, perlite, and vermiculite, are generally available. | |
| **Criticality Assessment** | Micas are primarily valued as insulators, due to their electrical and thermal characteristics; synthetic and natural substitutes are generally available. | |
| **US NNR Scarcity** | **Scarce in 2008: Yes** | **Permanently Scarce: Almost Certain** |
| **2008 US Import Reliance:** 18% | **2008 Domestic US Supply:** 82% | |
| **Historical US Import Trends** | Historically, the US has been both a net importer and a net exporter of scrap and flake mica; imports have increased significantly since 1984.<br><br>"Imported mica scrap and flake is primarily used for making mica paper and as a filler and reinforcer in plastics." (USGS, 2008) | |
| **Historical US Usage Trends** | Annual US scrap and flake mica utilization levels generally increased during the 20th century—in a cyclical manner—peaking temporarily in 1913, 1955, 1973, 1984, and 1998, before increasing into the new millennium. | |
| **US Peak Extraction Year (thru 2008):** 1984 | **US Peak Utilization Year (thru 2008):** 2006 | |
| **Potential Geopolitical US Supply Constraints** | None identified. | |
| **US Scarcity Assessment** | The US currently relies marginally on imported scrap and flake mica, the majority of which comes from Canada (35%) and China (33%). The quantities of scrap and flake mica supplied by foreign sources during 2008 accounted for 18% of the total 2008 US utilization level.<br><br>Available evidence supports the contention that domestic scrap and flake mica supplies will remain insufficient to completely address domestic requirements going forward:<br><br>• While US scrap and flake mica utilization increased into the new millennium, the annual US scrap and flake mica extraction level decreased by 36% since peaking (to date) in 1984—a compelling indicator that domestic economically viable scrap and flake mica extraction has peaked permanently;<br>• The US has become increasingly reliant on scrap and flake mica imports since 1984; and<br>• The quantity of scrap and flake mica produced domestically during 2008 amounted to only 82% of the total 2008 US utilization level—an indicator of America's increasing dependence on foreign NNRs.<br><br>Barring future reductions in the domestic (US) scrap and flake mica requirement trajectory and/or major new domestic economically viable discoveries, scrap and flake mica will almost certainly remain scarce domestically in the future. | |
| **Global NNR Scarcity** | **Scarce in 2008: Yes** | **Permanently Scarce: Unclear** |
| **Historical Global Extraction Trends** | "The United States [20%], Russia [28%], and Finland [20%] were major world producers of scrap and flake mica in 2007…" (USGS, 2008)<br><br>Annual global scrap and flake mica extraction levels generally increased during the 20th and 21st centuries, peaking temporarily in 1928, 1937, 1955, 1973, 1978 and 1987, before peaking permanently (to date) in 2005; annual global scrap and flake mica extraction increased 14% between 2000 and 2008. | |

| NNR Profile | Mica (Natural) Scrap and Flake (continued) | |
|---|---|---|
| **Global Peak Extraction Year (thru 2008):** 2005 | **Years to Global Reserve Exhaustion:** N/A | |
| **Projected Global Peak Extraction Year:** N/A | **Projected Global Peak Supply Year:** N/A | |
| **Interdependencies** | Scrap mica can be produced as a byproduct of feldspar and kaolin extraction. | |
| **Global Scarcity Assessment** | A 14% increase in the annual global scrap and flake mica extraction level between 2000 and 2008 implies an increase in global scrap and flake mica demand during the pre-recession period, and a corresponding increase in global scrap and flake mica supply in response to increased global demand.<br><br>The fact that the price of scrap and flake mica increased by 22% during the 2000-2008 period indicates that global scrap and flake mica supply, while increasing during the eight year period, remained insufficient to completely address global requirements in 2008.<br><br>Available evidence regarding the likelihood that global scrap and flake mica supplies will remain insufficient to completely address global requirements going forward is conflicting:<br><br>• An increase in the price of scrap and flake mica during the 2000-2008 period induced a nominal yet insufficient increase in scrap and flake mica supply— evidence of tight global supply in 2008; however<br>• Proven global scrap and flake mica reserves are considered by the USGS to be "more than adequate".<br><br>It is therefore unclear whether scrap and flake mica will remain scarce globally in the future, or whether globally available, economically viable scrap and flake mica supplies will be sufficient to completely address future global requirements. | |

1. "Mica", Wikipedia, 2011 - http://en.wikipedia.org/wiki/Mica.
2. "Mica (Scrap and Flake) Statistics", Historical Statistics for Mineral and Material Commodities in the United States, USGS, 2010 – http://minerals.usgs.gov/ds/2005/140/micascrap.xls.

| NNR Profile | Mica (Natural) Sheet | |
|---|---|---|
| **NNR Uses and Critical Applications** | | |
| **Primary Uses** | Micas are a group of sheet minerals having highly perfect basal cleavage; sheet mica, which is less abundant than scrap and flake mica, is used in electronic (capacitors) and in electrical (insulators) applications. | |
| **Critical Applications** | None identified. | |
| **NNR Criticality** | **NNR Criticality Classification: Declining** | |
| **Substitutes** | Economically viable synthetic and natural substitutes exist for all sheet mica applications. | |
| **Criticality Assessment** | Sheet mica serves several niche applications for which viable substitutes are readily available. | |
| **US NNR Scarcity** | **Scarce in 2008: Yes** | **Permanently Scarce: Almost Certain** |
| **2008 US Import Reliance:** 100% | **2008 Domestic US Supply:** 0% | |

| NNR Profile | Mica (Natural) Sheet (continued) |
|---|---|
| **Historical US Import Trends** | "These domestic [sheet mica] resources are uneconomic because of the high cost of hand labor required to mine and process sheet mica from pegmatites." (USGS, 2010)<br><br>With the exception of a few years in the late 1970s, the US has been reliant on sheet mica imports since the 1940s; the US has been totally reliant in sheet mica imports since 1977.<br><br>"Demand for sheet mica in 2007 increased for the second year in a row, following a 27% increase in imports in 2006." (USGS, 2008) |
| **Historical US Usage Trends** | Annual US sheet mica utilization levels varied considerably during the 20th and 21st centuries, peaking temporarily in 1913, 1929, 1937, and 1943, before peaking permanently (to date) in 1950 and generally declining—in a fluctuating manner—thereafter; the 2007 US sheet mica utilization level amounted to only 5% of the 1950 peak utilization level. |

| US Peak Extraction Year (thru 2008): 1943 | US Peak Utilization Year (thru 2008): 1950 |
|---|---|
| **Potential Geopolitical US Supply Constraints** | 23% of US sheet mica imports come from China; 20% come from Brazil, and 19% come from India. |
| **US Scarcity Assessment** | "Future [US sheet mica] supplies were expected to come increasingly from imports, primarily from Brazil, China, India, and Russia." (USGS, 2010)<br><br>That annual domestic sheet mica utilization decreased by 95% since peaking (to date) in 1950, is an indicator of declining American industrial preeminence and global economic competitiveness.<br><br>The US currently relies exclusively on imported sheet mica, the majority (60+%) of which comes from the BRIC countries (Brazil, Russia, India, and China).<br><br>Available evidence supports the contention that domestic sheet mica supplies will remain insufficient to completely address domestic requirements going forward:<br><br>• US sheet mica extraction ceased entirely in 1976—an indicator of America's increasing dependence on foreign NNRs, and a compelling indicator that domestic economically viable sheet mica extraction has peaked permanently; and<br>• US sheet mica reserves are considered by the USGS to be "very small" and "uneconomic".<br><br>Barring future reductions in the domestic (US) sheet mica requirement trajectory and/or major new domestic economically viable discoveries, sheet mica will almost certainly remain scarce domestically in the future.<br><br>"Prices for imported sheet mica also were expected to increase [in 2009], and good-quality sheet mica remained in short supply." (USGS, 2010) |

| Global NNR Scarcity | Scarce in 2008: No | Permanently Scarce: Unclear |
|---|---|---|
| **Historical Global Extraction Trends** | Annual global sheet mica extraction levels generally increased during the first three quarters of the 20th century, peaking temporarily in 1906, 1913, 1918, 1929, 1937, 1941, and 1951, before peaking permanently (to date) in 1975, and generally declining thereafter; annual global sheet mica extraction remained constant between 2000 and 2008. | |

| NNR Profile | Mica (Natural) Sheet (continued) |
|---|---|
| Global Peak Extraction Year (thru 2008): 1975 | Years to Global Reserve Exhaustion: N/A |
| Projected Global Peak Extraction Year: N/A | Projected Global Peak Supply Year: N/A |

| Interdependencies | Sheet mica is sometimes produced as a byproduct of gemstone and feldspar mining. |
|---|---|
| **Global Scarcity Assessment** | A constant annual global sheet mica extraction level between 2000 and 2008 implies stagnant global sheet mica demand and supply during the pre-recession period.<br><br>The fact that the price of sheet mica decreased by 17% during the 2000-2008 period indicates that the global supply of sheet mica in 2008 was sufficient to completely address 2008 global requirements.<br><br>Available evidence regarding the likelihood that global sheet mica supplies will remain sufficient to completely address global requirements going forward is conflicting:<br><br>• Assuming that annual sheet mica extraction did in fact remain constant between 2000 and 2008, a period of rapidly increasing global economic growth, and given that global sheet mica supplies were sufficient to completely address global requirements in 2008, it would seem likely that future global sheet mica supplies would remain sufficient to completely address global requirements going forward; however<br>• The annual global sheet mica extraction level decreased by 90% since reaching its peak (to date) level in 1975, although it is unclear whether this phenomenon resulted from declining global requirements, insufficient globally available, economically viable supply, or a combination of both; and<br>• The USGS expects future sheet mica scarcity, especially with regard to high quality sheet mica.<br><br>It is therefore unclear whether globally available, economically viable sheet mica supplies will remain sufficient to completely address future global requirements, or whether sheet mica will become scarce globally in the not-too-distant future. |

1. "Mica", Wikipedia, 2011 - http://en.wikipedia.org/wiki/Mica.
2. "Mica (Sheet) Statistics", Historical Statistics for Mineral and Material Commodities in the United States, USGS, 2010 – http://minerals.usgs.gov/ds/2005/140/micasheet.xls.

| NNR Profile | Molybdenum |
|---|---|
| **NNR Uses and Critical Applications** | |
| **Primary Uses** | Molybdenum is a silvery-white metal with a very high melting point, which is used as an alloy, superalloy, catalyst, lubricant, fertilizer, adhesive, and pigment; molybdenum is also a required element in higher life forms. |
| **Critical Applications** | High-strength steel alloy used in aircraft parts, electrical contacts, industrial motors, tool steels, and filaments. <br><br> "…molybdenum is widely utilized for its capacity to withstand high temperatures as well as high pressures. Molybdenum's high tensile strength makes it perfect for use in manufacturing steel alloys…" (Livestrong, 2010) |

| NNR Criticality | NNR Criticality Classification: Critical |
|---|---|
| **Substitutes** | While potential substitutes for molybdenum are being investigated, there are no currently viable substitutes in its primary application as a steel and cast iron alloy. |
| **Criticality Assessment** | "…because of the availability and versatility of molybdenum, industry has sought to develop new materials that benefit from the alloying properties of the metal." (USGS, 2010) <br><br> Molybdenum plays a key support role as an alloy in high strength, heat resistant iron and steel applications. <br><br> "Among the 80 naturally occurring metals, molybdenum is one of the 40 or so that can be considered as having major industrial importance." (HardAssets, 2008) |

| US NNR Scarcity | Scarce in 2008: No | Permanently Scarce: Unclear |
|---|---|---|
| **2008 US Import Reliance: 0%** | | **2008 Domestic US Supply:** 100% |
| **Historical US Import Trends** | The US has been a net exporter of molybdenum since 1939; however, annual US molybdenum net exports decreased since 1989, and decreased significantly during the new millennium. | |
| **Historical US Usage Trends** | Annual US molybdenum utilization levels generally increased—in a fluctuating manner—during the 20th and 21st centuries, peaking temporarily in 1903, 1918, 1942, 1954, 1968, 1973m 1979, 1988, and 1994, before increasing into the new millennium and peaking (to date) in 2006. | |
| **US Peak Extraction Year (thru 2008):** 1980 | | **US Peak Utilization Year (thru 2008):** 2006 |
| **Potential Geopolitical US Supply Constraints** | Nearly 40% of proven global molybdenum reserves are located in China (30% are located in the US); 52% of US ferromolybdenum imports come from China; however, the US is currently a net molybdenum exporter. <br><br> In 2010, China imposed a 25,500 metric ton quota on molybdenum exports. (Hague, 2010) | |

| NNR Profile | Molybdenum (continued) |
|---|---|
| **US Scarcity Assessment** | "U.S. mine output of molybdenum in concentrate in 2007 decreased slightly from that of 2006. U.S. imports for consumption increased an estimated 17% from those of 2006, while the U.S. exports increased only about 2% from those of 2006." (USGS, 2008)<br><br>The US is currently addressing its total requirement for molybdenum through domestic supplies.<br><br>Available evidence regarding the likelihood that domestic molybdenum supplies will remain sufficient to completely address domestic requirements going forward is conflicting:<br><br>• The 2008 US molybdenum extraction level exceeded the 2008 US molybdenum utilization level by 55%; however<br>• While US molybdenum utilization increased into the new millennium, the domestic molybdenum extraction level decreased by 18% since peaking (to date) in 1980—a compelling indicator that domestic economically viable molybdenum extraction has peaked permanently; and<br>• Net US molybdenum exports decreased by 61% since peaking in 1989.<br><br>It is therefore unclear whether domestically available, economically viable molybdenum supplies will remain sufficient to completely address future domestic requirements, or whether molybdenum will become scarce domestically in the not-too-distant future. |

| Global NNR Scarcity | Scarce in 2008: Yes | Permanently Scarce: Almost Certain |
|---|---|---|
| **Historical Global Extraction Trends** | "The majority of the world's moly [molybdenum] supply flows from two distinct types of mining operations:<br><br>• as a by-product - typically of copper mining (in Canada, Chile, Peru and the U.S.) - amounting to around 61% of total moly output (2007)<br>• as a primary product (in Canada, China and the U.S.)." (HardAssets, 2008)<br><br>Annual global molybdenum extraction/production levels generally increased during both the 20th and 21st centuries, peaking temporarily in 1918, 1928, 1943, 1960, 1980, and 1989, before increasing into the early years of the new millennium; annual global molybdenum extraction increased 61% between 2000 and 2008. | |

| Global Peak Extraction Year (thru 2008): 2008 | Years to Global Reserve Exhaustion: 20 |
|---|---|
| Projected Global Peak Extraction Year: 2025 | Projected Global Peak Supply Year: 2035 |

| **Interdependencies** | Molybdenum can be recovered as a byproduct of copper and tungsten processing. |
|---|---|

| NNR Profile | Molybdenum (continued) |
|---|---|
| **Global Scarcity Assessment** | "China's high level of steel production and consumption continued to generate strong internal consumption of molybdenum [in 2007]. This consumption, coupled with limited production in the Huludao area of Liaoning Province, led to reduced Chinese exports in 2006 and 2007, and continued to support historically high molybdenum prices." (USGS, 2008)<br><br>A 61% increase in the annual global molybdenum extraction/production level between 2000 and 2008 implies a robust increase in global molybdenum demand during the pre-recession period, and a correspondingly robust increase in global molybdenum supply in response to increased global demand.<br><br>The fact that the price of molybdenum increased by a phenomenal 795% during the 2000-2008 period indicates that global molybdenum supply, while increasing considerably during the eight year period, remained woefully insufficient to completely address global requirements in 2008.<br><br>Available evidence supports the contention that global molybdenum supplies will remain insufficient to completely address global requirements going forward:<br><br>• Proven global molybdenum reserves would exhaust in only 20 years, assuming the restoration of pre-recession utilization levels and growth rates;<br>• The global molybdenum extraction level is projected to peak in approximately 2025;<br>• The global molybdenum supply level is projected to peak in approximately 2035;<br>• The considerable increase in global molybdenum supply levels between 2000 and 2008 failed to prevent a phenomenal price increase during the period—compelling evidence of unaddressed global requirements in 2008; and<br>• It is questionable whether the robust 6.2% compound annual growth rate (CAGR) in global molybdenum production evidenced between 2000 and 2008—an interval during which molybdenum became scarce globally despite a significant increase in production—can be reestablished, much less increased, going forward. A 6.2% CAGR would necessitate a continuous doubling in the annual global production level of molybdenum every 11.5 years.<br><br>Barring future reductions in the global molybdenum requirement trajectory and/or major new economically viable discoveries, molybdenum will almost certainly remain scarce globally in the future.<br><br>"Molybdenum prices declined during the first quarter of 2009 only to begin a gradual increase in the third quarter." (USGS, 2010) |

1. "Molybdenum", Wikipedia, 2011 - http://en.wikipedia.org/wiki/Molybdenum.
2. "Molybdenum Statistics", Historical Statistics for Mineral and Material Commodities in the United States, USGS, 2010 – http://minerals.usgs.gov/ds/2005/140/molybdenum.xls.
3. "Objective Capital Rare Earth and Minor Metals Investment Summit: Strategic Metals – Policy and Power", slide 5; J. Kooroshy, The Hague Centre for Strategic Studies, 2010 -

http://www.slideshare.net/objectivecapital/objective-capital-rare-earth-and-minor-metals-investment-summit-strategic-metals-policy-and-power-jaakko-kooroshy.
4. "Why is Molybdenum an Important Metal?" Livestrong, 2010 -
http://www.livestrong.com/article/265150-why-is-molybdenum-an-important-metal/.
5. "Molybdenum: Mighty Tough", T. Vulcan, Hard Assets, 2008 -
http://www.hardassetsinvestor.com/features-and-interviews/1/927-molybdenum-tough-mighty-tough.html.

| NNR Profile | Natural Gas (Gas) |
|---|---|
| **NNR Uses and Critical Applications** | |
| **Primary Uses** | Natural gas is a colorless odorless "fossil fuel" used as a primary energy source, both domestically and globally. Natural gas is also a fertilizer feedstock, and is a source of hydrogen for various industrial applications (including hydrogen fuel cells). |
| **Critical Applications** | Natural gas is the largest source of cooking and central heating energy in the US (~50%); gas also plays a major role in domestic and global electricity generation, and as the primary feedstock for "fixed nitrogen" (ammonia) in NPK fertilizers. |

| NNR Criticality | NNR Criticality Classification: Indispensible |
|---|---|
| **Substitutes** | Other nonrenewable and renewable energy sources can be substituted for natural gas in most applications; although price/performance, scalability, and general availability vary per application. |
| **Criticality Assessment** | Unless and until alternative or renewable energy sources prove viable on a large scale, natural gas will remain a primary domestic and global energy source; natural gas is indispensible to modern industrial existence. |

| US NNR Scarcity | Scarce in 2008: Yes | Permanently Scarce: Likely |
|---|---|---|
| **2008 US Import Reliance:** 13% | **2008 Domestic US Supply:** 87% | |
| **Historical US Import Trends** | Historically, the US has been both a net exporter and a net importer of natural gas however, since 1958 the US has become an increasingly heavy net importer of natural gas. | |
| **Historical US Usage Trends** | Annual US natural gas utilization levels generally increased during the middle years of the 20th century, peaked temporarily in 1973, declined through the middle 1980s, then generally increased slowly but steadily thereafter. | |
| **US Peak Extraction Year (thru 2008):** 1973 | **US Peak Utilization Year (thru 2008):** 2008 | |
| **Potential Geopolitical US Supply Constraints** | Unlike coal and oil, which are easily transported internationally via tanker ship, natural gas is difficult and expensive to transport except by pipeline. The US is therefore unable to import large quantities of natural gas from countries other than Canada, even though global supplies may remain relatively plentiful well into the 2020s. | |

| NNR Profile | Natural Gas (Gas) continued |
|---|---|
| **US Scarcity Assessment** | "Average natural gas prices generally increase [between 2008 and 2035] in the Reference case [long term EIA forecast], as higher cost resources are brought on line to meet [US] demand growth." (EIA, 2010)<br><br>The US currently relies marginally on imported natural gas, a vast majority (nearly 100%) of which comes from Canada. The quantity of natural gas supplied by foreign sources during 2008 accounted for 13% of the total 2008 US utilization level.<br><br>Available evidence supports the contention that domestic natural gas supplies will likely remain insufficient to completely address domestic requirements going forward:<br><br>• While US natural gas utilization increased into the new millennium, the annual US natural gas extraction level decreased by 4% since peaking (to date) in 1973—an indicator that domestic natural gas extraction has likely peaked permanently;<br>• The US has become increasingly reliant on natural gas imports since 1958;<br>• The quantity of natural gas extracted domestically during 2008 amounted to only 89% of the total 2008 US utilization level—a primary indicator of America's increasing dependence on foreign NNRs; and<br>• The quantity of natural gas extracted domestically during 1973, the year of peak (to date) domestic natural gas extraction, amounted to only 93% of the 2008 total US utilization level.<br><br>Barring future reductions in the domestic (US) natural gas requirement trajectory and/or major new domestic economically viable discoveries, natural gas will likely remain scarce domestically in the future.<br><br>Under the most optimistic circumstances, the US natural gas extraction plateau might be extended until approximately 2020, as nonconventional domestic sources such as coal bed methane, tight sands, gas shales, and offshore fields temporarily offset declining US supplies of conventional onshore natural gas.<br><br>Note that the US Energy Information Administration (EIA) takes an opposing view regarding future domestic natural gas supplies:<br><br>"In December 2009 the US Energy Information Administration (EIA) projected US marketed [natural] gas production will have reached a first peak at 20.60 TCF [trillion cubic feet] in 2009, decline to 18.90 TCF in 2013, then rise again to 23.27 TCF in 2035..." (Wikipedia)<br><br>The EIA's 2009 US natural gas production total consists of 13 trillion cubic feet (63%) from conventional sources and 6.5 trillion cubic feet (37%) from unconventional (less accessible, riskier, and costlier) sources, such as offshore, coal bed methane, shale gas, and Alaskan gas. The EIA's 2035 projection consists of 9.1 trillion cubic feet (39%) from conventional sources and 14.2 trillion cubic feet (61%) from unconventional sources.<br><br>That conventional US natural gas supplies are in terminal decline is |

| | | | |
|---|---|---|---|
| | beyond dispute; whether economically viable US natural gas supplies from unconventional sources can be increased by 118%, from 6.5 to 14.2 trillion cubic feet, between 2009 and 2035 is highly questionable. | | |
| **Global NNR Scarcity** | **Scarce in 2008: Yes** | **Permanently Scarce: Almost Certain** | |
| **Historical Global Extraction Trends** | Annual global natural gas extraction levels generally increased in an uninterrupted manner during the latter portion of the 20th century; annual global gas extraction increased 24% between 2000 and 2008. | | |
| **Global Peak Extraction Year (thru 2008):** 2007 | | **Years to Global Reserve Exhaustion:** 34 | |
| **Projected Global Peak Extraction Year:** 2025* | | **Projected Global Peak Supply Year:** 2025* | |
| **Interdependencies** | Natural gas is sometimes recovered as a byproduct of oil extraction. | | |
| **Global Scarcity Assessment** | "According to David L. Goodstein, the worldwide rate of [natural gas] discovery peaked around 1960 and has been declining ever since. Exxon Mobil Vice President, Harry J. Longwell places the peak of global gas discovery around 1970 and has observed a sharp decline in natural gas discovery rates since then. The rate of [natural gas] discovery has fallen below the rate of consumption in 1980. The gap has been widening ever since. Declining gas discovery rates foreshadow future production decline rates because gas production can only follow gas discoveries." (Wikipedia [Peak Gas]) <br><br> A 24% increase in the annual global natural gas extraction level between 2000 and 2008 implies an increase in global natural gas demand during the pre-recession period, and a corresponding increase in global natural gas supply in response to increased global demand. <br><br> The fact that the price of natural gas increased by an extraordinary 156% during the 2000-2008 period indicates that global natural gas supply, while increasing during the eight year period, remained woefully insufficient to completely address global requirements in 2008. <br><br> Available evidence supports the contention that global natural gas supplies will remain insufficient to completely address global requirements going forward: <br><br> • Proven global natural gas reserves would exhaust in only 34 years, assuming the restoration of pre-recession utilization levels and growth rates; <br> • The global natural gas extraction (supply) level is projected to peak in approximately 2025; and <br> • An extraordinary increase in the price of natural gas during the 2000-2008 period could induce only a nominal increase in natural gas supply—compelling evidence that globally available, economically viable natural gas extraction may be at or near its permanent peak level. <br><br> Barring future reductions in the global natural gas requirement trajectory and/or major new economically viable discoveries, natural gas will almost certainly remain scarce globally in the future. | | |

*From On American Sustainability, page 46 - http://www.wakeupamerika.com/PDFs/On-American-Sustainability.pdf.

1. "Natural Gas", Wikipedia, 2011 - http://en.wikipedia.org/wiki/Natural_gas.
2. "Peak Gas", Wikipedia, 2011 - http://en.wikipedia.org/wiki/Peak_gas.

3. "Natural Gas Overview, 1949-2009, Table 6.1, US EIA, 2010 -
http://www.eia.doe.gov/emeu/aer/txt/stb0601.xls.
4. "World Dry Natural Gas Production, 1999-2008, Table 11.11, US EIA, 2010 -
http://www.eia.doe.gov/emeu/aer/txt/stb1111.xls.
5. "US Natural Gas Wellhead Price", Natural Gas Navigator, US EIA, 2010 -
http://www.eia.gov/dnav/ng/hist/n9190us3m.htm.
6. "World Proved Reserves of Oil and Natural Gas", US EIA, 2009 -
http://www.eia.doe.gov/emeu/international/reserves.html.
7. "Natural Gas Production by Source, 1990-2035, US EIA, 2010 -
http://www.eia.doe.gov/oiaf/aeo/excel/figure73_data.xls.
8. "Annual Energy Outlook 2010" (EIA, 2010), US EIA, 2010 -
http://www.eia.doe.gov/oiaf/archive/aeo10/execsummary.html.
9. "On American Sustainability—Anatomy of a Societal Collapse", pages 75-77; C. Clugston,
2009 - http://www.wakeupamerika.com/PDFs/On-American-Sustainability.pdf.

| NNR Profile | Nickel |
|---|---|
| **NNR Uses and Critical Applications** ||
| **Primary Uses** | Nickel is a hard, ductile, silvery-white metal used in batteries, as an alloy and superalloy, and as a catalyst; nickel is also used in plating, coinage, and magnet applications. |
| **Critical Applications** | As an alloy in nickel steels (stainless steel) and nickel cast irons; as the cathode in rechargeable batteries including nickel-cadmium, nickel-iron, nickel hydrogen, and nickel-metal hydride; and in the potentially critical application area of alkaline fuel cells.<br><br>"Stainless steel has traditionally accounted for two-thirds of primary nickel use worldwide..." (USGS, 2010) |
| **NNR Criticality** | **NNR Criticality Classification: Critical** |
| **Substitutes** | Increasingly viable nickel substitutes are being developed in both steel (chromium and titanium) and battery (lithium-ion) applications. |
| **Criticality Assessment** | While nickel plays an important supporting role in a variety of critical applications, its high cost is forcing substitution wherever possible. In the event that substitutes demonstrate price/performance superiority, the importance of nickel could decline.<br><br>"The commercial forms of nickel and nickel-base alloys are fully austenitic and are used/selected mainly for their resistance to high temperature and aqueous corrosion." (Key, 2010) |
| **US NNR Scarcity** | **Scarce in 2008: Yes** | **Permanently Scarce: Almost Certain** |
| **2008 US Import Reliance: 34%** || **2008 Domestic US Supply: 66%** |
| **Historical US Import Trends** | The US has been a net importer of nickel throughout the 20th and 21st centuries, often importing 100% of its annual supply. While no nickel has been extracted domestically since 1998, the US has been able to address a majority of its domestic nickel requirements through recycling and stock drawdowns. |

| NNR Profile | Nickel (continued) |
|---|---|
| **Historical US Usage Trends** | Annual US nickel utilization levels generally increased—in a fluctuating manner—during the first three quarters of the 20th century, peaking temporarily in 1901, 1906, 1912, 1918, 1929, 1944, 1956, and 1966, before peaking permanently (to date) in 1974. After generally declining through the middle 1990s, US nickel utilization increased into the early years of the new millennium; however, the 2008 US nickel utilization level still amounted to only 79% of the 1974 peak utilization level. |

| US Peak Extraction Year (thru 2008): 1997* | US Peak Utilization Year (thru 2008): 1974 |
|---|---|

| **Potential Geopolitical US Supply Constraints** | 44% of US nickel imports come from Canada; nearly 40% of proven global nickel reserves are located in Australia. |
|---|---|
| **US Scarcity Assessment** | "The United States did not have any active nickel mines in 2009. Limited amounts of byproduct nickel were recovered from copper and palladium-platinum ores mined in the Western United States." (USGS, 2010)<br><br>That annual domestic nickel utilization decreased by 21% since peaking (to date) in 1974, is a major indicator of declining American industrial preeminence and global economic competitiveness.<br><br>The US currently relies considerably on imported nickel, a large percentage (44%) of which comes from Canada. The quantity of nickel supplied by foreign sources during 2008 accounted for 34% of the total 2008 US utilization level.<br><br>Available evidence supports the contention that domestic nickel supplies will remain insufficient to completely address domestic requirements going forward:<br><br>• Domestic nickel extraction ceased entirely in 1999—a compelling indicator that domestic economically viable nickel extraction has peaked permanently; and<br>• The quantity of nickel extracted domestically during 1997, the year of peak (to date) domestic nickel extraction, amounted to only 8% of the 2008 total US utilization level—a significant indicator of America's increasing dependence on foreign NNRs.<br><br>Barring future reductions in the domestic (US) nickel requirement trajectory and/or major new domestic economically viable discoveries, nickel will almost certainly remain scarce domestically in the future. |

| Global NNR Scarcity | Scarce in 2008: Yes | Permanently Scarce: Likely |
|---|---|---|

| **Historical Global Extraction Trends** | "In 2005, Russia was the largest producer of nickel with about one-fifth world share closely followed by Canada, Australia and Indonesia, as reported by the British Geological Survey." (Wikipedia)<br><br>Global nickel extraction levels generally increased during both the 20th and 21st centuries, peaking temporarily in 1902, 1918, 1929, 1943 and 1977, before increasing into the new millennium; annual global nickel extraction increased 22% between 2000 and 2008.<br><br>"…as a result of significant increases in nickel prices between mid-2003 and mid-2007, a number of stainless steel producers substituted other less expensive input materials such as manganese for nickel…" (McCallum, 2009) |
|---|---|

| NNR Profile | Nickel (continued) | |
|---|---|---|
| **Global Peak Extraction Year (thru 2008):** 2007 | | **Years to Global Reserve Exhaustion:** 30 |
| **Projected Global Peak Extraction Year:** 2020 | | **Projected Global Peak Supply Year:** 2080 |
| **Interdependencies** | Nickel can be recovered as a byproduct of copper and palladium-platinum mining. | |
| **Global Scarcity Assessment** | "World nickel mine production was at an all time high in 2007... Nickel prices climbed to unprecedented levels in the first half of 2007..." (USGS, 2008) | |
| | A 22% increase in the annual global nickel extraction level between 2000 and 2008 implies an increase in global nickel demand during the pre-recession period, and a corresponding increase in global nickel supply in response to increased global demand. | |
| | The fact that the price of nickel increased by a robust 96% during the 2000-2008 period indicates that global nickel supply, while increasing during the eight year period, remained insufficient to completely address global requirements in 2008. | |
| | Available evidence, albeit somewhat conflicting, supports the contention that global nickel supplies will likely remain insufficient to completely address global requirements going forward: | |
| | <ul><li>The global nickel supply level is not projected to peak until approximately 2080; however</li><li>Proven global nickel reserves would exhaust in only 30 years, assuming the restoration of pre-recession utilization levels and growth rates;</li><li>The global nickel extraction level is projected to peak in approximately 2020; and</li><li>A robust increase in the price of nickel during the 2000-2008 period could induce only a nominal increase in nickel supply—evidence that globally available, economically viable nickel extraction may be at or near its permanent peak level.</li></ul> | |
| | Barring future reductions in the global nickel requirement trajectory and/or major new economically viable discoveries, nickel will likely remain scarce globally in the future. | |
| | "Although [nickel] consumption increased across the world, China exhibited the largest growth. Between 2000 and 2009, its domestic demand is estimated to have risen by an annual average rate of almost 25%. This phenomenal growth has seen China become the world's largest consumer of nickel. In 1995 China accounted for a modest 4% of world consumption, increasing to almost 30% in 2008." (Mineweb, 2010) | |

*The 1997 peak in US extraction was a one year "spike"; the previous peak was 1972.

1. "Nickel", Wikipedia, 2011 - http://en.wikipedia.org/wiki/Nickel.
2. "Nickel Statistics", Historical Statistics for Mineral and Material Commodities in the United States, USGS, 2010 – http://minerals.usgs.gov/ds/2005/140/nickel.xls.
3. "Nickel and Nickel Alloys", Key to Metals, 2010 - http://www.keytometals.com/Article9.htm.
4. "Global Nickel Market Demand to Return in 2010 – Roskill", Mineweb, 2010 - http://www.mineweb.com/mineweb/view/mineweb/en/page36?oid=95910&sn=Detail.

5. "Nickel", R. McCallum, Australian Commodities, abare.gov.au, 2009 - http://abare.gov.au/interactive/09ac_june/htm/nickel.htm.

| NNR Profile | Niobium |
|---|---|
| **NNR Uses and Critical Applications** | |
| **Primary Uses** | Niobium is a soft, ductile, gray metal used as an alloy (steel strengthening), a superalloy (in jet and rocket engines), and in superconducting magnets. |
| **Critical Applications** | As an alloy in high-grade structural steel used in autos and pipelines; as a superalloy in jet engines, gas turbines, and rocket subassemblies (Gemini and Apollo programs); in superconducting magnets (MRI scanners and particle accelerators); also being evaluated as a replacement for tantalum in capacitors. |

| NNR Criticality | NNR Criticality Classification: Critical |
|---|---|
| **Substitutes** | While niobium substitutes, including molybdenum, vanadium, tantalum, and titanium, are technically viable, most are price/performance inferior in their respective applications. |
| **Criticality Assessment** | Niobium plays a key support role in many critical industrial applications; and economically viable substitutes are generally not available.<br><br>"…the metal [niobium] is used in a variety of modern industries—particularly steel making, where it's a crucial ingredient in the construction of automobiles, oil pipelines and even airplanes." (Trading Report, 2010) |

| US NNR Scarcity | Scarce in 2008: Yes | Permanently Scarce: Almost Certain |
|---|---|---|
| **2008 US Import Reliance:** 100% | | **2008 Domestic US Supply:** 0% |
| **Historical US Import Trends** | The US has always been a net importer of niobium; the US has been increasingly reliant on niobium imports since the early 1960s. | |
| **Historical US Usage Trends** | Annual US niobium utilization levels generally increased during both the 20$^{th}$ and early 21$^{st}$ centuries, peaking temporarily in 1968, 1974, 1981, and 1988, before generally increasing into the new millennium. | |
| **US Peak Extraction Year (thru 2008):** 1959* | | **US Peak Utilization Year (thru 2008):** 2006 |
| **Potential Geopolitical US Supply Constraints** | 85% of US niobium imports come from Brazil; Brazil produces about 75% of the world's supply of niobium. | |

| NNR Profile | Niobium (continued) |
|---|---|
| **US Scarcity Assessment** | "No significant U.S. niobium mine production has been reported since 1959. Domestic niobium resources are of low grade, some are mineralogically complex, and most are not commercially recoverable." (USGS, 2010)<br><br>The US currently relies exclusively on imported niobium, the vast majority (85%) of which comes from Brazil.<br><br>Available evidence supports the contention that domestic niobium supplies will remain insufficient to completely address domestic requirements going forward:<br><br>• While US niobium utilization increased into the new millennium, domestic niobium extraction ceased entirely in 1960—a significant indicator of America's increasing dependence on foreign NNRs, and a compelling indicator that domestic economically viable niobium extraction has peaked permanently;<br>• US niobium import levels have generally increased since the early 1960s; and<br>• US niobium resources are not commercially viable.<br><br>Barring future reductions in the domestic (US) niobium requirement trajectory and/or major new domestic economically viable discoveries, niobium will almost certainly remain scarce domestically in the future. |

| Global NNR Scarcity | Scarce in 2008: Yes | Permanently Scarce: Almost Certain |
|---|---|---|
| **Historical Global Extraction Trends** | "According to the latest figures (2009) from the USGS, Brazil remains, by far, the world's largest producer of niobium [92% of global total]. Canada remains a small but significant producer as well." (Trading Report, 2010)<br><br>Annual global niobium extraction levels generally increased from the 1960s forward, peaking temporarily in 1974, 1980, and 1988, before increasing into the early years of the 21$^{st}$ century; annual global niobium extraction increased 154% between 2000 and 2008. | |

| Global Peak Extraction Year (thru 2008): 2008 | Years to Global Reserve Exhaustion: 15 |
|---|---|
| Projected Global Peak Extraction Year: N/A | Projected Global Peak Supply Year: N/A |

| Interdependencies | Niobium is a co-product with tantalum (common ores). |
|---|---|

| NNR Profile | Niobium (continued) |
|---|---|
| **Global Scarcity Assessment** | A 154% increase in the annual global niobium extraction level between 2000 and 2008 implies a substantial increase in global niobium demand during the pre-recession period, and a correspondingly substantial increase in global niobium supply in response to increased global demand.<br><br>The fact that the price of niobium increased by a robust 41% during the 2000-2008 period indicates that global niobium supply, while increasing substantially during the eight year period, remained insufficient to completely address global requirements in 2008.<br><br>Available evidence supports the contention that global niobium supplies will remain insufficient to completely address global requirements going forward:<br><br>• Proven global niobium reserves would exhaust in only 15 years, assuming the restoration of pre-recession utilization levels and growth rates;<br>• A robust increase in the price of niobium during the 2000-2008 period induced a substantial, but less than sufficient, increase in global niobium supply; and<br>• It is questionable whether the extremely robust 12.3% compound annual growth rate (CAGR) in global niobium extraction evidenced between 2000 and 2008—an interval during which niobium became scarce globally despite an extraordinary increase in extraction—can be reestablished, much less increased, going forward. A 12.3% CAGR would necessitate a continuous doubling in the annual global extraction level of niobium every 6 years.<br><br>Barring future reductions in the global niobium requirement trajectory and/or major new economically viable discoveries, niobium will almost certainly remain scarce globally in the future.<br><br>This assessment conflicts with that of the Tantalum-Niobium International Study Center (TIC):<br><br>"…the world's largest producer of niobium, Companhia Brasileira de Metalurgia e Mineracao (CBMM), owns the world's largest deposit of the mineral in Araxa, Brazil. According to TIC: 'The [niobium] reserves are enough to supply current world demand for about 500 years, about 460 million tons.'" [Note that the USGS lists total 2009 proven Brazilian niobium reserves at 2.9 million metric tons.] (Trading Report, 2010) |

*USGS data shows no US extraction from 1964 onward; 2010 Mineral Summaries statement says "no significant US production since 1959." There is no data claiming US extraction at any time.

1. "Niobium", Wikipedia, 2011 - http://en.wikipedia.org/wiki/Niobium.
2. "Niobium Statistics", Historical Statistics for Mineral and Material Commodities in the United States, USGS, 2010 – http://minerals.usgs.gov/ds/2005/140/niobium.xls.
3. "Niobium. Or Columbium?" The Trading Report, 2010 - http://www.thetradingreport.com/2010/06/22/niobium-or-columbium/.

| NNR Profile | Nitrogen (Ammonia) |
|---|---|

| **NNR Uses and Critical Applications** | |
|---|---|
| **Primary Uses** | Nitrogen is a colorless, odorless, tasteless gas used in the production of ammonia (produced on a commercial scale through the Haber-Bosch process, which combines atmospheric nitrogen and methane [natural gas]), which is one of the primary components (anhydrous ammonium sulfate and urea) of inorganic (NPK) fertilizers; nitrogen is also used in pharmaceuticals, explosives, and cleaning products; ammonia is essential to all living entities. |
| **Critical Applications** | Nitrogen (anhydrous ammonia) based inorganic NPK (nitrogen, phosphorous, and potassium) fertilizers are indispensible to modern industrial agriculture; ammonia is also a possible, though less energy dense, replacement fuel for gasoline and diesel. |

| **NNR Criticality** | **NNR Criticality Classification: Indispensible** |
|---|---|
| **Substitutes** | There is no substitute for nitrogen in living organisms; and there is no substitute for the Haber-Bosch process for producing "fixed" nitrogen* in fertilizers on a commercial scale. |
| **Criticality Assessment** | "It can be argued that ammonia is the man-made substance most critical to the existence of human society. The expansion of population since 1900 has been made possible by fertilizer driven agriculture, and modern nitrogen fertilizer is based on ammonia." (Quantum Sphere, 2010) <br><br> Ammonia (fixed nitrogen) is indispensible to agriculture on an industrial scale. However: <br><br> "Over fertilization and the subsequent runoff of excess fertilizer may contribute to nitrogen accumulation in watersheds. Nitrogen in excess fertilizer runoff was suspected to be a cause of the hypoxic zone [dead zone] in GOM {Gulf of Mexico]. (USGS, 2010) |

| **US NNR Scarcity** | **Scarce in 2008: Yes** | **Permanently Scarce: Almost Certain** |
|---|---|---|
| **2008 US Import Reliance:** 42% | | **2008 Domestic US Supply:** 58% |

| **Historical US Import Trends** | Historically, the US has been both a net exporter and a net importer of ammonia; since the middle 1970s, the US has become increasingly reliant on ammonia imports. |
|---|---|
| **Historical US Usage Trends** | Annual US ammonia utilization levels generally increased during the post WWII years of the 20th century, peaking temporarily in 1980 before peaking permanently (to date) in 1998. While domestic ammonia utilization recovered slightly during the 2000-2008 period, the 2008 US utilization level amounted to only 79% of the 1998 peak utilization level. |

| **US Peak Production Year (thru 2008):** 1980 | **US Peak Utilization Year (thru 2008):** 1998 |
|---|---|
| **Potential Geopolitical US Supply Constraints** | 55% of US ammonia imports come from Trinidad and Tobago. |

| NNR Profile | Nitrogen (Ammonia) [continued] |
|---|---|
| **US Scarcity Assessment** | "The high cost of natural gas combined with the reduction in U.S. production, has resulted in a dramatic increase in the cost of nitrogen fertilizers to U.S. farmers [2005 data]." (DOE, 2005)<br><br>That annual domestic ammonia utilization decreased by 21% since peaking (to date) in 1998, is a significant indicator of declining American industrial preeminence and global economic competitiveness.<br><br>The US currently relies considerably on imported ammonia, the majority of which (55%) comes from Trinidad and Tobago. The quantity of ammonia supplied by foreign sources during 2008 accounted for 42% of the total 2008 US utilization level.<br><br>Available evidence supports the contention that domestic ammonia supplies will remain insufficient to completely address domestic requirements going forward:<br><br>• The annual US ammonia production level decreased by 47% since peaking (to date) in 1980—a compelling indicator that domestic economically viable ammonia production has peaked permanently;<br>• The US has become increasingly reliant on ammonia imports since 1974; and<br>• The quantity of ammonia produced domestically during 2008 amounted to only 58% of the total 2008 US utilization level—a primary indicator of America's increasing dependence on foreign NNRs.<br><br>Barring future reductions in the domestic (US) ammonia requirement trajectory and/or major new domestic economically viable discoveries, ammonia will almost certainly remain scarce domestically in the future.<br><br>"In September [2007], the Kenai, AK, ammonia plant was closed because of a shortage of supply of natural gas from Alaska's Cook Inlet." (USGS, 2008) |

| Global NNR Scarcity | Scarce in 2008: Yes | Permanently Scarce: Almost Certain |
|---|---|---|
| **Historical Global Production Trends** | "China produced 32.0% of the worldwide [ammonia] production [in 2006] followed by India with 8.9%, Russia with 8.2%, and the United States with 6.5%." (Citizendium, 2010)<br><br>Annual global ammonia production levels increased dramatically during the mid/late decades of the 20th century, peaking temporarily in 1989 before resuming their upward trend into the new millennium; annual global ammonia production increased 23% between 2000 and 2008. | |

| Global Peak Production Year (thru 2008): 2008 | Years to Global Reserve Exhaustion: N/A |
|---|---|
| Projected Global Peak Production Year: N/A | Projected Global Peak Supply Year: N/A |

| **Interdependencies** | Methane (natural gas) is currently the feedstock of choice for the production of ammonia. |
|---|---|

| NNR Profile | Nitrogen (Ammonia) [continued] |
|---|---|
| **Global Scarcity Assessment** | A 23% increase in the annual global ammonia production level between 2000 and 2008 implies an increase in global ammonia demand during the pre-recession period, and a corresponding increase in global ammonia supply in response to increased global demand.<br><br>The fact that the price of ammonia increased by an extraordinary 179% during the 2000-2008 period indicates that global ammonia supply, while increasing during the eight year period, remained woefully insufficient to completely address global requirements in 2008.<br><br>Available evidence supports the contention that global ammonia supplies will remain insufficient to completely address global demand going forward:<br><br>• An extraordinary increase in the price of ammonia during the 2000-2008 period could induce only a nominal increase in ammonia supply—evidence that ammonia supply is nearing its permanent peak on a global level.<br>• The supply of ammonia is currently determined by the available supplies of natural gas that can be allocated to the production of ammonia. Unless a price/performance superior feedstock for ammonia is identified, ammonia will become increasing scarce globally as natural gas becomes increasingly scarce on the global level.<br><br>Barring future reductions in the global ammonia requirement trajectory and/or major new economically viable discoveries, ammonia will almost certainly remain scarce globally in the future.<br><br>"As expected, strong demand caused prices to rise: since June 2009, ammonia prices (FOB Yuzhniy, Russia) have advanced by 77%, from USD 173 to USD 305 per ton." (Finam, 2010) |

* To make nitrogen accessible to plants requires nitrogen fixation (conversion of atmospheric nitrogen to a plant-accessible form). "When nitrogen reacts spontaneously with a reagent, the net transformation is often called nitrogen fixation." (Wikipedia)

1. "Ammonia", Wikipedia, 2011 - http://en.wikipedia.org/wiki/Ammonia.
2. "Nitrogen", Wikipedia, 2011 - http://en.wikipedia.org/wiki/Nitrogen.
3. "Nitrogen Fertilizer", Wikipedia, 2011 - http://en.wikipedia.org/wiki/Nitrogen_fertilizer#Inorganic_fertilizers_.28mineral_fertilizer.29.
4. "Nitrogen Fixation", Wikipedia, 2011 - http://en.wikipedia.org/wiki/Nitrogen_fixation.
5. "Nitrogen Statistics", Historical Statistics for Mineral and Material Commodities in the United States, USGS, 2010 – http://minerals.usgs.gov/ds/2005/140/nitrogen.xls.
6. "Ammonia Production Picks Up", Finam, 2010 - http://www.finamrus.com/investments/daily00001021C1/default.asp.
7. "Chemical Production", Quantum Sphere, Inc. 2010 - http://www.qsinano.com/apps_ammonia.php.
8. "Ammonia Production", Citizendium, 2010 - http://en.citizendium.org/wiki/Ammonia_production.
9. "Impact of High Natural Gas Prices on the US Nitrogen Industry", US DOE, 2005 - http://www.fe.doe.gov/epact/Section_1818/The_Fertilizer_Institute_(2)_present_12-.pdf.

| NNR Profile | Oil |
|---|---|

### NNR Uses and Critical Applications

| | |
|---|---|
| **Primary Uses** | Oil is a (typically) black or dark brown liquid "fossil fuel" used in the production of motor fuels (gasoline, diesel, jet fuel), pharmaceuticals, plastics, pesticides, solvents, and myriad industrial and consumer products; oil is also used as an energy source for electricity generation and central heating in some areas. |
| **Critical Applications** | Oil is undoubtedly the most critical nonrenewable natural resource, both domestically and globally. It is indispensible as the feedstock for motor fuels, plastics, and pesticides among many other applications. |

### NNR Criticality — NNR Criticality Classification: Indispensible

| | |
|---|---|
| **Substitutes** | No viable substitutes exist for many oil applications, especially when scale and price/performance are considered. |
| **Criticality Assessment** | As oil becomes increasingly scarce and expensive, most other NNRs—the extraction, processing, and provisioning of which depend on oil derived products—will become increasingly expensive (and therefore increasingly scarce) as well. |

### US NNR Scarcity — Scarce in 2008: Yes — Permanently Scarce: Almost Certain

| **2008 US Import Reliance:** 57% | **2008 Domestic US Supply:** 43% |
|---|---|
| **Historical US Import Trends** | The US was a net importer of oil during the last half of the 20th century and the early years of the 21st century; net US oil imports generally increased steadily on an annual basis, in both absolute terms and as a percentage of total domestic utilization. |
| **Historical US Usage Trends** | Annual US oil utilization levels generally increased during the latter half of the 20th century and into the early 21st century, peaking temporarily in 1973, 1978, and 1988, before peaking permanently (to date) in 2005. |

| US Peak Extraction Year (thru 2008): 1970 | US Peak Utilization Year (thru 2008): 2005 |
|---|---|
| **Potential Geopolitical US Supply Constraints** | Approximately 80% of the world's proven oil reserves are located in the Middle East. |

| NNR Profile | Oil (continued) |
|---|---|
| **US Scarcity Assessment** | "M. King Hubbert created and first used the models behind peak oil in 1956 to accurately predict that United States oil production would peak between 1965 and 1970." (Wikipedia, [Peak Oil])<br><br>The US currently relies heavily on imported oil; the quantity of oil supplied by foreign sources during 2008 accounted for 57% of the total 2008 US utilization level.<br><br>Available evidence supports the contention that domestic oil supplies will remain insufficient to completely address domestic requirements going forward:<br><br>• While US oil utilization increased into the new millennium, the annual US oil extraction level decreased by 40% since peaking (to date) in 1970—a compelling indicator that domestic economically viable oil extraction has peaked permanently;<br>• Net US oil imports increased steadily since the 1950s;<br>• The quantity of oil extracted domestically during 2008 amounted to only 34% of the total 2008 US utilization level—a primary cause of America's lack of economic self-sufficiency; and<br>• The quantity of oil extracted domestically during 1970, the year of peak (to date) domestic oil extraction, amounted to only 58% of the 2008 total US utilization level;<br><br>Barring future reductions in the domestic (US) oil requirement trajectory and/or major new domestic economically viable discoveries, oil will almost certainly remain scarce domestically in the future.<br><br>The total (domestic and imported) supply of oil available to the US has plateaued between 7 billion and 7.5 billion barrels per year, as increasingly expensive nonconventional liquid fuel sources—i.e., offshore, deep water, natural gas plant liquids, tar sands, heavy oil, coal/gas to oil, and biofuels—temporarily displace declining sources of conventional onshore crude.<br><br>It is unlikely that the total supply of oil available to the US will increase going forward, given ever-increasing demand by emerging nations with ample foreign exchange, and ever-decreasing amounts of surplus oil available from traditional exporting countries.<br><br>(In 2008, the US ranked #1 globally in oil [all liquids] consumption [19.5 million barrels/day], #3 globally in oil [all liquids] production [8.5 million barrels/day], and #12 globally in proven oil reserves [21 billion barrels: enough to last for 3 years].) (EIA, 2010) |
| **Global NNR Scarcity** | **Scarce in 2008: Yes**   **Permanently Scarce: Almost Certain** |

| NNR Profile | Oil (continued) |
|---|---|
| **Historical Global Extraction Trends** | "China has emerged from being a net oil exporter in the early 1990s to become the world's third-largest net importer of oil in 2006." (EIA, 2010)<br><br>Annual global crude oil extraction levels generally increased during the latter half of the 20$^{th}$ century and into the 21$^{st}$ century, peaking temporarily in 1979 before peaking permanently (to date) in 2005; annual global crude oil extraction increased 8% between 2000 and 2008.<br><br>"The lighter grades of crude oil produce the best yields of these [petroleum based] products, but as the world's reserves of light and medium oil are depleted, oil refineries are increasingly having to process heavy oil and bitumen, and use more complex and expensive methods to produce the products required." (Wikipedia [Oil]) |

| Global Peak Extraction Year (thru 2008): 2005 | Years to Global Reserve Exhaustion: 39 |
|---|---|
| **Projected Global Peak Extraction Year: 2017** | **Projected Global Peak Supply Year: 2017** |

| **Interdependencies** | None identified. |
|---|---|
| **Global Scarcity Assessment** | "'By 2012, [global] surplus oil production capacity could entirely disappear, and as early as 2015, the shortfall in output could reach nearly 10 million barrels per day…'" (JOE 2010, 2010)<br><br>An 8% increase in the annual global oil extraction level between 2000 and 2008 implies an increase in global oil demand during the pre-recession period, and a corresponding increase in global oil supply in response to increased global demand.<br><br>The fact that the price of oil increased by an extraordinary 244% during the 2000-2008 period indicates that global oil supply, while increasing during the eight year period, remained woefully insufficient to completely address global requirements in 2008.<br><br>Available evidence supports the contention that global oil supplies will remain insufficient to completely address global requirements going forward:<br><br>• Proven global oil reserves would exhaust in only 39 years, assuming the restoration of pre-recession utilization levels and growth rates;<br>• The global oil extraction (supply) level is projected to peak in approximately 2017; and<br>• An extraordinary increase in the price of oil during the 2000-2008 period could induce only a nominal increase in oil supply—compelling evidence that globally available, economically viable oil extraction may be at or near its permanent peak level.<br><br>Barring future reductions in the global oil requirement trajectory and/or major new economically viable discoveries, oil will almost certainly remain scarce globally in the future.<br><br>"… as [oil] peaking is approached, liquid fuel prices and price volatility will increase dramatically, and, without timely mitigation, the economic, social, and political costs will be unprecedented." (Energy Bulletin, from Hirsh Report, 2011) |

*Per http://www.eia.doe.gov/emeu/aer/txt/stb0501.xls - EIA; 2008 import reliance is 74% if domestic crude only is considered; 65% if domestic crude and NGPLs are considered; and 60% if processing gains are included; and 57% if net imports are divided by total consumption.
**The difference between the 43% of total US oil supplied by domestic sources and the 35% of total US oil extracted (8%) is accounted for biofuels (3%) and stock changes and adjustments (5%).

1. "Oil", Wikipedia, 2011 - http://en.wikipedia.org/wiki/Oil.
2. "Petroleum", Wikipedia, 2011 - http://en.wikipedia.org/wiki/Petroleum.
3. "Peak Oil", Wikipedia, 2011 - http://en.wikipedia.org/wiki/Peak_oil.
4. "World Crude Oil Production, 1960-2009", Table 11.5, US EIA, 2009 – http://www.eia.doe.gov/emeu/aer/txt/stb1105.xls.
5. "Petroleum Overview, 1949-2008", Table 5.1, US EIA - http://www.eia.doe.gov/emeu/aer/txt/stb0501.xls.
6. "World Crude Oil Prices" (June 30, 2000 and May 31, 2008, June was unavailable); US EIA, 2011 - http://www.eia.gov/dnav/pet/pet_pri_wco_k_w.htm.
7. "World Proved Reserves of Oil and Natural Gas", US EIA, 2009 - http://www.eia.doe.gov/emeu/international/reserves.html.
8. "On American Sustainability—Anatomy of a Societal Collapse", pages 45-46 and accompanying notes; C. Clugston, 2009 - http://www.wakeupamerika.com/PDFs/On-American-Sustainability.pdf.
9. "China (Background)", US EIA, 2010 - http://www.eia.doe.gov/cabs/China/Background.html. EIA, quote on China's export/import flip-flop.
10. "Peak Oil Primer", Energy Bulletin, 2011 - http://www.energybulletin.net/primer.php. Hirsh quote
11. "Joint Operating Environment 2010", page 29, US Joint Forces Command, 2010 - http://www.peakoil.net/files/JOE2010.pdf.

| NNR Profile | Peat | |
|---|---|---|
| **NNR Uses and Critical Applications** | | |
| **Primary Uses** | Peat is an accumulation of partially decayed vegetation used primarily as a source of energy (fuel) in a limited number of regions; peat is also used horticulturally for soil improvement, as an oil absorbent, and as a filtration medium. | |
| **Critical Applications** | Cooking, domestic heating, and power generation on a limited basis. | |
| **NNR Criticality** | **NNR Criticality Classification: Declining** | |
| **Substitutes** | Peat is price/performance superior to alternatives such as organic materials, shredded paper, and straw in horticultural applications; viable peat substitutes, both nonrenewable and renewable, exist as energy sources. | |
| **Criticality Assessment** | Peat is harvested on an industrial scale in very few places—Ireland and Finland are examples—superior energy sources currently exist almost universally. | |
| **US NNR Scarcity** | **Scarce in 2008: Yes** | **Permanently Scarce: Almost Certain** |
| **2008 US Import Reliance: 57%** | | **2008 Domestic US Supply: 43%** |
| **Historical US Import Trends** | The US has been a net importer of peat (for horticultural uses) during both the 20th and 21st centuries; US peat imports as a percentage of total US utilization have increased continuously. | |

| NNR Profile | Peat (continued) |
|---|---|
| **Historical US Usage Trends** | Annual US peat utilization levels generally increased during the 20<sup>th</sup> and early 21<sup>st</sup> centuries, peaking temporarily in 1911, 1918, 1937, 1964, 1979, 1987, and 1999, before increasing into the new millennium.<br><br>"Peat is an important component of growing media, and the demand for peat generally follows that of horticultural applications." (USGS, 2010) |

| US Peak Extraction Year (thru 2008): 1987 | US Peak Utilization Year (thru 2008): 2005 |
|---|---|

| **Potential Geopolitical US Supply Constraints** | 97% of US peat imports come from Canada. |
|---|---|

| **US Scarcity Assessment** | The US currently relies heavily on imported peat, the majority of which (97%) comes from Canada. The quantity of peat supplied by foreign sources during 2008 accounted for 57% of the total 2008 US utilization level.<br><br>Available evidence supports the contention that domestic peat supplies will remain insufficient to completely address domestic requirements going forward:<br><br>• While US peat utilization increased into the new millennium, the annual US peat extraction level decreased by 29% since peaking (to date) in 1987—a compelling indicator that domestic economically viable peat extraction has peaked permanently;<br>• The US has become increasingly reliant on peat imports during the 20<sup>th</sup> and 21<sup>st</sup> centuries;<br>• The quantity of peat extracted domestically during 2008 amounted to only 43% of the total 2008 US utilization level—an indicator of America's increasing dependence on foreign NNRs; and<br>• The quantity of peat extracted domestically during 1987, the year of peak (to date) domestic peat extraction, amounted to only 60% of the 2008 total US utilization level.<br><br>Barring future reductions in the domestic (US) peat requirement trajectory and/or major new domestic economically viable discoveries, peat will almost certainly remain scarce domestically in the future. |
|---|---|

| Global NNR Scarcity | Scarce in 2008: No | Permanently Scarce: Unlikely |
|---|---|---|

| **Historical Global Extraction Trends** | Annual global peat extraction levels generally increased during the middle decades of the 20<sup>th</sup> century, peaking temporarily in 1940, 1967, and 1978, before peaking permanently (to date) in 1984; global peat extraction then declined dramatically in 1992. Annual global peat extraction increased 1% between 2000 and 2008. |
|---|---|

| Global Peak Extraction Year (thru 2008): 1984 | Years to Global Reserve Exhaustion: 50+ |
|---|---|
| Projected Global Peak Extraction Year: N/A | Projected Global Peak Supply Year: N/A |

| **Interdependencies** | None identified. |
|---|---|

| NNR Profile | Peat (continued) |
|---|---|
| **Global Scarcity Assessment** | A 1% increase in the annual global peat extraction level between 2000 and 2008 implies nearly stagnant global peat demand and supply during the pre-recession period.<br><br>The fact that the price of peat decreased by 22% during the 2000-2008 period indicates that the global supply of peat in 2008 was sufficient to completely address 2008 global requirements.<br><br>Available evidence supports the contention that global peat supplies will remain sufficient to completely address global requirements going forward:<br><br>• While global peat extraction levels have decreased dramatically since peaking (to date) in 1984, peat price levels have generally decreased since that time as well—evidence of sufficient global peat supplies;<br>• Proven global peat reserves are sufficient to last for over 100 years (assuming the restoration of pre-recession utilization levels and growth rates); and<br>• Proven global peat reserves are considered by the USGS to be quite large.<br><br>Barring future increases in the global peat requirement trajectory, globally available, economically viable peat supplies will likely remain sufficient to completely address global requirements going forward.<br><br>"The British Government is intending to eliminate peat used in horticulture applications, which includes using peat as a soil improver or growing media. However, other countries such as Russia and Ukraine are proposing to use additional peat as a fuel source." (USGS, 2010) |

1. "Peat", Wikipedia, 2011 - http://en.wikipedia.org/wiki/Peat.
2. "Peat Statistics", Historical Statistics for Mineral and Material Commodities in the United States, USGS, 2010 – http://minerals.usgs.gov/ds/2005/140/peat.xls.

| NNR Profile | Perlite | |
|---|---|---|
| **NNR Uses and Critical Applications** | | |
| **Primary Uses** | Perlite is a white (when expanded), amorphous, volcanic glass used in plasters, mortars, ceiling tiles, and insulation; also used as a horticultural aggregate and in filtration applications. | |
| **Critical Applications** | None identified. | |
| **NNR Criticality** | **NNR Criticality Classification: Important** | |
| **Substitutes** | Viable perlite substitutes, including diatomite, expanded clay and shale, pumice, slag, and vermiculite, exist in all application areas. | |
| **Criticality Assessment** | Perlite is useful in several niche residential and commercial construction application areas. | |
| **US NNR Scarcity** | **Scarce in 2008: Yes** | **Permanently Scarce: Almost Certain** |
| **2008 US Import Reliance: 26%** | **2008 Domestic US Supply: 74%** | |

| NNR Profile | Perlite (continued) |
|---|---|
| **Historical US Import Trends** | Prior to 1983, the US was self-sufficient in perlite supplies; the US became increasingly reliant on perlite imports from that point forward.<br><br>"The cost of rail transportation from the mines in the Western United States to some areas of the Eastern United States continued to burden domestic perlite producers with strong cost disadvantages compared with Greek perlite exporters." Note that it is less expensive to transport perlite from Greece than from the Western US.] (USGS, 2008) |
| **Historical US Usage Trends** | Annual US perlite utilization levels generally increased during the mid/late 20th century, peaking temporarily in 1956, 1958, 1969, 1974, and 1979 before peaking permanently (to date) in 2000. Domestic perlite utilization generally decreased thereafter; the 2008 US utilization level amounted to only 72% of the 2000 peak utilization level. |

| US Peak Extraction Year (thru 2008): 1999 | US Peak Utilization Year (thru 2008): 2000 |
|---|---|

| **Potential Geopolitical US Supply Constraints** | 100% of US perlite imports come from Greece. |
|---|---|
| **US Scarcity Assessment** | "Greece surpassed the United States in processed perlite production starting in 2003." (USGS, 2008)<br><br>That annual domestic perlite utilization decreased by 28% since peaking (to date) in 1999, is an indicator of declining American industrial preeminence and global economic competitiveness.<br><br>The US currently relies considerably on imported perlite, all of which (100%) comes from Greece. The quantity of perlite supplied by foreign sources during 2008 accounted for 26% of the total 2008 US utilization level.<br><br>Available evidence supports the contention that domestic perlite supplies will remain insufficient to completely address domestic requirements going forward:<br><br>• The annual US perlite extraction level decreased by 39% since peaking (to date) in 1999—an indicator that domestic perlite extraction has possibly peaked permanently;<br>• The US has become increasingly reliant on perlite imports since 1983; and<br>• The quantity of perlite extracted domestically during 2008 amounted to only 74% of the total 2008 US utilization level—an indicator of America's increasing dependence on foreign NNRs.<br><br>Barring future reductions in the domestic (US) perlite requirement trajectory and/or major new domestic economically viable discoveries, perlite will almost certainly remain scarce domestically in the future. |

| NNR Profile | Perlite (continued) | |
|---|---|---|
| **Global NNR Scarcity** | **Scarce in 2008: Yes** | **Permanently Scarce: Unclear** |
| **Historical Global Extraction Trends** | "Information for China and several other countries is unavailable, making it unclear whether or not Greece and the United States are the world's leading producers." (USGS, 2008)<br><br>Annual global perlite extraction levels generally increased during the latter decades of the 20th century, peaking temporarily in 1981 and 1989, before peaking permanently (to date) in 1999; annual global perlite extraction decreased 8% between 2000 and 2008. | |

| Global Peak Extraction Year (thru 2008): 1999 | Years to Global Reserve Exhaustion: 50+ |
|---|---|
| **Projected Global Peak Extraction Year: N/A** | **Projected Global Peak Supply Year: N/A** |

| Interdependencies | None identified. |
|---|---|
| **Global Scarcity Assessment** | An 8% decrease in the annual global perlite extraction level between 2000 and 2008 implies either a decrease in global perlite demand or insufficient global perlite supplies during the pre-recession period.<br><br>The fact that the price of perlite increased by 14% during the 2000-2008 period, indicates that the declining global supply of perlite was insufficient to completely address global requirements in 2008.<br><br>Available evidence regarding the likelihood that global perlite supplies will remain insufficient to completely address global requirements going forward is conflicting:<br><br>• The increased global perlite supply brought online between 2000 and 2008 was insufficient to prevent a price increase during the period—evidence of unaddressed global requirements in 2008; however<br>• Proven global perlite reserves would last for over 100 years (assuming the restoration of pre-recession utilization levels and growth rates).<br><br>It is therefore unclear whether perlite will remain scarce globally in the future, or whether globally available, economically viable perlite supplies will be sufficient to completely address future global requirements. |

1. "Perlite", Wikipedia, 2011 - http://en.wikipedia.org/wiki/Perlite.
2. "Perlite Statistics", Historical Statistics for Mineral and Material Commodities in the United States, USGS, 2010 – http://minerals.usgs.gov/ds/2005/140/perlite.xls.

| NNR Profile | Phosphate Rock |
|---|---|
| **NNR Uses and Critical Applications** | |
| **Primary Uses** | Phosphate rock (phosphorite) is a sedimentary rock that contains large quantities of phosphate, which is mined to obtain phosphorous, a primary component of NPK (nitrogen, phosphorous, potassium) fertilizers; phosphorous is also used in animal feed supplements and in industrial chemicals. |

| NNR Profile | Phosphate Rock (continued) |
|---|---|
| **Critical Applications** | NPK fertilizers are indispensible to mechanized agriculture, which is indispensible to modern industrial existence.<br><br>"95% of the U.S. phosphate rock mined was used to manufacture wet process phosphoric acid and super phosphoric acid, which were used as intermediate feedstocks in the manufacture of granular and liquid ammonium phosphate fertilizers and animal feed supplements." (USGS, 2010) |

| NNR Criticality | NNR Criticality Classification: Indispensible |
|---|---|
| **Substitutes** | "There are no substitutes for phosphorous in agriculture." (USGS, 2010) |
| **Criticality Assessment** | Phosphorous is indispensible to agriculture on an industrial scale. |

| US NNR Scarcity | Scarce in 2008: Yes | Permanently Scarce: Likely |
|---|---|---|

| 2008 US Import Reliance: 4% | 2008 Domestic US Supply: 96% |
|---|---|

| **Historical US Import Trends** | Throughout the 20th century, until 1995, the US was typically a heavy net exporter of phosphate rock (phosphorous); since that time America has become a net importer—the US ceased phosphorous exports entirely in 2004. |
|---|---|
| **Historical US Usage Trends** | Annual US phosphate rock utilization levels generally increased during the 20th century—in a fluctuating manner—peaking temporarily in 1911, 1917, 1920, 1930, 1937, 1967, 1980, 1984, and 1990, before peaking permanently (to date) in 1998; domestic phosphorous utilization declined relatively steadily since that time; the 2008 US utilization level amounted to only 81% of the 1998 peak utilization level. |

| US Peak Extraction Year (thru 2008): 1980 | US Peak Utilization Year (thru 2008): 1998 |
|---|---|

| **Potential Geopolitical US Supply Constraints** | "Most of the projected capacity growth for phosphoric acid and fertilizers will be captive production, as more countries attempt to limit reliance on imported fertilizers." (USGS, 2010)<br><br>100% of US phosphate rock imports come from Morocco; however, the US currently imports very little phosphorous material.<br><br>"…on June 23 [2009], the EU announced that both it and the U.S. 'had requested WTO consultations with China regarding China's export restrictions on a number of key raw materials, which it considers are in clear breach of international trade rules.<br><br>In the words of the EU announcement: 'European industries have raised concerns for a number of years on export restrictions - quotas, export duties and minimum export prices - which China applies on key raw materials, such as yellow phosphorous, bauxite, coke, fluorspar, magnesium, manganese, silicon metal, silicon carbide and zinc. Some of these resources cannot be found elsewhere.'" (Seeking Alpha, 2009) |
|---|---|

| NNR Profile | Phosphate Rock (continued) |
|---|---|
| **US Scarcity Assessment** | "The United States has only 12 phosphorus mines. The supplies from the most productive mine, in Florida, are declining rapidly -- it will be commercially depleted within 20 years." (Foreign Policy, 2010)<br><br>That annual domestic phosphorous (phosphate rock) utilization decreased by 19% since peaking (to date) in 1998, is a significant indicator of declining American industrial preeminence and global economic competitiveness.<br><br>The US currently relies marginally on imported phosphate rock, all of which (100%) comes from Morocco. The quantity of phosphate rock supplied by foreign sources during 2008 accounted for only 4% of the total 2008 US utilization level.<br><br>Available evidence supports the contention that domestic phosphate rock supplies will likely remain insufficient to completely address domestic requirements going forward:<br><br>• The annual US phosphate rock extraction level decreased by 44% since peaking (to date) in 1980—a compelling indicator that domestic economically viable phosphate rock extraction has peaked permanently;<br>• The US has become increasingly reliant on phosphate rock imports since 1996; and<br>• The quantity of phosphate rock extracted domestically during 2008 amounted to only 96% of the total 2008 US utilization level—an indicator of America's increasing dependence on foreign NNRs.<br><br>Barring future reductions in the domestic (US) phosphate rock requirement trajectory and/or major new domestic economically viable discoveries, phosphate rock will likely remain scarce domestically in the future.<br><br>"In 2007, U.S. phosphate rock production fell below 30 million tons for the first time in more than 40 years, owing to lower production in Florida." (USGS, 2008) |

| Global NNR Scarcity | Scarce in 2008: Yes | Permanently Scarce: Almost Certain |
|---|---|---|
| **Historical Global Extraction Trends** | "China has surpassed the United States as the leading producer of phosphate rock in the world." (USGS, 2008)<br><br>Annual global phosphate rock (phosphorous) extraction levels generally increased during most of the 20th century (especially since WWII), peaking temporarily in 1913, 1920, 1930, 1938, 1974, 1980,and 1988, before peaking permanently (to date) in 1988 and generally declining through the remainder of the century. Annual global phosphate rock extraction levels rebounded during the early years of the 21st century and increased 22% between 2000 and 2008.<br><br>"Worldwide, the resources of high-grade [phosphate rock] ore are declining..." (Wikipedia [Phosphate Rock]) | |

| Global Peak Extraction Year (thru 2008): 1988 | Years to Global Reserve Exhaustion: 48 |
|---|---|
| Projected Global Peak Extraction Year: 1988 | Projected Global Peak Supply Year: 2030 |

| Interdependencies | None identified. |
|---|---|

| NNR Profile | Phosphate Rock (continued) |
|---|---|
| **Global Scarcity Assessment** | "Some initial analyses from scientists with the 'Global Phosphorus Research Initiative' estimate that there will not be sufficient phosphorus supplies from mining to meet agricultural demand within 30 to 40 years." (Foreign Policy, 2010)<br><br>A 22% increase in the annual global phosphate rock extraction level between 2000 and 2008 implies an increase in global phosphate rock demand during the pre-recession period, and a corresponding increase in global phosphate rock supply in response to increased global demand.<br><br>The fact that the price of phosphate rock increased by an extraordinary 145% during the 2000-2008 period indicates that global phosphate rock supply, while increasing during the eight year period, remained woefully insufficient to completely address global requirements in 2008.<br><br>Available evidence supports the contention that global phosphate rock supplies will remain insufficient to completely address global requirements going forward:<br><br>• Proven global phosphate rock reserves would exhaust in only 48 years, assuming the restoration of pre-recession utilization levels and growth rates;<br>• The global phosphate rock supply level is projected to peak in approximately 2030; and<br>• An extraordinary increase in the price of phosphate rock during the 2000-2008 period could induce only a nominal increase in phosphate rock supply—compelling evidence that globally available, economically viable phosphate rock extraction may be near, at, or past its permanent peak level.<br><br>Barring future reductions in the global phosphate rock requirement trajectory and/or major new economically viable discoveries, phosphate rock will almost certainly remain scarce globally in the future.<br><br>"Our dwindling supply of phosphorus, a primary component underlying the growth of global agricultural production, threatens to disrupt food security across the planet during the coming century. This is the gravest natural resource shortage you've never heard of..." (Foreign Policy, 2010) |

1. "Phosphate Rock", Wikipedia, 2011 - http://en.wikipedia.org/wiki/Phosphate_rock.
2. "Phosphate", Wikipedia, 2011 - http://en.wikipedia.org/wiki/Phosphate.
3. "Phosphate Rock Statistics", Historical Statistics for Mineral and Material Commodities in the United States, USGS, 2010 – http://minerals.usgs.gov/ds/2005/140/phosphate.xls.
4. "Fluorspar: The Cool Metal, T. Vulcan, Seeking Alpha, 2009 - http://seekingalpha.com/article/160670-fluorspar-the-cool-mineral.
5. "Peak Phosphorous", B. Dery, B. Anderson; Energy Bulletin, 2007 - http://www.energybulletin.net/node/33164.
6. "Peak Phosphorous", J. Elser, S. White, Foreign Policy, 2010 - http://www.foreignpolicy.com/articles/2010/04/20/peak_phosphorus?page=0,0.

| NNR Profile | Platinum Group Metals (PGM) |
|---|---|

## NNR Uses and Critical Applications

| Primary Uses | Platinum Group Metals (PGM) are six wear-resistant precious metals—indium, osmium, ruthenium, rhodium, platinum, and palladium—that are used as catalysts, in the electronics industry, and in fine jewelry. |
|---|---|
| Critical Applications | In components of catalytic converters, fuel cells, electronic computer and communication devices, and nuclear reactors. |

| NNR Criticality | NNR Criticality Classification: Indispensible |
|---|---|
| Substitutes | Palladium is increasingly being substituted for platinum in catalytic converters. Substituting PGMs for each other or substituting base metals for PGMs often results in performance degradation. |
| Criticality Assessment | "One in four goods manufactured today either contain platinum group metals or had platinum group metals play a key role during their manufacturing process." (Wikipedia [Platinum Group Metals])<br><br>PGMs play critical supporting roles in a wide variety of industrial, defense, commercial, and consumer applications, both existing and emerging; PGMs are indispensible to modern industrial existence |

| US NNR Scarcity | Scarce in 2008: Yes | Permanently Scarce: Almost Certain |
|---|---|---|
| 2008 US Import Reliance: 89%** | | 2008 Domestic US Supply: 11% |
| Historical US Import Trends | The US has been heavily reliant on PGM imports since the early 20th century, increasingly so in the past several decades. | |
| Historical US Usage Trends | Annual US PGM utilization levels generally increased during the 20th century—in a fluctuating manner—peaking temporarily in 1906, 1913, 1919, 1929, 1939, 1944, 1956, 1968, 1974, 1979, 1986, and 1999; domestic PGM utilization increased significantly in 2007 and 2008. | |
| US Peak Extraction Year (thru 2008): 2002 | | US Peak Utilization Year (thru 2008): 2008 |
| Potential Geopolitical US Supply Constraints | 46% of US palladium imports come from Russia. | |

| NNR Profile | Platinum Group Metals (PGM) [continued] |
|---|---|
| **US Scarcity Assessment** | "The Stillwater and East Boulder Mines in south-central Montana were the only primary platinum-group metals (PGMs) mines in the United States [producing 2% of global platinum and 6% of global palladium in 2009]…" (USGS, 2010)<br><br>The US currently relies almost exclusively on imported PGMs; the quantity of PGMs supplied by foreign sources during 2008 accounted for 89% of the total 2008 US utilization level.<br><br>Available evidence supports the contention that domestic PGM supplies will remain insufficient to completely address domestic requirements going forward:<br><br>• While US PGM utilization increased into the new millennium, the annual US PGM extraction level decreased by 19% since peaking (to date) in 2002—an indicator that domestic PGM extraction has possibly peaked permanently;<br>• The US has been an increasingly reliant PGM net importer since the 1940s;<br>• The quantity of PGMs extracted domestically during 2008 amounted to only 5% of the total 2008 US utilization level—a primary indicator of America's increasing dependence on foreign NNRs; and<br>• The quantity of PGMs extracted domestically during 2002, the year of peak (to date) domestic PGM extraction, amounted to only 6% of the 2008 total US utilization level.<br><br>Barring future reductions in the domestic (US) PGM requirement trajectory and/or major new domestic economically viable discoveries, PGMs will almost certainly remain scarce domestically in the future. |

| Global NNR Scarcity | Scarce in 2008: No | Permanently Scarce: Unclear |
|---|---|---|

| **Historical Global Extraction Trends** | "South Africa, with vast platinum ore deposits in the Merensky Reef of the Bushveld complex, is the world's largest producer of platinum [79% in 2009], followed by Russia [11% in 2009]. Platinum and palladium are also mined commercially from the Stillwater igneous complex in Montana, USA [2% in 2009]." (Wikipedia and USGS, 2010 [figures])<br><br>Annual global PGM extraction/production levels generally increased during the 20th century (especially after WWII), peaking temporarily in 1911, 1945, 1957, 1981, and 1990, before resuming their upward trend into the new millennium; global PGM production/extraction increased by 28% between 2000 and 2008.<br><br>"The tightening of emissions standards in China, Europe, Japan, and other parts of the world is expected to lead to higher average platinum loadings on catalysts…" (USGS, 2010) |
|---|---|

| Global Peak Extraction Year (thru 2008): 2006 | Years to Global Reserve Exhaustion: 48 |
|---|---|
| **Projected Global Peak Extraction Year: 2005** | **Projected Global Peak Supply Year: 2110** |

| **Interdependencies** | PGMs can be recovered as a byproduct of nickel, copper, silver, and gold mining; ruthenium, rhodium, and palladium are also formed as a product of fission in nuclear reactors. |
|---|---|

| NNR Profile | Platinum Group Metals (PGM) [continued] |
|---|---|
| **Global Scarcity Assessment** | "Between March 2007 and March 2008, platinum prices have gone from about \$39/g to over \$67/g with more than half the increase occurring in the beginning of 2008. Not only has demand outpaced growth in primary capacity, but also, primary producers in South Africa have not been able to operate at full capacity due to country-wide power shortages." (IEEE Xplore, 2008)<br><br>A 22% increase in the annual global PGM extraction/production level between 2000 and 2008 implies an increase in global PGM demand during the pre-recession period, and a corresponding increase in global PGM supply in response to increased global demand.<br><br>The fact that the price of PGMs decreased by 29% during the 2000-2008 period indicates that the global supply of PGMs in 2008 was sufficient to completely address 2008 global requirements.<br><br>Available evidence regarding the likelihood that global PGM supplies will remain sufficient to completely address global requirements going forward is conflicting:<br><br>• While global PGM extraction/production levels have generally increased since the early 1980s, PGM price levels have generally decreased since that time, albeit in a fluctuating manner—evidence of sufficient global PGM supplies; and<br>• The global PGM supply level is not projected to peak until approximately 2110; however<br>• The price of PGMs increased by 39% between 2001 and 2008, which indicates PGM scarcity on a global level in 2008;<br>• The global PGM extraction/production level was projected to peak in 2005; and<br>• Proven global PGM reserves would exhaust in only 48 years, assuming the restoration of pre-recession utilization levels and growth rates.<br><br>It is therefore unclear whether globally available, economically viable PGM supplies will remain sufficient to completely address future global requirements, or whether PGMs will become scarce globally in the not-too-distant future.<br><br>"If western use does not decrease and Chinese use just doubles [between 2007 and 2017], there will be a severe shortage of platinum before 2017." (Lifton, 2007) |

*PGM include indium, osmium, ruthenium, rhodium, platinum, and palladium.
**Import reliance for platinum; 2008 import reliance for palladium was 79%.

1. "Platinum Group Metals", Wikipedia, 2011 -
http://en.wikipedia.org/wiki/Platinum_group_metals.
2. "Platinum", Wikipedia, 2011- http://en.wikipedia.org/wiki/Platinum.
3. "Palladium", Wikipedia, 2011- http://en.wikipedia.org/wiki/Palladium.
4. "Rhodium", Wikipedia, 2011 - http://en.wikipedia.org/wiki/Rhodium.

5. "Platinum Group Metals Statistics", Historical Statistics for Mineral and Material Commodities in the United States, USGS, 2010 – http://minerals.usgs.gov/ds/2005/140/platinum.xls.

6. "Strong Fundamentals Positive for Platinum Group Metals", Mineweb, 2010 - http://www.mineweb.com/mineweb/view/mineweb/en/page35?oid=107072&sn=Detail.

7. "The Dynamics of the Availability of Platinum Group Metals for Electronics Manufacturers" (Abstract), IEEE Xplore, 2008 - http://ieeexplore.ieee.org/xpl/freeabs_all.jsp?arnumber=4562861.

8. "Has Peak Platinum Production Been Reached? If so, How Will This Affect the American OEM Automotive Industry?" J. Lifton, 2007 - http://www.glgroup.com/News/Has-Peak-Platinum-Production-Been-Reached--If-so-How-Will-This-Affect-The-American-OEM-Automotive-Industry--19258.html.

| NNR Profile | Potash |
|---|---|
| **NNR Uses and Critical Applications** | |
| **Primary Uses** | Potash is the common name for the salts that contain potassium, a soft, silvery-white metal used the manufacture of NPK (nitrogen, phosphorous, and potassium) fertilizers; potash is also used in manufacturing soaps, glass, ceramics, chemical dyes, drugs, synthetic rubber, de-icing agents, water softeners and explosives. |
| **Critical Applications** | NPK (containing potassium) fertilizers are indispensible to industrial agriculture.* [See note below.] |

| NNR Criticality | NNR Criticality Classification: Indispensible |
|---|---|
| **Substitutes** | "There are no substitutes for potassium as an essential plant nutrient and an essential nutritional requirement for animals and humans." (USGS, 2010) |
| **Criticality Assessment** | Potassium is indispensible to agriculture on an industrial scale, and as such is indispensible to modern industrial existence. |

| US NNR Scarcity | Scarce in 2008: Yes | Permanently Scarce: Almost Certain |
|---|---|---|
| **2008 US Import Reliance:** 84% | | **2008 Domestic US Supply:** 16% |
| **Historical US Import Trends** | Historically, the US has been both a net importer and a net exporter of potash; since 1963, the US has become increasingly reliant on potash imports. | |
| **Historical US Usage Trends** | Annual US potash utilization levels generally increased during the 20th century, peaking temporarily in 1905, 1911, 1920, 1928, 1937, and 1959, before peaking permanently (to date) in 1979. Domestic potash utilization spiked in 2008, nearly eclipsing the 1979 peak (to date); the 2008 US utilization level amounted to 98% of the 1979 peak utilization level. | |
| **US Peak Extraction Year (thru 2008):** 1967 | | **US Peak Utilization Year (thru 2008):** 1979 |
| **Potential Geopolitical US Supply Constraints** | "The world's eight largest potash miners, whose market control already exceeds that of oil cartel OPEC, are poised to tighten their grip on prices of the crop fertilizer as proposed mergers consolidate sales channels." (Bloomberg, 2010)<br><br>86% of US potash imports come from Canada; over 50% of proven global potash reserves are located in Canada.<br><br>"The concentration of [potash] supplies is driving concern about a tight and politically charged market." (Financial Times, 2010) | |

| NNR Profile | Potash (continued) |
|---|---|
| **US Scarcity Assessment** | "More than 57 percent of [US] nitrogen and 86 percent of [US] potash was from imports in 2008. Because domestic production capacity is limited, any increase in fertilizer demand will have to be met largely by imports." (USDA, 2010)<br><br>That annual domestic potash utilization decreased by 2% since peaking (to date) in 1979, is an indicator of declining American industrial preeminence and global economic competitiveness.<br><br>The US currently relies almost exclusively on imported potash, the vast majority (86%) of which comes from Canada. The quantity of potash supplied by foreign sources during 2008 accounted for 84% of the total 2008 US utilization level.<br><br>Available evidence supports the contention that domestic potash supplies will remain insufficient to completely address domestic requirements going forward:<br><br>• The annual US potash extraction level decreased by 61% since peaking (to date) in 1967—a compelling indicator that domestic economically viable potash extraction has peaked permanently;<br>• The US has become increasingly reliant on potash imports since 1963;<br>• The quantity of potash extracted domestically during 2008 amounted to only 16% of the total 2008 US utilization level—a primary indicator of America's increasing dependence on foreign NNRs; and<br>• The quantity of potash extracted domestically during 1967, the year of peak (to date) domestic potash extraction, amounted to only 57% of the 2008 total US utilization level.<br><br>Barring future reductions in the domestic (US) potash requirement trajectory and/or major new domestic economically viable discoveries, potash will almost certainly remain scarce domestically in the future.<br><br>"A fivefold surge in potash prices over 2007-2008 led to at least eight class-action claims in the U.S. over alleged collusion, a charge the producers denied." (Bloomberg, 2010) |

| Global NNR Scarcity | Scarce in 2008: Yes | Permanently Scarce: Likely |
|---|---|---|
| **Historical Global Extraction Trends** | "Canada is the world's leading [potash] producer [30% of global production in 2008], followed by Russia [19%] and Belarus [14%]; the United States ranks seventh [3%]." (Wikipedia; USGS data)<br><br>Annual global potash extraction levels generally increased during the 20th century (especially since WWII), peaking temporarily in 1929, 1938, 1943, 1980 and 1989, before resuming their upward trend into the 21st century; global potash production increased by 29% between 2000 and 2008.<br><br>"As population growth drives demand for foodstuffs, and the arable land available to supply food shrinks, it is the mineral fertilizers farmers use that help cover the gap between consumer demand for calories and the productivity of farm land to supply it. Thus, the biggest consumers of potash are the hungriest - China and India…" (Asia Times, 2008) | | |

| NNR Profile | Potash (continued) | |
|---|---|---|
| **Global Peak Extraction Year (thru 2008):** 2007 | | **Years to Global Reserve Exhaustion:** 50+ |
| **Projected Global Peak Extraction Year:** N/A | | **Projected Global Peak Supply Year:** N/A |
| **Interdependencies** | None identified. | |
| **Global Scarcity Assessment** | "Potash demand and prices increased throughout the year [2007] domestically and worldwide as a result of more crop acres that required potash fertilizer being planted…" (USGS, 2008)<br><br>A 29% increase in the annual global potash extraction level between 2000 and 2008 implies an increase in global potash demand during the pre-recession period, and a corresponding increase in global potash supply in response to increased global demand.<br><br>The fact that the price of potash increased by an extraordinary 230% during the 2000-2008 period indicates that global potash supply, while increasing during the eight year period, remained woefully insufficient to completely address global requirements in 2008.<br><br>Available evidence, albeit somewhat conflicting, supports the contention that global potash supplies will likely remain insufficient to completely address global requirements going forward:<br><br>• Proven global potash reserves are sufficient to last for over 50 years (assuming the restoration of pre-recession utilization levels and growth rates); however<br>• An extraordinary increase in the price of potash during the 2000-2008 period could induce only a modest increase in potash supply—compelling evidence that globally available, economically viable potash extraction may be at or near its permanent peak level.<br><br>Barring future reductions in the global potash requirement trajectory and/or major new economically viable discoveries, potash will likely remain scarce globally in the future.<br><br>"With only 12 countries producing potash, supply is limited by potash's scarcity and expensive mining." (The Street, 2010) | |

\* "Demand for food and animal feed has been on the rise since 2000. The U.S. Department of Agriculture's Economic Research Service (ERS) attributes the trend to average annual population increases of 75 million people around the world. Geographically, population growth in Brazil, Russia, India and China, known collectively as "BRIC", greatly contributed to the increased use of potash-based fertilizer. Rising incomes in developing countries also was a factor in the growing potash and fertilizer use. With more money in the household budget, consumers added more meat and dairy products to their diets. This shift in eating patterns required more acres to be planted, more fertilizer to be applied and more animals to be fed – all requiring more potash." (Wikipedia [Potash])

1. "Potash", Wikipedia, 2011- http://en.wikipedia.org/wiki/Potash.
2. "Potassium", Wikipedia, 2011 - http://en.wikipedia.org/wiki/Potassium.
3. "Potash Statistics", Historical Statistics for Mineral and Material Commodities in the United States, USGS, 2010 – http://minerals.usgs.gov/ds/2005/140/potash.xls.
4. "July-December Imports of Nitrogen and Potash Decreased in 2009; Phosphate Exports Also Decreased", USDA, 2010 - http://www.ers.usda.gov/Data/FertilizerTrade/summary.htm.

5. "Food Production: Agriculture Wars", Financial Times, 2010 -
http://www.ft.com/cms/s/0/e5e74d66-b213-11df-b2d9-00144feabdc0.html.
6. China Caught in Potash Crunch", J. Helmer, Asia Times, 2008 -
http://www.atimes.com/atimes/China/JD22Ad02.html.
7. "Potash `Oligopoly' to Strengthen on Mergers as BHP Eyes Entry", Y. Humber, Bloomberg,
2010 - http://www.bloomberg.com/news/2010-10-04/potash-oligopoly-to-strengthen-on-
mergers-as-bhp-eyes-entry.html.
8. "Potash Stock Could Rise on Speculative Russian Merger", The Street, 2010 -
http://www.thestreet.com/story/10785050/potash-stock-could-rise-on-speculative-russian-
merger.html.

| NNR Profile | Pumice (and Pumicite) | |
|---|---|---|
| **NNR Uses and Critical Applications** | | |
| **Primary Uses** | Pumice is a pale colored volcanic rock used to manufacture light-weight concrete and cinder blocks; pumice is also used as an abrasive and an absorbent. | |
| **Critical Applications** | None identified. | |
| **NNR Criticality** | **NNR Criticality Classification: Important** | |
| **Substitutes** | Viable pumice substitutes, including crushed aggregates, diatomite, expanded shale and clay, and vermiculite, are readily available.<br><br>"The costs of transportation determine the maximum economic distance pumice and pumicite can be shipped and still remain competitive with alternative materials." (USGS, 2010) | |
| **Criticality Assessment** | Pumice is one of several substances that are suitable for addressing building and construction material applications. | |
| **US NNR Scarcity** | **Scarce in 2008: Yes** | **Permanently Scarce: Unclear** |
| **2008 US Import Reliance: 6%** | **2008 Domestic US Supply: 94%** | |
| **Historical US Import Trends** | While net US pumice imports decreased in 2007 and 2008 as a percentage of total domestic utilization, annual net US pumice imports typically ranged between 25% and 50% of total US utilization during the past four decades. | |
| **Historical US Usage Trends** | Annual US pumice utilization levels increased—in a fluctuating manner—during the 20th and 21st centuries (especially since WWII), peaking temporarily in 1906, 1929, 1942, 1957, 1964, 1977, and 1986, before peaking permanently (to date) in 2004. | |
| **US Peak Extraction Year (thru 2008): 2006** | **US Peak Utilization Year (thru 2008): 2004** | |
| **Potential Geopolitical US Supply Constraints** | 72% of US pumice imports come from Greece. | |

| NNR Profile | Pumice (and Pumicite) [continued] |
|---|---|
| **US Scarcity Assessment** | "…pumicite production is sensitive to mining and transportation costs, and if domestic production costs increase, imports and competing materials might replace pumice in many domestic markets." [Note that it is less expensive to import pumice from Greece than it is to transport it internally within the US.] (USGS, 2008)<br><br>The US currently relies marginally on imported pumice, the majority (72%) of which comes from Greece. While the quantity of pumice supplied by foreign sources during 2008 accounted for only 6% of the total 2008 US utilization level, the percentage of US pumice net imports has typically been considerably higher.<br><br>Available evidence regarding the likelihood that domestic pumice supplies will remain insufficient to completely address domestic requirements going forward is conflicting:<br><br>• US pumice net imports typically ranged between 25% and 50% of the total US utilization level since the 1960s (until 2005)—an indicator of America's increasing dependence on foreign NNRs; however<br>• The annual US pumice extraction level increased into the new millennium (through 2006); and<br>• Domestic pumice reserves are considered by the USGS to be "large".<br><br>It is therefore unclear whether pumice will remain scarce domestically in the future or whether domestically available, economically viable pumice supplies will be sufficient to completely address future domestic requirements.<br><br>"Although pumice and pumicite are plentiful in the Western United States, legal challenges and public land designations could limit access to known deposits." (USGS, 2010) |

| Global NNR Scarcity | Scarce in 2008: No | Permanently Scarce: Unlikely |
|---|---|---|
| **Historical Global Extraction Trends** | Annual global pumice extraction levels increased dramatically following WWII, peaking temporarily in 1964, 1972, and 1979, before resuming their upward trend during the late 1990s and into the new millennium; annual global pumice production increased 41% between 2000 and 2008. | |

| Global Peak Extraction Year (thru 2008): 2007 | Years to Global Reserve Exhaustion: N/A |
|---|---|
| Projected Global Peak Extraction Year: N/A | Projected Global Peak Supply Year: N/A |

| Interdependencies | None identified. |
|---|---|

| NNR Profile | Pumice (and Pumicite) [continued] |
|---|---|
| **Global Scarcity Assessment** | A 41% increase in the annual global pumice extraction level between 2000 and 2008 implies an increase in global pumice demand during the pre-recession period, and a corresponding increase in global pumice supply in response to increased global demand. <br><br> The fact that the price of pumice decreased by 11% during the 2000-2008 period indicates that the global supply of pumice in 2008 was sufficient to completely address 2008 global requirements. <br><br> Available evidence supports the contention that global pumice supplies will remain sufficient to completely address global requirements going forward: <br><br> • While global pumice extraction levels have generally increased since the early 1990s, pumice price levels have generally decreased since that time—evidence of sufficient global pumice supplies; and <br> • Proven global pumice reserves are considered by the USGS to be "large". <br><br> Barring future increases in the global pumice requirement trajectory, globally available, economically viable pumice supplies will likely remain sufficient—notwithstanding temporary local shortages—to completely address global requirements going forward. |

1. "Pumice", Wikipedia, 2011 - http://en.wikipedia.org/wiki/Pumice.
2. "Pumice Statistics", Historical Statistics for Mineral and Material Commodities in the United States, USGS, 2010 – http://minerals.usgs.gov/ds/2005/140/pumice.xls.

| NNR Profile | Quartz Crystal (Industrial) | |
|---|---|---|
| **NNR Uses and Critical Applications** | | |
| **Primary Uses** | Quartz crystal, cultured (synthetic) and natural, is a colorless (in its pure form) transparent or translucent mineral used primarily in electronics applications (filters, frequency controls, and timers); quartz crystal is also used in optical applications. | |
| **Critical Applications** | Frequency control oscillators and frequency filters in electronic circuits comprising computers, communication equipment, and other high-technology electronics equipment. | |
| **NNR Criticality** | **NNR Criticality Classification: Critical** | |
| **Substitutes** | Cultured quartz crystals continue to displace natural crystals; however, viable substitutes for quartz crystals in electronics applications such as frequency-control oscillators and frequency filters are generally unavailable. | |
| **Criticality Assessment** | Quartz crystal based electronic components are deployed in a wide range of electronics products, commercial and military. | |
| **US NNR Scarcity** | **Scarce in 2008: Yes** | **Permanently Scarce: Almost Certain** |
| **2008 US Import Reliance: 100%** | | **2008 Domestic US Supply: 0%** |
| **Historical US Import Trends** | Historically, the US has been both a net importer and a net exporter of quartz crystal; the US is currently 100% reliant on quartz crystal imports. | |

| NNR Profile | Quartz Crystal (Industrial) [continued] |
|---|---|
| Historical US Usage Trends | Annual US quartz crystal utilization levels fluctuated widely during the 20$^{th}$ century, peaking permanently (to date) in 1943 (spike), then peaking at lower levels in 1948, 1953, 1961, 1973, 1979, 1984, and 1990 (secondary peak); the 1998 (latest available USGS data) US utilization level amounted to only 11% of the 1943 peak utilization level. |

| US Peak Production Year (thru 2008): 1984* | US Peak Utilization Year (thru 2008): 1943** |
|---|---|

| Potential Geopolitical US Supply Constraints | Most US quartz crystal (cultured) imports come from China, Japan, and Russia (specific import data is not available form the USGS). |
|---|---|
| US Scarcity Assessment | "Lascas [cultured quartz crystal feedstock] mining and processing in Arkansas ended in 1997 and, in 2009, no U.S. firms reported the production of cultured quartz crystals." (USGS, 2010)<br><br>That annual domestic quartz crystal utilization decreased by 89% since peaking (to date) in 1943, is a significant indicator of declining American industrial preeminence and global economic competitiveness.<br><br>The US currently relies exclusively on imported quartz crystal, the vast majority of which comes from China, Japan, and Russia.<br><br>Available evidence supports the contention that domestic quartz crystal supplies will remain insufficient to completely address domestic requirements going forward:<br><br>• The annual US quartz crystal production level decreased by 59% between 1984 (domestic peak production year to date) and 2000 (last available USGS data)—a compelling indicator that domestic economically viable quartz crystal production has peaked permanently; and<br>• The US has not (apparently) produced quartz crystal domestically since the year 2000—an indicator of America's increasing dependence on foreign NNRs.<br><br>Barring future reductions in the domestic (US) quartz crystal requirement trajectory and/or major new domestic economically viable discoveries, quartz crystal will almost certainly remain scarce domestically in the future.<br><br>"Cultured [versus natural] quartz crystal production capacity still exists in the United States but would require considerable refurbishment to be brought online." (USGS, 2010) |

| Global NNR Scarcity | Scarce in 2008 and in the Future: Inconclusive |
|---|---|
| Historical Global Production Trends | Annual global quartz crystal production levels fluctuated widely during the 20$^{th}$ century, spiking in 1961, 1966 (peak to date), 1980, and 1984; annual global crystal production increased between the mid 1990s and the early 2000s (latest available USGS data is 2002). |

| Global Peak Production Year (thru 2008): 1966 | Years to Global Reserve Exhaustion: N/A |
|---|---|
| Projected Global Peak Production Year: N/A | Projected Global Peak Supply Year: N/A |

| Interdependencies | Lascas is the non-electronic grade quartz that is used as the feedstock for growing cultured quartz crystal. |
|---|---|

| NNR Profile | Quartz Crystal (Industrial) [continued] |
|---|---|
| **Global Scarcity Assessment** | Insufficient USGS production and pricing data are available to determine global quartz crystal scarcity in 2008. Regarding future global quartz crystal requirements... <br><br> "Trends indicate that demand for quartz crystal devices will continue to increase, and consequently, quartz crystal production is expected to remain strong well into the future." (USGS, 2010) |

*Ne USGS data after 2000.
**No USGS data after 1998.

1. "Quartz Crystal", Wikipedia, 2011 - http://en.wikipedia.org/wiki/Quartz_crystal.
2. "Quartz Crystal Statistics", Historical Statistics for Mineral and Material Commodities in the United States, USGS, 2010 – http://minerals.usgs.gov/ds/2005/140/quartzcrystal.xls.

| NNR Profile | Rare Earth Minerals (REM) |
|---|---|
| **NNR Uses and Critical Applications** | |
| **Primary Uses** | A rare earth mineral contains one or more of the rare earth elements—scandium, yttrium, and the 15 lanthanides—which are used in batteries, lasers, magnets, oil refining, superconductors, and phosphors; REMs are also used as alloys and catalysts. |
| **Critical Applications** | "The trend is for a continued increase in the use of rare earths in many applications, especially automotive catalytic converters, permanent magnets, and rechargeable batteries for electric and hybrid vehicles." (USGS, 2010) |
| **NNR Criticality** | **NNR Criticality Classification: Indispensible** |
| **Substitutes** | Viable REM substitutes are generally not available. |
| **Criticality Assessment** | REMs play key support roles in a variety of critical high technology application areas; REM based batteries and magnets are expected to be critical in ongoing renewable energy and electric transportation initiatives; REMs are indispensible to modern industrial existence. |
| **US NNR Scarcity** | **Scarce in 2008: Yes** | **Permanently Scarce: Almost Certain** |
| **2008 US Import Reliance: 100%** | | **2008 Domestic US Supply: 0%** |
| **Historical US Import Trends** | "In 2009, rare earths were not mined in the United States..." (USGS, 2010) <br><br> Historically, the US has been both a net exporter and a net importer of REMs; since 2001, the US has relied exclusively on imported REMs. | |
| **Historical US Usage Trends** | Annual US REM utilization levels generally increased during the 20th century (especially from the 1960s forward), peaking temporarily in 1905, 1917, 1929, 1937, 1954, 1974, and 1984, before peaking permanently (to date) in 1990. Following a usage spike in 1996, domestic REM utilization levels declined dramatically; the 2008 US utilization level amounted to only 27% of the 1990 peak utilization level. | |
| **US Peak Extraction Year (thru 2008): 1984** | | **US Peak Utilization Year (thru 2008): 1990** |

| NNR Profile | Rare Earth Minerals (REM) [continued] |
|---|---|
| **Potential Geopolitical US Supply Constraints** | "China's leading Rare Earth producers will set global prices for metals which are widely used in a number of electronic devices, digital displays and military applications…" (News, 2010)<br><br>91% of US REM imports come from China; China accounts for 95% of global REM extraction.<br><br>"On Sept. 1, 2009, China announced plans to reduce its [REM export] quota to 35,000 tons per year in 2010-2015 to conserve scarce resources and protect the environment." (Wikipedia) |
| **US Scarcity Assessment** | "The United States currently imports most of its rare earth minerals from China. However, China may stop exporting in the near future to assure its own needs. Unfortunately, the United States has very few rare earth mineral deposits." (geology.com, 2010)<br><br>That annual domestic REM utilization decreased by 73% since peaking (to date) in 1990, is a significant indicator of declining American industrial preeminence and global economic competitiveness.<br><br>The US currently relies exclusively on imported REMs, the overwhelming majority (91%) of which comes from China.<br><br>Available evidence supports the contention that domestic REM supplies will remain insufficient to completely address domestic requirements going forward:<br><br>• US REM extraction ceased entirely in 2001—a significant indicator of America's increasing dependence on foreign NNRs, and a compelling indicator that domestic economically viable REM extraction has peaked permanently;<br>• US REM import levels have generally increased since the late 1990s; and<br>• While REM extraction at the (under development) Mountain Pass, CA, Lehmi Pass, and Diamond Creek, ID mining ventures should contribute toward US requirements, it is not clear whether domestic REMs will be sufficient, in terms of mix and levels, to completely address US requirements.<br><br>Barring future reductions in the domestic (US) REM requirement trajectory and/or tremendous success at the Mountain Pass, Lehmi Pass, and/or Diamond Creek mines, REMs will almost certainly remain scarce domestically in the future.<br><br>"The United States was once self-reliant in domestically produced REEs, [Rare Earth Elements] but over the past 15 years has become 100% reliant on imports, primarily from China, because of lower-cost operations." (Humphries, 2010) |

| NNR Profile | Rare Earth Minerals (REM) [continued] | |
|---|---|---|
| **Global NNR Scarcity** | **Scarce in 2008: Yes** | **Permanently Scarce: Unclear** |
| **Historical Global Extraction Trends** | "China now produces over 97% of the world's rare earth supply, mostly in Inner Mongolia. All of the world's heavy rare earths (such as dysprosium) come from Chinese rare earth sources…" (Wikipedia)<br><br>Annual global REM extraction levels generally increased during the 20th and 21st centuries—often in a cyclical manner—peaking temporarily in 1909, 1917, 1938, 1944, 1954, 1969, 1974, and 1989, before resuming their upward trend into the new millennium; annual global REM extraction increased 47% between 2000 and 2008. | |
| **Global Peak Extraction Year (thru 2008): 2006** | **Years to Global Reserve Exhaustion: 49** | |
| **Projected Global Peak Extraction Year: 2078** | **Projected Global Peak Supply Year: 2088** | |
| **Interdependencies** | Most REMs are collocated, especially those in the "heavy" (yttrium) REM group and those in the "light" (cerium) REM group. | |
| **Global Scarcity Assessment** | "Prices were higher in 2007 than in 2006 for most rare-earth products amid increased demand and a stable [read "insufficient"] supply." (USGS, 2008)<br><br>A 47% increase in the annual global REM extraction level between 2000 and 2008 implies an increase in global demand during the pre-recession period, and a corresponding increase in REM supply in response to increased global demand.<br><br>The fact that the price of REMs increased by 50% during the 2000-2008 period indicates that global REM supply, while increasing during the eight year period, remained insufficient to completely address global requirements in 2008.<br><br>Available evidence regarding the likelihood that global REM supplies will remain insufficient to completely address global requirements going forward is conflicting:<br><br>• Proven global REM reserves would exhaust in only 49 years, assuming the restoration of pre-recession utilization levels and growth rates;<br>• The increased global REM supply brought online between 2000 and 2008 failed to prevent a price increase during the period—evidence of unaddressed global requirements in 2008; and<br>• It is questionable whether the robust 5% compound annual growth rate (CAGR) in global REM extraction evidenced between 2000 and 2008—an interval during which REMs became scarce globally, despite significant increases in production—can be reestablished, much less increased, going forward. A 5% CAGR would necessitate a continuous doubling in the annual global extraction level of REMs every 14 years; however<br>• The global REM extraction level is not projected to peak until approximately 2078; and<br>• The global REM supply level is not projected to peak until approximately 2088.<br><br>It is therefore unclear whether REMs will remain scarce globally in the future, or whether globally available, economically viable REM supplies will be sufficient to completely address future global requirements. | |

| | "World demand for rare earth elements is estimated at 134,000 tons per year [2009], with global production around 124,000 tons annually. The difference is covered by previously mined aboveground stocks. World demand is projected to rise to 180,000 tons annually by 2012, while it is unlikely that new mine output will close the gap in the short term." (Humphries, 2010) |
|---|---|

*Varies per REM depending on specific applications—requirements (demand) versus available supplies.

1. "Rare Earths", Wikipedia, 2011 - http://minerals.usgs.gov/ds/2005/140/rareearths.xls.
2. "Rare Earth Element", Wikipedia, 2011 - http://en.wikipedia.org/wiki/Rare_earth_element.
3. "Rare Earth Mineral Statistics", Historical Statistics for Mineral and Material Commodities in the United States, USGS, 2010 – http://minerals.usgs.gov/ds/2005/140/rareearths.xls.
4. "Rare Earth Elements: The Global Supply Chain", Summary and page 2, M. Humphries, Congressional Research Service, 2010 - http://www.fas.org/sgp/crs/natsec/R41347.pdf.
5. "Rare Earth Mineral Deposits in the US", geology.com, 2010 - http://geology.com/news/2010/u-s-rare-earth-mineral-deposits.shtml.
6. "U.S. Sits on Rare Supply of Tech-crucial Minerals", J. Hsu, MSNBC.com; 2010 - http://www.msnbc.msn.com/id/35782773/ns/technology_and_science-science/.
7. "China Rare Earth Producers to Set Joint Price Policy", Indium, Gallium, and Germanium News on the Web (News), 2010 - http://indiumsamplesblog.com/2010/08/10/china-rare-earth-producers-to-set-joint-price-policy/.

| NNR Profile | Rhenium | |
|---|---|---|
| **NNR Uses and Critical Applications** | | |
| **Primary Uses** | Rhenium is a silvery-white heavy metal used as a superalloy, a superconductor, and a chemical industry catalyst. | |
| **Critical Applications** | Catalyst in petroleum refining, and jet engine (F-15, F-16, F-22, and F-35) and industrial gas turbine engine blades. | |
| **NNR Criticality** | **NNR Criticality Classification: Critical** | |
| **Substitutes** | Viable substitutes in catalytic applications, including gallium, germanium, indium, iridium, selenium, silicon, tin, tungsten, and vanadium, are under evaluation; price/performance characteristics associated with rhenium substitutes in other applications vary. | |
| **Criticality Assessment** | Rhenium plays a vital role in several critical niche applications. In the event that viable substitutes are identified for its catalytic and superalloy applications, rhenium could decline in importance. | |
| **US NNR Scarcity** | **Scarce in 2008: Yes** | **Permanently Scarce: Almost Certain** |
| **2008 US Import Reliance: 85%** | **2008 Domestic US Supply: 15%** | |
| **Historical US Import Trends** | "Rhenium [2007] imports increased by about 15% owing to continued strong demand for superalloys in the gas turbine engine market and improved demand in the catalyst market." (USGS, 2008)<br><br>The US has been a net importer of rhenium since the 1960s; US rhenium net imports have increased dramatically over the past several decades. | |
| **Historical US Usage Trends** | Annual US rhenium utilization levels generally increased since the mid 1960s, peaking temporarily in 1971, 1978, and 1998, before resuming their upward trend into the early 21st century. | |
| **US Peak Production Year (thru 2008): 1991** | **US Peak Utilization Year (thru 2008): 2008** | |

| NNR Profile | Rhenium (continued) |
|---|---|
| **Potential Geopolitical US Supply Constraints** | 93% of US rhenium metal powder imports come from Chile, and 68% of ammonium perrhenate imports come from Kazakhstan; Chile has the largest proven rhenium reserves and is the world's largest rhenium producer (2005). |
| **US Scarcity Assessment** | "The United States continued to rely on imports for much of its supply of rhenium, and Chile and Kazakhstan supplied the majority of the imported rhenium." (USGS, 2008)<br><br>The US currently relies almost exclusively on imported rhenium, the vast majority (93% of metal powder) of which comes from Chile. The quantity of rhenium supplied by foreign sources during 2008 accounted for only 85% of the total 2008 US utilization level.<br><br>Available evidence supports the contention that domestic rhenium supplies will remain insufficient to completely address domestic requirements going forward:<br><br>• While US rhenium utilization increased into the new millennium, the annual US rhenium production level decreased by 59% since peaking (to date) in 1991—a compelling indicator that domestic economically viable rhenium extraction has peaked permanently;<br>• The US has become increasingly reliant on rhenium imports since the early 1990s;<br>• The quantity of rhenium produced domestically during 2008 amounted to only 15% of the total 2008 US utilization level—a significant indicator of America's increasing dependence on foreign NNRs; and<br>• The quantity of rhenium produced domestically during 1991, the year of peak (to date) domestic rhenium production, amounted to only 39% of the 2008 total US utilization level.<br><br>Barring future reductions in the domestic (US) rhenium requirement trajectory and/or major new domestic economically viable discoveries, rhenium will almost certainly remain scarce domestically in the future. |

| Global NNR Scarcity | Scarce in 2008: Yes | Permanently Scarce: Almost Certain |
|---|---|---|
| **Historical Global Production Trends** | Annual global rhenium production levels generally increased from the 1980s forward, peaking temporarily in 1991, and 2000, before generally increasing thereafter; global rhenium production increased 58% between 2000 and 2008.<br><br>"Owing to the scarcity and minor output of rhenium, its production and processing pose no known threat to the environment." (USGS, 2010) | |

| Global Peak Production Year (thru 2008): 2008 | Years to Global Reserve Exhaustion: 22 |
|---|---|
| **Projected Global Peak Production Year:** N/A | **Projected Global Peak Supply Year:** N/A |
| **Interdependencies** | Rhenium can be recovered as a byproduct of molybdenum and copper refinement. |

| NNR Profile | Rhenium (continued) |
|---|---|
| **Global Scarcity Assessment** | "Owing to strong demand [and obviously insufficient supply], APR [ammonium perrhenate—a rhenium compound] spot prices continued to rise…" (USGS, 2008)<br><br>A 58% increase in the annual global rhenium production level between 2000 and 2008 implies a robust increase in global rhenium demand during the pre-recession period, and a correspondingly robust increase in global rhenium supply in response to increased global demand.<br><br>The fact that the price of rhenium increased by a substantial 71% during the 2000-2008 period indicates that global rhenium supply, while increasing during the eight year period, remained insufficient to completely address global requirements in 2008.<br><br>Available evidence supports the contention that global rhenium supplies will remain insufficient to completely address global requirements going forward:<br><br>• Proven global rhenium reserves would exhaust in only 22 years, assuming the restoration of pre-recession utilization levels and growth rates;<br>• A robust increase in the price of rhenium during the 2000-2008 period induced a less than sufficient corresponding increase in global rhenium supply; and<br>• It is questionable whether the robust 5.9% compound annual growth rate (CAGR) in global rhenium production evidenced between 2000 and 2008—an interval during which rhenium became scarce globally despite a significant increase in production—can be reestablished, much less increased, going forward. A 5.9% CAGR would necessitate a continuous doubling in the annual global production level of rhenium every 12 years.<br><br>Barring future reductions in the global rhenium requirement trajectory and/or major new economically viable discoveries, rhenium will almost certainly remain scarce globally in the future.<br><br>"Demand for catalyst-grade APR, supported by the petroleum industry, was expected to continue to remain strong. Demand for rhenium in the aerospace industry, although more unpredictable, was also expected to remain strong." (USGS, 2010) |

1. "Rhenium", Wikipedia, 2011 - http://en.wikipedia.org/wiki/Rhenium.
2. "Rhenium Statistics", Historical Statistics for Mineral and Material Commodities in the United States, USGS, 2010 – http://minerals.usgs.gov/ds/2005/140/rhenium.xls.

| NNR Profile | Rubidium |
|---|---|
| **NNR Uses and Critical Applications** | |
| **Primary Uses** | Rubidium is a soft silvery-white metal used in chemical and electronic R&D applications. |
| **Critical Applications** | "Frequency standard" in cellular communication and GPS applications (atomic clocks). |

| NNR Criticality | | NNR Criticality Classification: Important |
|---|---|---|
| **Substitutes** | Cesium may be used interchangeably with rubidium in most applications. | |
| **Criticality Assessment** | In the event that new sources of rubidium are discovered, which in turn lead to the development of new applications and increased demand, rubidium's criticality could increase. | |

| US NNR Scarcity | Scarce in 2008: Yes | Permanently Scarce: Almost Certain |
|---|---|---|
| **2008 US Import Reliance:** 100% | | **2008 Domestic US Supply:** 0% |
| **Historical US Import Trends** | Rubidium containing ores are not mined in the US; all unrefined rubidium must be imported. | |
| **Historical US Usage Trends** | Annual US rubidium utilization levels have increased in recent years; a trend that the USGS expects to continue. | |
| **US Peak Production Year (thru 2008):** N/A | | **US Peak Utilization Year (thru 2008):** N/A |
| **Potential Geopolitical US Supply Constraints** | 100% of US rubidium is imported from Canada. | |
| **US Scarcity Assessment** | "Rubidium is not mined in the United States [in 2009]…" (USGS, 2010) <br><br> The US currently relies exclusively on imported rubidium, 100% of which comes from Canada. <br><br> Barring future reductions in the domestic (US) rubidium requirement trajectory and/or major new domestic economically viable discoveries, rubidium will almost certainly remain scarce domestically in the future. | |

| Global NNR Scarcity | Scarce in 2008 and in the Future: Inconclusive |
|---|---|
| **Historical Global Production Trends** | Global rubidium production data are not available from the USGS. |
| **Global Peak Production Year (thru 2008):** N/A | **Years to Global Reserve Exhaustion:** N/A |
| **Projected Global Peak Production Year:** N/A | **Projected Global Peak Supply Year:** N/A |
| **Interdependencies** | Rubidium is generally produced as a byproduct of cesium and lithium mining. |
| **Global Scarcity Assessment** | Global rubidium production and pricing data are not available from the USGS. However, from the USGS perspective: <br><br> "Demand [for rubidium] is limited by the lack of supply, but discovery of new sources of rubidium, increases in lithium exploration, as well as higher grade rubidium discoveries, may create new supplies leading to expanded commercial applications." (USGS, 2010) |

*Insufficient USGS data is available on a global level to make a valid assessment.

1. "Rubidium", Wikipedia, 2011 - http://en.wikipedia.org/wiki/Rubidium.

| NNR Profile | Salt |
|---|---|

## NNR Uses and Critical Applications

| Primary Uses | Salt (sodium chloride) is a white, gray, or pale pink mineral used as a food seasoning, in food preservation, and in cosmetic products; salt is also used for highway deicing (rock salt), as a chemical industry feedstock, and in water treatment; salt is essential to animal life. |
|---|---|
| Critical Applications | Chemical industry applications.<br><br>"The chemical industry is the largest consumer of salt using about 60% of total production. The industry predominantly converts the salt into chlorine, caustic and soda ash, without which petroleum refining, petrochemistry, organic synthesis, glass production, and so on would not be possible. (CEA, 2010) |

| NNR Criticality | NNR Criticality Classification: Critical |
|---|---|
| Substitutes | Salt substitutes are available, but are almost always price/performance inferior. |
| Criticality Assessment | Besides its more common applications as a food additive and highway deicer, salt plays several critical roles as a chemical industry feedstock. |

| US NNR Scarcity | Scarce in 2008: Yes | Permanently Scarce: Likely |
|---|---|---|

| 2008 US Import Reliance: 21% | 2008 Domestic US Supply: 79% |
|---|---|

| Historical US Import Trends | Despite its obvious abundance, the US has become an increasing net importer of salt since the 1960s. |
|---|---|
| Historical US Usage Trends | Annual US salt utilization levels generally increased during the 20th and 21st centuries, peaking temporarily in 1902, 1918, 1929, 1944, 1956, 1974, 1979, 1984, and 1996, before generally increasing during the early years of the new millennium. |

| US Peak Extraction Year (thru 2008): 2008 | US Peak Utilization Year (thru 2008): 2008 |
|---|---|

| Potential Geopolitical US Supply Constraints | 39% of US salt imports come from Canada, and 30% come from Chile.<br><br>"A major U.S. salt company was purchased for $1.68 billion by a German salt company in April [2009]. The acquisition made the German company the largest salt producer in the world." [Foreign ownership] (USGS, 2010) |
|---|---|
| US Scarcity Assessment | The US currently relies marginally on imported salt, the majority of which comes from Canada (39%) and Chile (30%). The quantity of salt supplied by foreign sources during 2008 accounted for 21% of the total 2008 US utilization level.<br><br>Available evidence, albeit somewhat conflicting, supports the contention that domestic salt supplies will likely remain insufficient to completely address domestic requirements going forward:<br><br>• Proven US salt reserves are considered by the USGS to be "large"; however<br>• Net US salt imports increased steadily since the 1960s; and<br>• The quantity of salt extracted domestically during 2008 amounted to only 79% of the total 2008 US utilization level—a significant indicator of America's increasing dependence on foreign NNRs.<br><br>Barring future reductions in the domestic (US) salt requirement trajectory and/or major new domestic economically viable discoveries, salt will likely remain scarce domestically in the future. |

| NNR Profile | Salt (continued) | |
|---|---|---|
| **Global NNR Scarcity** | **Scarce in 2008: Yes** | **Permanently Scarce: Unclear** |
| **Historical Global Extraction Trends** | "China surpassed the United States in 2006 as the leading producer of salt in the world." (USGS, 2008)<br><br>Annual global salt extraction levels generally increased during the 20th and 21st centuries, peaking temporarily in 1902, 1930, 1936, 1943, 1974, 1979, 1991, and 1997, before increasing into the new millennium; annual global salt extraction increased 32% between 2000 and 2008. | |

| Global Peak Extraction Year (thru 2008): 2006 | Years to Global Reserve Exhaustion: N/A |
|---|---|
| Projected Global Peak Extraction Year: N/A | Projected Global Peak Supply Year: N/A |

| **Interdependencies** | None identified. |
|---|---|
| **Global Scarcity Assessment** | A 32% increase in the annual global salt extraction level between 2000 and 2008 implies an increase in global salt demand during the pre-recession period, and a corresponding increase in global salt supply in response to increased global demand.<br><br>The fact that the price of salt increased by 25% during the 2000-2008 period indicates that global salt supply, while increasing during the eight year period, remained insufficient to completely address global requirements in 2008.<br><br>Available evidence regarding the likelihood that global salt supplies will remain insufficient to completely address global requirements going forward is conflicting:<br><br>• An increase in the price of salt during the 2000-2008 period induced a modest yet insufficient increase in salt supply—compelling evidence of tight global supply in 2008; however<br>• Proven global salt reserves are considered by the USGS to be "large".<br><br>It is therefore unclear whether salt will remain scarce globally in the future, or whether globally available, economically viable salt supplies will be sufficient to completely address future global requirements. |

1. "Salt", Wikipedia, 2011 - http://en.wikipedia.org/wiki/Salt.
2. "Salt Statistics", Historical Statistics for Mineral and Material Commodities in the United States, USGS, 2010 – http://minerals.usgs.gov/ds/2005/140/salt.xls.
3. "The Salt Industry Worldwide", CEA, 2010 - http://www.cea-life.com/minerals_health/salt_industry.htm.

| NNR Profile | Sand and Gravel (Construction) |
|---|---|
| **NNR Uses and Critical Applications** | |
| **Primary Uses** | Sand is composed of finely divided rock and mineral particles; gravel is "larger grained sand". Construction sand and gravel are used in applications such as brick making, road base and coverings, and concrete production. |
| **Critical Applications** | Concrete, road making, and brick making. |

| NNR Profile | Sand and Gravel (Construction) [continued] |
|---|---|
| **NNR Criticality** | **NNR Criticality Classification: Indispensible** |
| **Substitutes** | Crushed stone is a viable substitute for sand and gravel as a construction aggregate in some applications; recycled asphalt and concrete also substitute on a limited basis.<br><br>"Crushed stone, the other major construction aggregate, continues to replace natural sand and gravel, especially in more densely populated areas of the Eastern United States." (UGSS, 2010) |
| **Criticality Assessment** | While not particularly exotic, sand and gravel are indispensible construction materials for enabling modern industrial existence. |

| US NNR Scarcity | Scarce in 2008: No | Permanently Scarce: Unlikely |
|---|---|---|
| **2008 US Import Reliance: 0%** | | **2008 Domestic US Supply:** 100% |

| | |
|---|---|
| **Historical US Import Trends** | The US currently extracts sufficient construction sand and gravel domestically to completely address its internal requirements. |
| **Historical US Usage Trends** | Annual US construction sand and gravel utilization levels generally increased during both the 20th and 21st centuries, peaking temporarily in 1910, 1916, 1929, 1942, 1966, 1973, 1978, and 1988, before increasing into the new millennium.<br><br>"In response to changes in demand from the struggling residential construction industry, construction sand and gravel output decreased for the first time [in 2007] since 1991." (USGS, 2008) |

| US Peak Extraction Year (thru 2008): 2006 | US Peak Utilization Year (thru 2008): 2006 |
|---|---|
| **Potential Geopolitical US Supply Constraints** | 75% of US construction sand and gravel imports come from Canada; however, the US is not currently a net importer of construction sand and gravel. |

| NNR Profile | Sand and Gravel (Construction) [continued] |
|---|---|
| **US Scarcity Assessment** | "Construction sand and gravel valued at $8.0 billion was produced by an estimated 4,000 companies from about 6,300 operations in 50 States." (USGS, 2008)<br><br>The US is currently addressing its total requirement for construction sand and gravel through domestic supplies.<br><br>Available evidence supports the contention that domestic construction sand and gravel supplies will likely remain sufficient to completely address domestic requirements going forward:<br><br>• Domestic construction sand and gravel supplies were sufficient to completely address domestic requirements during the 2000-2008 period of rapid economic growth prior to the Great Recession; and<br>• Domestic construction sand and gravel reserves are considered by the USGS to be "large".<br><br>Barring future increases in the domestic (US) construction sand and gravel requirement trajectory, domestically available, economically viable construction sand and gravel supplies will likely remain sufficient—notwithstanding temporary local shortages—to completely address domestic requirements going forward.<br><br>"Movement of sand and gravel operations away from densely populated centers is expected to continue where environmental, land development, and local zoning regulations discourage them. Consequently, shortages of construction sand and gravel would support higher-than-average price increases in industrialized and urban areas." (USGS, 2010) |

| Global NNR Scarcity | | Scarce in 2008: Yes | Permanently Scarce: Unclear |
|---|---|---|---|
| **Historical Global Extraction Trends** | | "The United States was the world's leading producer and consumer of industrial sand and gravel based on estimated world production figures." (USGS, 2010)<br><br>USGS global construction sand and gravel extraction data are not available. | |

| Global Peak Extraction Year (thru 2008): N/A | Years to Global Reserve Exhaustion: N/A |
|---|---|
| Projected Global Peak Extraction Year: N/A | Projected Global Peak Supply Year: N/A |

| Interdependencies | None identified. |
|---|---|

| NNR Profile | Sand and Gravel (Construction) [continued] |
|---|---|
| **Global Scarcity Assessment** | While annual global extraction data associated with construction sand and gravel are unavailable from the USGS for the 2000-2008 pre-recession period, construction sand and gravel prices increased by 24% between 2000 and 2008, indicating that global industrial sand and gravel supplies were insufficient to completely address global requirements during 2008.<br><br>Available evidence regarding the likelihood that global construction sand and gravel supplies will remain insufficient to completely address global requirements going forward is conflicting:<br><br>• An increase in the price of industrial sand and gravel during the 2000-2008 period indicates some degree of global scarcity in 2008; however<br>• Proven global industrial sand and gravel resources are considered by the USGS to be "large".<br><br>It is therefore unclear whether construction sand and gravel will remain scarce globally in the future, or whether globally available, economically viable construction sand and gravel supplies will be sufficient to completely address future global requirements.<br><br>"Sand and gravel resources of the world are large. However, because of environmental restrictions, geographic distribution, and quality requirements for some uses, sand and gravel extraction is uneconomic in some cases." (USGS, 2010) |

1. "Sand", Wikipedia, 2011 - http://en.wikipedia.org/wiki/Sand.
2. "Gravel", Wikipedia, 2011 - http://en.wikipedia.org/wiki/Gravel.
3. "Sand and Gravel (Construction) Statistics", Historical Statistics for Mineral and Material Commodities in the United States, USGS, 2010 – http://minerals.usgs.gov/ds/2005/140/sandgravelconstruction.xls.
4. "Sand and Gravel", Mineral Information Institute (MII), 2011 - http://www.mii.org/Minerals/photosandgr.html.

| NNR Profile | Sand and Gravel (Industrial) | |
|---|---|---|
| **NNR Uses and Critical Applications** | | |
| **Primary Uses** | Sand is composed of finely divided rock and mineral particles; gravel is "larger grained sand". Industrial sand and gravel are used in glassmaking, in hydraulic fracturing applications, in foundries (casting), as an abrasive (sandblasting), on icy highways, and in water filtration applications. | |
| **Critical Applications** | Foundries (casting) and glass making. | |
| **NNR Criticality** | **NNR Criticality Classification: Indispensible** | |
| **Substitutes** | Industrial sand and gravel substitutes in glassmaking and foundry and molding applications include chromite, olivine, staurolite, and zircon sands. | |
| **Criticality Assessment** | While not particularly exotic, sand and gravel are indispensable industrial materials for enabling modern industrial existence. | |
| **US NNR Scarcity** | **Scarce in 2008: No** | **Permanently Scarce: Unlikely** |
| **2008 US Import Reliance:** 0% | **2008 Domestic US Supply:** 100% | |

| NNR Profile | Sand and Gravel (Industrial) [continued] |
|---|---|
| **Historical US Import Trends** | The US has been a net exporter of industrial sand and gravel since the early 1970s.<br><br>"The high level of [US industrial sand and gravel] exports was attributed to the high-quality and advanced processing techniques used in the United States for a large variety of grades of silica sand and gravel, meeting virtually every specification." (USGS, 2010) |
| **Historical US Usage Trends** | Annual US industrial sand and gravel utilization levels generally increased during the first three quarters of the 20th century, peaking temporarily in 1907, 1912, 1920, 1929, 1937, 1947, 1956, and 1970, before peaking permanently (to date) in 1979. Domestic industrial sand and gravel utilization declined in a fluctuating manner thereafter; the 2008 US utilization level amounted to 94% of the 1979 peak utilization level. |

| US Peak Extraction Year (thru 2008): 2005 | US Peak Utilization Year (thru 2008): 1979 |
|---|---|

| **Potential Geopolitical US Supply Constraints** | 54% of US industrial sand and gravel imports come from Canada; however, the US is a net exporter of industrial sand and gravel. |
|---|---|
| **US Scarcity Assessment** | That annual domestic industrial sand and gravel utilization decreased by 6% since peaking (to date) in 1979, is a significant indicator of declining American industrial preeminence and global economic competitiveness.<br><br>The US is however currently addressing its total requirement for industrial sand and gravel through domestic supplies.<br><br>Available evidence supports the contention that domestic industrial sand and gravel supplies will likely remain sufficient to completely address domestic requirements going forward:<br><br>• Domestic industrial sand and gravel supplies were sufficient to completely address domestic requirements during the 2000-2008 period of rapid economic growth prior to the Great Recession; and<br>• Domestic industrial sand and gravel reserves are considered by the USGS to be "large".<br><br>Barring future increases in the domestic (US) industrial sand and gravel requirement trajectory, domestically available, economically viable industrial sand and gravel supplies will likely remain sufficient—notwithstanding temporary local shortages—to completely address domestic requirements going forward.<br><br>"The industrial sand and gravel industry continued to be concerned with safety and health regulations and environmental restrictions in 2009. Local shortages were expected to continue to increase owing to local zoning regulations and land development alternatives." (USGS, 2010) |

| NNR Profile | Sand and Gravel (Industrial) [continued] | |
|---|---|---|
| **Global NNR Scarcity** | **Scarce in 2008: Yes** | **Permanently Scarce: Likely** |
| **Historical Global Extraction Trends** | Annual global industrial sand and gravel extraction levels fluctuated during the latter decades of the 20th century, peaking temporarily in 1988, before peaking permanently (to date) in 1995 and at the same level in 2007. Annual global industrial sand and gravel extraction increased 4% between 2000 and 2008. | |
| **Global Peak Extraction Year (thru 2008):** 2007 | **Years to Global Reserve Exhaustion:** N/A | |
| **Projected Global Peak Extraction Year:** N/A | **Projected Global Peak Supply Year:** N/A | |
| **Interdependencies** | None identified. | |
| **Global Scarcity Assessment** | A 4% increase in the annual global industrial sand and gravel extraction level between 2000 and 2008 implies an increase in global industrial sand and gravel demand during the pre-recession period, and a corresponding increase in global industrial sand and gravel supply in response to increased global demand.<br><br>The fact that the price of industrial sand and gravel increased by a robust 71% during the 2000-2008 period indicates that global industrial sand and gravel supply, while increasing during the eight year period, remained insufficient to completely address global requirements in 2008.<br><br>Available evidence, albeit somewhat conflicting, supports the contention that global industrial sand and gravel supplies will likely remain insufficient to completely address global requirements going forward:<br><br>• Proven global industrial sand and gravel reserves are considered by the USGS to be "large"; however<br>• A robust increase in the price of industrial sand and gravel during the 2000-2008 period induced only a nominal increase in industrial sand and gravel supply—evidence of tight global supply in 2008.<br><br>Barring future reductions in the global industrial sand and gravel requirement trajectory and/or major new economically viable discoveries, industrial sand and gravel will likely remain scarce globally in the future.<br><br>"Sand and gravel resources of the world are large. However, because of environmental restrictions, geographic distribution, and quality (grade) requirements for some uses, sand and gravel extraction is uneconomic in some cases." (USGS, 2010) | |

1. "Sand", Wikipedia, 2011 - http://en.wikipedia.org/wiki/Sand.
2. "Gravel", Wikipedia, 2011 - http://en.wikipedia.org/wiki/Gravel.
3. "Sand and Gravel (Industrial) Statistics", Historical Statistics for Mineral and Material Commodities in the United States, USGS, 2010 – http://minerals.usgs.gov/ds/2005/140/sandgravelindustrial.xls.

| NNR Profile | Selenium |
|---|---|
| **NNR Uses and Critical Applications** | |
| **Primary Uses** | Selenium is a dense, purplish-gray mineral used in glass making, chemicals (catalyst), and pigments; selenium is also used in photocells and solar cells, and as a nutritional supplement. Trace amounts of selenium are also necessary in mammals. |
| **Critical Applications** | Solar cells is an emerging selenium application.<br><br>"An increased interest in solar cell technologies has increased the consumption of selenium in CIGS [copper indium gallium (di) selenide] solar cells." (USGS, 2010) |

| NNR Criticality | NNR Criticality Classification: Important |
|---|---|
| **Substitutes** | Viable selenium substitutes are available in all application areas, including photovoltaics. |
| **Criticality Assessment** | Selenium plays a support role in a variety of niche applications; wide adoption of selenium based solar cells would increase its criticality. |

| US NNR Scarcity | Scarce in 2008: No | Permanently Scarce: Unclear |
|---|---|---|
| **2008 US Import Reliance: 0%*** | | **2008 Domestic US Supply:** 100%* |
| **Historical US Import Trends** | With the exception of 2007 and 2008 the US has been a net importer of selenium since the 1920s; at issue is whether the 2007 and 2008 metrics signal a trend reversal or an anomaly. | |
| **Historical US Usage Trends** | Annual US selenium utilization levels generally increased during the first ¾ of the 20th century, peaking temporarily in 1928, 1933, 1941, 1948, 1956, and 1969, before peaking permanently (to date) in 1969. Domestic selenium utilization fluctuated at declining levels since that time; the 2008 US utilization level amounted to only 58% of the 1969 peak utilization level.<br><br>"Domestic use [1n 2007] of selenium in glass remained unchanged, while its use in copiers continued to decline [declining application]." (USGS, 2010) | |
| **US Peak Production Year (thru 2008):** 1969 | | **US Peak Utilization Year (thru 2008):** 1969 |
| **Potential Geopolitical US Supply Constraints** | 46% of US selenium imports come from Belgium; however, the US is currently a net selenium importer. | |

| NNR Profile | Selenium (continued) |
|---|---|
| **US Scarcity Assessment** | That annual domestic selenium utilization decreased by 42% since peaking (to date) in 1969, is an indicator of declining American industrial preeminence and global economic competitiveness.<br><br>The US is however currently addressing its total requirement for selenium through domestic supplies, although this has only been the case since 2007.<br><br>Available evidence regarding the likelihood that domestic selenium supplies will remain sufficient to completely address domestic requirements going forward is conflicting:<br><br>• Because annual US selenium production data is unavailable since 1996, the percentage by which domestic selenium production exceeded domestic selenium utilization in 2008 cannot be determined—the percentage is assumed to be positive, given that the US was a net exporter of selenium in 2008; however<br>• The domestic selenium production level decreased by 33% between 1969 (peak year to date) and 1996 (latest available data)—a compelling indicator that domestic economically viable selenium production has peaked permanently; and<br>• The US was a heavy net selenium importer until 2007. [Given that only one company in Texas produced primary selenium (in 2009), it is unclear how the US transitioned from being a net importer of at least 50% of its total annual selenium requirement prior to 2007, to being a net exporter from 2007 forward.]<br><br>It is therefore unclear whether domestically available, economically viable selenium supplies will remain sufficient to completely address future domestic requirements, or whether selenium will become scarce domestically in the not-too-distant future. |

| Global NNR Scarcity | Scarce in 2008: Yes | Permanently Scarce: Almost Certain |
|---|---|---|
| **Historical Global Production Trends** | Annual global selenium extraction levels generally increased since WWII, peaking temporarily in 1941, 1957, 1964, 1970, and 1979, before peaking permanently (to date) in 1996, then declining precipitously and flattening into the new millennium; annual global selenium extraction increased 3% between 2000 and 2008. | |
| **Global Peak Production Year (thru 2008):** 1996 | | **Years to Global Reserve Exhaustion:** 50+ |
| **Projected Global Peak Production Year:** N/A | | **Projected Global Peak Supply Year:** N/A |
| **Interdependencies** | Typically produced [recovered] as a byproduct of copper, silver, and lead ores. | |

| NNR Profile | Selenium (continued) |
|---|---|
| **Global Scarcity Assessment** | A 3% increase in the annual global selenium production level between 2000 and 2008 implies an increase in global selenium demand during the pre-recession period, and a corresponding increase in global selenium supply in response to increased global demand.<br><br>The fact that the price of selenium increased by a phenomenal 572% during the 2000-2008 period indicates that global selenium supply, while increasing during the eight year period, remained woefully insufficient to completely address global requirements in 2008.<br><br>Despite the fact that proven global selenium reserves are sufficient to last for over 50 years (assuming the restoration of pre-recession utilization levels and growth rates), available evidence supports the contention that global selenium supplies will remain insufficient to completely address global requirements going forward:<br><br>• The global selenium production level peaked (to date) in 1997—evidence that globally available, economically viable selenium production may be near, at, or past its permanent peak level; and<br>• That such a phenomenal increase in the price of selenium during the 2000-2008 period was able to induce only a nominal increase in supply is compelling evidence that globally available, economically viable selenium supplies will remain insufficient to completely address global requirements going forward.<br><br>Barring future reductions in the global selenium requirement trajectory and/or major new economically viable discoveries, selenium will almost certainly remain scarce globally in the future.<br><br>"The supply of selenium is directly affected by the supply of the materials from which it is a byproduct—copper, and to a lesser extent, nickel." (USGS, 2010) |

*Potentially misleading; the US was a net importer of selenium every year but 2007 and 2008.

1. "Selenium", Wikipedia, 2011 - http://en.wikipedia.org/wiki/Selenium.
2. "Selenium Statistics", Historical Statistics for Mineral and Material Commodities in the United States, USGS, 2010 – http://minerals.usgs.gov/ds/2005/140/selenium.xls.

| NNR Profile | Silicon |
|---|---|
| **NNR Uses and Critical Applications** | |
| **Primary Uses** | Silicon is a strong, very brittle, lustrous gray metalloid used as an alloy (aluminum and steel), and in the production of semiconductors, glass, plastics, ceramics, and cement; silicon is also used as an abrasive, sealant, and bonding agent. Traces of silicon are required in all animal life. |
| **Critical Applications** | Construction, as the primary component of natural stone, cement, glass, and concrete; steel and iron manufacture, as an alloy; and electronics (high purity silicon), as the primary substrate in the manufacture of semiconductors. |

| NNR Profile | | Silicon (continued) | |
|---|---|---|---|
| **NNR Criticality** | | **NNR Criticality Classification: Indispensible** | |
| **Substitutes** | Aluminum, silicon carbide, and silicomanganese can be substituted for ferrosilicon in some applications; gallium arsenide and germanium can be substituted in some semiconductor applications. Price/performance is often an issue. | | |
| **Criticality Assessment** | In its various forms, silicon plays an integral role in the production of both basic and high-technology construction materials and industrial materials; silicon is indispensible to modern industrial existence. | | |
| **US NNR Scarcity** | **Scarce in 2008: Yes** | | **Permanently Scarce: Almost Certain** |
| **2008 US Import Reliance:** 52% (ferrosilicon) | | **2008 Domestic US Supply:** 48% | |
| **Historical US Import Trends** | The US has been an increasingly heavy net importer of silicon since the early 1970s. | | |
| **Historical US Usage Trends** | Annual US silicon utilization levels generally increased during the latter half of the 20$^{th}$ century (4/5 is ferrosilicon—aluminum and steel alloys), peaking temporarily in 1956, 1974, 1979, and 1988, before peaking permanently (to date) in 2000 and declining significantly thereafter; the 2008 US utilization level amounted to only 50% of the 2000 peak utilization level. "The annual growth rate for ferrosilicon demand usually falls in the range of 1% to 2%, in line with long-term trends in [US] steel production…" (USGS, 2008) | | |
| **US Peak Production Year (thru 2008):** 1979 | | **US Peak Utilization Year (thru 2008):** 2000 | |
| **Potential Geopolitical US Supply Constraints** | 29% of US of silicon imports (including 49% of ferrosilicon imports) come from China; China produced 65% of the world's silicon in 2008. "China's exports of ferrosilicon and silicon metal declined considerably because the Chinese Government imposed export tariffs in 2008 of 25% for ferrosilicon, 15% for metallurgical-grade silicon, and 10% for other silicon metal." (USGS, 2010) "…on June 23 [2009], the EU announced that both it and the U.S. 'had requested WTO consultations with China regarding China's export restrictions on a number of key raw materials, which it considers are in clear breach of international trade rules. In the words of the EU announcement: 'European industries have raised concerns for a number of years on export restrictions - quotas, export duties and minimum export prices - which China applies on key raw materials, such as yellow phosphorous, bauxite, coke, fluorspar, magnesium, manganese, silicon metal, silicon carbide and zinc. Some of these resources cannot be found elsewhere.'" (Seeking Alpha, 2009) | | |

| NNR Profile | Silicon (continued) |
|---|---|
| **US Scarcity Assessment** | "There are five major ferrosilicon producers in the world: China, Russia, Ukraine, Brazil, and Norway." (Asia Metal, 2008)<br><br>That annual domestic silicon utilization decreased by 50% since peaking (to date) in 2000, is a major indicator of declining American industrial preeminence and global economic competitiveness.<br><br>The US currently relies heavily on imported silicon, a considerable amount (29%) of which comes from China. The quantity of silicon (ferrosilicon) supplied by foreign sources during 2008 accounted for 52% of the total 2008 US utilization level.<br><br>Available evidence supports the contention that domestic silicon supplies will remain insufficient to completely address domestic requirements going forward:<br><br>• The annual US silicon production level decreased by 71% since peaking (to date) in 1979—a compelling indicator that domestic economically viable silicon production has peaked permanently;<br>• The US has become increasingly reliant on silicon imports since 1971; and<br>• The quantity of silicon produced domestically during 2008 amounted to only 48% of the total 2008 US utilization level—a significant indicator of America's increasing dependence on foreign NNRs.<br><br>Barring future reductions in the domestic (US) silicon requirement trajectory and/or major new domestic economically viable discoveries, silicon will almost certainly remain scarce domestically in the future. |

| Global NNR Scarcity | Scarce in 2008: Yes | Permanently Scarce: Likely |
|---|---|---|
| **Historical Global Production Trends** | "China was by far the leading producer of both ferrosilicon (2,700,000 tons) and silicon metal (780,000 tons) in 2009." (USGS, 2010)<br><br>Annual global silicon production levels generally increased during the latter half of the 20th century and into the 21st century, peaking temporarily in 1979 and 1990, before increasing into the new millennium. Annual global silicon production increased 76% between 2000 and 2008. | |

| Global Peak Production Year (thru 2008): 2008 | Years to Global Reserve Exhaustion: N/A |
|---|---|
| Projected Global Peak Production Year: N/A | Projected Global Peak Supply Year: N/A |

| Interdependencies | None identified. |
|---|---|

| NNR Profile | Silicon (continued) |
|---|---|
| **Global Scarcity Assessment** | A 76% increase in the annual global silicon production level between 2000 and 2008 implies a robust increase in global demand during the pre-recession period, and a correspondingly robust increase in global silicon supply in response to increased global demand.<br><br>The fact that the price of silicon increased by a substantial 59% during the 2000-2008 period indicates that global silicon supply, while increasing considerably during the eight year period, remained insufficient to completely address global requirements in 2008.<br><br>Available evidence, albeit somewhat conflicting, supports the contention that global silicon supplies will remain insufficient to completely address global requirements going forward:<br><br>• Proven global silicon reserves are considered by the USGS to be "ample in relation to demand"; however<br>• The considerable increase in global silicon supply brought online between 2000 and 2008 failed to prevent a substantial price increase during the period—compelling evidence of unaddressed global requirements in 2008; and<br>• It is questionable whether the robust 7.3% compound annual growth rate (CAGR) in global silicon production evidenced between 2000 and 2008—an interval during which silicon became scarce globally despite a significant increase in production—can be reestablished, much less increased, going forward. A 7.3 CAGR would necessitate a continuous doubling in the annual global production level of silicon every 10 years.<br><br>Barring future reductions in the global silicon requirement trajectory and/or major new economically viable discoveries, silicon will likely remain scarce globally in the future. |

1. "Silicon", Wikipedia, 2011 - http://en.wikipedia.org/wiki/Silicon.
2. "Silicon Statistics", Historical Statistics for Mineral and Material Commodities in the United States, USGS, 2010 – http://minerals.usgs.gov/ds/2005/140/silicon.xls.
3. "Fluorspar: The Cool Metal, T. Vulcan, Seeking Alpha, 2009 - http://seekingalpha.com/article/160670-fluorspar-the-cool-mineral.
4. "Silica", Mineral Information Institute (MII), 2010 - http://www.mii.org/Minerals/photosil.html.
5. "2008 Annual Report on Ferrosilicon Market", page 1, Asia Metal Ltd. 2009 - http://www.asianmetal.com/report/en/2008guitie_en.pdf.

| NNR Profile | Silver |
|---|---|
| **NNR Uses and Critical Applications** | |
| **Primary Uses** | Silver is a soft, white, highly conductive metal used in the production of ornaments, jewelry, utensils, and coins; silver is also used as an electrical conductor, a chemical catalyst, a dental amalgam, a germicide, a highly reflective optical coating, and in photographic films. |
| **Critical Applications** | Energy generation and storage. |

| NNR Profile | Silver (continued) |
|---|---|

| NNR Criticality | NNR Criticality Classification: Critical |
|---|---|
| **Substitutes** | Digital imagining is replacing photography and xerography processes requiring silver; metals such as tantalum, titanium, stainless steel, germanium, and aluminum are viable substitutes for silver in some other applications; however, silver also occupies a well defined niche as an investment grade precious metal. |
| **Criticality Assessment** | Silver is employed in a wide range of niche industrial applications for which viable substitutes often do not exist. In the event that silver becomes widely adopted in battery, solar cell, or other energy generation and storage applications, it will become more critical. |

| US NNR Scarcity | Scarce in 2008: Yes | Permanently Scarce: Almost Certain |
|---|---|---|

| 2008 US Import Reliance: 67% | 2008 Domestic US Supply: 33% |
|---|---|

| **Historical US Import Trends** | Historically, the US has been both a net exporter and a net importer of silver; the prevailing trend over the past several decades has been toward increasing US reliance on silver imports. |
|---|---|
| **Historical US Usage Trends** | Annual US silver utilization levels generally increased during the 20th and 21st centuries, often in a cyclical manner, peaking temporarily in 1911, 1929, 1955, 1945, 1966, 1976, and 1985, before peaking permanently (to date) in 2003; the 2008 US utilization level amounted to only 74% of the 2003 peak utilization level. |

| US Peak Production Year (thru 2008): 1916 | US Peak Utilization Year (thru 2008): 2003 |
|---|---|

| **Potential Geopolitical US Supply Constraints** | 54% of US silver imports come from Mexico. |
|---|---|
| **US Scarcity Assessment** | That annual domestic silver utilization decreased by 26% since peaking (to date) in 2003, is an indicator of declining American industrial preeminence and global economic competitiveness.<br><br>The US currently relies heavily on imported silver, the majority (54%) of which comes from Mexico. The quantity of silver supplied by foreign sources during 2008 accounted for 67% of the total 2008 US utilization level.<br><br>Available evidence supports the contention that domestic silver supplies will remain insufficient to completely address domestic requirements going forward:<br><br>• While US silver utilization increased into the new millennium, the annual US silver production level decreased by 50% since peaking (to date) in 1916—a compelling indicator that domestic economically viable silver production has peaked permanently;<br>• The US has become increasingly reliant on silver imports since 1998;<br>• The quantity of (primary) silver produced domestically during 2008 amounted to only 21% of the total 2008 US utilization level—an indicator of America's increasing dependence on foreign NNRs; and<br>• The quantity of silver produced domestically during 1916, the year of peak (to date) domestic potash production, amounted to only 41% of the 2008 total US utilization level.<br><br>Barring future reductions in the domestic (US) silver requirement trajectory and/or major new domestic economically viable discoveries, silver will almost certainly remain scarce domestically in the future. |

| NNR Profile | Silver (continued) | |
|---|---|---|
| **Global NNR Scarcity** | **Scarce in 2008: Yes** | **Permanently Scarce: Almost Certain** |

| **Historical Global Production Trends** | Annual global silver extraction/production levels generally increased during the 20th and 21st centuries, peaking temporarily in 1911, 1929, 1940, and 1989, before continuing their upward trend into the new millennium; annual global silver extraction/production increased 18% between 2000 and 2008. |
|---|---|

| Global Peak Production Year (thru 2008): 2008 | Years to Global Reserve Exhaustion: 11 |
|---|---|
| Projected Global Peak Production Year: 2010 | Projected Global Peak Supply Year: 2025 |

| **Interdependencies** | Most silver is produced as a byproduct of copper, gold, lead, and zinc refining. |
|---|---|

| **Global Scarcity Assessment** | "The deficit in world silver mine production as compared with world silver consumption was about 800 tons in 2007." (USGS, 2008)<br><br>An 18% increase in the annual global silver extraction/production level between 2000 and 2008 implies an increase in global silver demand during the pre-recession period, and a corresponding increase in global silver supply in response to increased global demand.<br><br>The fact that the price of silver increased by an extraordinary 146% during the 2000-2008 period indicates that global silver supply, while increasing during the eight year period, remained woefully insufficient to completely address global requirements in 2008.<br><br>Available evidence supports the contention that global silver supplies will remain insufficient to completely address global requirements going forward:<br><br>• Proven global silver reserves would exhaust in only 11 years, assuming the restoration of pre-recession utilization levels and growth rates;<br>• The global silver extraction/production level is projected to peak in approximately 2010;<br>• The global silver supply level is projected to peak in approximately 2025;<br>• An extraordinary increase in the price of silver during the 2000-2008 period induced only a nominal increase in silver supply—compelling evidence that globally available, economically viable silver extraction may be at or near its permanent peak level; and<br>• Investment demand for silver has been increasing during recent years as a hedge against excessive money printing by central banks from heavily indebted industrialized nations.<br><br>Barring future reductions in the global silver requirement trajectory and/or major new economically viable discoveries, silver will almost certainly remain scarce globally in the future. |
|---|---|

1. "Silver", Wikipedia, 2011 - http://en.wikipedia.org/wiki/Silver.
2. "Silver Statistics", Historical Statistics for Mineral and Material Commodities in the United States, USGS, 2010 – http://minerals.usgs.gov/ds/2005/140/silver.xls.

| NNR Profile | Soda Ash (Sodium Carbonate) |
|---|---|

## NNR Uses and Critical Applications

| Primary Uses | Soda ash is a white powdery mineral used in the production of glass, to neutralize acidity, as an electrolyte, and as a water softener. |
|---|---|
| Critical Applications | None identified. |

| NNR Criticality | NNR Criticality Classification: Important |
|---|---|
| Substitutes | Caustic soda is a viable soda ash substitute in some application areas (pulp and paper, water treatment, and certain chemical applications). |
| Criticality Assessment | Although some soda ash applications are pervasive, they are either non-critical (to industrialization) or they can be addressed effectively by soda ash substitutes. |

| US NNR Scarcity | Scarce in 2008: No | Permanently Scarce: Unlikely |
|---|---|---|

| 2008 US Import Reliance: 0% | 2008 Domestic US Supply: 100% |
|---|---|

| Historical US Import Trends | The US has been an increasingly heavy net exporter of soda ash since the 1960s. |
|---|---|
| Historical US Usage Trends | Annual US soda ash utilization levels generally increased during most of the 20th century, peaking temporarily in 1917, 1929, 1947, 1956, 1966, 1973, and 1979, before peaking permanently (to date) in 1990; the 2008 US utilization level amounted to only 86% of the 1990 peak utilization level. |

| US Peak Extraction Year (thru 2008): 2008 | US Peak Utilization Year (thru 2008): 1990 |
|---|---|

| Potential Geopolitical US Supply Constraints | None identified—however, foreign government actions can adversely impact US soda ash producers.<br><br>"The Chinese soda ash industry received some assistance from the government in the form of a 9 percent rebate on the Chinese soda ash export sales [in 2009]. By lowering the export price, Chinese soda ash manufacturers were able to increase export sales and maintain high operating rates. The lower priced Chinese soda ash exports adversely affected U.S. soda ash export sales causing domestic producers to reduce output levels for most of the year." (USGS, 2010) |
|---|---|

| NNR Profile | Soda Ash (Sodium Carbonate) [continued] |
|---|---|
| **US Scarcity Assessment** | "Soda ash is obtained from trona and sodium carbonate-rich brines. The world's largest deposit of trona is in the Green River Basin of Wyoming." (USGS, 2010) |
| | That annual domestic soda ash utilization decreased by 14% since peaking (to date) in 1990, is an indicator of declining American industrial preeminence and global economic competitiveness. |
| | The US is however currently addressing its total requirement for soda ash through domestic supplies. |
| | Available evidence supports the contention that domestic soda ash supplies will likely remain sufficient to completely address domestic requirements going forward: |
| | • Domestic soda ash supplies were sufficient to completely address domestic requirements during the 2000-2008 period of rapid economic growth prior to the Great Recession; and <br> • Domestic soda ash reserves are considered by the USGS to be practically inexhaustible. |
| | Barring future increases in the domestic (US) soda ash requirement trajectory, domestically available, economically viable soda ash supplies will likely remain sufficient to completely address domestic requirements going forward. |
| | "The five [US] producers have a combined annual nameplate capacity of 14.5 million tons [versus 6.8 million tons during 1990, the year of peak US soda ash utilization]." (USGS, 2010) |

| Global NNR Scarcity | Scarce in 2008: Yes | Permanently Scarce: Unclear |
|---|---|---|
| **Historical Global Extraction Trends** | Annual global soda ash extraction levels increased during the latter decades of the 20th century and into the 21st century, peaking temporarily in 1980 and 1990, before increasing into the new millennium; annual global soda ash extraction increased 32% between 2000 and 2008. <br><br> "The global economic problems in 2009 had a negative effect on most soda ash producers in the world, except in China." (USGS, 2010) | |

| Global Peak Extraction Year (thru 2008): 2008 | Years to Global Reserve Exhaustion: 50+ |
|---|---|
| Projected Global Peak Extraction Year: N/A | Projected Global Peak Supply Year: N/A |

| Interdependencies | Minerals such as salt, sodium sulfate, borax, can be extracted as coproducts with sodium carbonate (soda ash); sodium bicarbonate, sodium sulfite, and chemical caustic soda can be produced as byproducts of soda ash processing. |
|---|---|

| NNR Profile | Soda Ash (Sodium Carbonate) [continued] |
|---|---|
| **Global Scarcity Assessment** | A 32% increase in the annual global soda ash extraction level between 2000 and 2008 implies an increase in global demand during the pre-recession period, and a corresponding increase in global soda ash supply in response to increased global demand.<br><br>The fact that the price of soda ash increased by 48% during the 2000-2008 period indicates that global soda ash supply, while increasing during the eight year period, remained insufficient to completely address global requirements in 2008.<br><br>Available evidence regarding the likelihood that global soda ash supplies will remain insufficient to completely address global requirements going forward is conflicting:<br><br>• The increased global soda ash supply brought online between 2000 and 2008 failed to prevent a price increase during the period—evidence of unaddressed global requirements in 2008; however<br>• Proven global soda ash reserves are sufficient to last for over 50 years (assuming the restoration of pre-recession utilization levels and growth rates); and<br>• Proven global soda ash reserves are considered by the USGS to be practically inexhaustible.<br><br>It is therefore unclear whether soda ash will remain scarce globally in the future, or whether globally available, economically viable soda ash supplies will be sufficient to completely address future global requirements. |

1. "Soda Ash", Wikipedia, 2011 - http://en.wikipedia.org/wiki/Soda_ash.
2. "Soda Ash Statistics", Historical Statistics for Mineral and Material Commodities in the United States, USGS, 2010 – http://minerals.usgs.gov/ds/2005/140/sodaash.xls.

| NNR Profile | Sodium Sulfate | |
|---|---|---|
| **NNR Uses and Critical Applications** | | |
| **Primary Uses** | Sodium sulfate (dry) is a white solid mineral used in the manufacture of laundry detergents, textiles, and glass, and in paper pulping; sodium sulfate is also used as a feedstock in the production of soda ash. | |
| **Critical Applications** | Heat storage medium in solar heating applications (potentially significant). | |
| **NNR Criticality** | **NNR Criticality Classification: Important** | |
| **Substitutes** | With the exception of the glass making application, viable sodium sulfate substitutes are readily available. As an example, liquid laundry detergents, which contain no sodium sulfate, are displacing powdered detergents in some cases. | |
| **Criticality Assessment** | Two major sodium sulfate applications, powdered laundry detergent and paper pulping, are in decline as a result of more effective substitutes.<br><br>"The primary use of sodium sulfate worldwide is in powdered detergents. Sodium sulfate is a low cost, inert, white filler in home laundry detergents." (USGS, 2010) | |

| NNR Profile | Sodium Sulfate (continued) | |
|---|---|---|
| **US NNR Scarcity** | **Scarce in 2008: No** | **Permanently Scarce: Unclear** |
| **2008 US Import Reliance:** 0% | | **2008 Domestic US Supply:** 100% |
| **Historical US Import Trends** | While historically a net importer of sodium sulfate, the US became a net exporter in 1999. | |
| **Historical US Usage Trends** | "Sodium sulfate consumption in the domestic textile industry also has been declining because of imports of less expensive textile products." (USGS, 2010)<br><br>Annual US sodium sulfate utilization levels generally increased during the first three quarters of the 20th century, peaking temporarily in 1937, 1942, 1955, and 1968, before peaking permanently (to date) in 1973 and generally declining thereafter; the 2008 US utilization level amounted to only 17% of the 1973 peak utilization level. | |
| **US Peak Extraction Year (thru 2008):** 1968 | | **US Peak Utilization Year (thru 2008):** 1973 |
| **Potential Geopolitical US Supply Constraints** | 79% of US sodium sulfate imports come from Canada; however, the US is currently a net sodium sulfate exporter. | |
| **US Scarcity Assessment** | That annual domestic sodium sulfate utilization decreased by 83% since peaking (to date) in 1973, is an indicator of declining American industrial preeminence and global economic competitiveness.<br><br>However, as a result of continuously declining domestic demand for sodium sulfate, the US is currently addressing its total sodium sulfate requirement through domestic supplies, although this has only been the case since 1999.<br><br>Available evidence regarding the likelihood that domestic sodium sulfate supplies will remain sufficient to completely address domestic requirements going forward is conflicting:<br><br>• The 2008 US sodium sulfate extraction level exceeded the 2008 US domestic utilization level by nearly 14%; however<br>• The domestic sodium sulfate extraction level decreased by 76% since peaking (to date) in 1968—a compelling indicator that domestic economically viable sodium sulfate extraction has peaked permanently; and<br>• The US was a consistent sodium sulfate net importer until 1999.<br><br>It is therefore unclear whether domestically available, economically viable sodium sulfate supplies will remain sufficient to completely address future domestic requirements, or whether sodium sulfate will become scarce domestically in the not-too-distant future. | |
| **Global NNR Scarcity** | **Scarce in 2008: No** | **Permanently Scarce: Unlikely** |
| **Historical Global Extraction Trends** | Annual global sodium sulfate extraction/production levels increased during the latter decades of the 20th century, peaking temporarily in 1978 and 1990, before leveling off in the new millennium; annual global sodium sulfate extraction/production remained unchanged between 2000 and 2008. | |
| **Global Peak Extraction Year (thru 2008):** 2008 | | **Years to Global Reserve Exhaustion:** N/A |
| **Projected Global Peak Extraction Year:** N/A | | **Projected Global Peak Supply Year:** N/A |
| **Interdependencies** | Sodium sulfate can be recovered as a byproduct of hydrochloric acid production and from other manufacturing processes and products. | |

| NNR Profile | Sodium Sulfate (continued) |
|---|---|
| Global Scarcity Assessment | A constant annual global sodium sulfate extraction level between 2000 and 2008 implies stagnant global sodium sulfate demand and supply during the pre-recession period.

The fact that the price of sodium sulfate decreased by 6% during the 2000-2008 period indicates that the global supply of sodium sulfate in 2008 was sufficient to completely address 2008 global requirements.

Assuming that annual sodium sulfate extraction did in fact remain constant between 2000 and 2008, a period of rapidly increasing global economic growth; and given that global sodium sulfate supplies were sufficient to completely address global requirements in 2008, barring future increases in the global sodium sulfate requirement trajectory, globally available, economically viable sodium sulfate supplies will likely remain sufficient to completely address global requirements going forward.

It should be noted that in the event future global sodium sulfate requirements increase as the USGS expects, sufficient global supplies may not be universally available...

"World production and consumption of sodium sulfate have been stagnant but are expected to increase in the next few years, especially in Asia and South America." (USGS, 2010) |

1. "Sodium Sulfate", Wikipedia, 2011 - http://en.wikipedia.org/wiki/Sodium_sulfate.
2. "Sodium Sulfate Statistics", Historical Statistics for Mineral and Material Commodities in the United States, USGS, 2010 – http://minerals.usgs.gov/ds/2005/140/sodiumsulfate.xls.

| NNR Profile | Stone (Crushed) | |
|---|---|---|
| **NNR Uses and Critical Applications** | | |
| Primary Uses | Crushed stone* is a form of construction aggregate [see below for specifics] used for macadam road construction and cement manufacture; crushed stone is also used as riprap, railroad track ballast, filter stone, and soil conditioner (limestone and dolomite). | |
| Critical Applications | Road building. | |
| **NNR Criticality** | **NNR Criticality Classification: Indispensable** | |
| Substitutes | Suitable substitutes exist for road building and most construction applications— including sand and gravel, iron and steel slag, sintered or expanded clay or shale, and perlite or vermiculite. Substitutes may be more expensive and less scalable, given local availability considerations. | |
| Criticality Assessment | Although it is a basic raw material, crushed stone is widely deployed in a number of critical construction, agricultural, and industrial applications, primarily road building; crushed stone is indispensable to modern industrial existence. | |
| **US NNR Scarcity** | Scarce in 2008: No | Permanently Scarce: Unlikely |
| **2008 US Import Reliance: 1%** | 2008 Domestic US Supply: 99% | |

| NNR Profile | Stone (Crushed) [continued] |
|---|---|
| **Historical US Import Trends** | Historically, the US has been both a net exporter and a net importer of crushed stone. While the US is currently a net importer of crushed stone, and import levels have been increasing rapidly during the past several decades, net imports as a percentage of total US crushed stone utilization is still negligible—the US is essentially self-sufficient with respect to crushed stone supplies. |
| **Historical US Usage Trends** | Annual US crushed stone utilization levels generally increased during the 20th and 21st centuries, peaking temporarily in 1913, 1929, 1943, 1960, 1973, 1979, 1988, and 2001, before increasing into the new millennium. |

| US Peak Extraction Year (thru 2008): 2006 | US Peak Utilization Year (thru 2008): 2006 |
|---|---|

| **Potential Geopolitical US Supply Constraints** | 43% of US crushed stone imports come from Canada, and 38% come from Mexico; however, US is essentially self-sufficient with regards to crushed stone. |
|---|---|
| **US Scarcity Assessment** | "Crushed stone valued at $11 billion was produced by 1,600 companies operating 4,000 quarries, 86 underground mines, and 311 sales/distribution yards in 50 States." (USGS, 2010)<br><br>The US is essentially meeting its total requirement for crushed stone through domestic supplies.<br><br>Given that US crushed stone resources are considered by the USGS to be "adequate (except where special types are needed or where local shortages exist)"; barring future increases in the domestic (US) crushed stone requirement trajectory, domestically available, economically viable crushed stone supplies will likely remain sufficient—notwithstanding temporary local shortages—to completely address domestic requirements going forward.<br><br>"The crushed stone industry continued to be concerned with environmental, health, and safety regulations. Shortages in some urban and industrialized areas are expected to continue to increase owing to local zoning regulations and land-development alternatives." (USGS, 2010) |

| Global NNR Scarcity | Scarce in 2008: Yes | Permanently Scarce: Unclear |
|---|---|---|

| **Historical Global Extraction Trends** | Global USGS extraction data for crushed stone are not available.<br><br>"The demand for crushed stone is determined mostly by the level of construction activity, and, therefore, the demand for construction materials." (Wikipedia) |
|---|---|

| Global Peak Extraction Year (thru 2008): N/A | Years to Global Reserve Exhaustion: N/A |
|---|---|
| Projected Global Peak Extraction Year: N/A | Projected Global Peak Supply Year: N/A |

| **Interdependencies** | None identified. |
|---|---|

| NNR Profile | Stone (Crushed) [continued] |
|---|---|
| **Global Scarcity Assessment** | While annual global extraction data associated with crushed stone are unavailable from the USGS for the 2000-2008 pre-recession period, crushed stone prices increased by 39% between 2000 and 2008, indicating that global crushed stone supplies were insufficient to completely address global requirements during 2008.<br><br>Available evidence regarding the likelihood that global crushed stone supplies will remain insufficient to completely address global requirements going forward is conflicting:<br><br>• An increase in the price of crushed stone during the 2000-2008 period indicates global crushed stone scarcity in 2008; however<br>• Proven global crushed stone resources are considered by the USGS to be "very large".<br><br>It is therefore unclear whether crushed stone will remain scarce globally in the future, or whether globally available, economically viable crushed stone supplies will be sufficient to completely address future global requirements. |

*"…about 70% was limestone and dolomite; 14%, granite; 7%, traprock; and the remaining 9% was divided, in descending order of tonnage, among miscellaneous stone, sandstone and quartzite, marble, slate, calcareous marl, volcanic cinder and scoria, and shell. USGS, 2010

1. "Crushed Stone", Wikipedia, 2011 - http://en.wikipedia.org/wiki/Crushed_stone.
2. "Stone (Crushed) Statistics", Historical Statistics for Mineral and Material Commodities in the United States, USGS, 2010 – http://minerals.usgs.gov/ds/2005/140/stonecrushed.xls.

| NNR Profile | Stone (Dimension) |
|---|---|
| **NNR Uses and Critical Applications** | |
| **Primary Uses** | Dimension stone is natural stone* that has been trimmed, cut, drilled, or ground to specific shapes and/or sizes. Dimension stone uses include veneer, tile, kitchen counter tops, and monuments—i.e., construction and refurbishment applications in both commercial and residential markets. |
| **Critical Applications** | None identified. |
| **NNR Criticality** | **NNR Criticality Classification: Important** |
| **Substitutes** | Viable synthetic and natural building material substitutes, including aluminum, brick, ceramic tile, concrete, glass, plastics, resinagglomerated stone, and steel, exist for dimension stone in many application areas. |
| **Criticality Assessment** | While dimension stone fulfills a number of niche applications, viable substitutes exist in all cases. |
| **US NNR Scarcity** | **Scarce in 2008: Yes** / **Permanently Scarce: Almost Certain** |
| **2008 US Import Reliance: 87%** | **2008 Domestic US Supply: 13%** |
| **Historical US Import Trends** | The US has been primarily a net importer of dimension stone since the early 20th century; US imports have increased dramatically since the early 1980s.<br><br>"A current problem is how to consider stone quarried domestically, sent to China or Italy for finishing, and shipped back to be used in a project." (Wikipedia) [The issue from the perspective of US global competitiveness is: how and why can this process be less expensive than finishing the stone in the US?] |

| NNR Profile | Stone (Dimension) [continued] |
|---|---|
| **Historical US Usage Trends** | "The United States is the world's largest market for dimension stone." (USGS, 2010)<br><br>After fluctuating within a relatively tight range during the 20<sup>th</sup> century, and peaking temporarily in 1906, 1913, 1925, 1931, 1956, 1964, 1968, and 1989, annual US dimension stone utilization levels increased rapidly during the 21<sup>st</sup> century. |

| US Peak Extraction Year (thru 2008): 1931 | US Peak Utilization Year (thru 2008): 2007 |
|---|---|

| **Potential Geopolitical US Supply Constraints** | None identified. |
|---|---|
| **US Scarcity Assessment** | "Dimension stone was produced by 173 companies, operating 237 quarries, in 37 States." (USGS, 2010)<br><br>The US currently relies almost exclusively on imported dimension stone; the quantity of dimension stone supplied by foreign sources during 2008 accounted for 87% of the total 2008 US utilization level.<br><br>Available evidence supports the contention that domestic dimension stone supplies will remain insufficient to completely address domestic requirements going forward:<br><br>• While US dimension stone utilization increased into the new millennium, the annual US dimension stone extraction level decreased by 70% since peaking (to date) in 1931—a compelling indicator that domestic economically viable dimension stone extraction has peaked permanently;<br>• The US has become increasingly reliant on dimension stone imports since 1979;<br>• The quantity of dimension stone extracted domestically during 2008 amounted to only 13% of the total 2008 US utilization level—an indicator of America's increasing dependence on foreign NNRs; and<br>• The quantity of dimension stone extracted domestically during 1931, the year of peak (to date) domestic dimension stone extraction, amounted to only 45% of the 2008 total US utilization level.<br><br>Barring future reductions in the domestic (US) dimension stone requirement trajectory and/or major new domestic economically viable discoveries, dimension stone will almost certainly remain scarce domestically in the future. |

| Global NNR Scarcity | Scarce in 2008: No | Permanently Scarce: Unlikely |
|---|---|---|

| **Historical Global Extraction Trends** | Global USGS dimension stone extraction data are not available.<br><br>"…improved quarrying, finishing, handling technology, greater varieties of stone, and the rising costs of alternative construction materials, are among the factors that suggest the demand for dimension stone will continue to increase during the next 5 years [2008-2012]." (USGS, 2008) |
|---|---|

| Global Peak Extraction Year (thru 2008): N/A | Years to Global Reserve Exhaustion: N/A |
|---|---|
| Projected Global Peak Extraction Year: N/A | Projected Global Peak Supply Year: N/A |

| **Interdependencies** | None identified. |
|---|---|

| NNR Profile | Stone (Dimension) [continued] |
|---|---|
| **Global Scarcity Assessment** | While annual global extraction data associated with dimension stone are unavailable from the USGS for the 2000-2008 pre-recession period, dimension stone prices decreased by 24% between 2000 and 2008, indicating that global dimension stone supplies were sufficient to completely address global requirements during 2008.<br><br>Given that global dimension stone resources are considered by the USGS to be "sufficient"; barring future increases in the global dimension stone requirement trajectory, globally available, economically viable dimension stone supplies will likely remain sufficient—notwithstanding temporary local shortages—to completely address global requirements going forward.<br><br>"Dimension stone resources of the world are sufficient. Resources can be limited on a local level or occasionally on a regional level by the lack of a particular kind of stone that is suitable for dimension purposes." (USGS, 2010) |

\*"Approximately 34%, by tonnage, of dimension stone sold or used was limestone, followed by granite (26%), sandstone (19%), miscellaneous stone (18%), marble (2%), and slate (1%)." USGS, 2010

1. "Dimension Stone", Wikipedia, 2011 - http://en.wikipedia.org/wiki/Dimension_stone.
2. "Stone (Dimension) Statistics", Historical Statistics for Mineral and Material Commodities in the United States, USGS, 2010 – http://minerals.usgs.gov/ds/2005/140/stonedimension.xls.

| NNR Profile | Strontium | |
|---|---|---|
| **NNR Uses and Critical Applications** | | |
| **Primary Uses** | Strontium is a soft, silvery-white metal used in pyrotechnics and flares, in ceramic ferrite magnets, as an alloy (aluminum and magnesium), as pigments and fillers, and in CRT (cathode ray tube) glass; strontium is also used in niche medical and scientific applications. | |
| **Critical Applications** | Possibly ceramic ferrite magnets; CRTs are in decline. | |
| **NNR Criticality** | **NNR Criticality Classification: Important** | |
| **Substitutes** | While strontium substitutes are available (e.g., barium in ferrite ceramic magnets), most are price/performance inferior. | |
| **Criticality Assessment** | With the displacement of CRTs by flat panel computer and television screens, strontium's primary application is eroding. | |
| **US NNR Scarcity** | **Scarce in 2008: Yes** | **Permanently Scarce: Almost Certain** |
| **2008 US Import Reliance:** 100% | **2008 Domestic US Supply:** 0% | |
| **Historical US Import Trends** | The US has always been import dependent with respect to strontium; no strontium has been extracted domestically since 1956. | |
| **Historical US Usage Trends** | Annual US strontium utilization levels generally increased during the 20th century, peaking temporarily in 1917, 1923, 1937, 1943, 1948, 1956, 1964, 1971, 1979, 1984, and 1990, before peaking permanently (to date) in 1999 and declining dramatically thereafter; the 2008 US utilization level amounted to only 28% of the 1999 peak utilization level.<br><br>"…production facilities to manufacture CRTs for color televisions have shifted to other countries, causing the closure of all television glass plants in the United States, eliminating what was once the dominant U.S. market." (USGS, 2008) | |

| NNR Profile | Strontium (continued) | |
|---|---|---|
| **US Peak Extraction Year (thru 2008):** 1943 | | **US Peak Utilization Year (thru 2008):** 1999 |
| **Potential Geopolitical US Supply Constraints** | 93% of US strontium imports come from Mexico; China produces over two thirds of the world's strontium (2007). | |
| **US Scarcity Assessment** | That annual domestic strontium utilization decreased by 72% since peaking (to date) in 1999, is an indicator of declining American industrial preeminence and global economic competitiveness.<br><br>The US currently relies exclusively on imported strontium, the majority (93%) of which comes from Mexico.<br><br>Available evidence supports the contention that domestic strontium supplies will remain insufficient to completely address domestic requirements going forward:<br><br>• US strontium extraction ceased entirely in 1957—a compelling indicator that domestic economically viable strontium extraction has peaked permanently; and<br>• The quantity of strontium extracted domestically during 1943, the year of peak (to date) domestic strontium extraction, amounted to only 28% of the 2008 total US utilization level—an indicator of America's increasing dependence on foreign NNRs.<br><br>Barring future reductions in the domestic (US) strontium requirement trajectory and/or major new domestic economically viable discoveries, strontium will almost certainly remain scarce domestically in the future. | |
| **Global NNR Scarcity** | **Scarce in 2008: Yes** | **Permanently Scarce: Likely** |
| **Historical Global Extraction Trends** | "In descending order of production, China, Spain, and Mexico are the world's leading producers of celestite [the most common strontium mineral]…" (USGS, 2010)<br><br>Annual global strontium extraction levels increased dramatically during the latter half of the 20th century, peaking temporarily in 1956, 1964, 1971, 1989, and 1995, before increasing into the early 21st century; annual global strontium extraction increased 25% between 2000 and 2008. | |
| **Global Peak Extraction Year (thru 2008):** 2004 | | **Years to Global Reserve Exhaustion:** 12 |
| **Projected Global Peak Extraction Year:** N/A | | **Projected Global Peak Supply Year:** N/A |
| **Interdependencies** | None identified. | |

| NNR Profile | Strontium (continued) |
|---|---|
| **Global Scarcity Assessment** | A 25% increase in the annual global strontium extraction level between 2000 and 2008 implies an increase in global strontium demand during the pre-recession period, and a corresponding increase in global strontium supply in response to increased global demand.<br><br>The fact that the price of strontium increased by 13% during the 2000-2008 period indicates that global strontium supply, while increasing during the eight year period, remained insufficient to completely address global requirements in 2008.<br><br>Available evidence supports the contention that global strontium supplies will likely remain insufficient to completely address global requirements going forward:<br><br>• Proven global strontium reserves would exhaust in only 12 years, assuming the restoration of pre-recession utilization levels and growth rates; and<br>• The increased global strontium supply brought online between 2000 and 2008 failed to prevent a price increase during the period—evidence of unaddressed global requirements in 2008.<br><br>Barring future reductions in the global strontium requirement trajectory and/or major new economically viable discoveries, strontium will likely remain scarce globally in the future. |

1. "Strontium", Wikipedia, 2011 - http://en.wikipedia.org/wiki/Strontium.
2. "Ferrite (magnet)", Wikipedia, 2011 - http://en.wikipedia.org/wiki/Ferrite_(magnet).
3. "Strontium Statistics", Historical Statistics for Mineral and Material Commodities in the United States, USGS, 2010 – http://minerals.usgs.gov/ds/2005/140/strontium.xls.

| NNR Profile | Sulfur |
|---|---|
| **NNR Uses and Critical Applications** | |
| **Primary Uses** | Sulfur is a soft, bright yellow, crystalline mineral used primarily in fertilizer and fertilizer production (phosphate extraction); sulfur is also used in black gunpowder, matches, insecticides, and fungicides; sulfur is an essential element in living organisms. |
| **Critical Applications** | "Over 90% of global sulphur demand is for the production of sulphuric acid, the world's most widely produced and used inorganic chemical." (AFA, 2005)<br><br>Fertilizer (phosphoric acid from sulfuric acid) and fertilizer production. |
| **NNR Criticality** | **NNR Criticality Classification: Indispensible** |
| **Substitutes** | While other acids can be substituted for sulfuric acid in some cases, there are no viable sulfur substitutes for most applications, such as fertilizer. |

| NNR Profile | Sulfur (continued) |
|---|---|
| **Criticality Assessment** | "Approximately 85% [of extracted sulfur] (1989) is converted to sulfuric acid ($H_2SO_4$), which is of such prime importance to the world's economies that the production and consumption of sulfuric acid is an indicator of a nation's industrial development." (Wikipedia)<br><br>Sulfur is indispensible to agriculture on an industrial scale and to modern industrial existence. |

| US NNR Scarcity | Scarce in 2008: Yes | Permanently Scarce: Almost Certain |
|---|---|---|
| **2008 US Import Reliance:** 25% | | **2008 Domestic US Supply:** 75% |

| | |
|---|---|
| **Historical US Import Trends** | Historically, the US has been both a net exporter and a net importer of sulfur; the US has been an increasingly heavy net importer of sulfur since the mid 1970s. |
| **Historical US Usage Trends** | Annual US sulfur utilization levels generally increased during the 20th century, peaking temporarily in 1903, 1908, 1918, 1929, 1937, 1959, 1967, 1980, and 1991, before peaking permanently (to date) in 1995. Domestic sulfur utilization rebounded slightly during the early years of the new millennium; however, the 2008 US utilization level amounted to only 87% of the 1995 peak utilization level. |

| US Peak Extraction Year (thru 2008): 1981 | US Peak Utilization Year (thru 2008): 1995 |
|---|---|

| **Potential Geopolitical US Supply Constraints** | 71% of US elemental sulfur imports and 77% of US sulfuric acid imports come from Canada. |
|---|---|
| **US Scarcity Assessment** | That annual domestic sulfur utilization decreased by 13% since peaking (to date) in 1995, is a significant indicator of declining American industrial preeminence and global economic competitiveness.<br><br>The US currently relies considerably on imported sulfur, the majority (71%) of which comes from Canada. The quantity of sulfur supplied by foreign sources during 2008 accounted for 25% of the total 2008 US utilization level.<br><br>Available evidence supports the contention that domestic sulfur supplies will remain insufficient to completely address domestic requirements going forward:<br><br>• The annual US sulfur extraction level decreased by 21% since peaking (to date) in 1981—a compelling indicator that domestic economically viable sulfur extraction has peaked permanently;<br>• The US has become increasingly reliant on sulfur imports since 1974; and<br>• The quantity of sulfur extracted domestically during 2008 amounted to only 76% of the total 2008 US utilization level—a significant indicator of America's increasing dependence on foreign NNRs.<br><br>Barring future reductions in the domestic (US) sulfur requirement trajectory and/or major new domestic economically viable discoveries, sulfur will almost certainly remain scarce domestically in the future. |

| NNR Profile | Sulfur (continued) | |
|---|---|---|
| Global NNR Scarcity | Scarce in 2008: Yes | Permanently Scarce: Almost Certain |

| Historical Global Extraction Trends | "World sulfur production was relatively stable [in 2007], with Canada surpassing the United States as the leading global producer." (USGS, 2008)<br><br>Annual global sulfur extraction/production levels generally increased during the 20<sup>th</sup> century and into the 21<sup>st</sup> century, peaking temporarily in 1903, 1918, 1930, 1942, 1974, 1980, and 1988, before increasing into the new millennium. Annual global sulfur extraction/production increased 17% between 2000 and 2008.<br><br>"…increased production is expected from sulfur recovery at liquefied natural gas operations in the Middle East and expanded oil sands operations in Canada…" (USGS, 2010) |
|---|---|

| Global Peak Extraction Year (thru 2008): 2008 | Years to Global Reserve Exhaustion: N/A |
|---|---|
| Projected Global Peak Extraction Year: N/A | Projected Global Peak Supply Year: N/A |

| Interdependencies | Sulfur can be recovered as a byproduct of the petroleum refining process and natural gas processing; sulfuric acid can be recovered at nonferrous smelters. |
|---|---|

| Global Scarcity Assessment | "Worldwide sulfur prices increased throughout the year [2007] because of high demand in China and India." (USGS, 2008)<br><br>A 17% increase in the annual global sulfur extraction level between 2000 and 2008 implies an increase in global sulfur demand during the pre-recession period, and a corresponding increase in global sulfur supply in response to increased global demand.<br><br>The fact that the price of sulfur increased by a phenomenal 750% during the 2000-2008 period indicates that global sulfur supply, while increasing during the eight year period, remained woefully insufficient to completely address global requirements in 2008.<br><br>That such a phenomenal increase in the price of sulfur during the 2000-2008 period could induce only a nominal increase in supply is compelling evidence that global sulfur supplies will remain insufficient to completely address global requirements going forward.<br><br>Barring future reductions in the global sulfur requirement trajectory and/or major new economically viable discoveries, sulfur will almost certainly remain scarce globally in the future.<br><br>British Sulfur Consultants support this assessment: "the sulphur market could move into supply deficit within the next 10 years. This view is based on 3 key assumptions: |
|---|---|

- Increasing use will be made of the technique of acid gas re-injection as an alternative to sulphur recovery from sour natural gas.
- Demand for brimstone (elemental sulphur) will continue to grow strongly in China.
- Rising volumes of nickel metal will be produced by means of sulphuric acid leaching processes." (AFA, 2005)

|  | The USGS, who base their assessment on assumed abundant global fossil fuel reserves going forward, disagree:<br><br>"Reserves of sulfur in crude oil, natural gas, and sulfide ores are large. Because most sulfur production is a result of the processing of fossil fuels, supplies should be adequate for the foreseeable future." (USGS, 2010) |
|---|---|

1. "Sulfur", Wikipedia, 2011 - http://en.wikipedia.org/wiki/Sulfur.
2. "Sulfur Statistics", Historical Statistics for Mineral and Material Commodities in the United States, USGS, 2010 – http://minerals.usgs.gov/ds/2005/140/sulfur.xls.
3. "Crops Require Sulfur", L. Oldham, Mississippi State University (MSU), 2004 - http://msucares.com/crops/fertilizer/sulfur_required.html.
4. "AFA Sulfur Outlook", American Fertilizer Association (AFA), 2005 - http://www.afa.com.eg/upload/S3_003%20Sulphur%20Supply~Demand%20Balance_The%20Outlook%20to%202013.pdf.

| NNR Profile | Talc |
|---|---|
| **NNR Uses and Critical Applications** | |
| **Primary Uses** | Talc is a very soft white or gray mineral used as a cosmetic, lubricant, astringent, and filler in applications such as paper making, plastic, paint and coatings, rubber, food, electric cable, pharmaceuticals, and ceramics. |
| **Critical Applications** | None identified. |
| **NNR Criticality** | **NNR Criticality Classification: Declining** |
| **Substitutes** | Viable talc substitutes, including bentonite, chlorite, kaolin, pyrophyllite and mica, are readily available. |
| **Criticality Assessment** | While talc is used in a variety of commercial and industrial applications; viable substitutes exist in most cases; both US and global demand for talc are declining. |
| **US NNR Scarcity** | **Scarce in 2008: No** \| **Permanently Scarce: Unclear** |
| **2008 US Import Reliance:** 0% | **2008 Domestic US Supply:** 100% |
| **Historical US Import Trends** | Historically, the US has been primarily a net exporter of talc; US talc imports exceeded exports during six of the last ten years, but exports exceeded imports in 2008. |
| **Historical US Usage Trends** | Annual US talc utilization levels generally increased during most of the 20th century, peaking temporarily in 1907, 1917, 1929, 1937, 1951, 1956, 1959, 1964, 1969, 1973, and 1981, before peaking permanently (to date) in 1990 and generally declining since that time. The 2008 US talc utilization level amounted to only 62% of the 1990 peak utilization level. |
| **US Peak Extraction Year (thru 2008):** 1979 | **US Peak Utilization Year (thru 2008):** 1990 |
| **Potential Geopolitical US Supply Constraints** | 46% of US talc imports come from China; however, the US is currently a net talc exporter. |

| NNR Profile | Talc (continued) |
|---|---|
| **US Scarcity Assessment** | "The United States is self-sufficient in most grades of talc and related minerals." (USGS, 2010)<br><br>That annual domestic talc utilization decreased by 38% since peaking (to date) in 1990, is an indicator of declining American industrial preeminence and global economic competitiveness.<br><br>However, as a result of continuously declining domestic demand for talc, the US is currently addressing its total talc requirement through domestic supplies; although the US was a net talc importer during six out of the past 10 years (1999-2008).<br><br>Available evidence regarding the likelihood that domestic talc supplies will remain sufficient to completely address domestic requirements going forward is conflicting:<br><br>• The 2008 US talc extraction level exceeded the 2008 US domestic utilization level by nearly 8%; and<br>• Proven domestic talc reserves are considered by the USGS to be nearly 200 times the 2008 extraction level; however<br>• The domestic talc extraction level decreased by 47% since peaking (to date) in 1979—a compelling indicator that domestic economically viable talc extraction has peaked permanently; and<br>• The US has recently become a consistent net importer of talc—an indicator of America's increasing dependence on foreign NNRs.<br><br>It is therefore unclear whether domestically available, economically viable talc supplies will remain sufficient to completely address future domestic requirements, or whether talc will become scarce domestically in the not-too-distant future. |

| Global NNR Scarcity | Scarce in 2008: No | Permanently Scarce: Unclear |
|---|---|---|
| **Historical Global Extraction Trends** | "Europe's leading world producer of talc entered a joint venture to produce talc in Liaoning Province, China. … The move also was taken because many of the company's customers were relocating in Asia, where markets were expanding." (USGS, 2010)<br><br>Annual global talc extraction levels generally increased during the 20th century, peaking temporarily in 1907, 1913, 1917, 1927, 1937, 1942, 1974, 1980, and 1990, before peaking permanently (to date) in 1997; annual global talc extraction decreased 14% between 2000 and 2008. | |

| Global Peak Extraction Year (thru 2008): 1997 | Years to Global Reserve Exhaustion: 50+ |
|---|---|
| **Projected Global Peak Extraction Year:** N/A | **Projected Global Peak Supply Year:** N/A |
| **Interdependencies** | None identified. |

| NNR Profile | Talc (continued) |
|---|---|
| **Global Scarcity Assessment** | A 14% decrease in the annual global talc extraction level between 2000 and 2008 implies either a decrease in global talc demand or insufficient global talc supplies during the pre-recession period.<br><br>The fact that the price of talc, while fluctuating, remained essentially constant during the 2000-2008 period indicates generally declining global demand, and that 2008 global talc supplies were sufficient to completely address global requirements at that time.<br><br>Available evidence regarding the likelihood that global talc supplies will remain sufficient to completely address global requirements going forward is conflicting:<br><br>• The global talc extraction level decreased while the talc price level remained essentially constant between 2000 and 2008—evidence of sufficient global supplies; and<br>• Proven global talc reserves are sufficient to last for over 50 years (assuming the restoration of pre-recession utilization levels and growth rates); however<br>• The price of talc increased by 29% between 2005 and 2008—evidence of unaddressed global requirements in 2008;<br>• The global talc extraction level peaked (to date) in 1997—evidence that globally available, economically viable talc extraction may be at or near its permanent peak level; and<br>• The global talc extraction level declined by 28% since peaking (to date) in 1997, despite unprecedented global economic growth between 1997 and 2008—absent supply constraints, it seems intuitive that global talc extraction levels would have increased during this period.<br><br>It is therefore unclear whether globally available, economically viable talc supplies will remain sufficient to completely address future global requirements, or whether talc will become scarce globally in the not-too-distant future. |

1. "Talc", Wikipedia, 2011 - http://en.wikipedia.org/wiki/Talc.
2. "Talc Statistics", Historical Statistics for Mineral and Material Commodities in the United States, USGS, 2010 – http://minerals.usgs.gov/ds/2005/140/talc.xls.

| NNR Profile | Tantalum |
|---|---|
| **NNR Uses and Critical Applications** | |
| **Primary Uses** | Tantalum is a lustrous, hard, blue-gray metal used as an alloy, a superalloy, in electronic components, and in a variety of high technology niche applications. |
| **Critical Applications** | Electronics (capacitors) and alloys (carbide tools, jet engine components, nuclear reactor components, missile parts, and surgical instruments). |
| **NNR Criticality** | **NNR Criticality Classification: Critical** |
| **Substitutes** | While substitutes such as glass, niobium, platinum, titanium, zirconium, hafnium, iridium, molybdenum, rhenium, and tungsten, exist for various tantalum applications, they are typically price/performance inferior. |

| NNR Profile | Tantalum (continued) | | |
|---|---|---|---|
| **Criticality Assessment** | Tantalum capacitors are used in most computer and communication devices; tantalum alloy applications are diverse and significant; and substitutes in both application areas are typically price/performance inferior. | | |
| **US NNR Scarcity** | **Scarce in 2008: Yes** | **Permanently Scarce: Almost Certain** | |
| **2008 US Import Reliance:** 100% | | **2008 Domestic US Supply:** 0% | |
| **Historical US Import Trends** | The US has been totally reliant on tantalum imports since the 1960s. | | |
| **Historical US Usage Trends** | Annual US tantalum utilization levels fluctuated widely since the 1960s, peaking temporarily in 1967, before peaking permanently (to date) in 1974, and peaking at lower levels in 1984, 1998, and 2005; the 2008 US tantalum utilization level amounted to only 70% of the 1974 peak utilization level. | | |
| **US Peak Extraction Year (thru 2008):** 1959* | | **US Peak Utilization Year (thru 2008):** 1974 | |
| **Potential Geopolitical US Supply Constraints** | The vast majority of proven global tantalum reserves are located in Australia (36%) and Brazil (59%). "A key issue [in the tantalum market] is the continuing supply of low-cost columbite-tantalite (coltan) mined in Central Africa, mostly illegally, and sold to fund rebel militias. The major processors will not knowingly buy such material and almost all of it goes to China." (Roskill, 2009) | | |
| **US Scarcity Assessment** | "No significant U.S. tantalum mine production has been reported since 1959. Domestic tantalum resources are of low grade, some mineralogically complex, and most are not commercially recoverable." (USGS, 2010) That annual domestic tantalum utilization decreased by 30% since peaking (to date) in 1974, is a significant indicator of declining American industrial preeminence and global economic competitiveness. The US currently relies exclusively on imported tantalum. Available evidence supports the contention that domestic tantalum supplies will remain insufficient to completely address domestic requirements going forward: • US tantalum extraction ceased entirely in 1960—an indicator of America's increasing dependence on foreign NNRs, and a compelling indicator that domestic economically viable tantalum extraction has peaked permanently; and • US tantalum resources are not commercially viable. Barring future reductions in the domestic (US) tantalum requirement trajectory and/or major new domestic economically viable discoveries, tantalum will almost certainly remain scarce domestically in the future. | | |
| **Global NNR Scarcity** | **Scarce in 2008: No** | **Permanently Scarce: Unlikely** | |
| **Historical Global Extraction Trends** | "The primary mining of tantalum is in Australia [48% of global production in 2009]..." (Wikipedia and USGS [figures]) Annual global tantalum extraction levels fluctuated widely from the mid 1960s to the early 1990s, spiking in 1971, 1980, and 1991, before increasing dramatically into the new millennium; annual global tantalum extraction increased 9% between 2000 and 2008. | | |

| NNR Profile | Tantalum (continued) | |
|---|---|---|
| **Global Peak Extraction Year (thru 2008):** 2004 | | **Years to Global Reserve Exhaustion:** 50+ |
| **Projected Global Peak Extraction Year:** N/A | | **Projected Global Peak Supply Year:** N/A |
| **Interdependencies** | Tantalum is a co-product with niobium; it can also be recovered as a byproduct of tin mining. | |
| **Global Scarcity Assessment** | "A key characteristic of the tantalum industry in recent years has been that supply has nearly always been greater than demand. As a result, large material inventories have been built up at most levels of the supply chain…" (Roskill, 2009)<br><br>A 9% increase in the annual global tantalum extraction level between 2000 and 2008 implies an increase in global tantalum demand during the pre-recession period, and a corresponding increase in global tantalum supply in response to increased global demand.<br><br>The fact that the price of tantalum decreased by 12% during the 2001-2008 period (an enormous price spike occurred in 2000) indicates that the global supply of tantalum in 2008 was sufficient to completely address 2008 global requirements.<br><br>Available evidence supports the contention that global tantalum supplies will remain sufficient to completely address global requirements going forward:<br><br>• While global tantalum extraction levels have generally increased since the early 1980s, tantalum price levels have generally decreased since that time—evidence of sufficient global tantalum supplies; and<br>• Proven global tantalum reserves are sufficient to last for over 50 years (assuming the restoration of pre-recession utilization levels and growth rates).<br><br>Barring future increases in the global tantalum requirement trajectory, globally available, economically viable tantalum supplies will likely remain sufficient to completely address global requirements going forward.<br><br>"Tantalum will probably not be scarce until after 2030. But a U.S. government report notes that suppliers can easily hold capacitor makers hostage to price increases." (IEEE, 2008) | |

*Pre-1959 per the USGS.

1. "Tantalum", Wikipedia, 2011 - http://en.wikipedia.org/wiki/Tantalum.
2. "Tantalum Statistics", Historical Statistics for Mineral and Material Commodities in the United States, USGS, 2010 – http://minerals.usgs.gov/ds/2005/140/tantalum.xls.
3. "The Economics of Tantalum", 10th edition, Roskill, 2009 - http://www.roskill.com/reports/minor-and-light-metals/tantalum.
4. "Supply Risk, Scarcity, and Cellphones", S. Moore, IEEE Spectrum, 2008 - http://spectrum.ieee.org/telecom/wireless/supply-risk-scarcity-and-cellphones.

| NNR Profile | Tellurium |
|---|---|
| **NNR Uses and Critical Applications** | |
| **Primary Uses** | Tellurium is lustrous, brittle, silver-white metalloid used primarily as an alloy (with iron, steel, copper, and lead); tellurium is also used as a vulcanizing agent (rubber), and in solar panels, semiconductors, and early thermonuclear bombs. |
| **Critical Applications** | High efficiency (cadmium telluride) solar cells and various alloys. "Tellurium's major use is as an alloying additive in steel to improve machining characteristics." (USGS, 2010) |

| NNR Criticality | | NNR Criticality Classification: Critical |
|---|---|---|
| **Substitutes** | | Tellurium substitutes such as bismuth, calcium, lead, niobium, phosphorus, selenium, sulfur, and tantalum are generally price/performance inferior. |
| **Criticality Assessment** | | In addition to its solar panel application, tellurium also plays a key role in several industrial applications (as an alloy), and in several high tech optical and electronics applications including CDs, DVDs, memory chips, far-infrared detectors, and optical fibers (telecommunications). "National Renewable Energy Laboratory lab tests using this material [cadmium telluride] achieved some of the highest efficiencies for solar cell electric power generation." (Wikipedia) |

| US NNR Scarcity | Scarce in 2008: Yes | Permanently Scarce: Almost Certain |
|---|---|---|
| **2008 US Import Reliance: ~40%** | | **2008 Domestic US Supply: ~60%** |
| **Historical US Import Trends** | While the US has been both a net exporter and a net importer of tellurium, the trend since the 1960s has been toward increasingly heavy import reliance (US tellurium imports peaked in 2008). | |
| **Historical US Usage Trends** | Annual US tellurium utilization levels generally increased during the 20th century, peaking temporarily in 1930, 1941, 1952, 1959, and 1972, before peaking permanently (to date) in 1979 (data is not available after 1984). | |
| **US Peak Production Year (thru 2008): 1960*** | | **US Peak Utilization Year (thru 2008): 1979****** |
| **Potential Geopolitical US Supply Constraints** | 43% of US tellurium imports come from China. | |

340

| NNR Profile | Tellurium (continued) |
|---|---|
| **US Scarcity Assessment** | "In the United States, one firm produced commercial-grade tellurium at its refinery complex in Texas, mainly from copper anode slimes but also from lead refinery skimmings, both of domestic origin." (USGS, 2010)<br><br>That annual domestic tellurium utilization decreased by 52% (through 1984) since peaking (to date) in 1979, is an indicator of declining American industrial preeminence and global economic competitiveness.<br><br>The US currently relies heavily on imported tellurium, a large percentage (43%) of which comes from China. The quantity of tellurium supplied by foreign sources during 2006 was approximately 40% (My estimate for the 2006 US tellurium import percentage***; US tellurium production, utilization, and import percentage data were withheld).<br><br>Available evidence supports the contention that domestic tellurium supplies will remain insufficient to completely address domestic demand going forward:<br><br>• Annual US tellurium production has been sporadic since the middle 1970s—an indicator of America's increasing dependence on foreign NNRs, and an indicator that domestic tellurium production has likely peaked permanently; and<br>• The US has been generally reliant on net tellurium imports since the mid 1990s.<br><br>Barring future reductions in the domestic (US) tellurium requirement trajectory and/or major new domestic economically viable discoveries, tellurium will almost certainly remain scarce domestically in the future. |
| **Global NNR Scarcity** | **Scarce in 2008: No** — **Permanently Scarce: Unclear** |
| **Historical Global Production Trends** | "Tellurium is produced mainly in the United States, Canada, Peru and Japan. For the year 2006 the British Geological Survey gives the following numbers: Canada 11 t [metric tonnes], United States 50 t, Peru 37 t and Japan 24 t [the USGS withholds US tellurium production data]." (Wikipedia)<br><br>Annual global tellurium production levels generally increased in a widely fluctuating manner during the first three quarters of the 20th century, peaking temporarily in 1930, 1937, 1942, 1951, 1957, 1962, and 1969, before peaking permanently (to date) in 1974 and fluctuating downward since that time. Annual global tellurium production decreased by 14% between 2000 and 2003 (USGS global tellurium production data is unavailable after 2003).<br><br>"Growth in the global use of the leaching solvent extraction-electrowinning processes for copper extraction has limited the growth of tellurium supply [in 2009]." (UGSS, 2010) |
| **Global Peak Production Year (thru 2008): 1974** | **Years to Global Reserve Exhaustion: N/A** |
| **Projected Global Peak Production Year: 1970** | **Projected Global Peak Supply Year: 2100** |
| **Interdependencies** | Tellurium is typically obtained as a byproduct of copper, lead, and gold processing. |

| NNR Profile | Tellurium (continued) |
|---|---|
| **Global Scarcity Assessment** | "The price of tellurium increased in 2007 because growth in consumption worldwide was not matched by growth in production." (USGS, 2008)<br><br>A 14% decrease in the annual global tellurium production level between 2000 and 2003 (the last year of available USGS data), implies either a decrease in global tellurium demand or insufficient global tellurium supplies during the pre-recession period.<br><br>The fact that the price of tellurium decreased by 11% during the 2000-2003 period indicates generally declining global demand, and that 2003 global tellurium supplies were sufficient to completely address global requirements at that time.<br><br>Available evidence regarding the likelihood that global tellurium supplies will remain sufficient to completely address global requirements going forward is conflicting:<br><br>• Both the global tellurium production level and the tellurium price level decreased between 2000 and 2003—compelling evidence of sufficient global supplies; and<br>• The global tellurium supply level is not projected to peak until approximately 2100; however<br>• The price of tellurium increased by a phenomenal 453% between 2003 and 2008 (a period for which tellurium production data are unavailable)—compelling evidence of unaddressed global requirements in 2008;<br>• The global tellurium production level was projected to peak in 1970; and<br>• The global tellurium production level actually peaked (to date) in 1974—evidence that globally available, economically viable tellurium production may be near, at, or past its permanent peak level.<br><br>It is therefore unclear whether globally available, economically viable tellurium supplies will remain sufficient to completely address future global requirements, or whether tellurium will become scarce globally in the not-too-distant future.<br><br>"In his analysis, Ecclestone noted the ongoing debate 'on whether there is enough tellurium in the world to support the growing solar market, and how much costs would be added to the solar cell production if mines spend their resources to focus on tellurium production.'" (Mineweb, 2010) |

\* Through 1975.
\*\*Through 1984.
\*\*\*2006 tellurium imports were approximately 31 metric tonnes according to the USGS; 2006 US tellurium production was approximately 50 metric tonnes, according to the BGS; 31 is approximately 40% of 81.

1. "Tellurium", Wikipedia, 2011 - http://en.wikipedia.org/wiki/Tellurium.
2. "Tellurium Statistics", Historical Statistics for Mineral and Material Commodities in the United States, USGS, 2010 – http://minerals.usgs.gov/ds/2005/140/tellurium.xls.
3. "Western Industrial Users Seen as Hopeless at Securing Specialty Metals Supplies", Mineweb, 2010 -

http://www.mineweb.com/mineweb/view/mineweb/en/page72102?oid=107698&sn=Detail&pid
=65.

| NNR Profile | Thallium | |
|---|---|---|
| **NNR Uses and Critical Applications** | | |
| **Primary Uses** | Thallium is a soft, malleable, gray metal used primarily in electronics, medical imaging, pharmaceutical, and glass manufacturing applications; thallium is also used in infrared detectors, rat poisons, and insecticides. Ongoing research is being conducted into high temperature superconductor applications. | |
| **Critical Applications** | Superconductivity (potential). | |
| **NNR Criticality** | **NNR Criticality Classification: Important** | |
| **Substitutes** | While non-toxic thallium substitutes are available for many applications, thallium is still price/performance superior in most of its niche applications. | |
| **Criticality Assessment** | Thallium is used in a variety of niche industrial, medical, and scientific applications. In the event that thallium proves to be a widely deployed high temperature superconductor, its criticality will increase. | |
| **US NNR Scarcity** | **Scarce in 2008: Yes** | **Permanently Scarce: Almost Certain** |
| **2008 US Import Reliance:** 100% | **2008 Domestic US Supply:** 0% | |
| **Historical US Import Trends** | Historically, the US has been a net importer of thallium; the US has been totally reliant on thallium imports since 1982. | |
| **Historical US Usage Trends** | "Its [thallium's] use has been cut back or eliminated in many countries because of its nonselective toxicity." (Wikipedia)<br><br>Annual US thallium utilization levels have generally decreased—in a fluctuating manner—since peaking (to date) in 1970; the 2008 US thallium utilization level amounted to only 24% of the 1970 peak utilization level. | |
| **US Peak Production Year (thru 2008):** 1977 | **US Peak Utilization Year (thru 2008):** 1970 | |
| **Potential Geopolitical US Supply Constraints** | 78% of US thallium imports come from Russia.<br><br>"China continued its policy of eliminating toll trading tax benefits on exports of thallium that began in 2006, thus contributing to the shortage on the world market." (USGS, 2010) | |

| NNR Profile | Thallium (continued) |
|---|---|
| **US Scarcity Assessment** | "Although thallium was contained in ores mined or processed in the United States, it has not been recovered domestically since 1981." (USGS, 2010)<br><br>That annual domestic thallium utilization decreased by 76% since peaking (to date) in 1970, is an indicator of declining American industrial preeminence and global economic competitiveness, and of diminished domestic demand for thallium due to its toxicity.<br><br>The US currently relies exclusively on imported thallium.<br><br>Available evidence supports the contention that domestic thallium supplies will remain insufficient to completely address domestic requirements going forward:<br><br>• US thallium production ceased entirely in 1982—an indicator of America's increasing dependence on foreign NNRs, and a compelling indicator that domestic economically viable thallium production has peaked permanently; and<br>• Thallium is not produced in the US, despite the existence of (subeconomic) domestic thallium containing ores.<br><br>Barring future reductions in the domestic (US) thallium requirement trajectory and/or major new domestic economically viable discoveries, thallium will almost certainly remain scarce domestically in the future. |

| Global NNR Scarcity | Scarce in 2008: Yes | Permanently Scarce: Almost Certain |
|---|---|---|

| **Historical Global Production Trends** | "The Allchar deposit in southern Macedonia was the only area where thallium was ever actively mined." (Wikipedia)<br><br>Annual global thallium extraction/production levels peaked in 1989, and have declined on a graduated basis since that time; annual global thallium extraction decreased 33% between 2000 and 2008. |
|---|---|

| Global Peak Production Year (thru 2008): 1989 | Years to Global Reserve Exhaustion: 38* |
|---|---|
| Projected Global Peak Production Year: N/A | Projected Global Peak Supply Year: N/A |

| **Interdependencies** | Thallium is typically recovered through the processing of copper, lead, zinc, and other heavy metal ores.<br><br>"Thallium is a byproduct metal recovered in some countries from flue dusts and residues collected in the smelting of copper, zinc, and lead ores." (USGS, 2010) |
|---|---|

| NNR Profile | Thallium |
|---|---|
| **Global Scarcity Assessment** | "The price for thallium metal remained high in 2007 as the supply worldwide continued to be relatively tight…" (USGS, 2008)<br><br>A 33% decrease in the annual global thallium production level between 2000 and 2008 implies either a decrease in global thallium demand or insufficient global thallium supplies during the pre-recession period.<br><br>The fact that the price of thallium increased by an extraordinary 202% during the 2000-2008 period, indicates that the declining global supply of thallium was woefully insufficient to completely address global requirements in 2008.<br><br>Available evidence supports the contention that global thallium supplies will remain insufficient to completely address global requirements going forward:<br><br>• Proven global thallium reserves would exhaust in only 38 years, assuming that future annual utilization levels remain constant at the 2008 level;<br>• An extraordinary increase in the price of thallium during the 2000-2008 period could not induce an increase in global thallium supply—compelling evidence of unaddressed global requirements in 2008; and<br>• Annual global thallium production peaked (to date) in 1989—evidence that globally available, economically viable thallium production may be at or near its permanent peak level.<br><br>Barring future reductions in the global thallium requirement trajectory and/or major new economically viable discoveries, thallium will almost certainly remain scarce globally in the future.<br><br>"Higher internal demand for many metals, including thallium, has prompted China to begin importing greater quantities of thallium." (USGS, 2008) |

*Reserve to Production Ratio (2000-2008 extraction/production growth was negative)

1. "Thallium", Wikipedia, 2011 - http://en.wikipedia.org/wiki/Thallium.
2. "Thallium Statistics", Historical Statistics for Mineral and Material Commodities in the United States, USGS, 2010 – http://minerals.usgs.gov/ds/2005/140/thallium.xls.

| NNR Profile | Thorium |
|---|---|
| **NNR Uses and Critical Applications** | |
| **Primary Uses** | Thorium is a ductile, slightly-radioactive, slivery-white metal used historically in limited applications as a breeding source for nuclear fuel (in breeder reactors); non-energy thorium uses include alloys (magnesium), heat resistant ceramics, glass additive, welding electrodes, and catalyst. |

| NNR Profile | Thorium (continued) |
|---|---|
| **Critical Applications** | Potentially as a fuel source for nuclear reactors of various types. The thorium debate:<br><br>"…Thorium could be used with or as a substitute for Uranium in nuclear reactors. Thorium-powered nuclear reactors have the potential to be more efficient and produce less than 1 percent of the waste of today's Uranium nuclear reactors…" (Sestak, 2009)<br><br>"Much development work is still required before the thorium fuel cycle can be commercialized, and the effort required seems unlikely while (or where) abundant uranium is available." (World Nuclear Association, 2010) |

| NNR Criticality | | NNR Criticality Classification: Declining |
|---|---|---|
| **Substitutes** | | Viable, non-radioactive substitutes for thorium, including yttrium compounds and a magnesium alloy, generally exist (for non-nuclear reactor applications); uranium (primarily) and plutonium substitute as nuclear reactor fuels. |
| **Criticality Assessment** | | In the event that thorium becomes a viable nuclear fuel source, its criticality will increase substantially; its importance currently negligible, however, both domestically and globally.<br><br>"It is likely that thorium's use will continue to decline unless a low-cost disposal process is developed or new technology, such as a non-proliferative nuclear fuel, creates renewed demand." (USGS, 2010) |

| US NNR Scarcity | Scarce in 2008: Yes | Permanently Scarce: Almost Certain |
|---|---|---|
| **2008 US Import Reliance: 100%** | | **2008 Domestic US Supply: 0%** |
| **Historical US Import Trends** | | With very few exceptions, the US has been a net importer of thorium since the beginning of the 20th century. |
| **Historical US Usage Trends** | | "The use of thorium in the United States has decreased significantly since the 1980s, when consumption averaged 45 tons per year." (USGS, 2008)<br><br>Annual US thorium utilization levels fluctuated widely during the 20th century, peaking temporarily in 1917 (spike), 1922 (spike), 1950, 1960, and 1968, before peaking permanently (to date) in 1972 (spike) and declining dramatically since that time; the 2007 US thorium utilization level amounted to less than 1% of the 1972 peak utilization level.<br><br>"Thorium's use in most products has generally decreased because of its naturally occurring radioactivity." (USGS, 2010) |
| **US Peak Production Year (thru 2008): 1961** | | **US Peak Utilization Year (thru 2008): 1972** |
| **Potential Geopolitical US Supply Constraints** | | 100% of US monazite (thorium source) imports come from Canada; 72% of US thorium compound imports come from the UK. |

| NNR Profile | Thorium (continued) |
|---|---|
| **US Scarcity Assessment** | "Domestic mine production of thorium-bearing monazite ceased at the end of 1994 as world demand for ores containing naturally occurring radioactive thorium declined." (USGS, 2008)<br><br>That annual domestic thorium utilization decreased by 99% since peaking (to date) in 1972, is an indicator of repeated unsuccessful attempts to use thorium as a viable fuel source in nuclear reactors.<br><br>The US currently relies exclusively on imported thorium, a vast majority of which comes from Canada (100% of monazite) and the UK (72% of thorium compounds).<br><br>Available evidence supports the contention that domestic thorium supplies will remain insufficient to completely address domestic requirements, albeit significantly diminished requirements, going forward:<br><br>• Meaningful US thorium production ceased entirely in 1994—an indicator of America's increasing dependence on foreign NNRs, and a compelling indicator that domestic economically viable thorium production has peaked permanently; and<br>• Thorium is typically recovered from the same monazite minerals as rare earth minerals (REMs), which are not currently mined in the US (see Rare Earth Minerals).<br><br>Barring future reductions in the domestic (US) thorium requirement trajectory and/or major new domestic economically viable discoveries, thorium will almost certainly remain scarce domestically in the future. |

| Global NNR Scarcity | Scarce in 2008: Yes | Permanently Scarce: Unclear |
|---|---|---|
| **Historical Global Production Trends** | Available USGS global thorium data (1960-1977) are insufficient to assess current extraction/production trends. Annual global thorium extraction/production peaked temporary peak in 1963, before peaking permanently (to date) in 1972.<br><br>"Without demand for the rare earths [REMs], monazite would probably not be recovered for its thorium content. Other ore minerals with higher thorium contents, such as thorite, would be more likely sources if demand significantly increased." (USGS, 2010) | |

| Global Peak Production Year (thru 2008): 1972 | Years to Global Reserve Exhaustion: N/A |
|---|---|
| **Projected Global Peak Production Year: N/A** | **Projected Global Peak Supply Year: N/A** |

| Interdependencies | Thorium is typically recovered as a byproduct of rare earth mineral refining; the rare earth mineral source, monazite, is itself a byproduct of titanium and zirconium processing. |
|---|---|

| NNR Profile | Thorium (continued) |
|---|---|
| **Global Scarcity Assessment** | While annual global production data associated with thorium are unavailable from the USGS for the 2000-2008 pre-recession period, thorium prices increased by an extremely robust 93% between 2000 and 2008, indicating that global thorium supplies were insufficient to completely address global requirements during 2008.<br><br>Given the lack of USGS data, it is unclear whether thorium will remain scarce globally in the future, or whether globally available, economically viable thorium supplies will be sufficient to completely address future global requirements.<br><br>"Large thorium resources [not necessarily reserves] are found in Australia, Brazil, Canada, Greenland (Denmark), India, South Africa, and the United States." (USGS, 2010) |

*Global production/extraction data is not available past 1977.

1. "Thorium", Wikipedia, 2011 - http://en.wikipedia.org/wiki/Thorium.
2. "Thorium Statistics", Historical Statistics for Mineral and Material Commodities in the United States, USGS, 2010 – http://minerals.usgs.gov/ds/2005/140/thorium.xls.
3. "Thorium", World Nuclear Association, 2010- http://www.world-nuclear.org/info/inf62.html.
4. "Rep. Sestak Calls for a Thorium Study", EnergyFromThorium, 2009 - http://energyfromthorium.com/2009/06/30/rep-sestak-calls-for-thorium-study/.

| NNR Profile | Tin | | |
|---|---|---|---|
| **NNR Uses and Critical Applications** | | | |
| **Primary Uses** | Tin is a malleable, ductile, silvery-white metal used as an alloy (in bronze, pewter, and solder), as an anti-corrosive metal coating, in food packaging, and in the manufacture of window glass; also used in superconducting magnets. | | |
| **Critical Applications** | Solder, alloy, coating, food packaging, and superconductor.<br><br>"Developments continued in major tin-consuming countries to move to new lead-free solders that usually contain greater amounts of tin then do leaded solders." (USGS, 2010) | | |
| **NNR Criticality** | | **NNR Criticality Classification: Critical** | |
| **Substitutes** | Metallic and nonmetallic substitutes, including aluminum, glass, paper, plastic, tin-free steel, epoxy resins, aluminum alloys, and copper-base alloys, exist for many tin applications; price/performance characteristics vary per application. | | |
| **Criticality Assessment** | Tin is used in a wide variety of industrial, commercial, and scientific applications. While acceptable substitutes exist in many cases, tin still offers price/performance benefits in most cases. | | |
| **US NNR Scarcity** | **Scarce in 2008: Yes** | **Permanently Scarce: Almost Certain** | |
| **2008 US Import Reliance:** 80% | | **2008 Domestic US Supply:** 20% | |
| **Historical US Import Trends** | The US has been a net importer of tin since the beginning of the 20th century, often importing 100% of annual domestic requirements. Current domestically produced tin supplies come exclusively from recycling and previously accumulated stocks. | | |

| NNR Profile | Tin (continued) |
|---|---|
| **Historical US Usage Trends** | Annual US tin utilization levels generally increased through the first half of the 20th century, peaking temporarily in 1906, 1912, 1918, 1929, 1937, and 1945, before peaking permanently (to date) in 1950, and declining in a fluctuating manner until the early 1990s, after which domestic tin utilization increased slightly. The 2008 US tin utilization level amounted to only 43% of the 1950 peak utilization level. |

| US Peak Extraction Year (thru 2008): 1945 | US Peak Utilization Year (thru 2008): 1950 |
|---|---|

| **Potential Geopolitical US Supply Constraints** | 47% of US tin imports come from Peru; China and Indonesia each produce over 40% of the world's tin (2007). |
|---|---|

| **US Scarcity Assessment** | "Tin has not been mined or smelted in the United States since 1993 and 1989, respectively." (USGS, 2010)<br><br>That annual domestic tin utilization decreased by 57% since peaking (to date) in 1950, is a major indicator of declining American industrial preeminence and global economic competitiveness.<br><br>The US currently relies almost exclusively on imported tin, a large percentage (47%) of which comes from China. The quantity of tin supplied by foreign sources during 2008 accounted for 80% of the total 2008 US utilization level.<br><br>Available evidence supports the contention that domestic tin supplies will remain insufficient to completely address domestic requirements going forward:<br><br>• US tin extraction ceased entirely in 1990—a significant indicator of America's increasing dependence on foreign NNRs;<br>• The US has been heavily reliant on tin imports since the early 20th century; and<br>• The quantity of tin extracted domestically during 1945, the year of peak (to date) domestic tin extraction, amounted to only 69% of the 2008 total US utilization level—a compelling indicator that domestic economically viable tin extraction has peaked permanently.<br><br>Barring future reductions in the domestic (US) tin requirement trajectory and/or major new domestic economically viable discoveries, tin will almost certainly remain scarce domestically in the future.<br><br>"U.S. resources of tin, primarily in Alaska, were insignificant compared with those of the rest of the world." (USGS, 2010) |
|---|---|

| Global NNR Scarcity | Scarce in 2008: Yes | Permanently Scarce: Almost Certain |
|---|---|---|

| **Historical Global Extraction Trends** | "The major producers of tin are Malaysia, Thailand, Indonesia [33% of 2009 global production], Bolivia, Republic of Congo, Nigeria, and China [37% of 2009 global production]." (Group IVA and USGS [figures])<br><br>Annual global tin extraction levels generally increased during both the 20th and 21st centuries, peaking temporarily in 1913, 1929, 1937, 1941, 1957, 1972, 1980, and 1989, before generally increasing into the new millennium; annual global tin extraction increased 8% between 2000 and 2008.<br><br>"China continued as the world's leading tin producer from both mine and smelter sources…" (USGS, 2010) |
|---|---|

| NNR Profile | Tin (continued) | | |
|---|---|---|---|
| **Global Peak Extraction Year (thru 2008):** 2007 | | **Years to Global Reserve Exhaustion:** 18 | |
| **Projected Global Peak Extraction Year:** 2018 | | **Projected Global Peak Supply Year:** 2020 | |
| **Interdependencies** | None identified. | | |
| **Global Scarcity Assessment** | "The average monthly dealer price of tin rose steadily during the first 7 months of 2007…" (USGS, 2008) | | |
| | An 8% increase in the annual global tin extraction level between 2000 and 2008 implies an increase in global tin demand during the pre-recession period, and a corresponding increase in global tin supply in response to increased global demand. | | |
| | The fact that the price of tin increased by an extraordinary 145% during the 2000-2008 period indicates that global tin supply, while increasing during the eight year period, remained woefully insufficient to completely address global requirements in 2008. | | |
| | Available evidence supports the contention that global tin supplies will remain insufficient to completely address global requirements going forward: | | |
| | • Proven global tin reserves would exhaust in only 18 years, assuming the restoration of pre-recession utilization levels and growth rates;<br>• The global tin extraction level is projected to peak in approximately 2018;<br>• The global tin supply level is projected to peak in approximately 2020; and<br>• An extremely robust increase in the price of tin during the 2000-2008 period induced only a nominal increase in tin supply—compelling evidence that globally available, economically viable tin extraction may be at or near its permanent peak level. | | |
| | Barring future reductions in the global tin requirement trajectory and/or major new economically viable discoveries, tin will almost certainly remain scarce globally in the future. | | |
| | "Despite that increase in [2010 tin] demand, tin supplies in Indonesia have plummeted. The commodity's largest producer, its exports of redefined tin account for a third of the global market. … In part, that [decline] stems from a depletion of Indonesia's easily mined and high-grade reserves." (Investment U, 2010) | | |

1. "Tin", Wikipedia, 2011 - http://en.wikipedia.org/wiki/Tin.
2. "Tin Statistics", Historical Statistics for Mineral and Material Commodities in the United States, USGS, 2010 – http://minerals.usgs.gov/ds/2005/140/tin.xls.
3. "Tin", Group IVA - http://www.carondelet.pvt.k12.ca.us/Family/Science/GroupIVA/tin.htm.
4. "Investing in Tin: Portfolio Protection Against Corrosion", T. D'Altorio, Investment U. 2010 - http://www.investmentu.com/2010/August/investing-in-tin.html.

| NR Profile | Titanium Mineral Concentrates |
|---|---|

## NNR Uses and Critical Applications

| Primary Uses | Titanium mineral concentrates are titanium containing minerals; titanium mineral concentrates such as rutile and anatase are used in the production of titanium dioxide ($TiO_2$) pigments, which are used in paints, paper, toothpaste, and plastics; as a photocatalyst. Titanium mineral concentrates such as rutile, ilmenite, and leucoxene are the feedstocks for titanium metal. |
|---|---|
| Critical Applications | Rutile and ilmenite are the two economically viable feedstocks for titanium metal; titanium dioxide also offers potential as a photocatalyst in energy generation. |

| NNR Criticality | NNR Criticality Classification: Indispensible |
|---|---|
| Substitutes | Economically viable substitutes for rutile and ilmenite as feedstocks for producing titanium metal do not exist. |
| Criticality Assessment | Titanium mineral concentrates, especially rutile and ilmenite, are essential to the production of titanium metal, which plays a role in a number of critical industrial, military, chemical, scientific, and medical applications. |

| US NNR Scarcity | Scarce in 2008: Yes | Permanently Scarce: Almost Certain |
|---|---|---|

| 2008 US Import Reliance: 78% | 2008 Domestic US Supply: 22% |
|---|---|

| Historical US Import Trends | The US has been a net importer of titanium mineral concentrates since the early 20th century; annual US titanium net import levels have increased almost continuously since that time. |
|---|---|
| Historical US Usage Trends | Annual US titanium mineral concentrate utilization levels generally increased from the 1940s forward, peaking temporarily in 1956, 1969, 1974, and 1979, before peaking permanently (to date) in 1997, and decreasing in a fluctuating manner into the new millennium; the 2008 US titanium mineral concentrates utilization level amounted to only 82% of the 1997 peak utilization level. |

| US Peak Extraction Year (thru 2008): 1964 | US Peak Utilization Year (thru 2008): 1997 |
|---|---|

| Potential Geopolitical US Supply Constraints | 51% of US titanium mineral concentrate imports come from South Africa; nearly 50% of proven global rutile reserves are located in Australia.<br><br>"In the first half of 2009, new Government policies were implemented in Vietnam to stop ilmenite exports, control illegal mining, and promote the development of upgraded products." (USGS, 2010) |
|---|---|

351

| NR Profile | Titanium Mineral Concentrates (continued) |
|---|---|
| **US Scarcity Assessment** | "Two firms produced ilmenite and rutile concentrates from surface-mining operations in Florida and Virginia." (USGS, 2010)<br><br>That annual domestic titanium mineral concentrate utilization decreased by 18% since peaking (to date) in 1997, is a major indicator of declining American industrial preeminence and global economic competitiveness.<br><br>The US currently relies almost exclusively on imported titanium mineral concentrates, the majority (51%) of which comes from South Africa. The quantity of titanium mineral concentrates supplied by foreign sources during 2008 accounted for 78% of the total 2008 US utilization level.<br><br>Available evidence supports the contention that domestic titanium metal concentrate supplies will remain insufficient to completely address domestic requirements going forward:<br><br>• The annual US titanium metal concentrate extraction level decreased by 67% since peaking (to date) in 1964—a compelling indicator that domestic economically viable titanium mineral concentrate extraction has peaked permanently;<br>• The US has become increasingly reliant on titanium mineral concentrate imports since World War II;<br>• The quantity of titanium mineral concentrates extracted domestically during 2008 amounted to only 18% of the total 2008 US utilization level—a primary indicator of America's increasing dependence on foreign NNRs; and<br>• The quantity of titanium mineral concentrates extracted domestically during 1964, the year of peak (to date) domestic titanium mineral concentrate extraction, amounted to only 56% of the 2008 total US utilization level.<br><br>Barring future reductions in the domestic (US) titanium mineral concentrate requirement trajectory and/or major new domestic economically viable discoveries, titanium mineral concentrates will almost certainly remain scarce domestically in the future. |

| Global NNR Scarcity | Scarce in 2008: Yes | Permanently Scarce: Likely |
|---|---|---|
| **Historical Global Extraction Trends** | "Ilmenite is found mainly in Australia, Canada, Finland, South Africa and the U.S."; "Rutile, too, is commonly found in Australia and South Africa, but also India, Sri Lanka and Sierra Leone." (Seeking Alpha, 2010)<br><br>Annual global titanium mineral concentrate extraction levels generally increased during both the 20th and 21st centuries, peaking temporarily in 1940, 1957, 1970, 1974, 1980, 1984, and 1989, before increasing into the new millennium; annual global titanium mineral concentrate extraction increased 31% between 2000 and 2008.<br><br>"…: Ilmenite accounts for about 91% of the world's consumption of titanium minerals." (USGS, 2010) | |

| Global Peak Extraction Year (thru 2008): 2007 | Years to Global Reserve Exhaustion: 37 |
|---|---|
| **Projected Global Peak Extraction Year: 2025** | **Projected Global Peak Supply Year: 2050** |
| **Interdependencies** | None identified. |

| NR Profile | Titanium Mineral Concentrates (continued) |
|---|---|
| **Global Scarcity Assessment** | "Of these [titanium mineral concentrates] minerals, only rutile and ilmenite have any economic importance, yet even they are difficult to find in high concentrations." (Wikipedia)<br><br>A 31% increase in the annual global titanium mineral concentrate extraction level between 2000 and 2008 implies an increase in global demand during the pre-recession period, and a corresponding increase in titanium mineral concentrate supply in response to increased global demand.<br><br>The fact that the price of titanium mineral concentrates increased by 18% (for ilmenite; 8% for rutile) during the 2000-2008 period indicates that global titanium mineral concentrate supply, while increasing during the eight year period, remained insufficient to completely address global requirements in 2008.<br><br>Available evidence supports the contention that global titanium mineral concentrate supplies will likely remain insufficient to completely address global requirements going forward:<br><br>• Proven global titanium mineral concentrate reserves would exhaust in only 37 years, assuming the restoration of pre-recession utilization levels and growth rates,<br>• The global titanium mineral concentrate extraction level is projected to peak in approximately 2025;<br>• The global titanium mineral concentrate supply level is projected to peak in approximately 2050; and<br>• The increased global titanium mineral concentrate supply brought online between 2000 and 2008 failed to prevent a price increase during the period—evidence of unaddressed global requirements in 2008.<br><br>Barring future reductions in the global titanium mineral concentrate requirement trajectory and/or major new economically viable discoveries, titanium mineral concentrates will likely remain scarce globally in the future.<br><br>"The FFC Cambridge [refining] process may render titanium a less rare and expensive material for the aerospace industry and the luxury goods market, and could be seen in many products currently manufactured using aluminum and specialist grades of steel." (Wikipedia) |

1. "Titanium", Wikipedia, 2011 - http://en.wikipedia.org/wiki/Titanium.
2. "Titanium Dioxide", Wikipedia, 2011 - http://en.wikipedia.org/wiki/Titanium_dioxide.
3. "Titanium Mineral Concentrates Statistics", Historical Statistics for Mineral and Material Commodities in the United States, USGS, 2010 – http://minerals.usgs.gov/ds/2005/140/titaniummineral.xls.
4. "Mineral Commodity Summaries 2005" (for 2000 price), US Geological Survey, 2005 - http://minerals.usgs.gov/minerals/pubs/mcs/2005/mcs2005.pdf.
5. "Titanium: Mineral of the Gods", T. Vulcan, Seeking Alpha, 2010 - http://seekingalpha.com/article/194965-titanium-metal-of-the-gods.

| NNR Profile | Titanium Metal |
|---|---|

## NNR Uses and Critical Applications

| Primary Uses | Titanium is a strong, lustrous, corrosion-resistant, silver colored metal used as an alloy (e.g., with iron, molybdenum, vanadium, and aluminum) in aerospace (jet engines, missiles, and spacecraft), military, industrial process (chemicals and petro-chemicals, desalination plants, pulp, and paper), automotive, agricultural/food, medical prostheses, orthopedic implants, dental and endodontic instruments and files, dental implants, sporting goods, jewelry, mobile phones, and other applications. |
|---|---|
| Critical Applications | Titanium alloys are used in aircraft, armor plating, ships, spacecraft, missiles, and surgical implants. |

| NNR Criticality | NNR Criticality Classification: Indispensible |
|---|---|
| Substitutes | While materials such as aluminum, composites, intermetallics, steel, superalloys, nickel, specialty steels, and zirconium alloys are sometimes substituted for titanium metal, none possess titanium's strength-to-weight ratio and corrosion resistance. |
| Criticality Assessment | "The two most useful properties of the [titanium] metal form are corrosion resistance and the highest strength-to-weight ratio of any metal." (Wikipedia) <br><br> Titanium and titanium alloys are used in a broad range of critical commercial, industrial, and military applications; viable titanium substitutes are essentially nonexistent. Titanium metal is indispensible to modern industrial existence. |

| US NNR Scarcity | Scarce in 2008: Yes | Permanently Scarce: Almost Certain |
|---|---|---|

| 2008 US Import Reliance: 71% | 2008 Domestic US Supply: 29% |
|---|---|

| Historical US Import Trends | Historically, the US was primarily a net importer of titanium metal; US titanium metal imports have increased dramatically over the past two decades. |
|---|---|
| Historical US Usage Trends | Annual US titanium metal utilization levels generally increased in a widely fluctuating manner during the latter half of the 20th century, peaking temporarily in 1956, 1969, 1974, 1981, 1989, and 1997, before generally increasing into the new millennium. |

| US Peak Production Year (thru 2008): 1989* | US Peak Utilization Year (thru 2008): 2007 |
|---|---|

| Potential Geopolitical US Supply Constraints | 52% of US titanium sponge metal imports come from Kazakhstan. |
|---|---|

| NNR Profile | Titanium Metal (continued) |
|---|---|
| **US Scarcity Assessment** | The US currently relies heavily on imported titanium metal, the majority (52%) of which comes from Kazakhstan. The quantity of titanium metal supplied by foreign sources during 2008 accounted for 71% of the total 2008 US utilization level.<br><br>Available evidence supports the contention that domestic titanium metal supplies will remain insufficient to completely address domestic requirements going forward:<br><br>• While US titanium metal utilization increased into the new millennium, domestic titanium metal production apparently declined significantly since 1992 (given that recent US net import levels nearly equal US utilization levels)—a compelling indicator that domestic economically viable titanium metal production has peaked permanently;<br>• Net US titanium metal imports increased dramatically since the early 1990s; and<br>• The quantity of titanium metal extracted domestically during 1989, the year of peak (to date) domestic titanium metal extraction, amounted to only 75% of the 2008 total US utilization level—a primary indicator of America's increasing dependence on foreign NNRs.<br><br>Barring future reductions in the domestic (US) titanium metal requirement trajectory and/or major new domestic economically viable discoveries, titanium metal will almost certainly remain scarce domestically in the future. |

| Global NNR Scarcity | Scarce in 2008: Yes | Permanently Scarce: Unclear |
|---|---|---|
| **Historical Global Production Trends** | "While titanium mineral concentrates are to be found in a number of different regions around the globe, currently there are only six countries that actually produce titanium sponge from those concentrates (China [49,000 metric tons], Japan [40,000 metric tons], Russia [19,000 metric tons], Kazakhstan [16,000 metric tons], and Ukraine [6,000 metric tons] [US data was withheld by the USGS])." (Seeking Alpha, 2010; 2008 USGS data)<br><br>Global titanium production data is not available from the USGS. | |

| | | |
|---|---|---|
| **Global Peak Production Year (thru 2008):** N/A | **Years to Global Reserve Exhaustion:** N/A | |
| **Projected Global Peak Production Year:** N//A | **Projected Global Peak Supply Year:** N/A | |
| **Interdependencies** | None identified. | |

| NNR Profile | Titanium Metal (continued) |
|---|---|
| **Global Scarcity Assessment** | "Though titanium metal is expensive, its ore is actually quite abundant. The high cost comes from the difficulty of refining the metal, not its scarcity." (The Elements, 2009)<br><br>While annual global production data associated with titanium metal are unavailable from the USGS for the 2000-2008 pre-recession period, titanium metal prices increased by 43% between 2000 and 2008, indicating that global titanium metal supplies were insufficient to completely address global requirements during 2008.<br><br>Given the lack of USGS data, it is unclear whether titanium metal will remain scarce globally in the future, or whether globally available, economically viable titanium metal supplies will be sufficient to completely address future global requirements.<br><br>"Several concerted efforts to develop a low-cost method for producing titanium metal were ongoing." (USGS, 2008 and 2010) |

\* USGS data is not provided after 1991 (withheld)

1. "Titanium", Wikipedia, 2011 - http://en.wikipedia.org/wiki/Titanium.
2. "Titanium Statistics", Historical Statistics for Mineral and Material Commodities in the United States, USGS, 2010 – http://minerals.usgs.gov/ds/2005/140/titanium.xls.
3. "Titanium: Mineral of the Gods", T. Vulcan, Seeking Alpha, 2010 - http://seekingalpha.com/article/194965-titanium-metal-of-the-gods.
4. "The Elements: A Visual Exploration of Every Known Atom in the Universe, page 58; T. Gray, N. Mann, 2009 - http://books.google.com/books?id=XrjX_rbkg-0C&pg=PA59&lpg=PA59&dq=titanium+metal+scarcity&source=bl&ots=9EslQ0RicH&sig=tOOFZhPpt49EEeRMZlLCfFLEZrk&hl=en&ei=Cfi2TMbZGcH68AatmPjTCQ&sa=X&oi=book_result&ct=result&resnum=2&sqi=2&ved=0CBQQ6AEwAQ#v=onepage&q=titanium%20metal%20scarcity&f=false.

| NNR Profile | Tungsten | |
|---|---|---|
| **NNR Uses and Critical Applications** | | |
| **Primary Uses** | Tungsten is a brittle (in raw form) steel-gray metal used primarily in high temperature electrical and electronic applications; tungsten is also used in the fabrication of cutting and wear-resistant materials, in x-ray tubes, as wear-resistant and high temperature alloys and superalloys, in armaments, and as a catalyst. | |
| **Critical Applications** | Incandescent light bulb filament, rocket engines (nozzles), and turbine blades (hard metals and alloys). | |
| **NNR Criticality** | **NNR Criticality Classification: Critical** | |
| **Substitutes** | While tungsten substitutes exist—including molybdenum, titanium, ceramics, diamond, and uranium—most are price/performance inferior in their respective applications. | |

| NNR Profile | Tungsten (continued) |
|---|---|
| **Criticality Assessment** | Tungsten is used in a variety of applications, some of which are niche oriented, others of which (incandescent light bulb) are nearly ubiquitous.<br><br>"In recent years, the tungsten industry has increased its monitoring of proposed legislation and scientific research regarding the impact of tungsten on human health and the environment." (USGS, 2010) |

| US NNR Scarcity | Scarce in 2008: Yes | Permanently Scarce: Almost Certain |
|---|---|---|

| 2008 US Import Reliance: 60% | 2008 Domestic US Supply: 40% |
|---|---|

| **Historical US Import Trends** | With very few exceptions, the US has been a net importer of tungsten since the early 20th century; net imports have generally exceeded 50% of total domestic utilization for the past two decades. |
|---|---|
| **Historical US Usage Trends** | Annual US tungsten utilization levels increased in a widely fluctuating manner during the first half of the 20th century, peaking temporarily in 1918, 1929, 1937, and 1942, before peaking permanently (to date) in 1954. Domestic tungsten utilization continued to fluctuate, and gradually recovered toward the end of the 20th century and into the 21st century; the 2008 US tungsten utilization level amounted to only 80% of the 1954 peak utilization level. |

| US Peak Extraction Year (thru 2008): 1955 | US Peak Utilization Year (thru 2008): 1954 |
|---|---|

| **Potential Geopolitical US Supply Constraints** | 43% of US tungsten imports come from China; China produces 81% of the world's tungsten and 64% of proven global reserves are located in China.<br><br>"China's Government limited the number of exploration and mining licenses for tungsten, restricted the amounts of tungsten that could be produced and exported, imposed constraints on mining and processing tungsten ores, continued to shift the balance of export quotas to favor value-added downstream tungsten materials and products, and adjusted export taxes (the Chinese Government decreased export taxes on some tungsten materials and encouraged local governments to offer loans to producers in exchange for tungsten concentrates and products) on tungsten materials." (USGS, 2010) |
|---|---|

| NNR Profile | Tungsten (continued) |
|---|---|
| **US Scarcity Assessment** | "A mine in California produced tungsten concentrates in 2009." (USGS, 2010)<br><br>That annual domestic tungsten utilization decreased by 20% since peaking (to date) in 1950, is a significant indicator of declining American industrial preeminence and global economic competitiveness.<br><br>The US currently relies heavily on imported tungsten, a large percentage (43%) of which comes from China. The quantity of tungsten supplied by foreign sources during 2008 accounted for 60% of the total 2008 US utilization level.<br><br>Available evidence supports the contention that domestic tungsten supplies will remain insufficient to completely address domestic requirements going forward:<br><br>• Meaningful US tungsten extraction ceased in 1988—a compelling indicator that domestic economically viable tungsten extraction has peaked permanently;<br>• The US has become increasingly reliant on tungsten imports since the 1970s; and<br>• The quantity of tungsten extracted domestically during 1954, the year of peak (to date) domestic tungsten extraction, amounted to only 51% of the 2008 total US utilization level—a significant indicator of America's increasing dependence on foreign NNRs.<br><br>Barring future reductions in the domestic (US) tungsten requirement trajectory and/or major new domestic economically viable discoveries, tungsten will almost certainly remain scarce domestically in the future.<br><br>"…one small Canadian company, Malaga, is the sole listed stock that mines tungsten in the West." (Mineweb, 2010) |
| **Global NNR Scarcity** | **Scarce in 2008: Yes**    **Permanently Scarce: Almost Certain** |
| **Historical Global Extraction Trends** | "World tungsten supply was dominated by Chinese production [81% of 2009 global total] and exports." (USGS, 2010)<br><br>Annual global tungsten extraction levels generally increased during the 20th century, peaking temporarily in 1918, 1930, 1943, 1956, 1961,1980, and 1990, before increasing into the new millennium; annual global tungsten extraction increased 27% between 2000 and 2008.<br><br>"China ranks first in the world in terms of tungsten resources and reserves [64% of total proven global reserves in 2009] and has some of the largest deposits." (USGS, 2010) |
| **Global Peak Extraction Year (thru 2008): 2004** | **Years to Global Reserve Exhaustion: 32** |
| **Projected Global Peak Extraction Year: 2010** | **Projected Global Peak Supply Year: 2090** |
| **Interdependencies** | None identified. |

| NNR Profile | Tungsten (continued) |
|---|---|
| **Global Scarcity Assessment** | "The recent run up in APT [ammonium paratungstate] prices began in 2004, driven by rapidly increasing demand from China..." (Talking Tungsten, 2008)<br><br>A 27% increase in the annual global tungsten extraction level between 2000 and 2008 implies an increase in global tungsten demand during the pre-recession period, and a corresponding increase in global tungsten supply in response to increased global demand.<br><br>The fact that the price of tungsten increased by an extraordinary 239% during the 2000-2008 period indicates that global tungsten supply, while increasing during the eight year period, remained woefully insufficient to completely address global requirements in 2008.<br><br><ul><li>Proven global tungsten reserves would exhaust in only 32 years, assuming the restoration of pre-recession utilization levels and growth rates;</li><li>The global tungsten extraction level is projected to peak in approximately 2017; and</li><li>An extraordinary increase in the price of tungsten during the 2000-2008 period induced only a modest increase in tungsten supply—evidence that globally available, economically viable tungsten extraction may be at or near its permanent peak level</li></ul>Barring future reductions in the global tungsten requirement trajectory and/or major new economically viable discoveries, tungsten will almost certainly remain scarce globally in the future.<br><br>"To conserve its resources and meet increasing domestic demand, the Chinese Government was expected to continue to limit tungsten production and exports and to increase imports of tungsten. In addition, the Chinese tungsten industry was investing in mine development projects outside China and developing technologies to increase the use of tungsten scrap and the processing of underutilized ores." (USGS, 2010) |

1. "Tungsten", Wikipedia, 2011 - http://en.wikipedia.org/wiki/Tungsten.
2. "Tungsten Statistics", Historical Statistics for Mineral and Material Commodities in the United States, USGS, 2010 – http://minerals.usgs.gov/ds/2005/140/tungsten.xls.
3. "Objective Capital Rare Earth and Minor Metals Investment Summit: Strategic Metals – Policy and Power", slide 5; J. Kooroshy, The Hague Centre for Strategic Studies, 2010 - http://www.slideshare.net/objectivecapital/objective-capital-rare-earth-and-minor-metals-investment-summit-strategic-metals-policy-and-power-jaakko-kooroshy.
4. "Western Industrial Users Seen as Hopeless at Securing Specialty Metals Supplies", Mineweb, 2010 - http://www.mineweb.com/mineweb/view/mineweb/en/page72102?oid=107698&sn=Detail&pid=65.
5. "Talking Tungsten (Isn't It About Time?), slide 16; N. Bell, K. Campbell, Haywood Securities, 2008 - http://www.talkingtungsten.com/pdf/Talking-Tungsten-Presentation_Sep08.pdf.

| NNR Profile | Uranium |
|---|---|

## NNR Uses and Critical Applications

| Primary Uses | Uranium is a highly dense, weakly radioactive, silvery-white metal used as a fuel in the nuclear power industry and in the manufacture of weapons (including high density penetrators); uranium is also used in dating rocks and fossils. |
|---|---|
| Critical Applications | Nuclear power (electricity) generation and nuclear weapons. |

| NNR Criticality | NNR Criticality Classification: Critical |
|---|---|
| Substitutes | Both nonrenewable and renewable uranium substitutes exist as energy sources, although price/performance characteristics vary. While uranium substitutes exist in weaponry applications, few have the horrific destructive power associated with uranium. |
| Criticality Assessment | Nuclear energy currently represents relatively modest percentages of total energy utilization, both domestically (7.8%) and globally (5.5%) [2007 EIA numbers]. In the event that nuclear power assumes a greater role as a domestic and global energy source, uranium will become increasingly critical.<br><br>"…one pound of uranium would give as much energy as three million pounds of coal." (Blurt, 2010)<br><br>However:<br><br>"One of the major problem areas in the use of uranium nuclear fuel is the disposal of nuclear waste. Traditional nuclear reactors consume only 1-2% of uranium fuel." (Wikipedia) |

| US NNR Scarcity | Scarce in 2008: Yes | Permanently Scarce: Almost Certain |
|---|---|---|
| **2008 US Import Reliance: 65%** | | **2008 Domestic US Supply: 35%** |

| Historical US Import Trends | Historically, the US has been both a net exporter and a net importer of uranium, although imports have typically exceeded exports; over the past several decades, the US has become increasingly reliant on uranium imports. |
|---|---|
| Historical US Usage Trends | Annual US uranium utilization levels have varied widely since the 1950s, apparently peaking in 1960, before fluctuating in a generally downward direction until the 1990s, when domestic uranium utilization levels recovered slightly; the 2008 US uranium utilization level amounted to only 61% of the 1960 peak utilization level. |

| US Peak Extraction Year (thru 2008): 1981 | US Peak Utilization Year (thru 2008): 1960* |
|---|---|

| Potential Geopolitical US Supply Constraints | Canada, Australia, and Kazakhstan each produce approximately one quarter of the world's annual uranium supply.<br><br>"It appears global deals are being arranged on a country-to-country basis, and U.S. utilities are coming up short." (Seeking Alpha, 2007) |
|---|---|

| NNR Profile | Uranium (continued) |
|---|---|
| **US Scarcity Assessment** | "Small amounts [of uranium] are mined in the western United States, but the United States is largely reliant on overseas supplies. The United States also relies on Russia for half its fuel, under a "swords to ploughshares" [megatons to megawatts] deal…" (MITnews, 2007)<br><br>"…China, India and even Russia have plans for massive deployments of nuclear power and are trying to lock up supplies from countries on which the United States has traditionally relied." (MITnews, 2007)<br><br>That annual domestic uranium utilization decreased by 39% since peaking (to date) in 1960, is an indicator of America's continuously heavy reliance on fossil fuels as primary energy sources.<br><br>The US currently relies heavily on imported uranium, the vast majority of which comes from Russia (~50%) and Canada. The quantity of uranium supplied by foreign sources during 2008 accounted for 65% of the total 2008 US utilization level.<br><br>Available evidence supports the contention that domestic uranium supplies will remain insufficient to completely address domestic requirements going forward:<br><br>• The annual US uranium extraction level decreased by 90% since peaking (to date) in 1981—a compelling indicator that domestic economically viable uranium extraction has peaked permanently;<br>• The US has become increasingly reliant on uranium imports since the early 1980s;<br>• The quantity of uranium extracted domestically during 2008 amounted to only 8% of the total 2008 US utilization level—a significant indicator of America's increasing dependence on foreign NNRs; and<br>• The quantity of uranium extracted domestically during 1960, the year of peak (to date) domestic uranium extraction, amounted to only 75% of the 2008 total US utilization level.<br><br>Barring future reductions in the domestic (US) uranium requirement trajectory and/or major new domestic economically viable discoveries, uranium will almost certainly remain scarce domestically in the future.<br><br>"Based on average 1999-2008 consumption levels (uranium in fuel assemblies loaded into nuclear reactors), uranium reserves available at up to $100 per pound of U3O8 represented approximately 23 years worth of demand, while uranium reserves at up to $50 per pound of U3O8 represented about 10 years worth of demand." EIA [Reserve Estimates], 2010)<br><br>"The United States has experienced steep rises in mining claims [in the 2000s] even though almost all of the nation's identified reserves are of a quality that puts it on the more expensive end of process costs [i.e., low grade ores]." (CFR, 2010) |

| NNR Profile | Uranium (continued) | |
|---|---|---|
| **Global NNR Scarcity** | **Scarce in 2008: Yes** | **Permanently Scarce: Almost Certain** |
| **Historical Global Extraction Trends** | "More than half the world's uranium-mining production comes from Australia, Kazakhstan, and Canada. In December 2009, Kazakhstan announced it had pulled ahead of Australia to become the largest uranium producer in the world." (CFR, 2010)<br><br>Annual global uranium extraction levels fluctuated widely during the 20th century, peaking temporarily in 1958 before peaking permanently (to date) in 1982; annual global uranium extraction increased 23% between 2003 and 2008.<br><br>"The uranium market declined significantly through the 1980s and 1990s because of the end of the Cold War arms race as well as a cessation in construction of new nuclear plants." (CFR, 2010) | |
| **Global Peak Extraction Year (thru 2008): 1982** | | **Years to Global Reserve Exhaustion: 34** |
| **Projected Global Peak Extraction Year: 1982** | | **Projected Global Peak Supply Year: 1982** |
| **Interdependencies** | None identified. | |
| **Global Scarcity Assessment** | "Worldwide, uranium production meets only about 65 percent of current reactor requirements. ... 'Just as large numbers of new reactors are being planned, we are only starting to emerge from 20 years of underinvestment in the production capacity for the nuclear fuel to operate them.'" [MITnews [Neff quote], 2007)<br><br>A 23% increase in the annual global uranium extraction level between 2003 and 2008 implies an increase in global uranium demand during the pre-recession period, and a corresponding increase in global uranium supply in response to increased global demand.<br><br>The fact that the price of uranium increased by an extraordinary 215% during the 2003-2008 period indicates that global uranium supply, while increasing during the five year period, remained woefully insufficient to completely address global requirements in 2008.<br><br>Available evidence supports the contention that global uranium supplies will remain insufficient to completely address global requirements going forward:<br><br>• Proven global uranium reserves would exhaust in only 34 years, assuming the restoration of pre-recession utilization levels and growth rates;<br>• The global uranium supply level was projected to peak in 1982;<br>• An extraordinary increase in the price of uranium during the 2003-2008 period induced only a modest increase in uranium supply—compelling evidence that globally available, economically viable uranium extraction may be near, at, or past its permanent peak level; and<br>• It is questionable whether the robust 4.3% compound annual growth rate (CAGR) in global uranium extraction evidenced between 2003 and 2008—an interval during which uranium became scarce globally despite a significant increase in extraction—can be reestablished, much less increased, going forward. A 4.3% CAGR would necessitate a continuous doubling in the annual global extraction level of uranium every 16.5 years. | |

<table>
<tr><td></td><td>
Barring future reductions in the global uranium requirement trajectory and/or major new economically viable discoveries, uranium will almost certainly remain scarce globally in the future.

"'… the uranium market right now [2010] could be the world's most unbalanced commodity market. . . . the planet, by means of the nuclear power industry, consumes approximately 172 million pounds of uranium per year, as well as the planet only produces about 92 million pounds of uranium per year. The supply deficit is produced up through above-ground inventories, which are becoming worked down pretty quickly.'" (Energy Bulletin, 2010)

"Limited uranium supplies could be stretched if industry could recover five or six of these [U-235] atoms [versus the four U-235 atoms recovered through the current enrichment process], but there is not enough processing capacity worldwide to do so." (MITnews, 2007)
</td></tr>
</table>

*Domestic uranium utilization was calculated as domestic production plus imports minus exports. While these calculations fail to consider additions and subtractions from stocks, other possible utilization data were only available from 1991 forward.

1. "Uranium", Wikipedia, 2011 - http://en.wikipedia.org/wiki/Uranium.
2. "Uranium Overview, 1949-2008; US EIA, 2009 - http://www.eia.doe.gov/emeu/aer/txt/stb0903.xls.
3. "Uranium Ore Deposits", WISE Uranium Project, 2010 - http://www.wise-uranium.org/uod.html (used $130 (current price is only $46).
4. "Supply of Uranium", World Nuclear Association, 2010 - http://www.world-nuclear.org/info/inf75.html.
5. "Uranium Market", WISE Uranium Project, http://www.wise-uranium.org/umkt.html#PRICE.
6. "World Electric Nuclear Power Generation, 1980-2007", Table 2.7; US EIA, 2010- http://www.eia.doe.gov/pub/international/iealf/table27.xls.
7. "Summary Production Statistics of the US Uranium Industry", US EIA, 2009 - http://www.eia.doe.gov/cneaf/nuclear/dupr/usummary.html.
8. "US Uranium Reserves Estimates", US EIA, 2010 - http://www.eia.doe.gov/cneaf/nuclear/page/reserves/ures.html.
9. "World Energy Production by Source, 1970-2007, Table 11.1; US EIA, 2010 - http://www.eia.doe.gov/emeu/aer/txt/ptb1101.html.
10. "World Total Energy Consumption by Region and Fuel", Table A.2; US EIA, 2010 - http://www.eia.doe.gov/oiaf/ieo/pdf/ieorefcase.pdf.
11. "World Uranium Mining", World Nuclear Association, 2010 - http://www.world-nuclear.org/info/inf23.html.
12. "Describe the Importance of Uranium in the Contemporary World", Blurt, 2006 - http://www.blurtit.com/q561303.html.
13. "Peak Oil Review", T. Whipple (Powers), Energy Bulletin, 2010 - http://www.energybulletin.net/node/53724.
14. "Global Uranium Supply and Demand", T. Johnson, Council on Foreign Relations (CFR), 2010 - http://www.cfr.org/publication/14705/global_uranium_supply_and_demand.html.
15. "Lack of Fuel May Limit US Nuclear Power Expansion", MITnews, 2007 - http://web.mit.edu/newsoffice/2007/fuel-supply.html.
16. "US Utilities Quietly Worry About Uranium Supply", Seeking Alpha, 2007 - http://seekingalpha.com/article/32304-u-s-utilities-quietly-worry-about-uranium-supply.

| NNR Profile | Vanadium |
|---|---|
| **NNR Uses and Critical Applications** | |

| | |
|---|---|
| **Primary Uses** | Vanadium is a soft, silver-gray, ductile metal used primarily as an iron and steel alloy and in high speed tool steels; vanadium is also used as a catalyst in the production of sulfuric acid, in superconducting magnets, and in surgical instruments. |
| **Critical Applications** | Alloys in aerospace applications; possibly as an anode in lithium batteries.<br><br>"Beyond new uses for vanadium-based steel products, vanadium has interesting energy-storage properties and is being used in a new generation of batteries for electric cars and energy storage systems attached to wind or solar projects…" (Vanadium Investing News, 2010) |

| NNR Criticality | NNR Criticality Classification: Critical |
|---|---|
| **Substitutes** | Metals such as manganese, molybdenum, niobium, titanium, and tungsten, can substitute for vanadium as alloying elements in steel; and platinum and nickel can substitute as catalysts in some chemical processes. However, no viable substitute exists for vanadium in aerospace titanium alloys. |
| **Criticality Assessment** | In the event that vanadium becomes widely adopted as a battery component, its criticality will increase.<br><br>"Essentially, as an exceptionally versatile alloying element, using vanadium not only imparts to the steels strength, toughness and reliability, it also enables steel to be used effectively at extremes of both high and low temperature. In addition, where it is of vital importance, the strength-to-weight ratios of vanadium-containing steels can be of the highest order." (Seeking Alpha, 2009) |

| US NNR Scarcity | Scarce in 2008: Yes | Permanently Scarce: Almost Certain |
|---|---|---|
| **2008 US Import Reliance: 100%** | | **2008 Domestic US Supply: 0%** |

| | |
|---|---|
| **Historical US Import Trends** | Historically, the US was primarily a net importer of vanadium; US vanadium net imports have generally increased since 1993. |
| **Historical US Usage Trends** | Annual US vanadium utilization levels generally increased during the first three quarters of the 20th century, peaking temporarily in 1908, 1915, 1920, 1926, 1943, 1953, 1969, and 1974. Domestic vanadium utilization declined in a fluctuating manner thereafter, gradually increasing into the new millennium and spiking significantly in 2005—the only year during which US vanadium utilization exceeded the 1974 (previous peak) level; the 2008 US vanadium utilization level amounted to only 83% of the 1974 utilization level. |

| US Peak Production Year (thru 2008): 1981 | US Peak Utilization Year (thru 2008): 2005* |
|---|---|
| **Potential Geopolitical US Supply Constraints** | 70% of US ferrovanadium imports come from the Czech Republic; 42% of vanadium pentoxide imports come from South Africa; China and South Africa each account for approximately 40% of global vanadium production and approximately 40% of proven global reserves.<br><br>In 2009, China imposed a 30% export duty on vanadium exports. (Hague, 2010) |

| NNR Profile | Vanadium (continued) |
|---|---|
| **US Scarcity Assessment** | "While domestic resources and secondary recovery are adequate to supply a large portion of domestic needs, a substantial part of U.S. demand is currently met by foreign material [the US is 100% import reliant] because it is currently uneconomic to mine vanadium in the United States." (USGS, 2008)<br><br>That annual domestic vanadium utilization decreased by 17% since peaking (to date) in 1974 (the 2005 utilization level was an outlier), is a major indicator of declining American industrial preeminence and global economic competitiveness.<br><br>The US currently relies exclusively on imported vanadium, large percentages of which come from the Czech Republic (70% of ferrovanadium) and South Africa (42% of vanadium pentoxide).<br><br>Available evidence supports the contention that domestic vanadium supplies will remain insufficient to completely address domestic requirements going forward:<br><br>• Meaningful US vanadium production ceased in 1997—a significant indicator of America's increasing dependence on foreign NNRs, and a compelling indicator that domestic economically viable vanadium production has peaked permanently;<br>• US vanadium import levels have generally increased since the early 1990s; and<br>• Domestic vanadium resources are not commercially viable.<br><br>Barring future reductions in the domestic (US) vanadium requirement trajectory and/or major new domestic economically viable discoveries, vanadium will almost certainly remain scarce domestically in the future. |

| Global NNR Scarcity | Scarce in 2008: Yes | Permanently Scarce: Likely |
|---|---|---|
| **Historical Global Production Trends** | "South Africa [35% of 2009 global production], China [37% of 2009 global production] and Russia [26% of 2009 global production] remain the world's largest sources of vanadium." (Seeking Alpha, 2009 and USGS, 2010 [figures])<br><br>Annual global vanadium production levels generally increased during the 20th and 21st centuries, peaking temporarily in 1915, 1920, 1929, 1943, 1979, 1990, and 1998, before increasing into the new millennium; annual global vanadium production increased 37% between 2000 and 2008. | |

| Global Peak Production Year (thru 2008): 2007 | Years to Global Reserve Exhaustion: 50+ |
|---|---|
| Projected Global Peak Production Year: N/A | Projected Global Peak Supply Year: N/A |

| **Interdependencies** | Vanadium is typically recovered as a byproduct of petroleum and pig iron processing, and from spent catalyst and utility ash processing. |
|---|---|

| NNR Profile | Vanadium (continued) |
|---|---|
| **Global Scarcity Assessment** | "The rocketing vanadium price [in 2008] is no mystery. Demand is strong, while supplies are constrained. A big part of the supply constraint lies in South Africa. That's because a massive electricity shortage is preventing many mines from operating at full capacity." (Whiskey and Gunpowder, 2008)<br><br>A 37% increase in the annual global vanadium production level between 2000 and 2008 implies an increase in global vanadium demand during the pre-recession period, and a corresponding increase in global vanadium supply in response to increased global demand.<br><br>The fact that the price of vanadium increased by a phenomenal 547% during the 2000-2008 period indicates that global vanadium supply, while increasing during the eight year period, remained woefully insufficient to completely address global requirements in 2008.<br><br>Available evidence, albeit somewhat conflicting, supports the contention that global vanadium supplies will likely remain insufficient to completely address global requirements going forward:<br><br>• Proven global vanadium reserves are sufficient to last for over 50 years (assuming the restoration of pre-recession utilization levels and growth rates); however<br>• A phenomenal increase in the price of vanadium during the 2000-2008 period was able to induce only a modest increase in supply—compelling evidence of unaddressed global requirements in 2008; and<br>• It is questionable whether the robust 4% compound annual growth rate (CAGR) in global vanadium production evidenced between 2000 and 2008—an interval during which vanadium became scarce globally despite a significant increase in production—can be reestablished, much less increased, going forward. A 4% CAGR would necessitate a continuous doubling in the annual global production level of vanadium every 18 years.<br><br>Barring future reductions in the global vanadium requirement trajectory and/or major new economically viable discoveries, vanadium will likely remain scarce globally in the future.<br><br>"…analysts seem confident global demand for vanadium will continue to rise and that with vanadium's already tight supply picture and the growing trend towards micro-alloy steel and vanadium's performance in that area prices could climb." (Vanadium Investment News, 2010) |

*2005 US utilization was a spike; the previous peak utilization year was 1974.

1. "Vanadium", Wikipedia, 2011 - http://en.wikipedia.org/wiki/Vanadium.
2. "Vanadium Statistics", Historical Statistics for Mineral and Material Commodities in the United States, USGS, 2010 – http://minerals.usgs.gov/ds/2005/140/vanadium.xls.
3. "Objective Capital Rare Earth and Minor Metals Investment Summit: Strategic Metals – Policy and Power", slide 5; J. Kooroshy, The Hague Centre for Strategic Studies, 2010 - http://www.slideshare.net/objectivecapital/objective-capital-rare-earth-and-minor-metals-investment-summit-strategic-metals-policy-and-power-jaakko-kooroshy.

4. "Veni, Vidi, Vanadium – The Key to Steel", T. Vulcan, Seeking Alpha, 2009 - http://seekingalpha.com/article/139661-veni-vidi-vanadium-the-key-to-steel.
5. "Investing in Vanadium", C. Mayer, Whiskey and Gunpowder, 2008 - http://whiskeyandgunpowder.com/investing-in-vanadium/.
6. "Vanadium and Steel Bound Together?" D. McMahon, Vanadium Investing News, 2010 - http://vanadiuminvestingnews.com/357/vanadium-and-steel-bound-together/.

| NNR Profile | Vermiculite |
|---|---|
| **NNR Uses and Critical Applications** | |
| **Primary Uses** | Vermiculite is a limited expansion mineral used as an insulator in refractories and buildings; vermiculite is also used as a soil conditioner, packing material, fireproofing agent, absorbent, and lightweight concrete/plaster aggregate. |
| **Critical Applications** | None identified. |
| **NNR Criticality** | **NNR Criticality Classification: Declining** |
| **Substitutes** | Perlite and other substitute materials such as clay, shale, slag, slate, fiberglass, slag wool, sawdust, bark, and synthetic soil conditioners exist for various vermiculite applications; price/performance characteristics vary per application. |
| **Criticality Assessment** | While vermiculite is used in a variety of industrial applications, viable substitutes exist in nearly all cases. |
| **US NNR Scarcity** | **Scarce in 2008: Yes** — **Permanently Scarce: Almost Certain** |
| **2008 US Import Reliance:** 40% | **2008 Domestic US Supply:** 60% |
| **Historical US Import Trends** | The US was a net exporter of vermiculite during the 1970s and early 1980s; the US has become an increasingly heavy net importer of vermiculite since 1983. |
| **Historical US Usage Trends** | Annual US vermiculite utilization levels generally increased through the first three quarters of the 20th century, peaking temporarily in 1937, 1942, 1950, and 1955, before peaking permanently (to date) in 1973. Domestic utilization levels declined in a fluctuating manner since that time; the 2008 US vermiculite utilization level amounted to only 47% of the 1973 peak utilization level. |
| **US Peak Extraction Year (thru 2008):** 1973 | **US Peak Utilization Year (thru 2008):** 1973 |
| **Potential Geopolitical US Supply Constraints** | 59% of US vermiculite imports come from China, and 39% of US vermiculite imports come from South Africa. |

| NNR Profile | Vermiculite (continued) |
|---|---|
| **US Scarcity Assessment** | "Two companies with mining and processing facilities in South Carolina and Virginia produced vermiculite concentrate [in 2009]." (USGS, 2010) |
| | That annual domestic vermiculite utilization decreased by 53% since peaking (to date) in 1973, is a major indicator of declining American industrial preeminence and global economic competitiveness. |
| | The US currently relies considerably on imported vermiculite, the majority (98%) of which comes from China and South Africa. The quantity of vermiculite supplied by foreign sources during 2008 accounted for 40% of the total 2008 US utilization level. |
| | Available evidence supports the contention that domestic vermiculite supplies will remain insufficient to completely address domestic requirements going forward: |
| | • The annual US vermiculite extraction level decreased by 87% since peaking (to date) in 1973—a compelling indicator that domestic economically viable vermiculite extraction has peaked permanently;<br>• Net US vermiculite imports increased steadily since 1983; and<br>• The quantity of vermiculite extracted domestically during 2008 amounted to only 60% of the total 2008 US utilization level—an indicator of America's increasing dependence on foreign NNRs. |
| | Barring future reductions in the domestic (US) vermiculite requirement trajectory and/or major new domestic economically viable discoveries, vermiculite will almost certainly remain scarce domestically in the future. |

| Global NNR Scarcity | Scarce in 2008: No | Permanently Scarce: Unlikely |
|---|---|---|
| **Historical Global Extraction Trends** | Annual global vermiculite extraction levels generally increased during the latter half of the 20th century, peaking temporarily in 1955, 1974, and 1978, before peaking permanently (to date) in 1987. Global vermiculite extraction levels rebounded slightly during the new millennium, increasing 2% between 2000 and 2008.<br><br>"Although not all vermiculite contains asbestos, some products were made with vermiculite that contained asbestos until the early 1990s." (Wikipedia) | |

| Global Peak Extraction Year (thru 2008): 1987 | Years to Global Reserve Exhaustion: 50+ |
|---|---|
| Projected Global Peak Extraction Year: N/A | Projected Global Peak Supply Year: N/A |
| **Interdependencies** | None identified. |

| NNR Profile | Vermiculite (continued) |
|---|---|
| Global Scarcity Assessment | A 2% increase in the annual global vermiculite extraction level between 2000 and 2008 implies an increase in global vermiculite demand during the pre-recession period, and a corresponding increase in global vermiculite supply in response to increased global demand.<br><br>The fact that the price of vermiculite decreased by 21% during the 2000-2008 period indicates that the global supply of vermiculite in 2008 was sufficient to completely address 2008 global requirements.<br><br>Available evidence supports the contention that global vermiculite supplies will remain sufficient to completely address global requirements going forward:<br><br>• While global vermiculite extraction levels have generally decreased since peaking (to date) in 1987, vermiculite price levels have generally decreased since that time as well—evidence of sufficient global vermiculite supplies;<br>• Proven global vermiculite reserves are sufficient to last for over 50 years (assuming the restoration of pre-recession utilization levels and growth rates); and<br>• Proven global vermiculite reserves are considered by the USGS to be quite large.<br><br>Barring future increases in the global vermiculite requirement trajectory, globally available, economically viable vermiculite supplies will likely remain sufficient—notwithstanding temporary local shortages—to completely address global requirements going forward. |

1. "Vermiculite", Wikipedia, 2011 - http://en.wikipedia.org/wiki/Vermiculite.
2. "Vermiculite Statistics", Historical Statistics for Mineral and Material Commodities in the United States, USGS, 2010 – http://minerals.usgs.gov/ds/2005/140/vermiculite.xls.

| NNR Profile | Zinc |
|---|---|
| **NNR Uses and Critical Applications** | |
| Primary Uses | Zinc is a lustrous, bluish-white, non-corrosive metal used in galvanizing and diecasting, in batteries, as an alloy (with copper in brass, among others), as a dietary supplement, and in consumer products such as deodorant and shampoo; zinc is essential to human health. |
| Critical Applications | Galvanizing and alloys. |
| **NNR Criticality** | **NNR Criticality Classification: Indispensible** |
| Substitutes | While zinc substitutes, including aluminum, plastics, steel, magnesium, and cadmium, exist for various zinc applications, price/performance characteristics are often inferior. |

| NNR Profile | Zinc (continued) |
|---|---|
| **Criticality Assessment** | "Zinc is the fourth most common metal in use, trailing only iron, aluminum, and copper…" (Wikipedia)<br><br>Besides its primary use in galvanizing, zinc is alloyed with a wide variety of metals to address a broad range of construction, electronic, chemical, and manufacturing applications; zinc compounds are also used in a variety of medical applications. Zinc is indispensible to modern industrial existence.<br><br>"Other metals long known to form binary alloys with zinc are aluminum, antimony, bismuth, gold, iron, lead, mercury, silver, tin, magnesium, cobalt, nickel, tellurium and sodium." (Wikipedia) |

| US NNR Scarcity | Scarce in 2008: Yes | Permanently Scarce: Almost Certain |
|---|---|---|

| 2008 US Import Reliance: 71% | 2008 Domestic US Supply: 29% |
|---|---|

| **Historical US Import Trends** | The US was primarily a zinc net exporter until WWII; since that time US zinc net imports have increased continuously.<br><br>"U.S. firms soon [after WWII] lost their competitive position inter-nationally as the demand for lead and zinc expanded far faster than domestic production." (Reference for Business) |
|---|---|
| **Historical US Usage Trends** | Annual US zinc utilization levels generally increased during the 20$^{th}$ century, peaking temporarily in 1916, 1929, 1937, 1944, 1955, 1966, 1973, 1978, and 1988, before peaking permanently (to date) in 1999. Domestic zinc utilization generally declined since that time; the 2008 US zinc utilization level amounted to only 70% of the 1999 peak utilization level. |

| US Peak Extraction Year (thru 2008): 1969 | US Peak Utilization Year (thru 2008): 1999 |
|---|---|

| **Potential Geopolitical US Supply Constraints** | 68% of US zinc ore and concentrate imports come from Peru; 70% of US zinc metal imports come from Canada.<br><br>"…on June 23 [2009], the EU announced that both it and the U.S. 'had requested WTO consultations with China regarding China's export restrictions on a number of key raw materials, which it considers are in clear breach of international trade rules.<br><br>In the words of the EU announcement: 'European industries have raised concerns for a number of years on export restrictions - quotas, export duties and minimum export prices - which China applies on key raw materials, such as yellow phosphorous, bauxite, coke, fluorspar, magnesium, manganese, silicon metal, silicon carbide and zinc. Some of these resources cannot be found elsewhere.'" (Seeking Alpha, 2009) |
|---|---|

| NNR Profile | Zinc (continued) |
|---|---|
| **US Scarcity Assessment** | "The [US] lead and zinc industry consolidated operations gradually after production peaked in 1970: where 88 establishments existed in 1977, the number fell to 36 firms in 1996, and only 22 remained in 2003." (Reference for Business)<br><br>That annual domestic zinc utilization decreased by 30% since peaking (to date) in 1999, is a major indicator of declining American industrial preeminence and global economic competitiveness.<br><br>The US currently relies heavily on imported zinc, the majority of which comes from Peru (68% of zinc ore and concentrates) and Canada (70% of zinc metal). The quantity of zinc supplied by foreign sources during 2008 accounted for 71% of the total 2008 US utilization level.<br><br>Available evidence supports the contention that domestic zinc supplies will remain insufficient to completely address domestic requirements going forward:<br><br>• The annual US zinc extraction level decreased by 87% since peaking (to date) in 1969—a compelling indicator that domestic economically viable zinc extraction has peaked permanently;<br>• Net US zinc imports increased steadily since WWII; and<br>• The quantity of zinc extracted domestically during 2008 amounted to only 13% of the total 2008 US utilization level—a primary indicator of America's increasing dependence on foreign NNRs.<br><br>Barring future reductions in the domestic (US) zinc requirement trajectory and/or major new domestic economically viable discoveries, zinc will almost certainly remain scarce domestically in the future. |

| Global NNR Scarcity | Scarce in 2008: Yes | Permanently Scarce: Likely |
|---|---|---|
| **Historical Global Extraction Trends** | "There are zinc mines throughout the world, with the main mining areas being China (2.5 million metric tons), Australia (1.4 million metric tons) and Peru (1.2 million metric tons) [US produced 0.8 million metric tons]. China produced over one-fourth of the global zinc output in 2006." (Wikipedia [originally BGS] and Mansukh, 2007)<br><br>Annual global zinc extraction levels increased dramatically during the 20th and 21st centuries (especially following WWII), peaking temporarily in 1912, 1917, 1927, 1944, 1957, 1987, and 1991, before increasing into the new millennium; global zinc extraction increased 32% between 2000 and 2008. | |

| | | |
|---|---|---|
| **Global Peak Extraction Year (thru 2008):** 2008 | | **Years to Global Reserve Exhaustion:** 13 |
| **Projected Global Peak Extraction Year:** 2020 | | **Projected Global Peak Supply Year:** 2018 |
| **Interdependencies** | Zinc is typically recovered with copper, lead, and iron ores. | |

| NNR Profile | Zinc (continued) |
|---|---|
| **Global Scarcity Assessment** | "Strong demand for zinc, largely supported by China's growing economy and infrastructure, continued to outpace refined zinc production in 2007." (USGS, 2008)<br><br>A 32% increase in the annual global zinc extraction level between 2000 and 2008 implies an increase in global zinc demand during the pre-recession period, and a corresponding increase in global zinc supply in response to increased global demand.<br><br>The fact that the price of zinc increased by 28% during the 2000-2008 period indicates that global zinc supply, while increasing during the eight year period, remained insufficient to completely address global requirements in 2008.<br><br>Available evidence supports the contention that global zinc supplies will likely remain insufficient to completely address global requirements going forward:<br><br>• Proven global zinc reserves would exhaust in only 13 years, assuming the restoration of pre-recession utilization levels and growth rates,<br>• The global zinc extraction level is projected to peak in approximately 2020;<br>• The global zinc supply level is projected to peak in approximately 2018; and<br>• The increased global zinc supply brought online between 2000 and 2008 failed to prevent a price increase during the period—evidence of unaddressed global requirements in 2008.<br><br>Barring future reductions in the global zinc requirement trajectory and/or major new economically viable discoveries, zinc will likely remain scarce globally in the future. |

1. "Zinc", Wikipedia, 2011 - http://en.wikipedia.org/wiki/Zinc.
2. "Zinc Statistics", Historical Statistics for Mineral and Material Commodities in the United States, USGS, 2010 – http://minerals.usgs.gov/ds/2005/140/zinc.xls.
3. "Lead and Zinc Ores", Reference for Business - http://www.referenceforbusiness.com/industries/Mining/Lead-Zinc-Ores.html.
4. "Fluorspar: The Cool Mineral", T. Vulcan, Seeking Alpha, 2009 - http://seekingalpha.com/article/160670-fluorspar-the-cool-mineral.
5. Annual and Special Meeting, slide 15; Breakwater Resources, Ltd. 2010 - http://www.breakwater.ca/Theme/Breakwater/files/2010%20AGM%20Presentation.pdf.
6. "Zinc: Past, Present, and Future", Mansukh Investment and Trading Solutions, 2007 – (http://www.scribd.com/doc/903664/ZINC-REPORT-ORIGINAL.)

| NNR Profile | Zirconium |
|---|---|

## NNR Uses and Critical Applications

| | |
|---|---|
| **Primary Uses** | Zirconium is a lustrous, gray-white, corrosion-resistant metal used primarily as an alloying agent, in refractory and foundry applications, as an abrasive, in ceramics and armaments, and as a gemstone (diamond substitute). |
| **Critical Applications** | Nuclear power plants, space vehicles, and jet engine and stationary gas turbine blades.<br><br>"Zirconium metal producers were beginning to increase capacity [in 2009] in anticipation of a resurgence of nuclear energy plants." (USGS, 2010) |

| NNR Criticality | NNR Criticality Classification: Critical |
|---|---|

| | |
|---|---|
| **Substitutes** | Viable zirconium substitutes, including chromite, olivine, dolomite, niobium, stainless steel, tantalum, titanium, and synthetic materials, exist for some applications. |
| **Criticality Assessment** | In the event that nuclear power generation experiences resurgence, zirconium will become more critical.<br><br>"Zirconium has one physical property of special importance: It is transparent to neutrons." [...which makes it an optimal nuclear power plant material.] (Zirconium, 2006) |

| US NNR Scarcity | Scarce in 2008: No | Permanently Scarce: Unclear |
|---|---|---|

| 2008 US Import Reliance: 0% | | 2008 Domestic US Supply: 100% |
|---|---|---|
| **Historical US Import Trends** | The US was a net importer of zirconium until 1999, when it became a net exporter. | |
| **Historical US Usage Trends** | "Although consumption of zircon for use in television glass decreased significantly, consumption of zircon increased for ceramic, refractory, and chemical uses." (USGS, 2008)<br><br>Annual US zirconium utilization levels generally increased during the 20th century, peaking temporarily in 1905, 1918, 1927, 1937, 1942, 1950, 1957, 1961, (increased dramatically in 1966), 1973 and 1979, before peaking (spiking) permanently (to date) in 1988. Domestic zirconium utilization increased considerably during the new millennium, but did not exceed the 1988 level; the 2003 (the last year of data availability) US zirconium utilization level amounted to 96% of the 1988 peak utilization level. | |

| US Peak Extraction Year (thru 2008): 1989 | | US Peak Utilization Year (thru 2008): 1988 |
|---|---|---|
| **Potential Geopolitical US Supply Constraints** | 49% of US zirconium ore and concentrate imports come from Australia; 50% of unwrought zirconium imports come from France; however, the US is currently a net zirconium importer. | |

| NNR Profile | Zirconium (continued) |
|---|---|
| **US Scarcity Assessment** | "Two firms produced zircon from surface-mining operations in Florida and Virginia." (USGS, 2010)<br><br>The US is currently addressing its total requirement for zirconium through domestic supplies.<br><br>Available evidence regarding the likelihood that domestic zirconium supplies will remain sufficient to completely address domestic requirements going forward is conflicting (and limited due to the lack of USGS data):<br><br>• US net zirconium exports increased during past decade, indicating that current US zirconium supply is sufficient to completely address current domestic requirements; however<br>• The US was almost exclusively a net importer of zirconium during the 20th century.<br><br>It is therefore unclear whether domestically available, economically viable zirconium supplies will remain sufficient to completely address future domestic requirements, or whether zirconium will become scarce domestically in the not-too-distant future. |

| Global NNR Scarcity | Scarce in 2008: Yes | Permanently Scarce: Almost Certain |
|---|---|---|

| **Historical Global Extraction Trends** | "The principal commercial source of zirconium is the zirconium silicate mineral, zircon ($ZrSiO4$), which is found primarily in Australia [41% of 2009 global production, ex-US], Brazil, India, Russia, South Africa [32% of 2009 global production, ex-US], and the United States [the USGS withholds US zirconium production data]...." (Wikipedia)<br><br>Annual global zirconium extraction levels generally increased during the post WWII years of the 20th century, peaking temporarily in 1951, 1957, 1971, 1989 and 1995, before increasing into the new millennium; global zirconium extraction increased 75% between 2000 and 2008. |
|---|---|

| Global Peak Extraction Year (thru 2008): 2007 | Years to Global Reserve Exhaustion: 19 |
|---|---|
| Projected Global Peak Extraction Year: N/A | Projected Global Peak Supply Year: N/A |

| **Interdependencies** | Zircon (the zirconium-silicate mineral) s a coproduct of titanium and tin mining. |
|---|---|

| NNR Profile | Zirconium (continued) |
|---|---|
| **Global Scarcity Assessment** | "Prices for zircon concentrate increased to record-high levels [in 2007]." (USGS, 2008)<br><br>A 75% increase in the annual global zirconium extraction level between 2000 and 2008 implies a significant increase in global zirconium demand during the pre-recession period, and a correspondingly significant increase in global zirconium supply in response to increased global demand.<br><br>The fact that the price of zirconium increased by a robust 68% during the 2000-2008 period indicates that global zirconium supply, while significantly considerably during the eight year period, remained insufficient to completely address global requirements in 2008.<br><br>Available evidence supports the contention that global zirconium supplies will remain insufficient to completely address global requirements going forward:<br><br>• Proven global zirconium reserves would exhaust in only 19 years, assuming the restoration of pre-recession utilization levels and growth rates,<br>• The significant increase in global zirconium supply brought online between 2000 and 2008 failed to prevent a robust price increase during the period—compelling evidence of unaddressed global requirements in 2008; and<br>• It is questionable whether the robust 7.3% compound annual growth rate (CAGR) in global zirconium extraction evidenced between 2000 and 2008—an interval during which zirconium became scarce globally despite a significant increase in extraction—can be reestablished, much less increased, going forward. A 7.3% CAGR would necessitate a continuous doubling in the annual global extraction level of zirconium every 10 years.<br><br>Barring future reductions in the global zirconium requirement trajectory and/or major new economically viable discoveries, zirconium will almost certainly remain scarce globally in the future.<br><br>"…for a number of material resources the peak production is already in the past. An example is Zirconium, an element used for high temperature materials. Despite the ongoing need for Zirconium and rising prices, the extraction rate is declining." M2i, 2009) |

1. "Zirconium", Wikipedia, 2011 - http://en.wikipedia.org/wiki/Zirconium.
2. "Zirconium Statistics", Historical Statistics for Mineral and Material Commodities in the United States, USGS, 2010 – http://minerals.usgs.gov/ds/2005/140/zirconium.xls.
3. "Zirconium", Chemistry Explained, 2006 - http://www.chemistryexplained.com/elements/T-Z/Zirconium.html.
4. "Material Scarcity – an M2i Study, page 3; Stichting Materials Institute (M2i), 2009 - http://www.m2i.nl/images/stories/m2i%20material_scarcity%20report.pdf.

# Appendix B: 2000 and 2008 Global NNR Extraction/Production Levels and Price Levels

2000 and 2008 Global NNR Extraction/Production Levels and Price Levels

| NNR | Global NNR Extraction Levels | | | NNR Price Levels | | |
|---|---|---|---|---|---|---|
| | 2000 | 2008 | +/- | 2000 | 2008 | +/- |
| Abrasives (Manuf.) | N/A | N/A | N/A | $423 | $407 | -4% |
| Abrasives (Natural) | N/A | N/A | N/A | $210 | $98 | -53% |
| Aluminum | 24,300,000 | 39,000,000 | 60% | $1,550 | $2,020 | 30% |
| Antimony | 118,000 | 197,000 | 67% | $1,360 | $4,670 | 243% |
| Asbestos | 2,110,000 | 2,090,000 | -1% | $163 | $565 | 247% |
| Arsenic | 47,500 | 52,700 | 11% | $882 | $684 | -22% |
| Barite | 6,560,000 | 8,050,000 | 23% | $44 | $54 | 23% |
| Bauxite | 136,000,000 | 205,000,000 | 51% | $22 | $20 | -9% |
| Beryllium | 120 | 198 | 65% | $152,000 | $265,000 | 74% |
| Bismuth | 3,760 | 7,700 | 105% | $7,720 | $21,200 | 175% |
| Boron | 4,600,000 | 4,350,000 | -5% | $891 | $707 | -21% |
| Bromine | 542,000 | 669,000 | 23% | $852 | $1,120 | 31% |
| Cadmium | 20,300 | 19,600 | -3% | $343 | $4,480 | 1206% |
| Cement | 1,660,000,000 | 2,840,000,000 | 71% | $74 | $78 | 5% |
| Cesium | N/A | N/A | N/A | $59,900,000 | $44,200,000 | -26% |
| Chromium | 4,750,000 | 6,980,000 | 47% | $721 | $2,640 | 266% |
| Clays | N/A | N/A | N/A | $18 | $22 | 25% |
| Coal | 4,893,000,000 | 7,271,000,000 | 49% | $19 | $29 | 52% |
| Cobalt | 39,300 | 75,900 | 93% | $28,100 | $51,800 | 84% |
| Copper | 13,200,000 | 15,400,000 | 17% | $1,840 | $5,330 | 190% |
| Diamond (Industrial) | 97 | 942 | 871% | $2,020 | $894 | -56% |
| Diatomite | 1,890,000 | 2,170,000 | 15% | $242 | $170 | -30% |
| Feldspar | 9,540,000 | 21,900,000 | 130% | $57 | $50 | -12% |
| Fluorspar | 4,450,000 | 5,730,000 | 29% | $118 | $164 | 39% |
| Gallium | 90 | 111 | 23% | $606,000 | $438,000 | -28% |
| Garnet (Indus) | 456,000 | 1,310,000 | 187% | $258 | $206 | -20% |
| Gemstones | 13 | 17 | 30% | $42,000,000 | $40,100,000 | -5% |
| Germanium | 70 | 140 | 100% | $1,180 | $1,130 | -4% |
| Gold | 2,590 | 2,260 | -13% | $8,530,000 | $21,200,000 | 149% |
| Graphite | 846,000 | 1,120,000 | 32% | $506 | $625 | 24% |
| Gypsum | 108,000,000 | 159,000,000 | 47% | $14 | $31 | 115% |
| Hafnium | N/A | N/A | N/A | $177,000 | $260,000 | 47% |
| Helium | 19,800 | 29,500 | 49% | $9,940 | $9,690 | -3% |
| Indium | 335 | 573 | 71% | $178 | $519 | 192% |
| Iodine | 19,500 | 26,500 | 36% | $13,800 | $16,300 | 18% |

**2000 and 2008 Global NNR Extraction/Production Levels and Price Levels**

| NNR | Global NNR Extraction Levels | | | NNR Price Levels | | |
|---|---|---|---|---|---|---|
| | 2000 | 2008 | +/- | 2000 | 2008 | +/- |
| Iron Ore | 1,070,000,000 | 2,200,000,000 | 106% | $24 | $57 | 132% |
| Iron and Steel | 573,000,000 | 932,999,999 | 63% | 108 | 221 | 105% |
| Kyanite | 406,000 | 470,000 | 16% | $210 | $232 | 10% |
| Lead | 3,200,000 | 3,840,000 | 20% | $910 | $2,010 | 121% |
| Lime | 121,000,000 | 296,000,000 | 145% | $57 | $70 | 22% |
| Lithium | 204,000 | 382,000 | 87% | $4,230 | $3,360 | -21% |
| Magnesium Compounds | 12,700,000 | 18,300,000 | 44% | $384 | $391 | 2% |
| Magnesium Metal | 422,000 | 671,000 | 59% | $2,640 | $5,260 | 99% |
| Manganese | 6,960,000 | 13,300,000 | 91% | $551 | $1,800 | 227% |
| Mercury | 1,360 | 1,320 | -3% | $4,260 | $13,200 | 210% |
| Mica Scrap & Flake | 328,000 | 374,000 | 14% | $317 | $388 | 22% |
| Mica Sheet | 5,200 | 5,200 | 0% | $1,920 | $1,590 | -17% |
| Molybdenum | 135,000 | 218,000 | 61% | $5,330 | $47,700 | 795% |
| Natural Gas (tcf) | 88 | 110 | 24% | $3 | $9 | 156% |
| Nickel | 1,290,000 | 1,570,000 | 22% | $8,180 | $16,000 | 96% |
| Niobium | 24,800 | 62,900 | 154% | $19,700 | $27,773 | 41% |
| Nitrogen (fixed) | 108,000,000 | 133,000,000 | 23% | $145 | $405 | 179% |
| Oil (000 barrels) | 24,998,850 | 26,896,850 | 8% | $29 | $101 | 244% |
| Peat | 24,700,000 | 25,000,000 | 1% | $26 | $20 | -22% |
| Perlite | 1,940,000 | 1,790,000 | -8% | $32 | $36 | 14% |
| Phosphate Rock | 132,000,000 | 161,000,000 | 22% | $24 | $59 | 145% |
| PGM | 364 | 465 | 28% | $17,000,000 | $12,100,000 | -29% |
| Potash | 27,000,000 | 34,800,000 | 29% | $147 | $485 | 230% |
| Pumice | 13,700,000 | 19,300,000 | 41% | $17 | $15 | -11% |
| Quartz Crystal | 475 | N/A | N/A | N/A | N/A | N/A |
| REM | 90,900 | 134,000 | 47% | $6,110 | $9,160 | 50% |
| Rhenium | 36,000 | 57,000 | 58% | $873,000 | $1,540,000 | 76% |
| Rubidium | N/A | N/A | N/A | N/A | N/A | N/A |
| Salt | 195,000,000 | 258,000,000 | 32% | $23 | $28 | 25% |
| Sand & Gravel (Construction) | N/A | N/A | N/A | $5 | $6 | 24% |
| Sand & Gravel (Industrial) | 114,000,000 | 119,000,000 | 4% | $14 | $23 | 71% |
| Selenium | 1,460 | 1,510 | 3% | $8,020 | $53,900 | 572% |
| Silicon | 3,500,000 | 6,160,000 | 76% | $1,080 | $1,720 | 59% |
| Silver | 18,100 | 21,300 | 18% | $162,000 | $398,000 | 146% |
| Soda Ash | 34,500,000 | 45,500,000 | 32% | $69 | $102 | 48% |

**2000 and 2008 Global NNR Extraction/Production Levels and Price Levels**

| NNR | Global NNR Extraction Levels | | | NNR Price Levels | | |
|---|---|---|---|---|---|---|
| | 2000 | 2008 | +/- | 2000 | 2008 | +/- |
| Sodium Sulfate | 5,750,000 | 5,750,000 | 0% | $119 | $112 | -6% |
| Stone (Crushed) | N/A | N/A | N/A | $5 | $7 | 39% |
| Stone (Dimension) | N/A | N/A | N/A | $178 | $136 | -24% |
| Strontium | 396,000 | 496,000 | 25% | $830 | $942 | 13% |
| Sulfur | 59,300,000 | 69,600,000 | 17% | $23 | $199 | 750% |
| Talc | 8,730,000 | 7,510,000 | -14% | $107 | $108 | 1% |
| Tantalum | 1,070 | 1,170 | 9% | $91,600 | $80,300 | -12% |
| Tellurium | 110 | 95 | -14% | $32,600 | $29,100 | -11% |
| Thallium | 15,000 | 10,000 | -33% | $1,230,000 | $3,710,000 | 202% |
| Thorium | N/A | N/A | N/A | $78,100 | $151,000 | 93% |
| Tin | 278,000 | 299,000 | 8% | $7,730 | $18,900 | 145% |
| Titanium Concentrate | 7,350,000 | 9,640,000 | 31% | 94 | 111 | 18% |
| Titanium Metal | N/A | N/A | N/A | $8,240 | $11,800 | 43% |
| Tungsten | 44,000 | 55,900 | 27% | $7,840 | $26,600 | 239% |
| Uranium | 35,574 | 43,853 | 23% | $11 | $33 | 215% |
| Vanadium | 41,000 | 56,100 | 37% | $6,780 | $43,900 | 547% |
| Vermiculite | 521,000 | 530,000 | 2% | $135 | $106 | -21% |
| Zinc | 8,770,000 | 11,600,000 | 32% | $1,160 | $1,480 | 28% |
| Zirconium | 731,000 | 1,280,000 | 75% | $355 | $597 | 68% |

# Appendix C: NNR Scarcity Definitions

## Permanent Domestic (US) NNR Scarcity Definitions

- **Permanent Domestic NNR Scarcity is "Almost Certain":** available evidence (contained in the NNR Profile) supports the contention that future domestically available, economically viable NNR supplies will almost certainly be insufficient to completely address future domestic NNR requirements, barring future reductions in the domestic NNR requirements trajectory and/or major new economically viable discoveries—i.e., the US will almost certainly import some quantity of the NNR annually going forward;

- **Permanent Domestic (US) NNR Scarcity is "Likely":** available evidence (contained in the NNR Profile) supports the contention that future domestically available, economically viable NNR supplies will likely be insufficient to completely address future domestic (US) NNR requirements, barring future reductions in the domestic NNR requirements trajectory and/or major new economically viable discoveries—i.e., the US will likely import some quantity of the NNR annually going forward;

- **Permanent Domestic (US) NNR Scarcity is "Unclear":** available evidence (contained in the NNR Profile) regarding the likelihood that domestically available, economically viable NNR supplies will be sufficient to completely address future domestic NNR requirements is conflicting;

- **Permanent Domestic (US) NNR Scarcity is "Unlikely":** available evidence (contained in the NNR Profile) supports the contention that future domestically available, economically viable (US) NNR supplies will likely be sufficient to completely address future domestic NNR requirements, barring future increases in the domestic NNR requirements trajectory; and

- **Permanent Domestic (US) NNR Scarcity is "Inconclusive":** insufficient evidence exists regarding the likelihood that future domestically available, economically viable NNR supplies will be sufficient to completely address domestic NNR requirements.

## Permanent US Peak NNR Extraction/Production Level Definitions

- **Permanent Domestic (US) NNR Extraction/Production Peak is "Almost Certain":** the US relied on net imports every year since the peak (to date) extraction/production year, which preceded the year 2000;

- **Permanent Domestic (US) NNR Extraction/Production Peak is "Likely":** the US relied on net imports during some years since the peak (to date) extraction/production year, which preceded the year 2000;

- **Permanent Domestic (US) NNR Extraction/Production Peak is "Unclear":** the US has not relied on net imports since the peak (to date) extraction/production year, which preceded the year 2000; or domestic (US) peak-to-date extraction/production occurred in 2000 or later, and the US relied on net imports since the peak year;

- **Permanent Domestic (US) NNR Extraction/Production Peak is "Unlikely":** the US has not relied on net imports since the peak (to date) extraction/production year, which occurred in 2000 or later; and

- **Permanent Domestic (US) NNR Extraction/Production Peak is "Inconclusive":** insufficient domestic (US) extraction/production and/or import data exist to support an informed assessment.

## Permanent US Peak NNR Utilization Level Definitions

- **Permanent Domestic (US) NNR Utilization Peak is "Likely"**: the domestic (US) peak (to date) utilization year preceded the year 2000.
- **Permanent Domestic (US) NNR Utilization Peak is "Unclear"**: the domestic (US) peak (to date) utilization year occurred between 2000 and 2004.
- **Permanent Domestic (US) NNR Utilization Peak is "Unlikely"**: the domestic (US) peak (to date) utilization year occurred between the years 2005 and 2008.
- **Permanent Domestic (US) NNR Utilization Peak is "Inconclusive"**: insufficient domestic (US) NNR utilization data exist to support an informed assessment.

## Permanent Global NNR Scarcity Definitions

- **Permanent Global NNR Scarcity is "Almost Certain":** available evidence (contained in the NNR Profile) supports the contention that future globally available, economically viable NNR supplies will almost certainly be insufficient to completely address future global NNR requirements, barring future reductions in the global NNR requirements trajectory and/or major new economically viable discoveries;
- **Permanent Global NNR Scarcity is "Likely":** available evidence (contained in the NNR Profile) supports the contention that future globally available, economically viable NNR supplies will likely be insufficient to completely address future global NNR requirements, barring future reductions in the global NNR requirements trajectory and/or major new economically viable discoveries;
- **Permanent Global NNR Scarcity is "Unclear":** available evidence (contained in the NNR Profile) regarding the likelihood that globally available, economically viable NNR supplies will be sufficient to completely address future global NNR requirements is conflicting;
- **Permanent Global NNR Scarcity is "Unlikely":** available evidence (contained in the NNR Profile) supports the contention that future globally available, economically viable NNR supplies will likely be sufficient to completely address future global NNR requirements, barring future increases in the global NNR requirements trajectory; and
- **Permanent Global NNR Scarcity is "Inconclusive":** insufficient evidence exists regarding the likelihood that future globally available, economically viable NNR supplies will be sufficient to completely address global NNR requirements.

## Permanent Global Peak NNR Extraction/Production Level Definitions

- **Permanent Global Extraction/Production Peak is "Likely"**: the annual global peak (to date) extraction/production level occurred prior to the year 2000, and the NNR price level trended upward since the peak (to date) year;
- **Permanent Global Extraction/Production Peak is "Unclear"**: the annual global peak (to date) extraction/production level occurred in the 2000 or later, and the NNR price level trended upward since the peak (to date) year;
- **Permanent Extraction/Production Peak is "Unlikely"**: NNR price level trended downward since the peak (to date) year; and
- **Permanent Extraction/Production Peak is "Inconclusive"**: insufficient global extraction/production level and/or price level data exist to support an informed assessment.

# Chris Clugston Bio

Since 2006, I have conducted extensive independent research into the area of "sustainability", with a focus on nonrenewable natural resource (NNR) scarcity. NNRs are the fossil fuels, metals, and nonmetallic minerals that enable our modern industrial existence.

I have sought to quantify from a combined ecological and economic perspective the extent to which America and humanity are living unsustainably beyond our means, and to articulate the causes, magnitude, implications, and consequences associated with our "predicament".

My previous work experience includes thirty years in the high technology electronics industry, primarily with information technology sector companies. I held management level positions in marketing, sales, finance, and M&A, prior to becoming a corporate chief executive and later a management consultant.

I received an AB/Political Science, Magna Cum Laude and Phi Beta Kappa from Penn State University, and an MBA/Finance with High Distinction from Temple University.

Contact: coclugston@gmail.com

CPSIA information can be obtained
at www.ICGtesting.com
Printed in the USA
BVOW09s1002010318

509335BV00004B/75/P